THE GOOD HOTEL GUIDE 2014

GREAT BRITAIN & IRELAND

Editors:
Adam Raphael
Desmond Balmer
Nicola Davies

Editor in chief:
Caroline Raphael

THE GOOD HOTEL GUIDE LTD

The Good Hotel Guide Ltd

This edition first published in 2013 by
The Good Hotel Guide Ltd

Copyright © 2013 Adam and Caroline Raphael
Maps © 2013 David Perrott

Contributing editors:
Bill Bennett
Veronica Lee
Aileen Reid
Astella Saw

Production: Hugh Allan
Managing editor: Alison Wormleighton
Designer: Lizzy Laczynska
Text editor: Daphne Trotter
Researcher: Sophie McLean
Computer consultant: Vince Nacey
Website design and development: HeadChannel Ltd, London
Search engine optimisation: Oliver Stone

A CIP catalogue record for this book may be found in the British Library.

ISBN 978 0 9549404 8 5

Cover photograph: *The Castle at Taunton*, Taunton

Photographs on pp 18, 20, 28, 34, 36, 38, 39, 59, 331, 405, 455, 461 ©iStockphoto.com

Printed and bound in Spain by Graphy Cems

MIX
Paper from
responsible sources
FSC® C007507
FSC
www.fsc.org

'A good hotel is where the guest comes first'

Hilary Rubinstein, founding editor
(1926–2012)

Langar Hall, Langar

CONTENTS

INTRODUCTION

The *Good Hotel Guide* is the leading independent guide to hotels in Great Britain and Ireland. The print edition is at the heart of what we do because it is the guarantee of our independence. Hotels do not pay to be included: the editors select the entries on merit alone, making unbiased judgments based on reports from inspectors and readers. The only payment made is by the inspectors to the hotel for an anonymous visit.

The *Guide*'s website works in tandem with the print edition. It carries the entries for many, but not all, of our selected hotels. Hotels are asked to make a modest payment if they wish their entry to appear on the website. If they choose not to pay, the listing remains, but without the detail or photographs.

Many readers regularly report on their experiences at our selected hotels or on new places they think should be included. Unlike reader-review websites, which are open to abuse from unscrupulous hoteliers and guests with a grudge, these reports are carefully monitored by the editors. Most reports now come via email or the website; correspondents who prefer pen and paper can find report forms at the back of the book. The website has many tempting special offers from *Guide* hotels. It also has a growing selection of good hotels in mainland Europe.

One thing that doesn't change is the character of the places we select, which are as independent as the *Guide*. Most are small and family owned and managed. Our choices reflect the changing face of hospitality: pubs and restaurants-with-rooms are listed alongside simple B&Bs as well as many full-service hotels.

Desmond Balmer and Adam Raphael
July 2013

HOW TO USE THE *GOOD HOTEL GUIDE*

MAIN ENTRY

The 451 main entries, each of which is given a full page, are those we believe to be the best of their type in Great Britain and Ireland.

Colour bands identify each country; London has its own section.

An index at the back lists hotels by county; another index lists them by hotel name.

Hotels are listed alphabetically under the name of the town or village.

The maps at the back of the book are divided into grids for easy reference. A small house indicates a main entry, a triangle a Shortlist one.

The NEW symbol indicates that a hotel is making its first appearance, is returning after an absence, or has been upgraded from the Shortlist.

This hotel has agreed to give *Guide* readers a discount of 25% off their normal bed-and-breakfast rate for one night only. This is subject to availability, and terms and conditions apply.

We name readers who have endorsed a hotel. We do not name inspectors, readers who ask to remain anonymous, or those who have written a critical report.

The panels provide the contact details, the number of bedrooms and other facilities.

Sample entry panel:

896 ENGLAND

TUDDENHAM Suffolk   Map 2:B5

TUDDENHAM MILL [NEW]

On the Suffolk/Cambridgeshire border, the 18th-century mill (Grade II listed) has been given a modern make-over with bedrooms added in two wood-clad buildings. Owned by Agellus Hotels, a group of four hotels in East Anglia, it is managed by Lyndon Barrett-Scott. 'The style is luxurious, generous, thoughtful,' says the nominator. 'The mill has been nicely restored; open stonework, beams, the old mill race and grinding stones featured.' Her bedroom in one of the new buildings was 'light, modern; painted floorboards, crisp white linen, original art, minimal furniture; a really good bed; French windows opened on to a deck with seating'. The well-equipped bathroom had a 'powerful' walk-in shower; 'but nowhere to put storage bags'. The first-floor restaurant has outside decking overlooking the millpond. The chef, Paul Foster, serves 'interesting, delicious' dishes with 'delicate portions, well presented if slightly samey. We enjoyed ray wing, vanilla-poached chicory; beef cheek and loin, artichoke purée, pickled turnip.' Breakfast has 'freshly squeezed orange juice, real butter, chunky marmalade, thick bread toast; good cooked dishes'. (*Carol Jackson*)

25% DISCOUNT VOUCHERS

High Street, Tuddenham nr Newmarket IP28 6SQ

T: 01638-713552
E: info@tuddenhammill.co.uk
W: www.tuddenhammill.co.uk

BEDROOMS: 15, 12 in 2 separate buildings, 8 on ground floor, 1 suitable for &.
OPENS all year.
FACILITIES: bar, restaurant, 2 function rooms, free Wi-Fi, 12-acre grounds.
BACKGROUND MUSIC: 'modern' in bar and restaurant.
LOCATION: in village, 8 miles NE of Newmarket.
CHILDREN: all ages welcomed.
DOGS: allowed (£15 a night).
CREDIT CARDS: MasterCard, Visa.
PRICES: [2013] per room B&B £185–£395. À la carte £38. 1-night bookings refused weekends.

www.goodhotelguide.com

The wheelchair symbol is used to indicate whether or not a hotel can accommodate wheelchair users. This hotel has two bedrooms adapted for wheelchair use. If a hotel tells us it is not suitable for a wheelchair user, we say so in the panel.

We indicate whether the prices are given per person or per room for B&B (and D,B&B); in those cases where a hotel quotes for the room without breakfast, we give the room price alongside a separate breakfast charge. The à la carte price given for dinner is an estimate of the cost of three courses per person. The range of prices (from low season to high season) is given for 2014, or (when indicated) for 2013. These prices cannot be guaranteed – always check when booking.

HOW TO USE THE *GOOD HOTEL GUIDE*

SHORTLIST ENTRY

The Shortlist includes untested new entries and places we think should be appropriate in areas where we have limited choice. It also includes some hotels about which we have not had recent reports. There are no photographs; many of the hotels have chosen to be included on our website, where pictures are carried.

The wheelchair symbol indicates whether or not a hotel can accommodate wheelchair users. We recommend you phone the hotel to check details.

In some cases we list the entry under the nearest town.

These are abbreviated descriptions listing the essential facilities.

Dinner prices are either for a set menu or an estimate of the likely price of a three-course meal.

This hotel has agreed to give Guide readers a discount of 25% off their normal bed-and-breakfast rate for one night only. This is subject to availability, and terms and conditions apply.

Many readers tell us they find background music irritating. We tell you if music is played and where you might encounter it.

---

558 · SHORTLIST

Children welcomed (bunk beds; entertainment). Dogs welcomed (£15 per night). 96 bedrooms (12 suites; 1 room suitable for 6; plus 40 self-catering cottages in the grounds). Per room B&B £79–£389, D,B&B £129–£439.
25% DISCOUNT VOUCHERS

NORWICH Norfolk
Map 2:B5
NORFOLK MEAD, Church Loke, Coltishall, NR12 7DN. Tel 01603-737531, www.norfolkmead.co.uk. Transformed by new owners James Holliday and Anna Duttson, this hotel in a Georgian merchant's house has a sleek, modern design. It is in a 'near-perfect' position with eight-acre grounds running down to the river. Light and bright bedrooms are individually styled; Sloe has a cedar-wood sleigh bed and elevated views over the lawns; Hawthorn has bay windows and French doors leading to a private terrace. Anna Duttson cooks modern British menus with Asian influences, inspired by locally sourced produce. Lounge, bar, snug, restaurant; background music. Free Wi-Fi. Private dining. Walled garden; fishing lake; off-river mooring. Small conference/ wedding facilities. 7 miles NE of Norwich. Children, and dogs (in some rooms; £15 per night charge) welcomed. 13 bedrooms (some in cottage and summer house). Per room B&B £125–£175. Dinner £30.

OAKHILL Somerset
Map 2:D1
THE OAKHILL INN, Fosse Road, nr Radstock, BA3 5HU. Tel 01749-840442, www.theoakhillinn.com. In a pretty village with a long-standing history of brewing, there are real ales and log fires at this unpretentious, family-friendly pub-with-rooms owned by Charlie and Amanda Digney. Modern rustic rooms have bold colours and local art; two have a bathtub. Head chef Neil Creese cooks seasonal menus using local meat and produce; seafood is delivered daily from the Cornish coast. Breakfast, ordered the night before, has home-made Old Spot sausages and freshly baked pastries. 3 miles N of Shepton Mallet. 2 bars, restaurant; garden. Low-level background music. Free Wi-Fi. Parking. Children welcomed (family suite). 5 bedrooms. Per room B&B from £90.

OUNDLE Northamptonshire
Map 2:B3
LOWER FARM, Main Street, Barnwell, PE8 5PU. Tel 01832-273220, www. lower-farm.co.uk. On the edge of a pretty village three miles from Oundle, the old stables and milking parlour of a small arable farm have been converted into 'really nice', modern rooms, arranged around a central courtyard. A green philosophy has been followed: there are air source heat pumps, photovoltaic panels, under-floor heating, low-energy lighting and rainwater harvesting. Caroline Marriott, 'a friendly and accommodating hostess', looks after the B&B guests; her copious farmhouse breakfasts include a steak-and-eggs special. Husband John and his brother manage the farm, which has been in the Marriott family since the 1920s. Plenty of footpaths and cycleways in the area. Breakfast room (background music); courtyard garden with seating. Free Wi-Fi; no mobile phone signal. Children and dogs welcomed in some

CÉSARS 2014

We give our *César* awards to the ten best hotels of the year. Named after César Ritz, the most celebrated of hoteliers, these are the Oscars of hotel-keeping.

⚜ COUNTRY HOTEL OF THE YEAR

THE TRADDOCK, AUSTWICK

The Reynolds family have given their small hotel, an old manor house, the feel of a country home, not grand, not designerish, but supremely comfortable. The caring service is admired.

⚜ LUXURY HOTEL OF THE YEAR

THE BATH PRIORY, BATH

Elegant country house comfort, combined with impeccable service, exquisite modern cooking and a blissful lack of background music, makes Andrew and Christina Brownsword's luxury hotel a place to return to.

⚜ NORFOLK HOTEL OF THE YEAR

THE WHITE HORSE, BRANCASTER STAITHE

Above tidal sea marshes on the north Norfolk coast, Cliff Nye's small hotel has a relaxing ambience, delicious food, friendly staff; it is well managed by Christina Boyle.

⚜ DEVON HOTEL OF THE YEAR

THE OLD RECTORY, MARTINHOE

Huw Rees and Sam Prosser, who have given their old rectory a smart interior, run it with good humour and great attention to the needs of guests. Huw Rees's cooking is much praised.

⚜ RESTAURANT-WITH-ROOMS OF THE YEAR

THE BLACK SWAN, OLDSTEAD

In beautiful countryside, this delightful old pub has been meticulously restored by the Banks family, who are much in evidence. The innovative cooking of chef Adam Jackson is reason enough to visit.

❧ CORNISH B&B OF THE YEAR

ENNYS, ST HILARY

An exceptional place in a wonderful rural situation,
Gill Charlton's B&B, a 17th-century manor house, is
'a class act; definitely worth five stars'. Breakfast is
'well-nigh perfect'.

❧ NEWCOMER OF THE YEAR

THE CAT INN, WEST HOATHLY

Andrew Russell has created a welcoming atmosphere at
his immaculate 16th-century inn, opposite the church in
a pretty hilltop village in the Sussex Weald. The
cooking by chef Max Leonard is excellent.

❧ SCOTTISH HOTEL OF THE YEAR

KYLESKU HOTEL, KYLESKU

In an idyllic setting by a sea loch on the north-west
coast, this former coaching inn is run by the hands-on
owners, Tanja Lister, 'full of enthusiasm and energy',
and Sonia Virechauveix, who oversees the kitchen.

❧ WELSH GUEST HOUSE OF THE YEAR

BRYNIAU GOLAU, BALA

A haven for those who love peace and quiet, Katrina Le
Saux and Peter Cottee's Victorian home has a magical
setting overlooking Bala Lake. She is a caring host, he is
a talented cook.

❧ IRISH GUEST HOUSE OF THE YEAR

LORUM OLD RECTORY, BAGENALSTOWN

'A charming house in a scenic landscape; a wonderful
host and a most pleasant atmosphere.' Bobbie Smith
runs her Victorian rectory with an obvious passion for
detail, making it ever popular with readers.

REPORT OF THE YEAR COMPETITION

Readers' contributions are the lifeblood of the *Good Hotel Guide*. Everyone who writes to us is a potential winner of the Report of the Year competition. Each year a dozen correspondents are singled out for the helpfulness of their reports. They win a copy of the *Guide* and an invitation to our annual launch party in October. This year's winners are:

MAMIE ATKINS of Glan-Munchweiler, Germany
DR RICHARD BARRETT of Salisbury

KAY BIRCHLEY of Kington
DR ALEC FRANK of Lewes
DAVID JEROIS of Bovey Tracey
ANNIE LADE of Painswick
SUZANNE LYONS of Barnstaple
HELENA SHAW of North Harrow
ROBERT TURNER of Woolpit
LYNN WILDGOOSE of Romiley
ALAN AND EDWINA WILLIAMS of Southport
KEN AND PRISCILLA WINSLOW of Swindon

JOIN THE *GOOD HOTEL GUIDE* READERS' CLUB

Send us a review of your favourite hotel.
As a member of the club, you will be entitled to:
1. A pre-publication discount offer
2. Personal advice on hotels
3. Advice if you are in dispute with a hotel
4. Monthly emailed *Guide* newsletter

The writers of the 12 best reviews will each win a free copy of the *Guide* and an invitation to our launch party. And the winner of our monthly web competition will win a free night, dinner and breakfast for two at one of the *Guide*'s top hotels.

Send your review via:
our website: www.goodhotelguide.com
or email: editor@goodhotelguide.com
or fax: 020-7602 4182
or write to:

In the UK
Good Hotel Guide
Freepost PAM 2931
London W11 4BR
(no stamp needed)

From abroad
Good Hotel Guide
50 Addison Avenue
London W11 4QP
England

EDITOR'S CHOICE

A visit to a hotel should be a special occasion. Here are some of our favourite hotels in various categories. Turn to the full entry for the bigger picture.

BELLE TOUT LIGHTHOUSE
EASTBOURNE
On the chalk cliffs of Beachy Head, this decommissioned lighthouse has been restored as a B&B ('with a fantastic view'). Well-equipped bedrooms face the sea or the South Downs. A sitting room has a wraparound window looking out to the Seven Sisters. It is 'worth the effort' to climb the 80 steps up to the old light room with its 360-degree view.
Read more, page 152.

38 ST GILES
NORWICH
On a street of individual shops, this Georgian town house has a stylish interior; prints and drawings by local artists are displayed throughout. A magnificent central staircase leads to bedrooms, which have a mix of antiques and contemporary furniture. The leisurely breakfast, served on handmade crockery, has home-made bread and preserves, 'tasty' cooked dishes; extra toast and coffee.
Read more, page 237.

THE GREYHOUND ON THE TEST
STOCKBRIDGE
The River Test flows at the bottom of the garden of Lucy Townsend's old inn on the elegant high street of a Hampshire town. There are personal touches in the bedrooms, which are decorated in muted colours. Guests can take drinks from an honesty bar in the corridor or enjoy the buzz of the low-ceilinged bar. Candles glow on the wooden tables in the restaurant where Alan Haughie's daily-changing menu has 'interesting' dishes.
Read more, page 288.

THE HORSE GUARDS INN
TILLINGTON
Opposite the church in a conservation village in the South Downs national park, Sam Beard and his partner, Michaela Hofirkova, run their 350-year-old inn with an 'impressive can-do attitude'. The 'excellent' cooking of the chef, Mark Robinson, can be taken in the bar or the intimate dining room with its low beams and wood-burning stove. Two bedrooms are above the bar; the third is in an adjoining cottage.
Read more, page 303.

TUDDENHAM MILL
TUDDENHAM

The old mill race and grinding stones are featured in the stylish restoration of this Grade II listed, 18th-century mill on the Suffolk/Cambridgeshire border. Most of the modern bedrooms (painted floorboards, minimal furniture, original art) are in two recently added wood-clad buildings. Chef Paul Foster serves 'delicious', well-presented dishes in the first-floor restaurant in the old mill, which has outside decking overlooking the millpond.

Read more, page 306.

THE HACK & SPADE
WHASHTON

'Hospitable and enthusiastic hosts', Jane and Andy Ratcliffe, have created a 'quirky, interesting and unpretentious' restaurant-with-rooms at their renovated old pub in a tiny hilltop village in North Yorkshire's Swale valley. The uncluttered bedrooms have a cool, contemporary feel. Jane Ratcliffe serves 'tasty' dishes in the restaurant. No menu at breakfast, just the question 'What would you like?'

Read more, page 318.

THE LION INN
WINCHCOMBE

Owner Annie Fox-Hamilton has created a relaxed, modern air at her makeover of a 15th-century inn in a Saxon town in the Cotswolds. There are superb floral decorations in the public areas and the bedrooms which have been decorated in Scandinavian style. No television; bedrooms have books and board games. The cooking of Martyn Pearn impressed *Guide* inspectors.

Read more, page 321.

DUMFRIES HOUSE LODGE
CUMNOCK

The Prince of Wales led the consortium of charities which saved Dumfries House (built by Robert Adam for the Earl of Dumfries) from a private sale. A trust runs the house and the B&B accommodation in the former factor's lodge, which guests can treat as their country home. It is 'beautifully furnished' (many pieces come from the house). The manager, Mark Robson, cooks a delicious breakfast.

Read more, page 346.

BURRASTOW HOUSE
WALLS

Built in 1759 for the local laird, this remote guest house (*pictured opposite*) on the western edge of Shetland is run in personal style by the owner, Pierre Dupont, who creates each evening's menu from what is available locally. There is a comprehensive library, a drawing room with a wood-burning stove and a well-stocked drinks cabinet. Otters fish in the bay at the front of the house.

Read more, page 404.

OSBORNE HOUSE
LLANDUDNO

On the Victorian resort's promenade, this 'unusual and exciting' small hotel is the sister to a much larger establishment nearby. Each of the six bedrooms has a separate sitting room furnished with original Victorian pieces. Good 'gastropub' food is served all day in the café downstairs; a continental breakfast is brought to the bedroom in the morning. Guests have access to the pool and spa facilities at the larger hotel.

Read more, page 434.

CHURCH STREET HOTEL
LONDON

'A flamboyant, friendly place of great character', José and Mel Raido's idiosyncratic hotel in Camberwell Green is 'a one-off, giving good fun at reasonable prices'. The Greek/Spanish brothers have decorated in 'extravagant' Latino style. A stained-glass window of flying angels lights the entrance; the bedrooms have vivid colours, religious art. Tapas meals are served in the 'excellent' *Angels & Gypsies* restaurant. Per room B&B (continental) £60–£160. Dinner £28.
Read more, page 41.

THE FIELDING
LONDON

On a quiet pedestrianised street (lit by 19th-century gas lamps) in Covent Garden near the Royal Opera House, this small, privately owned hotel is a 'delightful treat for opera fans'. Up a narrow staircase, the rooms are 'modern, comfortable, clean and tidy'. Simply decorated, they have good storage space, tea- and coffee-making facilities. No public rooms, no meals; many eating places are nearby. Room (*excluding VAT*) £108–£240.
Read more, page 46.

BIGGIN HALL
BIGGIN-BY-HARTINGTON

James Moffett's unpretentious hotel within the Peak District national park has long been liked by walkers for the unfussy atmosphere and the 'real value for money'. The simple bedrooms are in the main house, the courtyard, the 'bothy' and the lodge. Traditional dishes are served in the candlelit dining room. Good walking in all directions. Per room D,B&B £118–£174.
Read more, page 91.

CASTLEMAN
CHETTLE

In a historic village in Dorset, this former dower house is run as an informal restaurant-with-rooms by Barbara Garnsworthy and her brother, Brendan, who runs the front-of-house. It is 'a straightforward country house where you are made to feel like friends'. There is an element of 'faded gentility' in the public rooms. The complete silence at night is much liked. Per room B&B £90–£105. Dinner £25–£28.
Read more, page 128.

THISTLEYHAUGH FARM
LONGHORSLEY

Enid Nelless's guest house in the rolling Cheviot hills is shielded from the world by a 720-acre organic sheep and cattle farm run by her husband, Henry. The bedrooms in the Georgian farmhouse are priced according to size; they have 'excellent' beds; 'masses of towels, all the goodies we needed'. The communal dinner is described as 'farmhouse cooking with flair'. Per person D,B&B from £70.

Read more, page 200.

LYDGATE HOUSE
POSTBRIDGE

Near the clapper bridge that spans the East Dart river, this whitewashed late Victorian house stands in extensive grounds with a footpath leading directly on to the moor. There is a wood-burning stove, a well-stocked library, and a small bar in the lounge. 'Dinners are of a good standard, with huge portions.' Per room B&B £45–£120. Dinner £27.50.

Read more, page 256.

THE BLACK SWAN
RAVENSTONEDALE

In a 'peaceful and attractive village' near Kirkby Stephen, Alan and Louise Dinnes's 'cosy pub' 'exudes warmth and friendliness'. The bedrooms, all different, are 'big, and refreshingly underpriced'. Chef Kev Hillyer's 'delicious artisan dishes' can be eaten in the bar or one of the two dining rooms. Smaller, cheaper portions are available for small appetites. Breakfasts are 'hearty'. Per room B&B £75–£125. Dinner £26.

Read more, page 259.

HOWTOWN HOTEL
ULLSWATER

On the quieter eastern shore of Lake Ullswater, the Baldry family's simple guest house 'evokes memories of times past'. It doesn't have a computer, let alone an email address. There is only one television (in a lounge); guests might choose not to watch it, as they are encouraged to talk to each other. Most of the simple bedrooms have lake views. A four-course dinner of traditional dishes is served six nights a week. Per person D,B&B £89.

Read more, page 308.

BEALACH HOUSE
DUROR

Jim and Hilary McFadyen's small guest house, a former farmhouse that is the only building remaining in the valley, is reached by a long forestry track. Bedrooms, if not large, 'had everything we needed'. Almost everything is home-made at dinner and breakfast which are taken communally. Per room B&B £90–£110. Dinner £30.

Read more, page 349.

PEN-Y-GWRYD HOTEL
NANT GWYNANT

The Pullee family's historic hotel (the training base for the climbers who conquered Everest in 1953) is a converted 19th-century farmhouse in the foothills of Snowdon. The bedrooms are small and simple; only five have a private bathroom. The food is 'good, honest fare, locally sourced and always fresh'. Per person B&B £42–£52. Set dinner £25–£30.

Read more, page 440.

WOOLLEY GRANGE
BRADFORD-ON-AVON

Part of the Luxury Family Hotels group, this Jacobean stone manor feels like 'the country home of a wealthy family friend'. There is much for children of all ages to do. The youngest have the Woolley Bears Den (a crèche with a baby area, playhouses, etc); older siblings have a playroom. The staff 'interact well with children', who share their parents' room for free.
Read more, page 103.

THE EVESHAM HOTEL
EVESHAM

Children (and 'well-behaved adults') are warmly welcomed at John and Sue Jenkinson's quirky, informal hotel. There is a huge playroom, an indoor swimming pool; slides and a trampoline in the 'lovely' gardens. Alice in Wonderland, a family suite, has a play nook under the beams. Children who share their parents' room are charged £2 a night for each year of their life; they can take early evening meals.
Read more, page 158.

AUGILL CASTLE
KIRKBY STEPHEN

Endless diversions are provided for children at Simon and Wendy Bennett's restored neo-Gothic Victorian castle. There are games and dressing-up paraphernalia in the drawing room; hens and ducks to feed in the grounds, a playground, a fort and a tree house. The laid-back atmosphere is praised: 'Our two-year-old daughter enjoyed running through the house.' Dinner is a sociable occasion.
Read more, page 185.

SWINTON PARK
MASHAM

On a large estate with a lake and a deer park, Mark and Felicity Cunliffe-Lister's mock-Gothic castle welcomes children of all ages. There are countless activities in the grounds: a boot room is filled with kites; an outdoor play area and parkland will offer hours of walking and playing. A playroom in the house, full of toys, converts into a private cinema. Nappies, wipes and baby powders are provided.
Read more, page 213.

BEDRUTHAN STEPS HOTEL
MAWGAN PORTH

Above a golden, sandy beach, this large family hotel has 'excellent facilities' for all ages. 'It catered perfectly for all our needs,' said a member of a family group, aged from eight months to 74 years old. There are indoor and outdoor swimming pools; 'a wonderful array of entertainment'; playgrounds, a jungle gym, tennis courts. Family meals can be taken in the 'relaxed' *Wild Café*.
Read more, page 214.

SOAR MILL COVE HOTEL
SOAR MILL COVE

'You don't get through three generations of Makepeace family business without gathering insider know-how about holidays with the crew,' says Keith Makepeace, the owner of this hotel in extensive grounds above a sandy cove. Children of all ages will be kept occupied in the indoor and outdoor play areas; or they can stroll down to the beach where learning to surf 'is surely a must'.
Read more, page 282.

CALCOT MANOR
TETBURY

'Child-friendly yet civilised for adults', this converted 14th-century farmhouse in the Cotswolds is popular with all generations. The youngest children have an Ofsted-registered *Playzone*; older ones have games consoles and computers in *The Mez*. Special times are allocated for children in the spa and swimming pool. Families dine together in the *Gumstool Inn* which 'buzzes with activity'.
Read more, page 301.

LOCH MELFORT HOTEL
ARDUAINE

Highland cattle, ducks and hens 'keep little ones interested' at Calum and Rachel Ross's country hotel in a 'peaceful setting', sheltered by woodland on Asknish Bay. Family-friendly meals are served in the *Chartroom II* bistro, which has a playground in front, and a box of toys and games. Extra beds are provided for children in some bedrooms. Guests can walk to a small beach.
Read more, page 332.

PORTH TOCYN HOTEL
ABERSOCH

'Some mothers coming here with their children came as children themselves,' say the Fletcher-Brewer family, who have been running their 'laid-back, homely' hotel on the Lleyn peninsula for three generations. Children are welcomed with a dedicated snug and a games conservatory. A casual, buzzy children's high tea is served at 5.30 pm; 'simple suppers' have been introduced for families seeking flexible dining.
Read more, page 409.

THE DRUIDSTONE
BROAD HAVEN

Favoured by those who seek informality and 'the feeling of total freedom', this late 19th-century stone house is on a cliff-top above a sandy beach. Terraces overlook the sea. 'We are first and foremost a relaxed, informal family hotel,' says Angus Bell, who is now in charge with his partner, Beth Wilshaw. Children have high tea around a big kitchen table. There are many activities locally: surfing, coasteering, sailing, canoeing and walking.
Read more, 416.

THE CARY ARMS
BABBACOMBE

Beside a beach beneath a steep cliff near Torquay, this small hotel (*pictured above*) has been given a nautical theme by Lana de Savary. All the bedrooms face the sea (some have a terrace or a balcony). They are decorated in New England style with panelled walls. The bar/dining area has stone walls, a wood and slate floor, a conservatory dining area. In warm weather there is alfresco dining in the garden which overlooks the bay.
Read more, page 73.

THE HENLEY
BIGBURY-ON-SEA

On a cliff above the tidal Avon estuary, this unpretentious Edwardian villa is run as a small hotel by Martyn Scarterfield and his wife, Petra Lampe. There are Lloyd Loom chairs and picture windows in the lounge where binoculars are provided for 'one of the best views in England', over the tidal Avon estuary. The five simple bedrooms are furnished in country style. Martyn Scarterfield's cooking is 'consistently good'.
Read more, page 90.

THE BLAKENEY
BLAKENEY

With views over salt marshes towards Blakeney Point (an area of outstanding natural beauty), this traditional hotel stands on the quayside of a tidal estuary. The first-floor lounge has a panoramic view (glorious sunsets). There are boat trips to take, sandy beaches to explore; good walking and cycling from the door.
Read more, page 95.

THE WHITE HORSE
BRANCASTER STAITHE

On the marshland coast of north Norfolk, Cliff Nye's small hotel is furnished in appropriate style for its seaside location. Eight bedrooms in a garden annexe that 'folds into the landscape thanks to a sedum roof' have the 'feel of a beach hut'. Decorated in seaside colours, each has a small patio. Fresh seafood (often Cyril's mussels harvested at the foot of the garden) features on Aurum Frankel's menus.
Read more, page 106.

HELL BAY HOTEL
BRYHER

There are sandy beaches at every turn on the smallest of the inhabited Isles of Scilly, which is reached by boat from St Mary's. Most of the bedrooms, decorated in coastal colours, face the sea and have a balcony, or a terrace from which you walk straight to a beach. At breakfast, you can watch egrets searching for their morning meal in a freshwater lake. For a castaway experience, take a boat (and a picnic) to the neighbouring uninhabited island, Samson.
Read more, page 114.

DRIFTWOOD HOTEL
PORTSCATHO

In an 'idyllic' setting overlooking Gerrans Bay on Cornwall's Roseland peninsula, Paul and Fiona Robinson's seaside-inspired hotel has everything needed for 'a comfortable stay'. Bedrooms (most have a sea view) are decorated in shades of sand and sky. Picnics can be provided for guests taking the steep steps that lead through woodland to a private beach.
Read more, page 255.

ST ENODOC
ROCK

In a fashionable north Cornish resort, this child-friendly if expensive hotel stands on a hill above the Camel estuary. It has a light Mediterranean decor with bright colours and original artwork. Nathan Outlaw, the high-profile Cornish chef, supervises two restaurants: the all-day *Outlaw's Seafood and Grill*, and *Restaurant Nathan Outlaw* which has an eight-course seafood tasting menu.
Read more, page 264.

WATERSMEET
WOOLACOMBE

The 'loveliness of the views' is matched by the 'graciousness of the accommodation' at this traditional hotel in a glorious setting above Woolacombe Bay. Tables are on three levels in the dining room to ensure that all guests can enjoy the 90-degree views of the bay. All but three of the bedrooms have a sea view; the best have a wooden balcony or garden terrace. There is a swimming pool in the gardens which lead down to the sea.
Read more, page 326.

THE COLONSAY
COLONSAY

In a 'wild and remote' location (an island off the west coast of Scotland), this renovated mid-18th-century inn is on a hill above the harbour. The 'well-maintained' garden has outdoor seating areas. Locally brewed beer is served in the bar, which is popular with islanders and visiting sailors. There are a dozen beaches around the island. Grey seals, otters, dolphins, even whales, can be spotted.
Read more, page 343.

THE DRUIDSTONE
BROAD HAVEN

Guests at this idiosyncratic 'family holiday centre' can enjoy all manner of beach activities (surfing, sailing, windsurfing, canoeing) on the huge sandy beach below. The informality ensures that they need not worry about sand in their shoes on their return to the cliff-top accommodation. There is much space in which to 'wander or just sit'. The accommodation is simple.
Read more, page 416.

LINTHWAITE HOUSE
BOWNESS-ON-WINDERMERE

Period features allied to contemporary comforts ensure that Mike Bevans's late Victorian hotel has a 'country house feel'. The 'relaxed and informal' atmosphere makes it an 'ideal place in which to recharge one's batteries'. Smart dress is required in the candlelit restaurant, where chef Chris O'Callaghan serves a 'delicious' modern British menu. The larger bedrooms (and public areas) have 'stunning' views over Lake Windermere. *Read more, page 102.*

FARLAM HALL
BRAMPTON

The Quinion family have run this restored Victorian manor house with 'professionalism and dedication' since 1975. Its sweeping driveway runs through woodland and landscaped gardens. The drawing rooms are extravagantly decorated with patterned wallpaper, knick-knacks and Victoriana. The bedrooms are spacious and well appointed. Barry Quinion's daily-changing menu of imaginative dishes is served in the dining room, where smart clothing is preferred. *Read more, page 105.*

GIDLEIGH PARK
CHAGFORD

On a large estate on the banks of the North Teign river, this luxurious country house hotel is managed by Andrew Foulkes for the owners, Andrew and Christina Brownsword. The Tudor-style building has panelled public rooms with Arts and Crafts features. Executive chef Michael Caines holds two *Michelin* stars for his elaborate French dishes. There is excellent walking in the grounds ('we didn't move the car once'). *Read more, page 126.*

GRAVETYE MANOR
EAST GRINSTEAD

Once owned by William Robinson, the pioneer of the English natural garden, this 16th-century Elizabethan manor house has been given an Arts and Crafts interior. Public areas, restored by the owners, Jeremy and Elizabeth Hosking, have dark wood panelling, bold floral displays. The atmosphere is 'not at all stuffy'. Much restoration work has been done in the gardens (*pictured above*). *Read more, page 149.*

HAMBLETON HALL
HAMBLETON

On a peninsula jutting into Rutland Water, Tim and Stefa Hart's mansion is run to the 'highest standards'. In the candlelit dining room, the chef, Aaron Patterson, has a *Michelin* star for his cooking of dishes that are 'attractive in their presentation and intense in their flavour'. Stefa Hart designed the sumptuous public rooms and the bedrooms, which vary in size and style. The best overlook Rutland Water.
Read more, page 170.

LIME WOOD
LYNDHURST

In extensive grounds in the New Forest, this Regency manor house has been given a modern makeover and is run as a 'relaxed' country house hotel under the guidance of Robin Hutson (who co-founded the Hotel du Vin group). The main dining room has been restyled this year as an informal restaurant with an Italian twist, supervised by Angela Hartnett: 'Much improved: vibrant, colourful and dynamic.'
Read more, page 209.

CHEWTON GLEN
NEW MILTON

The staff/guest ratio is three to one at this privately owned country house hotel in large grounds on the edge of the New Forest. Guests can 'play Tarzan and Jane' in twelve new tree houses ('great fun') which have been built on stilts in the grounds. They have a wood-burning stove, picture windows, a whirlpool bath on a wraparound terrace. Bedrooms in the main house have antiques and many have a terrace or balcony.
Read more, page 228.

GLENAPP CASTLE
BALLANTRAE

There are views to the sea and Ailsa Craig from this baronial castle which has been turned into a luxurious hotel by the owners, Graham and Fay Cowan. They have furnished it with fine paintings and antiques. The large bedrooms have swagged curtains, a wide bed; a spacious bathroom. Matt Worswick, the new chef, uses produce from the kitchen gardens for his seasonal six-course menus.
Read more, page 336.

BODYSGALLEN HALL
LLANDUDNO

In well-maintained grounds, this 'beautiful' 17th-century mansion is run by Historic House Hotels for the National Trust. The Grade I listed building has original oak panelling, stone mullioned windows; there are log fires and antique furniture in the entrance hall and drawing room. Some bedrooms are in cottages in the grounds; woodland walks, ponds, follies.
Read more, page 433.

LLANGOED HALL
LLYSWEN

In large grounds with the River Wye flowing through, this lovely 17th-century mansion (redesigned by Sir Clough Williams-Ellis) has been extensively renovated under new private ownership. Calum Milne has returned as manager. Afternoon tea is served in a drawing room that has 'a roaring fire and no annoying music'. Nick Brodie, the chef, serves modern dishes 'immaculately presented on lovely china'.
Read more, page 439.

THE ZETTER
LONDON

In fashionable Clerkenwell, this laid-back and quirky hotel is a conversion of a 19th-century warehouse which later became the headquarters of Zetter Pools. The bedrooms are decorated in bright colours and have retro furnishings (1960s chairs, bean bags) as well as all the latest technology. They vary greatly in size; each of the roof-top studios has a private patio. The crescent-shaped restaurant, *Bistrot Bruno Loubet*, overlooks St John's Square.
Read more, page 44.

THE ZETTER TOWNHOUSE
LONDON

Across the square from its sister hotel, *The Zetter* (see above), this intimate town house has an eccentric and original style, modelled as if it were the home of an eccentric aunt. Every surface is covered by her 'collection': antique ceramics, bronzes, old postcards, a stuffed kangaroo. The bedrooms have reclaimed and vintage furniture (headboards from fairgrounds).
Read more, page 45.

THE ROCKWELL
LONDON

The styling is minimalist without being spare (cream walls with splashes of colour, feature wallpaper) at this conversion of two stucco-fronted town houses in Earls Court (*pictured above*). Bedroooms have fitted light oak furniture. The large lobby/lounge has a huge bookcase, sofas and armchairs around a coffee table; the bar/dining room overlooks a south-facing courtyard garden (a suntrap in summer) accessed by a glass bridge.
Read more, page 47.

THE ARCH
LONDON

Colourful and modern, this sympathetic conversion of seven Georgian town houses is on a quiet street near Marble Arch. Comprehensively equipped bedrooms have hand-printed wallpaper and original sash windows; in-room facilities include a Nespresso coffee machine. An informal open-plan brasserie and bar has Philippe Starck stools, curtained booths. Striking modern artwork and installations can be seen throughout.
Read more, page 50.

NUMBER SIXTEEN
LONDON

On a leafy South Kensington street, this white stucco town house has been given an exuberant and lively interior by Kit Kemp, who owns the small Firmdale group with her husband, Tim. Well-fitted bedrooms have bold prints, a 'supremely comfortable' bed, excellent reading lights and a writing desk; bathrooms are handsome in granite and oak. Two light-filled drawing rooms have floor-to-ceiling windows; a conservatory opens on to the garden.
Read more, page 56.

THE QUEENSBERRY
BATH

Just off the Circus, this group of 18th-century town houses has been given a surprising minimalist interior which contrasts with the elegance of the street outside. The spacious bedrooms are decorated in muted tones with feature wallpapers, 'variously shaped cushions', throws. Modern dishes are served in the split-level *Olive Tree* restaurant in the basement.
Read more, page 82.

HOTEL DU VIN BRIGHTON
BRIGHTON

Between the Lanes and the seafront, this branch of the du Vin chain is a conversion of mock Tudor and Gothic revival buildings. The bar is in a vault-ceilinged hall which has a carved staircase and bizarre gargoyles. The bedrooms have a masculine decor (dark browns predominate); bathrooms have a stand-alone bath and a powerful drench shower.
Read more, page 108.

JESMOND DENE
NEWCASTLE-UPON-TYNE

Original Arts and Crafts features have been enhanced by modern designs and retro furnishings at this mansion in a wooded valley close to the city centre. The Great Hall and smart lounges have ornate fireplaces, stained glass, oak panelling; contemporary art. Bedrooms in the mansion have muted colours; suites in the recently built *New House* have a sitting room, a big bed and bolder colours.
Read more, page 231.

HART'S HOTEL
NOTTINGHAM

On the ramparts where the city's medieval castle once stood, Tim Hart has built a modern hotel with curved buttresses and lots of glass. His wife, Stefa, has designed the eye-catching interiors using bright colours; much art on the walls, a vast window in the lobby. The bedrooms are small but have high ceilings, plenty of natural light. Most have excellent views over the city.
Read more, page 238.

OLD BANK
OXFORD

Discreet and modern, Jeremy Mogford's hotel is a conversion of three old stone buildings (one was a bank) on the High, opposite All Souls. Vast canvases from the owner's extensive collection of contemporary art enliven the walls of *Quod*, the lively bar/brasserie, a favourite Oxford meeting place. Original artwork is also found in the bedrooms, which have muted colours, a marble bathroom. The best have views of the dreaming spires.
Read more, page 245.

THE ZETTER TOWNHOUSE
LONDON

Take an exotic cocktail (perhaps Fig French 75 – fig-infused cognac and champagne) in the eccentrically furnished bar of this intimate town house hotel on peaceful St John's Square in Clerkenwell. The bedrooms have equal character: an apartment has 'room to swing several cats'; a sunny sash window, a free-standing bath, and 'oodles of space to play'.
Read more, page 45.

THE PORTOBELLO
LONDON

A discreet hideaway on an elegant street in Notting Hill, this small, quirky hotel is favoured by celebrities from the world of music and fashion. When booking, ask for one of the special rooms, perhaps Room 6 on the lower ground floor which has French doors opening on to a garden; in its bathroom, the antique free-standing bath is draped with muslin curtains.
Read more, page 54.

BARNSLEY HOUSE
BARNSLEY

Once the home of Rosemary Verey, the noted gardener, this William and Mary house is liked for its 'relaxed country house feel'. For total privacy stay in the Secret Garden suite which is tucked away within the celebrated gardens. It has a glass facade facing a courtyard garden with a pond; an egg-shaped bath in the bedroom; a double shower and two basins in the bathroom.
Read more, page 74.

BURGH ISLAND HOTEL
BIGBURY-ON-SEA

'An experience like no other', this Grade II listed 1930s hotel is on a private island cut off by the tide twice a day. Restored as an 'Art Deco tour de force', it is run in 1930s style. Formal dress is not compulsory in the evening, but most guests enter into the spirit. The Garden Suite, reached by a private corridor, has a sitting room with French windows opening on to a secluded garden. The Beach House, built as a writer's retreat for Agatha Christie, stands away from the hotel above the shore. 'It must be the sexiest hotel room in the UK.'
Read more, page 89.

BELLE TOUT LIGHTHOUSE
EASTBOURNE

'A lovely and unusual place for a romantic getaway', this decommissioned lighthouse has an isolated setting on the cliffs of Beachy Head. Guests are given a choice between space or a view – the smaller rooms have the view (two larger rooms face the South Downs). The Captain's Cabin overlooks the present lighthouse; a double bed in a loft (reached by the original ladder) is a feature of the intimate Lighthouse Keepers' Room. *Read more, page 152.*

COMBE HOUSE
GITTISHAM

Ken and Ruth Hunt's 'stunning renovation' of a Grade I listed Elizabethan manor house is reached by a mile-long drive through rolling parkland. The most romantic room is in a thatched cottage in a private walled garden near the entrance. Original features have been enhanced by contemporary furnishings in shades of natural linen. The interiors of the main house are 'seductively traditional'. *Read more, page 164.*

LE MANOIR AUX QUAT'SAISONS
GREAT MILTON

The grounds of Raymond Blanc's luxury hotel in a pretty Oxfordshire village are as romantic as the bedrooms. There is a Japanese tea garden and an English water garden. M. Blanc has collaborated with leading designers to style the romantic themed suites. Opium has an oriental decor with wood panelling, scarlet fabrics, a low-level bed and an original Ming stone carving. Its private walled garden has a water feature. *Read more, page 167.*

LAVENHAM PRIORY
LAVENHAM

Dating from the 13th century, this half-timbered former Benedictine priory has been restored in the style of the Elizabethan merchant's mansion it later became. The bedchambers, reached by oak staircases, have many original features: braced crown posts, wall paintings, massive oak floorboards. Guests have use of the Great Hall with its brick floor and enormous inglenook fireplace. *Read more, page 190.*

THE OLD RAILWAY STATION
PETWORTH

A fantasy fulfilled for lovers of the golden age of the railways. This disused railway station near Goodwood has intimate but well-furnished bedrooms in four Pullman carriages on a disused track bed. Two to a carriage, they have a 'surprisingly spacious' bathroom with a proper bath. Two larger bedrooms are in the restored station building. Check-in is at the ticket desk. *Read more, page 250.*

ARDANAISEIG
KILCHRENAN

Possibly the 'most peaceful hotel in Britain', this late Georgian baronial mansion lies in wooded grounds down more than ten miles of winding track. Guests seeking romance need look no further than the split-level converted Boat Shed on the shore of Loch Awe. It has its own boat, allowing couples to explore the tiny islands on the loch. *Read more, page 367.*

LITTLE BARWICK HOUSE
BARWICK
Tim (the chef) and Emma Ford promise 'a true foodie experience, modern English, without froths, foams and excessive twiddliness', at their popular restaurant-with-rooms (*pictured above*) near the Somerset/Dorset border. His menu of innovative (but not elaborate) dishes, which varies daily, might include confit of pork belly, roasted with honey and Chinese five spice, braised flageolet beans, Calvados sauce.
Read more, page 76.

THE WATERSIDE INN
BRAY
Chef/patron Alain Roux and his 'attentive, ever-smiling' manager, Diego Masciaga, run this renowned restaurant-with-rooms on the River Thames. The unwary might be shocked by the prices, but 'you get what you pay for, and more'. The glass-fronted restaurant (which overlooks the river) has held three *Michelin* stars since 1985 for the classic French cooking; a typical dish might be pan-fried medallion of veal, carrots, crispy calf's head fritter, white wine veal jus.
Read more, page107.

READ'S
FAVERSHAM
Liked for the combination of 'informality alongside splendour', Rona and David Pitchford's restaurant-with-rooms is a 'beautiful' Georgian manor house near an old market town. She is 'consistently keen to help guests' front-of-house'; he is the chef. Fresh local ingredients 'come to the fore' in dishes like roast loin of Kentish lamb with glazed apricots, croustillant of slow-braised shoulder, Savoy cabbage, carrot purée.
Read more: page 160.

THE GREAT HOUSE
LAVENHAM
Owners Régis and Martine Crépy have run this fine Georgian house on the market square of a medieval town for many years as a restaurant-with-rooms with a Gallic feel. The cooking of chef Enrique Bilbault is 'wonderful': his classic dishes might include steamed and seared monkfish tail on the bone, crushed garden peas with pancetta, white vermouth sauce. The service mainly by young French waiters, is 'charming, attentive, not at all snooty'.
Read more, page 189.

MR UNDERHILL'S
LUDLOW

The restaurant and the accommodation have been restyled this year at Christopher and Judy Bradley's restaurant-with-rooms on the banks of the River Teme. He is a self-taught chef whose cooking is 'playful' and imaginative. His eight-course set menu (no choice until dessert) might include white fish velouté, marmalade ice cream; lemon sole, chorizo crust, old amontillado and smoked almond.
Read more, page 205.

MORSTON HALL
MORSTON

The 'high-quality' cooking of Galton Blackiston attracts foodies to this Jacobean flint-and-brick mansion on the north Norfolk coast. He runs it as a restaurant-with-rooms with his wife, Tracy. Dinner, taken at a single sitting at 8 pm, has a no-choice four-course menu. Typical dishes: Morston Hall-style cock-a-leekie; locally farmed rabbit (rack, saddle, ravioli), carrot and cumin, chestnuts, pickled celeriac, Armagnac jus.
Read more, page 222.

JSW
PETERSFIELD

'The food is always excellent' at Jake Watkins's smart restaurant-with-rooms, a former coaching inn near the centre of a busy market town. He 'allows the ingredients to speak for themselves' in his simple dishes like scallops, cauliflower purée, cep vinaigrette; local wild seabass, samphire, Jersey Royals, sauce vierge. The chocolate truffles served with the coffee are 'unmissable'.
Read more, page 249.

THE PEAT INN
PEAT INN

In a hamlet near St Andrews, Geoffrey and Katherine Smeddle's restaurant-with-rooms is a 'real treat, worth saving for'. In the candlelit restaurant, he serves seasonal modern Scottish/French dishes, eg, maple-glazed breast of Gartmorn duck, Savoyarde potatoes, broad beans, pickled peaches, Madeira jus.
Read more, page 383

TYDDYN LLAN
LLANDRILLO

A reader warns against eating too many of the 'best-ever' canapés before dining at Bryan and Susan Webb's restaurant-with-rooms, a pretty Georgian country house with a shaded veranda on two sides. He cooks seasonal Welsh dishes, eg, crubeens (stuffed pig's trotters), piccalilli, Wirral watercress salad; roast turbot, leek risotto, red wine sauce. 'Great service' is provided by an 'efficient, young staff'.
Read more, page 432

PLAS BODEGROES
PWLLHELI

In a Georgian house on the remote Lleyn peninsula, Chris and Gunna Chown's restaurant-with-rooms is liked for the 'warmth of the welcome, and the relaxing ambience'. In a dining room decorated with modern Welsh paintings, Chris Chown and Hugh Bracegirdle, the chefs, prepare 'beautifully presented' modern interpretations of traditional dishes: perhaps broccoli soup, almond cappucino; breast of organic chicken, legmeat sausage, butternut squash tortellini, thyme sauce.
Read more: page 448.

THE VICTORIA
LONDON

Celebrity chef Paul Merrett and restaurateur Greg Bellamy own this pub-with-rooms with 'a nice local atmosphere' near Richmond Park. The conservatory restaurant has 'imaginative' menus with dishes like seared bass, laksa, roasted peanuts, chilli and lime. A light supper (charcuterie board, cheese board, salmon plate) is served on Sunday nights in the winter months; the summer brings evening barbecues.

Read more, page 53.

THE DEVONSHIRE ARMS AT BEELEY
BEELEY

Chef/patron Alan Hill runs this 'delightful pub', a 17th-century coaching inn on the Chatsworth estate, for the Duke and Duchess of Devonshire. In the brasserie extension, he serves a seasonally changing menu of 'gastro classics' (eg, potted duck; beer-battered fish and chips) in 'generous portions'; and daily specials, perhaps assiette of Youlgreave pork (fillet, belly, ham), pudding, beetroots and apple.

Read more, page 86.

THE BILDESTON CROWN
BILDESTON

Suffolk farmer James Buckle has restored this old coaching inn in a sleepy Suffolk village; his herd of Red Poll cattle supplies the kitchen with beef. The 'exceptional' cooking of chef Chris Lee can be taken in two bar areas and the formal *Ingrams* restaurant. Traditional dishes are brought up to date on his 'classics' menu; a 'select' menu has more elaborate choices, eg, poached and roasted breast of guineafowl, sprouts, chestnuts, watercress.

Read more, page 92.

THE HORSE AND GROOM
BOURTON-ON-THE-HILL

Brothers Tom and Will (the chef) Greenstock are the cheerful hosts at this former coaching inn in a Cotswold village of honey-stone houses. In the open-plan bar and restaurant, the blackboard menu has daily specials. Will Greenstock uses local produce and vegetables from the garden for dishes like home-cured salt beef, beetroot and horseradish relish; griddled Dexter sirloin steak, garlic, parsley and shallots.

Read more, page 100.

THE TROUT AT TADPOLE BRIDGE
BUCKLAND MARSH

Popular with locals and boating visitors (six moorings are free if you dine in the restaurant), Gareth and Helen Pugh's old stone pub (*pictured opposite*) stands by a narrow bridge over the River Thames. In the informal restaurant and bar, chef Pascal Clavaud cooks modern dishes like bubble and squeak, poached egg, Hollandaise sauce; confit of duck leg, black pudding mash, red onion gravy.
Read more, page 116.

THE SUN INN
DEDHAM

Piers Baker's discreetly restored 15th-century coaching inn stands opposite St Mary's Church on Dedham's main street. In the open-plan dining room, chefs Ugo Simonelli and Ewan Naylon serve a daily-changing modern menu with an Italian twist. Typical dishes: handmade pasta stuffed with pork, partridge, pancetta, juniper and sage; grilled salt marsh lamb, roasted red and yellow beetroots, salsa verde.
Read more, page 146.

THE SWAN INN
SWINBROOK

In a 'delightful' rural village near Burford, this lovely old inn has been styled in homage to the Mitford sisters, with large black-and-white pictures of the family and associated memorabilia. In the bar and restaurant, 'excellent' meals are served on a seasonal menu. It might include smoked mackerel with beetroot salad; shredded venison confit, haricot blanc, thyme and black pudding.
Read more, page 294.

THE GURNARD'S HEAD
ZENNOR

'Oozing character and generosity', Charles and Edmund Inkin's laid-back inn is 'homely and likeable'. There are open fires and wooden tables in the bar and restaurant. Chef Bruce Rennie's seasonal menu is led by what his suppliers bring to the back door: 'fish from day boats, greenery from small growers'. It might include wild garlic soup, scallop, salted almonds; lamb rump and breast, parsley risotto, oyster mushrooms.
Read more, page 329.

THE FELIN FACH GRIFFIN
FELIN FACH

Julie Bell manages this old coaching inn near Brecon for Charles and Edmund Inkin (who also own *The Gurnard's Head*, see above). The chef, Ross Bruce, turns to the kitchen gardener, Joe Hand, for vegetables, herbs and soft fruit. His short, seasonal supper menu has dishes like tomato and mozzarella on ciabatta, basil and red wine dressing; coins of monkfish, new potatoes, corn, pancetta.
Read more, page 425.

THE BELL AT SKENFRITH
SKENFRITH

By a bridge over the River Monnow, this refurbished 17th-century coaching inn is run by owners Janet and William Hutchings. In the 'elegant, well-run' dining room, chef Kieran Gough's modern dishes use local produce, heritage vegetables from the large kitchen garden. A typical dish: rump of Welsh lamb, smoked mashed potato, sautéed bacon and cabbage, apricot purée.
Read more, page 451.

BLAGDON MANOR
ASHWATER
'They made us really welcome, as did their chocolate Labradors.' Cassie and Mace, the resident canines, 'always look forward to meeting new friends'. Visiting dogs to Liz and Steve Morey's 17th-century manor house are given a fleece blanket, dog bowl and treats 'to make their stay as comfortable as yours'. There is excellent walking in 17 acres of open fields around the manor.
Read more, page 68.

COMBE HOUSE
GITTISHAM
Dog-owners are given a K9 survival pack and an illustrated booklet of dog-friendly walks at Ken and Ruth Hunt's Grade I listed Elizabethan manor house on a large estate of woodland and pastures. Pets can safely play in the walled garden of a thatched cottage in the grounds. Guests are asked for their dog's name when booking, to ensure canines are properly greeted on arrival.
Read more, page 164.

OVERWATER HALL
IREBY
'Perfect for dogs, on or off the leash', this castellated Georgian mansion is in an isolated part of the northern Lake District. Dog-owners need not venture beyond the 18-acre grounds to exercise their best friends. Pets are allowed to sit in one of the lounges ('not on chairs, please') and in the bedrooms. A dog-sitting service is offered for days when an owner might wish to visit a museum or art gallery.
Read more, page 183.

THE COTTAGE IN THE WOOD
MALVERN WELLS
Up to two well-behaved dogs ('or any other pets') are welcomed in the ground-floor rooms in *The Pinnacles*, 100 yards from the main building of this Georgian house. Dogs are 'made to feel at home' and provided with a bed, biscuits and a water bowl. Paths across the Malvern Hills can be accessed from the door.
Read more, page 210.

PLUMBER MANOR
STURMINSTER NEWTON
'It is easy to take your dog for a walk whenever necessary,' say the Prideaux-

Brune family, who welcome canines to four courtyard bedrooms at their 17th-century manor house. These rooms have direct access to the gardens. Dogs are not allowed in the main house. There are long country walks from the door. *Read more, page 292.*

PRINCE HALL
TWO BRIDGES

Fi and Chris Daly and their resident canine hostess, Polo, promise 'doggy decadence' at this small hotel high on Dartmoor. Dog-friendly bedrooms have space for 'a pet bed or two'; doggie treats are provided. Polo can advise on the 'best spots to curl up while the owners enjoy lunch or dinner'. There are extensive grounds in which to romp and roam. An outside tap, a sponge and towels are provided to keep muddy paws clean. Emergency supplies of dog food are available. *Read more, page 307.*

HOLBECK GHYLL
WINDERMERE

Dogs are given their own welcome pack at this former hunting lodge in large grounds overlooking Lake Windermere. The hotel has teamed up with Mungo and Maud, the 'edgy' pet outfitters, to provide a VIC package for Very Important Canines. It includes a luxury dog bed, a blanket, a bowl, a bag of organic treats and a toy to take home. The resident dog, Daisy, 'will generously allow you to tickle her ears'. *Read more, page 323.*

THE BONHAM
EDINBURGH

Guests wishing to travel with their four-legged friends can take advantage of a 'doggy dreams' package at this town house hotel in a quiet square near the West End. It includes a welcome toy and treat, and an in-room meal 'prepared by our chefs' (perhaps a luxury bowl of meat, pasta and vegetables, though regular dog food can be provided for fussy eaters). A dog bed guarantees a comfortable night's sleep. *Read more, page 352.*

KILCAMB LODGE
STRONTIAN

Milly, the resident pooch at this old stone lodge on the shore of Loch Sunart, has her own Facebook page with helpful advice for visiting dogs. She recommends walks in the ancient forests, and splashing in the loch. Extra towels, bags, mats for feeding bowls and treats are provided. Four pet-friendly rooms are close to an exit that leads directly into the grounds for 'calls of nature'. *Read more, page 395, even if you don't have a dog!*

RATHMULLAN HOUSE
RATHMULLAN

'We hate leaving our own dogs in the kennels when we go on holiday,' says Mark Wheeler who provides a superior doggy room in the courtyard extension of this handsome white mansion on the shores of Lough Swilly. The room, adjoining the human bedroom, has a bed, doggie pics and a coat hook. Company is on hand 'courtesy of our own Jack Russell, Brushie, but be warned, she is known as the MD'. There is good walking on the beach. *Read more, page 494.*

Each of these hotels has a tennis court (T) and/or a swimming pool (S)

LONDON
One Aldwych,
  Strand (S)

ENGLAND
Deans Place,
  Alfriston (S)
Hartwell House,
  Aylesbury (T,S)
Bath Priory,
  Bath (S)
Park House,
  Bepton (T,S)
Burgh Island,
  Bigbury-on-Sea (T,S)
Blakeney,
  Blakeney (S)
Hell Bay,
  Bryher (S)
Gidleigh Park,
  Chagford (T)
Tor Cottage,
  Chillaton (S)
Treglos,
  Constantine Bay (S)
Corse Lawn House,
  Corse Lawn (T,S)
Rectory,
  Crudwell (S)
Dart Marina,
  Dartmouth (S)
Old Whyly,
  East Hoathly (T,S)

Starborough Manor,
  Edenbridge (S)
Summer Lodge,
  Evershot (T,S)
Evesham,
  Evesham (S)
Stock Hill House,
  Gillingham (T)
Hambleton Hall,
  Hambleton (T,S)
Augill Castle,
  Kirkby Stephen (T)
Feathers,
  Ledbury (S)
Lime Wood,
  Lyndhurst (S)
Bedruthan Steps,
  Mawgan Porth (T,S)
Scarlet,
  Mawgan Porth (S)
Budock Vean,
  Mawnan Smith (T,S)
Eshott Hall,
  Morpeth (T)
Mullion Cove,
  Mullion Cove (S)
TerraVina,
  Netley Marsh (S)
Chewton Glen,
  New Milton (T,S)
Newick Park,
  Newick (T,S)
Old Rectory,
  Norwich (S)

Hotel Penzance,
  Penzance (S)
St Enodoc,
  Rock (S)
Rose Vale,
  St Agnes (S)
Ennys,
  St Hilary (T,S)
Star Castle,
  St Mary's (T,S)
Tides Reach,
  Salcombe (S)
Soar Mill Cove,
  Soar Mill Cove (T,S)
Plumber Manor,
  Sturminster Newton (T)
Calcot Manor,
  Tetbury (T,S)
Nare,
  Veryan-in-Roseland (T,S)
Holbeck Ghyll,
  Windermere (T)
Watersmeet,
  Woolacombe (S)
Middlethorpe Hall,
  York (S)

SCOTLAND
Glenapp Castle,
  Ballantrae (T)
Isle of Eriska,
  Eriska (T,S)
Inverlochy Castle,
  Fort William (T)
Ardanaiseig,
  Kilchrenan (T)
New Lanark Mill,
  Lanark (S)
Kirroughtree House,
  Newton Stewart (T)
Skirling House,
  Skirling (T)

WALES
Trefeddian,
  Aberdyfi (T,S)

Porth Tocyn,
  Abersoch (T,S)
Glangrwyney Court,
  Crickhowell (T)
Gliffaes,
  Crickhowell (T)
Bodysgallen Hall and Spa,
  Llandudno (T,S)
St Tudno,
  Llandudno (S)
Lake,
  Llangammarch Wells (T,S)
Portmeirion,
  Portmeirion (S)

CHANNEL ISLANDS
White House,
  Herm (T,S)
Atlantic,
  St Brelade (T,S)
Longueville Manor,
  St Saviour (T,S)

IRELAND
Cashel House,
  Cashel Bay (T)
Rathsallagh House,
  Dunlavin (T)
Marlfield House,
  Gorey (T)
Shelburne Lodge,
  Kenmare (T)
Rosleague Manor,
  Letterfrack (T)
Currarevagh House,
  Oughterard (T)
Rathmullan House,
  Rathmullan (T,S)
Coopershill,
  Riverstown (T)
Ballymaloe House,
  Shanagarry (T,S)
Ardtara,
  Upperlands (T)

Each of these hotels has at least one bedroom equipped for a visitor in a wheelchair. You should telephone to discuss individual requirements

LONDON

Montague on the Gardens,
 Bloomsbury
Zetter,
 Clerkenwell
Arch,
 Marble Arch
Victoria,
 Mortlake
One Aldwych,
 Strand
Goring,
 Victoria

ENGLAND

Wentworth,
 Aldeburgh
Deans Place,
 Alfriston
Rothay Manor,
 Ambleside
Hartwell House,
 Aylesbury
Bath Priory,
 Bath
Park House,
 Bepton
Bildeston Crown,
 Bildeston
du Vin Birmingham,
 Birmingham

Millstream,
 Bosham
Woolley Grange,
 Bradford-on-Avon
White Horse,
 Brancaster Staithe
Brooks,
 Bristol
Hell Bay,
 Bryher
Pendragon Country House,
 Camelford
Blackmore Farm,
 Cannington
Gidleigh Park,
 Chagford
Captain's Club,
 Christchurch
Beech House & Olive Branch,
 Clipsham
Treglos,
 Constantine Bay
Hipping Hall,
 Cowan Bridge
Clow Beck House,
 Croft-on-Tees
Coach House at Crookham,
 Crookham

Dart Marina,
 Dartmouth
Dedham Hall,
 Dedham
Summer Lodge,
 Evershot
Evesham,
 Evesham
Le Manoir,
 Great Milton
Stag and Huntsman,
 Hambleden
Battlesteads,
 Hexham
Byfords,
 Holt
Slaughters Country Inn,
 Lower Slaughter
Lime Wood,
 Lyndhurst
Cottage in the Wood,
 Malvern Wells
Swinton Park,
 Masham
Bedruthan Steps,
 Mawgan Porth
Scarlet,
 Mawgan Porth
Midland,
 Morecambe

Manor House,
Moreton-in-Marsh
Redesdale Arms,
Moreton-in-Marsh
TerraVina,
Netley Marsh
Chewton Glen,
New Milton
Jesmond Dene House,
Newcastle upon Tyne
Newick Park,
Newick
Beechwood,
North Walsham
Hart's,
Nottingham
Grange at Oborne,
Oborne
Old Bank,
Oxford
Old Parsonage,
Oxford
Elephant,
Pangbourne
Old Railway Station,
Petworth
Black Swan,
Ravenstonedale
Burgoyne,
Reeth
Rose Vale,
St Agnes
Titchwell Manor,
Titchwell
Tuddenham Hall,
Tuddenham
Nare,
Veryan-in-Roseland
Holbeck Ghyll,
Windermere
Watersmeet,
Woolacombe

Middlethorpe Hall,
York

SCOTLAND
Boath House,
Auldearn
Dunvalanree in Carradale,
Carradale
Killoran House,
Dervaig
**Three Chimneys and
House Over-By,**
Dunvegan
Bonham,
Edinburgh
Lovat,
Fort Augustus
New Lanark Mill,
Lanark
Langass Lodge,
Locheport
Sunny Brae,
Nairn
Craigatin House,
Pitlochry
Green Park,
Pitlochry
Viewfield House,
Portree
Skirling House,
Skirling
Torridon,
Torridon

WALES
Harbourmaster,
Aberaeron
Ye Olde Bulls Head,
Beaumaris
Penbontbren,
Glynarthen

Hand at Llanarmon,
Llanarmon Dyffryn
Ceiriog
Tyddan Llan,
Llandrillo
Bodysgallen Hall and Spa,
Llandudno
Lake,
Llangammarch Wells
Hafod Elwy Hall,
Pentrefoelas
Portmeirion,
Portmeirion

IRELAND
**Mustard Seed at Echo
Lodge,**
Ballingarry
Stella Maris,
Ballycastle
Seaview House,
Ballylickey
Quay House,
Clifden
Rayanne House,
Holywood
No. 1 Pery Square,
Limerick
Sheedy's,
Lisdoonvarna
Rathmullan House,
Rathmullan
Ardtara,
Upperlands

LONDON

Whitehall seen from St James's Park

BLOOMSBURY

THE MONTAGUE ON THE GARDENS

Near the British Museum, this Georgian town house hotel is liked for its warm, personal touch: 'The staff don't speak like trained robots.' It is managed by Dirk Crokaert for the Red Carnation group. The public rooms are lavishly decorated: a bold red lounge has draped curtains and crystal chandeliers; a striking conservatory mixes stripes and graphic floral prints. With patterned wallpaper, gilded mirrors and hand-crafted furniture, the individually styled bedrooms can be equally flamboyant; extra touches ('unusual at this price range') include complimentary mineral water, 'proper' coffee, fresh fruit. Children are welcomed with games, DVDs, their own slippers and bathrobe. In the informal *Blue Door* bistro, chef Martin Halls serves a seasonal menu which might include spring pea soup, smoked bacon; seared beef fillet, sautéed morels, baby carrots. There are light meals and snacks at the *Terrace* bar, and summer barbecues on the wood-deck. Afternoon tea may be taken on the terrace overlooking the private gardens of Bedford Square. 'This is the sort of place that restores your faith in London.' More reports, please.

15 Montague Street
London WC1B 5BJ

T: 020-7637 1001
F: 020-7637 2516
E: bookmt@rchmail.com
W: www.montaguehotel.com

BEDROOMS: 100, 1 suitable for &.
OPEN: all year.
FACILITIES: lobby, lounge, 2 conservatories, *Terrace* bar, *Blue Door* bistro, free Wi-Fi, civil wedding licence, terrace.
BACKGROUND MUSIC: classic contemporary in public areas, pianist in *Terrace* bar in evening except Sun.
LOCATION: Bloomsbury, underground Russell Square.
CHILDREN: all ages welcomed.
DOGS: not allowed in dining rooms.
CREDIT CARDS: all major cards.
PRICES: [2013] per room B&B single £216–£360, double £234–£666. Set menu from £24.50 (*plus 12½% discretionary service charge*).

SEE ALSO SHORTLIST

CAMBERWELL GREEN

CHURCH STREET HOTEL

'A flamboyant, friendly place of great character that makes a refreshing change from the usual London hotel experience.' José and Mel Raido's idiosyncratic hotel in Camberwell Green 'may not be perfect', say *Guide* inspectors (visiting in 2013), but 'it is a one-off, giving good fun at reasonable prices'. The Greek/Spanish brothers have decorated in 'extravagant' Latino style. A stained-glass window of flying angels lights the entrance; the bedrooms have vivid colours, religious art. 'Our high-ceilinged room above the restaurant had electric-blue walls, white-painted furnishings; niches on the wall held crucifixes, bottles of rum; there were complimentary bars of chocolate and interesting books on a small table; the bathroom was a riot of Mexican tiles.' There may be some noise from the corridor and the busy road ('double glazing and earplugs help'). Eight of the smaller – and cheaper – rooms have shared bathrooms. The 'excellent' *Angels & Gypsies* restaurant is popular locally for its tapas menu: it has exposed brick walls, wooden tables on a wooden floor ('busy and buzzy'). The continental breakfast is taken at communal tables in the residents' lounge.

29–33 Camberwell Church Street
London SE5 8TR

T: 020-7703 5984
F: 020-7358-4110
E: info@churchstreethotel.com
W: www.churchstreethotel.com

BEDROOMS: 28.
OPEN: all year, restaurant closed 24/25 Dec, 1/2 Jan.
FACILITIES: lounge/breakfast room, free Wi-Fi, restaurant, unsuitable for &.
BACKGROUND MUSIC: 'easy listening' in public areas.
LOCATION: Camberwell Green, underground Oval.
CHILDREN: all ages welcomed.
DOGS: not allowed.
CREDIT CARDS: Amex, MasterCard, Visa.
PRICES: per room B&B (continental) £60–£160. À la carte £28.

SEE ALSO SHORTLIST

CHELSEA

THE DRAYCOTT

The union flag flies above this luxury hotel, part of Adrian Gardiner's Mantis group. It is a conversion of three adjoining Edwardian town houses in a quiet street close to Sloane Square. Melissa Stoman is the manager. 'It is expensive, but a good base for anyone who can afford it: the impeccable service lives up to the cost,' said inspectors. Nina Campbell was responsible for the refurbishment of the 'charming' drawing room and the breakfast room. Afternoon tea, champagne and hot chocolate (served in the drawing room) are included in the room rates. Each of the original houses has a 'fine' wooden staircase; a warren of corridors and small lifts provide access to the bedrooms. Edwardian features are retained in rooms which are 'not the least bit designerish'. A room with a moulded ceiling and floor-to-ceiling windows with heavy curtains had a sofa in front of a gas fire, a drinks cupboard, a desk, table and chairs for meals; 'a lived-in feel'. There is no restaurant (many eating places are close by); guests can dine in from a 24-hour room-service menu.

25% DISCOUNT VOUCHERS

26 Cadogan Gardens
London SW3 2RP

T: 020-7730 6466
F: 020-7730 0236
E: reservations@draycotthotel.com
W: www.draycotthotel.com

BEDROOMS: 35.
OPEN: all year.
FACILITIES: drawing room, library, breakfast room, free Wi-Fi, 1-acre garden, unsuitable for &.
BACKGROUND MUSIC: classical in breakfast room.
LOCATION: Chelsea, underground Sloane Square.
CHILDREN: all ages welcomed.
DOGS: not allowed in breakfast room.
CREDIT CARDS: all major cards.
PRICES: [2013] per room B&B £165–£470, D,B&B £215–£520. Set menus £40–£65. 1-night bookings sometimes refused.

SEE ALSO SHORTLIST

CHELSEA

Map 2:D4

SAN DOMENICO HOUSE

In a residential street close to Sloane Square, the Melpignano family's boutique hotel is spread across two Victorian red brick houses. It has been extended and renovated throughout. 'Decorations and fittings reveal impeccable taste,' said an inspector. 'The entrance hall is imposing; there is a luxurious, inviting lounge. The staff are personable and obliging.' The walls and corridors are hung with 'prints of the famous from previous centuries'. The bedrooms, individually decorated, are furnished with 'beautiful and distinguished antiques' (perhaps a carved bedhead, a gilded mirror, a chaise longue). Each has a 'well-lit' marble bathroom (dressing gowns and slippers supplied). The modern facilities (air conditioning, free Wi-Fi, illuminated wardrobe with safe) are 'high class'. Some rooms have a balcony with a small terrace overlooking Chelsea. There is no restaurant, but a room-service menu (salads, sandwiches, etc) is available. Breakfast, in a basement room with white walls, a marble fireplace, has 'good' coffee and bacon, freshly squeezed orange juice. The hotel has 'a most pleasing and relaxing ambience and an emphasis on comfort and service. It will not disappoint.'

25% DISCOUNT VOUCHERS

29–31 Draycott Place
London SW3 2SH

T: 020-7581 5757
F: 020-7584 1348
E: info@sandomenicohouse.com
W: www.sandomenicohouse.com

BEDROOMS: 17.
OPEN: all year.
FACILITIES: lounge, breakfast room, roof terrace, free Wi-Fi, unsuitable for &.
BACKGROUND MUSIC: classical in lounge.
LOCATION: Chelsea, underground Sloane Square.
CHILDREN: all ages welcomed.
DOGS: not allowed.
CREDIT CARDS: all major cards.
PRICES: [2013] (*excluding VAT*) room £255–£390. Breakfast (*including VAT*) £14.40–£21.60.

SEE ALSO SHORTLIST

CLERKENWELL

Map 2:D4

THE ZETTER

'Laid back and quirky', this contemporary conversion of a Victorian warehouse (later the headquarters of a pools company) is in fashionable Clerkenwell. 'It is not a design hotel as such, just an easy-going place with imaginative styling,' said an inspector. The staff are 'exceptionally friendly; a porter, who carted our bag to the room, explained how everything worked; later he rescued me with a smile when I failed to work the coffee machine in the corridor'. The bedrooms come in various sizes, from 'compact' rooms to roof-top studios and suites, each of which has a private patio. They are decorated in bright colours and have retro furnishings (1960s chairs, bean bags). The hotel's much-praised *Bistrot Bruno Loubet* overlooks St John's Square. At breakfast, a 'superb' continental buffet has freshly squeezed orange juice, crunchy home-made granola; large loaves of fresh bread, pastries and croissants; a wide selection of cooked dishes. A green ethos is followed; drinking water is pumped from a well below the building; air conditioning switches off when a window is opened. The owners, Mark Sainsbury and Michael Benyan, also developed the *Zetter Townhouse* (see next entry).

86–88 Clerkenwell Road
London EC1M 5RJ

T: 020-7324 4444
F: 020-7324 4445
E: reservations@thezetter.com
W: www.thezetter.com

BEDROOMS: 59, 2 suitable for &.
OPEN: all year.
FACILITIES: 2 lifts, ramps, cocktail bar/lounge, restaurant, 2 function/meeting rooms, free Wi-Fi.
BACKGROUND MUSIC: 'low-volume' eclectic mix.
LOCATION: Clerkenwell, by St John's Sq, NCP garage 5 mins' walk, underground Farringdon.
CHILDREN: all ages welcomed.
DOGS: only guide dogs allowed.
CREDIT CARDS: Amex, MasterCard, Visa.
PRICES: [2013] room (*excluding VAT*) from £185. Continental breakfast £9.50, à la carte £30.

SEE ALSO SHORTLIST

CLERKENWELL

Map 2:D4

THE ZETTER TOWNHOUSE

🏆*César award in 2012*

On St John's Square, Michael Benyan and Mark Sainsbury's intimate town house hotel is 'welcoming and comfortable, a real find in London', say fellow *Guide* hoteliers: 'It has the small hotel feel in spades.' Other praise in 2013: 'I love its original style, so unlike faceless chain hotels.' The ground floor is designed as if it were the home of an eccentric aunt ('we call her Wilhelmina'): every surface is covered by her 'collection': antique ceramics, bronzes, old postcards, a stuffed kangaroo. There are velvet sofas and armchairs, huge vases of fresh flowers, in the 'excellent' cocktail bar. The 'wit and flair', attention to detail and 'outstanding' service are praised. The bedrooms have reclaimed and vintage furniture; headboards from fairgrounds, antique walnut wardrobes. 'Good bedside lighting'. There are huge drench showers. Breakfast can be taken in the bedroom (cooked dishes from the room-service menu); the bar has a continental selection. Or cross the square to the *Bruno Loubet* restaurant ('excellent and surprisingly good value') in the sister *Zetter* hotel (see previous entry). (*David and Heather Armstrong, Nick Patton, and others*)

49–50 St John's Square
London EC1V 4JJ

T: 020-7324 4567
F: 020-7324 4456
E: reservations@thezetter.com
W: www.thezettertownhouse.com

BEDROOMS: 13.
OPEN: all year.
FACILITIES: cocktail lounge, private dining room, games room, free Wi-Fi.
BACKGROUND MUSIC: in public areas.
LOCATION: Clerkenwell, underground Farringdon.
CHILDREN: all ages welcomed.
DOGS: only guide dogs allowed.
CREDIT CARDS: Amex, MasterCard, Visa.
PRICES: [2013] room (*excluding VAT*) from £205. Continental breakfast £9.50.

SEE ALSO SHORTLIST

COVENT GARDEN

THE FIELDING

'A delightful treat for opera fans', this privately owned small hotel is steps away from the Royal Opera House. It is liked for the location and the 'friendly' staff; Grace Langley is the manager. 'Superb photographs of ballet adorn the walls; other decorations reflect the history of the area,' says a visitor in 2013. After nightfall, fairy lights strung about the Georgian facade add a 'romantic' air. Up a narrow staircase, the bedrooms are simply decorated in shades of sage, cream and burgundy. They are 'modern, comfortable, clean and tidy'. 'Our second-floor room had plenty of storage space, and was equipped with everything one could need, like air conditioning. Slippers and black eye shades were provided, a nice touch. The bathroom had a large shower cubicle, simple but high-quality toiletries; a toothbrush and toothpaste.' Another comment: 'The most peaceful night we have ever had in London.' *The Fielding* has no public rooms, and no meals are served, but there is a wide choice of restaurants and cafés in the neighbourhood. Guests have free access to a nearby health centre. (*Penelope Visman, Richard James*)

4 Broad Court
Bow Street
London WC2B 5QZ

T: 020-7836 8305
F: 020-7497 0064
E: reservations@
thefieldinghotel.co.uk
W: www.thefieldinghotel.co.uk

BEDROOMS: 25.
OPEN: all year.
FACILITIES: no public rooms, free Wi-Fi, unsuitable for &.
BACKGROUND MUSIC: none.
LOCATION: central, underground Covent Garden.
CHILDREN: all ages welcomed.
DOGS: not allowed.
CREDIT CARDS: all major cards.
PRICES: [2013] room (*excluding VAT*) £108–£240.

SEE ALSO SHORTLIST

EARLS COURT

Map 2:D4

THE ROCKWELL

'The atmosphere is relaxed' (say inspectors) at this contemporary hotel, a conversion of two stucco-fronted town houses in Earls Court. Owned by Michael Squire (an architect) and Tony Bartlett, it is managed by Ocky Paller. The bedrooms vary greatly in size from small single rooms to split-level mezzanine suites. 'The styling is minimalist without being spare; cream walls with splashes of colour (a mauve bed cover, two blue armchairs); furnishings and fittings were in light oak; a big headboard had built-in side tables (lighting was excellent). Turndown in the evening revealed sheets and blankets on the large bed; mineral water and robes were provided (but no tea tray – 24-hour room service). Double glazing eliminated traffic noise.' The large lobby/lounge has a huge fitted bookcase, sofas and armchairs around a coffee table with newspapers and magazines. The bar/dining room overlooks a south-facing courtyard garden accessed by a glass bridge. Breakfast has a 'good' continental buffet (a freshly baked loaf for toast); cereals, croissants, pastries; salamis and cheese. 'The prices are modest for such a good position close to the museums and good shopping.'

181 Cromwell Road
London SW5 0SF

T: 020-7244 2000
F: 020-7244 2001
E: enquiries@therockwell.com
W: www.therockwell.com

BEDROOMS: 40, 1 on ground floor.
OPEN: all year.
FACILITIES: lift, ramps, lobby, lounge, bar, restaurant, conference room, free Wi-Fi, garden.
BACKGROUND MUSIC: in bar.
LOCATION: 1 mile SW of Marble Arch, opposite Cromwell Hospital, underground Earls Court.
CHILDREN: all ages welcomed.
DOGS: not allowed.
CREDIT CARDS: Amex, MasterCard, Visa.
PRICES: room £90–£176. Breakfast £9.50–£12.50, à la carte £28.

SEE ALSO SHORTLIST

KNIGHTSBRIDGE

Map 2:D4

THE CAPITAL

🏅 *César award in 2008*

Minutes from Hyde Park and Harrods, David Levin's tradition-steeped stone and red-brick town house hotel has welcomed a new member to the family. In a Nina Campbell-designed dining room, chef Nathan Outlaw – who runs Britain's only *Michelin*-starred fish restaurant, in Cornwall – has opened *Outlaw's at The Capital*, specialising in seafood (eg, citrus-cured bream, horseradish yogurt, fennel; or brill, anchovy potato, kale). 'Dinner was outstanding, with Mr Levin's Sauvignon [from his organic Loire valley vineyard] to wash it down. The staff were very good, even finding out where the butter had been sourced.' Lighter meals can be taken in the bar. The hotel holds fast to its heritage: individually styled bedrooms have hand-stitched mattresses, elegant English fabrics, and antiques and original artwork from the Levin collection. Some rooms can be interconnected for a family. There are hot chocolate and home-made jams and marmalades at breakfast; afternoon tea, with home-baked scones and pastries, is served daily in the sitting room. 'Mr Levin clearly sets high standards.' He also owns *The Levin*, next door (see entry). (*Robert and Shirley Lyne*)

22–24 Basil Street
London SW3 1AT

T: 020-7589 5171
F: 020-7225 0011
E: reservations@capitalhotel.co.uk
W: www.capitalhotel.co.uk

BEDROOMS: 49.
OPEN: all year (restaurant closed Sun).
FACILITIES: lift, sitting room, bar, restaurant, brasserie/bar next door, only restaurant suitable for ♿, free Wi-Fi.
BACKGROUND MUSIC: soft jazz in bar in evenings.
LOCATION: central, underground Knightsbridge, private car park.
CHILDREN: all ages welcomed.
DOGS: small dogs, on request.
CREDIT CARDS: all major cards.
PRICES: [2013] per room B&B (continental, excluding VAT) £270–£600, D,B&B £370–£700. Cooked breakfast £19.50 per person, à la carte £50, tasting menu £70 (*plus 12½% discretionary service charge*).

SEE ALSO SHORTLIST

KNIGHTSBRIDGE

Map 2:D4

THE LEVIN

'An ideal base for consumer therapy' (close to the Knightsbridge shops), David Levin's small town house hotel is 'immaculate', say visitors in 2013. 'Mr Levin clearly sets high standards; everything is just about perfect. The staff are interested and interesting, remembering previous conversations.' Harald Duttine is the manager. A dramatic threaded light installation hangs from the ceiling to the floor of the stairwell in the small lobby, which has an honesty bar and seating with newspapers. There are just 12 bedrooms: 'Our standard room was not large, but was well appointed; the bed was comfortable, and the lighting was good (we could actually read in bed); an excellent bathroom.' In the basement, meals are served from 7.30 am until late evening in *Le Metro* bar and bistro. Breakfast has a lavish buffet with 'especially good croissants and pastries from the owner's bakery'; a wide variety of cooked dishes (extra charge). The dining menu has classics (eg, fish and chips) and 'grazing' dishes like tempura king prawns. The wine list includes a Sauvignon Blanc from David Levin's Loire valley vineyard. (*Robert and Shirley Lyne, and others*)

28 Basil Street
London SW3 1AS

T: 020-7589 6286
F: 020-7823 7826
E: reservations@thelevinhotel.co.uk
W: www.thelevinhotel.co.uk

BEDROOMS: 12.
OPEN: all year, restaurant closed Sun after 5.30 pm.
FACILITIES: lobby, library, honesty bar, bar/brasserie (*Le Metro*), free Wi-Fi, access to nearby health club/spa, unsuitable for &.
BACKGROUND MUSIC: in restaurant.
LOCATION: central, underground Knightsbridge (Harrods exit), private car park (£40 a night).
CHILDREN: all ages welcomed.
DOGS: not allowed.
CREDIT CARDS: all major cards.
PRICES: [2013] per room B&B (continental) £360–£660.
À la carte £30.

SEE ALSO SHORTLIST

MARBLE ARCH

Map 2:D4

THE ARCH

On a surprisingly quiet street near Marble Arch, this colourful modern hotel is liked for its 'excellent' restaurant, 'unfailingly helpful' staff and 'well-thought-through details'. A sympathetic conversion of seven Georgian town houses and two mews homes, 'it has an intimate feel for its size', *Guide* inspectors say. It is owned by Abraham Bejerano; Grant Powell is the manager. 'Comprehensively equipped' bedrooms have hand-printed wallpaper and original sash windows; in-room offerings are commended: fresh milk, a Nespresso coffee machine, complimentary soft drinks. A returning guest found a standard room 'pleasant but small', with a 'handsome' shower room ('though it overflowed'). In the 'informal' open-plan brasserie, chef Lawrence Glyzer's modern dishes might include terrine of foie gras, fig chutney, sourdough toast; pan-fried sea bass, braised fennel, razor clams; a 'wonderful' Earl Grey martini impressed. 'We received superb service and splendid food every evening from a small but comprehensive menu.' Breakfast is praised: 'especially good home-made muesli; eggs on sourdough toast; small jars of home-made preserves; proper butter'. (*WA, and others*)

50 Great Cumberland Place
London W1H 7FD

T: 020-7724 4700
F: 020-7724 4744
E: info@thearchlondon.com
W: www.thearchlondon.com

BEDROOMS: 82, 2 suitable for ⌷.
OPEN: all year.
FACILITIES: lobby, bar, brasserie, library, champagne salon, gym, free Wi-Fi.
BACKGROUND MUSIC: in public areas, all day and night.
LOCATION: near Marble Arch, underground Marble Arch.
CHILDREN: all ages welcomed.
DOGS: allowed.
CREDIT CARDS: Amex, MasterCard, Visa.
PRICES: [2013] room (*excluding VAT*) from £230. Breakfast £18.50–£21.50, à la carte £54 (*plus 12½% discretionary service charge*).

SEE ALSO SHORTLIST

MARBLE ARCH

Map 2:D4

THE GRAZING GOAT

With its natural wood tones, open fires and shades of ash and moss, this stylish pub-with-rooms brings a rustic feel to a 'peaceful little zone' near Marble Arch. Owned by the small Cubitt House group, it 'will appeal to the young at heart', say inspectors in 2013. 'It is not cheap but you get a thoughtfully furnished bedroom and exceptional bathroom in a good location.' Under the watch of two stuffed, bearded goats, the ground-floor bar 'heaves' with after-work drinkers; it has a long bar with stools and a decent cocktail list (a British Bellini is made with elderflower liqueur and Prosecco). The bedrooms are on the top three floors (no lift), with views of the neighbouring rooftops: 'Our room had a huge bed, a ceiling-height freestanding mirror, lots of storage.' Service in the panelled first-floor dining room is 'prompt and efficient'; the British bistro menu includes modern dishes such as cider-braised pork belly, white bean casserole, crackling. The 28-day-aged Castle of Mey steaks are 'particularly recommended'. A 'good' breakfast (charged extra) has 'splendid' bacon and eggs with sourdough toast.

6 New Quebec Street
London W1H 7RQ

T: 020-7724 7243
E: reservations@
thegrazinggoat.co.uk
W: www.thegrazinggoat.co.uk

BEDROOMS: 8.
OPEN: all year.
FACILITIES: bar, dining room, free Wi-Fi, unsuitable for &.
BACKGROUND MUSIC: in bar and dining room.
LOCATION: central, underground Marble Arch.
CHILDREN: all ages welcomed.
DOGS: allowed on ground floor only, not in bedrooms.
CREDIT CARDS: Amex, MasterCard, Visa.
PRICES: [2013] room £195–£225. Cooked breakfast from £6.50, à la carte £32 (plus 12½% discretionary service charge).

SEE ALSO SHORTLIST

MARYLEBONE

Map 2:D4

DURRANTS

🏵 *César award in 2010*

Decorated with antiques, fresh flowers and the odd pair of Staffordshire china dogs, this 'nicely traditional, very British' hotel has been owned by the Miller family for nearly 100 years. Ian McIntosh is the long-serving manager; the staff are 'very friendly'. The hotel occupies a conversion of four terraced houses with a Georgian facade: inside, the lounges have original paintings, engravings, and armchairs upholstered in tartans and florals. 'We loved the cosy bar with its coal fire.' The bedrooms (some have been refurbished this year) have classic English fabrics and a 'first-rate', handmade bed. They are 'well kitted out' but vary in size and style: one visitor liked his 'extremely pleasant' room at the front of the hotel while another room was thought 'small and dark'. In the wood-panelled restaurant, chef Cara Baird's menu is based on seasonally available produce, perhaps beetroot tart, horseradish crème fraîche; pan-fried sea bass, mussel and basil broth. Afternoon tea in the *Wallace Room* is 'excellent'. Breakfasts are 'properly cooked – not the ubiquitous buffet'. 'This is the type of personal, slightly eccentric hotel we like.' (*RC, and others*)

26–32 George Street
London W1H 5BJ

T: 020-7935 8131
F: 020-7487 3510
E: enquiries@durrantshotel.co.uk
W: www.durrantshotel.co.uk

BEDROOMS: 92, 7 on ground floor.
OPEN: all year, restaurant closed 25 Dec evening.
FACILITIES: lifts, ramp, bar, restaurant, lounge, 5 function rooms, Wi-Fi (£10 per 24 hours).
BACKGROUND MUSIC: none.
LOCATION: off Oxford Street, underground Bond Street, Baker Street.
CHILDREN: all ages welcomed.
DOGS: only guide dogs allowed.
CREDIT CARDS: Amex, MasterCard, Visa.
PRICES: [2013] room from £185. Set dinner (Sun–Fri) £17.50–£19.50, à la carte £50 (*excluding 'optional' 12½% service charge*).

SEE ALSO SHORTLIST

MORTLAKE

THE VICTORIA

In a leafy residential neighbourhood, this 'cheerful' pub-with-rooms has 'a nice local atmosphere'. It is owned by celebrity chef Paul Merrett and restaurateur Greg Bellamy. The cosy bar has dark woods, vintage Penguin paperbacks and a log fire; the conservatory restaurant has 'imaginative' menus, perhaps seared Cornish squid, spiced chickpea purée, Alejandro chorizo, coriander yogurt. A light supper (charcuterie board, cheese board, salmon plate) is served on Sunday nights in the winter months; the summer brings evening barbecues. The simple, modern bedrooms, in a separate building reached by a covered walkway, have a flat-screen TV, an iPod docking system and, in the bathroom, an 'efficient' shower. The pub is 'very family-friendly, especially in summer, when the large courtyard can be enjoyed'. A varied children's menu includes fresh fruit smoothies, hummus and grilled chicken sandwiches; a play area outside has swings and a climbing frame. Richmond Park, where herds of red and fallow deer roam the woodland, is just five minutes' walk away. Mortlake station, ten minutes' walk, is 25 minutes by train from London Waterloo.

25% DISCOUNT VOUCHERS

10 West Temple Sheen
London SW14 7RT

T: 020-8876 4238
F: 020-8878 3464
E: bookings@thevictoria.net
W: www.thevictoria.net

BEDROOMS: 7, 3 on ground floor, 1 suitable for &.
OPEN: all year.
FACILITIES: bar, restaurant, free Wi-Fi, garden.
BACKGROUND MUSIC: 'easy listening' throughout.
LOCATION: Mortlake (10 mins' walk) to Waterloo/Clapham Jct, car park.
CHILDREN: all ages welcomed.
DOGS: allowed in bar.
CREDIT CARDS: MasterCard, Visa.
PRICES: [2013] per room B&B (continental) single £120–£130, double £130–£160 (higher in Wimbledon weeks). Cooked breakfast from £8.50 per person, à la carte £35 (*plus 12½% discretionary service charge*).

SEE ALSO SHORTLIST

NOTTING HILL   Map 2:D4

THE PORTOBELLO

'The opposite of bland: there is nothing conventional about the *Portobello*.' *Guide* inspectors welcomed the 'enjoyable eccentricity' of Tim Herring and Johnny Ekperigin's 'discreet' hotel on an 'elegant' street in Notting Hill. Bedrooms vary considerably in size and style: guests should discuss their choice before booking (staff are 'frank' in their descriptions). The cheapest 'cabin' rooms are also the smallest; one of the best 'special' rooms has a small conservatory. 'In our quirky, Moroccan-themed room on the top floor, mirrors were cleverly used to create a feeling of light and space. There was a large, low bed, a window seat with cushions, an antique writing desk; excellent lighting. A claw-footed bath stood at one end of the room; the neat bathroom (tiny but perfectly formed) had a modern shower.' Breakfast can be taken in bed or in the 'charming' drawing room facing the garden ('alas, not open to guests'); orange juice is freshly squeezed; toast and pastries were 'unremarkable'. A 24-hour room-service menu is available; guests get a discount at nearby *Julie's*, the restaurant under the same ownership.

22 Stanley Gardens
London W11 2NG

T: 020-7727 2777
F: 020-7792 9641
E: info@portobellohotel.com
W: www.portobellohotel.com

BEDROOMS: 21 (smoking allowed in 5).
OPEN: all year except 24–28 Dec.
FACILITIES: lift, small bar, foyer/lounge, free Wi-Fi, access to nearby health club, unsuitable for &.
BACKGROUND MUSIC: none.
LOCATION: Notting Hill, meter parking, underground Notting Hill Gate.
CHILDREN: all ages welcomed.
DOGS: allowed.
CREDIT CARDS: Amex, MasterCard, Visa.
PRICES: [2013] per room B&B (continental, *excluding VAT*) £145–£320.

SEE ALSO SHORTLIST

SOHO

Map 2:D4

HAZLITT'S

❦*César award in 2002*

'The staff are helpful, everything is immaculate and the ambience is relaxing.' *Guide* inspectors this year were impressed by Peter McKay's quirky B&B hotel in Soho. Spread across a group of historic buildings, *Hazlitt's* is named after the essayist who lived in one of them. 'Unsurprisingly, there are books everywhere.' There is no signage on the entrance; 'admission is gained by a bell-push, but the welcome is warm'. The bedrooms are traditionally furnished: 'Our room, entered by a lobby with a wardrobe (free-range hangers), had a huge wooden bed with ceiling-high carved oak bedhead; the supremely comfortable bed was fitted with sheets and blankets as we requested. There were oil paintings on the dark panelled walls; damask curtains with tie-backs on the two windows; a desk, small table and two chairs; a deep large bath in the bathroom. Triple glazing cut out noise from the street.' A narrow passage downstairs leads from the entrance lobby to a library with an honesty bar and a sitting room. A simple breakfast of fruit salad, pastries and rolls is brought to the bedroom.

6 Frith Street
London W1D 3JA

T: 020-7434 1771
F: 020-7439 1524
E: reservations@hazlitts.co.uk
W: www.hazlittshotel.com

BEDROOMS: 30, 2 on ground floor.
OPEN: all year.
FACILITIES: lift, 2 sitting rooms, meeting room, free Wi-Fi, unsuitable for &.
BACKGROUND MUSIC: none.
LOCATION: Soho (front windows triple glazed, rear rooms quietest), NCP nearby, underground Tottenham Court Road, Leicester Square.
CHILDREN: all ages welcomed.
DOGS: not allowed.
CREDIT CARDS: all major cards.
PRICES: [2013] room (*excluding VAT*) £185–£750. Breakfast £11.95.

SEE ALSO SHORTLIST

SOUTH KENSINGTON

NUMBER SIXTEEN

♀ *César award in 2011*

'Courteous' staff create 'a personal, home-from-home feeling' at this modern hotel, part of the small Firmdale Hotels group. It is 'well situated' on a quiet side street near South Kensington's shops and museums. The bedrooms have bold prints, a 'wonderfully comfortable' bed, 'excellent' reading lights and a writing desk. 'No bland corporate anonymity here,' say visitors in 2013. 'Full marks for the good-sized, well-equipped bathroom.' Extra touches include an overnight shoe-cleaning service. Downstairs, 'colourful', light-filled drawing rooms have floor-to-ceiling windows; a conservatory opens on to the garden. There is a well-stocked honesty bar in the library. No restaurant, but a 24-hour room-service menu, served in bedrooms and public areas, includes classics such as Caesar salad, steak sandwiches and crab linguine. Children are welcomed with books, DVDs and popcorn, and their own bathrobe and toiletries; babysitting can be arranged. A comprehensive breakfast menu, normally charged extra, has healthy options such as organic porridge cooked with soya milk. (*Harry and Annette Medcalf, and others*)

16 Sumner Place
London SW7 3EG

T: 020-7589 5232
F: 020-7584 8615
E: sixteen@firmdale.com
W: www.firmdale.com

BEDROOMS: 41, 5 on ground floor.
OPEN: all year.
FACILITIES: drawing room, library, conservatory, free Wi-Fi, civil wedding licence, garden.
BACKGROUND MUSIC: none.
LOCATION: Kensington, underground South Kensington.
CHILDREN: all ages welcomed.
DOGS: not allowed.
CREDIT CARDS: all major cards.
PRICES: [2013] room (*excluding VAT*) £180–£375. Breakfast £18.50–£24.50 per person (*plus 12½% discretionary service charge*).

SEE ALSO SHORTLIST

STRAND

Map 2:D4

ONE ALDWYCH

✪César award in 2005

A striking conversion of the Edwardian offices of the *Morning Post* newspaper, *One Aldwych* is larger than the average *Guide* hotel, and more expensive. It keeps its entry because of continuing praise for the service: 'At last we have found a London hotel that we really like,' says a regular correspondent (based in California). 'Everyone was friendly and helpful; dinner was superb.' Drinks, bar food and afternoon tea are served in the double-height lobby, an 'elegant, large and light space with comfortable seating'; it has huge flower arrangements, a giant statue of an oarsman; 'a peaceful place for morning coffee'. There are two dining choices. *Indigo*, a 'relaxed' restaurant on a balcony, has a modern European menu. *Axis*, on the lower ground floor, has been renovated with modern colours, Thai silk panels. The chef, Dominic Teague, cooks seasonal dishes, perhaps sea bass, parsnip, marsh samphire, confit lemon. The 'comfortable' bedrooms have original art, fibre-optic reading lights; flowers and fruit are delivered daily. Guests have access to a health club (the chlorine-free swimming pool has underwater music). (*H Richard Lamb*)

1 Aldwych
London WC2B 4BZ

T: 020-7300 1000
F: 020-7300 0501
E: reservations@onealdwych.com
W: www.onealdwych.com

BEDROOMS: 105, 6 suitable for &.
OPEN: all year, *Axis* closed Sat lunch/Sun/Mon.
FACILITIES: lifts, bar, 2 restaurants, free Wi-Fi, function facilities, screening room, health club (18-metre swimming pool, spa, sauna, gym), civil wedding licence.
BACKGROUND MUSIC: in *Axis*, lobby.
LOCATION: Strand, valet parking, underground Covent Garden, Charing Cross, Waterloo.
CHILDREN: all ages welcomed.
DOGS: only guide dogs allowed.
CREDIT CARDS: all major cards.
PRICES: [2013] rooms and suites (*excluding VAT*) £250–£1,430, breakfast £23, pre- and post-theatre menu £19.75–£23.75, à la carte (*Indigo*) £35, (*Axis*) £40.

SEE ALSO SHORTLIST

VICTORIA

Map 2:D4

THE GORING

❦ César award in 1994

The favoured choice for royal visitors to nearby Buckingham Palace long before it became the Middleton family base for the wedding of the decade, this 'expensive but excellent' hotel has been run by the Goring family since it was built in 1910. Jeremy Goring is in charge; David Morgan-Hewitt is the managing director. 'It stands out amongst its peers for the attention to detail,' say visitors this year. Among the 'finer points' are: complimentary shoe cleaning that is 'a joy to behold'; the 'polite but firm' reminders to guests that mobile phones and laptop computers are not welcome in the public rooms; full waiter service at breakfast – 'hot toast and tea/coffee exactly when you want them'. The timing of the housekeeping was less appreciated: 'Twice our room was not serviced until well into the afternoon; on our final day, a maid knocked on the door at 7.55 am to ask what time we were leaving.' All bedrooms have rich fabrics (silks from the house of Gainsborough), bespoke and antique furniture; many face the private garden. (*David Carment, Harry and Annette Medcalf*)

Beeston Place
Grosvenor Gardens
London SW1W 0JW

T: 020-7396 9000
F: 020-7834 4393
E: reception@thegoring.com
W: www.thegoring.com

BEDROOMS: 69, 2 suitable for ♿.
OPEN: all year.
FACILITIES: lifts, ramps, lounge bar, terrace room, restaurant, function facilities, Wi-Fi (£15.75 for 24 hours), civil wedding licence.
BACKGROUND MUSIC: none.
LOCATION: near Victoria Station, garage, mews parking, underground Victoria.
CHILDREN: all ages welcomed.
DOGS: not allowed.
CREDIT CARDS: all major cards.
PRICES: [2013] per room (*excluding 12.5% service*) B&B £400–£655. Breakfast £30, set lunch £38, set dinner £49.50, à la carte £75.

SEE ALSO SHORTLIST

ENGLAND

Peak District, Derbyshire

ABBOTSBURY Dorset

Map 1:D6

THE ABBEY HOUSE

In a beautiful position next to a fragment of an 11th-century abbey, this 14th-century house stands in well-kept gardens, with wide lawns sloping down to a millpond. It is run as a small guest house by Jonathan and Maureen Cooke, whose 'kindness' and 'impeccable standards' have won them much praise over many years from *Guide* readers. The decor is for those who enjoy a traditional style: there are flagstone floors, panelled doors, original windows; a cosy lounge with plenty of books; much chintz and knick-knacks. The 'very comfortable' bedrooms differ in size and style: Benedictine is spacious and has a double and a single bed; it faces south over the garden. St Nicholas also has a double and a single bed, plus a separate lounge area with TV and easy chairs. The 'excellent' breakfast is served in a room with a beamed ceiling and large fireplace, thought to have been the abbey infirmary. No evening meals, but the Cookes have a comprehensive list of local eating places. The village is noted for its ancient swannery and its subtropical gardens.

Church Street
Abbotsbury DT3 4JJ

T: 01305-871330
E: info@theabbeyhouse.co.uk
W: www.theabbeyhouse.co.uk

BEDROOMS: 5.
OPEN: all year, tea room open for lunches Apr–Sept, dinners for house parties only.
FACILITIES: reception, lounge, breakfast/tea room, free Wi-Fi, 1½-acre garden (stage for opera), sea 15 mins' walk, unsuitable for &.
BACKGROUND MUSIC: classical, sometimes.
LOCATION: village centre.
CHILDREN: not under 12.
DOGS: not allowed.
CREDIT CARDS: none.
PRICES: [2013] per room B&B £75–£110. 1-night bookings sometimes refused.

ALDEBURGH Suffolk

Map 2:C6

THE WENTWORTH

The 'personal attention of the owner and staff' is liked by 'addicts' who return regularly to Michael Pritt's traditional hotel on a quiet road opposite a shingle beach. 'Everything is comfortable, attractive and fresh thanks to a continuous programme of renewal,' say visitors; this year the main lounges have been renovated. Another comment: 'Always reliable, long-serving staff; nothing changes.' A sea-facing bedroom on the first floor was 'bright, airy and very clean; a tiny bathroom'. A single room was 'quiet, well appointed; no unnecessary fussiness'. Seven bedrooms in *Darfield House* have light oak furniture, neutral colours; a modern bathroom. Saurav Kumar joined as head chef in 2013. 'Breakfast is excellent; delicious muesli, good cooked (fine black pudding), superb bread and croissants,' say visitors who were admonished for sitting at the wrong table and 'marched to another one'. *The Wentworth* is 'well attuned' to concerts at nearby Snape Maltings, with the 'civilised and practical' option of taking a pre-concert starter and main course, returning for a post-concert pudding. (*Richard Parish, John and Margaret Speake, Simon Rodway*)

25% DISCOUNT VOUCHERS

Wentworth Road
Aldeburgh IP15 5BD

T: 01728-452312
F: 01728-454343
E: stay@wentworth-aldeburgh.co.uk
W: www.wentworth-aldeburgh.com

BEDROOMS: 35, 7 in *Darfield House* opposite, 5 on ground floor, 1 suitable for ♿.
OPEN: all year.
FACILITIES: ramps, 2 lounges, bar, restaurant, private dining room, conference room, free Wi-Fi, 2 terrace gardens, shingle beach 200 yds.
BACKGROUND MUSIC: none.
LOCATION: seafront, 5 mins' walk from centre.
CHILDREN: all ages welcomed.
DOGS: not allowed in restaurant.
CREDIT CARDS: all major cards.
PRICES: per room B&B £150–£280, D,B&B £188–£311. Set dinner £25. 1-night bookings refused Sat.

ALFRISTON East Sussex

Map 2:E4

DEANS PLACE

NEW

On the banks of the Cuckmere river, Michael Clinch's country hotel is on the outskirts of a pretty village at the foot of the South Downs national park. It is upgraded to a full entry in the *Guide* thanks to a positive report by a regular contributor who had 'a happy and relaxing stay'. Inspectors, who 'would return', were impressed with 'the right mix of fine dining and child-friendliness. The decor might be dated, but it had a nice traditional feel.' James Dopson is now the manager. There is plenty of space in the public areas: a 'well-decorated' bar, lounge and a garden room with full-length windows. In the formal *Harcourts* restaurant, the chef, Stuart Dunley, serves 'delicious' modern dishes, perhaps chicken and pesto terrine; salmon, Pernod sauce, dauphinoise potatoes. 'Our large bedroom was comfortably furnished; its bed was made up with sheets and blankets; it had a hospitality tray and a well-laid-out information pack. Everything was clean.' There is much to do in the area ('great attractions for children'). Good walking all around. Picnic hampers can be arranged for Glyndebourne. (*Simon Rodway, and others*)

25% DISCOUNT VOUCHERS

Seaford Road
Alfriston BN26 5TW

T: 01323-870248
F: 01323-870918
E: reception@deansplacehotel.co.uk
W: www.deansplacehotel.co.uk

BEDROOMS: 36, 1 suitable for ♿.
OPEN: all year.
FACILITIES: lounge, bar, restaurant, meeting rooms, free Wi-Fi, civil wedding licence, heated outdoor swimming pool (10 by 5 metres, May–Sept), 3-acre garden.
BACKGROUND MUSIC: classical, jazz in restaurant.
LOCATION: edge of village.
CHILDREN: all ages welcomed.
DOGS: allowed.
CREDIT CARDS: Amex, MasterCard, Visa.
PRICES: [2013] per room B&B £100–£160, D,B&B £165–£225. Set meals £28–£35.

SEE ALSO SHORTLIST

ALKHAM Kent

THE MARQUIS AT ALKHAM

'A superb stay; fabulous food, wine and service, and a lovely suite.' Praise comes from a visitor ('en route to Champagne') for this restaurant-with-rooms close to Dover and the Channel Tunnel. The 200-year-old inn stands above a sloping cricket pitch in a pretty village at the southern end of the Kent Downs. The exterior may be timeless; the interior has been given a modern look with exposed brickwork, wooden floors, up-to-date fabrics and furnishings. Bedrooms are graded from 'standard' to 'suite'. There are large pocket-sprung beds, under-floor heating, TV and DVD-players, and Alkham valley views. 'We had a spacious suite, super bathroom, nice bedding and a decent coffee machine.' The building is on a busy road; rooms at the back are the quietest. Chef Charles Lakin's Kentish menu might include mackerel, beetroot, sea radish, cockles; slow-roast shoulder of venison, hunter's pie, parsnip. Breakfast has an extensive buffet with seasonal fruits, cured meats, fish and cheese; cooked choices include waffles with cinnamon butter and honey. 'We're planning on returning and I have even recommended the place to my mother-in-law.' (*RM-P*)

25% DISCOUNT VOUCHERS

Alkham Valley Road
Alkham, Dover
CT15 7DF

T: 01304-873410
F: 01304-873418
E: reception@
    themarquisatalkham.co.uk
W: www.themarquisatalkham.co.uk

BEDROOMS: 10, 3 in 2 cottages 3 mins' drive away.
OPEN: all year, restaurant closed Mon lunch.
FACILITIES: bar, lounge, dining room, free Wi-Fi, civil wedding licence, small garden.
BACKGROUND MUSIC: ambient in public areas.
LOCATION: 4 miles W of Dover.
CHILDREN: all ages welcomed, not under 8 in restaurant after 6 pm.
DOGS: not allowed.
CREDIT CARDS: Amex, MasterCard, Visa.
PRICES: [2013] per person B&B £44.50–£134.50, D,B&B £74.50–£169. Set menu from £30.

AMBLESIDE Cumbria

Map 4: inset C2

THE REGENT

'A first-class, friendly hotel; the owning family are much in evidence,' says a returning visitor this year. Opposite a slipway and pier on Lake Windermere, this white-fronted hotel is owned by Christine Hewitt and managed by her son, Andrew. Bedrooms vary considerably in size and shape. Garden rooms, which are on the first floor, have a spa bath, king-size bed, a large sitting area and a private terrace. Courtyard rooms are ideal for dog owners (£10 a night charge). The Sail Loft Room has a private wooden terrace with a lake view. Smaller rooms are 'comfortable and well equipped'. All rooms have TV, CD-player, tea- and coffee-making facilities, a PlayStation. In the split-level restaurant, chef John Mathers serves a seasonal menu which might include red pepper parfait with goat's cheese; slow-roast shoulder of pork filled with Cumberland sausage. 'The food is excellent, with a wide choice.' Breakfast, available from 8 am until noon, has an unusually wide range of dishes, from the Full Lakelander (egg, bacon, sausage, mushrooms, tomato, black pudding) to a Lakeland rarebit or Belgian waffles. (*David RW Jervois*)

25% DISCOUNT VOUCHERS

Waterhead Bay
Ambleside LA22 0ES

T: 015394-32254
F: 015394-31474
E: info@regentlakes.co.uk
W: www.regentlakes.co.uk

BEDROOMS: 30, 10 in courtyard, 5 in garden, 7 on ground floor.
OPEN: all year, except Christmas.
FACILITIES: ramp, lounge, sun lounge, bar, restaurant, free Wi-Fi in public areas, courtyard, ¼-acre garden, on Lake Windermere.
BACKGROUND MUSIC: classical/modern in public rooms.
LOCATION: on A591, S of centre, at Waterhead Bay.
CHILDREN: all ages welcomed.
DOGS: not allowed in public rooms.
CREDIT CARDS: MasterCard, Visa.
PRICES: [2013] per person B&B £52–£79, D,B&B £79–£114. À la carte £28.

SEE ALSO SHORTLIST

AMBLESIDE Cumbria

Map 4: inset C2

ROTHAY MANOR

César award in 1992

'I've never known it in better heart; as always very comfortable with admirable staff; the food is better than ever.' Praise comes this year from a regular visitor (and *Guide* reader) for the Nixon family's traditional hotel, which has earned an entry in every edition of the *Guide*. It has a 'delightful setting', in large gardens a short walk from the head of Lake Windermere. The bedrooms at the front have views across the gardens to Wansfell Pike; those at the back look out over the River Rothay. Superior rooms, many with a balcony, have a more modern decor; all are spacious with good storage. In the restaurant, which overlooks the gardens, long-standing head chef Jane Binns serves a daily-changing menu using locally sourced ingredients. Her dishes might include pan-fried chicken livers, Parmesan mash, red-onion gravy; venison braised with wild mushrooms, shallots, herbs, Coniston ale. Breakfast 'sets you up for the day'; juices, yogurts and cereals are on a buffet; hot food is cooked to order. Children are welcomed, and have their own menu in a family dining room. (*John Borron*)

25% DISCOUNT VOUCHERS

Rothay Bridge
Ambleside LA22 0EH

T: 015394-33605
F: 015394-33607
E: hotel@rothaymanor.co.uk
W: www.rothaymanor.co.uk

BEDROOMS: 19, 2 in annexe, 2 suitable for ♿.
OPEN: all year except 17 Jan–2 Feb.
FACILITIES: ramp, 2 lounges, bar, 2 dining rooms, meeting/conference facilities, free Wi-Fi, 1-acre garden (croquet), free access to local leisure centre.
BACKGROUND MUSIC: none.
LOCATION: ¼ mile SW of Ambleside.
CHILDREN: all ages welcomed.
DOGS: not allowed.
CREDIT CARDS: MasterCard, Visa.
PRICES: [2013] per room B&B £125–£280, D,B&B £175–£350. À la carte £32.50.

SEE ALSO SHORTLIST

AMPLEFORTH North Yorkshire

Map 4:D4

SHALLOWDALE HOUSE

César award in 2005

'As relaxing as ever', Phillip Gill and Anton van der Horst's small guest house on the southern edge of the North York Moors national park has many fans. 'It is absolutely true that Phillip and Anton treat their guests as if they were friends,' says a returning visitor this year. Other reporters, on their seventh visit, found the hosts 'as hospitable and thoughtful as ever'. 'Wonderful; so reliable,' is another comment. The building, on a south-facing hillside, has been designed to make the most of the perspective. All three bedrooms have picture windows; two have a king-size bed and an en suite bathroom, the third has a private bathroom across the corridor. 'Our room was large, comfortable, and had fabulous views over the countryside.' Guests are asked to give 48 hours' notice for dinner, a four-course set meal (preferences discussed); dishes might be local asparagus; duck breasts with endives and Marsala. 'Phillip's cooking is as good as some of the best restaurants in the country; his apricot tart was the finest dessert of our entire summer trip.' (*Frances Thomas, John and Christine Moore, Richard Creed*)

West End, Ampleforth
nr York, YO62 4DY

T: 01439-788325
F: 01439-788885
E: stay@shallowdalehouse.co.uk
W: www.shallowdalehouse.co.uk

BEDROOMS: 3.
OPEN: all year except Christmas/New Year, occasionally at other times.
FACILITIES: drawing room, sitting room, dining room, free Wi-Fi, 2½-acre grounds, unsuitable for &.
BACKGROUND MUSIC: none.
LOCATION: edge of village.
CHILDREN: not under 12.
DOGS: not allowed.
CREDIT CARDS: MasterCard, Visa.
PRICES: per room B&B single £95–£110, double £115–£140. Set dinner £39.50. 1-night bookings occasionally refused weekends.

ARUNDEL West Sussex

Map 2:E3

THE TOWN HOUSE

'Stuffiness is taboo' at this Grade II listed Regency building at the top of Arundel's steep High Street. It is run as a restaurant-with-rooms by Lee Williams (also the chef) and his wife, Katie. There is no dress code: 'It is like being at a casual dinner party with friends,' say the owners. *Guide* inspectors were impressed by the welcome and 'dazzled' by the food. 'We were warmly greeted by the owner, who carried our case to our room.' Bedrooms on the second floor have 'splendid' views of the castle and battlements; a suite has a small balcony. 'Our room had hand-painted original coving and panelling; a Venetian-style mirror above a modern oak desk; plenty of storage and a side table with tea- and coffee-making kit. Housekeeping was good.' In the restaurant, which has an Italian 16th-century gilded ceiling, Lee Williams serves 'interesting' modern dishes. 'Exceptional home-made focaccia with a dip of olive oil and balsamic vinegar; warm chorizo and goat's cheese salad; excellent roast loin of venison.' Breakfast has home-baked bread; 'very good bacon' in the full English.

25% DISCOUNT VOUCHERS

65 High Street
Arundel BN18 9AJ

T: 01903-883847
E: enquiries@thetownhouse.co.uk
W: www.thetownhouse.co.uk

BEDROOMS: 4.
OPEN: all year except 25/26 Dec, 1 Jan, 2 weeks Easter, 2 weeks Oct, restaurant closed Sun/Mon.
FACILITIES: restaurant, free Wi-Fi, unsuitable for &.
BACKGROUND MUSIC: 'easy listening' in restaurant.
LOCATION: top end of High Street.
CHILDREN: all ages welcomed.
DOGS: not allowed.
CREDIT CARDS: Diners, MasterCard, Visa.
PRICES: [2013] per room B&B £95–£130, D,B&B (midweek) £135–£170. Set dinner £23.50–£29. 1-night bookings refused weekends in high season.

ASHWATER Devon

Map 1:C3

BLAGDON MANOR

❦César award in 2006

A 'great place to chill out', this Grade II listed mansion in rolling countryside near Dartmoor is run as a restaurant-with-rooms by Liz and Steve Morey. 'They made us really welcome, as did their chocolate Labradors,' says a guest this year (visiting dogs are given a fleece blanket, a towel and treats). The public rooms have much character: polished flagstone floors, oak beams, huge walk-in fireplaces. The bedrooms vary in size and view. 'Ours had ancient beams, a smart sitting area and a big bedroom with a king-size bed; we liked the biscuits, chocolates and decanter of sherry.' A bath 'with a view over the valley' was enjoyed. This year a suite has been created out of two smaller bedrooms. Steve Morey's 'wonderful' cooking is praised: 'I particularly liked pearled spelt risotto with mushrooms and truffle oil; breast of guineafowl was accompanied by an amazing black pudding.' Breakfast is 'generous'. The menu names the staff 'from sous-chef to housekeepers, a helpful touch'. There are 'lots of maps and local information' in the bedrooms; excellent walking in the immediate vicinity. (*Steven Hur*)

25% DISCOUNT VOUCHERS

Ashwater EX21 5DF

T: 01409-211224
E: stay@blagdon.com
W: www.blagdon.com

BEDROOMS: 6.
OPEN: all year Wed–Sun, except Jan.
FACILITIES: ramps, lounge, library, snug, bar, conservatory, restaurant, private dining room, free Wi-Fi in lounge, 20-acre grounds (3-acre gardens, croquet, giant chess, gazebo, pond), unsuitable for &.
BACKGROUND MUSIC: none.
LOCATION: 8 miles NE of Launceston.
CHILDREN: not under 12.
DOGS: not allowed in restaurant, £8.50 charged per night.
CREDIT CARDS: MasterCard, Visa.
PRICES: [2013] per room B&B £145–£250. Set dinner £35–£40. 1-night bookings refused Christmas.

AUSTWICK North Yorkshire

Map 4:D3

AUSTWICK HALL

On a wooded hillside on the edge of a pretty village, this old manor house is run as an upmarket B&B by 'enthusiastic hosts' Michael Pearson and Eric Culley. They have renovated the Elizabethan house with sympathy, filling it with a 'clever mix of the old and new': antiques, heirlooms, an 'ever-expanding' collection of ethnic artwork. The 'relaxing' lounge has sofas and armchairs, bookcases, a wood-burning stove. The huge entrance hall, dominated by a rosewood table, has an impressive central staircase which opens on to two landings. The 'grand' bedrooms have old floorboards, antique furnishings, many original features; they are well equipped with a hospitality tray, bottled water, a full-screen TV, DVD/CD-player. Dinner is no longer served (information is provided on local eating places). 'No need to be up at the crack of dawn' for the 'very good' breakfast which is served until 10 am (it can also be taken in bed). There is a help-yourself selection of fruits, juices, fruit salad, cereals, 'buttery' croissants; local dried-cured bacon in the full English. The house and gardens are open to the public on Mondays in summer.

Townhead Lane
Austwick LA2 8BS

T: 01524-251794
E: austwickhall@austwick.org
W: www.austwickhall.co.uk

BEDROOMS: 5.
OPEN: all year except 3–31 Jan.
FACILITIES: hall, sitting room, drawing room, dining room, free Wi-Fi, civil wedding licence, 13-acre gardens, unsuitable for &.
BACKGROUND MUSIC: none.
LOCATION: edge of village.
CHILDREN: not under 16.
DOGS: not allowed.
CREDIT CARDS: MasterCard, Visa.
PRICES: [2013] per room B&B single £140–£170, double £155–£185. 1-night bookings refused weekends.

AUSTWICK North Yorkshire

Map 4:D3

🌱 THE TRADDOCK

César award: country hotel of the year

In this 'genuine, untouristy' village amid tranquil hills and green fields, this old manor house is run by the Reynolds family as a small hotel. 'It has the feel of a comfortable country home, not grand, not designerish, not shabby either,' say *Guide* inspectors, who liked the 'caring' service and the welcome given to children (and dogs). 'Paul Reynolds, who gave us a warm greeting, showed us around, carried our bags, moved our car.' There are three lounges with 'big sofas, lots of chairs, board games'; one opens on to a terrace with chairs and tables 'where we took tea with delicious scones'. In the two dining rooms, chef John Pratt serves 'good' modern dishes, perhaps rack of Mansergh Hall lamb, roast vegetable clapshot, colcannon potatoes; 'an amazing prune and Armagnac soufflé'. The 'pretty' bedrooms are individually styled: 'Ours had swagged curtains, lots of cushions, a chandelier; a claw-footed bath and basin in the room.' Four more rooms have been renovated this year and one room was expanded into a suite. A 'fantastic' breakfast has 'thick toast', 'enormous' full English, 'an excellent kipper'.

25% DISCOUNT VOUCHERS

Austwick, Settle
LA2 8BY

T: 01524-251224
F: 01524-251796
E: info@austwicktraddock.co.uk
W: www.thetraddock.co.uk

BEDROOMS: 12, 1 on ground floor.
OPEN: all year.
FACILITIES: 3 lounges, bar, 2 dining rooms, function facilities, free Wi-Fi, 1½-acre grounds (sun deck), only public rooms accessible to ♿.
BACKGROUND MUSIC: in 2 lounges and dining rooms.
LOCATION: 4 miles NW of Settle, train Settle, bus.
CHILDREN: all ages welcomed.
DOGS: allowed in bedrooms, public rooms on lead, not in restaurant.
CREDIT CARDS: MasterCard, Visa.
PRICES: [2013] per person B&B £45–£95, D,B&B £75–£130. À la carte £30.1-night bookings refused weekends in season.

AYCLIFFE VILLAGE Co. Durham

Map 4:C4

THE COUNTY

NEW

The 'lovely atmosphere' impressed the nominator of this restaurant-with-rooms, a former pub opposite the green in a village off the A1(M) north of Darlington. It is owned, and managed with 'plenty of attention to detail', by Colette Farrell and Stuart Dole. 'They are experienced hoteliers and it shows.' The 'welcoming' open-plan restaurant, which is busy with locals ('always a good sign'), is 'decorated in modern New England style, with pale painted walls'. Stuart Dole is the chef: 'His short menu had flavourful chicken terrine and jumbo prawns; an excellent steak pie; lamb shank that fell off the bone. Much was home-made, like the bread and the onion marmalade.' The accommodation is in a building next door, which has a small residents' lounge. 'Our lovely bedroom overlooked the village green; it had a large bed, two comfy leather chairs, excellent lighting; a walk-through dressing area led to a huge bathroom.' Both owners were on duty at breakfast. 'We had excellent eggs Benedict, and an anything-but-humble bacon sandwich with good dry-cured bacon on home-made bloomer bread.' (*Lynn Wildgoose*)

13 The Green
Aycliffe Village
Newton Aycliffe
DL5 6LX

T: 01325-312273
E: info@thecountyaycliffevillage.com
W: www.thecountyaycliffevillage.com

BEDROOMS: 7 in annexe.

OPEN: all year except 25/26 Dec, 1 Jan.

FACILITIES: bar, restaurant, free Wi-Fi, unsuitable for ♿.

BACKGROUND MUSIC: 'easy listening'.

LOCATION: in village 5 miles N of Darlington.

CHILDREN: all ages welcomed.

DOGS: not allowed.

CREDIT CARDS: Amex, MasterCard, Visa.

PRICES: [2013] per room B&B single £49, double £70–£110. À la carte £25.

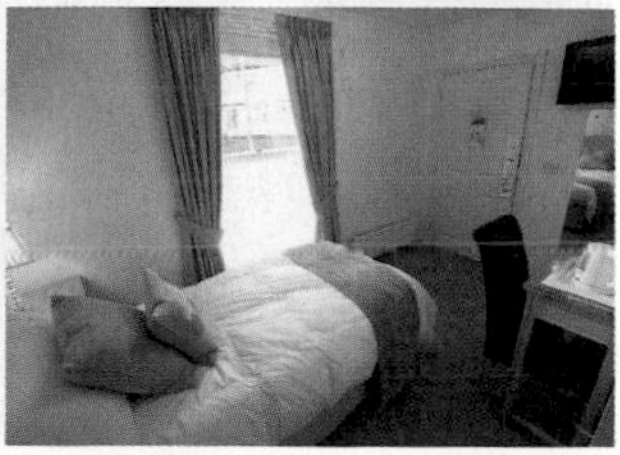

AYLESBURY Buckinghamshire

Map 2:C3

HARTWELL HOUSE

César award in 1997

'We were very impressed: the staff were courteous and always attentive; a great stay though you certainly pay for it.' Praise this year for this stately home in 'stunning' grounds, which is run by Richard Broyd's Historic House Hotels for the National Trust; Jonathan Thompson is the long-serving manager. The Grade I listed house was famously the residence in exile of Louis XVIII of France. 'We were blown away by the size of our royal four-poster room, larger than most of the public rooms. It had a beautiful, very large and comfortable bed, sofas, a dressing table; a well-appointed bathroom. We were surprised to read in the room notes that Louis's queen hated staying in it.' There are four 'sumptuous' drawing rooms with fine plasterwork, antiques and marble fireplaces. Most bedrooms and suites are in the main house, others are in a converted coach house or the Old Rectory. 'Pleasant' pre-dinner drinks and canapés in the lounge were enjoyed: 'Our smoked salmon starter was fine but the main courses were not exciting; coffee in the drawing room was lovely.' (*Olivia Howes Smith, and others*)

25% DISCOUNT VOUCHERS

Oxford Road
nr Aylesbury HP17 8NR

T: 01296-747444
F: 01296-747450
E: info@hartwell-house.com
W: www.hartwell-house.com

BEDROOMS: 46, 16 in stable block, some on ground floor, 2 suitable for &.
OPEN: all year.
FACILITIES: lift, ramps, 4 drawing rooms, bar, 3 dining rooms, conference facilities, free Wi-Fi, civil wedding licence, spa (swimming pool, 8 by 16 metres), 90-acre grounds (tennis).
BACKGROUND MUSIC: none.
LOCATION: 2 miles W of Aylesbury.
CHILDREN: not under 4.
DOGS: allowed in some bedrooms.
CREDIT CARDS: Amex, MasterCard, Visa.
PRICES: [to 31 Mar 2014] per room B&B single £175–£196, double £205–£700. D,B&B from £125 per person, set dinner £24.95, à la carte £60.

BABBACOMBE Devon

Map 1:D5

THE CARY ARMS

In a dramatic setting below a steep cliff near Torquay, this small hotel has been given a modern make-over with a nautical theme by Lana de Savary. It is approached down a narrow, vertiginous road; the 'welcoming' young staff will unload luggage and drive visitors' cars to a private car park. The bar/dining area is a 'contemporary take on the original 19th-century inn': stone walls, wood and slate floor, wooden tables in alcoves; a conservatory dining area. In the restaurant, chef Ben Kingdon serves 'good gastropub food' using locally sourced fish and meat. His menus might include smoked mackerel, beetroot and horseradish relish; fillet of Devon beef, Parmentier potatoes and spring onions, shallot and red wine sauce. All the bedrooms face the sea; some have a private terrace or balcony. A large room with light panelled walls had 'a big, comfy bed; a good bathroom'. Breakfast is 'very good, wholesome but not over the top': on the bar a buffet with fresh fruit, jugs of freshly squeezed juices, ham on the bone, smoked salmon. 'Good' cooked dishes brought to the table. (*CJ, and others*)

Beach Road
Babbacombe TQ1 3LX

T: 01803-327110
F: 01803-323221
E: enquiries@caryarms.co.uk
W: www.caryarms.co.uk

BEDROOMS: 8, 2 on ground floor, plus 4 self-catering cottages.
OPEN: all year.
FACILITIES: lounge, bar, restaurant, conservatory, free Wi-Fi, civil wedding licence, garden, terrace, treatment room.
BACKGROUND MUSIC: occasional live jazz.
LOCATION: by beach.
CHILDREN: all ages welcomed.
DOGS: not allowed in 6 bedrooms.
CREDIT CARDS: Amex, MasterCard, Visa.
PRICES: [2013] per room B&B £175–£375. À la carte £29. 1-night bookings refused weekends.

BARNSLEY Gloucestershire

Map 3:E6

BARNSLEY HOUSE

In a 'beautiful setting' among celebrated gardens, this William and Mary house is liked for its 'relaxed country house feel'. Once the home of Rosemary Verey, the noted gardener, it is now a luxury hotel run by the owners of *Calcot Manor*, Tetbury (see entry). Inspectors liked the 'smell of wood burning in the cosy lounges', and the 'friendly, not obsequious staff'. They were less impressed with a duplex room in a stable block, which had a bedroom up a steep flight of stairs, and a bath 'the size of a small swimming pool'. On asking, they were moved 'without demur' to a 'lovely' room in the main house: 'The charming bedroom had a view of the garden through a porthole window.' Guests can dine in the *Potager* restaurant ('a pleasant meal in a lovely long room with tall windows') or at *The Village Pub*, a short walk away (see Shortlist), which is under the same ownership. Breakfast has a 'good buffet, nice chunky toast, excellent cooked dishes; but surely at these prices they should squeeze their own orange juice'.

Barnsley, nr Cirencester
GL7 5EE

T: 01285-740000
F: 01285-740925
E: reception@barnsleyhouse.com
W: www.barnsleyhouse.com

BEDROOMS: 18, 6 in stableyard, 5 in courtyard, 1 in cottage, 1 on ground floor.
OPEN: all year.
FACILITIES: lounge, bar, restaurant, meeting room, free Wi-Fi, civil wedding licence, terrace, 11-acre garden (spa), unsuitable for &.
BACKGROUND MUSIC: in restaurant.
LOCATION: 5 miles NE of Cirencester.
CHILDREN: not under 14.
DOGS: allowed in stableyard rooms, not in grounds.
CREDIT CARDS: all major cards.
PRICES: [2013] per room B&B £280–£660. Set menus £21–£24, à la carte £40. 1-night bookings sometimes refused at weekends.

SEE ALSO SHORTLIST

BARNSTAPLE Devon

Map 1:B4

BROOMHILL ART HOTEL **NEW**

In a heavily wooded valley in north Devon, this Victorian house is the centre of an unusual arts enterprise that embraces a sculpture park, an art gallery, a café/restaurant and a small hotel. It was created 16 years ago by a 'hard-working' Dutch couple, Rinus and Aniet Van De Sande. *Guide* inspectors this year 'greatly enjoyed' their stay: 'Behind a scruffy exterior lies a quirky small hotel, professionally run by the hands-on owners. The greeting was warm and our bags were carried to a large room with a bay window overlooking the grounds with their colourful sculptures. The beds were comfortable (though bedside lights were dim), storage was good; a sofa, armchair and coffee table were set in the bay window; a small shower room had everything we needed.' Evening meals are served from Wednesday to Saturday in the 'well-appointed' restaurant ('candles, fresh flowers, a great ambience'). 'We enjoyed a mini-soup appetiser (parsnip and cumin); Exe Valley mussels; confit of duck with spicy orange sauce, lentil salad with chorizo; plenty, too, for vegetarians.' The 'good' breakfast has Greek yogurt, fresh fruit salad; 'excellent coffee and scrambled eggs'.

Muddiford Road
Barnstaple EX31 4EX

T: 01271-850262
F: 01271-850575
E: info@broomhillart.co.uk
W: www.broomhillart.co.uk

BEDROOMS: 6.
OPEN: all year except 18 Dec–10 Jan, restaurant closed evening Sun–Tues.
FACILITIES: restaurant, library, gallery, free Wi-Fi, civil wedding licence, 10-acre grounds with sculpture park, unsuitable for &.
BACKGROUND MUSIC: varied in public areas.
LOCATION: 4 miles N of Barnstaple.
CHILDREN: all ages welcomed.
DOGS: allowed by arrangement, not in public rooms.
CREDIT CARDS: MasterCard, Visa.
PRICES: [2013] per room B&B single £50, double £75, D,B&B (Fri/Sat 2-night rate) single £175, double £245. Set dinner £24.95. 1-night bookings generally refused at weekends in high season.

BARWICK Somerset

Map 1:C6

LITTLE BARWICK HOUSE

25% DISCOUNT VOUCHERS

César award in 2002

'Tim and Emma Ford are hosts par excellence' at their restaurant-with-rooms, a listed Georgian dower house close to the Somerset/Dorset border. 'Emma is welcoming and attentive; Tim's cooking sets the standard for us,' say regular visitors this year. 'It all contributes to a relaxing and enjoyable stay.' In the restaurant, ingredients are 'locally sourced, well presented but not over-elaborate; Tim's menus have some variation every day, which is much appreciated for a stay of a number of nights'. The Fords say they 'offer a true foodie experience, modern English, without froths, foams and excessive twiddliness'. Typical dishes: grilled Cornish red mullet, aubergine caviar; roasted breast of maize-fed guinea fowl, wild mushrooms, Madeira sauce. Emma Ford has an 'encyclopaedic' knowledge of the wine list; many wines are available by the glass. The individually furnished bedrooms have fresh flowers, flat-screen TV, radio, home-made shortbread, cafetière coffee/tea tray. There is a choice of blankets or duvet, and an evening turn-down service. 'Much to see and do in the area.' (*Bryan and Mary Blaxall*)

Barwick, nr Yeovil
BA22 9TD

T: 01935-423902
F: 01935-420908
E: reservations@barwick7.fsnet.co.uk
W: www.littlebarwickhouse.co.uk

BEDROOMS: 6.
OPEN: all year except 2 weeks Christmas, 1 week Aug, restaurant closed Sun evenings, Mon.
FACILITIES: ramp, 2 lounges, restaurant, conservatory, free Wi-Fi, 3½-acre garden (terrace, paddock), unsuitable for &.
BACKGROUND MUSIC: none.
LOCATION: ¾ mile outside Yeovil.
CHILDREN: not under 5.
DOGS: allowed in public rooms subject to other guests' approval.
CREDIT CARDS: Amex, MasterCard, Visa.
PRICES: [2013] per person B&B £70–£90, D,B&B £110–£145. Set dinner £43.95. 1-night bookings sometimes refused.

BASLOW Derbyshire

Map 3:A6

THE CAVENDISH

🏆 *César award in 2002*

Overlooking the Chatsworth estate, this 250-year-old former coaching inn is run as a traditional country hotel for the Devonshire trustees by Eric Marsh (who also owns *The George Hotel*, Hathersage – see entry) and Philip Joseph (the manager). 'Mr Marsh was much in evidence and made himself known to all the guests,' says a visitor who was 'impressed'. *The Cavendish* is on a busy road, but the bedrooms are at the back; all have a view of the Chatsworth estate. The largest rooms are in the original *Peacock Inn*, the oldest part of the building; others are in the Mitford wing. Ten rooms have been refurbished this year. 'We enjoyed the view from our room, which was quiet and spacious. Fresh milk in the minibar was replenished daily.' In the *Gallery* restaurant and the conservatory *Garden Room*, chef Mike Thomson serves modern British dishes, eg, organic salmon fillet. caramelised shallots, smoked pancetta, wild mushrooms. 'Our dinner was excellent, innovative and well presented.' Breakfasts have 'a good selection of cereals and fresh fruits; substantial cooked dishes'. (*DR, and others*)

Church Lane
Baslow DE45 1SP

T: 01246-582311
F: 01246-582312
E: info@cavendish-hotel.net
W: www.cavendish-hotel.net

BEDROOMS: 24, 2 on ground floor.
OPEN: all year.
FACILITIES: lounge, bar, 2 restaurants, 2 meeting rooms, free Wi-Fi, ½-acre grounds (putting), river fishing nearby.
BACKGROUND MUSIC: classical in *Garden Room* restaurant.
LOCATION: on A619, in Chatsworth grounds.
CHILDREN: all ages welcomed.
DOGS: not allowed.
CREDIT CARDS: Amex, MasterCard, Visa.
PRICES: [2013] room £133–£286. Breakfast £18.90 per person, set meals £45 (*5% 'service levy' included in all prices*). 1-night bookings sometimes refused.

BASLOW Derbyshire

Map 3:A6

FISCHER'S BASLOW HALL

♀ *César award in 1998*

'A great favourite' with those who like 'innovative cooking' combined with 'a degree of luxury', this Edwardian manor house is run as a restaurant-with-rooms by Max and Susan Fischer. Guests in 2013 enjoyed 'friendly service and excellent food'. It stands on a winding tree-lined drive in a village on the edge of the Chatsworth estate. Returning visitors 'were greeted almost like long-lost friends'. Mr Fischer and head chef Rupert Rowley have a *Michelin* star for their menus, which might include dishes like mosaic of rabbit wrapped in carrot; spiced monkfish, roast cauliflower; Derbyshire beef cooked over coal). 'We had the tasting menu with accompanying wines. Fantastic.' There is a wide range of vegetarian options. Bedrooms in the main house are traditional, with 'lavish fabrics and ornate plasterwork ceilings'; those in the *Garden House* are 'very spacious and well equipped'. Breakfast has freshly squeezed juices, fresh fruit, home-made granola and 'generous smoked salmon portions offset by fluffy scrambled eggs; good cafetière coffee'. 'The place is as near to perfection as you can get.'
(*David Craig, and others*)

Calver Road
Baslow DE45 1RR

T: 01246-583259
F: 01246-583818
E: reservations@fischers-
   baslowhall.co.uk
W: www.fischers-baslowhall.co.uk

BEDROOMS: 11, 5 in *Garden House*.
OPEN: all year except 25/26 and 31 Dec evening.
FACILITIES: lounge/bar, breakfast room, 3 dining rooms, function facilities, free Wi-Fi, civil wedding licence, 5-acre grounds, unsuitable for &.
BACKGROUND MUSIC: none.
LOCATION: edge of village.
CHILDREN: not under 12 in restaurant after 7 pm.
DOGS: not allowed.
CREDIT CARDS: Amex, MasterCard, Visa.
PRICES: [2013] per person B&B £77.50–£112.50. Set dinner £48–£72. 1-night bookings refused for superior rooms Sat in season.

BASSENTHWAITE LAKE Cumbria

THE PHEASANT

'We have visited *The Pheasant* on many occasions and it never disappoints. It remains my ideal country hotel – warm, comfortable, good food, log fires and charming staff.' This year's praise for a 17th-century coaching inn (a favourite of the legendary huntsman John Peel), which is at the unspoilt northern end of the Lake District. Owned by the trustees of the Inglewood estate, it is managed by the 'ever-present' Matthew Wylie. Bedrooms vary in size and aspect: 'Our superior room was well appointed, with a good view of the garden.' Other rooms overlook woodlands. A visitor who raised housekeeping issues was given an immediate apology and a refund. There are 'plenty of comfortable public spaces' where guests can have the 'excellent afternoon tea'. In *The Fell* restaurant, chef Alan O'Kane's dishes might include roulade of wild rabbit, apricot, beignet, blackberry and beetroot jelly; roast rack of Cumbrian lamb, shank ragout, confit potato and jus. More hearty fare is available in the informal bistro, which is frequented by locals. Breakfast 'is full of choices'. Popular with visitors on a walking holiday. (*RJ Ruffell, and others*)

Bassenthwaite Lake
nr Cockermouth
CA13 9YE

T: 017687-76234
F: 017687-76002
E: info@the-pheasant.co.uk
W: www.the-pheasant.co.uk

BEDROOMS: 15, 2 on ground floor in lodge.
OPEN: all year except 25 Dec.
FACILITIES: 3 lounges, bar, dining room, bistro, free Wi-Fi, 10-acre grounds, lake 200 yds (fishing), unsuitable for &.
BACKGROUND MUSIC: none.
LOCATION: 5 miles E of Cockermouth, ¼ mile off A66 to Keswick.
CHILDREN: not under 8.
DOGS: allowed in lodge bedrooms and public rooms.
CREDIT CARDS: MasterCard, Visa.
PRICES: [2013] per room B&B £120–£200, D,B&B £140–£220. Set dinner £35. 1-night bookings sometimes refused Sat.

BATH Somerset

APSLEY HOUSE

'Anybody contemplating running a B&B should come here to see how it should be done,' says a visitor this year to Claire and Nicholas Potts's elegant Georgian house, built by the Duke of Wellington for his mistress. 'It lived up to its billing: comfortable, good housekeeping, attractive furniture, helpful staff,' is another comment. The Pottses, who are on hand most days, are assisted by two sets of managers: David and Stephanie Cowley, and Louise Vincent and Pablo Palma. Bedrooms are 'well appointed', with a modern bathroom. Mornington, on the lower ground floor, is a 'light room with steps up to the elegant garden'. The house is set back from a busy road. The 'spacious' lounge, with tall windows overlooking the garden and distant countryside, has an honesty bar. No dinner, but the hosts have an extensive list of recommended restaurants which 'cater for so many different cultures'. The 'generous' and 'perfect, freshly prepared' breakfast has cereals, fresh fruit, yogurt; cooked options include a daily special. It is a 'pleasant walk into town'; a good bus service for the uphill return. (*Jean Chothia, Kenneth and Mary Moore*)

141 Newbridge Hill
Bath BA1 3PT

T: 01225-336966
F: 01225-425462
E: info@apsley-house.co.uk
W: www.apsley-house.co.uk

BEDROOMS: 12, 1 on ground floor, plus 1 self-catering apartment.
OPEN: all year except 24/25/26 Dec.
FACILITIES: drawing room, bar, dining room, free Wi-Fi, ¼-acre garden.
BACKGROUND MUSIC: Classic FM in dining room.
LOCATION: 1¼ miles W of city centre.
CHILDREN: all ages welcomed (under-2s free).
DOGS: only guide dogs allowed.
CREDIT CARDS: Amex, MasterCard, Visa.
PRICES: [2013] per room B&B single £125–£180, double £140–£195. 1-night bookings refused Sat.

SEE ALSO SHORTLIST

BATH Somerset

⚜ THE BATH PRIORY

César award: luxury hotel of the year

Ilegant country house comfort, combined with impeccable service, exquisite modern cooking and a blissful lack of background music, make this a place to return to.' Praise from *Guide* inspectors in 2013 for this luxury hotel ('expensive but it delivers real quality'), part of Andrew and Christina Brownsword's small group (see also *Gidleigh Park*, Chagford, and *The Slaughters Country Inn*, Lower Slaughter). Set back from a busy road, the 'graceful' buildings back on to a 'large and beautiful garden'. A 'charming' bedroom facing the garden had a 'pleasant country house decor; a separate sitting area; the many thoughtful touches included a plethora of free-range coat-hangers'. There are two dining rooms: a large, carpeted room overlooking the gardens, and a more intimate room. Tables are 'well spaced and the atmosphere is calm' in the larger restaurant: Sam Moody's dishes are 'all very nouvelle and pretty; small enough portions to allow you to manage three courses'. Breakfast has a 'good buffet, leaf tea; an excellent kipper'. There is 'not a whiff of the obsequious about the perfect service'.

Weston Road
Bath BA1 2XT

T: 01225-331922
F: 01225-448276
E: mail@thebathpriory.co.uk
W: www.thebathpriory.co.uk

BEDROOMS: 33, 6 in annexe, 3 on ground floor, 1 suitable for ♿.
OPEN: all year.
FACILITIES: ramps, lounge bar, library, drawing room, 2 dining rooms, free Wi-Fi, civil wedding licence, spa (heated indoor pool, 9 by 5 metres), 4-acre grounds (heated outdoor pool, 11 by 4 metres).
BACKGROUND MUSIC: none.
LOCATION: 1½ miles W of centre.
CHILDREN: no under-12s in restaurant at night.
DOGS: allowed in 2 bedrooms, not in public rooms.
CREDIT CARDS: all major cards.
PRICES: [2013] per room B&B £310–£1,050, D,B&B £460–£1,200. À la carte £75. 1-night bookings refused weekends.

SEE ALSO SHORTLIST

BATH Somerset

Map 2:D1

THE QUEENSBERRY

In a handsome street just off the Circus, Laurence and Helen Beere's boutique hotel is a contemporary conversion of four 18th-century town houses. The minimalist decor evokes mixed reactions from readers: some enjoy the contrast with the elegance of the street; others find the neutral colours 'drab and out of keeping with a Georgian house'. All agree that the staff are 'attentive, happy, informal, but professional'. The spacious bedrooms are decorated in muted tones with feature wallpapers, 'variously shaped cushions', throws; 'poor reading lights'. All rooms have flat-screen TV, DAB radio and CD-player; the suites have an iPod docking station and a wet room; there are roll-top baths and huge shower heads. Chris Cleghorn was appointed chef in 2013 for the split-level *Olive Tree* restaurant: he serves modern dishes on his short menus, perhaps roasted cauliflower soup, mussels, hazelnut and coriander; confit duck leg, parsnip and vanilla purée. We would welcome reports on his cooking. Lighter meals (sandwiches, snacks) can be taken in the *Old Q* bar. Breakfast is 'good, especially the cooked dishes'. A car-parking scheme 'works astonishingly well'. (*Alec Frank*)

25% DISCOUNT VOUCHERS

4–7 Russel Street
Bath BA1 2QF

T: 01225-447928
F: 01225-446065
E: reservations@
   thequeensberry.co.uk
W: www.thequeensberry.co.uk

BEDROOMS: 29, some on ground floor.
OPEN: all year, restaurant closed Mon–Thurs lunch.
FACILITIES: lift, 2 drawing rooms, bar, restaurant, meeting room, free Wi-Fi, 4 linked courtyard gardens, unsuitable for &.
BACKGROUND MUSIC: in restaurant and bar.
LOCATION: near Assembly Rooms.
CHILDREN: all ages welcomed.
DOGS: not allowed.
CREDIT CARDS: Amex, MasterCard, Visa.
PRICES: [2013] per room B&B £150–£250. Set dinner £33, à la carte £44. 1-night bookings sometimes refused Sat.

SEE ALSO SHORTLIST

BATH Somerset

Map 2:D1

TASBURGH HOUSE

'An illustration of why owner-managed places are so much better than manager-run ones.' A *Guide* inspector appreciated the 'personal touch' at Susan Keeling's red brick Victorian guest house; Dalila Nasri is the manager. 'Everyone was friendly and kind: Susan left a welcoming note, booked taxis, brought drinks.' The imposing house stands on the slope of a hill facing Bath ('wonderful views'); the terraced gardens at the back lead down to a canal. Each named after an English author, the bedrooms (two have been refurbished this year) vary in size: John Keats can accommodate three people, Percy Shelley five. Two are on the ground floor; a family suite is on the second floor. Tennyson is 'a delightful double, all green and gold, with an original fireplace and views across the garden and the valley to Bath. A nice bathroom, too, with a window.' Music plays all day in the 'charming' lounge and the conservatory. A continental buffet breakfast, included in the price, has freshly squeezed orange juice, yogurt, cafetière coffee, fruit. Cooked dishes cost extra. A three-course evening meal can be provided, by arrangement, for groups of eight or more.

Warminster Road
Bath BA2 6SH

T: 01225-425096
F: 01225-463842
E: stay@tasburghhouse.co.uk
W: www.tasburghhouse.co.uk

BEDROOMS: 12, 2 on ground floor.
OPEN: 14 Jan–21 Dec.
FACILITIES: drawing room, dining room, conservatory, free Wi-Fi, terrace, 7-acre grounds (canal walks, mooring), unsuitable for &.
BACKGROUND MUSIC: 'classical/jazz when appropriate'.
LOCATION: on A36 to Warminster, ½ mile E of centre.
CHILDREN: not under 6.
DOGS: only guide dogs allowed.
CREDIT CARDS: MasterCard, Visa.
PRICES: [2013] per room B&B (continental breakfast) single £95, double £120–£180. Cooked breakfast £8.50, set dinner (Mon–Thurs for groups of 8 or more by prior arrangement) £35. 1-night bookings sometimes refused Sat.

SEE ALSO SHORTLIST

BEAMINSTER Dorset

Map 1:C6

BRIDGEHOUSE

'A lovely hotel with friendly staff.' Mark and Joanna Donovan's 13th-century priest's house stands by a bridge in a 'pleasant' market town. 'The charm of the old building is combined with plenty of modern comfort,' say returning visitors. 'You are made to feel welcome from the moment you arrive.' Dinner, in an elegant Georgian dining room, is a 'highlight'. The cooking of the chef, Stephen Pielesz, is praised: 'Starters are interesting, and main courses, such as venison with a small game pie, are imaginative; the shared platter of desserts is highly recommended.' Breakfast and light lunches are taken in a conservatory by the walled garden. The largest bedrooms are in the main house. Four smaller rooms are in a converted coach house at the back. Also in the coach house is a family suite which children can share with their parents. The public rooms, in the oldest part of the building, have thick walls, mullioned windows; there are log fires in inglenook fireplaces, oak beams. 'A good base for exploring west Dorset; much walking close to hand.' (*Stephen and Beverly Potts*)

25% DISCOUNT VOUCHERS

3 Prout Bridge
Beaminster DT8 3AY

T: 01308-862200
F: 01308-863700
E: enquiries@bridge-house.co.uk
W: www.bridge-house.co.uk

BEDROOMS: 13, 4 in coach house, 4 on ground floor.
OPEN: all year.
FACILITIES: hall/reception, lounge, bar, conservatory, restaurant, free Wi-Fi, civil wedding licence, ¼-acre walled garden, alfresco dining.
BACKGROUND MUSIC: light jazz and classical.
LOCATION: 100 yds from centre.
CHILDREN: all ages welcomed.
DOGS: allowed in coach house, in bar except during food service.
CREDIT CARDS: Amex, MasterCard, Visa.
PRICES: [2013] per room B&B £125–£220. À la carte £35. 1-night bookings refused weekends and bank holidays.

BEAULIEU Hampshire

Map 2:E2

MONTAGU ARMS

'A most enjoyable stay; the staff were friendly and efficient and the food was excellent.' Praise in 2013 from regular *Guide* correspondents for this much-extended 17th-century country house, formerly an inn, in beautiful gardens in the New Forest national park. The wisteria-clad, brick-faced building is traditionally furnished, with wood-panelled public rooms; chintz armchairs, sofas and a log fire in the lounge. A wicker-furnished conservatory looks on to the gardens. Bedrooms, some of which overlook Beaulieu Palace, are individually decorated and vary in size. 'Our very comfortable room had its own sitting room.' Early morning tea or coffee can be delivered to the room. In the *Michelin*-starred *Terrace* restaurant, the chef, Matthew Tomkinson, uses local seasonal ingredients for his menus, in dishes like chilled fennel gazpacho, home-smoked organic salmon; roast fillet of beef, red chicory, sweet shallots and smoked bacon. Meals may be taken alfresco on the patio in fine weather. Simpler fare (eg, fish pie, steaks) is available in the less formal *Monty's Inn*. Guests can use the SenSpa at a sister hotel, *Careys Manor*, nearby. (*Mary and Bryan Blaxall, and others*)

Palace Lane
Beaulieu SO42 7ZL

T: 01590-612324
F: 01590-612188
E: reservations@montaguarms.co.uk
W: www.montaguarmshotel.co.uk

BEDROOMS: 22.
OPEN: all year, *Terrace* restaurant closed Mon.
FACILITIES: lounge, conservatory, bar/brasserie, restaurant, free Wi-Fi, civil wedding licence, garden, access to nearby spa, only public rooms suitable for &.
BACKGROUND MUSIC: none.
LOCATION: village centre.
CHILDREN: all ages welcomed (under-3s stay free).
DOGS: not allowed.
CREDIT CARDS: Amex, MasterCard, Visa.
PRICES: [2013] per person B&B £114–£189, D,B&B £149–£224. À la carte £72. 1-night bookings refused Sat in season.

BEELEY Derbyshire

THE DEVONSHIRE ARMS AT BEELEY

'A delightful pub in a quiet village', this 17th-century coaching inn on the Chatsworth estate is run by chef/patron Alan Hill for the Duke and Duchess of Devonshire; Oliver Fry is the manager. The original bar, which serves local ales, has oak beams, flagged floor, log fires; the brasserie extension has a colourful, contemporary decor. Alan Hill serves a seasonally-changing menu of 'gastro classics' (eg, potted duck, ham 'n' eggs, beer-battered fish and chips) in 'generous portions'; and daily specials, perhaps pot roast estate partridge, root vegetable and wild mushroom tart. The emphasis is on locally sourced food: 'We were amused by the board offering to barter fresh garden produce in exchange for coffee or a drink.' The contemporary bedrooms are in the main building, *Brookside House* next door, and the 'delightful' *Dove Cottages* across the road. 'Our room in *Brookside House* was beautifully decorated and had an exceptionally comfortable bed; housekeeping was excellent.' A 'best-ever' breakfast has unusual dishes like Emma's posh sandwich (Parma ham, warm tomato, brown sauce, truffle fried eggs). (*JD, P and JH*)

Devonshire Square
Beeley, nr Matlock DE4 2NR

T: 01629-733259
F: 01756-710498
E: res@devonshirehotels.co.uk
W: www.devonshirebeeley.co.uk

BEDROOMS: 14, 4 in annexe, 6 in cottages across the road, 5 on ground floor.
OPEN: all year.
FACILITIES: bar, brasserie, malt vault, free Wi-Fi.
BACKGROUND MUSIC: 'soft ambient' in bar.
LOCATION: 5 miles N of Matlock, off B6012.
CHILDREN: all ages welcomed.
DOGS: allowed in *Brookside* bedrooms, not in public rooms.
CREDIT CARDS: Amex, MasterCard, Visa.
PRICES: [2013] per room B&B £129–£239. À la carte £30.

BEPTON West Sussex

Map 2:E3

PARK HOUSE

'A perfect size: large enough for you to find plenty to do, but small enough to feel intimate and homely.' This country hotel at the foot of the South Downs, which is managed by Rebecca Coonan for the O'Brien family, is 'much recommended' by a *Guide* inspector this year. The staff are 'extremely kind, and went out of their way to be helpful'. The Victorian house (with medieval roots) has been thoroughly renovated: it stands in 'gorgeous, colourful' gardens; 'lots of tables and benches set in different spots'. 'Our bedroom was lovely, large windows on two sides, with views of the croquet lawn; the furnishings were country house – curtains with pelmets. The nice bathroom had generous products.' In the formal dining room and a conservatory, Callum Keir is the new chef, serving a modern menu of dishes like wild rabbit loin, crushed salad potatoes, watercress; pan-fried salmon, with samphire, saffron potatoes. 'We enjoyed a superb lunch.' The 'lavish' breakfast has 'lots of fresh juice, fruit and muesli', with 'tasty' cooked dishes. 'There is great walking on the South Downs nearby.' (*Mary Woods, and others*)

Bepton Road
Bepton
Midhurst GU29 0JB

T: 01730-819000
F: 01730-819099
E: reservations@parkhousehotel.com
W: www.parkhousehotel.com

BEDROOMS: 21, 5 on ground floor, 1 suitable for ♿, 9 in cottages in grounds.
OPEN: closed Christmas.
FACILITIES: drawing room, bar, dining room, conservatory, free Wi-Fi, civil wedding licence, 9-acre grounds, spa, indoor and outdoor swimming pools (both heated, 15 metres), tennis, pitch and putt.
BACKGROUND MUSIC: in dining room.
LOCATION: 2½ miles SW of Midhurst.
CHILDREN: all ages welcomed.
DOGS: allowed in 2 bedrooms, not in dining room.
CREDIT CARDS: Amex, MasterCard, Visa.
PRICES: [2013] per person B&B £67.50–£180. Set dinner £37.50. 1-night bookings refused weekends.

BIDEFORD Devon

Map 1:C4

YEOLDON HOUSE

25% DISCOUNT VOUCHERS

'A warm personal letter of welcome' impressed a visitor to Brian and Jennifer Steele's 'venerable' 18th-century gabled house on the banks of the River Torridge. They run it as a small country hotel. 'It's a class act,' says a visitor in 2013. A 'delectable' garden, with a fish pond and a waterfall, 'falls down a steep slope' to the river. Inside, the decor is traditional ('like something out of an Agatha Christie novel') with lots of artefacts, old stained glass and suitcases on the stairs. Each of the ten bedrooms is individually styled. Lady Dawe has a four-poster bed; the split-level Hubbastone has a balcony with a river view. 'Our room was dual-aspect, with good lighting and an antique dressing table.' In the river-facing restaurant, *Soyer's*, dinner is 'conducted with old-world courtesy'. Mr Steele serves a seasonally appropriate menu of 'exquisitely cooked local fare', perhaps ham hock terrine with Cumberland sauce; pan-fried fillet of turbot, fennel and saffron cream. 'The restaurant illustrates how Devon farmers and fishermen produce the UK's most bountiful harvest. My only complaint was that the appetite was well and truly dulled for the sumptuous breakfast.' (*Peter Anderson, and others*)

Durrant Lane
Northam, nr Bideford
EX39 2RL

T: 01237-474400
F: 01237-476618
E: yeoldonhouse@aol.com
W: www.yeoldonhousehotel.co.uk

BEDROOMS: 10.
OPEN: all year except 21 Dec–5 Jan, restaurant closed midday and Sun evening.
FACILITIES: lounge/bar, restaurant, free Wi-Fi, civil wedding licence, 2-acre grounds, beach 5 mins' drive, unsuitable for &.
BACKGROUND MUSIC: classical evenings in public rooms.
LOCATION: 1 mile N of Bideford.
CHILDREN: all ages welcomed.
DOGS: allowed, but not left unattended and not in restaurant.
CREDIT CARDS: Diners, MasterCard, Visa.
PRICES: [2013] per room B&B £125–£140, D,B&B £175–£190. Set menu £35. 1-night bookings sometimes refused in summer.

BIGBURY-ON-SEA Devon

Map 1:D4

BURGH ISLAND HOTEL

César award in 2012

'An experience like no other', this Grade II listed 1930s hotel is on a private island cut off by the tide twice a day. It has been restored as an 'Art Deco tour de force' by the owners Deborah Clark and Tony Orchard. 'It is quirky but magnificent; the house rules become part of the charm after you have been in residence for a couple of days,' says a visitor. A reporter who 'balked' at the black-tie dress code for dinner (encouraged but not obligatory) found it 'made perfect sense; it is run with a proper sense of period fun'. In the beamed, candlelit dining room, chef Tim Hall serves a daily-changing menu of modern dishes, perhaps Brixham crab, broad bean and citrus salad; chicken breast, sweetcorn panna cotta, spring greens, smoked almonds. The 1930s background music played in the beautiful public rooms 'seemed appropriate'. The bedrooms, named after famous guests (Noël Coward, Josephine Baker, Amy Johnson), vary greatly: the Garden Suite has a sitting room with French windows onto the garden; the Artist's Studio is in a room above the neighbouring *Pilchard Inn*. (*RA, MW*)

Burgh Island
Bigbury-on-Sea TQ7 4BG

T: 01548-810514
E: reception@burghisland.com
W: www.burghisland.com

BEDROOMS: 25, 1 suite in Beach House, apartment above *Pilchard Inn*.
OPEN: all year, limited closure 2 weeks in Jan.
FACILITIES: lift, sun lounge, *Palm Court* bar, dining room, ballroom, children's games room, spa, free Wi-Fi, civil wedding licence, 17-acre grounds on 26-acre island (30-metre natural sea swimming pool, tennis).
BACKGROUND MUSIC: 1930s in public areas, live Wed, Sun with dinner.
LOCATION: 5 miles S of Modbury, private garages on mainland.
CHILDREN: not under 5, no under-12s at dinner.
DOGS: only assistance dogs allowed.
CREDIT CARDS: MasterCard, Visa.
PRICES: [to 31 Mar 2014] per room D,B&B single £310, double £400–£640. 1-night bookings sometimes refused Sat/Sun at bank holidays.

BIGBURY-ON-SEA Devon

Map 1:D4

THE HENLEY

❦ *César award in 2003*

In an 'idyllic spot' on a cliff above the tidal Avon estuary, this unpretentious Edwardian villa is now a small hotel run by the owners, Martyn Scarterfield and his wife, Petra Lampe. It has long been popular for the informality and the 'high standards' of the host's cooking. 'We enjoyed ourselves as much as ever,' say returning visitors. 'Petra greeted us warmly and offered a tray of tea in the garden, which must have one of the best views in England.' In the lounge there are comfortable chairs, lots of books and magazines (and binoculars to enjoy the views). The five simple bedrooms are furnished in country style: Room 2 has double-aspect windows, all have sea views, TV, free Wi-Fi, tea-making facilities and bathrobes. Guests assemble for pre-dinner drinks in the lounge, where the menu is 'recited with flair' by Petra Lampe. The short menu might include braised pork belly, seared scallops, sweetcorn purée; fillet steak with Madeira and peppercorn sauce. Breakfast, served at a time agreed with guests, is 'excellent'. (*John and Christine Moore, and others*)

Folly Hill
Bigbury-on-Sea TQ7 4AR

T/F: 01548-810240
E: thehenleyhotel@btconnect.com
W: www.thehenleyhotel.co.uk

BEDROOMS: 5.
OPEN: mid-Mar–Oct.
FACILITIES: 2 lounges, bar, conservatory dining room, free Wi-Fi, small garden (steps to beach, golf, sailing, fishing), Coastal Path nearby, unsuitable for &.
BACKGROUND MUSIC: jazz, classical in the evenings in lounge, dining room.
LOCATION: 5 miles S of Modbury.
CHILDREN: not under 12.
DOGS: well-behaved dogs in lounge only.
CREDIT CARDS: Amex, MasterCard, Visa.
PRICES: [2013] per room B&B single £85, double £120–£145. D,B&B (3 nights min.) £25 added per person, set dinner £36. 1-night bookings sometimes refused weekends.

BIGGIN-BY-HARTINGTON Derbyshire   Map 3:B6

BIGGIN HALL

There are footpaths in all directions over beautiful countryside from the grounds of James Moffett's unpretentious hotel within the Peak District national park. It has long been liked by walkers for the unfussy atmosphere and the 'real value for money'. The Grade II* listed 17th-century building has antiques, narrow mullioned windows, massive fireplaces; there are two sitting rooms and a library. James Moffett tells us that in response to comments about 'impersonal service', he has changed the evening mealtime routine: guests now have a choice of dinner times between 6.30 and 8 pm. 'This has been well received and has resulted in improved service,' he says. There are fresh flowers on the tables in the candlelit dining room where traditional dishes (eg, smoked bacon and Brie salad; roasted shoulder of Derbyshire lamb, onion sauce) are served; 'the cheeseboard is impressive'. The simple bedrooms are in the main house, the courtyard, the 'bothy' and the lodge. A 'first-rate' breakfast, taken between 8 and 9 am, has a hot and cold buffet. Packed lunches are provided. Cycle storage is now available. (*Michael and Patricia Blanchard, and others*)

Biggin-by-Hartington
Buxton SK17 0DH

T: 01298-84451
E: enquiries@bigginhall.co.uk
W: www.bigginhall.co.uk

BEDROOMS: 21, 13 in annexes, some on ground floor.
OPEN: all year.
FACILITIES: sitting room, library, dining room, meeting room, free Wi-Fi (in sitting rooms), civil wedding licence, 8-acre grounds (croquet), River Dove 1½ miles, unsuitable for &.
BACKGROUND MUSIC: classical, in dining room.
LOCATION: 8 miles N of Ashbourne.
CHILDREN: not under 12.
DOGS: allowed in courtyard and bothy bedrooms, not in public rooms.
CREDIT CARDS: MasterCard, Visa.
PRICES: [2013] per room B&B £86–£142, D,B&B £118–£174. Set dinner £22.50. 1-night bookings sometimes refused.

BILDESTON Suffolk

Map 2:C5

THE BILDESTON CROWN

Suffolk farmer James Buckle has 'handsomely restored' this old coaching inn in a sleepy Suffolk village. More a restaurant-with-rooms than an inn ('a must for foodies,' said a *Guide* inspector), it is run by Chris Lee, the chef, and his wife, Hayley, the manager. There are beamed ceilings and walls throughout: drinks and meals can be taken in the two bar areas (blue walls, wooden tables and chairs, an open fire). A classics menu has traditional dishes 'brought up to date' (eg, game pie; fish and chips). More formal dining is available in *Ingrams* restaurant, which has a separate entrance, a small lounge, and a courtyard for alfresco eating. Chris Lee serves elaborate dishes on his 'select' and tasting menus, perhaps Red Poll tongue, confit cod cheek, horseradish and watercress; sea bass, warm lobster Caesar, bacon, anchovy dressing. 'Good food, well presented.' A winding landing ('beware of low beams') leads to the 'well-equipped' bedrooms. They have a modern decor: some guests find the 'luxury' Black Fuchsia room overpowering; a modest rear room had a 'soft, comfortable king-size bed, a luxury sound system, large wardrobe'.

104 High Street
Bildeston IP7 7EB

T: 01449-740510
E: reception@thebildestoncrown.com
W: www.thebildestoncrown.com

BEDROOMS: 13, 1 suitable for &.
OPEN: all year, except 25, 26 Dec and 1 Jan (restaurant is open for lunch on all three).
FACILITIES: lift, bar, lounge, restaurant, 2 meeting rooms, free Wi-Fi, civil wedding licence, courtyard.
BACKGROUND MUSIC: 'jazz/chill-out' in bar and restaurant.
LOCATION: village centre.
CHILDREN: all ages welcomed.
DOGS: allowed (£10 charge).
CREDIT CARDS: Amex, MasterCard, Visa.
PRICES: [2013] per room B&B single (Sun–Thurs) £70–£120, double £100–£195. À la carte £45.

BIRMINGHAM West Midlands

Map 2:B2

HOTEL DU VIN BIRMINGHAM

In the revitalised Jewellery quarter of the city (within walking distance of the cathedral, shops, galleries and museums), this branch of the du Vin chain is a conversion of an ornate red brick early Victorian building (once the city's eye hospital). 'It might not be particularly personal, but the staff are excellent, the situation is superb and the food is fine,' said a *Guide* inspector. The entrance is 'grand': four giant pillars, offset by tromp l'oeil stonework and a ceiling fresco, lead to an open square courtyard with an automatic cover in case of rain. A sweeping staircase leads to the bedrooms (each named after a wine or winery), which vary considerably in size and price. Each has a large bed with wooden surrounds, a dark decor (black, brown and beige); a large bathroom with a stand-alone bath, a 'huge', powerful shower; a small fridge with fresh milk and drinks. The welcome from the young staff is 'courteous, and service is prompt'. In the 'charming' dining room ('wooden tables, shining glasses, lots of pictures'), the menu has bistro classics, eg, French onion soup; rack of lamb, confit tomato; steaks.

25 Church Street
Birmingham B3 2NR

T: 0121-200 0600
E: info.birmingham@
  hotelduvin.com
W: www.hotelduvin.com

BEDROOMS: 66, 3 suitable for &.
OPEN: all year.
FACILITIES: lift, bistro, 2 bars, billiard room, free Wi-Fi, civil wedding licence, spa, courtyard.
BACKGROUND MUSIC: in public areas.
LOCATION: central, near St Philip's Cathedral.
CHILDREN: all ages welcomed.
DOGS: not allowed in bar/bistro.
CREDIT CARDS: Amex, MasterCard, Visa.
PRICES: [2013] room only £125–£365. Breakfast £10–£14.95, à la carte £35.

BIRMINGHAM West Midlands

Map 2:B2

SIMPSONS

One of only three *Michelin* star restaurants in Birmingham, *Simpsons* has four bedrooms to which guests can 'retreat' after a 'staggeringly good meal'. Chef/patron Andreas Antona has given this Georgian mansion in leafy Edgbaston a Greek-style landscaped garden which reflects his background (he was born into a Greek Cypriot family in north London). The staff are 'welcoming, helpful'. The cooking is classical with Mediterranean influences: typical dishes might be roast pigeon, carrots, date purée, toasted cracked wheat, feta; sea bass, salt-baked celeriac, burnt butter. 'One of the best meals we have ever had,' said a trusted reporter. In warm months, alfresco meals can be taken on a terrace facing the garden. The bedrooms (available from Tuesday to Saturday) are 'very comfortable and well equipped; a good bathroom'. Venetian has an antique bed, lots of velvet, reds and golds; French has plaster mouldings, hand-painted cream and gold furnishings. The rooms are supplied with a basket of fruit, mineral water, coffee-making facilities. The continental breakfast has freshly squeezed orange juice, fruit salad, home-made yogurt: 'As delicious as dinner, all beautifully presented.' (*VL*)

20 Highfield Road
Edgbaston
Birmingham B15 3DU

T: 0121-454 3434
F: 0121-454 3399
E: info@simpsonsrestaurant.co.uk
W: www.simpsonsrestaurant.co.uk

BEDROOMS: 4.
OPEN: all year except bank holidays, restaurant closed Sun evening, accommodation Tues–Sat only.
FACILITIES: lounge, 3 restaurant areas, private dining room, Wi-Fi (chargeable), cookery school, terrace (alfresco dining), garden, only restaurant suitable for &.
BACKGROUND MUSIC: none.
LOCATION: 1 mile from centre.
CHILDREN: all ages welcomed (no special facilities).
DOGS: only guide dogs allowed.
CREDIT CARDS: Amex, MasterCard, Visa.
PRICES: [2013] per room B&B (continental) £160–£225. À la carte £60.

BLAKENEY Norfolk

Map 2:A5

THE BLAKENEY HOTEL

'A happy ship, unpompous, with charming staff.' There is much praise this year for the Stannard family's traditional quayside hotel. Its views over the river and marshes are 'second to none'. 'The friendly atmosphere and general efficiency is no doubt due to the family ownership,' says a regular correspondent who observed a 'mature clientele' in the off season; *The Blakeney* is busy with families during the school holidays. Taking afternoon tea in the first-floor lounge, which has a panoramic outlook over the tidal estuary, is 'a treat not to be missed'. In the dining room, chef Martin Sewell prepares 'honest British food', with dishes like grilled fillet of plaice, crushed potatoes, caper and lemon dressing. 'While not pretending to be haute cuisine, it is of a consistent quality.' The best bedrooms have the views: 'Our triple-aspect room was large and well appointed; an excellent bathroom with a roll-top bath and separate shower.' A visitor who, 'as requested', left comments, was 'impressed to receive a satisfactory reply on two negative issues, written within days'. (*Shawn Kholucy, Bryan and Mary Blaxall, Sara Hollowell, David Craig*)

Blakeney
nr Holt NR25 7NE

T: 01263-740797
F: 01263-740795
E: reception@blakeneyhotel.co.uk
W: www.blakeneyhotel.co.uk

BEDROOMS: 64, 16 in *Granary* annexe opposite, some on ground floor.
OPEN: all year.
FACILITIES: lift, ramps, lounge, sun lounge, bar, restaurant, free Wi-Fi, function facilities, heated indoor swimming pool (12 by 5 metres), steam room, sauna, mini-gym, games room, ¼-acre garden.
BACKGROUND MUSIC: none.
LOCATION: on quay.
CHILDREN: all ages welcomed.
DOGS: allowed in some bedrooms, not in public rooms.
CREDIT CARDS: Amex, MasterCard, Visa.
PRICES: [2013] per person B&B £81–£143, D,B&B £93–£161. Set dinner £29, à la carte £29–£45. 1-night bookings sometimes refused Fri/Sat, bank holidays.

BLEDINGTON Oxfordshire

Map 3:D6

THE KING'S HEAD INN

Ducks and hens roam the gravelled drive of this 400-year-old Cotswold stone inn which has a 'special setting' by a green of a handsome village. It is run by the hands-on owners, Archie and Nicola Orr-Ewing; Nick Jermanic is the manager, Matt Laughton is the chef. Unlike some pubs-with-rooms, guests may check in during the afternoon. The bedrooms are above the bar and in an annexe across a courtyard. Inn rooms, the smaller and cheaper, have a mix of antiques and painted furniture. A double-aspect courtyard room, decorated in beige and cream, has a feature wall with a bold metallic design; a 'functional' bathroom with mosaic tiles. 'It was wonderfully quiet at night.' The 'sense of being a proper pub' is maintained in the inn, where 'locals wander in with their dogs for a pint'. There is a series of interconnecting rooms with old beams, rugs on flagstone floors, settles, wooden tables; the separate dining room is plainer in style. Modern dishes are served on a seasonal menu, which might include baked Cornish scallops, Cheddar and parsley crust; grilled Barnsley chop, black pudding, mint and balsamic jus.

The Green
Bledington OX7 6XQ

T: 01608-658365
F: 01608-658902
E: info@kingsheadinn.net
W: www.thekingsheadinn.net

BEDROOMS: 12, 6 in annexe, some on ground floor.
OPEN: all year.
FACILITIES: 2 bars, restaurant, free Wi-Fi, courtyard.
BACKGROUND MUSIC: occasionally.
LOCATION: on village green.
CHILDREN: all ages welcomed.
DOGS: not allowed in bedrooms.
CREDIT CARDS: MasterCard, Visa.
PRICES: per room B&B £95–£135. À la carte £30. 1-night bookings refused Sat.

BLOCKLEY Gloucestershire

Map 3:D6

LOWER BROOK HOUSE

In a Cotswold village once noted for its silk production, this converted 17th-century mill (Grade II listed) is approached through 'delightful' gardens. 'Full of character', it is run as a small hotel by owners Julian and Anna Ebbutt. 'A lot of thought' has been put into the well-being of guests, said an inspector who was 'enchanted' by candles lit in the windows ('the traditional sign of welcome rarely remembered these days'). The bedrooms, which vary in size, are decorated in 'plain, modern style'. Colebrook, a large double room, has a freestanding steel bath and separate shower in its bathroom. All rooms have fresh fruit, home-made biscuits, tea- and coffee-making facilities, a Thermos of fresh milk. There are flagstone floors and exposed beams in the two sitting areas, which have 'bold colours, a medley of personal objects'. A short supper menu, available from Monday to Saturday, can be taken in your room or in the small dining room. Anna Ebbutt is the cook: her traditional dishes might include confit of pork belly, herb and apple crust. Breakfast is 'very good'.

25% DISCOUNT VOUCHERS

Lower Street
Blockley GL56 9DS

T: 01386-700286
F: 01386-701400
E: info@lowerbrookhouse.com
W: www.lowerbrookhouse.com

BEDROOMS: 6.
OPEN: all year except Christmas, dining room closed Sun night.
FACILITIES: lounge (with free Wi-Fi), restaurant, 1-acre garden, unsuitable for &.
BACKGROUND MUSIC: in restaurant at night.
LOCATION: centre of village.
CHILDREN: not under 10.
DOGS: not allowed.
CREDIT CARDS: Amex, MasterCard, Visa.
PRICES: per room B&B £80–£190. À la carte £20. 1-night bookings usually refused Sat.

BOSCASTLE Cornwall

Map 1:C3

THE OLD RECTORY

The welcome is personal ('a cup of tea in the sitting room and a chat') at Chris and Sally Searle's slate-hung house in a valley near the north Cornwall coast. A returning visitor this year noted many improvements to the house: a 'lovely' outside terrace; a renovation of the conservatory (where evening meals are taken) and the 'magnificent' gardens (a walled kitchen garden provides fruit and vegetables for the meals). The writer Thomas Hardy met his future wife, Emma Gifford, the rector's sister, while staying at the rectory, and returned to write some of his best poetry after her death. The bedrooms are decorated in period style: Emma's room has 'such character, especially the little corridor leading to the shower and the Victorian loo'. Breakfast has compotes from the Searles's fruit, eggs from their hens and ducks, bacon and sausages from their pigs. 'Full English was enlivened by peppers from the garden.' The Searles's daughter, Anna, will cook a set two-course meal in the evening (bring your own bottle, no corkage). 'Everything is green, from solar panels in a field to waste disposal.' (*Canon Michael Bourdeaux*)

St Juliot, nr Boscastle
PL35 0BT

T: 01840-250225
E: sally@stjuliot.com
W: www.stjuliot.com

BEDROOMS: 4, 1 in stables (linked to house).
OPEN: all year.
FACILITIES: sitting room, breakfast room, conservatory, 3-acre garden (croquet lawn, 'lookout'), unsuitable for &.
BACKGROUND MUSIC: none.
LOCATION: 2 miles NE of Boscastle.
CHILDREN: not under 10.
DOGS: only allowed in stables.
CREDIT CARDS: MasterCard, Visa.
PRICES: [2013] per room B&B £75–£102. 1-night bookings refused weekends and busy periods.

BOSHAM West Sussex

Map 2:E3

THE MILLSTREAM

In a historic village, this popular hotel, originally a collection of workmen's cottages, stands in a large garden with a gazebo and a fast-flowing stream. Returning visitors consider it 'like an old friend'. A fire is lit in the bar in cool months; on warm days, guests sit under sunshades on the lawn. Pretty bedrooms have bold floral prints; a hospitality tray with biscuits and fresh fruit. 'In an understated way, it gets a lot of things right: a silent fridge with mineral water and fresh milk; a face flannel is a nice extra.' Across the footbridge over the millstream, two suites in the thatched Waterside Cottage each have French windows that lead to a private garden. The restaurant was refurbished in late 2012 and given new tables and chairs. The chef, Neil Hiskey, serves 'ambitious' modern dishes on a daily-changing menu, perhaps smoked haddock and leek open ravioli, quail's egg; fillet of bream, coriander gnocchi. *Marwick's Brasserie*, which is also open to non-residents, has a more casual atmosphere. Breakfast has an extensive menu; an express breakfast is served in the lounge until 11.30 am. (*PJ, SK*)

Bosham Lane
Bosham, nr Chichester
PO18 8HL

T: 01243-573234
F: 01243-573459
E: info@millstreamhotel.com
W: www.millstreamhotel.com

BEDROOMS: 35, 2 in cottage, 7 on ground floor, 1 suitable for &.
OPEN: all year.
FACILITIES: lounge, bar, restaurant (pianist Fri and Sat), brasserie, conference room, free Wi-Fi, civil wedding licence, 1¼-acre garden, Chichester Harbour 300 yards.
BACKGROUND MUSIC: 'mixed' music 10.30 am–10.30 pm in lounge and restaurant.
LOCATION: 4 miles W of Chichester.
CHILDREN: all ages welcomed, £20 B&B to share adult's room.
DOGS: only guide dogs allowed.
CREDIT CARDS: all major cards.
PRICES: [2013] per room B&B single £99–£139, double £159–£229. D,B&B (min. 2 nights) £95–£122 per person, set dinner £26.50–£34, à la carte £45. 1-night bookings refused Sat.

BOURTON-ON-THE-HILL Gloucestershire   Map 3:D6

THE HORSE AND GROOM

♀ *César award in 2012*

'Delightful, warm, welcoming; you get the feeling
of being in a well-organised establishment
where everyone knows their job and gets on
with it cheerfully.' Praise in 2013 from visitors
returning to Tom and Will Greenstock's former
coaching inn in a Cotswold village of honey-
stone houses. Tom is 'much in evidence' front-
of-house; his brother, Will, is the chef whose
blackboard menu is 'tweaked regularly'.
'Evesham asparagus was served with shrimps
one evening, bacon another; chicken breast with
roast sweet potato one day, aubergine purée
the next (each so different and delicious).' The
bedrooms are 'spacious and have all the
essentials'. A room overlooking the garden had a
'good bed, very nice bathroom; June's scrummy
home-made flapjacks and a Thermos of fresh
milk with the tea tray. June also makes the pièce
de résistance at breakfast: gorgeous, buttery
croissants.' There is no lounge: 'It's the bar or
bedroom, but you can sit comfortably and read
in all the bedrooms.' Some road noise during
the day from the busy A44; quieter at night
('heavy curtains provided soundproofing').
(*Jill and Mike Bennett*)

25% DISCOUNT VOUCHERS

Bourton-on-the-Hill
nr Moreton-in-Marsh
GL56 9AQ

T/F: 01386-700413
E: greenstock@
     horseandgroom.info
W: www.horseandgroom.info

BEDROOMS: 5.
OPEN: all year except 25/31 Dec,
restaurant closed Sun eve.
FACILITIES: bar/restaurant, free Wi-
Fi, 1-acre garden, unsuitable for &.
BACKGROUND MUSIC: none.
LOCATION: village centre.
CHILDREN: all ages welcomed.
DOGS: not allowed.
CREDIT CARDS: MasterCard, Visa.
PRICES: [2013] per room B&B
£96–£170. À la carte £26. 1-night
bookings refused weekends.

BOWNESS-ON-WINDERMERE Cumbria   Map 4: inset C2

LINDETH FELL

❧*César award in 2009*

'The owners and their youthful team of charming staff could not have made us feel more at home and relaxed.' This year's praise for a much-loved hotel, on the fells above Lake Windermere, owned and run by Diana Kennedy and her daughter, Sheena. 'It is one of those rare places where guests are valued as individuals and are always addressed by their surname,' said a trusted correspondent. 'Feel free to let us know what you think of our bedrooms,' say the Kennedys, who have a 'rolling programme of refurbishment'. 'It was sometimes hard to leave our newly spruced-up, palatial room,' said one guest. There are two drawing rooms: the larger, which has 'stunning' views over the gardens and the lake, has deep sofas; the smaller is for those who want to read (books and magazines are provided). There is also seating in the oak-panelled hall. Brian Parsons is the new chef in 2013; his menus might include ham hock terrine, fig and apple chutney; lemon- and herb-crusted salmon, new potatoes, mangetout. (*Peter Hayes and Sarah Marshall, Gwyn Morgan, I and FW*)

25% DISCOUNT VOUCHERS

Lyth Valley Road
Bowness-on-Windermere
LA23 3JP

T: 015394-43286
F: 015394-47455
E: kennedy@lindethfell.co.uk
W: www.lindethfell.co.uk

BEDROOMS: 14, 1 on ground floor.
OPEN: all year except Jan.
FACILITIES: ramp, hall, 2 lounges, dispense bar, 3 dining rooms, free Wi-Fi, 7-acre grounds (gardens, croquet, putting, bowls, tarn, fishing permits).
BACKGROUND MUSIC: none.
LOCATION: 1 mile S of Bowness on A5074.
CHILDREN: all ages welcomed, but no under-7s in dining rooms in evening.
DOGS: only assistance dogs allowed.
CREDIT CARDS: MasterCard, Visa.
PRICES: [2013] per person B&B £65–£105, D,B&B £100–£140. Set dinner £36. 1-night bookings sometimes refused weekends, bank holidays.

SEE ALSO SHORTLIST

BOWNESS-ON-WINDERMERE Cumbria   Map 4: inset C2

LINTHWAITE HOUSE

'Unlike some hotels in the area which have gone ultra-modern and lost the style we visit the lakes for, *Linthwaite* combines the contemporary with period features to retain a country house feel.' Praise this year for Mike Bevans's creeper-covered white and stone late Victorian hotel in a 'stunning setting with breathtaking views over Lake Windermere'. Andrew Nicholson is the manager: the staff 'are there when you need them, but not in your face'. The atmosphere is 'relaxed and informal; an ideal place in which to recharge one's batteries'. Bedrooms vary in size and outlook; larger rooms overlook the lake, others have a garden view; 'Our favourite room is modern, warm, cosy; in the bathroom the towels are soft and thick.' Smart dress is required in the candlelit restaurant, where chef Chris O'Callaghan serves a 'delicious' modern British menu of 'beautifully presented' food. His dishes might include gin-cured salmon, lemon purée, tonic sorbet; poached guineafowl breast, braised baby gem, saffron consommé. Breakfast has an extensive buffet (cereals, fruit, creamy yogurt, compotes); home-made croissants; a wide choice of cooked dishes. (*Susan McCosh, and others*)

Crook Road
Bowness-on-Windermere
LA23 3JA

T: 015394-88600
F: 015394-88601
E: stay@linthwaite.com
W: www.linthwaite.com

BEDROOMS: 30, some on ground floor.
OPEN: all year.
FACILITIES: ramp, lounge/bar, conservatory, 3 dining rooms, function facilities, free Wi-Fi, civil wedding licence, 14-acre grounds.
BACKGROUND MUSIC: in bar and dining room.
LOCATION: ¾ mile S of Bowness.
CHILDREN: no under-7s in dining rooms after 7 pm.
DOGS: allowed in two bedrooms.
CREDIT CARDS: Amex, MasterCard, Visa.
PRICES: [2013] per person B&B £99–£305, D,B&B £139–£345. À la carte £52. 1-night bookings sometimes refused weekends.

BRADFORD-ON-AVON Wiltshire

Map 2:D1

WOOLLEY GRANGE NEW

Back in the ownership of the founder, Nigel Chapman, this Jacobean stone manor is part of the Luxury Family Hotels group. We sent inspectors with young children to check it out. 'Like the country home of a wealthy family friend, *Woolley Grange* is a bit shabby around the edges; charmingly so if you have the right attitude. More effort is needed on the luxury side, but there is a happy, relaxed attitude; the staff interact well with children.' Clare Hammond, the manager, 'was warm and ever-present; she always addressed our girls by name. They loved every minute with an infectious pleasure; we had a blast in the indoor swimming pool and enjoyed exploring the grounds.' The staff in the crèche, a light-filled space, were 'expert at putting parents' minds at rest'. Children share their parents' bedroom (some are a suite) for free: 'Our beamed room had lots of storage, a large bouncy bed with an eye-catching headboard; no outlook and some noise from the kitchen area.' In the *Orangery* conservatory, there was a good variety of 'tasty' dishes for children. 'We ate well in the restaurant in the evening.'

Woolley Green
Bradford-on-Avon BA15 1TX

T: 01225-864705
E: info@woolleygrangehotel.co.uk
W: www.woolleygrangehotel.co.uk

BEDROOMS: 25, 11 in annexes, 2 on ground floor.
OPEN: all year.
FACILITIES: 2 drawing rooms, 2 restaurants, cinema, free Wi-Fi, civil wedding licence, crèche, spa, heated indoor and outdoor swimming pools (12 metres), 14-acre grounds.
BACKGROUND MUSIC: none.
LOCATION: 1 mile NE of Bradford-on-Avon.
CHILDREN: all ages welcomed.
DOGS: not allowed in restaurants.
CREDIT CARDS: Amex, MasterCard, Visa.
PRICES: [2013] per room B&B £120–£430, D,B&B £190–£515. À la carte £39.

BRAITHWAITE Cumbria

THE COTTAGE IN THE WOOD

'Lovely people who offer excellent service', Kath and Liam Berney run their restaurant-with-rooms in a converted 17th-century whitewashed coaching inn. It stands within the forest on Whinlatter Pass, looking down to the Skiddaw mountain range. The bedrooms vary in size: smaller rooms are decorated in cottage style with brass and light oak fittings; the Garden Room has an 'amazing' wet room and a sitting area; Spruce, an attic suite, has a roll-top bath and separate shower. In the conservatory restaurant, which has been refurbished and extended this year, chef Ryan Blackburn uses local and foraged produce for his modern daily-changing menus. His dishes might include line-caught mackerel, beetroot, watercress and horseradish; braised cheek of beef, roasted carrots, chicory and monk's beard. Breakfast has fruit juices, cereals, yogurt; local bacon and sausages (and eggs from 'the happiest hens you have ever come across'); home-made jam and marmalade. Guests have a cosy sitting room with a wood-burner, walking magazines, books and games; in summer they can sit on a terrace or in the small garden. 'Ideal for walkers and mountain bikers; good value.' (*PH*)

Magic Hill
Whinlatter Forest
Braithwaite CA12 5TW

T: 017687-78409
E: relax@thecottageinthewood.co.uk
W: www.thecottageinthewood.co.uk

BEDROOMS: 9.
OPEN: Feb–Dec (except Mon), restaurant closed Sun/Mon.
FACILITIES: lounge, bar, restaurant, free Wi-Fi, 5-acre grounds (terraced garden).
BACKGROUND MUSIC: none.
LOCATION: 5 miles NW of Keswick.
CHILDREN: not under 10.
DOGS: not allowed.
CREDIT CARDS: Amex, MasterCard, Visa.
PRICES: [2013] per room B&B £110–£190. Set menu £40. 1-night bookings refused weekends.

BRAMPTON Cumbria

Map 4:B3

FARLAM HALL

César award in 2001

'There is a firm hand on the tiller here: the Quinion family have owned and run this hotel since 1975, and their professionalism and dedication show.' Solid praise this year for this traditional country hotel (Relais & Châteaux), occupying a restored Victorian manor home in large, lush grounds. 'It is pleasant to arrive up the sweeping driveway, through the gardens, to this ivy-covered hotel. We were welcomed at the door and our luggage was promptly taken.' 'Comfy', extravagantly decorated drawing rooms have open fires and 'a relaxing ambience'; drinks can be served in the lounges, garden or bedroom. 'Our large, well-appointed room had lots of storage, and views of the garden; the decent-sized bathroom had good shelf space.' Smart dress is preferred in the elegant dining room, where Barry Quinion's daily-changing menu might include timbale of West Coast crab; Lancashire guineafowl breast, mushroom duxelle. Outside, 'the pretty gardens, with a pond and a stream running through woodland, are worth exploring'. Hadrian's Wall is easily accessible; trout fishing and birdwatching are close by. 'We would return.' (*ST*)

25% DISCOUNT VOUCHERS

Brampton CA8 2NG

T: 01697-746234
F: 01697-746683
E: farlam@farlamhall.co.uk
W: www.farlamhall.co.uk

BEDROOMS: 12, 1 in stables, 2 on ground floor.
OPEN: all year except 25–30 Dec, 5–21 Jan; restaurant closed midday (light lunches by arrangement) except New Year's Day, Mothering and Easter Sun.
FACILITIES: ramps, 2 lounges, restaurant, free Wi-Fi, civil wedding licence, 8-acre grounds, unsuitable for &.
BACKGROUND MUSIC: none.
LOCATION: on A689, 2½ miles SE of Brampton (not in Farlam village).
CHILDREN: not under 5.
DOGS: not allowed unattended in bedrooms.
CREDIT CARDS: Amex, MasterCard, Visa.
PRICES: [2013] per person B&B £107–£137, D,B&B £150–£180. Set dinner £45–£47.50. 1-night bookings refused New Year's Eve.

BRANCASTER STAITHE Norfolk

🏵 THE WHITE HORSE

César award: Norfolk hotel of the year

'A lovely hotel with a relaxing ambience, delicious food, friendly staff and good management.' *Guide* inspectors 'would readily return' to Cliff Nye's small hotel above tidal sea marshes on the north Norfolk coast. Christina Boyle, the manager, is a 'reassuring presence'. The public areas have a well-stocked bar, a lounge with Lloyd Loom chairs and sofas, and a conservatory restaurant with a decked area (for alfresco drinks and meals on mild days). 'There is a warm atmosphere with good lighting, wooden tables.' Fresh fish (often Cyril's mussels harvested at the foot of the garden) features on Aurum Frankel's menus: 'Substantial portions of modern dishes; a lovely squash and pomegranate salad; delicious stone bass; service was prompt.' Eight of the bedrooms are in a garden annexe that 'folds into the landscape thanks to a sedum roof'; each has a small terrace with chairs and a table. 'Ours was spacious and light, with matting and laminated flooring at the entrance; seaside colours and a simple decor appropriate to the position.' These rooms are popular with dog owners and walkers. Breakfast 'has all the right elements'.

Brancaster Staithe
PE31 8BY

T: 01485-210262
F: 01485-210930
E: reception@
     whitehorsebrancaster.co.uk
W: www.whitehorsebrancaster.co.uk

BEDROOMS: 15, 8 on ground floor in annexe, 1 suitable for ♿.
OPEN: all year.
FACILITIES: 2 lounge areas, public bar, conservatory restaurant, dining room, free Wi-Fi, ½-acre garden (covered sunken garden), harbour sailing.
BACKGROUND MUSIC: 'subtle' at quiet times, not when busy or in summer.
LOCATION: centre of village just E of Brancaster.
CHILDREN: all ages welcomed.
DOGS: allowed in annexe rooms (£10) and bar.
CREDIT CARDS: MasterCard, Visa.
PRICES: [2013] per room B&B £130–£170, D,B&B (Nov–Mar only) £170. À la carte £28. 1-night bookings sometimes refused weekends.

BRAY Berkshire

Map 2:D3

THE WATERSIDE INN

In a 16th-century Berkshire village on the banks of the River Thames, this restaurant-with-rooms is run by the chef/patron, Alain Roux, and his 'attentive, ever-smiling' manager, Diego Masciaga. Gourmets have long been drawn by the cooking; the restaurant has held three *Michelin* stars since 1985. 'It would be silly to report without reference to cost,' says a regular correspondent. 'The unwary could get a shock, but you get what you pay for, and more.' Meals are taken in a glass-fronted restaurant overlooking the river, to encourage a 'relaxed environment'. A two- or three-course 'menu gastronomique', available at lunchtime, has classic French dishes, perhaps clams and sweetcorn velouté; slices of spit-roasted beef rump, a celeriac lasagne. The seven-course 'menu exceptionnel', which must be taken by the entire table, is recommended. The 'impeccable' bedrooms are French in style. One room above the restaurant has a trompe-l'oeil mural. Two rooms share a riverside terrace ('ideal' for couples travelling together); the newest room in a nearby cottage has 'his and hers' bathrooms. A continental breakfast is brought to the bedroom in a wicker tray.

Ferry Road
Bray SL6 2AT

T: 01628-620691
E: reservations@waterside-inn.co.uk
W: www.waterside-inn.co.uk

BEDROOMS: 11, 3 in cottage.
OPEN: 24 Jan–24 Dec, closed Mon/Tues.
FACILITIES: restaurant, private dining room (with drawing room and courtyard garden), free Wi-Fi, civil wedding licence, riverside terrace (launch for drinks/coffee), unsuitable for &.
BACKGROUND MUSIC: none.
LOCATION: 3 miles SE of Maidenhead.
CHILDREN: not under 12.
DOGS: not allowed.
CREDIT CARDS: all major cards.
PRICES: [2013] per room B&B £200–£750. Set lunch £59.50–£79.50, à la carte £140, menu exceptionnel £152.

BRIGHTON East Sussex

Map 2:E4

HOTEL DU VIN BRIGHTON

Between the Lanes and the seafront, this branch of the du Vin chain (an interesting conversion of mock Tudor and Gothic revival buildings) is a 'favourite in Brighton' for some *Guide* readers. A trusted reporter staying on a 'good Sunday-night deal' agreed: 'They continue to do many things very well: you can count on a big, comfortable bed, an excellent bathroom; the continental breakfast buffet is state-of-the-art.' The staff are 'well motivated and trained; everyone makes an effort to help you'. The decor ('masculine – dark browns predominate') might be 'beginning to show its age', but the bathroom is 'as good as you will get anywhere: a huge stand-alone bath, a powerful shower'. In the lively bistro (wooden floors and tables, banquettes), the seasonal menu might include prawn and crayfish cocktail; half Normandy chicken, jus rôti. The adjacent *Pub du Vin* has a simpler menu. The wine list is 'varied and interesting'. The breakfast buffet has 'delicious fresh breads, pastries, crisp croissants; two types of fresh fruit salad, a fruit compote, a wonderful treacly granola; a big jug of freshly squeezed orange juice. Good cooked dishes.' (*DB*)

2–6 Ship Street
Brighton BN1 1AD

T: 01273-718588
E: info.brighton@hotelduvin.com
W: www.hotelduvin.com

BEDROOMS: 49, 6 in courtyard, 11 in connected *Pub du Vin*.
OPEN: all year.
FACILITIES: lounge/bar, bistro, billiard room, function rooms, free Wi-Fi, civil wedding licence, unsuitable for ⅁.
BACKGROUND MUSIC: 'easy listening' in bar all day.
LOCATION: 50 yds from seafront.
CHILDREN: all ages welcomed.
DOGS: allowed.
CREDIT CARDS: Amex, MasterCard, Visa.
PRICES: [2013] room £149–£300. Breakfast £10–£14.95, à la carte £31. 1-night bookings sometimes refused in summer.

SEE ALSO SHORTLIST

BRISTOL

Map 1:B6

BROOKS GUESTHOUSE

25% DISCOUNT VOUCHERS

Recommended for 'younger guests wanting to explore the city', Carla and Andrew Brooks's simple, modern hotel is a converted former hostel. The situation – by St Nicholas Market, close to the main shopping areas – is 'excellent'. A visitor this year found the staff were 'welcoming and helpful'. Entry is through wrought iron gates into a large, paved courtyard with an 'inspiring' mural painted by Banksy's friends. Modern watercolour prints decorate the corridors which lead to the bedrooms, which vary in size (and price). They have a bright contemporary decor; hooks and coat-hangers provide the storage (which for one guest 'did not compensate for the lack of a wardrobe'). Bedlinen is 'comfortable and clean'. 'Everything functioned silently' in the small bathroom. Courtyard rooms are quieter than those facing the street, which might suffer from noise as the pubs empty. There are sofas, armchairs, an honesty bar, newspapers and magazines in a lounge/dining room; an open-plan stainless steel kitchen gives 'a homely feel'. Breakfast has 'excellent' freshly squeezed orange juice, yogurt, muesli, cereals, 'great' eggs and bacon; 'good' coffee. (*RR, and others*)

Exchange Avenue
Bristol BS1 1UB

T: 0117-930 0066
F: 0117-929 9489
E: info@
 brooksguesthousebristol.com
W: www.brooksguesthouse
 bristol.com

BEDROOMS: 23, 1 on ground floor suitable for &.
OPEN: all year except 22–26 Dec.
FACILITIES: lounge/dining room, free Wi-Fi, courtyard garden.
BACKGROUND MUSIC: 'easy listening' in lounge.
LOCATION: central.
CHILDREN: all ages welcomed.
DOGS: not allowed.
CREDIT CARDS: Amex, MasterCard, Visa.
PRICES: per room B&B £70–£120.

BRISTOL

NUMBER THIRTY EIGHT CLIFTON

♞ *César award in 2013*

With 'wonderful views down to Bristol and beyond', this luxury B&B occupies a refurbished five-storey Georgian merchant's house 'right at the top of Clifton'. Adam Dorrien-Smith is the owner; the 'charming and cheerful' managers are Shona Smillie and Jarek Eliasz. The hotel has 'a stunning contemporary interior' inspired by Bristol's seafaring history: there are copper baths, wood-panelled walls, seagrass carpets. 'Our room, No. 3, was done in classic boutique style: minimalist decor, designer blinds and the occasional carefully chosen object, such as a retro Roberts radio. The bathroom had an old-fashioned roll-top bath big enough for two, set in a window with a view. We loved it.' The ground-floor lounge has 'comfortable sofas and armchairs, coffee tables with magazines, local information'; sculptures by Cornish artist Tom Leaper are a 'special' touch. Breakfast is 'inspiring' ('we were asked how we liked our bacon cooked – a first'); but the room in which it is served lacked 'space for everyone at the same time'. No evening meals; restaurants and bars are within walking distance. (*David Berry*)

38 Upper Belgrave Road
Clifton, Bristol BS8 2XN

T: 0117-946 6905
E: info@number38clifton.com
W: www.number38clifton.com

BEDROOMS: 10.
OPEN: all year.
FACILITIES: lounge, breakfast room, free Wi-Fi, terrace, unsuitable for ♿.
BACKGROUND MUSIC: light jazz at breakfast.
LOCATION: on edge of Clifton Downs.
CHILDREN: not under 12.
DOGS: not allowed.
CREDIT CARDS: all major cards.
PRICES: [2013] per room B&B £125–£210.

BROADWAY Worcestershire

Map 3:D6

THE BROADWAY HOTEL **NEW**

Opposite the green of a handsome Cotswold village, this half-stone, half-timber 16th-century building has been renovated by the small Cotswold Inns and Hotels group. 'Exceptional value in a fantastic location; everything is immaculate,' say *Guide* inspectors in 2013. In the oldest part of the building, the 'stunning' high-ceilinged bar has a minstrels' gallery along one side; a huge open log fire on the other. There are oak beams and mullioned windows in the 'comfortably furnished' sitting room. 'The atmosphere is warm in *Tattersalls Brasserie*, where we had a lovely table on a raised section. Dinner was excellent with a good choice and decent-sized portions: a fine goat's cheese and beetroot salad; rack of lamb (served exactly as requested), gratin potato, fennel and shallot salsa.' The bedrooms are individually furnished and decorated. 'Our room, of adequate size, had a built-in hanging wardrobe, chairs, drawers, good lighting; an extremely comfortable mattress ensured a good night's sleep. The well-lit bathroom had a large mirror.' Breakfast has a generous buffet; an extensive range of hot dishes includes 'all the options' for eggs, haddock and kippers, cold meats and cheese.

25% DISCOUNT VOUCHERS

The Green
Broadway WR12 7AA

T: 01386-852401
F: 01386-853879
E: info@broadwayhotel.info
W: www.cotswold-inns-hotels.co.uk/broadway

BEDROOMS: 19, 1 on ground floor.
OPEN: all year.
FACILITIES: bar, sitting room, brasserie, free Wi-Fi, small garden.
BACKGROUND MUSIC: gentle in public areas.
LOCATION: village centre.
CHILDREN: all ages welcomed.
DOGS: allowed in some bedrooms, on leads in public rooms (£10 charge).
CREDIT CARDS: all major cards.
PRICES: [2013] per room B&B single £120–£160, double £160–£220. D,B&B £26 added per person, à la carte £28.

BROADWAY Worcestershire

Map 3:D6

RUSSELL'S

♀ *César award in 2006*

'Excellent in all respects,' says a visitor in 2013 to this restaurant-with-rooms on the wide main street of this Cotswold village. Once the showroom of Sir Gordon Russell, the Arts and Crafts furniture designer, it was renovated by the owner, Andrew Riley. He has retained original features (inglenook fireplaces, beams, an old oak staircase) while adding contemporary artwork and gadgets. The bedrooms have a clean modern look and are well equipped: a coffee machine was 'a welcome extra'. 'Our room was large, clean and light; a big bath and a shower cubicle; an honesty bar on the landing.' A room at the top of the house has A-frame beams, two brown armchairs at the foot of a king-size bed. The L-shaped bistro-style dining room is 'stylish; china, glass, all top quality, modern cutlery'. The cooking of the chef, Neil Clarke, is thought 'first rate'. His daily-changing modern British menu, using produce from the Vale of Evesham, might include ham hock and leek ballottine, soused carrots, piccalilli, crisp quail's egg; canon of Lighthorne lamb, herb crust, fondant potato, spinach, wild mushrooms. (*Richard Smith*)

The Green, 20 High Street
Broadway WR12 7DT

T: 01386-853555
F: 01386-853964
E: info@russellsofbroadway.co.uk
W: www.russellsofbroadway.co.uk

BEDROOMS: 7, 3 in adjoining building, 2 on ground floor.
OPEN: all year, restaurant closed Sun night.
FACILITIES: ramp, residents' lobby, bar, restaurant, private dining room, free Wi-Fi, patio (heating, meal service).
BACKGROUND MUSIC: 'ambient' in restaurant.
LOCATION: village centre.
CHILDREN: all ages welcomed.
DOGS: not allowed.
CREDIT CARDS: Amex, MasterCard, Visa.
PRICES: per room B&B £115–£305, D,B&B (seasonal) £150–£245. Set menus £18.95–£26.95, à la carte £42. 1-night bookings refused weekends.

BROCKENHURST Hampshire

Map 2:E2

THE PIG

'A country house hotel with attitude', this former hunting lodge in the New Forest is 'relaxed and stylish'. A visitor arriving in darkness for dinner in 2013 thought the 'beautifully lit' building was 'magical': 'Walking into the hallway, warmly greeted by charming staff, felt like an event: the lounge and bar are immaculately furnished, and have wall chandeliers and eye-catching boars' heads.' A carved wooden sideboard serves as the bar ('the only downside was obtrusive music'); there are board games and books, a pool table. The 'beautiful' conservatory restaurant has 'a superb patchwork tiled floor', tables of different sizes with candles, pots of herbs. Produce from the kitchen garden, greenhouses (and the forager) drive the 'tempting' 25-mile menus of chef James Golding. 'Generous portions of delicious food; rocket and Hampshire salami risotto; turbot with sorrel Béarnaise; new season forced rhubarb Pavlova.' Bedrooms are in the main house and in a stable block by the kitchen garden: a stable room had 'wooden floorboards, brick walls mainly painted white; a large bed with good soft pillows'. A sister hotel, *The Pig in the Wall*, has opened in Southampton (see entry).

Beaulieu Road
Brockenhurst SO42 7QL

T: 01590-622354
E: info@thepighotel.com
W: www.thepighotel.co.uk

BEDROOMS: 26, 10 in stable block (100 yds), some on ground floor.
OPEN: all year.
FACILITIES: 2 lounges, bar, restaurant, free Wi-Fi, Potting Shed spa, kitchen garden, 14-acre grounds.
BACKGROUND MUSIC: in restaurant and lounges.
LOCATION: 2 miles E of Brockenhurst.
CHILDREN: all ages welcomed.
DOGS: allowed in 1 bedroom, some public areas.
CREDIT CARDS: all major cards.
PRICES: [2013] room £125–£265. Breakfast £10–£15, full alc £35. 1-night bookings refused at weekends.

BRYHER Isles of Scilly

Map 1: inset C1

HELL BAY HOTEL

On the smallest, and southernmost, of the inhabited Scilly Isles, Robert Dorrien-Smith's hotel, built in the style of cottages, faces the Atlantic Ocean and the jagged rocks of Hell Bay. Visitors arrive from the mainland (by air or boat) at the main island, St Mary's, and take the short sea journey to Bryher, where they will be met at the quay. The hotel's enormous lounge has a lofty ceiling, with 'tree-like' supports echoed in the curved wooden top of the fireplace. A 'wonderful art collection' of modern Cornish work is displayed; a good collection of art books. The bedrooms, decorated in bright seaside colours, are off an open internal courtyard. Most face the sea and have a balcony or a terrace (from which you walk straight to the beach). In the dining rooms, chef Richard Kearsley cooks a short menu of modern dishes like grilled fillet of Cornish mackerel, English asparagus; braised shoulder and roasted loin of lamb, butternut squash fondant, spiced lentils. At breakfast, you can watch egrets searching for their morning meal in a freshwater lake. Guests can explore other beaches on the island.

Bryher, Isles of Scilly
Cornwall TR23 0PR

T: 01720-422947
F: 01720-423004
E: contactus@hellbay.co.uk
W: www.hellbay.co.uk

BEDROOMS: 25 suites, in 5 buildings, some on ground floor, 1 suitable for &.

OPEN: 15 Mar–3 Nov.

FACILITIES: lounge, games room, bar, 2 dining rooms, free Wi-Fi, gym, sauna, large grounds (heated swimming pool, 15 by 10 metres, children's playground, par 3 golf course), beach 75 yds.

BACKGROUND MUSIC: none.

LOCATION: W coast of island, boat from Tresco (reached by boat/helicopter from mainland) or St Mary's.

CHILDREN: all ages welcomed (high tea at 5.30).

DOGS: not allowed in public rooms except games room.

CREDIT CARDS: MasterCard, Visa.

PRICES: [2013] per person B&B £100–£285, D,B&B £135–£320. Set dinner £39.

BUCKDEN Cambridgeshire

Map 2:B4

THE GEORGE

On the main street of a pretty Cambridgeshire village, this 19th-century former coaching inn has been given a 'smart, stylish' make-over by owners Anne, Richard and Becky Furbank; Cynthia Schaeffer is the manager. The 'nice old inn' has 'charming' public areas: there's a spacious bar lounge and a conservatory-style dining room ('full of cheerful diners'). The chef, José Graziosi, has a modern British style, with dishes like tempura-battered squid, black onion seeds, rocket and harissa sauce; fillet of venison, braised red cabbage, butternut squash purée, spiced red wine jus. Meals can also be taken in the bar and lounge, and alfresco on the terrace in summer. The bedrooms are named after famous Georges (Stubbs, Best, Handel, etc). 'Washington was spacious; lots of brown in the decor; surprisingly poor storage – no drawers apart from the bedside tables; the big bed had blankets and sheets as we requested; a good bathroom with a bath. We liked the green commitment shown by the note in the room that said the sheets are changed every three days.' Breakfast has freshly squeezed orange juice, yogurt and honey; 'beautifully cooked eggs'.

25% DISCOUNT VOUCHERS

High Street
Buckden PE19 5XA

T: 01480-812300
F: 01480-813920
E: mail@thegeorgebuckden.com
W: www.thegeorgebuckden.com

BEDROOMS: 12.
OPEN: all year.
FACILITIES: lift, bar, lounge, restaurant, private dining room, free Wi-Fi, civil wedding licence, courtyard.
BACKGROUND MUSIC: jazz in all public areas.
LOCATION: village centre.
CHILDREN: all ages welcomed, baby-changing facilities.
DOGS: not allowed in public rooms.
CREDIT CARDS: Amex, MasterCard, Visa.
PRICES: [2013] per room B&B £95–£150. D,B&B £75–£125 per person, à la carte £35.

BUCKLAND MARSH Oxfordshire

Map 2:C2

THE TROUT AT TADPOLE BRIDGE

Beside a narrow bridge over the River Thames, Gareth and Helen Pugh's 'unpretentious' 17th-century pub/restaurant is liked for the 'great' food and 'friendly' staff. It is popular with locals and boating visitors; six moorings are free if you dine in the restaurant. The atmosphere is informal and the decor 'unfussy': contemporary colour schemes combined with traditional materials. The Pughs, who have two young sons, welcome visiting children with toys and games. Young Charlie Pugh (who likes plain and simple cooking) helped design a children's menu (dishes like sausages and mash, onion gravy). His brother, Alexander ('bon viveur in the making'), suggested 'we offer smaller portions of most things including mussels'. Chef Pascal Clavaud prepares modern dishes, perhaps trio of Kelmscott pork, parsnip dauphinoise, curly kale. Bedrooms are 'thoughtfully' decorated and equipped. A reader who enjoyed the cooking this year thought his room looked 'tired'; other visitors thought their room 'the best pub accommodation we have stayed in'. Breakfast has home-made bread, a well-stocked sideboard and interesting cooked choices. (*K and PW, and others*)

Buckland Marsh
SN7 8RF

T: 01367-870382
F: 01367-870912
E: info@trout-inn.co.uk
W: www.trout-inn.co.uk

BEDROOMS: 6, 3 in courtyard.
OPEN: all year except 25/26 Dec.
FACILITIES: bar, dining area, breakfast area, free Wi-Fi, 2-acre garden (river, moorings).
BACKGROUND MUSIC: none.
LOCATION: 2 miles N of A420, halfway between Oxford and Swindon.
CHILDREN: all ages welcomed.
DOGS: allowed.
CREDIT CARDS: MasterCard, Visa.
PRICES: [2013] per room B&B £130, D,B&B £190. À la carte £28. 1-night bookings refused Sat.

BUDE Cornwall

Map 1:C3

THE BEACH AT BUDE

In a 'great' position above Summerleaze beach, this upmarket B&B has 'lovely sea views' from a terrace that has been extended by the new owner, William Daniel. He has also added two bedrooms and a bar. Sara Whiteman is the manager. 'It is very good indeed; we were made most welcome,' says a visitor this year. A stainless steel-and-chrome lift leads to the bedrooms, which are decorated in New England seaside style (limed oak furnishings, Lloyd Loom chairs). The bathrooms have a 'fantastic powerful shower'. 'It was nice to have mineral water and fresh milk in a fridge.' The best rooms overlook the beach – five have a private terrace. In a 'large and airy' breakfast room, there is 'a good display of cereals, fruit juices, fresh fruit, croissants, etc'. Porridge with jam, honey or Cornish clotted cream is available. Cooked choices ('of good quality') include a bacon baguette, scrambled eggs and smoked salmon, as well as a full breakfast. 'Loud' pop music was not appreciated. There is a store for surfboards. Help is given with booking restaurants. (*Annie Lade, and others*)

Summerleaze Crescent
Bude EX23 8HL

T: 01288-389800
F: 01288-389820
E: enquiries@thebeachatbude.co.uk
W: www.thebeachatbude.co.uk

BEDROOMS: 17, 3 on ground floor.
OPEN: all year except 22 Dec–5 Jan.
FACILITIES: lift, bar, lounge, conservatory, dining room, free Wi-Fi, terrace.
BACKGROUND MUSIC: various.
LOCATION: above Summerleaze beach.
CHILDREN: not under 8.
DOGS: not allowed.
CREDIT CARDS: Amex, MasterCard, Visa.
PRICES: [2013] per room B&B single £105–£155, double £125–£175.

BURFORD Oxfordshire

Map 2:C2

BURFORD HOUSE

'Just the sort of hotel you would hope to find in this picturesque town; characterful, charming, with good attention to detail.' Praise in 2013 for this 17th-century house, owned by Thomas Peter Hawkins, and run by his son, Ian. There are two lounges: the 'more formal' at the front has 'tasteful furnishings'; a rear room with 'soft armchairs, a fine grandfather clock' opens on to a courtyard garden, where alfresco meals can be taken in warm weather. The *Centre Stage* restaurant has 'immaculately dressed' tables, theatrical posters; 'the joyful addition of white damask tablecloths and napkins'. Dinner is available from Wednesday to Saturday: the British menu of the chef, Zoë Amos, might include Devonshire crab cake, sweet chilli jam; pepper beef fillet, rosemary fondant potato, cauliflower purée. (Music from the shows is played in the evening, light classical at other meals.) 'Our quiet bedroom had good furniture, notably a wooden four-poster bed; a beautifully clean bathroom.' 'Breakfast, such an important meal, is a delight: orange juice is freshly squeezed; perfectly cooked smoked haddock with a poached egg.' (*Angy Kirker, and others*)

99 High Street
Burford OX18 4QA

T: 01993-823151
F: 01993-823240
E: stay@burfordhouse.co.uk
W: www.burfordhouse.co.uk

BEDROOMS: 8, 2 in adjoining coach house, 1 on ground floor.
OPEN: all year, restaurant closed Sun–Tues nights.
FACILITIES: 2 lounges, restaurant, free Wi-Fi, small courtyard garden, unsuitable for &.
BACKGROUND MUSIC: in 1 lounge and restaurant.
LOCATION: central.
CHILDREN: all ages welcomed.
DOGS: allowed in ground-floor bedroom, 1 lounge.
CREDIT CARDS: all major cards.
PRICES: [2013] per room B&B £125–£220. Set dinner £30–£35. 1-night bookings refused weekends in season, bank holidays.

SEE ALSO SHORTLIST

BURFORD Oxfordshire

Map 2:C2

THE LAMB INN

'A classic Cotswold inn', the *Lamb* has flagstoned floors, beamed ceilings, log fires, polished copper and brass, antiques. The mellow stone building, originally a row of 15th-century weavers' cottages, is part of a small group (see also *The Manor House*, Moreton-in-Marsh); Bill Ramsay is the manager. The small public bar, which serves light lunches and snacks, leads into two large lounges with settees, chairs and books. In summer, guests can sit in the enclosed garden with its gravel paths and lawns among well-planted borders; wooden tables and chairs in private corners. The restaurant has 'well-dressed' tables, bold floral displays: the chef, Sean Ducie, serves contemporary dishes like Sambuca salmon, celery cress; hay-smoked fillet steak, truffled dauphinoise potatoes, shallot purée, cèpes. There is also a 'delicious' eight-course tasting menu. The bedrooms, 'comfortable, rather than stylish', are furnished with antiques; several have been refurbished this year. Allium (the largest) overlooks Burford Priory, and can be connected to Rosie to create family accommodation. Preserves are made in the kitchen for breakfast, which has an 'excellent' buffet; a large choice of cooked dishes. (*BB*)

25% DISCOUNT VOUCHERS

Sheep Street
Burford OX18 4LR

T: 01993-823155
F: 01993-822228
E: manager@lambinn-burford.co.uk
W: www.cotswold-inns-hotels.co.uk/lamb

BEDROOMS: 17.
OPEN: all year.
FACILITIES: 2 lounges, bar, restaurant, free Wi-Fi, courtyard, ½-acre garden, unsuitable for &.
BACKGROUND MUSIC: 'gentle' in restaurant.
LOCATION: 150 yds from centre.
CHILDREN: all ages welcomed.
DOGS: allowed, in allocated bedrooms, on lead in restaurant.
CREDIT CARDS: all major cards.
PRICES: [2013] per person B&B £80–£155, D,B&B £112.50–£187.50. Set menus £32.50–£39, tasting menu £55 (*10% service added to restaurant bills*). 1-night bookings sometimes refused Sat.

SEE ALSO SHORTLIST

BURNHAM MARKET Norfolk

Map 2:A5

THE HOSTE `NEW`

In the centre of a lovely village with a plethora of upmarket shops, this 300-year-old inn returns to the *Guide* under new ownership: Brendan and Bee Hopkins have commissioned much renovation. Iris Rillaerts has joined as manager. 'It is a well-run hotel, with helpful staff and excellent food,' say inspectors. The bar is a popular local watering hole; there is good artwork in the panelled dining room where 'service was especially good'. The chef, Gemma Arnold, cooks an extensive menu of modern dishes: 'The fish was excellent: a fine seafood chowder; Thai-crusted halibut with oriental noodles was delicious.' The bedrooms are in the main building, a courtyard wing, *Vine House* across the green, and *Railway House* ten minutes' walk away. A courtyard room had 'silver furnishings, silvery wallpaper, floor-to-ceiling curtains with tassels and pelmets: slightly over the top but the essentials were right. A large comfortable bed, quality bedlinen, excellent lighting, a decent bathroom.' Breakfast 'was above average: a wonderful buffet table (constantly replenished) had jugs of freshly squeezed juice, interesting cereals, two fruit purées; exceptionally good sausages'.

The Green
Burnham Market PE31 8HD

T: 01328-738777
F: 01328-730103
E: reception@thehoste.com
W: www.thehoste.com

BEDROOMS: 61, 6 on ground floor, 6 in courtyard wing, 7 in *Vine House*, 8 in *Railway House*.
OPEN: all year.
FACILITIES: bar, conservatory, restaurant, free Wi-Fi, spa, terrace garden (at *Vine House*).
BACKGROUND MUSIC: in public areas.
LOCATION: village centre.
CHILDREN: all ages welcomed.
DOGS: allowed in some rooms.
CREDIT CARDS: all major cards.
PRICES: per room B&B £120–£230, D,B&B £180–£290. À la carte £35. 1-night bookings sometimes refused weekends.

BURPHAM West Sussex

Map 2:E3

BURPHAM COUNTRY HOUSE NEW

In a lovely village in the Arun valley, this former 18th-century hunting lodge is run as a 'relaxed' guest house by Steve and Jackie Penticost. 'They are lovely people, chatty, upfront and always on hand,' says an inspector. 'She carried a heavy bag upstairs for us, despite our protests.' The house has an ecclesiastical porch and a wooden veranda. 'It is nicely decorated with well-chosen furniture, pictures and pottery; there is comfortable seating in the pleasant lounge which has an honesty bar, a wood fire in winter. Our bedroom had a four-poster bed (very comfortable), two decent chairs, a padded window seat; plenty of storage; an interesting mirrored wardrobe reflected light inwards; a modern bathroom (with noisy electric shower).' The tables are well spaced in the dining room; Steve Penticost is the 'confident and competent' chef: dishes enjoyed this year included scallops, pea and mint purée; duck with Puy lentils, chorizo sauce, carrots. Breakfast, taken in a 'charming' conservatory, has help-yourself cereals, juice, etc; 'a superb cooked choice includes eggs (from hens in the garden) any way you like; I went for Eggs Royale, poached on muffin with smoked salmon'.

The Street
Burpham BN18 9RJ

T: 01903-882160
E: info@ burphamcountryhouse.com
W: www.burphamcountryhouse.com

BEDROOMS: 9, 1 on ground floor.
OPEN: all year except Christmas, Jan.
FACILITIES: 2 lounges, dining room, conservatory, free Wi-Fi, ¼-acre garden, unsuitable for &.
BACKGROUND MUSIC: in restaurant.
LOCATION: in village 3 miles NE of Arundel.
CHILDREN: all ages welcomed.
DOGS: allowed in ground-floor room by arrangement.
CREDIT CARDS: MasterCard, Visa.
PRICES: [2013] per person B&B £35–£70. À la carte £40. 1-night bookings refused Sat in season.

CAMELFORD Cornwall

Map 1:C3

PENDRAGON COUNTRY HOUSE

'A good place to stay', this former Victorian rectory is run as a small guest house by Sharon and Nigel Reed. 'We really liked this place,' said a *Guide* inspector in 2013. 'Nigel is a splendid, informally dressed host.' The Reeds have 'filled the lovely house with antique furniture and well-chosen pictures; the sitting rooms have plenty of comfortable seating, books, board games and cards. An honesty bar is a good idea.' Bedrooms vary in size: 'Ours had everything we could wish for: high-quality bedding, huge fluffy towels and immense bathrobes; a full tea tray with a mini cafetière and a proper teapot, milk in a fridge on the landing. The decor was elegant with nice paintings, heavy damask curtains; lots of hanging space; gallons of hot water in the bathroom.' Nigel Reed is the chef, preparing a set meal (no choices but preferences identified). 'He cooks well, giving us a beautifully prepared ham hock terrine with delicious plum compote; baked hake, beurre blanc, roast potatoes, and super fresh veg bundled round with a leek leaf.' Sharon Reed makes all jams and marmalade for breakfast.

Davidstow
Camelford PL32 9XR

T: 01840-261131
E: enquiries@
   pendragoncountryhouse.com
W: www.pendragoncountryhouse.
   com

BEDROOMS: 7, 1 on ground floor suitable for &.
OPEN: all year except 24–26 Dec, restaurant closed Sun.
FACILITIES: sitting room, bar, *Orangery* breakfast/dining room, private dining room, free Wi-Fi, civil wedding licence, 1¼-acre grounds.
BACKGROUND MUSIC: if requested.
LOCATION: 3½ miles NE of Camelford.
CHILDREN: all ages welcomed.
DOGS: allowed in downstairs bedroom.
CREDIT CARDS: all major cards.
PRICES: per room B&B single £60–£65, double £90–£100. D,B&B £22.50 added per person, set meals £25.

CAMPSEA ASHE Suffolk

Map 2:C6

THE OLD RECTORY

'We had a warm welcome from Mrs Sally Ball, the owner of this lovely old house and garden, who promptly gave us tea by a log fire.' There is much enthusiasm this year for this former rectory (which dates to 1750), by a church in a village near the Suffolk coast. It stands in large gardens: 'The only sounds you will hear are the birds and the occasional chime of the church bells,' says Sally Ball. She has 'decorated the building beautifully'. There's an honesty bar in the sitting room. A three-course set menu is served on three evenings a week (by arrangement for parties of eight or more on other nights), and might include spicy beetroot soup, herb dressing; pan-fried pheasant breast, pearl barley, wild mushrooms. 'The food was fresh, local and delicious.' Bedrooms are individually designed: Maple has furniture from Macau and overlooks the 16th-century church; Garden Cottage, next to the main building, has its own front door and small terrace; Oak has a super king-size sleigh bed. Breakfast may be taken in the conservatory in warm weather. (*AD and J Lloyd, Anne Clarke*)

Station Road
Campsea Ashe
nr Woodbridge IP13 0PU

T: 01728-746524
E: mail@theoldrectorysuffolk.com
W: www.theoldrectorysuffolk.com

BEDROOMS: 7, 1 in garden cottage on ground floor, 1 in coach house.
OPEN: all year except Christmas/New Year, restaurant closed lunch, Sun/Tues/Thurs/Sat except for parties of 8 or more by arrangement.
FACILITIES: sitting room, dining room, conservatory, free Wi-Fi, terrace, garden, unsuitable for &.
BACKGROUND MUSIC: none.
LOCATION: in village 8 miles NE of Woodbridge.
CHILDREN: all ages welcomed.
DOGS: allowed in garden cottage and coach house, not in main house.
CREDIT CARDS: MasterCard, Visa.
PRICES: [2013] per person B&B £45–£70. Set dinner £28. 1-night bookings refused weekends at busy times.

CANNINGTON Somerset

Map 1:B5

BLACKMORE FARM

'Wonderful value and excitement' is given to visitors at Ann and Ian Dyer's 15th-century Grade I listed manor house on their working dairy farm at the foot of the Quantock hills. The 'energetic, friendly' couple invite guests to watch milking from a special room; their enterprise extends to a farm shop selling local meat and dairy products, including their own award-winning ice cream. Light lunches and cream teas are served in their café ('with Mrs Dyer's gorgeous puddings'). B&B guests enter the house by an ancient door which opens on to the Great Hall where breakfast is taken communally at a large oak table. There are oak beams, stone archways and huge open fireplaces. Each of the bedrooms has its own character: the Gallery has original wall panelling, a sitting room up a steep flight of steps; a small bathroom (lavatory in a medieval garderobe). The Solar has a large double bedroom, a single bed in a closet leading off it. Two bedrooms are in a converted barn. Children are made welcome and will enjoy the farm animals and the lack of formality.

Blackmore Lane
Cannington
nr Bridgwater TA5 2NE

T: 01278-653442
E: dyerfarm@aol.com
W: www.blackmorefarm.co.uk

BEDROOMS: 5, 2, in ground-floor barn, suitable for ♿.
OPEN: all year.
FACILITIES: lounge/TV room, hall/breakfast room, free Wi-Fi, 1-acre garden (stream, coarse fishing).
BACKGROUND MUSIC: none.
LOCATION: 3 miles NW of Bridgwater.
CHILDREN: all ages welcomed.
DOGS: not allowed.
CREDIT CARDS: Diners, MasterCard, Visa.
PRICES: [2013] per person B&B £50–£55. 1-night bookings refused bank holiday weekends.

CARTMEL Cumbria

Map 4: inset C2

AYNSOME MANOR

🐾 *César award in 1998*

'For value and high standards *Aynsome Manor* must be one of the bargains of the Lake District.' Chris and Andrea Varley (second-generation owners) attract many returning visitors to their 17th-century stone manor house close to the ancient village of Cartmel. Long-term fans were 'welcomed like long-lost friends' in 2013. David Autef now runs front-of-house. Log fires cheer visitors in the two comfortable lounges. Ten bedrooms are around a flagged courtyard and in the main house; two others are in a nearby cottage converted from a 16th-century stone-built stable. Rooms are well equipped, with TV, radio alarm clock, free Wi-Fi and tea/coffee facilities. The Georgian dining room, candlelit in the evenings, has panelled walls and a finely moulded ceiling; views of the countryside are 'outstanding'. Chef Gordon Topp's daily-changing menu might include pan-fried breast of guineafowl, sautéed pak choi. 'Good food, cooked simply, giving maximum taste,' is a typical comment; as is 'The manor has a wonderful atmosphere and is neither stuffy nor pretentious. We will return.' (*CC Schofield, Ken and Mildred Edwards*)

25% DISCOUNT VOUCHERS

Cartmel
nr Grange-over-Sands
LA11 6HH

T: 01539-536653
F: 01539-536016
E: aynsomemanor@btconnect.com
W: www.aynsomemanorhotel.co.uk

BEDROOMS: 12, 2 in cottage (with lounge) across courtyard.
OPEN: all year except 25/26 Dec, 3–31 Jan, lunch served Sun only, Sun dinner for residents only.
FACILITIES: 2 lounges, bar, dining room, free Wi-Fi, ½-acre garden, unsuitable for ♿.
BACKGROUND MUSIC: none.
LOCATION: ½ mile outside village.
CHILDREN: no under-5s at dinner.
DOGS: not allowed in public rooms.
CREDIT CARDS: Amex, MasterCard, Visa.
PRICES: per room B&B single £85–£140, double £99–£140. D,B&B £76–£92 per person, set dinner £24–£37. 1-night bookings sometimes refused weekends.

CHAGFORD Devon

Map 1:C4

GIDLEIGH PARK

'A wonderful place to stay. The atmosphere is everything one could wish for, the staff the best possible. I would like to live at *Gidleigh*.' A visitor enjoyed 'a very happy stay' this year at this Tudor-style country house hotel (Relais & Châteaux), on a large estate within Dartmoor national park. It is managed by Andrew Foulkes for the owners, Andrew and Christina Brownsword. 'We arrived to the warmest welcome, and didn't move the car once; excellent walking in the grounds.' The panelled public rooms have Arts and Crafts features; the bedrooms are individually decorated. 'Our beautiful room had large windows overlooking the gardens and the surging River Teign. The bathroom was excellent, with roll-top bath and huge walk-in shower.' On the same floor is a pantry which guests may use day or night, with a coffee machine, tea, milk and 'delicious' biscuits. 'So civilised.' Executive chef Michael Caines has two *Michelin* stars for his 'elaborate' cooking (a typical dish: Brixham scallops, caramelised cauliflower purée, sweet raisin vinaigrette, cumin velouté). The Brownswords' small group of hotels includes *The Bath Priory*, Bath (see entry). (*Barbara Watkinson*)

Chagford TQ13 8HH

T: 01647-432367
F: 01647-432574
E: gidleighpark@gidleigh.co.uk
W: www.gidleigh.com

BEDROOMS: 24, 2 in annexe (75 yds), 2 in cottage (375 yds), 3 on ground floor, 1 suitable for &.
OPEN: all year.
FACILITIES: ramps, drawing room, hall, bar, loggia, conservatory, 3 dining rooms, free Wi-Fi, civil wedding licence, 107-acre grounds (gardens, tennis).
BACKGROUND MUSIC: none.
LOCATION: 2 miles from Chagford.
CHILDREN: no under-8s at dinner.
DOGS: allowed in 3 bedrooms, not in public rooms.
CREDIT CARDS: all major cards.
PRICES: [2013] per person B&B £172.50–£597.50, D,B&B £282.50–£707.50. À la carte £110. 1-night bookings sometimes refused at weekends.

SEE ALSO SHORTLIST

CHAGFORD Devon

Map 1:C4

PARFORD WELL

'A sophisticated town house in the most beautiful countryside.' A visitor returning this year praises Tim Daniel's small B&B in the Teign valley. Within the Dartmoor national park, it is well placed for touring and walking. The host, formerly manager of one of London's first town house hotels, 'lives in a discreet semi-detached part of the property: you can sit in the lounge at night and imagine that you own the place'. The lounge (where arriving guests are given afternoon tea and home-made cake) has a wood-burning stove, books, games, paintings. The three bedrooms overlook the garden; two have an en suite bathroom; the third has its own bathroom across the landing. Visitors can take breakfast privately in a side room or join 'the other interesting guests' at a communal table. There is freshly prepared fruit salad, prunes, yogurt with honey; a choice of cereals and porridge; 'everything is cooked to order, not a bain-marie in sight'. Smoked salmon is often available. A short walk away is a 'good, sensibly priced' pub; there is a restaurant in the village. (*David Charlesworth*)

Sandy Park
nr Chagford TQ13 8JW

T: 01647-433353
E: tim@parfordwell.co.uk
W: www.parfordwell.co.uk

BEDROOMS: 3.
OPEN: all year.
FACILITIES: sitting room, 2 breakfast rooms, free Wi-Fi, ½-acre garden, unsuitable for &.
BACKGROUND MUSIC: none.
LOCATION: in hamlet 1 mile N of Chagford.
CHILDREN: not under 8.
DOGS: not allowed.
CREDIT CARDS: none.
PRICES: per room B&B £85–£100. 1-night bookings sometimes refused weekends in season.

SEE ALSO SHORTLIST

CHETTLE Dorset

CASTLEMAN

César award in 2004

In a historic village in Dorset, this former dower house is run as an informal, even quirky, restaurant-with-rooms by Barbara Garnsworthy and her brother, Brendan, who is front-of-house. 'You may find damaged paintwork and a mishmash of coat-hangers in the bedrooms, but this is a straightforward country house where you are made to feel like friends,' say trusted reporters. There is an element of 'faded gentility' in the public rooms: a galleried hall, a Regency-style drawing room, and a Victorian oak-panelled drawing room with a Jacobean ceiling. The eight bedrooms are decorated in a range of styles; superior ones are 'very large, with plenty of storage, tables and sofas'. 'Do not expect room service or a minibar.' Barbara Garnsworthy cooks modern dishes with Richard Morris, perhaps scallop and spinach gratin; roast rack of lamb, wild garlic and onion cream sauce. 'We appreciate breakfast (more or less anything you ask for), which is served until 10 am. There is complete silence here; no notices or rules; delightful country walks from the door.' (*J and DA, and others*)

25% DISCOUNT VOUCHERS

Chettle
nr Blandford Forum
DT11 8DB

T: 01258-830096
F: 01258-830051
E: enquiry@castlemanhotel.co.uk
W: www.castlemanhotel.co.uk

BEDROOMS: 8 (1 family).
OPEN: Mar–Jan, except 25/26 Dec, 31 Dec, restaurant closed midday except Sun.
FACILITIES: 2 drawing rooms, bar, restaurant, free Wi-Fi, 2-acre grounds (stables for visiting horses), riding, fishing, shooting, cycling nearby, only restaurant suitable for &.
BACKGROUND MUSIC: none.
LOCATION: village, 1 mile off A354 Salisbury–Blandford, hotel signposted.
CHILDREN: all ages welcomed.
DOGS: not allowed.
CREDIT CARDS: MasterCard, Visa.
PRICES: [2013] per room B&B £90–£105. À la carte £25–£28.

CHICHESTER West Sussex

Map 2:E3

ROOKS HILL

Close to the cathedral city of Chichester and to Goodwood, this Grade II listed former farmhouse is run as an upmarket B&B by owners Ron and Lin Allen. Guests are 'warmly' welcomed: help is given with baggage, and tea or coffee provided in the part-panelled lounge. The house is 'full of fresh flowers, and furnishings are of high quality'. In the three bedrooms (one is on the ground floor), windows are triple glazed to dampen noise from the fairly busy road. Beds have a pocket-sprung mattress, a feather and down duvet (sheets and blankets can also be provided), feather pillows. Bathrooms are modern, with a thermostatically controlled shower. There is a good supply of books in the lounge (many connected with racing). Breakfast, served in an oak-beamed, double-aspect room, has home-baked bread, fresh fruit, cereals, free-range eggs and oak-smoked salmon; preserves are made from organic fruit grown in the garden. The cooked dishes have 'excellent ingredients' from local suppliers. The *Earl of March* pub opposite is good for meals, and there are many restaurants in Chichester (a five-minute drive away). More reports, please.

Lavant Road
Mid Lavant, Chichester PO18 0BQ

T: 01243-528400
E: info@rookshill.co.uk
W: www.rookshill.co.uk

BEDROOMS: 3, 1 on ground floor.
OPEN: all year, except 25 Dec, 1 Jan.
FACILITIES: lounge, breakfast room, free Wi-Fi, courtyard garden, unsuitable for &.
BACKGROUND MUSIC: classical in breakfast room.
LOCATION: 2 miles N of city centre.
CHILDREN: not under 12.
DOGS: not allowed.
CREDIT CARDS: Amex, MasterCard, Visa.
PRICES: [2013] per person B&B £75–£165. 1-night bookings refused weekends Apr–Oct.

SEE ALSO SHORTLIST

CHILLATON Devon

TOR COTTAGE

In a private and secluded mid-Devon valley, Maureen Rowlatt's upmarket B&B stands in extensive wooded grounds surrounded by hillsides where deer roam. 'She is a lovely, gentle host who made our stay a joy,' says a visitor this year. 'On arrival we were offered tea with fresh scones, jam and clotted cream.' Four of the bedrooms, each with private terrace, are in the garden. Each has a wood-burning stove and a well-equipped kitchenette (fridge, microwave/grill, cutlery and crockery). The Garden Room, a conversion of a stone cart house, has a vaulted ceiling with original beams, antique double bed and sitting area with a log fire. Laughing Waters, furnished in New England style, has maple furnishings, a black stove, a gypsy caravan, a hammock. The Cottage Wing, upstairs in the main house, also has a hospitality area. Guests can prepare simple meals in their room; a picnic platter can be provided. A 'magnificent' breakfast, ordered the evening before, has 'home-made muesli and an endless supply of hot toast, ginger marmalade; pots of tea'; a wide choice for vegetarians alongside the usual cooked dishes. (*Paul Powell-Jackson*)

Chillaton, nr Lifton
PL16 0JE

T: 01822-860248
F: 01822-860126
E: info@torcottage.co.uk
W: www.torcottage.co.uk

BEDROOMS: 5, 4 in garden.
OPEN: Feb–Dec except Christmas/New Year, do not arrive before 4 pm.
FACILITIES: sitting room, large conservatory, breakfast room, free Wi-Fi, 28-acre grounds (2-acre garden, heated swimming pool, 13 by 6 metres, May–Sept, barbecue, stream, bridleway, walks), river (fishing ½ mile), unsuitable for &.
BACKGROUND MUSIC: in conservatory.
LOCATION: ½ mile S of Chillaton.
CHILDREN: not under 14.
DOGS: only guide dogs allowed.
CREDIT CARDS: MasterCard, Visa.
PRICES: per person B&B (min. 2 nights) £75–£77.50. Picnic platter £16. 1-night bookings sometimes refused.

CHRISTCHURCH Dorset

Map 2:E2

CAPTAIN'S CLUB HOTEL   NEW

In a 'lovely setting' on the banks of the River Stour, this dramatic metal-and-glass spa hotel is 'modern but with character'. Owned by Robert Wilson and Timothy Lloyd, it is upgraded to a full entry after positive reports by two regular *Guide* correspondents. 'They couldn't have looked after us better; we liked the personalised welcome card in our room from the hotel director.' The open-plan public areas have doors on to a riverside terrace with tables for drinks and meals, 'delightful when the sun shines'. Tables are 'immaculately laid' in *Tides* restaurant where chef Andrew Gault's dishes might include seared scallops, roast chorizo and apple; rump of lamb, spinach, crispy shallot. 'The quality and presentation were excellent.' Standard bedrooms are 'large, and have a delightful view over the river'. A suite, with a separate lounge and kitchen, was 'fabulous; two bathrooms, floor-to-ceiling windows; a good hospitality tray'. The hotel accommodation has direct access to the spa (robes and slippers supplied). Breakfast has fresh-cut fruit segments, Dorset cereals, croissants; hot dishes cooked to order. River trips can be arranged. (*Ian Malone, Peter Chadwick*)

Wick Ferry
Wick Lane
Christchurch BH23 1HU

T: 01202-475111
F: 01202-490111
E: enquiries@captainsclubhotel.com
W: www.captainsclubhotel.com

BEDROOMS: 29, 2 suitable for ♿.
OPEN: all year.
FACILITIES: lounge, bar, restaurant, function facilities, free Wi-Fi, terrace, spa (hydrotherapy pool, sauna, treatments).
BACKGROUND MUSIC: 'easy listening' in public areas.
LOCATION: on Christchurch quay.
CHILDREN: all ages welcomed.
DOGS: allowed in suites.
CREDIT CARDS: Amex, MasterCard, Visa.
PRICES: [2013] per room B&B from £249, D,B&B from £307. À la carte £32.

SEE ALSO SHORTLIST

CLEARWELL Gloucestershire

TUDOR FARMHOUSE NEW

In a quiet village in the Royal Forest of Dean, this farmhouse (parts of which date back to the 13th century) and converted outbuildings is run as a small hotel by the owners, Hari and Colin Fell. 'We had a very pleasant stay,' say regular reporters this year, upgrading *Tudor Farmhouse* to a full entry. 'The house and the outbuildings have been attractively converted, retaining oak beams and original features; the gardens are pretty, the staff are helpful, the meals tasty and well presented.' Martin Adams, who joined as chef in 2013, uses local suppliers for his menus which might include sourdough Welsh rarebit, pickled vegetables; Crooked End farm lamb shoulder, roasted garlic dauphine, cabbage, celeriac, golden raisins. Five of the bedrooms are in the main house: 'Our small room was up a steep spiral staircase.' Level access is available for bedrooms in a converted barn. Sustainable English oak has been used by local artisans in the conversion of the old cider house; the loft suite has a vaulted ceiling; a cast iron bath and walk-in shower in the bathroom. (*Jane and Martin Bailey*)

25% DISCOUNT VOUCHERS

High Street
Clearwell GL16 8JS

T: 01594-833046
E: info@tudorfarmhousehotel.co.uk
W: www.tudorfarmhousehotel.co.uk

BEDROOMS: 23, 5 on ground floor, 11 in barn, 7 in cider house.
OPEN: all year except Christmas.
FACILITIES: 2 lounges, restaurant, free Wi-Fi, 14-acre grounds.
BACKGROUND MUSIC: in restaurant.
LOCATION: 7 miles SE of Monmouth.
CHILDREN: all ages welcomed.
DOGS: not allowed.
CREDIT CARDS: MasterCard, Visa.
PRICES: [2013] per person B&B £95–£210. À la carte £35–£40. 1-night bookings refused weekends May–Sept.

CLEE STANTON Shropshire

Map 3:C5

TIMBERSTONE

25% DISCOUNT VOUCHERS

'A very welcoming couple', Tracey Baylis and Alex Read, go from 'strength to strength' at their B&B. A restored stone cottage in the Clee hills, it is five miles from Ludlow. 'They gave us tea and coffee when we arrived, and when we returned from walks,' say visitors this year. 'They could not be kinder or warmer,' say returning guests. In a peaceful hamlet reached by narrow lanes ('difficult to find but they give good directions'), the cottage has been 'lovingly' extended. Bedrooms in the main house have old beams, an iron bedstead; two rooms are in a 'beautifully crafted' extension. 'Our very comfortable room had good lighting, nice linen.' A large, light public room has a sitting area at one end, a dining table at the other. It has a wood-burning stove, books, maps, board games and jigsaw puzzles. Tracey Baylis will cook an evening meal by arrangement (recommended), which is taken at a communal table. 'A delicious dinner, elegantly served, with canapés and choice for each course.' Breakfast has home-made preserves, freshly squeezed orange juice; a wide choice of cooked dishes. (*Josie Mayers, David Bartley*)

Lackstone Lane
Clee Stanton
Ludlow SY8 3EL

T: 01584-823519
E: timberstone1@hotmail.com
W: www.timberstoneludlow.co.uk

BEDROOMS: 4 (plus summerhouse retreat in summer).
OPEN: all year except 25 Dec and 1 Jan.
FACILITIES: lounge/dining room, free Wi-Fi, ½-acre garden, treatment room, unsuitable for &.
BACKGROUND MUSIC: in lounge/dining room ('if guests request it').
LOCATION: 5 miles NE of Ludlow.
CHILDREN: all ages welcomed.
DOGS: not allowed.
CREDIT CARDS: MasterCard, Visa.
PRICES: [2013] per room B&B £90. À la carte £30.50.

CLIPSHAM Rutland

Map 2:A3

BEECH HOUSE & OLIVE BRANCH

César award in 2012

The atmosphere is 'beautifully cosy' in this relaxed pub/restaurant in a pretty Rutland village. The owners, Sean Hope (the chef) and Ben Jones, have given it a rustic look with stained beams, warm terracotta walls, open fires; a mix of antique and pine tables, chairs and benches. The bedrooms are in a renovated Georgian house, a short walk across the road (umbrellas provided). Apple, on the first floor, is a pretty room decorated in creams and greens; it has a French painted chest of drawers, good lighting, a large bed. A ground-floor room 'was tastefully appointed, with a beautiful carved Jacobean-style headboard, quality reproduction furniture; a small sitting room with a sofa'. The only public area is the landing, which has a fridge (with milk for the hospitality tray in the room), magazines, books and local information. Sean Hope seeks the ingredients for his menus from as close to the pub as possible. Typical dishes: Campanelle pasta, Cropwell Bishop stilton; honey-roast pork belly, cider fondant, stem broccoli. The 'very good' breakfast is taken in a restored barn. (*RG*)

25% DISCOUNT VOUCHERS

Main Street
Clipsham LE15 7SH

T: 01780-410355
F: 01780-410000
E: info@theolivebranchpub.com
W: www.theolivebranchpub.com

BEDROOMS: 6, 2 on ground floor, family room (also suitable for &) in annexe.
OPEN: all year.
FACILITIES: ramps, pub, dining room, breakfast room, free Wi-Fi, small front garden.
BACKGROUND MUSIC: in pub.
LOCATION: in village 7 miles NW of Stamford.
CHILDREN: all ages welcomed.
DOGS: allowed in downstairs bedrooms and bar.
CREDIT CARDS: MasterCard, Visa.
PRICES: [2013] per room B&B £115–£195. Set dinner £24.50, à la carte £30.50.

COLWALL Worcestershire

Map 3:D5

COLWALL PARK HOTEL

'An extremely friendly hotel with a charm all of its own, due to the rural setting and, even more, to the staff and owners.' Praise in 2013 for Iain and Sarah Nesbitt's country hotel in a village on the western flanks of the Malvern hills. Part black-and-white timbered, part red brick, the Edwardian building is 'ideal for a walking or sightseeing holiday'. The two residents' lounges have open fires, comfortable sofas and chairs. Individually decorated bedrooms range in size and style: 'Our standard room was pleasantly furnished, and had home-made shortbread biscuits on the tea tray. Fresh milk is available from Reception.' In the *Seasons* restaurant (light oak panelling, leather chairs, linen cloths), the cooking of chef James Garth is much admired: he uses local suppliers for his modern dishes such as grilled goat's cheese and red onion tartlet; slow-cooked spare rib of Hereford beef. Lighter meals and snacks are served in the *Lantern Bar*, which is popular with locals. Breakfast has home-made pastries and rolls. 'Very good value.' The railway station on the doorstep has good links to Hereford, Birmingham and London. (*Judith Waller, and others*)

25% DISCOUNT VOUCHERS

Colwall, nr Malvern
WR13 6QG

T: 01684-540000
F: 01684-540847
E: hotel@colwall.com
W: www.colwall.co.uk

BEDROOMS: 22.
OPEN: all year.
FACILITIES: ramp, 2 lounges (1 with TV), library, bar, restaurant, ballroom, free Wi-Fi, business facilities, 1-acre garden, only public rooms suitable for &.
BACKGROUND MUSIC: blues in bar, jazz in restaurant.
LOCATION: halfway between Malvern and Ledbury on B4218, train Colwall.
CHILDREN: all ages welcomed.
DOGS: allowed in bar only.
CREDIT CARDS: MasterCard, Visa.
PRICES: [2013] per room B&B £100–£190. D,B&B £80–£125 per person, à la carte £35. 1-night bookings sometimes refused weekends.

CONSTANTINE BAY Cornwall

Map 1:D2

TREGLOS HOTEL

'A good, well-run hotel with a warm welcome,' says a visitor in 2013 to this traditional hotel which is popular with families during the holidays; teenagers should feel comfortable here, say readers, finding friends of their own age group. Owned by Jim and Rose Barlow for more than 40 years, it stands in landscaped gardens overlooking the white sandy beach of Constantine Bay. The Barlow family have 'moved with the times', say visitors. The dress code for dinner in the restaurant has been relaxed to smart casual (no shorts or T-shirts). The chef, Carl Quible, serves a daily-changing menu of dishes like fish and shellfish bisque; chargrilled chicken breast, bacon and sausage roulade, mushroom sauce. The public rooms are 'peaceful and well furnished, with open fires'. Many of the bedrooms, decorated in blue and beige, have views over Constantine Bay; some have a balcony. There is much for all ages to do: a children's playground, a games and snooker room, a spa pool and beauty treatment facilities. The Barlow family also owns Merlin Golf and Country Club (ten minutes' drive away). Small dogs are allowed in some bedrooms (£12 charge). (*BF*)

25% DISCOUNT VOUCHERS

Constantine Bay
Padstow PL28 8JH

T: 01841-520727
F: 01841-521163
E: stay@tregloshotel.com
W: www.tregloshotel.com

BEDROOMS: 42, 1 on ground floor, 2 suitable for &.
OPEN: mid-Feb–end Nov.
FACILITIES: ramps, 2 lounges (pianist twice weekly), bar, restaurant, children's den, snooker room, free Wi-Fi (signal strength varies), beauty treatments, indoor swimming pool (10 by 5 metres), 1-acre grounds.
BACKGROUND MUSIC: in bar.
LOCATION: 4 miles W of Padstow.
CHILDREN: no under-5s in restaurant after 6.30 pm.
DOGS: allowed in some bedrooms, not in public rooms.
CREDIT CARDS: MasterCard, Visa.
PRICES: [2013] per room B&B £165–£209, D,B&B £209–£249. Set dinner £32.

CORNHILL ON TWEED Northumberland   Map 4:A3

COLLINGWOOD ARMS

'I could not fault it; the welcome from Kevin Kenny, the manager, was extremely friendly. He remembered me, perhaps because I may have broken a shower when I stayed three years ago.' A visitor returning this year praises Lindie and Richard Cook's 200-year-old former coaching inn beside the River Tweed in Scottish border country. Restored by local craftsmen working alongside architects and historians, the Grade II listed Georgian building has been updated throughout. There is an open log fire in the entrance hall, a 'spacious and well-kept' library. Wi-Fi access is confined to the public rooms. The 'superb' bedrooms, each named after a ship in Vice-Admiral Collingwood's van at the battle of Trafalgar, have antique furnishings, a large, 'comfortable' bed; 'shelf space for all one's bits and pieces' in the bathroom. There are local beers in the 'relaxed' bar, informal eating in the adjacent brasserie. In the dining room, chef Gordon Campbell serves a daily-changing menu of dishes like applewood-smoked duck breast, pear chutney; whole lemon sole on the bone, sautéed potatoes, braised fennel. Good fishing in the Tweed. (*Richard Bright, and others*)

25% DISCOUNT VOUCHERS

Main Street
Cornhill on Tweed
TD12 4UH

T: 01890-882424
F: 01890-883098
E: enquiries@collingwoodarms.com
W: www.collingwoodarms.com

BEDROOMS: 15, 1 on ground floor.
OPEN: all year.
FACILITIES: hall, library, bar/brasserie, dining room, free Wi-Fi in public areas only, 3-acre garden.
BACKGROUND MUSIC: in brasserie.
LOCATION: village centre.
CHILDREN: all ages welcomed.
DOGS: allowed in kennels, only guide dogs in restaurant.
CREDIT CARDS: MasterCard, Visa.
PRICES: [2013] per room B&B £130–£190, D,B&B from £175. Set menus £29–£35, à la carte £20.

CORSE LAWN Gloucestershire

Map 3:D5

CORSE LAWN HOUSE

🦢 *César award in 2005*

'Outstandingly good: the staff, many of them long-serving, are enormously helpful.' Praise this year for Baba Hine's hotel and restaurant, a Queen Anne Grade II listed building fronted by a large ornamental pond, in the Severn valley near Tewkesbury. 'Baba is a great character, supported by her efficient manager, Gilles Champier.' In the extensive grounds are 'well-tended gardens', a croquet lawn and an all-weather tennis court. There are open fires and antiques in the two drawing rooms. 'Our large bedroom on the first floor was furnished in old-fashioned country house style, which we rather like; everything was well thought out.' 'It was refreshing to have real tea leaves and fresh milk in our room.' Meals can be taken in a formal dining room or a more relaxed bistro. The chef, Martin Kinahan, serves French/English dishes in both areas, perhaps Mediterranean fish soup, rouille croutons; best end of lamb, olive-crushed potato. 'It was good to have our breakfast entirely served at table.' Dogs are 'welcomed and, pleasingly, not charged for'. (*Simon Rodway, and others*)

25% DISCOUNT VOUCHERS

Corse Lawn GL19 4LZ

T: 01452-780771
F: 01452-780840
E: enquiries@corselawn.com
W: www.corselawn.com

BEDROOMS: 18, 5 on ground floor.
OPEN: all year except 24–26 Dec.
FACILITIES: lounge, bar lounge, bistro/bar, 2 restaurants, free Wi-Fi, 2 conference/private dining rooms, civil wedding licence, 12-acre grounds (croquet, tennis, covered heated swimming pool, 20 by 10 metres).
BACKGROUND MUSIC: none.
LOCATION: 5 miles SW of Tewkesbury on B4211.
CHILDREN: all ages welcomed.
DOGS: on lead in public rooms.
CREDIT CARDS: all major cards.
PRICES: [2013] per room B&B single £100, double £160–£190, D,B&B from £185. Set dinner £20–£33.50, à la carte £35–£40.

COWAN BRIDGE Lancashire

Map 4: inset D2

HIPPING HALL

Q César award in 2008

'The atmosphere is smart but pleasantly informal,' say trusted correspondents returning to Andrew Wildsmith's small hotel/restaurant, a 17th-century house in mature gardens in a village near Kirkby Lonsdale. 'He is a skilful host who spends time talking to his guests, as do his young, well-trained staff.' The stone buildings have been 'renovated with flair, combining simplicity with luxury'. Andrew Wildsmith takes orders for dinner and 'table-hops' during the meal in the 'spectacular' dining room, a 15th-century Great Hall (linked by a conservatory). 'Dinner is flexible: you can choose dishes from chef Brent Hulena's three menus – a short carte, a tasting and a vegetarian tasting. The style is well presented and modern, technically impeccable.' Typical dishes: cod, pepper, tomato, courgette; cheek and belly of Cumbrian pork, orange, choucroute. The 'comfortable' bedrooms have a minimal style; natural stone in the modern bathrooms. No 'mediocre buffet' at breakfast, which is served at table with 'similar care' to dinner. Orange juice is freshly squeezed, a home-made smoothie is available; leaf tea'. (*David and Kate Wooff, Robert Cooper*)

Cowan Bridge
nr Kirkby Lonsdale LA6 2JJ

T: 015242-71187
E: info@hippinghall.com
W: www.hippinghall.com

BEDROOMS: 9, 3 in cottage, 1, on ground floor, suitable for &.
OPEN: all year.
FACILITIES: lounge, bar, restaurant, free Wi-Fi, civil wedding licence, 3-acre garden.
BACKGROUND MUSIC: jazz in dining hall, bar.
LOCATION: 2 miles SE of Kirkby Lonsdale, on A65.
CHILDREN: all ages welcomed.
DOGS: allowed in 2 bedrooms, not in public rooms.
CREDIT CARDS: MasterCard, Visa.
PRICES: [2013] per room B&B £119–£229. D,B&B £40 added per person, set dinner £55–£65. 1-night bookings normally refused Sat.

CROFT-ON-TEES Co. Durham

Map 4:C4

CLOW BECK HOUSE

🏵 *César award in 2007*

'Friendly and hospitable' Heather and David Armstrong 'make their guests feel special' at their small hotel and restaurant, a cluster of converted farm buildings close to the River Tees. 'Pretentious we are not,' say the Armstrongs, who have created flamboyant bedrooms in stone outbuildings around gardens created from the family's farmland. Some are as flowery as their name (Lily, Fleur), another has a Japanese theme. They have 'every extra you could imagine'. In the beamed restaurant, David Armstrong, the chef, serves 'good and wholesome' British dishes like chicken breast strips in spicy tomato sauce; rack of Yorkshire lamb, a rich blackcurrant and port gravy. 'Our menu is only a suggestion,' he says. Children are welcomed; they have games on the lawn, a play area, puzzles and crayons; their menu includes boiled eggs and soldiers, and chocolate spread ('don't tell the adults'). Breakfast has home-made preserves, unusual breads and toast, 'excellent' grilled items (including many specials). There is good walking in open countryside from the door (ten minutes' drive to Darlington town centre). (*RM, and others*)

Monk End Farm
Croft-on-Tees
nr Darlington DL2 2SP

T: 01325-721075
F: 01325-720419
E: david@clowbeckhouse.co.uk
W: www.clowbeckhouse.co.uk

BEDROOMS: 13, 12 in garden buildings, 1 suitable for &.
OPEN: all year except Christmas/New Year.
FACILITIES: ramps, lounge, restaurant, free Wi-Fi, small conference facilities, 2-acre grounds in 100-acre farm.
BACKGROUND MUSIC: classical in restaurant.
LOCATION: 3 miles S of Darlington.
CHILDREN: all ages welcomed.
DOGS: not allowed in bedrooms, public rooms.
CREDIT CARDS: Amex, MasterCard, Visa.
PRICES: per room B&B single £85, double £135. À la carte £37.

CROOKHAM Northumberland

Map 4:A3

THE COACH HOUSE AT CROOKHAM

'Simple, but good value', this informal guest house is a complex of buildings including a Grade II listed 17th-century dower house and a smithy. It is 'well run' by owners Toby and Leona Rutter, who are 'charming', say visitors this year. Another comment: 'Good, homely service; a friendly welcome.' Guests are given complimentary tea and cakes on arrival, in the beamed residents' lounge which has an open fire and honesty bar. In the evening, tables in the dining rooms are dressed with crisp linen, and dinner is served on fine china. The hostess is the cook: her three-course dinner has a wide choice of starters but just one main course. A typical meal might include garlic mushrooms on toasted brioche; roast topside of Aberdeen Angus beef. Bedrooms in the main house are traditionally furnished; one has a private staircase. Those in the courtyard have twin beds or a king-size bed, leather furniture and widescreen TV. 'We appreciated the little things like fresh milk in the fridge and the complimentary mineral water.' Breakfast has 'good kippers and porridge'. (*Robert Cooper, and others*)

Crookham
Cornhill-on-Tweed
TD12 4TD

T: 01890-820293
F: 01890-820284
E: stay@coachhousecrookham.com
W: www.coachhousecrookham.com

BEDROOMS: 10, 7 around courtyard, 3 suitable for &.
OPEN: Feb–Nov.
FACILITIES: lounge, 2 dining rooms, free Wi-Fi in dining rooms, terrace, orchard.
BACKGROUND MUSIC: none.
LOCATION: On A697, 3 miles N of Milfield.
CHILDREN: all ages welcomed.
DOGS: allowed in courtyard bedrooms, not in public rooms.
CREDIT CARDS: MasterCard, Visa (*2% surcharge each*).
PRICES: per person B&B £40–£55, D,B&B £63.95–£78.95. Set dinner £23.95. 1-night bookings sometimes refused.

CRUDWELL Wiltshire

Map 3:E5

THE RECTORY HOTEL

In 'beautiful grounds' with a walled garden and an outdoor swimming pool, this 'homely hotel with a quality finish' is owned by Jonathan Barry (formerly with Hotel du Vin) and antiques dealer Julian Muggridge. Manager Jenna Tomblin's team provides 'informal, attentive, anything-you-need service', says a visitor. Children are welcomed, which is appropriate for a Cotswold stone building that once was home to the village rector and his 14 children. 'Our young son loved roaming the grounds; he was well looked after at mealtimes, and a travel cot and baby monitor were provided.' Dogs are welcomed too. There are upholstered armchairs, magazines and a log fire in the sitting room. Simply decorated bedrooms, in pastel shades, have antiques, books, a Roberts radio; some have original beams. In the wood-panelled restaurant overlooking the garden and sunken baptism pool, chef Peter Fairclough's menus have local, organic and foraged produce, typically roasted guineafowl, wild garlic risotto. (Meals can be served in the garden in summer.) The market towns of Tetbury and Nailsworth are nearby; the 'wonderful' *Potting Shed* pub (under the same ownership) is up the street. (*GP*)

Crudwell, nr Malmesbury
SN16 9EP

T: 01666-577194
F: 01666-577853
E: info@therectoryhotel.com
W: www.therectoryhotel.com

BEDROOMS: 12.
OPEN: all year, restaurant closed lunchtime.
FACILITIES: lounge, bar, dining room, free Wi-Fi, meeting facilities, civil wedding licence, 3-acre garden (heated swimming pool, 10 by 5 metres), unsuitable for &.
BACKGROUND MUSIC: 'light background' in bar and dining room.
LOCATION: 4 miles N of Malmesbury.
CHILDREN: all ages welcomed.
DOGS: not allowed in dining room.
CREDIT CARDS: Amex, MasterCard, Visa.
PRICES: per room B&B £105–£205. Set dinner £32.50 per person. 1-night bookings refused bank holidays.

DARTMOUTH Devon

Map 1:D4

DART MARINA

'Absolutely marvellous; warm, cosy and inviting.' Close to the town centre, Richard Seton's 'very well-run' hotel is liked for the 'air of calm' in the smart public rooms, which have 'huge, immaculately cleaned windows through which we watched the higher ferry ply to and fro across the Dart estuary'. Paul Downing, the manager, is 'efficient, friendly, and he listens to comments; the charming staff care about the guests'. Three new rooms were added in 2013; they are designed in colours that reflect the tree-lined river views. All rooms overlook the river. 'Ours was beautifully prepared and squeakily clean.' 'When we were upgraded to a balcony room, they remembered that we had requested blankets and sheets and immediately made the change while we had a delicious afternoon tea,' said inspectors. In the light *River* restaurant, the cooking of chef Tom Woods is 'second to none; his dishes are imaginative and tasty. One that stood out was caramelised scallops, pea purée, pancetta foam.' Breakfast has a 'generous' buffet of compotes, fruit salads, yogurts, etc. 'My Manx granny would have approved of the quality of the kipper.' A new garden (with a maritime theme) has been created. (*Mary Woods, and others*)

Sandquay Road
Dartmouth
TQ6 9PH

T: 01803-832580
F: 01803-835040
E: reception@dartmarina.com
W: www.dartmarina.com

BEDROOMS: 52, 3 on ground floor, 1 suitable for &.
OPEN: all year.
FACILITIES: lounge/bar, bistro, restaurant, free Wi-Fi, river-front terrace, spa (heated indoor swimming pool, 8 by 4 metres, gym).
BACKGROUND MUSIC: in lounge and bar daytime, in restaurant evenings.
LOCATION: on waterfront.
CHILDREN: all ages welcomed.
DOGS: in ground-floor rooms (£10), not during meal times in public rooms.
CREDIT CARDS: MasterCard, Visa.
PRICES: [2013] per room B&B £140–£200, D,B&B £194–£260. Set dinner £30–£37.50. 1-night bookings refused Sat, bank holiday weekends.

SEE ALSO SHORTLIST

DARTMOUTH Devon

NONSUCH HOUSE

🌶 *César award in 2000*

It would be difficult to better the views from Kit and Penny Noble's Edwardian house at the top of a hill opposite Dartmouth. From the conservatory/dining room and the bedroom windows there is a panorama of sea, harbour, the town and the River Dart, on which there is constant activity. There is a residents' lounge with a log fire, comfortable chairs and masses of books and magazines. The Nobles are 'charming' hosts; welcoming and knowledgeable. The four spacious bedrooms are south-facing; they are well equipped, with large bed, TV, DVD/CD-player, bathrobes, chairs and writing desk. Chilled water and fresh milk are provided. Dinner, prepared by Kit Noble, is available on four nights a week; guests are encouraged to discuss likes and dislikes. No liquor licence, bring your own wine; 'We will provide the fridge, the ice, the lemon and the nibbles for pre-dinner drinks.' Breakfast has home-made bread, muesli, fruit compotes; local produce is used for cooked dishes and fish is home smoked. Although the hill is steep, the Nobles say there are 'gentle ways' of getting up and down. (*SH*)

Church Hill, Kingswear
Dartmouth TQ6 0BX

T: 01803-752829
F: 01803-752357
E: enquiries@nonsuch-house.co.uk
W: www.nonsuch-house.co.uk

BEDROOMS: 4.
OPEN: all year, dining room closed midday, evening Tues/Wed/Sat.
FACILITIES: ramps, lounge, dining room/conservatory, free Wi-Fi, ¼-acre garden (sun terrace), rock beach 300 yds (sailing nearby), membership of local gym and spa.
BACKGROUND MUSIC: none.
LOCATION: 5 mins' walk from ferry to Dartmouth.
CHILDREN: not under 12.
DOGS: not allowed.
CREDIT CARDS: MasterCard, Visa.
PRICES: [2013] per room B&B single £85–£155, double £110–£180. D,B&B £37.50 per person added. 1-night bookings usually refused weekends.

SEE ALSO SHORTLIST

DEDHAM Essex

Map 2:C5

DEDHAM HALL & FOUNTAIN HOUSE RESTAURANT

'A tranquil setting, lovely staff, fabulous gardens,' says a visitor this year to Jim and Wendy Sarton's 'quirky' guest house, a 15th-century manor house in the landscape painted by Constable. Guests on art courses run by the Sartons in the winter months stay in rooms around a converted 14th-century barn. Bedrooms in the main house are traditionally furnished: 'We had a large comfortable bed in a room that overlooked a field and lavender bushes; the sun shone, the bees buzzed; it was wonderfully quiet.' The cooking in the *Fountain House* restaurant, which overlooks the pond in the 'well-kept' gardens ('informal and English in style'), is much praised: 'Excellent; generous portions (none of your itsy-bitsy nouvelle cuisine). My guineafowl came with delicious stuffing; the wines were well priced.' Dinner is provided for hotel guests when the restaurant is closed. An earlier comment: 'Wonderfully warm: everyone who looked after us came from nearby.' The lounge has oak beams, books, and paintings by artists who have attended the courses. There are many walks from the door. (*Beverley Smith, Julia de Waal*)

Brook Street, Dedham
nr Colchester CO7 6AD

T: 01206-323027
E: sarton@dedhamhall.demon.co.uk
W: www.dedhamhall.co.uk

BEDROOMS: 20, 16 in annexe, some on ground floor, suitable for &.
OPEN: all year except Christmas/New Year, restaurant closed Sun/Mon.
FACILITIES: ramps, 2 lounges, 2 bars, dining room, restaurant, studio, free Wi-Fi, 6-acre grounds (pond, gardens).
BACKGROUND MUSIC: none.
LOCATION: end of High Street.
CHILDREN: all ages welcomed.
DOGS: not allowed.
CREDIT CARDS: MasterCard, Visa.
PRICES: per person B&B £55–£65, D,B&B £85–£95. Set menu £35.

DEDHAM Essex

THE SUN INN

The owner, Piers Baker, has discreetly restored this 15th-century coaching inn, giving it a classic country pub atmosphere ('preferable to the favoured minimalist style'). The yellow-painted inn stands opposite St Mary's Church, which has Constable's *Ascension* on permanent display. In the bar (also painted yellow) are old oak floorboards and beams, log fires, window seats, sofas, club chairs, board games, books, lots of local information. The drawing room, with its large fireplace, is in country house style. In the open-plan dining room, chefs Ugo Simonelli and Ewan Naylon serve a daily-changing modern menu with an Italian influence, which might include Old Spot pork loin, braised black cabbage, Spello lentils. Bedrooms are in more modern style; furniture is a mix of antique and repro; beds are large; there are neutral fabrics and quirky touches (old packing cases for bedside tables). Two rooms are reached by an external Elizabethan staircase at the back of the building. Breakfast has help-yourself cereals, fruit compote, cured meats; American-style pancakes with seasonal fruit coulis as an alternative to a fry-up or an omelette. More reports, please.

High Street, Dedham
nr Colchester CO7 6DF

T: 01206-323351
E: office@thesuninndedham.com
W: www.thesuninndedham.com

BEDROOMS: 7.
OPEN: all year except 25/26 Dec, 5/6 Jan.
FACILITIES: lounge, bar, dining room, free Wi-Fi, 1-acre garden (covered terrace, children's play area), unsuitable for &.
BACKGROUND MUSIC: jazz/blues in bar.
LOCATION: central, 5 miles NE of Colchester.
CHILDREN: all ages welcomed.
DOGS: not allowed in bedrooms.
CREDIT CARDS: MasterCard, Visa.
PRICES: per room B&B £90–£150, D,B&B £160–£220. À la carte 27.50.

DODDISCOMBSLEIGH Devon

Map 1:C4

THE NOBODY INN

'A lovely old pub in a wonderful hidden valley.'
Guide inspectors were greeted warmly ('first by
a friendly chef in the car park') at Sue Burdge's
17th-century inn in a rural village near Exeter. It
has two connected beamed bars with wooden
tables, one with books and board games ('busy
on a Friday night'). It has cask beers, Devon
ciders, 'an enormous selection of whiskies'.
Meals can be taken in either bar from two
menus ('classics' including 'the best-ever steak-
and-ale pie', and 'specials') or in a small
adjoining restaurant which has 'linen cloths,
crisp napkins'. The chef, Adam Parnham, has a
'passion for using locally sourced produce': 'We
enjoyed excellent starters (crisp belly pork, pea
purée; Brie and parsley soufflé): main courses
were rich and generous.' The bedrooms are
above the bars ('some noise until closing time,
but this is a pub'): 'Ours was a reasonable size,
beamed but light and bright; a good built-in
wardrobe (captive hangers, alas) and a small,
functional shower room.' Breakfast, ordered the
evening before, is served at an agreed time.
(*Peter Anderson, and others*)

Doddiscombsleigh EX6 7PS

T: 01647-252394
F: 01647-252978
E: info@nobodyinn.co.uk
W: www.nobodyinn.co.uk

BEDROOMS: 5.
OPEN: all year, restaurant closed
Sun/Mon evening.
FACILITIES: 2 bars, restaurant, free
Wi-Fi (may be patchy), small
garden, patio, unsuitable for &.
BACKGROUND MUSIC: none.
LOCATION: in village 6 miles SW of
Exeter.
CHILDREN: not under 14 in bar.
DOGS: not allowed in restaurant,
bedrooms.
CREDIT CARDS: MasterCard, Visa.
PRICES: [2013] per room B&B single
£65, double £90. À la carte £30–£35.

DODDISCOMBSLEIGH Devon

Map 1:C4

TOWN BARTON

In this 'blissfully quiet' Domesday village,
hidden in the fold of hills west of Exeter, Nick
Borst-Smith runs his old manor house as a 'very
good value' B&B. 'It is a lovely place and
seriously underpriced,' says a visitor this year.
Two of the four spacious bedrooms are on the
ground floor. 'Ours was exceedingly comfortable
and very well furnished, with a huge bed; its
well-appointed bathroom had excellent soap and
shampoo.' The rooms are generously equipped:
fresh milk in the fridge, a jug of distilled water,
a cafetière with ground coffee and 'fine' teas.
The two rooms at the back overlook the
medieval church whose stained glass survives
because Henry VIII's wreckers couldn't find
the village. Nick Borst-Smith will leave a
continental breakfast tray in the room overnight
('excellent orange juice, splendid jam and
marmalade, sliced bread for the toaster'). He
will book a table for dinner at the nearby
Nobody Inn, which he used to own (see previous
entry); a cooked breakfast can also be taken at
the inn. (*Peter Anderson, Andrew Kleissner*)

Doddiscombsleigh
nr Exeter EX6 7PT

T: 01647-252005
E: rooms@townbarton.co.uk
W: www.townbarton.co.uk

BEDROOMS: 4, 2 on ground floor.
OPEN: all year.
FACILITIES: free Wi-Fi, 4-acre
gardens.
BACKGROUND MUSIC: none.
LOCATION: in village 6 miles SW of
Exeter.
CHILDREN: all ages welcomed.
DOGS: not allowed.
CREDIT CARDS: MasterCard, Visa.
PRICES: room £50–£75. Breakfast
£5–£10.95 per person.

EAST GRINSTEAD West Sussex

Map 2:D4

GRAVETYE MANOR

The pioneer of the English natural garden, William Robinson, created the fine gardens and gave the interiors of this 16th-century Elizabethan manor house an Arts and Crafts style. The owners, Jeremy and Elizabeth Hosking, have invested heavily in a restoration of both house and garden that has been true to Robinson's vision. It is run as a luxury hotel (Relais & Châteaux) by Andrew Thomason, the managing director. The public areas have dark wood panelling, thick carpets, bold floral displays; the smell of wood smoke from open fires. The staff are 'charming', creating an atmosphere that is 'not at all stuffy'. Bedrooms, named after tree species found on the estate, have rich fabrics, antiques and hand-crafted beds. They vary in size; all have the latest technology. Tables are well spaced in the formal candlelit dining room (no background music in the evening, 'please leave your mobile phone at reception'). Chef Rupert Gleadow serves a modern British menu of dishes like chicken consommé, chicken and leek tortellini; braised pork belly, mashed potatoes, merguez sausage. Breakfast has freshly squeezed juices, 'lovely preserves' and an 'excellent' full English.

Vowels Lane
East Grinstead RH19 4LJ

T: 01342-810567
F: 01342-810080
E: info@gravetyemanor.co.uk
W: www.gravetyemanor.co.uk

BEDROOMS: 17.
OPEN: all year.
FACILITIES: 3 lounges, bar, restaurant, private dining room, free Wi-Fi, civil wedding licence, 35-acre grounds, only restaurant suitable for &.
BACKGROUND MUSIC: classic in restaurant at breakfast.
LOCATION: 5 miles SW of East Grinstead.
CHILDREN: not under 7 in restaurant.
DOGS: not allowed.
CREDIT CARDS: Amex, MasterCard, Visa.
PRICES: [2013] per room B&B £240–£430, D,B&B £370–£420. Set dinner £25–£40, à la carte £60.

EAST HOATHLY East Sussex

Map 2:E4

OLD WHYLY

'Very civilised', this 'beautiful' Grade II listed
Georgian manor house (with a history dating
back to the 12th century) is run as an upmarket
B&B (with evening meals available) by the
owner, Sarah Burgoyne. She warmly greeted
Guide inspectors in 2013. They were given tea
and home-made cake in a 'nicely proportioned
drawing room with a large open fire, fine
furniture, many books'. A first-floor bedroom
was 'small but pleasant; sheets and blankets on
the comfortable bed; a wardrobe and chest of
drawers; a good shower room'. A jug of fresh
milk was left on the tea/coffee tray during
evening turn-down. 'We joined another couple
in the lounge for aperitifs and canapés before
dining together in the candlelit dining room.
Sarah, an accomplished cook, gave us a beetroot
and goat's cheese starter; fillet of cod on a bed of
beans and herbs; a home-made tart. The short
wine list was reasonably priced. She joined us
with her spaniel, Puzzle, for coffee. Breakfast,
also taken communally, had 'freshly squeezed
orange juice, poached pears, the usual full
English'. Picnic hampers can be supplied for
nearby Glyndebourne.

London Road
East Hoathly BN8 6EL

T: 01825-840216
E: stay@oldwhyly.co.uk
W: www.oldwhyly.co.uk

BEDROOMS: 4.
OPEN: all year.
FACILITIES: drawing room, dining
room, free Wi-Fi, 3-acre garden in
30-acre grounds, heated outdoor
swimming pool (10 by 5 metres),
tennis, unsuitable for &.
BACKGROUND MUSIC: none.
LOCATION: 1 mile N of village.
CHILDREN: all ages welcomed.
DOGS: not allowed.
CREDIT CARDS: none.
PRICES: [2013] per person B&B
£47.50–£70. Set dinner £32.50,
Glyndebourne hamper £38. 1-night
bookings sometimes refused
weekends in high season.

EAST LAVANT West Sussex

Map 2:E3

THE ROYAL OAK

In a village near Chichester with views over the South Downs towards Goodwood, Charles Ullmann's 200-year-old whitewashed flint-stone inn is popular with *Guide* readers. Many original features are retained in the bar/restaurant (an open fire, exposed brickwork, beams); good linen napkins on the rustic wooden tables. This year there is a new chef, Daniel Ward, whose menu might include seared Scottish scallops, crisp belly pork, pickled ginger; pan-fried brill with fennel and crab croquettes. There is a daily list of blackboard specials. We would welcome reports on his cooking. In fine weather, meals may be taken outside on the terrace or in a small garden. 'It might look like a pub, but the bedrooms are well fitted,' said one visitor. They are in the main building and a converted cottage and barn overlooking fields behind the inn. Some have inglenook and exposed beams; all have a modern bathroom with 'lots of nice touches'. Breakfast has a 'good choice of cereals and lovely fresh fruit'; the usual cooked dishes. Busy during Goodwood events and with theatre-goers at Chichester. (*JB, DV*)

Pook Lane
East Lavant PO18 0AX

T: 01243-527434
E: rooms@royaloakeastlavant.co.uk
W: www.royaloakeastlavant.co.uk

BEDROOMS: 5, 3 in adjacent barn and cottage, 2 self-catering cottages nearby.
OPEN: all year, except 25 Dec.
FACILITIES: bar/restaurant, free Wi-Fi, terrace (outside meals), small garden, unsuitable for &.
BACKGROUND MUSIC: jazz in restaurant.
LOCATION: 2 miles N of Chichester.
CHILDREN: all ages welcomed.
DOGS: not allowed in bedrooms.
CREDIT CARDS: all major cards.
PRICES: [2013] per room B&B £125–£220. À la carte £35. 1-night bookings refused weekends, bank holidays.

EASTBOURNE East Sussex

Map 2:E4

BELLE TOUT LIGHTHOUSE NEW

'A lovely and unusual place for a romantic getaway.' On the chalk cliffs of Beachy Head, this decommissioned lighthouse has been sympathetically restored by the owner, David Shaw, and is run as a B&B ('with a fantastic view'). Ian Noall is the manager. 'I was asked if I wanted space or a view; I chose the view,' said a *Guide* inspector. 'My small double room was dual-aspect, facing the present lighthouse on one side and grazing sheep on the other. It was all white, with colour provided by artwork, blinds, cushions and throws; plenty of storage, good reading lights, two director's chairs. The tiny bathroom had good water pressure, fluffy towels, everything I needed.' Two larger rooms face the South Downs. The sitting room, with 'comfy chairs and sofas', has a wraparound window looking out to the Seven Sisters. A 'generous' breakfast has home-made muesli and muffins, fresh and dried fruits; a long list of local ingredients for the full English, plus daily specials (perhaps eggs Benedict). There is a 360-degree view from the former light room, which is reached by 80 steps ('worth the effort').

Beachy Head Road
Eastbourne BN20 0AE

T: 01323-423185
E: info@belletout.co.uk
W: www.belletout.co.uk

BEDROOMS: 6.
OPEN: all year, except 15 Dec–16 Jan.
FACILITIES: 2 lounges, breakfast room, free Wi-Fi, terrace, garden, unsuitable for &.
BACKGROUND MUSIC: none.
LOCATION: 3 miles W of Eastbourne.
CHILDREN: not under 16.
DOGS: not allowed.
CREDIT CARDS: MasterCard, Visa.
PRICES: [2013] per room B&B £145–£220. Min. 2-night stay, 1-night bookings only accepted 7–10 days in advance.

SEE ALSO SHORTLIST

EDENBRIDGE Kent

Map 2:D4

STARBOROUGH MANOR

'A beautiful building in attractive grounds', this 18th-century manor house is run as a luxury B&B by Lynn and Jonathan Mathias. 'They are excellent hosts, combining professionalism with warmth,' says a visitor this year. A 'delightful' sitting room on the first floor has a television, games, DVDs and a library of books. A second sitting room offers peace and quiet. Bedrooms, individually furnished in traditional country style, have flat-screen TV, complimentary water and a hospitality tray. 'We had a large room with good bed and lighting; a huge bathroom.' Two rooms share a bathroom and are let as a family suite. Breakfast is taken communally in the kitchen or, for larger parties, in the dining room. It has generous portions of fresh fruit; cereals and yogurts on the table; 'excellent' smoked salmon and scrambled eggs, or perhaps hash browns and baked beans. No evening meals: a kitchen and dining room are available (for a charge of £15) for those who wish to prepare their own – 'a bonus'). A heated swimming pool in the grounds is available in the summer. (*Vicky Maltby*)

Moor Lane, Marsh Green
Edenbridge TN8 5QY

T: 01732-862152
E: lynn@starboroughmanor.co.uk
W: www.starboroughmanor.co.uk

BEDROOMS: 4.
OPEN: all year.
FACILITIES: 2 sitting rooms, dining room, free Wi-Fi, 14-acre grounds, heated outdoor pool (5 by 10 metres), unsuitable for &.
BACKGROUND MUSIC: none.
LOCATION: 1½ miles W of Edenbridge.
CHILDREN: all ages welcomed.
DOGS: by prior arrangement.
CREDIT CARDS: MasterCard, Visa.
PRICES: [2013] per room B&B single £90–£100, double £140. 1-night bookings sometimes refused weekends in summer.

EGTON BRIDGE North Yorkshire

Map 4:C5

BROOM HOUSE

In an 'attractive' setting down a country lane and close to the River Esk in the North York Moors national park, this small guest house is 'a relaxing place to stay'. Owned and run by David and Maria White, the restored Victorian farmhouse has sofas and an open fire in the residents' lounge. 'Comfortable' bedrooms have 'a modern decor' and views over the gardens or the Esk valley; a small double room on the ground floor has a private patio leading to the lawn. A twin room, overlooking the garden, had 'good lighting, and lots of hanging and drawer space'. In the candlelit restaurant, Maria White uses home-grown vegetables and fruit and local produce in her menus, for dishes like potted pork, apple crackling salad; daube of beef, horseradish mash. (Vegetarians are 'well catered for'.) 'The food was good,' say visitors in 2013, though they would have preferred a daily-changing menu to the carte. The 'excellent' breakfast has local honey, and smoked fish from nearby Whitby. The heritage North Yorkshire Moors Railway steam train occasionally puffs by at the end of the garden. (*John and Eileen Avison, and others*)

25% DISCOUNT VOUCHERS

Broom House Lane
Egton Bridge YO21 1XD

T: 01947-895279
F: 01947-895657
E: mw@broom-house.co.uk
W: www.egton-bridge.co.uk

BEDROOMS: 8, 1 on ground floor, 2 in cottage.
OPEN: Mar–Nov, restaurant closed Sun, Mon nights.
FACILITIES: lounge, dining room, restaurant, free Wi-Fi, ½-acre garden.
BACKGROUND MUSIC: in restaurant.
LOCATION: ½ mile W of village.
CHILDREN: all ages welcomed.
DOGS: not allowed.
CREDIT CARDS: MasterCard, Visa.
PRICES: [2013] per room B&B £83–£140, D,B&B £120–£170. À la carte £24. 1-night bookings sometimes refused bank holidays.

EMSWORTH Hampshire

36 ON THE QUAY

🦢 *César award in 2011*

On the quayside of a quiet town on the border of Hampshire and West Sussex, this 17th-century former fishermen's inn is run as a restaurant-with-rooms by Karen and Ramon Farthing. It 'has a lot to recommend it, not least the location'. She is in charge of the 'quietly efficient' service in the dining room, which faces Emsworth harbour. Her husband is the *Michelin*-starred chef, whose cooking has long been admired by *Guide* readers. He is 'not afraid of contrasting textures and seasonings' in his modern French dishes, perhaps cold pressed pork cheek, pumpkin, mushrooms, crisp pork, lemon miso; supreme of turbot, caponata, steamed leeks and roasted salsify, basil and orange beignet, light chicken infusion. His tasting menu is 'faultless'. Five bedrooms are above the restaurant (Vanilla has a sofa in the sitting area positioned to overlook the harbour); a cottage across the road has a bedroom, lounge and mini-kitchen. Continental breakfast can be taken in the bedroom or in a small breakfast room. It has cereals, fresh fruit, brioches and croissants, home-made jams. (*B and MB, K and PW*)

47 South Street
Emsworth PO10 7EG

T: 01243-375592
E: bookings@36onthequay.co.uk
W: www.36onthequay.co.uk

BEDROOMS: 6, 1 in cottage (with lounge) across road (can be let weekly).
OPEN: all year except 24–26 Dec, first 2 weeks Jan, 1 week May, 1 week Oct, restaurant closed Sun/Mon.
FACILITIES: lounge area, bar area, restaurant, free Wi-Fi, terrace, only restaurant suitable for ♿.
BACKGROUND MUSIC: none.
LOCATION: on harbour.
CHILDREN: all ages welcomed.
DOGS: allowed in cottage, by arrangement.
CREDIT CARDS: MasterCard, Visa.
PRICES: [2013] per room B&B £100–£200. Set dinner £57.95.

ERMINGTON Devon

Map 1:D4

PLANTATION HOUSE

'Attention to detail makes this small hotel feel
very special.' In a Georgian rectory overlooking
the River Erme, Richard Hendey is both owner
and much-praised chef. 'Richard creates a
wonderful atmosphere when front-of-house,
often opening a special bottle as a house wine.'
The building is 'tastefully decorated in muted
tones'; there is a log fire in the lounge in winter,
and a terrace for summer aperitifs. Bedrooms
have 'everything one wants', including hot-
water bottles and flowers from the garden. 'Our
spacious master suite had a large, comfortable
bed, a modern bathroom, and far-reaching
views of the Devon countryside. Lovely extra
touches: fruit and biscuits, fresh milk in the
minibar, a small decanter of brandy – all
replenished each day.' 'We enjoyed some
stunning meals: home-smoked salmon, apple
and hawthorn sorbet; tender, melting duck with
an incredibly crispy skin.' 'Every meal was
outstanding, with wonderful flavours and a
beautiful presentation.' Breakfast has freshly
squeezed orange juice, 'good, crisp croissants',
'real leaf tea, a joy', eggs from the house's own
hens. 'My husband raved about the smoked
haddock.' (*Linda McGivern, Stephen Parish, GC*)

Totnes Road
Ermington, nr Plymouth
PL21 9NS

T: 01548-831100
E: info@plantationhousehotel.co.uk
W: www.plantationhousehotel.co.uk

BEDROOMS: 9.
OPEN: all year, restaurant closed
midday, some Sundays.
FACILITIES: lounge/bar, 2 dining
rooms, free Wi-Fi, terrace, garden,
unsuitable for &.
BACKGROUND MUSIC: if required.
LOCATION: 10 miles E of Plymouth.
CHILDREN: 'well-behaved' children
welcomed.
DOGS: allowed in 1 bedroom, not in
public rooms.
CREDIT CARDS: Amex, MasterCard,
Visa.
PRICES: per room B&B single £70,
double £100–£230. D,B&B £39
per person added, set dinner £39.
1-night bookings occasionally
refused bank holidays.

EVERSHOT Dorset

Map 1:C6

SUMMER LODGE

In large grounds in a pretty Dorset village, this creeper-clad, Georgian country house was enlarged by Thomas Hardy (an architect by profession) for his friend, the 6th Earl of Ilchester. It is run as a luxury hotel and spa (Relais & Châteaux) by the Red Carnation group, which also owns the 16th-century *Acorn Inn* in the village (see Shortlist). Public rooms are opulently furnished with heavy drapes, a chandelier, settees; scatter cushions in the lounge; dark wood furniture with subdued lighting in the bar. Guests with simpler tastes will find relief in the sunny conservatory/breakfast room. The bedrooms have rich fabrics, antiques and bold prints. Towels and linen are refreshed twice daily and there is a turn-down service. A suite designed by Hardy now has an open fireplace and two bathrooms (plus all the latest technology). In the restaurant, chef Steven Titman cooks elaborate dishes with a French influence; the carte includes his 'signature dish' – pan-seared Lyme Bay scallops, trio of pumpkin, pumpkin seed dressing. Guests may borrow bicycles to explore the village, which was adopted by Hardy as the setting for *Tess of the d'Urbervilles*.

9 Fore Street
Evershot DT2 0JR

T: 01935-482000
F: 01935-482040
E: summerlodge@rchmail.com
W: www.summerlodgehotel.com

BEDROOMS: 24, 9 in coach house and courtyard house, 4 in lane, 1 on ground floor suitable for &.
OPEN: all year.
FACILITIES: ramps, drawing room, lounge/bar, restaurant, free Wi-Fi, indoor swimming pool (11 by 6 metres), civil wedding licence, 4-acre grounds (tennis).
BACKGROUND MUSIC: 'easy listening' in lounge/bar.
LOCATION: 10 miles NW of Dorchester.
CHILDREN: all ages welcomed.
DOGS: allowed in some bedrooms.
CREDIT CARDS: all major cards.
PRICES: [2013] per room B&B £235–£650, D,B&B £315–£730. Set dinner £45, à la carte £60. 1-night bookings refused some weekends July–Oct, some bank holidays.

SEE ALSO SHORTLIST

EVESHAM Worcestershire

THE EVESHAM HOTEL

❦ *César award in 1990*

John Jenkinson, who owns and runs this small hotel with his wife Sue, delights in off-beat jokes and wearing comedy ties (the *César* award was for 'utterly acceptable mild eccentricity'). Visitors who can put up with teddy-bear key fobs and the talking mirrors in the lavatories will discover a hotel 'where they go the extra mile to suit everyone's needs'. Children (and 'well-behaved adults') are warmly welcomed: there is a huge playroom, an 'ideal' indoor swimming pool, a trampoline in the 'lovely' gardens. Sue Jenkinson is responsible for the bedrooms, some of which are themed. Alice in Wonderland, a family suite, has a play nook under the beams. The Gaudí room has a mosaic headboard, the Tropical room a fish tank; South Pacific has an aquarium under the basin. All rooms have a silent fridge, a fan; double doors minimise corridor noise. Many of the staff are long-serving ('hospitality is faultless'). Tom Brooks was appointed head chef in June 2013. In the Georgian dining room, the menus have an extensive choice. (*Lee and Lorraine Prince*)

25% DISCOUNT VOUCHERS

Cooper's Lane, off Waterside
Evesham WR11 1DA

T: 01386-765566
F: 01386-765443
E: reception@eveshamhotel.com
W: www.eveshamhotel.com

BEDROOMS: 39, 11 on ground floor, 2 suitable for ♿.
OPEN: all year except 25/26 Dec.
FACILITIES: 2 lounges, bar, restaurant, private dining room, free Wi-Fi, indoor swimming pool (5 by 12 metres), 2½-acre grounds (croquet, putting, swings, trampoline).
BACKGROUND MUSIC: none.
LOCATION: 5 mins' walk from centre, across river.
CHILDREN: all ages welcomed.
DOGS: only guide dogs allowed in public rooms.
CREDIT CARDS: Amex, MasterCard, Visa.
PRICES: per room B&B single £82–£92, double £133–£179. D,B&B £82–£92 per person, à la carte £27.50. 1-night bookings refused Sat for Cheltenham Gold Cup, New Year, occasionally Sat at other times.

EXFORD Somerset

Map 1:B4

THE CROWN

'A working village inn; the hotel and pub have separate entrances with a door from hotel reception opening on to the pub. You can enjoy village life simply by walking through.' There is much praise this year for Sara and Dan Whittaker's 17th-century coaching inn in a pretty Exmoor village. 'It is welcoming and relaxing, not smart or intimidating, which suited our sons who enjoyed going on to the moor to see the deer.' Another comment: 'What a find: comfortable, with excellent food; friendly staff and management.' *The Crown* has a gun safe; it is 'very dog friendly'; stabling can be provided for horses. A fire burns in the lobby, which is 'nicely furnished for flopping'. In the smart restaurant, chef Olivier Certain serves modern dishes such as twice-baked cheese soufflé; gilt-head sea bream, ratatouille, braised fennel. Meals can also be taken in the bar. Bedrooms are individually styled and vary in size. The only early-morning noise in a front room 'was agricultural, interesting rather than intrusive'. (*Mrs M Mitchell, Kay and Peter Rogers, Gwyn Morgan*)

Exford
Exmoor National Park
TA24 7PP

T: 01643-831554
F: 01643-831665
E: info@crownhotelexmoor.co.uk
W: www.crownhotelexmoor.co.uk

BEDROOMS: 16.
OPEN: all year.
FACILITIES: lounge, cocktail bar, public bar, restaurant, meeting room, free Wi-Fi, 3-acre grounds (trout stream, water garden, terrace garden), stabling, unsuitable for &.
BACKGROUND MUSIC: in bar and restaurant.
LOCATION: on village green.
CHILDREN: all ages welcomed.
DOGS: not allowed in restaurant.
CREDIT CARDS: MasterCard, Visa.
PRICES: [2013] per person B&B £55–£80, D,B&B £75–£115. Set menu £27.50–£35.

FAVERSHAM Kent

READ'S

🏵 *César award in 2005*

A 'beautiful' Georgian manor house near an old market town, Rona and David Pitchford's restaurant-with-rooms is liked for the combination of 'informality alongside splendour'. Rona Pitchford is 'consistently keen to help guests' front-of-house; her husband is the chef, using local produce (fish from Whitstable, vegetables and herbs from the walled garden) for his classic seasonal dishes on a flexible menu, perhaps halibut, caramelised cauliflower purée, pomegranate, caper and golden raisin dressing. 'The ambience is delightful in the dining room; no background music, a gentle hum of conversation, elegantly dressed tables.' The bedrooms have a 'traditional but not dated' decor: 'Our spacious room had window seats overlooking a magnificent cedar tree; heaps of good taste, rich fabrics, plush, thick curtains; a seating area with a coffee table, magazines, a decanter of sherry; an impeccable bathroom.' A well-stocked fridge in the pantry is available on an honesty basis. Breakfast has croissants, home-made jams; 'delicious home-pressed apple juice'; 'excellent' cooked choices. (*A and BB*)

Macknade Manor
Canterbury Road
Faversham ME13 8XE

T: 01795-535344
F: 01795-591200
E: enquiries@reads.com
W: www.reads.com

BEDROOMS: 6.
OPEN: all year except 25/26 Dec, restaurant closed Sun/Mon.
FACILITIES: sitting room/bar, restaurant, private dining room, free Wi-Fi, civil wedding licence, 4-acre garden (terrace, outdoor dining), only restaurant suitable for &.
BACKGROUND MUSIC: none.
LOCATION: 1 mile SE of Faversham.
CHILDREN: all ages welcomed.
DOGS: not allowed in public rooms.
CREDIT CARDS: Amex, MasterCard, Visa.
PRICES: [2013] per room B&B single £125–£185, double £165–£195. D,B&B £135–£240 per person. Set dinner £60.

FOWEY Cornwall

Map 1:D3

THE OLD QUAY HOUSE

🏅 *César award in 2013*

'An experience of serene charm.' A trusted reporter found 'everything just right' at Jane and Roy Carson's stylish conversion of a Victorian seamen's mission on the waterfront of this pretty town. Anthony Chapman manages the 'hard-working, well-trained staff'. Visitors arriving by car are encouraged to drop off baggage before parking up the hill (cost included) in a town of steep narrow streets. 'Our light bedroom had a gorgeous view of the estuary; a king-size bed, an excellent wardrobe, two comfortable chairs; a freestanding bath and a separate walk-in shower.' Several bedrooms have a small balcony. A fridge on the landing has fresh milk. The restaurant has glass doors opening on to a waterside terrace. Ashley Wright is now the chef: his modern menu might include soused mackerel, beetroot marshmallow, horseradish panna cotta; fillet and blade of beef, turnip, spinach, onion marmalade. Breakfast has a buffet of cereals, yogurt, fresh fruit, croissants; 'individually prepared cooked dishes were excellent'. 'It was a pleasure every time to enter my restful bedroom.' (*Eithne Scallan, Ken and Priscilla Winslow*)

28 Fore Street
Fowey PL23 1AQ

T: 01726-833302
F: 01726-833668
E: info@theoldquayhouse.com
W: www.theoldquayhouse.com

BEDROOMS: 11.
OPEN: all year, restaurant closed Mon/Tues Jan/Feb.
FACILITIES: open-plan lounge, bar, restaurant with seating area, free Wi-Fi, civil wedding licence, waterside terrace, unsuitable for &.
BACKGROUND MUSIC: 'relaxed' at mealtimes.
LOCATION: central, on waterfront.
CHILDREN: not under 13.
DOGS: not allowed.
CREDIT CARDS: Amex, MasterCard, Visa.
PRICES: [2013] per room B&B £120–£325. D,B&B £37.50 per person added, set dinner £37.50, à la carte £35–£40. 1-night bookings refused peak season weekends and bank holidays.

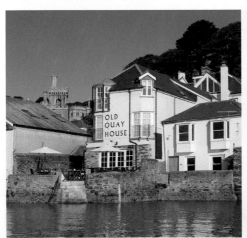

GATESHEAD Tyne and Wear

Map 4:B4

ESLINGTON VILLA

In gardens with mature shrubs and trees (and plenty of seating), Nick and Melanie Tulip's Victorian hotel is 'convenient for Newcastle's city centre and the surrounding countryside'. Visitors praise the 'relaxed' atmosphere in which 'you feel at home'. Colin Edgar is the manager. The public areas have 'good' antiques, Victorian decorative pieces and traditional as well as modern artwork; background jazz is played throughout. The bedrooms are named after shrubs and trees. Those in the older part of the house have a traditional decor (Chestnut has a four-poster bed and a large bathroom with a corner bath). Rooms in an extension have a lighter, more contemporary touch. There is a 'proper' bar with sofas and leather chairs. The traditional restaurant has a conservatory extension along the front of the house. The chef, Jamie Walsh, cooks modern British dishes with a French twist, perhaps goat's cheese crottin, beetroot and walnut salad; Gressingham duck breast, dauphinoise potatoes, juniper berry sauce. The East Coast railway line, which runs along the bottom of the garden, is shielded by trees ('not obtrusive'). (*JC, and others*)

8 Station Road, Low Fell
Gateshead NE9 6DR

T: 0191-487 6017
F: 0191-420 0667
E: home@eslingtonvilla.co.uk
W: www.eslingtonvilla.co.uk

BEDROOMS: 18, 3 with separate entrance on ground floor.
OPEN: all year except 25/26 Dec, 1 Jan.
FACILITIES: ramp, lounge/bar, conservatory, restaurant, private dining room, conference/function facilities, free Wi-Fi, 2-acre garden (patio).
BACKGROUND MUSIC: jazz in public rooms.
LOCATION: 2 miles from centre, off A1.
CHILDREN: all ages welcomed.
DOGS: not allowed.
CREDIT CARDS: Amex, MasterCard, Visa.
PRICES: [2013] per room B&B single £59.50–£79.50, double £74.50–£99.50. Set dinner £21.95–£25.95.

GILLINGHAM Dorset

Map 2:D1

STOCK HILL HOUSE

'Why do we keep going back? Along with every other guest, we are made to feel so welcome. The cuisine is delicious.' A long-term fan explains why he has followed Peter and Nita Hauser's 'journey from their early days in Sark to the present day in Dorset', where they run this imposing late Victorian house as a small hotel/restaurant. Another returning guest said this year: 'Standards are as immaculate now as on my first visit; service in both hotel and restaurant is superb.' Peter Hauser's daily-changing menu, which reflects his Austrian heritage, has 'a splendid combination of the tried and tested with more innovative dishes', perhaps supreme of chicken filled with Viennese sausage and Swiss chard. 'Peter uses the finest produce; his delicate touch enhances the quality into a rare treat.' The bedrooms, individually decorated, have antiques, curios, rich furnishings, bold fabrics. 'Yummy' breakfasts include freshly squeezed juices, home-made yogurts, muesli and cereals; full English or fish. The house, with 'lovely' landscaped grounds, was the summer home of the cartoonist Osbert Lancaster. (*Ian Culley, David Ward*)

Stock Hill
Gillingham SP8 5NR

T: 01747-823626
F: 01747-825628
E: reception@stockhillhouse.co.uk
W: www.stockhillhouse.co.uk

BEDROOMS: 9, 3 in coach house, 3 on ground floor.
OPEN: all year.
FACILITIES: ramp, 2 lounges, restaurant, breakfast room, private dining room, free Wi-Fi, 11-acre grounds (tennis, croquet, small lake), unsuitable for &.
BACKGROUND MUSIC: none.
LOCATION: 1 mile W of Gillingham.
CHILDREN: not under 7.
DOGS: not allowed.
CREDIT CARDS: MasterCard, Visa.
PRICES: [2013] per room D,B&B single £175, double £265–£325. Set dinner £45.

GITTISHAM Devon

Map 1:C5

COMBE HOUSE

🏆 *César award in 2007*

'A delight; seductively traditional inside with modern overtones in the garden.' More praise this year for Ken and Ruth Hunt's 'stunning renovation' of a Grade I listed Elizabethan manor house. 'First impressions are glorious: a beautiful old house in rolling parkland, log fire alight in the hall.' Guests may explore the kitchen garden which supplies vegetables and fruit for the modern menus of chef Hadleigh Barrett. His 'excellent' meals might include wood pigeon, sweet potato, nuts and seeds; seared brill, ragout of mussels, leeks and chard, lemon oil and chives. The bedrooms are individually styled in rich colours: 'Our room, up a half stair, had a sofa, chair, coffee table and desk; French doors opened on to the garden.' There is a choice between sheets and a duvet. 'What bliss to find a hot-water bottle in our bed when we returned from dinner.' A thatched cottage with a private garden in the grounds is a secluded hideaway for a couple. An adjoining house is being converted into accommodation for up to eight guests. 'Good circular walks from the door.' (*Wendy Ashworth, Frances Thomas, Mrs BM Watkinson*)

25% DISCOUNT VOUCHERS

Gittisham
nr Honiton EX14 3AD

T: 01404-540400
E: stay@combehousedevon.com
W: www.combehousedevon.com

BEDROOMS: 16, 1 in cottage.
OPEN: all year except 2 weeks in Jan.
FACILITIES: ramp, sitting room, Great Hall, bar, restaurant, private dining rooms, free Wi-Fi, civil wedding licence, 10-acre garden in 3,500-acre estate (helipad), only public rooms suitable for ♿.
BACKGROUND MUSIC: occasionally in hall and bar.
LOCATION: 4 miles SW of Honiton.
CHILDREN: all ages welcomed.
DOGS: allowed in public rooms except restaurant, some bedrooms.
CREDIT CARDS: MasterCard, Visa.
PRICES: [2013] per person B&B £107.50–£215. Set dinner £52. 1-night bookings sometimes refused Fri/Sat.

GRASMERE Cumbria

Map 4: inset C2

THE GRASMERE HOTEL `NEW`

On the edge of a pretty village, this three-storey Victorian house has been extensively renovated by the new owners, Rob van der Palen and Anton Renac, who had a dedicated following among *Guide* readers at their previous hotel in Rosthwaite. 'It is a lovely place; they provide everything one needs in the way of hospitality, attention and comfort,' say the nominators in 2013. All the bedrooms have been given a modern bathroom. 'Our spacious room had a king-size bed, two comfortable armchairs, a generous dressing table and a wardrobe. The impressive bathroom was a joy; we would love to have transported it home.' Dinner orders are taken over drinks and amuse-bouche in the 'comfortable' lounge. Tables are well spaced in the dining room. It overlooks the small garden, which is bordered by the River Rothay. Anton Renac, the chef, produces European dishes, perhaps home-smoked duck breast, orange and walnut dressing; oven-baked cod loin, saffron sauce. 'He has not lost his touch; everything was perfectly cooked and presented; the muzak was subdued.' Breakfast is 'as good as it could be'. (*Tom and Sarah Mann*)

Broadgate
Grasmere LA22 9TA

T: 015394-35277
E: info@grasmerehotel.co.uk
W: www.grasmerehotel.co.uk

BEDROOMS: 11.
OPEN: all year except 6–19 Dec, 2–30 Jan.
FACILITIES: lounge, restaurant, free Wi-Fi, ½-acre garden, unsuitable for &.
BACKGROUND MUSIC: 'easy listening'.
LOCATION: village centre.
CHILDREN: not under 10.
DOGS: allowed in some bedrooms, not in public rooms.
CREDIT CARDS: MasterCard, Visa.
PRICES: per person B&B £57–£69, D,B&B £77–£89. À la carte £30. 1-night bookings generally refused Sat.

SEE ALSO SHORTLIST

GRASMERE Cumbria

OAK BANK

'Wonderful value for money in a great location for touring the lakes.' The 'modest' appearance of Glynis and Simon Wood's small hotel 'belies high standards' (an inspector's view). 'The hands-on owners and their staff are 'friendly and hard-working'. There is a 'warm' atmosphere in the two lounges, which have plenty of comfortable seating. One has a converted range, the other a bar and an open fire. The three inter-connected dining rooms (one in a conservatory) are 'attractively laid out', with fresh flowers on well-spaced tables. Darren Comish joined as chef in 2013. His daily-changing menu of modern dishes might include warm ham hock, two-hour poached duck egg; plaice, razor clam, mussels, purple potatoes, confit tomato, clam velouté. Ingredients are sourced within Cumbria 'where possible'; bread, pasta, sorbets and ice creams are 'made on the premises'. The 'nice touches' in the bedrooms are liked: a small decanter of sherry for a pre-dinner drink, 'first-class' toiletries. 'We were so comfortable in our warm, well-furnished room that we slept in for breakfast.' (*Carol Hendry, Mel Irwin, Christine McDonald, and others*)

Broadgate
Grasmere LA22 9TA

T: 015394-35217
F: 015394-35685
E: info@lakedistricthotel.co.uk
W: www.lakedistricthotel.co.uk

BEDROOMS: 14, 1 on ground floor.
OPEN: all year except 22–26 Dec, 3-16 Jan, 3–15 Aug.
FACILITIES: lounge, bar, dining room, conservatory dining room, free Wi-Fi, unsuitable for &.
BACKGROUND MUSIC: during dinner in bar lounge and dining rooms.
LOCATION: outskirts of village.
CHILDREN: all ages welcomed.
DOGS: allowed in 3 bedrooms, 1 lounge.
CREDIT CARDS: MasterCard, Visa.
PRICES: per person B&B £32.75–£84, D,B&B £52.75–£104. Set dinner £33.50, à la carte £30.50–£38.95. 1-night bookings usually refused weekends.

SEE ALSO SHORTLIST

GREAT MILTON Oxfordshire

Map 2:C3

LE MANOIR AUX QUAT'SAISONS

🏆 *César award in 1985*

The extensive gardens are among the glories of Raymond Blanc's luxury hotel, a manor house in a pretty Oxfordshire village. M. Blanc supervised the restoration of the grounds, which have an English water garden, a Japanese garden (with a tea house), an orchard of 800 apple and pear trees, and a two-acre vegetable garden which provides 90 varieties for the kitchen. Co-owned with Orient Express Hotels, *Le Manoir* has long been managed by Philip Newman-Hall. A porter meets hotel guests in the car park; luggage is delivered to the bedrooms, which are in the house and in garden buildings. Many are themed: Art Deco Arabesque is styled with mirrored and dark glass, Italian furniture; a mirrored tiled bath in the bathroom; Lemongrass is inspired by South-East Asia, and has a bathroom with a 'vast' walk-in shower and a steam room with stone relaxation beds. Even standard rooms are large, with a luxurious bathroom. The conservatory restaurant has held two *Michelin* stars for almost 30 years. There are two set lunch menus; for a special occasion, try the nine-course menu découverte.

Church Road
Great Milton OX44 7PD

T: 01844-278881
F: 01844-278847
E: lemanoir@blanc.co.uk
W: www.manoir.com

BEDROOMS: 32, 22 in garden buildings, some on ground floor, 1 suitable for ♿.
OPEN: all year except 6/7 Jan.
FACILITIES: ramps, 2 lounges, champagne bar, restaurant, private dining room, free Wi-Fi, cookery school, civil wedding licence, 27-acre grounds.
BACKGROUND MUSIC: in the lounges.
LOCATION: 8 miles SE of Oxford.
CHILDREN: all ages welcomed.
DOGS: not allowed in house, kennels provided.
CREDIT CARDS: Amex, MasterCard, Visa.
PRICES: [2013] per room B&B (French breakfast) £515–£1,680, D,B&B (Sun–Thurs) £850–£2,210. Set dinner £160, à la carte £150.

HALNAKER West Sussex

THE OLD STORE

'Standards remain the highest' at Patrick and Heather Birchenough's B&B, an 18th-century Grade II listed house in a village in the Goodwood estate. 'After a tiring journey, it is such a delight to be welcomed with a cup of tea and a slice of home-made cake.' There's a reception room with a grandfather clock, and a lounge with a model train built in 1894 ('it still works, in theory'). One bedroom is on the ground floor; the others are reached by fairly steep stairs; a family room is large enough for four. 'Our room had been recently redecorated, everything was modern, fresh and tasteful. Beds are very comfortable, and triple glazing ensures a good night's sleep despite the nearness of a main road.' Breakfast has 'Heather's home-made preserves, her own bread, and a delicious selection of hot food cooked to order; every item tastes good'. The garden has herbaceous borders and a semicircle of lawn. The *Anglesey Arms*, across the road, is open for evening meals, and nearby Chichester has many places to eat. 'Extremely good value for money.' (*Mary Woods*)

Stane Street, Halnaker,
nr Chichester PO18 0QL

T: 01243-531977
E: theoldstore4@aol.com
W: www.theoldstoreguesthouse.com

BEDROOMS: 7, 1 on ground floor.
OPEN: 15 Mar–21 Dec.
FACILITIES: lounge, breakfast room, free Wi-Fi, ⅓-acre garden with seating, unsuitable for &.
BACKGROUND MUSIC: none.
LOCATION: 4 miles NE of Chichester.
CHILDREN: all ages welcomed.
DOGS: not allowed.
CREDIT CARDS: MasterCard, Visa.
PRICES: [2013] per person B&B £35–£50 (higher for Goodwood 'Festival of Speed' and 'Revival' meetings). 1-night bookings refused weekends in high season.

HAMBLEDEN Buckinghamshire

Map 2:D3

THE STAG & HUNTSMAN NEW

In an 'enchanting' village in the Chiltern hills, this old pub has been carefully restored by the Culden Faw estate. It is run as a pub-with-rooms by Christoph Brooke's Hillbrooke group; Peter Stevens is the manager. *Guide* inspectors were impressed: 'They have maintained the atmosphere of a proper village pub; the food is good and the bedrooms are nicely decorated. The welcome was warm, the service attentive. When we asked details of local walks, a laminated book was immediately brought to our room.' The bedrooms vary in size: 'Our large room had a vaulted ceiling and interesting mismatched painted and limed wood furniture. Its large wardrobe had free-range hangers; good tea and cafetiere coffee on a tray; a feature wall of William Morris wallpaper. The bedside lighting was dim; plenty of storage in a huge bathroom.' An 'unpretentious' menu of pub classics (with some daily specials) is served in the linked bar and dining areas, which have dark-green painted walls. 'Our steaks were tender and cooked precisely to order.' In warm months, meals can be taken in the small garden (which has a barbecue).

Rectory Hill
Hambleden RG9 6RP

T: 01491-571227
F: 01491-520810
E: enquiries@
 thestagandhuntsman.co.uk
W: www.thestagandhuntsman.co.uk

BEDROOMS: 9, 1 on ground floor suitable for &.
OPEN: all year.
FACILITIES: lounge, 4 bars, free Wi-Fi, small garden.
BACKGROUND MUSIC: none.
LOCATION: centre of village, 3 miles NE of Henley-on-Thames.
CHILDREN: all ages welcomed.
DOGS: allowed.
CREDIT CARDS: Amex, MasterCard, Visa.
PRICES: [2013] per room B&B £100–£200, D,B&B £150–£250. À la carte £30. 1-night bookings sometimes refused.

HAMBLETON Rutland

Map 2:B3

HAMBLETON HALL

❧ *César award in 1985*

'It remains an all-time favourite. The location, rooms and service are faultless.' Praise in 2013 for Tim and Stefa Hart's luxury hotel on a peninsula jutting into Rutland Water. Another comment: 'The food and accommodation are of the highest standard.' In the candlelit dining room, which has golden damask on the walls, the chef, Aaron Patterson, has a *Michelin* star. 'The dishes are so attractive in their presentation and intense in their flavour,' is a comment in 2013. 'Delicious hors d'oeuvres (pumpkin, smoked salmon); crab, cèpes, beef and pheasant heralded the way for a never-to-be-forgotten tarte Tatin; a hedonistic experience.' Stefa Hart oversees the decor: the drawing room has fine fabrics, antiques, open fires, plumped cushions on deep sofas. The spacious bedrooms are individually decorated. The best overlook Rutland Water. Tim Hart's popular Hambleton bakery supplies 'divine' bread for dinner and the 'leisurely' breakfast, which includes home-made granola, fruit compotes, yogurt and freshly squeezed juices. He also owns *Hart's Hotel* in Nottingham (see entry). (*Robert Gower, Roderic Rennison*)

Hambleton
Oakham LE15 8TH

T: 01572-756991
F: 01572-724721
E: hotel@hambletonhall.com
W: www.hambletonhall.com

BEDROOMS: 17, 2-bedroomed suite in pavilion.
OPEN: all year.
FACILITIES: lift, ramps, hall, drawing room, bar, restaurant, 2 private dining rooms, free Wi-Fi, civil wedding licence, 17-acre grounds (swimming pool, heated May–Sept, tennis).
BACKGROUND MUSIC: none.
LOCATION: 3 miles SE of Oakham.
CHILDREN: only children 'of a grown-up age' in restaurant in evening.
DOGS: not allowed in public rooms, nor unattended in bedrooms.
CREDIT CARDS: all major cards.
PRICES: [2013] per room B&B £255–£430. Set dinner £65. 1-night bookings sometimes refused weekends.

HAROME North Yorkshire

Map 4:D4

THE STAR INN

🏆 *César award in 2004*

In a village on the edge of the moors, this converted medieval cruck-framed longhouse is a 'watering hole for foodies' tempted by the modern cooking of chef/director Andrew Pern. They can stay in eight smart bedrooms in *Cross House Lodge*, across the road (behind the inn's corner shop). These have quirky features: one has a bath at the end of the bed, another a bathroom with a view; there's a rope-slung bed, a room with a snooker table (it converts to a normal table), another with a piano. All are provided with a tea tray, fresh fruit and home-made fudge. An additional room was due to open in autumn 2013. Andrew Pern, who was brought up on a farm in the nearby Esk valley, sources Yorkshire ingredients for his 'interesting' seasonal menus which might include twice-baked Hawes Wensleydale cheese soufflé, Waldorf vinaigrette; posh North Sea fish pie, English mustard velouté, lobster and flat parsley salad. Meals can be taken in the garden in warm weather. Breakfast is a communal affair around an octagonal table in the 'rustic' *Wheelhouse* in the lodge.

Harome, nr Helmsley
YO62 5JE

T: 01439-770397
E: reservations@
  thestarinnatharome.co.uk
W: www.thestaratharome.co.uk

BEDROOMS: 8 in *Cross House Lodge* opposite, 3 on ground floor.
OPEN: all year, restaurant closed Mon lunch.
FACILITIES: lounge, coffee loft, bar, breakfast room, restaurant, private dining room, civil wedding licence, free Wi-Fi, terrace, 2-acre garden, unsuitable for ♿.
BACKGROUND MUSIC: 'gentle jazz in public areas'.
LOCATION: village centre.
CHILDREN: all ages welcomed (children's menu).
DOGS: by arrangement, not in public rooms.
CREDIT CARDS: MasterCard, Visa.
PRICES: [2013] per room B&B £150–£260. Set meal £20–£25, à la carte £45.

HARWICH Essex

Map 2:C5

THE PIER AT HARWICH

On the quayside of the busy port, Paul Milsom's conversion of two historic buildings houses two restaurants and a hotel. The restaurants and seven of the bedrooms are in the main building, built in the 1850s in the style of a Venetian palazzo as a waiting room for ferry passengers; the other rooms and a beamed guest lounge are in the adjacent former *Angel* pub, built in the 17th century. Bedrooms are individually decorated: those at the front have panoramic views over the quayside and the Stour and Orwell estuaries, where 'ferries and fishing boats come and go'. 'Room 3 is our favourite, with windows to the front and side.' In the first-floor *Harbourside* restaurant (minimalist decor, a polished pewter champagne and oyster bar), chef Tom Bushell's speciality is locally landed seafood, perhaps skate wing with brown shrimp, capers and French parsley. Simpler dishes (eg posh fish and shellfish pie) and sandwiches are served in the ground-floor *Ha' Penny* bistro. 'The breakfast selection has improved, giving more choice, including bacon or sausage sandwiches, smoked salmon with scrambled egg.' (*Lynn Wildgoose*)

25% DISCOUNT VOUCHERS

The Quay
Harwich CO12 3HH

T: 01255-241212
F: 01255-551922
E: pier@milsomhotels.com
W: www.milsomhotels.com

BEDROOMS: 14, 7 in annexe, 1 on ground floor.
OPEN: all year.
FACILITIES: ramps, lounge (in annexe), restaurant, bistro, free Wi-Fi, civil wedding licence, small front terrace.
BACKGROUND MUSIC: 'easy listening'.
LOCATION: on quay.
CHILDREN: all ages welcomed.
DOGS: not allowed in public rooms.
CREDIT CARDS: All major cards.
PRICES: [2013] per room B&B £115–£225. À la carte £39.50.

HASTINGS East Sussex

Map 2:E5

BLACK ROCK HOUSE

'A delightful and relaxing place to stay.' On a quiet residential street on a hill above the town, this privately owned B&B, in a 'handsome' Victorian villa, remains in 'pristine condition' after changing hands in 2012, say inspectors. 'The house is immaculate: wooden floors, a warm and inviting lounge, a bowl of red apples on the hall table.' Yuliya Vereshchuk, the manager, is 'helpful in all respects'. Individually styled bedrooms are light and airy; two have sea views. 'Our room, the Turret, had a restrained modern look and excellent lighting. The huge bathroom was splendid: a window at either end, a powerful shower, a dressing area, ample storage.' Attention to detail is praised: 'We had fresh milk, home-made biscotti; a carafe of filtered water. There was a torch in the bedside drawer, a library of books, magazines and DVDs in the hallway.' A 'just right' breakfast, served until 10 am (11 at weekends), has proper napkins: home-made granola, a seasonal fruit compote, freshly squeezed juice, chunky toast, 'delicious' home-made strawberry jam. An 'excellent' cooked dish had 'the loveliest mushrooms'.

10 Stanley Road
Hastings TN34 1UE

T: 01424-438448
E: enquiries@
   black-rock-hastings.co.uk
W: www.black-rock-hastings.co.uk

BEDROOMS: 5.
OPEN: all year.
FACILITIES: lounge, breakfast room, free Wi-Fi, terrace, unsuitable for &.
BACKGROUND MUSIC: lounge and breakfast room.
LOCATION: central.
CHILDREN: not under 10, family room available.
DOGS: not allowed.
CREDIT CARDS: MasterCard, Visa.
PRICES: [2013] per room B&B single £85–£90, double £125–£140. 1-night bookings refused bank holidays, weekends.

HASTINGS East Sussex

Map 2:E5

SWAN HOUSE

Two minutes' walk from the seafront, in the interesting older part of Hastings, this white-painted, black-beamed cottage dates back to 1490. It is run as an upmarket B&B by 'thoughtful' host, Brendan McDonagh, and his partner, Lionel Copley. 'Brendan supplied tea and biscuits free of charge to friends who came to visit us.' The bedrooms are individually styled in muted colours. There are large beds and a mix of modern and vintage furniture. 'Our stay was extremely comfortable,' says a visitor this year. 'Our room, Renaissance, was large and light, with a small terrace. It had a big squashy sofa, and iPod dock; high-quality toiletries in the shower.' A smaller ground-floor room in a Victorian extension is 'good for people who cannot manage the stairs'. The house is filled with curios and antiques collected by the owners. Breakfast has Greek yogurt with prunes and honey; kippers and haddock come from Peter's Eastern Fish Shop in the old town. 'A bonus is the two delightful dogs, Daisy and Matilda.' A sister guest house, *The Old Rectory*, is in a nearby 18th-century building. (*Pat Woodward*)

1 Hill Street
Hastings, TN34 3HU

T: 01424-430014
E: res@swanhousehastings.co.uk
W: www.swanhousehastings.co.uk

BEDROOMS: 4, 1 on ground floor.
OPEN: all year except Christmas.
FACILITIES: lounge/breakfast room, courtyard garden, civil wedding licence, free Wi-Fi, unsuitable for &.
BACKGROUND MUSIC: none.
LOCATION: in old town, near seafront.
CHILDREN: not under 5.
DOGS: not allowed.
CREDIT CARDS: Amex, MasterCard, Visa.
PRICES: per room B&B single £80–£120, double £120–£150.

HATCH BEAUCHAMP Somerset

Map 1:C6

FROG STREET FARMHOUSE

At the end of a no-through-road deep in the Somerset countryside ('don't trust satnav'), this wisteria-clad longhouse (which dates back to the 15th century) is run as a small guest house by Louise and David Farrance. They have restored the building with sympathy, retaining the traditional character – Jacobean panelling, exposed beams and open inglenook fireplaces – while adding a fresh and 'stylish' look. 'Just a wonderful place to be,' says a visitor, 'with the most lovely hosts.' The lounge has leather seating, a large television, books and games, and a wood-burning stove, 'lit every afternoon ready for our return from our days out'. Louise Farrance, 'a good cook', will prepare a simple evening meal by arrangement, with dishes like prawn and avocado, Marie Rose sauce; breast of chicken, creamy mango sauce, mushrooms and onions. The bedrooms, 'extremely comfortable and well designed', have a large bed, the latest technology. The Orchard Suite is ideal for families; the Snug has its own lounge and a log-burning fire. Breakfast includes home-made bread and preserves, local produce (free-range eggs from the farm) for the cooked dishes. (*FG, and others*)

Hatch Beauchamp
nr Taunton TA3 6AF

T: 01823-481883
E: frogstreet@hotmail.com
W: www.frogstreet.co.uk

BEDROOMS: 4.
OPEN: all year except Christmas.
FACILITIES: 2 lounges, dining room, free Wi-Fi, 150-acre grounds, unsuitable for &.
BACKGROUND MUSIC: optional.
LOCATION: 4 miles NW of Ilminster.
CHILDREN: all ages welcomed.
DOGS: not allowed.
CREDIT CARDS: all major cards (charges may apply).
PRICES: per room B&B single £70–£80, double £90–£120. Set dinner £22.50–£27.50.

SEE ALSO SHORTLIST

HATHERSAGE Derbyshire

Map 3:A6

THE GEORGE HOTEL

'*The George* carries on admirably in the tradition of an old coaching inn; a place to arrive with pleasure, stay in comfort and travel from satisfied.' There is praise this year from regular correspondents for Eric Marsh's 15th-century grey-stone building in a Peak District village popular with walkers and climbers. 'We were given a super welcome, with help immediately on hand with our luggage; the whole atmosphere felt right.' The bedrooms at the back are the quietest; front rooms have double-glazed windows. 'Our room was spacious, with comfortable armchairs, a good reading lamp; a modern bathroom with slightly eccentric plumbing.' In the candlelit dining room, the cooking of the chef, Helen Heywood, is 'first rate: sea bass with a barley and wild mushroom risotto was very tasty'. Breakfast was 'good, with fruit salad, a choice of cereal, the usual cooked dishes but also American pancakes with a blueberry compote'. 'My only regret was that I forgot to buy a jar of the chef's excellent large-cut marmalade.' Eric Marsh also runs *The Cavendish* in Baslow (see entry). (*Peter and Kay Rogers, Peter Anderson*)

Main Road
Hathersage S32 1BB

T: 01433-650436
F: 01433-650099
E: info@george-hotel.net
W: www.george-hotel.net

BEDROOMS: 24.
OPEN: all year.
FACILITIES: lounge/bar, restaurant, 2 function rooms, free Wi-Fi, civil wedding licence, courtyard, only restaurant suitable for &.
BACKGROUND MUSIC: light jazz in restaurant.
LOCATION: in village centre, parking.
CHILDREN: all ages welcomed.
DOGS: only guide dogs allowed.
CREDIT CARDS: Amex, MasterCard, Visa.
PRICES: [2013] per room B&B £70–£198, D,B&B £106.50–£271. Set dinner £36.50 (5% *'service levy' included in all prices*). 1-night bookings occasionally refused.

HEXHAM Northumberland

Map 4:B3

BATTLESTEADS `NEW`

On the edge of a village in the North Tyne valley, this extended 18th-century farmhouse is run as a small hotel and restaurant by Dee and Richard Slade, the 'very welcoming, hands-on' owners. 'An excellent pub/hotel in a sparsely populated area,' say regular *Guide* correspondents, whose commendation upgrades *Battlesteads* to a full entry. Close to Hadrian's Wall and the moors, it is popular with ramblers. Its mainly local staff are 'friendly, professional'. *Battlesteads* has been named green hotel of the year for its environmental practice: 'Visitors are invited to tour the organic gardens and inspect the biomass boiler which, supplemented by solar panels, provides limitless hot water.' Polytunnels in the gardens supply fruit, vegetables and herbs for the 'generous' dishes on the local and seasonal menus of chef Eddie Shilton, perhaps game terrine, beetroot chutney; lamb shank, leek, rosemary and redcurrant jus, creamy mash. 'Our bedroom was well fitted, though more storage space would have helped.' A large communal drying room is 'useful for walkers', as are the 'excellent sandwiches for picnics, with generous filling, and flavour'. 'Very good value for money.' (*Stephen and Pauline Glover, D Morrell*)

Wark-on-Tyne
nr Hexham NE48 3LS

T: 01434-230209
F: 01434-230039
E: info@battlesteads.com
W: www.battlesteads.com

BEDROOMS: 17, 4 on ground floor, 2 suitable for &.
OPEN: all year.
FACILITIES: bar, dining room, function facilities, free Wi-Fi, civil wedding licence, 2-acre grounds.
BACKGROUND MUSIC: jazz in public areas.
LOCATION: edge of village, 12 miles N of Hexham.
CHILDREN: all ages welcomed.
DOGS: allowed in public rooms, by arrangement in bedrooms.
CREDIT CARDS: Amex, MasterCard, Visa.
PRICES: [2013] per room B&B £115–£145, D,B&B from £160. Set meals £23.50–£27.50.

SEE ALSO SHORTLIST

HOLT Norfolk

BYFORDS

'The enthusiasm of the young staff at all times' impressed a *Guide* inspector visiting Iain and Clair Wilson's 'interesting conversion of an ironmongery' in the centre of a small market town. The 'higgledy-piggledy' building has narrow doorways, brickwork, oak floorboards. It is run as a 'posh B&B' with a small deli selling frozen meals and take-away pizzas. An all-day café becomes a restaurant in the evening. Its large menu has tapas-style grazing dishes, pizzas and burgers. 'This is not gourmet food, just simple cooking.' The bedrooms, of different sizes and shapes, are 'beautifully furnished and generously equipped'. A superior room was 'long rather than wide, with a sloping attic roof; darkish, though there was a skylight; fine in winter, perhaps less good in summer'. The bathrooms are modern: 'Well designed, with a double-ended bath and separate shower. Little details make the difference: a vase of lilies, good towels, wonderful toiletries.' Breakfast is 'first class': a vast buffet has jugs of fruit juices, prune compote, fresh fruit salad, good toast and home-made preserves; dishes include Cley Smokehouse fish. Limited parking at the rear.

1–3 Shirehall Plain
Holt NR25 6BG

T: 01263-711400
E: queries@byfords.org.uk
W: www.byfords.org.uk

BEDROOMS: 16, 3 on ground floor, 1 suitable for &.
OPEN: all year.
FACILITIES: ramps, 5 internal eating areas, free Wi-Fi, deli.
BACKGROUND MUSIC: none.
LOCATION: central, private secure parking.
CHILDREN: all ages welcomed.
DOGS: only guide dogs allowed.
CREDIT CARDS: Amex, MasterCard, Visa.
PRICES: [2013] per room B&B single £110–£125, double £145–£215, D,B&B single £130–£145, double £185–£255. À la carte £35. 1-night bookings refused Sat.

HOPE Derbyshire

Map 3:A6

UNDERLEIGH HOUSE

In a 'beautiful' setting, on a private lane, outside a Domesday-old village, Vivienne and Philip Taylor's B&B is 'excellent value for money', says a visitor in 2013. 'We were made very welcome, and greatly enjoyed the afternoon tea.' The long, low, creeper-covered building is a conversion of a 19th-century barn and cottage. The 'well-fitted' bedrooms vary in size (some are small). The Thornhill Suite has a bedroom with a round window overlooking the valley, an adjoining lounge with a stable door opening on to a stone staircase to the garden. Townhead, on the ground floor, has glazed doors on two sides, one of which faces the rose garden. All rooms have a comprehensive information pack, bottled water, fresh fruit, tea- and coffee-making equipment. The prize-winning breakfast is taken communally at a long oak table in a room with a beamed ceiling and flagstone floor. There is home-made bread, preserves made by Philip Taylor (perhaps apricot and amaretto), and a wide range of cooked dishes. The Taylors are happy to advise on the excellent walking locally. 'They took trouble to make a dinner reservation for us.' (*Jenny Ferguson*)

Lose Hill Lane
off Edale Road
Hope S33 6AF

T: 01433-621372
F: 01433-621324
E: info@underleighhouse.co.uk
W: www.underleighhouse.co.uk

BEDROOMS: 5.
OPEN: all year except Christmas, Jan.
FACILITIES: lounge, breakfast room, free Wi-Fi, ¼-acre garden, unsuitable for &.
BACKGROUND MUSIC: none.
LOCATION: 1 mile N of Hope.
CHILDREN: not under 12.
DOGS: allowed by arrangement.
CREDIT CARDS: MasterCard, Visa (*both 3% surcharge*).
PRICES: [2013] per room B&B £90–£110. 1-night bookings refused Fri/Sat, bank holidays.

SEE ALSO SHORTLIST

HOUGH-ON-THE-HILL Lincolnshire

Map 2:A3

THE BROWNLOW ARMS   NEW

There's 'a good feeling' about this stone-built
18th-century inn in a quiet country village. It
has been run for many years as a restaurant-
with-rooms by the owners, Paul and Lorraine
Willoughby. 'The delicious food is a big draw
locally,' said a *Guide* inspector in 2013, 'and the
accommodation is equally appealing.' Four of
the 'charming' bedrooms are in the main
building; three ground-floor rooms are in a
neighbouring barn conversion. 'Our spacious
room had a lobby/dressing area with a
wardrobe; an inviting bed with a red sofa at its
foot; red and gold tapestry curtains were
matched by the bed drape and cushions; good
lighting from the large bedside table lights;
interesting old coaching prints on the walls, a
shame about the artificial flowers.' The dining
rooms have a 'grand, informal air – like a smart
country house party'; the chef, Oliver Snell,
cooks an 'excellent' dinner: 'So many good
things to choose from; we had a nicely presented
goat's cheese and chicory salad; sea bass, mussels
and frites; breast of Barbary duck. Service was
efficient on a busy evening.' Breakfast was
'equally good'.

High Road
Hough-on-the-Hill NG32 2AZ

T: 01400-250234
E: armsinn@yahoo.co.uk
W: www.thebrownlowarms.com

BEDROOMS: 7, 3 on ground floor in
barn conversion.
OPEN: all year except 24–26 Dec,
first 2 weeks Jan, restaurant closed
Sun evening, Mon.
FACILITIES: bar, 3 restaurants, free
Wi-Fi, unsuitable for &.
BACKGROUND MUSIC: in public
areas.
LOCATION: in village 7 miles N of
Grantham.
CHILDREN: not under 8.
DOGS: not allowed.
CREDIT CARDS: MasterCard, Visa.
PRICES: [2013] per room B&B single
£65, double £99. Set dinner £21.95,
à la carte £40.

HUNSTANTON Norfolk

ROSE-FITT HOUSE `NEW`

On a quiet sea-facing square, this Victorian house has been renovated by Paul and Barbara Bamfield, who run it as a B&B. 'They have clearly done their homework,' says the nominator. 'It is rare to have no grumbles, but we left after four nights struggling to think of anything that could have been better.' The 'high standards' are maintained in the bedrooms, which are 'clean and well appointed': 'considerate' touches include trays for sandy shoes (a beach is close by), bottled water, a hospitality tray, dressing gowns, DVDs, etc. On each floor is a family suite which has a double bedroom and a separate twin-bedded room. Only children older than five are welcomed. Breakfast, ordered the evening before for an agreed time, is a 'treat'. 'Everything you would expect' for cereals, juices, toast and croissants; a wide choice of cooked dishes includes kippers, myriad egg options, sausages and black pudding. 'Paul is a fount of useful advice on the area and will recommend places to eat and attractions to explore.' Sandringham, Holkham Hall, and the RSPB reserve at Titchwell are nearby. (*John Aglionby*)

Northgate
Hunstanton PE36 6DR

T: 01485-534776
E: rosefitthouse@mail.com
W: www.rose-fitt-house-hunstanton.co.uk

BEDROOMS: 6.
OPEN: all year except Dec/Jan.
FACILITIES: dining room, free Wi-Fi, unsuitable for ♿.
BACKGROUND MUSIC: radio at breakfast.
LOCATION: central.
CHILDREN: not under 5.
DOGS: not allowed.
CREDIT CARDS: MasterCard, Visa.
PRICES: per room B&B £65–£82. 1-night bookings sometimes refused.

HUNTINGDON Cambridgeshire

Map 2:B4

THE OLD BRIDGE

By a medieval bridge on the River Ouse, this creeper-clad 18th-century town house hotel is owned by John Hoskins, a Master of Wine who runs a wine shop on the premises. 'We really enjoyed our stay; excellent room, good bathroom; superb food, friendly staff,' says a visitor this year. Nina Rhodes is the manager. In the large, light *Terrace* restaurant (with an oval cupola), chef James Claydon serves a monthly-changing menu of modern dishes alongside 'classics' (eg, home-cured wagyu beef, savoy cabbage, beetroot and horseradish dressing; Jimmy Butler's pork and leek sausages, mashed potato, mustard sauce). Children under twelve have their own menu. John Hoskins's wife, Julia, is responsible for the design of the bedrooms and for maintenance ('18th-century buildings demand a lot of TLC'). Rooms have a contemporary look and are well thought through ('plenty of mirrors, good hanging space'). A small room was thought 'impeccable' by a recent visitor. The building is hedged by a busy traffic system; bedrooms have triple glazing and air conditioning. Wine tastings and dinners are held; functions are confined to a self-contained area. (*Richard Lamb*)

25% DISCOUNT VOUCHERS

1 High Street
Huntingdon PE29 3TQ

T: 01480-424300
F: 01480-411017
E: oldbridge@huntsbridge.co.uk
W: www.huntsbridge.com

BEDROOMS: 24, 2 on ground floor.
OPEN: all year.
FACILITIES: ramps, lounge, bar, restaurant, private dining room, wine shop, business centre, civil wedding licence, free Wi-Fi, 1-acre grounds (terrace, garden), river (fishing, jetty, boat trips), unsuitable for &.
BACKGROUND MUSIC: none.
LOCATION: 500 yds from centre, parking, station 10 mins' walk.
CHILDREN: all ages welcomed.
DOGS: not allowed in restaurant.
CREDIT CARDS: MasterCard, Visa.
PRICES: per room B&B single £89–£130, double £160–£230, D,B&B £199–£260. À la carte £30.

IREBY Cumbria

Map 4: inset B2

OVERWATER HALL

In an isolated part of the northern Lake District, this castellated Grade II listed Georgian mansion is run as a small hotel in personal style by the owners, Stephen Bore and Angela Hyde ('hands-on' front-of-house) and her husband, Adrian (the chef). The house has no reception desk, just a 'greeting', say visitors. Children are welcomed: an extra bed can be provided; there's a high chair and a baby monitor. The under-fives, who are not allowed in the restaurant in the evening, can take high tea. Dogs are 'genuinely' welcomed (no charge): they can sit ('not on chairs, please') with their owners in one of the boldly decorated lounges. The bedrooms also have a bold decor; extras include bathrobes, flowers, a fruit bowl and mineral water. Bathrooms are well equipped, some have a walk-in shower. In the elegantly laid dining room, smart casual dress is required. Adrian Hyde uses Cumbrian produce for his modern dishes, perhaps cream risotto of Solway crab with mascarpone; beef fillet, fondant potato, braised shin, spinach, Marsala jus. There is good walking in the large grounds, where red squirrels can be seen. (*WR*)

Overwater, nr Ireby
CA7 1HH

T: 017687-76566
F: 017687-76921
E: welcome@overwaterhall.co.uk
W: www.overwaterhall.co.uk

BEDROOMS: 11, 1 on ground floor.
OPEN: all year.
FACILITIES: drawing room, lounge, bar area, restaurant, free Wi-Fi, civil wedding licence, 18-acre grounds, Overwater tarn 1 mile.
BACKGROUND MUSIC: classical in restaurant.
LOCATION: 2 miles NE of Bassenthwaite Lake.
CHILDREN: all ages welcomed, not under 5 in restaurant (high tea at 5.30 pm).
DOGS: allowed except in 1 lounge, restaurant.
CREDIT CARDS: MasterCard, Visa.
PRICES: per person B&B £70–£100, D,B&B £100–£140. Set dinner £45. 1-night bookings refused Sat.

KIRKBY LONSDALE Cumbria

Map 4: inset C2

SUN INN

On a narrow street in a Cumbrian market town, this 'homely' white-painted 17th-century inn is managed in hands-on style by the owners, Lucy and Mark Fuller. It is a 'well-run place where everyone knows how to make guests feel welcome and wanted', said a visitor. 'The staff were excellent throughout.' Traditional features (flagstone and wood floors, panelling, exposed beams) are combined with contemporary design in the restaurant and bedrooms. Lunch in the bar this year 'was nicely served on big plates, proper linen napkins; we had delicious tomato and pepper soup with good bread; excellent fish and chips, a lovely summer pudding'. In the restaurant, a short seasonal menu might include locally made haggis and black pudding, neeps, whisky sauce; slow-roasted shoulder of lamb, roasted garlic mash, root vegetables, braised cabbage. The bedrooms, individually designed, have 'elegant' furnishings, modern bathroom. Breakfast includes home-made granola, fruit, croissants and freshly squeezed orange juice; butter and preserves are 'unpackaged'; the sausages and bacon come from the butcher next door but one. Parking is awkward in the interesting town. (*HN, and others*)

6 Market Street
Kirkby Lonsdale LA6 2AU

T: 015242-71965
F: 015242-72485
E: email@sun-inn.info
W: www.sun-inn.info

BEDROOMS: 11.
OPEN: all year, bar and restaurant closed Mon lunch.
FACILITIES: bar, restaurant, free Wi-Fi.
BACKGROUND MUSIC: in bar.
LOCATION: town centre.
CHILDREN: all ages welcomed.
DOGS: allowed in 8 bedrooms, bar.
CREDIT CARDS: MasterCard, Visa.
PRICES: [2013] per room B&B £110–£168. Set dinner £26.95.

KIRKBY STEPHEN Cumbria

Map 4:C3

AUGILL CASTLE

'I loved this welcoming castle with its laid-back atmosphere and friendly staff. We were greeted as if we were family friends; our two-year-old daughter enjoyed running through the building.' There is much praise this year for Wendy and Simon Bennett's informal neo-Gothic Victorian castle between the Lake District and the Yorkshire Dales. A group of 29 visitors (from children to pensioners) was 'blown away by its charm, the warm welcome and the quality of the food and accommodation'. There are endless diversions for children, from a drawing room with games and dressing-up paraphernalia to a playground, a tree house and a cinema. Bedrooms are decorated with bold colours and furnished with a mix of antiques and contemporary pieces; some have a four-poster bed. 'Our room was comfortable, clean, with fabulous views and a huge bath.' Dinner, booked in advance, is taken communally at a huge oak table; meals are 'sociable occasions, with no whispering over the consommé'. The no-choice set menu might include terrine of chicken and baby leeks; fillet of Cumbrian lamb rolled in black pepper. Breakfast is 'a leisurely affair'. (*Marielle Sheffield, Caroline Falkus*)

South Stainmore
nr Kirkby Stephen CA17 4DE

T: 01768-341937
E: enquiries@stayinacastle.com
W: www.stayinacastle.com

BEDROOMS: 14, 2 on ground floor, 4 in Stable House, 2 in Orangery.
OPEN: all year except Christmas, dinner by arrangement, lunch for groups by arrangement.
FACILITIES: hall, cinema, drawing room, library (honesty bar), music (sitting) room, dining room, civil wedding licence, 15-acre grounds (landscaped garden, tennis).
BACKGROUND MUSIC: none.
LOCATION: 3 miles NE of Kirkby Stephen.
CHILDREN: all ages welcomed.
DOGS: not allowed.
CREDIT CARDS: Amex, MasterCard, Visa.
PRICES: per room B&B £160–£200, D,B&B £220–£260. Set dinner £30. 2-night bookings preferred weekends.

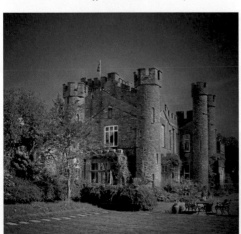

LACOCK Wiltshire

Map 2:D1

AT THE SIGN OF THE ANGEL

César award in 1989

In an atmospheric National Trust village often used as the backdrop for films and television, this 'enchanting' 15th-century half-timbered inn is owned and run by Lorna and George Hardy. Doorways are low, walls are uneven, but 'so what if the floor boards creak and the doors are quaintly off-side, because character abounds'. Public rooms have log fires, exposed beams, flagstone floors; the lounge has 'two wonderfully large leather chairs, a sofa, lots of old books'. Bedrooms have all been recently upgraded; one has a 'magnificent' four-poster, another an enormous carved bed that once belonged to Isambard Kingdom Brunel. Bathrooms are modern. Tables are laid with silverware in the three interconnecting medieval dining rooms, where Lorna Hardy serves traditional English dishes, perhaps a whole dressed Cornish crab with chilli mayonnaise; individual steak and kidney pudding. 'The menu is one of the best we have sampled, locally sourced and cooked to perfection.' The bread and the preserves for breakfast are made in the kitchen; there is stewed fruit, Wiltshire bacon, eggs from hens in the garden.

25% DISCOUNT VOUCHERS

6 Church Street
Lacock, nr Chippenham SN15 2LB

T: 01249-730230
F: 01249-730527
E: angel@lacock.co.uk
W: www.lacock.co.uk

BEDROOMS: 6.
OPEN: all year except 24–26 Dec, closed Mon lunch except bank holidays.
FACILITIES: ramps, lounge, bar, restaurant, free Wi-Fi.
BACKGROUND MUSIC: none.
LOCATION: village centre, 3 miles S of Chippenham.
CHILDREN: all ages welcomed.
DOGS: not allowed in public rooms.
CREDIT CARDS: all major cards.
PRICES: [2013] per room B&B single £85, double £129–£159. D,B&B from £82.95 per person, set dinner £17.95, à la carte £32.

LANGAR Nottinghamshire

LANGAR HALL

César award in 2000

'The ultimate reason for visiting the East Midlands', Imogen Skirving's informal small hotel in the Vale of Belvoir has long been liked by readers for its informality and character. The honey-stoned Georgian house has been the Skirving family home for more than 150 years (Imogen Skirving first took in guests to make ends meet when she inherited the house). Family portraits line the stairs that lead to the bedrooms, which are themed and named after people who have stayed in the house. Cartland (in grey, black and white – not pink) for the novelist; Agnew's, a chalet in the garden, is the preferred room for the BBC cricket correspondent when commentating at Trent Bridge; Barrister, a masculine room with painted panelling, reflects *Langar Hall*'s popularity with the legal profession. The hands-on owner likes to meet her guests in the bar (which has prints associated with Paul Smith, the Nottingham-based designer), the white sitting room, or in the restaurant. Chefs Gary Booth and Ross Jeffrey serve seasonal dishes, perhaps Langar lamb, rosemary potato millefeuille. (*PJ, and others*)

25% DISCOUNT VOUCHERS

Church Lane
Langar NG13 9HG

T: 01949-860559
F: 01949-861045
E: info@langarhall.co.uk
W: www.langarhall.com

BEDROOMS: 14, 1 on ground floor, 1 in garden chalet, 2 in the *Lodge*.
OPEN: all year.
FACILITIES: ramps, sitting room, study, library, bar, garden room, restaurant, civil wedding licence, 20-acre grounds (gardens, children's play area, croquet, ponds, fishing), unsuitable for &.
BACKGROUND MUSIC: none.
LOCATION: 12 miles SE of Nottingham.
CHILDREN: all ages welcomed by arrangement.
DOGS: small dogs on a lead allowed by arrangement, not unaccompanied.
CREDIT CARDS: MasterCard, Visa.
PRICES: [2013] per room B&B single £90–£140, double £109–£199. D,B&B (Sun and Mon) £70–£115 per person, set dinner (not on Sat) £25–£30, à la carte £35.

LASTINGHAM North Yorkshire

Map 4:C4

LASTINGHAM GRANGE

César award in 1991

'Staying at *Lastingham Grange* is a truly remarkable experience, like being in an Agatha Christie novel. It seemed that the majority of the guests had been coming for decades.' Perhaps this is explained by the 'outstanding service' received by a visitor this year to the Wood family's traditional hotel, a converted 17th-century farmhouse on the edge of the North Yorkshire Moors. 'Everyone knows your name immediately, and staff are constantly checking if you need anything, and bringing tea and coffee.' It is a family affair: Bertie Wood is helped by his mother, Jane, and brother, Tom. Not all guests are elderly: children are welcomed; under-twelves share their parents' room for no charge; there's an adventure playground and special meals. The bedrooms are 'small and old-fashioned but spotlessly clean and comfortable'. In the dining room, chef Paul Cattaneo serves food 'which is traditional but very good' (typical dishes: chilled melon with Parma ham; roast duckling, sage and onion stuffing). 'Superb walking on the moors from the door; a truly charming hotel, unusual in this day and age.' (*Val Ferguson*)

Lastingham YO62 6TH

T: 01751-417345
F: 01751-417358
E: reservations@
   lastinghamgrange.com
W: www.lastinghamgrange.com

BEDROOMS: 12, plus cottage in village.
OPEN: Mar–Nov.
FACILITIES: ramps, hall, lounge, dining room, laundry facilities, free Wi-Fi, 12-acre grounds (terrace, garden, adventure playground, croquet, boules), unsuitable for &.
BACKGROUND MUSIC: none.
LOCATION: 5 miles NE of Kirkbymoorside.
CHILDREN: all ages welcomed.
DOGS: not allowed in public rooms.
CREDIT CARDS: Amex, MasterCard, Visa.
PRICES: [2013] per person B&B £75–£100, D,B&B £110–£140. Set dinner £39.95, à la carte £25.

LAVENHAM Suffolk

Map 2:C5

THE GREAT HOUSE

🏆 *César award in 2009*

On the market square of this medieval town, this fine Georgian house is run with Gallic flair as a restaurant-with-rooms by owners Régis and Martine Crépy. It has been sympathetically restored to combine the centuries-old atmosphere (low beams, creaking floorboards) with contemporary flair: the public areas and the bedrooms are decorated in contemporary colours, discreet modern furnishings; fresh flowers. In a courtyard, a recently added dining area has a retractable canopy. The service in the restaurant, mainly by young French waiters, is 'charming, attentive, not at all snooty'. The cooking of chef Enrique Bilbault is 'wonderful': his classic dishes might include spiced cauliflower mousse, lightly smoked cod, chive and dill lobster jelly; guineafowl breast, morel, shallot and sage mousseline, port sauce. A 'lovely' loft room had 'an aura of great comfort'; 'We slept well in a bed that was soft and supportive; excellent pillows, one thick and one thin, allowing us to configure them as we wished, a welcome detail.' At breakfast, 'good cheese made me glad I had not chosen the cheeseboard the evening before'. (*A and MK*)

Market Place
Lavenham CO10 9QZ

T: 01787-247431
F: 01787-248007
E: info@greathouse.co.uk
W: www.greathouse.co.uk

BEDROOMS: 5.
OPEN: Feb–Dec, restaurant closed Sun night, Mon, Tues midday.
FACILITIES: lounge/bar, restaurant, free Wi-Fi, patio dining area, ½-acre garden, unsuitable for ⅃.
BACKGROUND MUSIC: French.
LOCATION: by Market Cross, near Guildhall, public car park.
CHILDREN: all ages welcomed.
DOGS: not allowed.
CREDIT CARDS: MasterCard, Visa.
PRICES: [2013] per person B&B £62.50–£112.50, D,B&B £94.50–£160.50. Set dinner £33.50, à la carte £58. 1-night bookings sometimes refused Sat.

SEE ALSO SHORTLIST

LAVENHAM Suffolk

Map 2:C5

LAVENHAM PRIORY

César award in 2012

In one of the best-preserved medieval wool villages in England, this half-timbered former Benedictine priory (Grade I listed) dates from the 13th century. 'It's a privilege to sleep in such a historic building,' said one visitor. The owners, Tim and Gilli Pitt, have restored the priory in the style of the merchant's house it became during its Elizabethan period. Guests approach the 'wonderful facade' through a mini-parterre, with herbs and old roses. The bedchambers, reached by oak staircases, have many original features: braced crown posts, wall paintings, massive oak floorboards. 'What a special room,' wrote an inspector. 'It had beams on the terracotta-painted walls; brocade curtains and matching bedspread; a sitting area with armchairs, and an incongruous plasma television.' Guests are encouraged to make full use of the centre-piece of the building, the Great Hall, which has a log fire in an enormous inglenook fireplace, and rugs on the brick floor. There is also a smaller sitting room. Breakfast, a communal affair at a large table with white damask cloth and napkins, has freshly squeezed orange juice, DIY toast, cooked dishes to order.

Water Street
Lavenham CO10 9RW

T: 01787-247404
F: 01787-248472
E: mail@lavenhampriory.co.uk
W: www.lavenhampriory.co.uk

BEDROOMS: 6.
OPEN: all year except Christmas/New Year.
FACILITIES: Great Hall/sitting room, snug, breakfast room, free Wi-Fi, 3-acre garden (medieval courtyard, herb garden), unsuitable for &.
BACKGROUND MUSIC: none.
LOCATION: central.
CHILDREN: not under 10.
DOGS: not allowed in house.
CREDIT CARDS: Diners, MasterCard, Visa.
PRICES: per room B&B single £87–£92, double £120–£156. 1-night bookings refused Sat.

SEE ALSO SHORTLIST

LEAMINGTON SPA Warwickshire

Map 2:B2

EIGHT CLARENDON CRESCENT

'My bedroom was one of the most beautifully decorated and richly furnished rooms I have slept in, far superior to hotel rooms that cost four times as much.' David and Christine Lawson's upmarket B&B, in a Grade II listed Regency house in a quiet crescent, was 'everything I could hope for', says a regular *Guide* reporter this year. 'It retained its generous Regency proportions. At night, comfortable between crisp linen sheets, I was surprised how few sounds entered through the open window; I would never have thought I was close to the centre of town.' Three of the bedrooms have an en suite bathroom, the fourth a private bathroom across the corridor. There are 'beautiful arrangements of fresh flowers' in the house, which has 'many fine antiques'. Guests are asked to indicate on a clipboard what time they wish to take breakfast and to 'tick the items they would like'. Christine Lawson cooks and serves the 'universally excellent' meal around a large circular table. 'Fresh fruit and yogurts, home-made bread, perfectly cooked bacon and eggs; tea and coffee in silver pots.' (*Trevor Lockwood*)

8 Clarendon Crescent
Leamington Spa CV32 5NR

T: 01926-429840
F: 01926-424641
E: lawson@lawson71.fsnet.co.uk
W: www.8clarendoncrescent.co.uk

BEDROOMS: 4.
OPEN: all year except Christmas, New Year, Easter, occasional holidays.
FACILITIES: drawing room, dining room, free Wi-Fi, garden, 1-acre with private dell, unsuitable for &.
BACKGROUND MUSIC: none.
LOCATION: close to centre.
CHILDREN: all ages welcomed.
DOGS: not allowed.
CREDIT CARDS: none.
PRICES: [2013] per room B&B single £50, double £80.

LEDBURY Herefordshire

Map 3:D5

THE FEATHERS

'A lovely old building', David Elliston's 16th-century black-and-white timbered coaching inn is a 'great' town hotel 'with many locals passing through'. There is a 'nice' old-fashioned reception area, and a beamed lounge. A visitor who entered by the bar 'was given excellent advice on the range of eating options'. *Fuggles Brasserie*, which is thickly hung with hops on the ceiling, is the informal option: a 'fine' risotto and 'good' fishcakes were enjoyed; service was 'friendly and efficient'. In *Quills*, which has chandeliers and leather seating, Suzie Isaacs is the chef: her modern British menu might include pan-fried scallops, chorizo crisps; Cotswold venison loin, goose-fat Parmentier potatoes, roasted beetroot. Much of the original character of the building is retained in the bedrooms, which have beamed walls and ceilings and antique furniture. Number 5 is the biggest, with a king-size bed and a seating area; another room has an antique four-poster and looks over the town centre. Breakfast had 'a good choice of fruit and cereals and a very tasty full English'. (*RC, and others*)

25% DISCOUNT VOUCHERS

High Street
Ledbury HR8 1DS

T: 01531-635266
F: 01531-638955
E: enquiries@feathers-ledbury.co.uk
W: www.feathers-ledbury.co.uk

BEDROOMS: 22, 1 suite in cottage, also self-catering apartments.
OPEN: all year.
FACILITIES: lounge, bar, brasserie, restaurant, free Wi-Fi, function/conference/wedding facilities, spa (swimming pool, 11 by 6 metres, whirlpool, gym), civil wedding licence, courtyard garden (fountain, alfresco eating), unsuitable for &.
BACKGROUND MUSIC: none.
LOCATION: town centre, parking.
CHILDREN: all ages welcomed.
DOGS: allowed, only guide dogs in restaurant and brasserie.
CREDIT CARDS: all major cards.
PRICES: [2013] per room B&B single £97.50–£132.50, double £148–£250, D,B&B double £172.50–£192.50. Set menu £22, à la carte £29. 1-night bookings sometimes refused weekends.

LEDBURY Herefordshire

Map 3:D5

THE NOVERINGS

NEW

In extensive grounds with woodland, meadows and gardens, this handsome Edwardian house is run as a small B&B (with simple evening meals available) by the owners, Peter and Heather Clark. 'They are professional, friendly and informal, going out of their way to ensure we were comfortable,' said the nominator (a long-time *Guide* correspondent). The 'substantial' house has a 'beautiful' oak staircase, a huge hall, and a billiard room (with a full-size table), which doubles as the breakfast room. Each of the three bedrooms has a sitting area (there is no residents' lounge): 'Ours, the Venetian room, was palatial (the biggest we have ever been given); on a cold night, it was warm; the bed was enormous; the bathroom had a roll-top bath and a walk-in shower. The Clarks will serve a two-course supper ('simple and delicious') by arrangement: it might include chicken with Marsala and mushrooms; seasonal fruit crumble. Meals are served at separate tables; no licence – guests are encouraged to 'bring your favourite tipple with you'. The 'excellent' breakfast can be taken on a terrace in warm weather. (*Alec Frank*)

Brook Lane, Bosbury
Ledbury HR8 1QD

T: 01531-641785
E: info@thenoverings.co.uk
W: www.thenoverings.co.uk

BEDROOMS: 3.
OPEN: Apr–Nov.
FACILITIES: dining room, billiard room, free Wi-Fi, 1-acre garden in 17 acres of woodland, unsuitable for &.
BACKGROUND MUSIC: none.
LOCATION: 5 miles N of Ledbury.
CHILDREN: not under 16.
DOGS: not allowed.
CREDIT CARDS: MasterCard, Visa (*4% surcharge for credit cards*).
PRICES: [2013] per room B&B £85–£120. Set menu £20. 1-night bookings sometimes refused at weekends.

LEDBURY Herefordshire

Map 3:D5

VERZON HOUSE

25% DISCOUNT VOUCHERS

The hospitality is 'of the old school', say inspectors in 2013 visiting this 'lovely' old red brick farmhouse. It is run as a small hotel by Peter and Audrey Marks. These 'charming owners' have 'cleverly blended' traditional features in the interesting building with 'striking contemporary furnishings'. An 'impressive' steel-and-chrome chandelier hangs in the stairwell in the hallway, by a galleried staircase with inlaid wood. 'Our large bedroom, which had gorgeous views of countryside towards the Malvern hills, had smart swagged curtains, a huge bed, steel-and-glass furniture, bright modern pictures; a small fridge with water and fresh milk for the hospitality tray in the large wardrobe; good lighting in the white-tiled bathroom.' Drinks and canapés are taken in a 'real bar with leather stools, original brickwork, unusual pictures and lamps'. Peter Marks, the chef, serves a short menu in the dining room: 'Good, careful cooking of top-quality ingredients: an excellent cup of sweetcorn soup; fresh and tasty smoked haddock fishcakes with tartare sauce; delicious organic salmon. Service was spot on; Mr Marks came round to check that all was well.'

Hereford Road, Trumpet
Ledbury
HR8 2PZ

T: 01531-670381
F: 01531-670830
E: info@verzonhouse.com
W: www.verzonhouse.com

BEDROOMS: 8.
OPEN: Feb–Dec, restaurant closed Sun evening/Mon.
FACILITIES: bar, lounge, dining room, free Wi-Fi, civil wedding licence, terrace, 4-acre grounds, only public areas suitable for &.
BACKGROUND MUSIC: in bar.
LOCATION: 2 miles W of Ledbury.
CHILDREN: welcomed, no under-8s at dinner.
DOGS: only guide dogs allowed.
CREDIT CARDS: Amex, MasterCard, Visa.
PRICES: per room B&B single from £105, double from £165. D,B&B £145 per person. À la carte £40. 1-night bookings rarely refused.

LEONARD STANLEY Gloucestershire

Map 3:E5

THE GREY COTTAGE

César award in 1999

The welcome is 'warmer than warm' at Rosemary Reeves's small guest house in the Cotswolds which has long been popular with *Guide* readers. 'There is nothing nicer than to return after a day out to find Rosemary waiting with a fresh pot of tea, cake and a chat,' says a visitor travelling on her own. Another comment in 2013: 'Rosemary's service and attention to detail is outstanding.' Mrs Reeves tells us that one bedroom has a new bathroom ('beautifully done' is a comment); the other two have a new vanity unit. All rooms have 'fresh flowers, fruit, lots of extras' – shoehorn, bottle opener, chocolates, etc. 'Memorable' dinners are provided by arrangement; no choice (preferences are discussed on booking). 'Chargrilled fillet steak, which melted in the mouth, came with tomato and tarragon sauce, steamed new potatoes, leaf spinach; rhubarb and ginger crumble with ice cream could not be faulted.' Breakfast is a 'gigantic feast': freshly squeezed orange juice, fresh and dried fruit, cereals and yogurt, do-it-yourself toast, butter balls; full English, eggs 'cooked how you like them'. (*Sue Raymond, Jill Belton, Gordon Franklin*)

Bath Road, Leonard Stanley
Stonehouse GL10 3LU

T: 01453-822515
E: rosemary.reeves@
    btopenworld.com
W: www.greycottage.co.uk

BEDROOMS: 3.
OPEN: all year except Christmas/New Year, occasional holidays.
FACILITIES: sitting room with TV, conservatory, dining room, Wi-Fi on request, ¼-acre garden, unsuitable for &.
BACKGROUND MUSIC: 'no, never!'
LOCATION: 3 miles SW of Stroud.
CHILDREN: not under 10.
DOGS: not allowed.
CREDIT CARDS: none.
PRICES: B&B per room single £55, double £65–£85 (5% reduction for 3-night stays). Set dinner £23–£25.

LICHFIELD Staffordshire

Map 2:A2

NETHERSTOWE HOUSE

'A huge effort is made by the staff to ensure your stay is memorable,' said inspectors visiting Ben Heathcote's small hotel in this cathedral city. A converted 19th-century mill, the Grade II listed half-timbered building is approached through a housing estate. 'Within minutes, the houses disappear; you enter the dense tree-lined drive and the outside world vanishes.' There is an imposing fireplace in the entrance hall/ lounge; public rooms are 'spacious and comfortable'. The piped music in the public areas is 'awful'. There are nine bedrooms in the main house, varying in size. 'Ours was large and long, with a bathroom at the end, off which a separate shower and loo opened in turn.' The Penthouse has its own lounge and dining area. A modern wing houses eight apartments, 'well furnished and tastefully decorated'. Tables have white linen cloths and napkins in the elegant *Ivy* dining room, where Stephen Garland, the new chef, cooks 'classic dishes with a modern twist'. His menu lists 'food miles', eg, breast of Packington Farm duck, orange, wild mushroom and sultana fricassée (seven miles). There is a vaulted cellar steakhouse for less formal dining. (*R and CS, and others*)

Netherstowe Lane
Lichfield WS13 6AY

T: 01543-254270
F: 01543-419998
E: info@netherstowehouse.com
W: www.netherstowehouse.com

BEDROOMS: 9, plus 8 serviced apartments in annexe.
OPEN: all year.
FACILITIES: 2 lounges, bar, 3 dining rooms, free Wi-Fi, cellar, gymnasium, 2-acre grounds, unsuitable for &.
BACKGROUND MUSIC: in public rooms.
LOCATION: 2 miles N of city centre.
CHILDREN: over 12 in hotel, all ages welcomed in apartments.
DOGS: guide dogs only allowed.
CREDIT CARDS: MasterCard, Visa.
PRICES: per room B&B £95–£195, D,B&B £170–£230. Set dinner £29–£35, à la carte £35.

LIFTON Devon

Map 1:C3

THE ARUNDELL ARMS

🏆 *César award in 2006*

'An excellent combination of relatively simple accommodation and outstanding cooking,' says a visitor returning to this sporting inn for the first time since Adam Fox-Edwards took over from his mother, Anne Voss Bark. We are sorry to record her death, aged 84, in November 2012. Her son 'is much in evidence, greeting guests in the evenings'. Another comment (in 2013): 'This remains an excellent hotel.' Fishing is an important attraction (the hotel has 20 miles of rights on the Tamar and tributaries); non-fishing guests were 'made very welcome'. The main dining room, once the village assembly room, 'has been refurbished in a style in keeping with the scale of the space'; Steve Pidgeon is the chef. 'Delicious canapés came with aperitifs. We enjoyed an assiette of fish (crab, scallop and red mullet) served on an impractical slate; fillet of lamb, pink kidneys and baby vegetables, all cooked perfectly.' The *Courthouse* bar is 'a more vernacular alternative', with pub favourites. Bedrooms (three are new this year) are decorated in country house style. 'Breakfast shared the freshness and elegance of dinner.' (*Richard Parish, David RW Jervois*)

Fore Street
Lifton PL16 0AA

T: 01566-784666
F: 01566-784494
E: reservations@arundellarms.com
W: www.arundellarms.com

BEDROOMS: 26, 4 on ground floor.
OPEN: all year, except Christmas (food only).
FACILITIES: ramp, lounge, cocktail bar, public bar, 2 dining rooms, conference/meeting rooms, games room, free Wi-Fi, skittle alley, civil wedding licence, ½-acre garden, 20 miles fishing rights on River Tamar and tributaries, fishing school.
BACKGROUND MUSIC: varied in restaurant and bar.
LOCATION: 3 miles E of Launceston.
CHILDREN: all ages welcomed.
DOGS: not allowed in restaurant.
CREDIT CARDS: MasterCard, Visa.
PRICES: [2013] per room B&B single £90, double £180–£200. D,B&B £130–£140 per person, set dinner £43, à la carte £50.

LODDISWELL Devon

HAZELWOOD HOUSE

On a wooded hillside in an area of outstanding natural beauty, this quirky guest house is run in informal style by the owners, Gillian Kean, Anabel Farnell-Watson and Jane Bowman. Visitors are encouraged to 'make full use of communal space' in a house that is liked for the 'sense of hospitality' and 'lack of rules'. Weekends devoted to yoga, folk music and the arts are regularly held. The public rooms and bedrooms are painted in bright colours and decorated with eclectic artwork (Jane Bowman paints watercolours). Larger bedrooms with an en suite bathroom are on the first floor: an inspector's room, decorated in lilac, had a queen-size bed with a brass bedstead; 'lashings of hot water' in the bathroom. Rooms on the second floor are smaller; they have shared bathrooms nearby. In the evening, guests gather by a wood-burning stove in the lounge; pre-dinner drinks are a sociable affair with interaction among guests and the hosts. The chef, Alex Sandu, cooks imaginative dishes, perhaps goat's cheese parcel, home-made damson relish; baked skate wing, lemon and brown butter. (*SK, and others*)

Loddiswell
nr Kingsbridge TQ7 4EB

T: 01548-821232
F: 01548-821318
E: info@hazelwoodhouse.com
W: www.hazelwoodhouse.com

BEDROOMS: 14, 7 with facilities en suite.
OPEN: all year (closed Wed/Thurs off-season).
FACILITIES: hall with piano, drawing room, study/TV room, dining room, function/conference facilities, civil wedding licence, 67-acre grounds (river, boathouse, chapel), only restaurant suitable for &.
BACKGROUND MUSIC: on request.
LOCATION: 2 miles N of Loddiswell.
CHILDREN: all ages welcomed.
DOGS: allowed in bedrooms, on leads in public rooms.
CREDIT CARDS: MasterCard, Visa.
PRICES: per room B&B single £48–£115, double £75–£160. Set dinner £25–£28.

LODSWORTH West Sussex

Map 2:E3

THE HALFWAY BRIDGE `NEW`

In the South Downs, this traditional country inn has been given a contemporary make-over by Sam and Janet Bakose; Helen Totton is the manager. 'The atmosphere is warm and friendly; the service exemplary, and the bedrooms are stylish,' wrote a *Guide* inspector in 2013. The beamed bedrooms are in converted barns in a former stable yard behind the main building. 'Our suite had a sitting room to one side of the lobby with full-length windows and shutters, a settee, desk and leather chair; a spacious bedroom on the other side had a subdued colour scheme, a full-length mirror on one wall; a large wardrobe with a small fridge (fresh milk, hooray). The bathroom had a bath and a separate shower cabinet. Housekeeping was of the highest standard.' The bedrooms are quiet; there may be some noise outside from the busy A272. The inn has a large bar, and a series of intimate dining areas with brick walls, wood-burning stoves. 'We enjoyed upmarket pub food: substantial portions of cottage pie; calf's liver and bacon; a delicious clementine sponge pudding; a range of good wines by the carafe.'

Lodsworth
Petworth GU28 9BP

T: 01798-861281
E: enquiries@halfwaybridge.co.uk
W: www.halfwaybridge.co.uk

BEDROOMS: 7, in converted barns.
OPEN: all year.
FACILITIES: bar, restaurant, free Wi-Fi, terrace, unsuitable for &.
BACKGROUND MUSIC: light jazz in bar and restaurant.
LOCATION: 3 miles W of Petworth.
CHILDREN: all ages welcomed.
DOGS: allowed in bar, not in bedrooms.
CREDIT CARDS: Amex, MasterCard, Visa.
PRICES: [2013] per room B&B £120–£190. Set meals £19.50–£23.50, à la carte £35.

LONGHORSLEY Northumberland

Map 4:B3

THISTLEYHAUGH FARM

❦ César award in 2011

'What a peaceful spot: we were well looked after and enjoyed our time on the farm.' Enid Nelless's guest house in the rolling Cheviot hills is shielded from the world by a 720-acre organic sheep and cattle farm run by her husband, Henry. The only disturbance might be the sheepdogs 'rounding up the squealing pigs; great fun to watch'. The Georgian farmhouse, which dates back to 1780, has open fires, many original features; a well-tended garden. The bedrooms are individually decorated and priced by size: there are 'excellent' beds; 'masses of towels, all the goodies we needed', and 'lots of hot water' in the bathrooms. Complimentary sherry is served before dinner in the garden room before guests dine communally in the dining room at 7 pm. Enid Nelless's daughter-in-law, Zoë, is the chef: she uses ingredients from the farm for her set menu, which might include roasted red pepper and tomato soup; organic roast lamb shoulder, creamed potatoes, cabbage, roasted carrots. 'Farmhouse cooking with flair,' one visitor called it. Breakfast has a 'well-stocked' buffet; Craster kipper with scrambled eggs. (*SP*)

Longhorsley, nr Morpeth
NE65 8RG

T/F: 01665-570629
E: thistleyhaugh@hotmail.com
W: www.thistleyhaugh.co.uk

BEDROOMS: 5.
OPEN: all year except January, dining room closed Sat eve.
FACILITIES: 2 lounges, dining room, free Wi-Fi, 720-acre farm, 1-acre garden (summer house), fishing, shooting, golf, riding nearby, unsuitable for &.
BACKGROUND MUSIC: none.
LOCATION: 10 miles N of Morpeth, W of A697.
CHILDREN: all ages welcomed.
DOGS: not allowed (kennels nearby).
CREDIT CARDS: MasterCard, Visa.
PRICES: per person B&B £45–£85, D,B&B from £70.

LOOE Cornwall

THE BEACH HOUSE

'In a perfect location on the seafront at Hannafore, near the harbour entrance', Rosie and David Reeve's white-fronted B&B is popular with readers. 'Rosie and David are excellent hosts, with an in-depth knowledge of where to go and what to do in the area.' A visitor this year was 'warmly greeted – halfway down the drive – and offered a tray of tea and fresh home-made cake'. Bedrooms are 'comfortable and well appointed, with every facility'. Cawsand (which has bay windows) and Whitsand have extensive sea views; Kynance has an en suite shower room. Two bedrooms at the back of the house have access to a sea-facing sitting room across the hall. Breakfast, ordered the night before and served between 7.45 and 9.15 am, is 'excellent': fruit juices, cereals and fresh fruit are on the sideboard. Alternatives to the standard fry-up include French toast (sweet with fruits) and pancakes with fruits and maple syrup. Holistic therapies and beauty treatments are available in the Top Deck treatment room. 'Recommended to anyone who would like a well-run, friendly stay in Looe.' (*Michael Gill, Stan Hollands*)

Marine Drive, Hannafore
Looe PL13 2DH

T: 01503-262598
F: 01503-262298
E: enquiries@
   thebeachhouselooe.co.uk
W: www.thebeachhouselooe.co.uk

BEDROOMS: 5.
OPEN: all year except Christmas.
FACILITIES: garden room, breakfast room, free Wi-Fi, terrace, ⅓-acre garden, beach opposite, unsuitable for &.
BACKGROUND MUSIC: classical in dining room.
LOCATION: ½ mile from centre.
CHILDREN: children over 16 welcomed.
DOGS: not allowed.
CREDIT CARDS: MasterCard, Visa.
PRICES: [2013] per person B&B £45–£70. 1-night bookings refused weekends, high season.

SEE ALSO SHORTLIST

LORTON Cumbria

Map 4: inset C2

NEW HOUSE FARM

Ideally placed for touring the northern lakes, this Grade II listed farmhouse dating from the 1650s is run as a guest house by owner Hazel Thompson. Readers recommend it for those who 'wish to avoid pretentiousness' and who look for 'comfort and welcoming hospitality'. During renovation many fine period pieces – flagged floors, oak beams and open stone fireplaces – were discovered and restored. Views are 'spectacular' and there are open fields, woods and streams for visitors to explore, and a garden hot tub to enjoy. Each of the bedrooms has an individual character: the ground-floor Stable Room has a solid oak four-poster bed and a double airbath; Whiteside, on the first floor, has a king-size brass bed. 'Our bedroom was excellent; the superb bathroom had a middle-of-room bath.' Meals are cooked on the Aga by Mrs Thompson, using local ingredients when possible; main courses might include roast pheasant or locally caught salmon. 'The food was very good.' Lunches and teas are served in the adjacent converted byre. Breakfast has freshly baked croissants, fruit, porridge and dishes cooked to order. (*GM, and others*)

Lorton
nr Cockermouth CA13 9UU

T: 07841-159818
E: hazel@newhouse-farm.co.uk
W: www.newhouse-farm.com

BEDROOMS: 5, 1 in stable, 1 in Old Dairy.
OPEN: all year.
FACILITIES: 3 lounges, dining room, free Wi-Fi, civil wedding licence, 17-acre grounds (garden, hot tub, streams, woods, field, lake and river, safe bathing, 2 miles), unsuitable for &.
BACKGROUND MUSIC: none.
LOCATION: 2 miles S of Lorton.
CHILDREN: not under 6.
DOGS: not allowed in public rooms.
CREDIT CARDS: MasterCard, Visa.
PRICES: per person B&B £55–£85, D,B&B £32 added. Set dinner £35.

LOWER BOCKHAMPTON Dorset

Map 1:C6

YALBURY COTTAGE

Once the homes of the shepherd and the keeper of the water meadows, these 350-year-old thatched cottages are in a pretty hamlet in Thomas Hardy country: the writer's birthplace is within walking distance. They are run as a small hotel/restaurant by Ariane (the 'pleasant' hostess) and Jamie Jones (the chef). 'We couldn't fault the friendly service,' says a visitor this year. The 'highlight' is dinner in the oak-beamed restaurant in the oldest section of the building. 'A delicious dressed Portland crab was served with crisp bruschetta and lemon mayonnaise; the tastiest aged beef steak with rösti potato, spiced butternut purée, wild mushroom sauce; lovely home-made bread rolls.' A maze of corridors through the original four cottages leads to the bedrooms, which have a rural decor: 'Our room was clean, neat and comfortable; it overlooked farmland and horses in a nearby field.' Housekeeping is praised. Breakfast, which 'maintains the standards of dinner', has apricots steeped in honey and cinnamon, prunes in apple juice; black and white pudding, local mushrooms in the full English; eggy brioche with raisins and orange maple syrup. (*Steven Hur*)

25% DISCOUNT VOUCHERS

Lower Bockhampton
nr Dorchester DT2 8PZ

T: 01305-262382
E: enquiries@yalburycottage.com
W: www.yalburycottage.com

BEDROOMS: 8, 6 on ground floor.
OPEN: all year except Christmas/New Year.
FACILITIES: lounge, restaurant, free Wi-Fi, unsuitable for &.
BACKGROUND MUSIC: 'easy listening' in lounge at dinner time.
LOCATION: 2 miles E of Dorchester.
CHILDREN: all ages welcomed, but not in restaurant after 8 pm.
DOGS: allowed in bedrooms, lounge.
CREDIT CARDS: MasterCard, Visa.
PRICES: [2013] per room B&B single £70–£85, double £95–£120, D,B&B single £99–£115, double £160–£180. Set dinner £31–£36.

LOWER SLAUGHTER Gloucestershire

Map 3:D6

THE SLAUGHTERS COUNTRY INN

NEW

In a Domesday village of Cotswold stone cottages, this 17th-century building (once a crammer for Eton, later a hotel) has been revamped as a country inn by Andrew and Christina Brownsword. Stuart Hodges is the manager. Trusted *Guide* correspondents in 2013 were 'impressed' by the renovations and the 'well-kept' gardens, which border the River Eye. 'It is comfortable, relaxing; the staff create an informal, friendly atmosphere.' The bar, which is open all day and often busy with locals, has 'large sofas, armchairs and coffee tables; plenty of books and magazines'. It has its own menu. The restaurant is a 'bright room with mirrored walls giving each of the well-spaced tables a garden view'. Chris Fryer is the chef. 'We enjoyed a crab risotto with rocket and Parmesan; good grilled sea bream, lyonnaise potatoes, spinach and basil oil.' The bedrooms are in the main house and in cottages in the grounds. 'Ours had a sloping ceiling and beams; two armchairs and a coffee table with a good information book; poor reading lights, alas; a brightly lit bathroom.' Breakfast has 'good scrambled eggs'. (*Pat and Jeremy Temple*)

Lower Slaughter GL54 2HS

T: 01451-822143
F: 01451-821485
E: info@theslaughtersinn.co.uk
W: www.theslaughtersinn.co.uk

BEDROOMS: 30, 11 in annexe, 3 on ground floor, 1 suitable for &.
OPEN: all year.
FACILITIES: bar, restaurant, function rooms, free Wi-Fi, civil wedding licence, terrace, 4-acre gardens.
BACKGROUND MUSIC: in public areas.
LOCATION: in village, 3 miles SW of Stow-on-the-Wold.
CHILDREN: all ages welcomed.
DOGS: not allowed in restaurant.
CREDIT CARDS: all major cards.
PRICES: [2013] per room B&B £85–£305, D,B&B £155–£375. À la carte £30. 1-night bookings refused Sat.

LUDLOW Shropshire

Map 3:C4

MR UNDERHILL'S

♥ *César award in 2000*

At the foot of the castle ramparts on the banks of the River Teme, Chris and Judy Bradley's restaurant-with-rooms has many fans. A recent comment: 'We loved our stay: the service was unpretentious, warm and attentive.' The Bradleys tell us that the restyling of the restaurant and the accommodation is now complete: 'All the niggles we had to live with are gone.' Chris Bradley has a *Michelin* star for his innovative cooking. Self-taught, he serves an eight-course set menu (no choice until the dessert, likes and dislikes discussed). Typical dishes: duck liver custard, sweetcorn cream, lemongrass and ginger glaze; slow-roasted fillet of Marches beef, braised beefburgers, tarragon and shallot jus; cone of chocolate, blackcurrant and fruit sweeties. The service, supervised by Judy Bradley, gives a 'sense of occasion without being stuffy'. The three spacious suites are decorated in neutral tones. Two have a separate sitting room; the third has an open-plan sitting area and two bathrooms. The timber-framed Shed in the garden is 'attractive and hi-tech'. Breakfast is 'excellent'. (*E and TB, and others*)

Dinham Weir
Ludlow SY8 1EH

T: 01584-874431
W: www.mr-underhills.co.uk

BEDROOMS: 4, 1 in annexe.
OPEN: all year except Christmas/New Year, 10 days June, 10 days Oct, restaurant closed Mon/Tues.
FACILITIES: small lounge, restaurant, function facilities, free Wi-Fi, ½-acre courtyard, riverside garden (fishing, swimming), unsuitable for &.
BACKGROUND MUSIC: none.
LOCATION: below castle, on River Teme, station ½ mile, parking.
CHILDREN: not 2–8.
DOGS: not allowed.
CREDIT CARDS: MasterCard, Visa.
PRICES: per room B&B £235–£365. Set menus £62.50–£72.50. 1-night bookings sometimes refused Sat.

SEE ALSO SHORTLIST

LYDFORD Devon

Map 1:C4

THE DARTMOOR INN

🏵 *César award in 2007*

'On the doorstep of Dartmoor', this old inn on a busy road is run as a small restaurant-with-rooms by Karen and Philip Burgess, 'conscientious hosts'. In the restaurant (a series of interconnecting rooms) and bar, Andrew Honey and Philip Burgess are the chefs, serving 'innovative' modern British dishes on a short monthly-changing set menu or a longer carte. Typical dishes: pork rillette, smoked paprika; wild sea bass, herb crust, celeriac purée, mash. Vegetarian guests were given 'plenty of choice'. There are local ales and a log fire in the small bar, which has its own simpler menu (eg, fish and chips, home-made mayonnaise). A cold supper is served on a Sunday evening. Karen Burgess has decorated the inn with references to Sweden and New England (Swedish linen is among the items sold in a small boutique on the premises). The bedrooms, which have antiques and hand-painted furniture from England and France, are individually styled; each has a sitting area. 'Plenty of hot water in the bathroom.' Breakfast is 'outstanding'. 'We were able to walk all the day in the area.' (*JB, and others*)

Moorside
Lydford, nr Okehampton
EX20 4AY

T: 01822-820221
F: 01822-820494
E: info@dartmoorinn.co.uk
W: www.dartmoorinn.com

BEDROOMS: 3.
OPEN: all year, restaurant closed Sun evening.
FACILITIES: 2 bars, restaurant, free Wi-Fi, shop, small sunken garden, unsuitable for &.
BACKGROUND MUSIC: none.
LOCATION: 6 miles E of Tavistock on A386 to Okehampton, train Exeter/Plymouth, parking.
CHILDREN: all ages welcomed.
DOGS: not allowed in bedrooms.
CREDIT CARDS: Amex, MasterCard, Visa.
PRICES: [2013] per room B&B from £95, D,B&B from £125. Set menu £16.95, à la carte £28.50.

LYME REGIS Dorset

Map 1:C6

THE MARINERS

From Jane Austen's novel *Persuasion* to John Fowles's *The French Lieutenant's Woman*, Lyme Regis, in a designated area of natural beauty on the Dorset coast, has considerable literary connections. This evocative 17th-century former coaching inn, renovated by the owner, William Jeremy Ramsdale, has played its part in history: it was the home of the three fossil-hunting Philpott sisters, and is the place where Beatrix Potter was inspired to write *The Tale of Little Pig Robinson*. The 'attractive decor' is admired by visitors, and it has 'a good garden with a terrace and fine views of Lyme Bay'. Some of the bedrooms have the sea view; all are 'well lit', and have a flat-screen television, tea- and coffee-making facilities. Extras such as fresh flowers, hand-made chocolates and champagne can be provided. In the beamed restaurant, chef Richard Reddaway uses local produce for his 'best of British' menus, with dishes like mussels with shallot, garlic and white wine sauce; chargrilled Dorset sirloin steak, wild mushrooms. 'A good standard of cooking,' one guest wrote. There is also a bar menu and, in fine weather, alfresco dining on the terrace. (*J and TS*)

Silver Street
Lyme Regis DT7 3HS

T: 01297-442753
E: enquiries@hotellymeregis.co.uk
W: www.hotellymeregis.co.uk

BEDROOMS: 14.
OPEN: all year.
FACILITIES: lounge, bar, restaurant, free Wi-Fi, garden, unsuitable for &.
BACKGROUND MUSIC: in restaurant and bar.
LOCATION: central.
CHILDREN: all ages welcomed.
DOGS: allowed.
CREDIT CARDS: MasterCard, Visa.
PRICES: [2013] per person B&B £34.50–£75, D,B&B £59.50–£100. Set dinner £18.95–£24.95, à la carte £25. 1-night bookings sometimes refused high season.

SEE ALSO SHORTLIST

LYMINGTON Hampshire

Map 2:E2

BRITANNIA HOUSE

'An ideal base for exploring this lively seaside town', Tobias Feilke's unusual B&B is formed of two houses opposite each other, close to a marina, cobbled streets and smart shops. *Guide* inspectors in 2013 were charmed: 'Tobias is an enthusiastic, amiable host who has created a warm and homely environment with quirky decorative furnishings and good attention to detail.' An eclectic collection of hats greets visitors in the hall of the older building (which dates from 1865); a 'bright and cheerful' lounge overlooks one of the town's two marinas. 'Our ground-floor bedroom was lavishly decorated in a neo-classical style: brocade curtains with swags and tassels, a large painted wardrobe, Doric columns, classical prints and pistachio walls; good-quality bedlinen, lovely, comfy pillows. The small bathroom had a good shower, fluffy towels.' A room opposite 'was more plainly done with plaid furnishings'. Rooms in the modern building opposite have a neutral decor. All rooms have tea-making facilities. Breakfast is taken around two communal tables in a country-style kitchen: 'We enjoyed a hearty dish of eggs, delicious local bacon, mushrooms, tomatoes.'

Station Street
Lymington SO41 3BA

T: 01590-672091
E: enquiries@britannia-house.com
W: www.britannia-house.com

BEDROOMS: 5, 2 on ground floor.
OPEN: all year.
FACILITIES: lounge, kitchen/breakfast room, free Wi-Fi, courtyard garden, unsuitable for &.
BACKGROUND MUSIC: none.
LOCATION: 2 mins' walk from High Street/quayside, parking.
CHILDREN: not under 8.
DOGS: not allowed.
CREDIT CARDS: MasterCard, Visa.
PRICES: [2013] per room B&B £85–£95. 1-night bookings refused weekends.

LYNDHURST Hampshire

Map 2:E2

LIME WOOD

This 'stunning place', a Regency manor house, has been given a modern make-over and is run as a 'relaxed' country house hotel under the guidance of Robin Hutson (who founded the Hotel du Vin group). 'The staff are extremely friendly and professional,' says a visitor returning in 2013. Kenneth Speirs has joined as general manager from *The Halkin* in London (see Shortlist). The main dining room has been restyled as an informal restaurant, *Hartnett Holder & Co*: Angela Hartnett joined the chef Luke Holder to create a menu of dishes with New Forest ingredients given an Italian twist. 'It is very much improved: vibrant, colourful and dynamic; the food, especially the fish, is delicious.' The *Scullery* is now used for breakfast and private parties: 'An excellent buffet table and atmosphere (we stayed well away from the noise of the radio).' The bedrooms are in the main house and three 'beautifully designed' buildings in the grounds. 'Our small room, the cheapest, was well appointed, except that it had an uncomfortable chaise longue but no armchair – the only fault we could find. A lovely bathroom.' (*Barbara Watkinson*)

Beaulieu Road
Lyndhurst SO43 7FZ

T: 02380-287177
F: 02380-287199
E: info@limewood.co.uk
W: www.limewoodhotel.co.uk

BEDROOMS: 29, 5 on ground floor, 2 suitable for &, 5 in *Crescent*, 5 in *Coach House*, 5 in *Pavilion*.
OPEN: all year, restaurant closed for lunch Mon.
FACILITIES: lifts, ramps, bar, 2 lounges, library, 2 restaurants, private dining rooms, civil wedding licence, free Wi-Fi, spa (16-metre swimming pool), 14-acre gardens.
BACKGROUND MUSIC: in communal areas.
LOCATION: in New Forest, 12 miles SW of Southampton.
CHILDREN: all ages welcomed.
DOGS: allowed in selected bedrooms.
CREDIT CARDS: Amex, MasterCard, Visa.
PRICES: [2013] room £245–£775. Breakfast £13.50 or £18.50, à la carte £45.1-night bookings sometimes refused weekends, bank holidays.

MALVERN WELLS Worcestershire

Map 3:D5

THE COTTAGE IN THE WOOD

❦César award in 1992

'There can be few places more delightful than the terrace of this late Georgian house, with its magnificent view over the Severn valley.' The Pattin family's hotel on a plateau on the Malvern hills continues to win friends: 'Attentive staff and an excellent welcome'; 'All very good again,' are other comments. It is owned by John and Sue Pattin; their son, Dominic, is the chef; daughter Maria Taylor is the operations director. The bedrooms are in the main house (they vary in size), the purpose-built *Pinnacles* (the largest), 100 yards from the main building, and four in *Beech Cottage*, each with its own front door. 'The little touches make them special: free mineral water, home-made biscuits, good reading lights, a full-size bottle of handcream, the Wi-Fi code clearly displayed.' The meals are 'beautifully presented and delicious; we had goat's cheese risotto; seared sea bass; superb white chocolate and raspberry cheesecake'. 'Not only was our carnivore happy; the vegetarian was well catered for.' Breakfasts were 'up to the standard of dinner'. (*Trevor Lockwood, Linda Darlison, Stephen and Pauline Glover*)

Holywell Road
Malvern Wells
WR14 4LG

T: 01684-588860
F: 01684-560662
E: reception@
  cottageinthewood.co.uk
W: www.cottageinthewood.co.uk

BEDROOMS: 30, 4 in *Beech Cottage*, 70 yds, 19 (1 suitable for ♿) in *The Pinnacles*, 100 yds.
OPEN: all year.
FACILITIES: lounge, bar, restaurant, function facilities, free Wi-Fi, 7-acre grounds.
BACKGROUND MUSIC: none.
LOCATION: 3 miles S of Great Malvern.
CHILDREN: all ages welcomed.
DOGS: guide dogs welcomed, other dogs on ground floor in *The Pinnacles* only.
CREDIT CARDS: Amex, MasterCard, Visa (*2% surcharge on credit cards*).
PRICES: [2013] B&B per room £99–£198. D,B&B (min. 2 nights) £66–£126 per person. À la carte £25–£40. 1-night bookings sometimes refused Sat.

MARAZION Cornwall

Map 1:E1

MOUNT HAVEN HOTEL & RESTAURANT

'All the warmth and comfort you would expect from staying with good friends,' were enjoyed by a visitor in 2013 to Mike and Orange Trevillion's hotel in a village overlooking St Michael's Mount. 'The owners were slightly on the eccentric side, but truly outstanding hosts. The entire hotel is spotless, and the friendly staff are eager to please.' The building has a contemporary feel with overtones of the Orient but 'no ostentation'. There are silks from Mumbai, caskets from Bhutan, the aroma of incense in the lobby. Most of the bedrooms have a wood and glass balcony overlooking the sea; the rooms on the top floor have panoramic views of Mount's Bay. 'Ours was lovely, tastefully decorated and with a comfy bed, small balcony and well-appointed bathroom.' The dining room has been renovated this year and given new banquette seating. Glass doors open on to a terrace with tables and chairs. Lee Groves joined as chef in 2013. The extensive breakfast menu includes fresh fruit, yogurt, cereals; cooked dishes include French toast, kedgeree, omelettes, as well as full English. (*Lauren McCann, and others*)

25% DISCOUNT VOUCHERS

Turnpike Road
Marazion TR17 0DQ

T: 01736-710249
F: 01736-711618
E: reception@mounthaven.co.uk
W: www.mounthaven.co.uk

BEDROOMS: 18, some on ground floor.
OPEN: all year.
FACILITIES: lounge/bar, restaurant, free Wi-Fi in all public areas and some bedrooms, healing room (holistic treatments), sun terrace, ½-acre grounds (rock/sand beaches 100 yds), unsuitable for &.
BACKGROUND MUSIC: bar, restaurant all day.
LOCATION: 4 miles E of Penzance, car park.
CHILDREN: all ages welcomed.
DOGS: allowed in public rooms only.
CREDIT CARDS: MasterCard, Visa.
PRICES: [2013] per room B&B £130–£220, D,B&B £190–£280. À la carte £30–£35. Min. 2 nights on bank holidays.

MARTINHOE Devon

Map 1:B4

✤ THE OLD RECTORY

César award: Devon hotel of the year

The house and garden have an allure all of their own,' says a visitor this year to Huw Rees and Sam Prosser's small hotel in the Exmoor national park. Part Georgian and part Victorian, it was built as the rectory for Martinhoe's 11th-century church. The garden is 'a riot of smartly pruned rhododendrons, cut lawns and a brook brimming with bulrushes'. The house is 'smarter still, not exactly modern or boutique but a long way from chintz'. Bedrooms are in the main building and a converted coach house. 'Ours, Heddon, was a study in beige, with a large, hedonistic bed, a huge bath and carefully chosen furniture. The effect was restful without being soporific.' Huw Rees is the much-praised cook: visitors arriving late were given 'bowls of stunning red pepper soup, fresh rolls and well-chosen cheeses'. 'The best part of our stay was the attention paid by our hosts whose laughter ripples through the house (though never at the expense of guests). The sternest test for a country hotel is when the weather is poor. *The Old Rectory* passed with distinction.' (*David Berry*)

Martinhoe EX31 4QT

T: 01598-763368
E: info@oldrectoryhotel.co.uk
W: www.oldrectoryhotel.co.uk

BEDROOMS: 11, 2 on ground floor, 2 in coach house.
OPEN: Mar–Nov.
FACILITIES: 2 lounges, conservatory, dining room, free Wi-Fi, 3-acre grounds.
BACKGROUND MUSIC: in dining room.
LOCATION: 4 miles SW of Lynton.
CHILDREN: not under 14.
DOGS: not allowed.
CREDIT CARDS: Amex, MasterCard, Visa.
PRICES: [2013] per room B&B from £160, D,B&B from £200. 1-night bookings refused high season and weekends.

MASHAM North Yorkshire

Map 4:D4

SWINTON PARK

🏵 *César award in 2011*

'Elegant, even luxurious, but never stuffy', Mark and Felicity Cunliffe-Lister's mock-Gothic castle in the Yorkshire Dales is 'impressive'. It stands in 200 acres of 'truly beautiful grounds' with a lake and a deer park. Tom Lewis is the manager. There are countless activities in the grounds for adults and children (all ages are welcomed). Visitors trapped indoors by bad weather 'relaxed reading newspapers and magazines in the elegant public rooms'. There's a spa and fitness centre and a snooker room; a private cinema. The bedrooms and suites are on the first and second floors (a lift is available). 'We were surprised by the size of our room and the general level of comfort; we had everything we could ever need,' is one comment. Another reader was impressed with his king-size bed, 'suitable for a ménage à trois'. In the dining room ('tables properly laid, our meal was unhurried and perfectly served'), chef Simon Crannage has a modern style, with dishes like middle white pork, crispy herb buckwheat, treacle roasted carrot. (*Ken and Mildred Edwards, WK Wood, and others*)

25% DISCOUNT VOUCHERS

Masham, nr Ripon
HG4 4JH

T: 01765-680900
F: 01765-680901
E: reservations@swintonpark.com
W: www.swintonpark.com

BEDROOMS: 31, 4 suitable for ♿.
OPEN: all year, restaurant closed midday Mon.
FACILITIES: lift, ramps, 3 lounges, library, bar, restaurant, free Wi-Fi, banqueting hall, spa, games rooms, cinema, civil wedding licence, 200-acre grounds (many activities).
BACKGROUND MUSIC: in bar and dining room.
LOCATION: 1 mile SW of Masham.
CHILDREN: all ages welcomed.
DOGS: not allowed in public rooms, unattended in bedrooms.
CREDIT CARDS: Diners, MasterCard, Visa.
PRICES: [2013] per person B&B £97.50–£207.50, D,B&B £132.50–£242.50. Set dinner £52. 1-night bookings sometimes refused Sat.

MAWGAN PORTH Cornwall

Map 1:D2

BEDRUTHAN STEPS HOTEL

César award in 2012

'Wonderful: spotless rooms, caring staff and excellent facilities, especially for families.' Praise in 2013 for this large white hotel, which is owned and managed by sisters Emma Stratton, Deborah Wakefield and Rebecca Whittington. 'It catered perfectly for all our needs,' says a member of a family group aged from eight months to 74 years old. 'We were worried that the new dining arrangements of an allowance towards meals for each guest might be complicated. It worked: the adults rarely spent their allowance while the eight-year-old certainly did. The food was excellent in both restaurants: the *Herring* was sophisticated with an emphasis on fish; the *Wild Café* with its board menu was relaxed.' There's much to do for all ages; swimming pools, playgrounds, a jungle gym for the children and a spa for their parents. Visitors without children had 'a lovely adult experience; the hotel managed to keep contact with children to a minimum'. 'The fantastic breakfasts have roasted button mushrooms, local sausages and bacon; home-made granola and muesli.' *The Scarlet* (see next entry) is a child-free sister hotel. (*Tracy McGrail, Monica Crosby*)

Mawgan Porth
TR8 4BU

T: 01637-861200
F: 01637-860714
E: stay@bedruthan.com
W: www.bedruthan.com

BEDROOMS: 101, 1 suitable for &.
OPEN: all year except 22–28 Dec, 3–21 Jan.
FACILITIES: lift, 2 lounges, 2 bars, *Herring* restaurant, *Wild Café*, free Wi-Fi, poolside snack bar, ballroom, 4 children's clubs, spa (indoor swimming pool), civil wedding licence, 5-acre grounds (heated swimming pools, tennis, playing field).
BACKGROUND MUSIC: 'relaxed' in bar, spa and restaurants.
LOCATION: 4 miles NE of Newquay.
CHILDREN: all ages welcomed.
DOGS: allowed in some public areas.
CREDIT CARDS: MasterCard, Visa.
PRICES: [2013] per room B&B £75 (single)–£490 (double). À la carte £30. 7-night bookings required in school holidays.

MAWGAN PORTH Cornwall

Map 1:D2

THE SCARLET

'An escape for grown-ups', this striking modern hotel was built by sisters Emma Stratton, Deborah Wakefield and Rebecca Whittington to be 'luxurious without costing the planet'. They run it on eco-friendly lines: sustainable initiatives include grey water recycling; table cloths have been removed from its restaurant to lessen the laundry load; an annual reduction of ten per cent in the carbon footprint. It stands in a spectacular position down the hill from the sisters' other hotel, the family-friendly *Bedruthan Steps* (see previous entry). 'Exceptional service, beautiful rooms, delicious food,' says a visitor this year. The bedrooms are in five categories, from 'just right' to 'indulgent'; each has an outside space and a sea view. 'Our wonderful room was filled with light, and had the most amazing views whatever the weather.' In the restaurant, chef Tom Hunter uses locally sourced ingredients in sophisticated dishes like braised pig's cheek and ham hock beignets, celeriac remoulade; fillet of brill, saffron gnocchi, leek, beetroot, herb fish cream. There is a 'sumptuous' spa with 'reassuring therapists'. Breakfast, from a daily-changing menu, is 'exceptional'. (*Jinder Jhuti, Louise Arnold*)

25% DISCOUNT VOUCHERS

Tredragon Road
Mawgan Porth TR8 4DQ

T: 01637-861800
F: 01637-861801
E: stay@scarlethotel.co.uk
W: www.scarlethotel.co.uk

BEDROOMS: 37, 2 suitable for &.
OPEN: all year except Jan.
FACILITIES: lift, lobby, bar, lounge, library, restaurant, free Wi-Fi, civil wedding licence, spa (indoor swimming pool, 4 by 13 metres, steam room, hammam, treatment room), natural outdoor swimming pool (40 sq metres), seaweed baths.
BACKGROUND MUSIC: all day in bar and restaurant.
LOCATION: 4 miles NE of Newquay.
CHILDREN: normally not under 16.
DOGS: not allowed in restaurant or bar, some bedrooms.
CREDIT CARDS: MasterCard, Visa.
PRICES: [2013] per room B&B £195–£460, D,B&B £280–£525. Set dinner £42.50. 1-night bookings refused Fri/Sat.

MAWNAN SMITH Cornwall

Map 1:E2

BUDOCK VEAN

'Excellent quality, well managed,' says a visitor this year to Martin Barlow's resort hotel on the banks of the Helford river. It is run on traditional lines: 'A bit old-fashioned, reminiscent of the 1940s; it suits us perfectly as we love the requirement for men to wear a jacket and tie at dinner.' Another comment (in 2013): 'The very pleasant staff remember you from your previous visit.' There are 'delightful' public rooms: four lounges, a snooker room, conservatory and two bars. The bedrooms might have a traditional decor but they boast the latest technology: a flat-screen TV, 'superfast' Wi-Fi. 'My excellent room had views of the golf course.' In the formal main restaurant, 'we appreciated the entertainment provided by a pianist during and after dinner'. The chef, Darren Kelly, serves a daily-changing menu of 'excellent' dishes, perhaps pan-seared Falmouth Bay scallops; loin of Cornish wild venison. The same menu can be taken in the more informal *Country Club*. There are many facilities for all ages in the large grounds: a nine-hole golf course, tennis; a spa and an indoor swimming pool. (*John and Eileen Avison, Douglas and Margaret Smith, David RW Jervois*)

Helford Passage, Mawnan Smith
nr Falmouth TR11 5LG

T: 01326-252100
F: 01326-250892
E: relax@budockvean.co.uk
W: www.budockvean.co.uk

BEDROOMS: 57, 4 self-catering cottages.
OPEN: all year except 2–20 Jan.
FACILITIES: lift, ramps, 3 lounges, conservatory, 2 bars, restaurant, *Country Club*, snooker room, free Wi-Fi, civil wedding licence, 65-acre grounds (covered heated swimming pool, 15 by 8 metres), health spa, 9-hole golf course, tennis.
BACKGROUND MUSIC: live in restaurant.
LOCATION: 6 miles SW of Falmouth.
CHILDREN: no under-7s in dining room after 7 pm.
DOGS: not allowed in public rooms.
CREDIT CARDS: all major cards.
PRICES: [2013] per person B&B £71–£163, D,B&B £86–£178. Set dinner £39.95, à la carte £34.50. 1-night bookings refused high season weekends.

MILTON ABBOT Devon

Map 1:D3

HOTEL ENDSLEIGH

Built in 1810 by the Duke and Duchess of Bedford, this shooting and fishing lodge has been restored as a luxurious country hotel by Olga Polizzi of *Tresanton*, St Mawes (see entry). 'The quality of peace and comfort is almost magical,' says a correspondent who has been reporting to the *Guide* for 25 years. 'You are swept into an atmosphere of attention and care. The house is designed for your comfort: you can lounge around all day reading a book or newspaper without feeling that the staff want you out of their way to do their work.' Helen Costello, the manager, 'leads a young team who are always on hand to meet your every need. When the wind blows, fires are lit, and tea and coffee and home-made biscuits are available, not forgetting the delight of afternoon tea.' The house has original panelling and Victorian artefacts alongside modern furniture and contemporary works of art. In the evening, hundreds of tea-lights are lit. Chef Christopher Dyke serves a short modern menu of dishes like venison, Puy lentil salsa, raisin purée, chocolate; salmon, pomme dauphine, red pepper purée. (*Ruth West*)

Milton Abbot
nr Tavistock PL19 0PQ

T: 01822-870000
F: 01822-870578
E: mail@hotelendsleigh.com
W: www.hotelendsleigh.com

BEDROOMS: 16, 1 on ground floor, also 1 in lodge (1 mile from main house).
OPEN: all year except 18–31 Jan.
FACILITIES: drawing room, library, card room, bar, 2 dining rooms, free Wi-Fi, civil wedding licence, terraces, 108-acre estate (fishing, ghillie available).
BACKGROUND MUSIC: none.
LOCATION: 7 miles NW of Tavistock, train/plane Plymouth.
CHILDREN: all ages welcomed.
DOGS: not allowed in restaurant, or 'near afternoon tea table'.
CREDIT CARDS: all major cards.
PRICES: [2013] per room B&B £185–£360. Set dinner £40. 1-night bookings refused weekends.

MORECAMBE Lancashire

Map 4:D2

THE MIDLAND [NEW]

Built as a railway hotel in Art Deco style in the 1930s, in a 'superb' seafront position, this Grade II listed building fell into disrepair. Now 'sympathetically' restored by the small English Lakes group, it was recommended to the *Guide* by regular contributors: 'Excellent; the friendly staff know their business.' We sent an inspector: 'Morecambe may be rough around the edges, but the seafront has been regenerated; *The Midland*, the classiest building in town, is a popular meeting place for locals.' A large open-plan lounge, a bar, and the *Sun Terrace* restaurant are on the ground floor. The bedrooms are off either side of a curved corridor. 'The compact rooms are laid out as if on a ship; everything folds away or is hidden from view; very comfortable beds, though no bedside light.' Each of the sea-facing rooms has a balcony. Tables are well spaced in the restaurant, which has floor-to-ceiling windows. 'There is plenty of choice on the menu: a particularly good salad of Bury black pudding, pear and Mrs Kirkham's cheese; baked hake was perfectly cooked.' (*Margaret West, Anthony Bradbury, and others*)

Marine Road West
Morecambe LA4 4BU

T: 01524-424000
F: 01524-424054
E: themidland@englishlakes.co.uk
W: www.englishlakes.co.uk

BEDROOMS: 44, 2 suitable for &.
OPEN: all year.
FACILITIES: lift, lounge, bar/café, restaurant, free Wi-Fi, function rooms, civil wedding licence.
BACKGROUND MUSIC: 1930s/1950s music in bar, restaurant.
LOCATION: on seafront.
CHILDREN: all ages welcomed.
DOGS: not allowed in restaurant.
CREDIT CARDS: Amex, MasterCard, Visa.
PRICES: [2013] per room B&B £94–£348. D,B&B £27 per person added. À la carte £33.

MORETON-IN-MARSH Gloucestershire   Map 3:D6

THE MANOR HOUSE

'Attractive and welcoming', this old mansion is on the edge of this old Cotswold market town. Inspectors and readers have praised the welcome from its 'unfailingly polite and helpful' staff. It is managed by Simon Stanbrook for the small Cotswold Inns and Hotels group (see entry for *The Lamb Inn*, Burford). The entrance porch (dated 1688 though parts of the building are older) opens on to a spacious lobby with a cosy nook with a log fire and seating to one side. The long reception desk is backed by bold patterned wallpaper. The walls are hung with pictures of dogs painted by a local artist, a theme continued in the *Beagle* bar with its huge mural of beagles. Informal meals can be taken here. There are views of the garden from the formal *Mulberry* restaurant. The chef, Nick Orr, serves elaborate dishes like rabbit bolognaise tortellini; blackened halibut, saffron potato espuma, crisp seaweed, mussel cream. 'Food as theatre,' said an inspector. The bedrooms, reached by winding corridors, are 'thoughtfully furnished and well equipped'. Popular with weddings at weekends (check when booking).

25% DISCOUNT VOUCHERS

High Street
Moreton-in-Marsh
GL56 0LJ

T: 01608-650501
F: 01608-651481
E: info@manorhousehotel.info
W: www.cotswold-inns-hotels.co.uk/manor

BEDROOMS: 35, 1 in cottage, 1 on ground floor suitable for &.
OPEN: all year.
FACILITIES: library, lounge, bar, brasserie, restaurant, function rooms, free Wi-Fi, civil wedding licence, ½-acre garden.
BACKGROUND MUSIC: in bar.
LOCATION: on edge of market town.
CHILDREN: all ages welcomed.
DOGS: 'well-behaved dogs' allowed in allocated bedrooms, 'on leads' in public rooms.
CREDIT CARDS: all major cards.
PRICES: [2013] per person B&B £79–£175, D,B&B £111–£207. Set dinner £39 (£32 if booked in advance). 1-night bookings sometimes refused Sat.

SEE ALSO SHORTLIST

MORETON-IN-MARSH Gloucestershire

Map 3:D6

THE REDESDALE ARMS

On the main street of this pretty Cotswold market town, this 17th-century inn, with its honey-coloured Georgian facade, is run by Robert Smith, the co-owner and manager. 'His welcome is warm and he has a hands-on style,' says a visitor in 2013. 'The service is terrific.' There are original beams, old passages in the bars, and a lounge with leather seating. The new chef, Daniel Ciobotiaru, has brought 'young, exciting ideas' (says Robert Smith) to his modern menus. His 'excellent' menu might include sautéed mushrooms, creamy garlic sauce, melted Gruyère cheese; trio of Old Spot sausages, herb- and bacon-mashed potato. Bedrooms in the main building are traditionally styled; those at the front have double glazing. Rooms in a converted stable block off the courtyard at the back and in the recently completed mews have contemporary furnishings. 'Close attention to detail is shown, especially the lighting.' 'Our Mews room was comfortable and spacious.' The 'little extra touches' – good toiletries, a decanter of sherry, umbrella – are appreciated. Breakfast is a 'generous' buffet. 'A typical town hotel; busy with lots of people chatting in the bar and eating in the dining room.' (*John Frood, and others*)

High Street
Moreton-in-Marsh
GL56 0AW

T: 01608-650308
F: 01608-651843
E: info@redesdalearms.com
W: www.redesdalearms.com

BEDROOMS: 32, 25 in annexe across courtyard, 1 suitable for &.
OPEN: all year.
FACILITIES: 3 lounge bars, 2 restaurants, heated open dining area, free Wi-Fi.
BACKGROUND MUSIC: in all public areas.
LOCATION: town centre.
CHILDREN: all ages welcomed.
DOGS: allowed on lead in bar, not in bedrooms or restaurant.
CREDIT CARDS: MasterCard, Visa.
PRICES: [2013] per room B&B £79–£149, D,B&B £129–£179. À la carte £30. 1-night bookings refused Sat Apr–Oct.

SEE ALSO SHORTLIST

MORPETH Northumberland

Map 4:B4

ESHOTT HALL

The owners, Robert and Gina Parker, have 'tastefully' modernised this 'beautiful period house' on an extensive estate in deep Northumberland countryside. Laura Blakey and Annabel Garven are the managers: they and the 'skilled, friendly' staff have created a 'profound country house atmosphere', says a visitor this year. Period features (a rare William Morris stained-glass window and a flying staircase in the hall) have been retained in the renovation of the 17th-century crenellated house. There are original fireplaces in the elegant lounge and the library which has leather sofas and chairs. The cooking of chef Chris Wood 'is beyond expectation' (a 2013 comment): 'A dish of pink lamb loin and a mini shepherd's pie was sublime; the desserts were equally memorable, with interesting flavours that worked together – elderflower panna cotta, puffed rice shortbread, Eshott rhubarb.' The bedrooms combine contemporary colours with traditional furnishing. Some rooms can accommodate children; dogs are allowed in others. Breakfast has kippers from Seahouses, smoked salmon from Craster. 'We watched the red squirrels on the lawn.' (*D Morrell, Keith Makepeace*)

Morpeth NE65 9EN

T: 01670-787454
F: 01670-786011
E: info@eshotthall.co.uk
W: www.eshotthall.co.uk

BEDROOMS: 11, plus 5 in *Dove Cottage* annexe.
OPEN: all year.
FACILITIES: drawing room, library, 2 dining rooms, free Wi-Fi in library, civil wedding licence, 35-acre estate, tennis, unsuitable for &.
BACKGROUND MUSIC: classical in dining rooms.
LOCATION: 6 miles N of Morpeth.
CHILDREN: all ages welcomed.
DOGS: allowed in 2 bedrooms, not in public rooms.
CREDIT CARDS: Amex, MasterCard, Visa.
PRICES: [per room] B&B £120–£200, D,B&B £170–£270. À la carte £35.

MORSTON Norfolk

Map 2:A5

MORSTON HALL

♔*César award in 2010*

'This very well-run restaurant-with-rooms works smoothly, unobtrusively and without hitch.' Much praise this year from regular correspondents for Tracy and Galton Blackiston's Jacobean flint-and-brick mansion on the north Norfolk coast. Other comments: 'A lovely atmosphere and high-quality cooking'; 'Galton Blackiston is a brilliant chef.' Guests gather at 7.30 pm for drinks and canapés in two candlelit lounges. Dinner is a no-choice four-course menu (allergies and dislikes catered for), taken at a single sitting at 8 pm. 'Fresh local ingredients are allowed to shine; a starter of sage, roasted celeriac with truffle was simple, brilliant.' Bedrooms in the main building are decorated in country house style. 'Our spacious room was well equipped and had lovely views over the garden; a superb bathroom.' Suites in the pavilion have a more modern style: 'No trendy touches, just good taste enhanced by thoughtful extras.' Breakfast has a 'delicious warm beignet to start, an excellent full English; very good home-made bread and a good croissant meant a long walk was needed'. (*David Hampshire, Richard and Jill Burridge, Wolfgang Stroebe*)

Morston, Holt
NR25 7AA

T: 01263-741041
F: 01263-740419
E: reception@morstonhall.com
W: www.morstonhall.com

BEDROOMS: 13, 6 in garden pavilion on ground floor.
OPEN: all year except Christmas/New Year, 1–29 Jan, restaurant closed midday except Sun.
FACILITIES: hall, lounge, sunroom, conservatory, restaurant, free Wi-Fi, 3½-acre garden (pond, croquet).
BACKGROUND MUSIC: None.
LOCATION: 2 miles W of Blakeney.
CHILDREN: all ages welcomed.
DOGS: not allowed in public rooms.
CREDIT CARDS: all major cards.
PRICES: per person D,B&B £170–£195. Set dinner £65. 1-night bookings sometimes refused Sat.

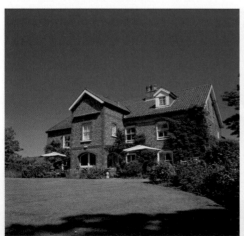

MOUSEHOLE Cornwall

Map 1:E1

THE OLD COASTGUARD **NEW**

'Highly recommended for the very relaxed
atmosphere,' says a regular *Guide* correspondent
in 2013, earning a full entry for this informal
seaside hotel and restaurant. It is managed by
Kay Bolt for the owners, Charles and Edmund
Inkin. The brothers have continued renovation,
bringing the trademark features of their other
hotels (the *Felin Fach Griffin* in Felin Fach,
Wales, and *The Gurnard's Head*, Zennor, see
entries). Most bedrooms now have a tongue-
and-groove panelled headboard, mustard yellow
walls, sale-room finds; there are books, a Roberts
radio but no TV. 'Our room had the wacky
feature of a bath in the window; it was a treat to
lie in it watching the sun rise over the sea.' A
lower lounge runs the length of the building;
'guests were sitting here reading, playing board
games, snoozing'. A snack menu is served in the
afternoon. Well-spaced tables in the dining
room also have the view over a subtropical
garden to the sea. Chef Tom Symons serves a
seasonal menu of dishes like crab rarebit, toast;
lamb shoulder shepherd's pie, minted peas.
Radio 4 plays at breakfast which otherwise 'hits
all the buttons'. (*Kay Birchley*)

Mousehole
Penzance TR19 6PR

T: 01736-731222
E: enquiries@oldcoastguardhotel.
  co.uk
W: www.oldcoastguardhotel.co.uk

BEDROOMS: 14.
OPEN: all year except 4 days in Dec,
24/25 Dec.
FACILITIES: bar, sun terrace, dining
room, free Wi-Fi in bar only, small
garden.
BACKGROUND MUSIC: Radio 4 at
breakfast, selected music during
meals.
LOCATION: edge of village, 2 miles S
of Newlyn.
CHILDREN: all ages welcomed.
DOGS: not allowed in dining room.
CREDIT CARDS: MasterCard, Visa.
PRICES: [2013] per room B&B £110–
£195, D,B&B £150–£235. À la carte
£24. 1-night bookings sometimes
refused Sat.

MULLION COVE Cornwall

Map 1:E2

MULLION COVE HOTEL

The hands-on Grose family run this former railway hotel on a cliff-top on the Lizard peninsula with their 'friendly, non-intrusive staff'. There are floor-to-ceiling windows looking out to the sea, easy chairs and settees in the lounges. In the *Atlantic View* restaurant, the 'daily-changing menu was a delight'; fresh fish and seafood feature in dishes like tempura-fried salmon goujons, avocado and pea shoot salad; grilled fillet of St Ives skate wing, brown shrimp, parsley butter. 'The staff went out of their way to help a visitor with significant dietary requirements.' More informal meals can be taken in the Art Deco-inspired *Glenbervie* bar. Most of the renovated bedrooms face the sea. 'We had fabulous views from triple-aspect bay windows in our room in a round tower. Housekeeping was excellent; we had fresh fruit in the room every day, plus delicious home-made flapjacks.' The breakfast buffet selection is 'very good indeed'; in addition to the usual cooked dishes, there are eggs Benedict and grilled kippers. Dogs are welcomed (free off-season): they are given a welcome pack and have outdoor washing facilities. (*MTS, and others*)

25% DISCOUNT VOUCHERS

Mullion
Helston TR12 7EP

T: 01326-240328
F: 01326-240998
E: enquiries@mullion-cove.co.uk
W: www.mullion-cove.co.uk

BEDROOMS: 30, some on ground floor.
OPEN: all year.
FACILITIES: lift, 3 lounges, bar, restaurant, free Wi-Fi, 3-acre garden, heated outdoor swimming pool (11 by 5.5 metres).
BACKGROUND MUSIC: 'easy listening' in bar.
LOCATION: on edge of village.
CHILDREN: all ages welcomed.
DOGS: allowed in some bedrooms, 1 lounge.
CREDIT CARDS: Amex, MasterCard, Visa.
PRICES: [2013] per room B&B £100–£320, D,B&B £150–£370. Set dinner £36.

NEAR SAWREY Cumbria

Map 4: inset C2

EES WYKE COUNTRY HOUSE

'Beautiful views, excellent food, friendly atmosphere' were enjoyed this year by a guest on his fifth visit to Richard and Margaret Lee's 'good-value' hotel overlooking the scenic forests and fells of the Lake District. The white-painted Georgian house was once rented by Beatrix Potter, author of the Peter Rabbit books. Six of the simple bedrooms have en suite facilities: two have a private bathroom across a landing (dressing gowns provided). The two lounges have comfortable chairs and sofas, a log fire in winter; orders are taken here in a 'friendly country atmosphere' for dinner. It is served at 7.30 pm in a room which looks over the grounds to Esthwaite Water. Richard Lee's daily-changing five-course menu of English/French dishes is 'highly recommended'. It might include pork and apricot terrine with pistachio nuts; sea bass roasted with red onion, pancetta, tarragon and garlic. The wine list is 'reasonably priced'. The award-winning breakfast has a buffet of cereals, fruit, compotes, yogurt, home-made bread and croissants; honey in the comb; cooked choices include locally made sausages and dry-cured bacon, Loch Fyne kippers or poached Finnan haddock. (*ET, and others*)

25% DISCOUNT VOUCHERS

Near Sawrey
Ambleside LA22 0JZ

T: 015394-36393
E: mail@eeswyke.co.uk
W: www.eeswyke.co.uk

BEDROOMS: 8, 1 on ground floor.
OPEN: all year.
FACILITIES: 2 lounges, restaurant, free Wi-Fi, veranda, 1-acre garden, unsuitable for &.
BACKGROUND MUSIC: none.
LOCATION: edge of village 2½ miles SE of Hawkshead on B5286.
CHILDREN: not under 12.
DOGS: not allowed.
CREDIT CARDS: MasterCard, Visa.
PRICES: per room B&B £90–£150. Set dinner £35. 1-night bookings sometimes refused.

NETHER WESTCOTE Oxfordshire

Map 3:D6

THE FEATHERED NEST

♥ *César award in 2013*

'Blissfully rural; the sense of quiet was profoundly nourishing.' A reporter reviewing the *Guide's César* award in 2013 to this country pub/restaurant in a hillside Cotswold village was impressed. Once a malthouse, the old inn has been renovated 'with a sure touch' by the owners, Tony and Amanda Timmer. The view of the verdant Evenlode valley is 'alone worth the journey'. 'The service is flawless,' said an inspector who arrived to find Tony Timmer on his knees lighting a log fire. The bar, popular with locals, has flagstone floors, quirky saddle stools; there is a separate bar menu. In the dining room, where French doors 'bring the light flooding in', the cooking of chef Kuba Winkowski also 'lights up the experience': his seasonal menu of elaborate dishes might include sea bass, razor clam, cauliflower purée, chorizo and haricot beans, minestrone consommé. 'Every morsel was delicious.' The bedrooms are 'beautifully done and thoughtfully equipped'; neutral painted walls; patterned fabrics for blinds, cushions and bedhead adding a splash of colour; 'a smashing double-aspect bathroom'. Breakfast was 'of the highest quality'.

Nether Westcote
Chipping Norton OX7 6SD

T: 01993-833030
F: 01993-833031
E: info@thefeatherednestinn.co.uk
W: www.thefeatherednestinn.co.uk

BEDROOMS: 4.
OPEN: all year except 25 Dec, restaurant closed Mon except bank holidays.
FACILITIES: bar, dining room, garden room, free Wi-Fi, civil wedding licence, unsuitable for &.
BACKGROUND MUSIC: soft in public areas.
LOCATION: in village.
CHILDREN: all ages welcomed.
DOGS: not allowed.
CREDIT CARDS: Amex, MasterCard, Visa.
PRICES: [2013] per room B&B single £105–£135, double £150–£200. À la carte £55. 1-night bookings refused weekends.

NETLEY MARSH Hampshire

Map 2:E2

HOTEL TERRAVINA

🔖 *César award in 2009*

'This hotel deserved its award from the *Guide*; it uplifts the spirits with its sunny modern decor and the warm welcome from the staff.' Praise in 2013 from a regular correspondent for Gérard and Nina Basset's small hotel in the New Forest. The red brick Victorian building has been given a bright interior with warm Mediterranean colours, glass panels, natural wood or slate flooring. In the dining room, George Blogg is the head chef, cooking modern dishes with 'a Californian influence', perhaps treacle-cured salmon, citrus and potato salad; guineafowl breast, mashed potato, coq au vin garnish. The 'delicate flavours' and extensive wine list (Gérard Basset is an award-winning sommelier) were admired this year. Menus were 'cheerfully adapted' for a visitor with a dairy intolerance. A new fine-dining restaurant has opened (Saturday to Monday). Bedrooms are 'attractively furnished, if somewhat quirky; several have a bath in the bedroom'. Many have a patio or terrace; all are decorated in neutral colours and have state-of-the-art fittings, air conditioning, espresso coffee machine; a deluge rain shower in the bathroom. (*Jane Bailey*)

174 Woodlands Road
Netley Marsh
nr Southampton SO40 7GL

T: 02380-293784
F: 02380-293627
E: info@hotelterravina.co.uk
W: www.hotelterravina.co.uk

BEDROOMS: 11, some on ground floor, 1 suitable for ♿.
OPEN: all year.
FACILITIES: ramp, lounge, bar, restaurant, private dining room, free Wi-Fi, civil wedding licence, 1-acre grounds (heated outdoor swimming pool).
BACKGROUND MUSIC: none.
LOCATION: NW of Southampton, 2 miles W of Totton.
CHILDREN: all ages welcomed.
DOGS: not allowed.
CREDIT CARDS: Amex, MasterCard, Visa.
PRICES: [2013] per room B&B £155–£265, D,B&B £215–£245. Set menu £21–£27, tasting menu £65, à la carte £45–£50. 2-night bookings preferred at weekends (check with hotel).

NEW MILTON Hampshire

CHEWTON GLEN

'An impressive place, very well run; your name is remembered and staff greet you when you pass them.' In large grounds on the edge of the New Forest, this privately owned country house hotel, managed by Andrew Stembridge, has a staff/guest ratio of three to one. 'Attention to detail is excellent; everyone is extremely helpful and polite,' is a comment in 2013. The 12 new tree-house suites on stilts in the grounds are 'great fun'. They have a wood-burning stove, picture windows, a whirlpool tub on a wrap-around terrace. 'The view from our bed was of trees and greenery; you can play Tarzan and Jane. Continental breakfast arrived through a hatch while we slept.' Bedrooms in the main house have antiques, modern fabrics ('alas, lighting too dim for reading'). Many have a terrace or balcony. In the contemporary *Vetiver* restaurant, Luke Matthews uses vegetables and herbs from the walled garden, fish landed at nearby Mudeford quay, for his 'eclectic' dishes, perhaps roast halibut, fennel purée, brown shrimp. There's much to do in the grounds ('it's like a resort hotel'). Children are welcomed. (*Natalie Fiorentino, and others*)

Christchurch Road
New Milton BH25 6QS

T: 01425-275341
F: 01425-272310
E: reservations@chewtonglen.com
W: www.chewtonglen.com

BEDROOMS: 70, 14 on ground floor, 12 tree-house suites in grounds, 1 suitable for &.
OPEN: all year.
FACILITIES: 3 lounges, bar, restaurant, function rooms, free Wi-Fi, civil wedding licence, spa, indoor 17-metre swimming pool, 130-acre grounds, outdoor 15-metre swimming pool, tennis centre, par-3 golf course.
BACKGROUND MUSIC: in public areas.
LOCATION: on S edge of New Forest national park.
CHILDREN: all ages welcomed.
DOGS: allowed in some bedrooms.
CREDIT CARDS: all major cards.
PRICES: [to Mar 2014] room £325–£2,250. Breakfast £26, set dinner £60, à la carte £55. 1-night bookings refused weekends.

NEW ROMNEY Kent

Map 2:E5

ROMNEY BAY HOUSE

♀ *César award in 2012*

In a spectacular position by a pebble beach on the Kent coast, this distinctive three-storey house was designed by Sir Clough Williams-Ellis of Portmeirion fame. Today it is run as a small hotel by Clinton and Lisa Lovell, who have a 'sure sense of detail'. Full of nooks and crannies, the house has a large main lounge with white settees, antique tables and candlesticks; a log fire. A first-floor lounge has a library, games and a telescope ('you can see France on a clear day'). The bedrooms face either the sea or a links golf course immediately behind the house. They are equipped with 'everything you need'; thoughtful extras include a sewing cushion, field glasses. The host cooks a four-course dinner, served in a conservatory dining room, on four evenings a week. There is no choice but ingredients are discussed in advance; his menu might include wild sea bass, saffron risotto; rump of Romney Marsh lamb, fondant potato. 'The food is very good indeed,' said one visitor. A 'faultless' breakfast has a 'good' buffet; freshly prepared hot dishes. (*ES, DL*)

25% DISCOUNT VOUCHERS

Coast Road, Littlestone
New Romney TN28 8QY

T: 01797-364747
E: romneybayhouse@hotmail.co.uk
W: www.romneybayhousehotel.co.uk

BEDROOMS: 10.
OPEN: all year except 1 week Christmas, 1 week early Jan, dining room closed midday, Sun/Mon/Thurs evenings.
FACILITIES: 2 lounges, bar, conservatory, dining room, free Wi-Fi, small function facilities, 1-acre garden, unsuitable for ♿.
BACKGROUND MUSIC: none.
LOCATION: 1½ miles from New Romney.
CHILDREN: not under 14.
DOGS: not allowed.
CREDIT CARDS: Amex, MasterCard, Visa.
PRICES: per room B&B single from £75, double £110–£164. Set dinner £45. 1-night advance bookings refused weekends.

NEWBIGGIN-ON-LUNE Cumbria

Map 4:C3

BROWNBER HALL

'A place for dog lovers to note', this 'sizeable' Victorian country house is reached by a private drive that runs alongside a nature reserve. The 'personable' owner, Hilary Reid, 'came out to meet us in the dark, and offered help with my bag', said a visitor. 'Our three border terriers received a genuine welcome and an edible treat each; they were as pampered as we were.' The bedrooms on the first floor are reached by a 'fine' staircase or a lift. A south-facing room has 'Stag furniture (wardrobe and dresser), two wing chairs, a small bed with a comfortable mattress and soft pillows; good bedside lights; richly coloured curtains; a walk-in shower in the spotless bathroom'. There's a wood-burning stove and wing chairs in the large rectangular lounge; a long table with folders of up-to-date information on the area; a library and an honesty bar. In the smart dining room, breakfast is taken at separate tables: juice, cereals and yogurt on a sideboard; 'excellent' ingredients for the cooked dishes; home-made bread, and marmalade in a dish. Good walking from the door. (RG)

Newbiggin-on-Lune
CA17 4NX

T/F:015396-23208
E: enquiries@brownberhall.co.uk
W: www.brownberhall.co.uk

BEDROOMS: 10.
OPEN: all year except Christmas.
FACILITIES: lounge, dining room, free Wi-Fi, terrace, garden, unsuitable for ♿.
BACKGROUND MUSIC: none.
LOCATION: outside village, 5 miles SW of Kirkby Stephen.
CHILDREN: not under 10.
DOGS: allowed (numbers are limited).
CREDIT CARDS: MasterCard, Visa.
PRICES: [2013] per room B&B single £35–£55, double £70–£90. 1-night bookings refused bank holiday weekends.

NEWCASTLE UPON TYNE Tyne and Wear Map 4:B4

JESMOND DENE HOUSE

❦César award in 2013

At the head of a wooded valley yet just three stops on the metro from the city centre, Peter Candler's Arts & Crafts mansion is 'a very good hotel' (the judgment of a trusted reporter). Original features (ornate fireplaces, stained glass, oak panelling) have been preserved in the Great Hall and the two smart lounges; they stand alongside striking contemporary art and retro furnishings. Scott Davidson is the manager. 'The staff strike the right balance between efficiency and friendliness.' Bedrooms in the mansion have muted colours; suites in the recently built *New House* have a sitting room, big bed, bolder colours. All rooms are 'generously equipped: bathrobes, slippers, bowl of fruit, magazines, and an information pack'. Some ground-floor rooms have direct access to the garden. The cooking of the chef, Michael Penaluna, is much praised. His 'interesting, sometimes unusual, and reasonably priced' dishes might include braised ox tongue, pickled oysters; halibut, couscous, lemon marmalade, bitter cress. 'As we were leaving, a young staff member crossed our path and insisted on carrying our bag.' (*D and KW, P and JT*)

Jesmond Dene Road
Newcastle upon Tyne
NE2 2EY

T: 0191-212 3000
F: 0191-212 3001
E: info@jesmonddenehouse.co.uk
W: www.jesmonddenehouse.co.uk

BEDROOMS: 40, 8 in adjacent annexe, 2 suitable for ♿.
OPEN: all year.
FACILITIES: lift, 2 lounges, cocktail bar, restaurant, conference/function facilities, free Wi-Fi, civil wedding licence, 2-acre garden.
BACKGROUND MUSIC: in public areas.
LOCATION: 5 mins' drive from centre via A167.
CHILDREN: all ages welcomed.
DOGS: only guide dogs allowed.
CREDIT CARDS: all major cards.
PRICES: [2013] per room B&B £130–£400. À la carte £50, tasting menu £55–£65.

SEE ALSO SHORTLIST

NEWICK East Sussex

Map 2:E4

NEWICK PARK

'A beautiful place', this Georgian Grade II*
listed mansion in a huge estate of parkland and
woodland is run as a country house hotel by the
owners, Michael and Virginia Childs. Andrew
Hawkes is their manager. They have restored
the building 'beautifully'. The four 'light and
spacious' lounges have antiques, log fires;
'something for everyone'. In the 'breathtaking'
dining room, chef Chris Moore serves modern
European menus using organic fruit and
vegetables from the hotel's walled garden, and
game in season from the estate; pheasant is a
speciality. His dishes might include ballottine of
pheasant, pear and mustard purée; slow-cooked
pork belly, lentil purée, sage and onion bhaji,
apple and black pudding. Bedrooms, which
overlook the estate and gardens or the South
Downs, vary in size; most have a king-size bed,
Egyptian linens and large windows. Two have a
four-poster, and one has an eight-foot-wide bed.
All are 'well appointed'; smaller rooms have a
shower only. Each of the three rooms in the
Granary, a short walk from the main house,
has a sitting room; two have doors opening on
to a patio. (*PA*)

Church Road
Newick BN8 4SB

T: 01825-723633
F: 01825-723969
E: bookings@newickpark.co.uk
W: www.newickpark.co.uk

BEDROOMS: 16, 3 on ground floor
suitable for &, 3 in *Granary*.
OPEN: all year.
FACILITIES: lounges, bar, study,
library, restaurant, free Wi-Fi,
conference facilities, civil wedding
licence, 255-acre grounds, heated
outdoor swimming pool (12 by 6
metres).
BACKGROUND MUSIC: classical in
public areas.
LOCATION: 2 miles S of Newick.
CHILDREN: not under 3 in
restaurant.
DOGS: allowed in 4 bedrooms, not in
public rooms.
CREDIT CARDS: Amex, MasterCard,
Visa.
PRICES: [2013] per room B&B
£165–£285. D,B&B from £105 per
person. Set menu £42.50.

NEWLANDS Cumbria

Map 4: inset C2

SWINSIDE LODGE

At the foot of Cat Bells, five minutes' walk from Derwentwater, Mike and Kath Bilton's small Georgian Lakeland house is much liked for the 'friendly and attentive service'. It is especially popular with walkers: 'Our stay was peaceful and spoiling; they took unending trouble to explain the most rewarding walks,' say visitors this year. Bedrooms come in three sizes. 'Our superior room at the top was immaculate, with thrilling views of Cat Bells; the pastoral sounds of newborn lambs and birdlife started our day.' Evening turn-down is available; all rooms have a hospitality tray, guidebooks, a sewing kit. There are two 'inviting' sitting rooms. In the candlelit dining room, which is open to non-residents, chef Clive Imber serves a set four-course dinner, which changes daily. His British/French dishes might include butternut squash, sage and garlic soup; slow-braised daube of beef, beef fillet, foie gras, pancetta, gratin potato, sage pesto. 'High-quality cooking, beautifully served.' There's an 'informative and extensive' wine list. The 'yummy' breakfast has local bacon and free-range eggs, home-made breads and chutneys. (*Sarah Marshall and Peter Hayes*)

Grange Road
Newlands
nr Keswick CA12 5UE

T: 017687-72948
F: 017687-73312
E: info@swinsidelodge-hotel.co.uk
W: www.swinsidelodge-hotel.co.uk

BEDROOMS: 7.
OPEN: all year except Dec, Jan.
FACILITIES: 2 lounges, dining room, free Wi-Fi, ½-acre garden, unsuitable for &.
BACKGROUND MUSIC: in Reception.
LOCATION: 2 miles SW of Keswick.
CHILDREN: not under 12.
DOGS: not allowed in house (dry store available).
CREDIT CARDS: MasterCard, Visa.
PRICES: [2013] per room B&B £134–£234, D,B&B £184–£284. Set dinner £38.

NORTH MOLTON Devon

HEASLEY HOUSE

🏆 *César award in 2010*

'There is a deep well of calm to be drawn on' at Jan and Paul Gambrill's small hotel in a 'delightful' hamlet where water meadows run down to the River Mole. The back garden of the white-painted Grade II Georgian dower house fringes Exmoor national park. Original features have been preserved in the house including the fireplace and ceiling. 'Fabulous; the Gambrills are brilliant hosts,' says a visitor in 2013. 'There are wonderful touches: beautiful pictures of Exmoor; fresh flowers on the table at dinner; daily home-made breads.' Paul Gambrill is the 'brilliant' chef, serving a seasonal menu with dishes like butternut squash, ginger and lemongrass soup; breast of duckling, prune and Armagnac sauce, gratin potatoes. There is a 'short, well-balanced wine list with a modest mark-up'. The bedrooms are individually styled: 'Our lovely room had a separate sitting area; the spacious bathroom had every conceivable extra.' Breakfast has freshly squeezed orange juice, cereals, yogurts, 'perfect cooked dishes'. 'A good place to yomp through the fields before sleeping soundly.' (*Simon Rodway*)

Heasley Mill
North Molton EX36 3LE

T: 01598-740213
E: enquiries@heasley-house.co.uk
W: www.heasley-house.co.uk

BEDROOMS: 8.
OPEN: all year except Christmas, private parties only at New Year, Feb, Mar 13/14.
FACILITIES: lounge, bar, restaurant, free Wi-Fi, ¼-acre garden, unsuitable for ♿.
BACKGROUND MUSIC: none.
LOCATION: N of N Molton.
CHILDREN: all ages welcomed.
DOGS: not allowed in restaurant.
CREDIT CARDS: MasterCard, Visa.
PRICES: per room B&B £160, D,B&B £224. Set dinner £26–£32.

NORTH WALSHAM Norfolk

Map 2:A6

BEECHWOOD HOTEL

There are echoes of a 'gentler era' at Lindsay
Spalding and Don Birch's small hotel, a creeper-
clad Georgian house that was once Agatha
Christie's Norfolk retreat. 'Don and Lindsay are
hands-on owners who take an interest in every
guest,' says a visitor this year. 'They are in
evidence most days. Even when they are not,
standards are maintained by a professional and
friendly staff.' The public areas are 'immaculate'.
Tables are well spaced in the restaurant where
the chef, Steven Norgate, serves a short menu
with daily specials. Ingredients are sourced
within ten miles for dishes like medley of
halibut, plaice, monkfish and salmon, crayfish
risotto, tomato dressing. 'Everything is
beautifully cooked and presented: a vegetarian
was given a special menu with delicious dishes.'
Ipod docking stations have been installed in the
bedrooms this year. Rooms in a new wing
overlook the 'well-kept garden'. Evening turn-
down is appreciated. The resident Airedale
terriers, Duke and Tess, 'appear after their walk
at night'. The hosts, who celebrate 20 years at
Beechwood in 2013, 'try to make single guests
especially welcome'. (*Judith and John Albutt,
Andrew Aitken, and others*)

25% DISCOUNT VOUCHERS

20 Cromer Road
North Walsham
NR28 0HD

T: 01692-403231
F: 01692-407284
E: info@beechwood-hotel.co.uk
W: www.beechwood-hotel.co.uk

BEDROOMS: 17, some on ground
floor, 1 suitable for ♿.
OPEN: all year, except Christmas,
restaurant closed midday Mon–Sat.
FACILITIES: 2 lounges, bar,
restaurant, free Wi-Fi, 1-acre
garden (croquet).
BACKGROUND MUSIC: none.
LOCATION: near town centre.
CHILDREN: not under 10.
DOGS: allowed (3 'dog' bedrooms).
CREDIT CARDS: MasterCard, Visa.
PRICES: per person B&B £50–£80,
D,B&B £65–£100. Set dinner £39.
1-night bookings sometimes
refused Sat.

NORWICH Norfolk

THE OLD RECTORY

In mature gardens overlooking the River Yare, this Grade II listed, creeper-clad Georgian rectory with adjoining Victorian coach house is the family home of Chris and Sally Entwistle. Aided by their Birman cats, Rolo and Milli, they run it as a country hotel in the leafy conservation area just east of the city. The 'friendly welcome' was commended this year. Afternoon tea can be taken by a log fire in the drawing room or on the pool terrace. Most bedrooms have south-facing views over the gardens; those in the main house are large, some with a fireplace; those in the coach house have sloping beams and their own entrance leading to the terrace. 'Our standard room had a luxurious bathroom and separate shower.' A visitor this year was troubled by noise from trains. In the conservatory-style dining room, candlelit at night, chef James Perry serves a daily-changing dinner menu using local and seasonal produce. Dishes might include lemon- and herb-cured organic salmon fillet; roasted marinated Shropham pork fillet, cider-braised Puy lentils. Breakfast has a 'wide choice of freshly cooked dishes'. (*B and MB, and others*)

103 Yarmouth Road
Thorpe St Andrew
Norwich NR7 0HF

T: 01603-700772
F: 01603-300772
E: enquiries@oldrectorynorwich.com
W: www.oldrectorynorwich.com

BEDROOMS: 8, 3 in coach house.
OPEN: all year except Christmas/New Year, restaurant closed Sun.
FACILITIES: drawing room, conservatory, dining room, free Wi-Fi, 1-acre garden, unheated swimming pool (9 by 3 metres, summer only), unsuitable for &.
BACKGROUND MUSIC: in evenings.
LOCATION: 2 miles E of Norwich.
CHILDREN: all ages welcomed.
DOGS: only guide dogs allowed.
CREDIT CARDS: all major cards.
PRICES: [2013] per room B&B £130–£200, D,B&B £180–£250 (min. 2 nights). Set dinner £30. 1-night bookings refused weekends (spring and summer).

SEE ALSO SHORTLIST

NORWICH Norfolk

Map 2:B5

38 ST GILES `NEW`

On a street of independent shops, this Georgian town house is styled by the owner, William Cheeseman, as a 'boutique B&B'. 'It meets the two essential features for this claim,' says a *Guide* inspector this year. 'The fine building has stylish interiors and the breakfast, with tasty home-made things, is of the highest quality.' A discreet entrance opens on to a wide lobby and two flights of an 'unexpectedly magnificent central staircase with an interesting modern chandelier'. There are contemporary prints and drawings by local artists everywhere. 'My enormous bedroom ran the length of the house; it was furnished with a mix of antiques (a lovely Chinese wedding cabinet as a wardrobe) and contemporary – dark wood, an eastern-style bed and table, quality silk curtains; a bathroom with tiles and walnut panelling.' A smaller room ('still of a good size') has a shower room. Breakfast, served on delicate handmade crockery in a room off the lobby, was 'a cut above': 'Delicious home-made bread and preserves; light and fluffy buttermilk pancakes with Norfolk bacon and maple syrup; extra toast and coffee was provided; no pressure to leave.'

38 St Giles Street
Norwich NR2 1LL

T: 01603-662944
E: 38stgiles@gmail.com
W: www.38stgiles.co.uk

BEDROOMS: 6, 1 on ground floor.
OPEN: all year.
FACILITIES: breakfast room, free Wi-Fi.
BACKGROUND MUSIC: Radio 3 at breakfast.
LOCATION: central.
CHILDREN: all ages welcomed.
DOGS: allowed by appointment, not in public rooms.
CREDIT CARDS: MasterCard, Visa.
PRICES: per room B&B single £90, double £130–£160. 2-night bookings 'encouraged' at weekends.

SEE ALSO SHORTLIST

NOTTINGHAM Nottinghamshire

Map 2:A3

HART'S HOTEL

❧ *César award in 2007*

In a 'great position' overlooking the city, Tim Hart's striking, purpose-built hotel rises where the ramparts of Nottingham's medieval castle once stood. Adam Worthington is the manager. The 'lovely, modern' bedrooms are 'small but well equipped'; each of six garden rooms has a private terrace. There is no air conditioning in the rooms, 'but a system of louvred shutters works very well'. Dan Burridge is the chef in *Hart's* restaurant, a short walk away; his modern British menus might include veal shin croquette, soft-boiled quail's egg, spring vegetable salad; roast cod, smoked bacon and mustard bulgar wheat, braised leeks. More casual meals are served in the *Park Bar* (which also caters for room service); afternoon tea and pre-dinner drinks may be taken in the hotel's secluded garden. Breakfast has locally produced yogurt, eggs from free-range hens, and breads from Tim Hart's *Hambleton Bakery* in nearby Rutland. 'Breakfast could perhaps have been cooked to order rather than a buffet,' say visitors this year. Tim Hart also owns *Hambleton Hall*, Hambleton (see entry). (*Richard Bright, and others*)

Standard Hill, Park Row
Nottingham NG1 6GN

T: 0115-988 1900
F: 0115-947 7600
E: reception@hartshotel.co.uk
W: www.hartsnottingham.co.uk

BEDROOMS: 32, 2 suitable for ♿.
OPEN: all year.
FACILITIES: lift, ramps, reception/lobby, bar, restaurant (30 yds), free Wi-Fi, conference/banqueting facilities, small exercise room, civil wedding licence, small garden, private car park with CCTV.
BACKGROUND MUSIC: light jazz in bar.
LOCATION: city centre.
CHILDREN: all ages welcomed.
DOGS: not allowed in public rooms, or unattended in bedrooms.
CREDIT CARDS: Amex, MasterCard, Visa.
PRICES: [2013] room £125–£265. Breakfast £9–£14 per person, set dinner £24, à la carte £27–£46.

OBORNE Dorset

Map 1:C6

THE GRANGE AT OBORNE

Reached by a country lane where ducks roam free beside a stream, this 200-year-old former manor house is now a family-run hotel. Owned by Karenza and Ken Mathews, it is managed by their daughter, Jennifer, and her husband, Jonathan Fletcher. 'The family are very much in evidence,' says a visitor in 2013. The public rooms are 'well furnished' in traditional style. In the candlelit dining room, chef Nick Holt serves contemporary English dishes like West Bay crab cannelloni; chicken supreme, wild garlic mousseline, creamed potato. His seasonal menu changes every ten days. The bedrooms have a mixture of styles: some have silk throws and the original fireplace; others are more contemporary. Some have a balcony, or French windows opening on to the garden. 'Full marks for our large room and its fully tiled bathroom.' Facilities for the disabled are 'set up well'. The extensive breakfast has cereals, compotes, fruit salad on a buffet table; a wide choice of cooked dishes includes omelettes, kippers or a full English. The Mathewses have written a guide to Wessex to give guests an 'unbiased' insight into nearby attractions (Stonehenge, Hardy Country, Cadbury Castle). (*K and ME*)

25% DISCOUNT VOUCHERS

Oborne, nr Sherborne
DT9 4LA

T: 01935-813463
F: 01935-817464
E: reception@thegrange.co.uk
W: www.thegrangeatoborne.co.uk

BEDROOMS: 18, 1 suitable for ♿.
OPEN: all year.
FACILITIES: lounge, bar, restaurant, 2 function rooms, free Wi-Fi, civil wedding licence, ¾-acre garden.
BACKGROUND MUSIC: 'easy listening' all day, in public rooms.
LOCATION: 2 miles NE of Sherborne by A30.
CHILDREN: all ages welcomed.
DOGS: only guide dogs allowed.
CREDIT CARDS: Amex, MasterCard, Visa.
PRICES: [2013] per room B&B single £88–£169, double £107–£188, D,B&B single £121–£202, double £173–£254. Set dinner £28–£35. 1-night bookings sometimes refused Sat in summer.

OLD HUNSTANTON Norfolk

Map 2:A5

THE NEPTUNE

A short stroll from the beach, this creeper-clad 18th-century former coaching inn on the north Norfolk coast is a restaurant-with-rooms run by chef/patron Kevin Mangeolles and his wife, Jacki. 'A modest man without airs or graces, he could have been the hired help rather than the *Michelin*-starred chef,' said an inspector who was greeted in person by the chef at the entrance. Inside, the doors are low and there are many steps along the narrow corridors. There is a bar/lounge area with slate flagstones and subdued lighting; pre-dinner drinks and 'delicious' canapés are taken here. 'The food is the thing; and it is really good.' In the 'elegant' dining room with its 'nicely laid tables', Kevin Mangeolles uses local seasonal produce for his menus which might include pan-fried scallops, toasted-rice broth, ginger; breast of Gressingham duck, butternut squash purée, red cabbage. 'The service, by Jacki (occasionally helped by Kevin), was professional and friendly.' Bedrooms are 'compact', some bathrooms 'weeny'; they are 'nicely done up with pleasant fabrics'; 'fine for an overnight stay'. Everything is served at table at the 'exemplary' breakfast.

85 Old Hunstanton Road
Old Hunstanton PE36 6HZ

T: 01485-532122
E: reservations@theneptune.co.uk
W: www.theneptune.co.uk

BEDROOMS: 6, all with shower.
OPEN: all year, except 25/26 Dec, 3 weeks Jan, 10 days Nov, Mon.
FACILITIES: residents' lounge, bar, restaurant, free Wi-Fi, unsuitable for &.
BACKGROUND MUSIC: jazz in bar.
LOCATION: village centre, on A149.
CHILDREN: not under 10.
DOGS: not allowed.
CREDIT CARDS: Amex, MasterCard, Visa.
PRICES: per person B&B £60–£75, D,B&B £105–£125. À la carte £55. 1-night bookings sometimes refused weekends.

OLDSTEAD North Yorkshire

Map 4:C4

⚜ THE BLACK SWAN AT OLDSTEAD

NEW

César award: restaurant-with-rooms of the year

'A real winner; in beautiful countryside, this delightful old pub is now a restaurant-with-rooms with fantastic food.' *Guide* inspectors in 2013 'can't wait to return' to this once rundown pub in a village at the foot of the Hambleton hills. It was bought by the Banks family, who have farmed for generations locally, and meticulously restored. Tom and Ann Banks often work in the bar and restaurant; their eldest son, James, is the manager. In the restaurant, 'a warm, relaxing room with polished antique tables set with gleaming glasses and slate mats', chef Adam Jackson has a *Michelin* star for his innovative cooking. 'Dishes are simply described, which brings an element of surprise on arrival: delicious local asparagus with a warm salad of rocket, Jersey Royals, tomatoes, goat's cheese; perfectly cooked halibut with spinach and basil pesto. Portions just right, presentation superb.' Each of the bedrooms in a rear extension has a private terrace. 'Our lovely room was furnished with antiques that retained a contemporary feel; a striking cast iron bedstead; a leather sofa; a well-above-average hospitality tray.'

Oldstead
York YO61 4BL

T: 01347-868387
E: enquiries@blackswanoldstead.co.uk
W: www.blackswanoldstead.co.uk

BEDROOMS: 4, on ground floor in annexe.
OPEN: all year except 1 week Jan, restaurant closed lunch Mon–Wed.
FACILITIES: bar, restaurant, private dining room, free Wi-Fi, small garden.
BACKGROUND MUSIC: in bar and restaurant.
LOCATION: in village 7 miles E of Thirsk.
CHILDREN: not under 10.
DOGS: not allowed.
CREDIT CARDS: MasterCard, Visa.
PRICES: [2013] per room D,B&B £270–£350. Set meals £25–£70, à la carte £45.

ORFORD Suffolk

THE CROWN AND CASTLE

César award in 2013

Beside the castle in a beautiful and quiet Suffolk village, this red brick inn is owned and run by TV presenter Ruth Watson, her husband, David, and Tim Sunderland, the partner/ manager. The owners 'clearly know how to hire, and keep, good staff', said a reporter this year. A reader agrees: 'The staff are well trained, always anxious to help.' 'You feel they really want you to be there,' is a comment in 2013. Bedrooms in the main house have sea views; each of the rooms in the garden (umbrellas are provided) has a terrace facing the castle. 'Our room was warm and inviting; in bad weather it is a pleasure to stay in and read.' Two terrace rooms which interconnect through a common lobby are new. Ruth Watson, who oversees the cooking, has been joined by a new head chef, Charlene Gavazzi. A new menu was introduced in June 2013 with Italian dishes (risotto alla Milanese) alongside British favourites (steak and kidney pie, mash, buttered cabbage). Breakfast is 'a rural feast'. (*John Saul, CH, and others*)

Orford, nr Woodbridge
IP12 2LJ

T: 01394-450205
E: info@crownandcastle.co.uk
W: www.crownandcastle.co.uk

BEDROOMS: 21, 10 (all on ground floor) in garden, 3 (on ground floor) in terrace.
OPEN: all year.
FACILITIES: lounge/bar, restaurant, private dining room, gallery (with Wi-Fi), 1-acre garden.
BACKGROUND MUSIC: none.
LOCATION: market square.
CHILDREN: not under 8 in hotel and *Trinity* restaurant (any age at lunch).
DOGS: allowed in bar, 5 garden rooms.
CREDIT CARDS: MasterCard, Visa.
PRICES: per room B&B £130–£245, D,B&B £199–£315. À la carte £32. 1-night bookings refused Fri/Sat.

OSWESTRY Shropshire

Map 3:B4

PEN-Y-DYFFRYN

♥ *César award in 2003*

In 'beautiful countryside' on the last hill in
Shropshire (a stream below marks the border
with Wales), this former Georgian rectory is
now a small country hotel owned by Miles and
Audrey Hunter. 'Everyone from guests, to the
owners and staff was smiling, which made the
experience relaxed and stress free,' one visitor
found. Complimentary tea is given to arriving
guests, on the terrace in fine weather or in front
of a log fire on chillier days. Many of the
'delightful' bedrooms are south facing; each of
the four rooms in the coach house has a stone-
walled patio which opens on to the garden
(useful for walkers and dog owners). A visitor
with poor mobility liked a ground-floor
bedroom, 'which despite being between the
lounge and dining room was pleasingly quiet'.
In the restaurant, with its huge south-facing sash
windows, chef David Morris serves a daily-
changing menu which might include twice-baked
goat's cheese soufflé; roasted breast of
guineafowl with a vegetable and herb broth.
'Dinners were superb.' 'There was an extensive
wine list with sensible prices.' (*CB, and others*)

25% DISCOUNT VOUCHERS

Rhydycroesau
Oswestry SY10 7JD

T: 01691-653700
E: stay@peny.co.uk
W: www.peny.co.uk

BEDROOMS: 12, 4, each with patio, in
coach house, 1 on ground floor.
OPEN: all year except Christmas.
FACILITIES: 2 lounges, bar,
restaurant, free Wi-Fi, 5-acre
grounds (dog-walking area),
unsuitable for &.
BACKGROUND MUSIC: light classical
in evening.
LOCATION: 3 miles W of Oswestry.
CHILDREN: not under 3.
DOGS: not allowed in public rooms
after 6 pm.
CREDIT CARDS: MasterCard, Visa.
PRICES: per person B&B £63–£90,
D,B&B £88–£124. Set dinner £37.
1-night bookings sometimes
refused Sat.

OXFORD Oxfordshire

Map 2:C2

OLD BANK

🏵 *César award in 2011*

'Everything is of the highest quality; the service is brilliant,' says a visitor in 2013 to this modern hotel on the High Street opposite All Souls College. The 'stylish, well-run and discreetly luxurious property' is a conversion of three old stone buildings, one of which was once a bank. Ben Truesdale is the manager. Vast canvases from owner Jeremy Mogford's extensive collection of contemporary art enliven the walls of *Quod*, the lively bar/brasserie, which is regarded as 'an excellent Oxford meeting place'. On one side of a large central bar is a sitting area for 'chatting and drinking'; on the other are tightly packed tables: 'The food is well cooked, and service by the young, well-mannered staff is attentive.' The menu has pizzas, hamburgers and steaks from the grill, and dishes of the day, perhaps 'a delicious risotto of goat's cheese, peas and broad beans'. The bedrooms are decorated in muted modern colours; a spacious room had an 'excellent marble bathroom'. The best rooms have a view of colleges and spires. The *Old Parsonage* hotel (see next entry) is under the same ownership. (*Derek Lambert, and others*)

92–94 High Street
Oxford OX1 4BJ

T: 01865-799599
F: 01865-799598
E: reception@oldbank-hotel.co.uk
W: www.oldbank-hotel.co.uk

BEDROOMS: 42, 1 suitable for ♿.
OPEN: all year.
FACILITIES: lift, residents' lounge/bar, bar/grill, dining terrace, 2 meeting/private dining rooms, free Wi-Fi, small garden.
BACKGROUND MUSIC: jazz in library/bar in evenings.
LOCATION: central (windows facing High St double glazed), access to rear car park.
CHILDREN: all ages welcomed.
DOGS: not allowed.
CREDIT CARDS: Amex, MasterCard, Visa.
PRICES: [2013] per room B&B £165–£461, D,B&B £225–£521. Set lunch/early supper menu (Mon–Fri) £12.95, à la carte £30 (*discretionary service charge 12% added*). 1-night bookings often refused weekends.

SEE ALSO SHORTLIST

OXFORD Oxfordshire

Map 2:C2

OLD PARSONAGE

'One can truly escape the pressures of the twenty-first century here.' Jeremy Mogford's wisteria-covered hotel, built in 1660, stands behind high stone walls in St Giles. It was due to be closed for four months from November 2013 for a 'top-to-bottom' make-over. 'We will upgrade to a higher level without compromising all that the *Old Parsonage* personifies,' we are told. Sally Conran will oversee the design of seven new bedrooms, and the remodelling of the existing rooms, which will be given new furnishings and a bathroom. A roof terrace will be converted into a residents' sitting room, and the gardens will be redesigned. The original, iron-studded oak door will be retained, and the bar/restaurant and club-like lounge will keep their character – with new Bloomsbury period prints. Tom Mansfield is the chef; his menu of classic British dishes might include smoked haddock kedgeree; baby chicken, fondant potatoes, wild mushrooms. Bicycles can be borrowed to explore the cycling-friendly city and complimentary walking tours can be arranged. In-room beauty treatments are available. Jeremy Mogford also owns the *Old Bank* (see previous entry). (*RG, PV*)

1 Banbury Road
Oxford OX2 6NN

T: 01865-310210
F: 01865-311262
E: reservations@oldparsonage-
   hotel.co.uk
W: www.oldparsonage-hotel.co.uk

BEDROOMS: 30 (35 from March 2014), 10 on ground floor, 1 suitable for &.
OPEN: all year except Nov 2013–Mar 2014.
FACILITIES: lounge, bar/restaurant, free Wi-Fi, civil wedding licence, terrace, roof garden, small garden.
BACKGROUND MUSIC: 'quiet' jazz in bar/restaurant area.
LOCATION: NE end of St Giles.
CHILDREN: all ages welcomed.
DOGS: allowed.
CREDIT CARDS: Amex, MasterCard, Visa.
PRICES: [2013] per room B&B from £162, D,B&B from £222. Set lunch/early supper £15.95–£18.95, à la carte £33.25 (*12½% discretionary service charge added*). 1-night bookings sometimes refused weekends.

SEE ALSO SHORTLIST

PANGBOURNE Berkshire

Map 2:D3

THE ELEPHANT

'The staff were friendly and helpful, the food was excellent,' say visitors this year to Christoph Brooke's informal hotel in a busy Thames valley village. Another comment: 'It has a pleasant air; very much a town hotel, popular locally for functions and events.' Christoph Brooke offers 'a return to the opulence of the Empire' in the decor. The public areas have handcrafted Indian furniture, oriental rugs and delicate fabrics. There are overstuffed sofas, quirky furniture – 'many elephant references'. Bedrooms are individually decorated, with some eccentric touches. 'We had an excellently furnished room, giving on to the most attractive garden, which was kept in immaculate order.' 'Our room had a beautiful, large Indian bed (cream-painted, carved wood), interesting furnishings and fittings and a good hospitality tray.' Barry Liversidge, the chef, focuses on locally sourced, seasonal produce for his dishes served in the two dining areas. *BaBar* has a bistro feel; the menu at *Christoph's* might include smoked salmon roulade, avocado and chilli salsa; guineafowl supreme, baby onions and chestnut mushrooms. (*Jane and Christopher Couchman, and others*)

Church Road
Pangbourne
RG8 7AR

T: 01189-842244
F: 01189-767346
E: reception@elephanthotel.co.uk
W: www.elephanthotel.co.uk

BEDROOMS: 22, 8 in annexe, 4 on ground floor, 1 suitable for &.
OPEN: all year.
FACILITIES: bar, 2 lounges, restaurant, conference rooms, free Wi-Fi, civil wedding licence, garden.
BACKGROUND MUSIC: variety.
LOCATION: in village, 6 miles NW of Reading.
CHILDREN: all ages welcomed.
DOGS: allowed.
CREDIT CARDS: Amex, MasterCard, Visa.
PRICES: [2013] per person B&B £77.50, D,B&B £107.50. À la carte £27.50.

PENZANCE Cornwall

Map 1:E1

THE ABBEY HOTEL

César award in 1985

'What a lovely, relaxed place.' This Georgian town house in the oldest part of the town is run as a small B&B hotel by the Cox family. 'It is as low-key as you might expect for a place run by Thaddeus Cox, a charming, laid-back host,' said *Guide* inspectors this year. The building has a vivid blue exterior; the interiors are equally bold – scarlet walls and carpets in the halls and corridors. The quirky bedrooms are individually styled: 'Our spacious first-floor room was beautifully proportioned; the lavatory and shower were in a cupboard behind faux bookcases, and a washbasin was concealed in another cupboard. There were two lovely armchairs, thick curtains and shutters for the large sash windows which overlooked the harbour.' The largest room has floor-to-ceiling windows overlooking the bay; a bathroom facing the *Abbey*'s private garden. Afternoon tea and pre-supper drinks can be taken in a 'wonderful' drawing room with three-seater sofas, books and magazines. Breakfast, in an oak-panelled dining room, is 'well done'. No evening meals in the hotel: the Cox family also owns the restaurant/bar next door, *Slipway*.

Abbey Street
Penzance TR18 4AR

T: 01736-366906
E: hotel@theabbeyonline.co.uk
W: www.theabbeyonline.co.uk

BEDROOMS: 6, also 2 apartments in adjoining building.
OPEN: Mar–Jan, except Christmas.
FACILITIES: drawing room, dining room, free Wi-Fi, garden, unsuitable for &.
BACKGROUND MUSIC: none.
LOCATION: 300 yds from centre, parking.
CHILDREN: all ages welcomed.
DOGS: not allowed in dining room.
CREDIT CARDS: Amex, MasterCard, Visa.
PRICES: [2013] per room B&B single £75–£120, double £100–£200. 1-night bookings refused bank holidays.

PENZANCE Cornwall

Map 1:E1

HOTEL PENZANCE

'As comfortable as it is good looking', Stephen and Yvonne Hill's small hotel stands on a hill above the harbour. It 'exceeded expectations' this year. Another comment: 'The welcome was warm; throughout my stay I was treated like a friend.' The hotel is a conversion of two Edwardian merchants' houses in a quiet residential area; there is a heated swimming pool in the subtropical gardens. Many of the bedrooms have the views; four have a Juliet balcony. All have bright colours, bathrobes, fresh coffee and a range of teas. 'Everything was spotless in our room (No. 17), which had wonderful views of St Michael's Mount on one side and the harbour on the other.' In the *Bay* restaurant, chef Ben Reeve serves a seasonal menu of modern dishes like sesame-roasted tuna, pickled wild mushrooms; pan-fried breast of wild pigeon and partridge. A lobster and shellfish menu is available (at 24 hours' notice) as is a vegan selection. There is an exhibition of work by local artists. Breakfast (which has home-made bread, a buffet of cereals and fruit, a 'fine grill') is of 'particular note'.

25% DISCOUNT VOUCHERS

Britons Hill
Penzance TR18 3AE

T: 01736-363117
F: 01736-350970
E: reception@hotelpenzance.com
W: www.hotelpenzance.com

BEDROOMS: 25, 2 on ground floor.
OPEN: all year.
FACILITIES: ramps, 3 lounges, bar/restaurant, free Wi-Fi, civil wedding licence, ½-acre garden, terrace, 15-metre swimming pool, rock beach.
BACKGROUND MUSIC: in restaurant.
LOCATION: on hill, ½ mile from centre.
CHILDREN: all ages welcomed.
DOGS: not allowed in restaurant.
CREDIT CARDS: Amex (2½% *surcharge*), MasterCard, Visa.
PRICES: [2013] per room B&B single £89–£94, double £145–£205. D,B&B £30 per person added, set dinner from £25, à la carte £36.

PETERSFIELD Hampshire

Map 2:E3

JSW

'The food is always excellent,' says a trusted reporter in 2013 visiting Jake Watkins's smart restaurant-with-rooms near the centre of this busy market town. The owner/chef has a *Michelin* star for his modern British cooking. The 17th-century former coaching inn has old beams, a cellar (stocked with 900 wine choices) and three tunnels to other buildings in the town. In the cream-coloured dining room, tables are 'generously' spaced; there is outdoor seating under cream umbrellas in the rear courtyard. Cooking is kept simple 'to allow the ingredients to speak for themselves'. 'We enjoyed a winter vegetable soup with Parmesan croutons; guineafowl with sweetcorn. Best of all were Jake's chocolate truffles that accompanied coffee.' There are five- and seven-course tasting menus with optional matching wines, and a separate vegetarian menu. Three of the bedrooms overlook the street, the fourth faces the rear courtyard. Decorated in shades of cream and brown, all have LCD TV, shower cabinet (no bath). A continental breakfast, delivered to the room, has muesli, freshly squeezed orange juice, pastries from a Parisian market, home-made bread and preserves. (*BB*)

20 Dragon Street
Petersfield GU31 4JJ

T: 01730-262030
E: jsw.restaurant@btconnect.com
W: www.jswrestaurant.com

BEDROOMS: 4.
OPEN: all year except Sun/Mon, 2 weeks Jan and Aug.
FACILITIES: restaurant, free Wi-Fi, courtyard, unsuitable for &.
BACKGROUND MUSIC: none.
LOCATION: town centre.
CHILDREN: over-5s welcomed as long as well behaved, not allowed at dinner Fri/Sat.
DOGS: not allowed.
CREDIT CARDS: all major cards.
PRICES: [2013] per room B&B single £80–£105, double £95–£120, D,B&B £185–£310. Set dinner £27.50–£32.50, à la carte £49.50. 1-night bookings refused Fri, Sat.

PETWORTH West Sussex

THE OLD RAILWAY STATION

King Edward VII used this railway station on visits to nearby Goodwood. Now the old wooden building and four Pullman carriages on the disused track bed form a B&B with a difference. It is run by the owners, Gudmund Olafsson and Catherine Stormont. Reception is at the ticket window; tea and coffee are served in the old waiting room, which has leather-buttoned sofas and chairs, 'intriguing railwayana including a display about the station's history'. In warm weather, drinks can be taken on the platform. The two largest bedrooms are in the main building (one is up a spiral staircase); eight rooms are in the carriages, each divided into two bedrooms, each with a separate entrance. 'Our room, the Alicante, was somewhat narrow but well furnished; it had a surprisingly spacious bathroom; guests will need a certain amount of agility to stay in such a room.' Breakfast, 'splendid and unhurried', has 'excellent' ingredients; 'a platter of cold meats and a vegetarian dish are alternatives to the cooked choices'. It can be taken in the waiting room or in the carriage. (*A and MK*)

Petworth GU28 0JF

T: 01798-342346
F: 01798-343066
E: info@old-station.co.uk
W: www.old-station.co.uk

BEDROOMS: 10, 8 in Pullman carriages, 1 suitable for &.
OPEN: all year except 24–26 Dec.
FACILITIES: lounge/bar/breakfast room, free Wi-Fi, platform/terrace, 2-acre garden.
BACKGROUND MUSIC: soft 1940s–1960s in waiting room.
LOCATION: 1½ miles S of Petworth.
CHILDREN: not under 10.
DOGS: not allowed.
CREDIT CARDS: Amex, MasterCard, Visa.
PRICES: [2013] per room B&B £78–£230. 1-night bookings refused weekends and during Goodwood events.

PICKERING North Yorkshire

Map 4:D4

THE WHITE SWAN INN

The hub of community life on the main street of a 'nice old market town', this 16th-century former coaching inn is managed by Catherine Feather for Victor and Marion Buchanan, the owners for 28 years. They guarantee that the 'sound of piped music won't intrude on your drink' in the small wood-panelled bar (or indeed the rest of the building). Hotel guests can sit in the *Bothy*, a converted barn which has a wood-burning stove, sofas, complimentary tea, coffee and biscuits, newspapers and magazines and a television. The bedrooms on the first and second floors of the main building are traditionally styled; rooms in the *Hideaway*, converted stables across an open courtyard, are more contemporary; Superior rooms have a separate sitting area; one has a TV you can watch from the bath. The information pack is 'a masterpiece of amusing comments'. In the dining room, the long-serving chef, Darren Clemmit, serves 'honest food'; perhaps roast confit of duck leg, orange and apricot chutney; Whitby fish and chips, posh peas and tartare sauce. Breakfast has 'very good marmalade', cereals, fruit, and cooked options. More reports, please.

Market Place
Pickering YO18 7AA

T: 01751-472288
F: 01751-475554
E: welcome@white-swan.co.uk
W: www.white-swan.co.uk

BEDROOMS: 21, 9 in annexe.
OPEN: all year.
FACILITIES: ramps to ground-floor facilities, lounge, bar, club room, restaurant, private dining room, conference/meeting facilities, free Wi-Fi, small terrace (alfresco meals), 1½-acre grounds.
BACKGROUND MUSIC: none.
LOCATION: central.
CHILDREN: all ages welcomed.
DOGS: not allowed in restaurant.
CREDIT CARDS: Amex, MasterCard, Visa.
PRICES: [2013] per room B&B single £105–£139, double £139–£179. D,B&B £30 added per person, à la carte £36.

PICKHILL North Yorkshire

THE NAG'S HEAD

'Everything an English inn should be', Edward and Janet Boynton's 300-year-old coaching inn on the main street of a pretty Domesday village attracts many returning visitors. 'The welcome from the hard-working proprietors is always warm; their obliging staff give excellent service without pretension,' says a visitor this year. Another comment (from a reader on his 14th visit): 'I have never been disappointed.' The bedrooms are simply furnished. 'We stayed in the Suite, on the first floor of a separate building adjacent to the pub; pine furniture, large comfy bed; a peaceful sleep is guaranteed.' Pre-dinner drinks are taken in the *Tap Room* (popular with locals), where Janet Boynton takes food orders. The 'lovely' restaurant has 'a huge bookshelf crammed with old books, big mirrors and a fireplace'. The 'large and varied' daily-changing menu might include roast Holme-on-Swale wood pigeon en croûte, dauphinoise potatoes, shallot purée, red wine reduction. Breakfast has 'proper butter', 'hot croissants, good toast'; poached eggs, smoked haddock among the many cooked options. Ask for directions when booking. (*Ian Malone, Alan Parsons, JBH*)

Pickhill, nr Thirsk
YO7 4JG

T: 01845-567391
F: 01845-567212
E: enquiries@
   nagsheadpickhill.co.uk
W: www.nagsheadpickhill.co.uk

BEDROOMS: 12, 6 in annexe, 3 on ground floor.
OPEN: all year except 25 Dec.
FACILITIES: ramps, lounge, bar, restaurant, free Wi-Fi, meeting facilities, lawn (croquet).
BACKGROUND MUSIC: in lounge, bar and restaurant.
LOCATION: 5 miles SE of Leeming.
CHILDREN: all ages welcomed.
DOGS: allowed in some bedrooms.
CREDIT CARDS: Amex, MasterCard, Visa.
PRICES: [2013] per room B&B single £60–£75, double £80–£97. À la carte £28.

PORLOCK Somerset

Map 1:B5

THE OAKS

'Excellent, can't be faulted for service, comfort and food,' says a visitor this year to Tim and Anne Riley's small hotel in an elevated position above Porlock Bay. The imposing Edwardian house stands among wide lawns and oak trees within Exmoor national park. The Rileys, 'a delightful couple', greet guests with tea and cakes on arrival; luggage is carried to the room. The atmosphere of 'old-fashioned courtesy' is appreciated by readers, many of whom are on a return visit. It is 'the kind of place you would expect to see Bertie Wooster pop up from behind a pot plant', say the owners, who are proud of the house's period features. There are two lounges, which have antiques, pictures and coastal views; just the place for 'after-dinner coffee or after-walk collapse'. All the bedrooms have views across Porlock village to the sea. In the *Oaks* dining room, Anne Riley cooks a daily-changing, 'unpretentious', four-course menu which might include smoked bacon, cheese and mushroom flan; breast of local duckling, port wine, ginger and green peppercorns. There is a 'good choice' at breakfast. (*John and Eileen Avison, and others*)

Porlock TA24 8ES

T: 01643-862265
E: info@oakshotel.co.uk
W: www.oakshotel.co.uk

BEDROOMS: 7.
OPEN: Apr–Nov, Christmas/New Year.
FACILITIES: 2 lounges, bar, restaurant, free Wi-Fi, 2-acre garden, pebble beach 1 mile, unsuitable for &.
BACKGROUND MUSIC: classical during dinner.
LOCATION: edge of village.
CHILDREN: not under 8.
DOGS: not allowed.
CREDIT CARDS: MasterCard, Visa.
PRICES: per room B&B £165, D,B&B £230. Set dinner £37.50.

PORT ISAAC Cornwall

PORT GAVERNE HOTEL

In a quiet cove with a shingle beach and a handful of small boats, this unpretentious inn is run by 'caring' owners, Graham and Annabelle Sylvester, with their 'accommodating' staff. Once frequented by the crews of the slate vessels which traded in the port until the advent of the railways, the bar has traditional features: wooden beams, slate floors, cosy corners. It is often busy with locals, and visitors and their dogs (the Sylvesters have four dogs of their own). A narrow staircase leads to the simple bedrooms (several have been upgraded this year): they have traditional furnishings and a hospitality tray. A 'cosy' lounge on the first floor is for hotel guests only. Long-serving chef Ian Brodey serves simple meals (eg, ham, egg and chips) in the bar and the snugs; children have their own menu. In the separate dining room (which has paintings by local artists – for sale) his short menu might include steamed asparagus wrapped in smoked salmon; baked chicken, coriander rice, Thai green curry sauce. The busier village of Port Isaac is reached by a short (uphill) walk to the next bay.

Port Gaverne
nr Port Isaac
PL29 3SQ

T: 01208-880244
FP: 0500 657867
F: 01208-880151
E: graham@
    port-gaverne-hotel.co.uk
W: www.port-gaverne-hotel.co.uk

BEDROOMS: 16.
OPEN: all year except Christmas, 2 weeks Feb.
FACILITIES: lounge, 2 bars, restaurant, free Wi-Fi, beer garden, golf, fishing, surfing, sailing, riding nearby, unsuitable for &.
BACKGROUND MUSIC: none.
LOCATION: ½ mile N of Port Isaac.
CHILDREN: all ages welcomed.
DOGS: not allowed in restaurant, certain bedrooms.
CREDIT CARDS: MasterCard, Visa.
PRICES: per person B&B £50–£60. À la carte £30.

PORTSCATHO Cornwall

Map 1:E2

DRIFTWOOD HOTEL

🔊 *César award in 2010*

'Top marks in every category.' In an 'idyllic'
setting overlooking Gerrans Bay on the
Roseland peninsula, Paul and Fiona Robinson's
seaside-inspired hotel has 'helpful, well-trained
staff', everything for 'a comfortable stay'. There
are books, magazines and board games in the
sitting rooms; children have a games room.
Bedrooms, decorated in shades of sand and sky,
have 'top-quality' linens and towels. 'Our sea-
view room was light and airy. Full-length
double windows opened up to an even better
view of the gardens and sea. The large bathroom
had a window – always a bonus.' Morning tea is
brought to the room with a newspaper (tea-
making facilities, with fresh milk, can be left at
the door). There are 'lots of lovely resting places'
in the terraced gardens; a path leads to a private
beach. In the dining room, *Michelin*-starred chef
Chris Eden's modern European menu might
include an 'outstanding' crispy shoulder of lamb.
'Dinner had a selection of home-made breads,
an amuse-bouche and a pre-dessert. Quite a
feast.' There are home-baked muffins, local
honey and 'superb' cooked dishes at breakfast.
(*Ken and Priscilla Winslow*)

Rosevine
nr Portscatho TR2 5EW

T: 01872-580644
F: 01872-580801
E: info@driftwoodhotel.co.uk
W: www.driftwoodhotel.co.uk

BEDROOMS: 15, 4 in courtyard, also
2 in cabin (2 mins' walk).
OPEN: 3 Feb–9 Dec.
FACILITIES: 2 lounges, bar,
restaurant, children's games room,
free Wi-Fi, 7-acre grounds (terraced
gardens, private beach, safe bathing),
unsuitable for ♿.
BACKGROUND MUSIC: jazz in
restaurant and bar.
LOCATION: N side of Portscatho.
CHILDREN: all ages welcomed, early
supper for children, no very young
children in restaurant in evenings.
DOGS: not allowed.
CREDIT CARDS: Amex, MasterCard,
Visa.
PRICES: [2013] per room B&B
£180–£260, D,B&B £210–£280. Set
dinner £50, à la carte £50. 1-night
bookings refused weekends.

POSTBRIDGE Devon

LYDGATE HOUSE

'In the middle of nowhere', this whitewashed late Victorian house, reached by a private lane, stands in extensive grounds with a footpath leading directly on to the moor. The 'confident, experienced hosts', Stephen and Karen Horn, maintain 'high standards', say visitors. Near the clapper bridge that spans the East Dart river, the south-facing house has exceptional views down the valley. There is a wood-burning stove, a well-stocked library, and a small bar in the lounge. The bedrooms, each named after a bird, are individually decorated: Wagtail and Dipper each have a small sitting room; Kingfisher has an en suite shower. Heron is a double-aspect room (facing both valley and river) with mahogany furniture, an original fireplace; Buzzard is a spacious room with a sleigh bed. In the conservatory dining room, Karen Horn makes much use of local produce. Her daily-changing menu might include grilled goat's cheese with a raspberry vinaigrette; breast of Creedy Carver duck, plum sauce. 'Dinners, of a good standard, have huge portions'; breakfast is 'excellent'. 'Delicious' cream teas are popular with non-residents. 'Very good value.' (*HA, JT, and others*)

25% DISCOUNT VOUCHERS

Postbridge, Dartmoor
PL20 6TJ

T: 01822-880209
E: info@lydgatehouse.co.uk
W: www.lydgatehouse.co.uk

BEDROOMS: 7, 1 on ground floor.
OPEN: all year except 5–25 Jan, restaurant closed Sun/Mon.
FACILITIES: lounge/bar, snug, dining room, free Wi-Fi, terrace, 36-acre grounds (moorland, paddock, river, private access for guests), fishing, swimming, unsuitable for &.
BACKGROUND MUSIC: none.
LOCATION: on edge of hamlet, 8 miles SW of Moretonhampstead.
CHILDREN: not under 12.
DOGS: not allowed in public rooms.
CREDIT CARDS: MasterCard, Visa.
PRICES: per room B&B single £45–£55, double £85–£120. Set menu £27.50.

PURTON Wiltshire

Map 3:E5

THE PEAR TREE AT PURTON

Church End
Purton, nr Swindon SN5 4ED

T: 01793-772100
F: 01793-772369
E: stay@peartreepurton.co.uk
W: www.peartreepurton.co.uk

In large grounds with 'pleasant' walks, a vineyard and a wild-flower meadow, this 16th-century former vicarage on the outskirts of a Saxon village has long been run as a small hotel by Francis and Anne Young. 'Good food and good care' were enjoyed by a visitor this year. The Youngs supervised the conversion of the sandstone building, adding more bedrooms in an extension. The original building has a panelled library with a stone fireplace and a door opening on to the garden. In the formal dining room, spread over two conservatories, the chef, Alan Postill, serves modern dishes like griddled Scottish beef medallions, chargrilled shallots, Puy lentils. White wine from the vines in the garden, Cuvée Alix (named after their daughter), is available. The traditionally decorated bedrooms are well equipped; some have a balcony or terrace; many have a spa bath. There is honey from the hosts' hives and preserves from the village for the award-winning breakfast which highlights local products. The Youngs, who have an 'infectious enthusiasm' for their house and garden, are proud to be 'consciously green'. (*MB, and others*)

BEDROOMS: 17, some on ground floor.
OPEN: all year except 26 Dec.
FACILITIES: ramps, lounge/bar, library, restaurant, free Wi-Fi, function/conference facilities, civil wedding licence, 7½-acre grounds (vineyard, croquet, pond, jogging route).
BACKGROUND MUSIC: none.
LOCATION: 5 miles NW of Swindon.
CHILDREN: all ages welcomed.
DOGS: not unattended in bedrooms.
CREDIT CARDS: all major cards.
PRICES: per room B&B double £125–£200, D,B&B from £196. Set dinner £35.50, à la carte £35.50.

RAMSGILL-IN-NIDDERDALE N. Yorkshire   Map 4:D3

THE YORKE ARMS

♛ *César award in 2000*

'Of course one goes for the food' at Bill and Frances Atkins's restaurant-with-rooms. Their rural inn has a timeless setting on the green of a village in a beautiful Yorkshire dale. Frances Atkins holds a *Michelin* star for her innovative cooking: she uses the Dales as her larder, and grows herbs and vegetables in a field behind the inn. 'When you look at the menu, you think you will have to stay a few days to experience the different temptations,' says a visitor. The 'inspirations from the seasons' menu might include seared tuna, lemon and Caesar, broad beans and squid; squab pigeon, pistachio tapenade, lime jelly, asparagus, morel. Bill Atkins is in charge of front-of-house, creating 'a country house-party atmosphere' in the busy flagstoned bar and the beamed dining room. 'The service is efficient but friendly; people seem to care.' The bedrooms are 'also to be recommended: they may not all be spacious, but they are comfortable; modern bathrooms are well equipped'. Four suites are in a courtyard building; two rooms are in a nearby cottage. (*DH, and others*)

Ramsgill-in-Nidderdale
nr Harrogate HG3 5RL

T: 01423-755243
F: 01423-755330
E: enquiries@yorke-arms.co.uk
W: www.yorke-arms.co.uk

BEDROOMS: 16, 4 in courtyard, 2 in *Ghyll Cottage*.
OPEN: all year, Sun dinner for residents only.
FACILITIES: ramp, lounge, bar, 2 dining rooms, free Wi-Fi, function facilities, 2-acre grounds, unsuitable for &.
BACKGROUND MUSIC: in dining rooms.
LOCATION: centre of village, train from Harrogate.
CHILDREN: not under 12.
DOGS: allowed by arrangement in 1 bedroom, bar area.
CREDIT CARDS: Diners, MasterCard, Visa.
PRICES: [2013] per room D,B&B £290–£430. Tasting menu £85, à la carte £70.

RAVENSTONEDALE Cumbria

Map 4:C3

THE BLACK SWAN

🏵 *César award in 2013*

In a 'peaceful and attractive village' near Kirkby Stephen, Alan and Louise Dinnes's 'cosy pub' is popular with locals and regular visitors. 'It continues to exude warmth and friendliness,' says a returning guest who 'immediately felt at home'. The welcome is 'charming without being effusive'; 'the friendliness of the staff is reason enough to plan a return'. The bedrooms, all different, are 'big, and refreshingly underpriced'. An extra room has been added this year; those on the ground floor have been renovated. 'Ours was comfortable and convenient. An added pleasure was the view of the garden, with daily visits from a red squirrel.' It is 'fun to hear the locals chatting' in the two bars, perhaps over a pint of Black Sheep bitter. Chef Kev Hillyer's 'artisan dishes' can be taken in either bar or the dining room. 'Dinners were delicious: trio of salmon, a tasty starter; memorable lamb and beef bourguignon.' The menu 'is sufficiently varied, so I didn't need to eat the same dish over five days'. Smaller, cheaper portions are available for small appetites. Breakfasts are 'hearty'.
(*Sue Pethen, Trevor Lockwood, Gwyn Morgan*)

25% DISCOUNT VOUCHERS

Ravenstonedale
Kirkby Stephen CA17 4NG

T/F: 015396-23204
E: enquiries@blackswanhotel.com
W: www.blackswanhotel.com

BEDROOMS: 15, 2 in ground-floor annexe, 1 suitable for ♿.
OPEN: all year.
FACILITIES: bar, lounge, 2 dining rooms, free Wi-Fi, beer garden, tennis and golf in village.
BACKGROUND MUSIC: optional 'easy listening' in bar, restaurant.
LOCATION: in village 5 miles SW of Kirkby Stephen.
CHILDREN: all ages welcomed.
DOGS: allowed in 3 ground-floor bedrooms, not in restaurant.
CREDIT CARDS: All major cards.
PRICES: [2013] per room B&B £75–£125. À la carte £26.

REETH North Yorkshire

THE BURGOYNE

'The perfect place to wind down', this Grade II listed Georgian country house is run as a small hotel by the owners, Mo and Julia Usman. It has a 'commanding' position on the upper edge of a village green in Swaledale. 'We were greeted by the chef in his whites,' said inspectors, who commented that the staff were 'well dressed, well trained, and happy in their work'. One of the two lounges is 'clubby', the other more formal: they have original features, cut flowers, magazines, books and games. Seven of the bedrooms are at the front, with south-facing views of the dale. 'Ours was exceptionally comfortable, with a large bed, settee, writing desk and generous hospitality tray.' In the dining room, which overlooks the village, chef Paul Salonga cooks in traditional English style 'with a modern twist': his 'delicious' dishes on a daily-changing menu might include fresh asparagus wrapped in Parma ham, grilled hollandaise; pan-fried Gressingham duck breast, apple purée and orange liqueur sauce. Breakfast has a wide choice of cooked dishes, 'from kippers to eggs Benedict and a full English'.

On the Green, Reeth
nr Richmond DL11 6SN

T/F: 01748-884292
E: enquiries@theburgoyne.co.uk
W: www.theburgoyne.co.uk

BEDROOMS: 8, 1 on ground floor suitable for &.
OPEN: all year, except Christmas.
FACILITIES: ramp, 2 lounges, dining room, free Wi-Fi, ½-acre garden.
BACKGROUND MUSIC: 'quietly' in evening in public rooms.
LOCATION: village centre.
CHILDREN: by arrangement.
DOGS: allowed.
CREDIT CARDS: MasterCard, Visa.
PRICES: [2013] per room B&B £100–£210, D,B&B £150–£288. Set dinner £39.

RICHMOND North Yorkshire

Map 4:C3

MILLGATE HOUSE

César award in 2011

'As good as ever: a house and garden full of interest.' Austin Lynch and Tim Culkin's early Georgian home remains popular with readers. Typical comments this year: 'The owners are full of information about the area and are eager to tell the visitor about everything local, usually at leisure over tea.' 'Their attention to detail extended to putting a bottle of white wine in the fridge for our return from dinner, a gesture much appreciated by our driver.' Guests have 'full use of the magnificent drawing room', which is filled with antiques, fine silver and china, souvenirs and paintings. These 'eclectic collections' extend to the three bedrooms which have 'comfy' chairs, lots of books: the largest has double-aspect windows overlooking the castle and the River Swale. A 'stupendous' breakfast has an extensive buffet of fresh fruit, cereals, seeds and croissants; hot dishes are cooked to order. The house, just off the market square, has award-winning gardens which are open to the public from April to October. A set dinner is available for groups of 16 or more. (*Sir John Johnson, Michael Brown*)

Richmond DL10 4JN

T: 01748-823571
E: oztim@
   millgatehouse.demon.co.uk
W: www.millgatehouse.com

BEDROOMS: 3, also self-catering facilities for 12.
OPEN: all year.
FACILITIES: hall, drawing room, dining room, free Wi-Fi, ½-acre garden, unsuitable for &.
BACKGROUND MUSIC: occasional classical in hall.
LOCATION: town centre.
CHILDREN: all ages welcomed.
DOGS: not in public rooms.
CREDIT CARDS: none.
PRICES: [2013] per person B&B £55–£72.50.

RICHMOND-UPON-THAMES Surrey

Map 2:D3

BINGHAM

A few steps through a garden from the River Thames, this smart hotel/restaurant occupies two extensively renovated Grade II listed Georgian houses. Samantha Trinder is the owner; the manager is Erick Kervaon. The 'opulent' public rooms – the bar a soft silver, the restaurant gold – overlook the river, 'making the most of a wonderful setting'. In summer, French doors are opened to the riverside balcony for alfresco dining. The individually designed bedrooms have Art Deco-inspired furniture and modern touches (DVD-player, an iPod docking station, a built-in music system); best rooms have river views. 'Our compact room had a sofa at the end of the large bed; lighting too dim for reading; a well-equipped bathroom.' Service is 'attentive' in the 'elegant' dining room, where head chef Shay Cooper cooks 'superb' modern dishes, perhaps oxtail and bone marrow, sautéed cèpes, pickled onion. (Vegetarians have their own menu; children choose from a sophisticated selection.) 'We enjoyed a delicious meal with distinct flavours coming through in elaborate dishes.' With fruit smoothies, home-baked bread and fine leaf tea, breakfast 'lived up to the standard of dinner'.

25% DISCOUNT VOUCHERS

61–63 Petersham Road
Richmond-upon-Thames
TW10 6UT

T: 020-8940 0902
E: info@thebingham.co.uk
W: www.thebingham.co.uk

BEDROOMS: 15.
OPEN: all year, restaurant closed Sun evening.
FACILITIES: bar, restaurant, function room, free Wi-Fi, civil wedding licence, terrace, garden, unsuitable for &.
BACKGROUND MUSIC: 'relaxed, elegant' or 'upbeat' in restaurant.
LOCATION: ½ mile S of centre, underground Richmond.
CHILDREN: all ages welcomed.
DOGS: not allowed.
CREDIT CARDS: all major cards.
PRICES: [2013] per room B&B £190–£305. D,B&B £137.50–£195 per person, set dinner £45–£65, à la carte £45 (*plus 12½% discretionary service charge*).

RIPLEY North Yorkshire

Map 4:D4

THE BOAR'S HEAD

♦ *César award in 1999*

On the edge of the Yorkshire Dales, the old village of Ripley was rebuilt in the 1830s based on a French model village, but this 18th-century coaching inn could not be anything but British. Traditionally furnished with antiques, paintings and period furniture, it is part of the Ripley Castle estate owned by Sir Thomas and Lady Ingilby; guests have free access to the castle and gardens. Bedrooms are spread between the main building, the courtyard area and the adjacent *Birchwood House*, which has six 'superior' rooms. There are mixed reports from *Guide* regulars this year; one couple thought the White Room, in the main building, 'very comfortable'; others described the same room as 'cold, shabby with dismal lighting'. Earlier guests liked their 'dog-friendly room, complete with basket and drinking bowl'. Visitors can eat from a lengthy brasserie-style menu with daily blackboard specials in the 'relaxed' bistro and bar or the more formal main dining room. A typical dish: slow-roasted belly pork, braised cheek, mustard-mashed potatoes. Popular with shooting parties, weddings, etc. (*John and Margaret Speake, and others*)

Ripley Castle Estate, Ripley
nr Harrogate HG3 3AY

T: 01423-771888
F: 01423-771509
E: reservations@
  boarsheadripley.co.uk
W: www.boarsheadripley.co.uk

BEDROOMS: 25, 10 in courtyard, 6 in *Birchwood House* adjacent, some on ground floor.
OPEN: all year.
FACILITIES: ramps, 2 lounges, bar/bistro, restaurant, free Wi-Fi, civil wedding licence (in castle), 150-acre estate (deer park, lake, fishing, 20-acre garden).
BACKGROUND MUSIC: 'easy listening' in restaurant and bistro.
LOCATION: 3 miles N of Harrogate.
CHILDREN: all ages welcomed.
DOGS: allowed.
CREDIT CARDS: all major cards.
PRICES: per room B&B single £85–£125, double £100–£150. À la carte £28–£30.

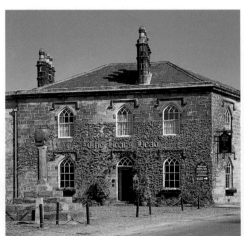

ROCK Cornwall

ST ENODOC NEW

'There's a real feeling of a family operation where everyone cares,' says a regular correspondent restoring a full entry for this child-friendly if expensive hotel in a fashionable north Cornish resort. Kate Simms is the manager. Nathan Outlaw, the high-profile Cornish chef, supervises two restaurants at *St Enodoc*: the all-day *Outlaw's Seafood and Grill*, and *Restaurant Nathan Outlaw* (which has two *Michelin* stars for its eight-course seafood tasting menu). 'We went for the food and found the *Grill* alone worth a detour: outstanding brill with a sauce of potted shrimps. The hotel itself was a pleasant surprise.' A cluster of houses on a hill above the Camel estuary, it has a light, Mediterranean decor with bright colours and original artwork. 'Our well-equipped room had a lovely estuary view; good touches were the comfortable bed, plenty of storage with proper hangers (hallelujah); two armchairs. A decent bathroom with local toiletries and good lighting.' Children have a games room; tea in the grill at 5 pm. 'Breakfasts are very good: an excellent buffet, delicious porridge, plump and succulent kippers.' (*David Hampshire, and others*)

Rock
nr Wadebridge PL27 6LA

T: 01208-863394
F: 01208-863970
E: info@enodoc-hotel.co.uk
W: www.enodoc-hotel.co.uk

BEDROOMS: 20.
OPEN: all year except Jan.
FACILITIES: lounge, library, billiard room, 2 restaurants, free Wi-Fi, spa, heated outdoor swimming pool (May–Sept, 9 by 4.5 metres), terrace, garden, only restaurants suitable for &.
BACKGROUND MUSIC: none.
LOCATION: outskirts of village.
CHILDREN: all ages welcomed.
DOGS: not allowed.
CREDIT CARDS: Amex, MasterCard, Visa.
PRICES: [2013] per room B&B £175–£495. D,B&B (not high season) from £230 per person, tasting menu (*Restaurant*) £99, à la carte (*Seafood & Grill*) £40. 1-night bookings refused weekends.

ROMALDKIRK Co. Durham

Map 4:C3

THE ROSE AND CROWN

In November 2012, this 18th-century coaching inn, opposite the green of a Teesdale village, was bought by Thomas and Cheryl Robinson, local farmers who also own *Headlam Hall*, Darlington (see Shortlist). Henny Crosland has joined as head chef, working alongside Andrew Lee, who has stayed. We sent inspectors in 2013 who reported: 'A lovely hotel and staff; everything in the building, which is most attractive inside and out, was polished and gleaming; the welcome was friendly.' The downstairs area is divided between the main restaurant with a nearby lounge (comfy sofas and chairs, plenty of magazines), and a traditional bar with a bistro area, which serves light meals all day. The restaurant has a 'good-value' set menu: 'We had an excellent parsley and honey soup; asparagus with quail's eggs; delicious sea bream with spinach and new potatoes.' The bedrooms in the main house are traditional in style: 'A large, firm bed, plenty of drawer space, reasonable lighting; a pity about the captive hangers.' More contemporary rooms in a rear courtyard have direct access to the car park (popular with dog owners and ramblers). Breakfast is 'good'.

Romaldkirk
nr Barnard Castle DL12 9EB

T: 01833-650213
E: hotel@rose-and-crown.co.uk
W: www.rose-and-crown.co.uk

BEDROOMS: 12, 5 in rear courtyard, some on ground floor.
OPEN: all year except 23–27 Dec.
FACILITIES: residents' lounge, lounge bar, *Crown Room* (bar meals), restaurant, free Wi-Fi, fishing (grouse shooting, birdwatching) nearby.
BACKGROUND MUSIC: jazz/swing in brasserie.
LOCATION: village centre.
CHILDREN: all ages welcomed.
DOGS: allowed in bar, not unattended in bedrooms.
CREDIT CARDS: Amex, MasterCard, Visa.
PRICES: [2013] per person B&B £75–£95, D,B&B £110–£130. Set dinner £35, à la carte £32.

ROSS-ON-WYE Herefordshire

Map 3:D5

WILTON COURT

Once a magistrates' court where legal battles were fought, Helen and Roger Wynn's restaurant-with-rooms today has 'a peaceful atmosphere' in a 'lovely situation on the River Wye'. 'The standards remain high: more refurbished bedrooms, new china, lovely food, silky-smooth service,' say returning guests (fellow hoteliers) in 2013. Many original features of the part-Elizabethan building have been retained: there are beams, leaded windows, uneven floors, 16th-century stone fireplaces; an ancient mulberry tree stands in the sheltered garden. Decorated with handsome patterned wallpaper, bedrooms overlook the gardens or the river. In the conservatory dining room, head chef Martyn Williams's 'first-class' cooking reinterprets English cuisine 'with a twist', typically Barbary duck breast, fondant potato, summer greens. (Small portions are available for children.) 'The food, which was always good, seems to have got even better. I had the best-ever king prawn starter with horseradish croutons.' (A dissenter, however, deplored the 'repetitive opera music'.) (*Christopher Beadle, Richard Morgan-Price, Huw Thomas, Peter Adam*)

25% DISCOUNT VOUCHERS

Wilton Lane, Ross-on-Wye
HR9 6AQ

T: 01989-562569
F: 01989-768460
E: info@wiltoncourthotel.com
W: www.wiltoncourthotel.com

BEDROOMS: 10.
OPEN: all year except 2–15 Jan.
FACILITIES: sitting room, bar, restaurant, private dining room, conference facilities, free Wi-Fi, civil wedding licence, 1-acre grounds (riverside garden, fishing), only restaurant suitable for &.
BACKGROUND MUSIC: classical at mealtimes in restaurant/bar.
LOCATION: ½ mile from centre.
CHILDREN: all ages welcomed.
DOGS: not allowed in restaurant.
CREDIT CARDS: Amex, MasterCard, Visa.
PRICES: [2013] per person B&B single £100–£155, double £67.50–£82.50, D,B&B £92.50–£175. Set dinner £29–£32, à la carte £40. 1-night bookings refused weekends Apr–Oct.

SEE ALSO SHORTLIST

RUSHLAKE GREEN East Sussex

Map 2:E4

STONE HOUSE

'Well cared for and on good form.' Praise in 2013 from a trusted reporter for Jane and Peter Dunn's country hotel (Tudor with Georgian additions) on the Sussex Weald. The manor house, which has been in the family's hands for more than five centuries, stands in extensive grounds with parkland, a farm, two lakes and a 'truly wonderful' walled fruit and vegetable garden. Another comment this year: 'I cannot fault it: all was perfection. Not for those who favour minimalism, it has beautiful antique furniture, decorative china, family portraits, lovely fabrics.' 'We were greeted at our taxi door by a woman with an impressive manner, friendly without being imposing; she carried our bags and brought fresh milk for our room.' Jane Dunn is the much-praised chef: 'A top-notch dinner with fresh ingredients and simple recipes. The highlights were a cured salmon starter and brown bread ice cream.' The 'delightful' bedrooms are in a grand Georgian wing and the older Tudor section, which has smaller rooms with beams, a sloping ceiling. Breakfast had 'a particularly good fruit compote'. (*Anna Brewer, Zara Elliott*)

25% DISCOUNT VOUCHERS

Rushlake Green
Heathfield TN21 9QJ

T: 01435-830553
F: 01435-830726
W: www.stonehousesussex.co.uk

BEDROOMS: 6, plus 2 in coach house.
OPEN: all year except 22 Dec–3 Jan, 20 Feb–20 Mar.
FACILITIES: hall, drawing room, library, dining room, billiard room, free Wi-Fi, 1,000-acre estate (5½-acre garden, farm, woodland, croquet, shooting, pheasant/clay-pigeon shooting, 2 lakes, rowing, fishing), unsuitable for &.
BACKGROUND MUSIC: none.
LOCATION: 4 miles SE of Heathfield, by village green.
CHILDREN: not under 9.
DOGS: not allowed in public rooms.
CREDIT CARDS: MasterCard, Visa.
PRICES: [2013] per room B&B single £110–£140, double £148–£280. Set dinner from £30. 1-night bookings refused Sat.

RYE East Sussex

JEAKE'S HOUSE

❦ *César award in 1992*

'It is smiles all the way' at Jenny Hadfield's B&B in this famous old town ('a microcosm of English history, full of interest and landmarks'). Visitors this year 'had a happy, comfortable stay'. Created from three adjoining buildings (one a former Quaker meeting house, later a Baptist chapel), *Jeake's House* has uneven wooden flooring that might creak during the night. 'Everything works' in the bedrooms, which are named after literary and artistic visitors who came when the house was owned by the American poet Conrad Aitken. They are reached along a warren of corridors with steep stairs in places (luggage is always carried). Some rooms have low beams; five have a four-poster bed. A 'well-used and well-priced' honesty bar is available to guests in the lounge, which stocks sample menus from local restaurants. Breakfast, 'a treat', is taken in a galleried room. There is a sideboard buffet of cereals, juices and fruit; alternatives to the traditional full English include buttered kipper fillets with fresh lemon; smoked wild salmon with scrambled eggs. (*Alec Frank*)

Mermaid Street
Rye TN31 7ET

T: 01797-222828
E: stay@jeakeshouse.com
W: www.jeakeshouse.com

BEDROOMS: 11.
OPEN: all year.
FACILITIES: parlour, bar/library, breakfast room, free Wi-Fi, unsuitable for &.
BACKGROUND MUSIC: classical in breakfast room.
LOCATION: central, car park (£3 per 24 hours, advance booking needed).
CHILDREN: not under 8.
DOGS: allowed, on leads 'and always supervised'.
CREDIT CARDS: MasterCard, Visa.
PRICES: per person B&B £45–£64. 1-night bookings sometimes refused weekends.

SEE ALSO SHORTLIST

ST AGNES Cornwall

Map 1:D2

ROSE IN VALE

NEW

In a peaceful wooded valley, this Georgian manor house is a country hotel run by owners James and Sara Evans. 'It is very traditional and charming (no edgy decor here),' says a *Guide* inspector in 2013. 'The standards of comfort and service are high; the staff were efficient without ever seeming to hurry us.' An extension has been added: 'It is totally in keeping; the effect is of a comfortable country house rather than a formal stately home.' A large bedroom in the extension had 'a superb, comfy bed, good bedlinen; a well-appointed tea tray with a teapot (bliss); two good armchairs and glossy magazines made it a cosy retreat'. In the *Valley* restaurant, the chef, Anthony Theobald, uses local produce for seasonal dishes like chicken and thyme risotto; roast Cornish brill, smoked haddock and shellfish chowder, buttered spinach. 'Dinner was excellent; presentation was pleasantly straightforward.' There are well-planted gardens, woodland walks and an outdoor swimming pool in the grounds. The drawing room has 'deep chairs and sofas, an open fire'. Breakfast includes fresh fruit, compotes, 'lots of lovely toast; irresistible smoked salmon and scrambled eggs'.

25% DISCOUNT VOUCHERS

Mithian
St Agnes TR5 0QD

T: 01872-552202
F: 01872-552700
E: reception@rose-in-vale-hotel.co.uk
W: www.rose-in-vale-hotel.co.uk

BEDROOMS: 23, 7 on ground floor, 2 suitable for &, 3 in garden annexes.
OPEN: all year except 2 weeks in Jan.
FACILITIES: lift, bar, drawing room, restaurant, free Wi-Fi, civil wedding licence, 10-acre grounds, swimming pool (10 by 20 metres).
BACKGROUND MUSIC: classical in restaurant.
LOCATION: 2 miles E of St Agnes.
CHILDREN: not under 12.
DOGS: allowed in some bedrooms, not in restaurant.
CREDIT CARDS: MasterCard, Visa.
PRICES: [2013] per room B&B £120–£255, D,B&B £175–£310. Set dinner £32.50.

ST HILARY Cornwall

Map 1:E1

❦ENNYS

César award: Cornish B&B of the year

'A class act: an exceptional place in a wonderful rural situation.' *Guide* inspectors share a reader's view that Gill Charlton's B&B, a 17th-century manor house, is 'definitely worth five stars'. 'Gill bought the house in a down-trodden state and has lavished much care on restoring it and the surrounding buildings.' The furnishing throughout the house is 'appropriate to its age'; an elegant drawing room is filled with artefacts and original art. Afternoon tea is laid out daily in a lovely old kitchen with an Aga. 'Our bedroom, furnished in country house style, had a huge, extremely comfortable bed, a built-in cupboard with proper hangers, fresh flowers; a small but well-appointed bathroom. The only sound at night was the hooting of owls. Breakfast, at properly laid tables, was well-nigh perfect; a personal jug of freshly squeezed orange juice; on the sideboard were home-made muesli, fresh-cut fruit salad, mini-croissants; tasty thick bacon and a meaty sausage; home-made marmalade and jam.' Guests are encouraged to use the grass tennis court and outdoor swimming pool at all times of day.

Trewhella Lane, St Hilary
nr Penzance TR20 9BZ

T: 01736-740262
F: 01736-740055
E: ennys@ennys.co.uk
W: www.ennys.co.uk

BEDROOMS: 5, 2 in barn, 3 self-catering apartments (can be B&B off-season).
OPEN: Apr–Oct.
FACILITIES: sitting room, breakfast room, free Wi-Fi, 3-acre grounds (grass tennis court, 13-metre heated swimming pool), unsuitable for ♿.
BACKGROUND MUSIC: none.
LOCATION: 5 miles E of Penzance.
CHILDREN: not under 12.
DOGS: not allowed.
CREDIT CARDS: MasterCard, Visa.
PRICES: per room B&B £105–£195. 1-night bookings occasionally refused high season, bank holidays.

ST IVES Cornwall

Map 1:D1

BOSKERRIS HOTEL

'There is a good feeling at the *Boskerris*: a refreshing attitude of "what can we do to help?"' Praise from *Guide* inspectors this year for Jonathan and Marianne Bassett's small hotel above Carbis Bay. A reader agrees: 'We loved the relaxed attitude; the decor suited the setting.' The hotel has been redecorated throughout; the open-plan lounge and bar have been updated with new furniture, rugs and lamps. There are sofas, chairs and much local information. Glass doors open on to a 'delightful' decked terrace overlooking the bay. Simple suppers (with a 'hint of the Mediterranean') are served in the dining room. Most of the bedrooms have a sea view: 'Our room at the front was immaculate, decorated in shades of white and cream; a spotless modern bathroom.' All rooms have been given bathrobes and slippers, extra-large towels; mineral water and a tea and coffee tray. Breakfast has 'wonderful' home-made muesli; fresh fruit salad and freshly squeezed orange juice; 'delicious' cooked dishes. A short walk down a steep hill leads to the station for the short train journey to St Ives. (*Teresa Biggs, and others*)

Boskerris Road
Carbis Bay
St Ives TR26 2NQ

T: 01736-795295
E: reservations@boskerrishotel.co.uk
W: www.boskerrishotel.co.uk

BEDROOMS: 15, 1 on ground floor.
OPEN: Mar–Nov, restaurant closed Sun.
FACILITIES: lounge, bar, restaurant, private dining/meeting room, free Wi-Fi, decked terrace, 1½-acre garden.
BACKGROUND MUSIC: jazz/Latin.
LOCATION: 1½ miles from centre (5 mins by local train), car park.
CHILDREN: not under 7.
DOGS: not allowed.
CREDIT CARDS: Amex (5% *surcharge*), MasterCard, Visa.
PRICES: [2013] per room B&B £125–£255. À la carte £29. 1-night bookings refused bank holidays, sometimes in high season.

ST IVES Cornwall

Map 1:D1

THE TIDE HOUSE   `NEW`

On a side street close to the harbour, this granite-fronted building, which dates back to the 16th century, was renovated over 18 months by David and Suzy Fairfield, who run it as a small hotel. He is an 'excellent host'. An interior designer, she was responsible for the styling. 'Gorgeous; you could be in Martha's Vineyard; it is very well run, and most enjoyable,' said a *Guide* inspector who wrote of 'light, airy open spaces with exposed granite walls, limed rather than just painted; old carved stone lintels, lovely pictures by local artists; large, comfy modern furniture, big vases of lilies'. The living room has a wood-burning stove; there's an honesty bar in the snug; children (there's a family room) have a den with a PlayStation ('non-aggressive' games), toys, books. 'Our large room had windows on three sides – a great view over rooftops of the harbour; a superb bed.' Breakfast has 'very good ingredients (fresh figs, lychees and pomegranates in the fruit bowl), well-sourced breads, jams and marmalade'; organic bacon, thyme-roasted tomatoes, sautéed mushrooms, fried or scrambled eggs, etc. Evening meals are not normally provided as the hotel is in the centre of town.

Skidden Hill
St Ives TR26 2DU

T: 01736-791803
E: enquiries@thetidehouse.co.uk
W: www.thetidehouse.co.uk

BEDROOMS: 6, 1 on ground floor.
OPEN: all year except 22–29 Dec.
FACILITIES: sitting room, snug/library, breakfast room, children's den, free Wi-Fi, small terrace, unsuitable for &.
BACKGROUND MUSIC: 'low volume' in sitting room.
LOCATION: central.
CHILDREN: all ages welcomed.
DOGS: not allowed.
CREDIT CARDS: MasterCard, Visa.
PRICES: [2013] per room B&B £115–£240. 1-night bookings refused peak season.

SEE ALSO SHORTLIST

ST LEONARDS-ON-SEA East Sussex

Map 2:E4

HASTINGS HOUSE

'Immaculately clean, with modern, stylish decor', Seng and Elisabeth Loy's seafront B&B, a white stuccoed Victorian house facing a garden square, is 'highly recommended' by readers. The bedrooms, which have large windows and high ceilings, are individually designed, and decorated in rich colours. Each has a large bed, flat-screen TV, DVD-player (with free film selection), hairdryer, minibar, bathrobes and tea- and coffee-making kit. Some have a sea view. Room 3 has high bay windows, long-drop curtains; the colour scheme mixes aubergine, dark browns, cream and gold. Room 6, at the top, has dark wood and shades of orange and gold. The lounge has a marble-topped bar, a widescreen TV with DVDs; the dining room, which overlooks the garden with sea views, has dark wood tables, leather chairs, linen napkins. Breakfast includes organic apple juice, freshly cut fruits, cereals; 'a great choice of eggs' and cooked dishes; freshly baked bread from a local bakery. Afternoon tea, 'light bites' and an evening meal can be arranged if requested when booking and in summer a picnic hamper is available for guests heading to the beach.

9 Warrior Square
St Leonards-on-Sea TN37 6BA

T: 01424-422709
F: 01424-420592
E: info@hastingshouse.co.uk
W: www.hastingshouse.co.uk

BEDROOMS: 8.
OPEN: all year.
FACILITIES: bar/lounge, dining room, free Wi-Fi, small terrace, unsuitable for &.
BACKGROUND MUSIC: jazz in bar/lounge.
LOCATION: seafront, 1 mile from town centre.
CHILDREN: all ages welcomed.
DOGS: allowed in public areas only.
CREDIT CARDS: Amex, MasterCard, Visa.
PRICES: per room B&B single £80–£110, double £95–£145. 1-night bookings refused weekends and bank holidays.

ST LEONARDS-ON-SEA East Sussex

ZANZIBAR INTERNATIONAL HOTEL

The owner, Max O'Rourke, has drawn on his extended travels to give this once run-down Victorian town house in a seafront terrace of faded grandeur an international style. 'It is typical South Coast boho; white-painted walls and original wide pine polished floorboards tie it together to give a restful feel, on the right side of camp,' said a *Guide* inspector. The themed bedrooms are named after the countries and continents visited by the owner. Antarctica with 'snow-soft' furnishings has floor-to-ceiling windows with a panoramic view of the sea; Manhattan is a 'swanky' loft apartment in Art Deco style; India has big table lamps (good for reading), a vast bed, an antique mirror, an 'extensive' hospitality tray, fresh milk and water in a minibar; a spacious bathroom with twin basins, bathrobes. In the restaurant, *Pier Nine at Zanzibar*, chef Ben Krikorian serves dishes with 'interesting flavour combinations', perhaps breaded scallops, grilled haloumi, pear purée; sweet potato and pea curry, slow-braised coconut rice. Breakfast has 'tasty' porridge; 'good bread'; 'the full English came in large or small portions, a nice touch'.

9 Eversfield Place
St Leonards-on-Sea
TN37 6BY

T: 01424-460109
E: info@zanzibarhotel.co.uk
W: www.zanzibarhotel.co.uk

BEDROOMS: 8, 1 on ground floor.
OPEN: all year.
FACILITIES: lounge, bar, restaurant, free Wi-Fi, garden, beach across road, unsuitable for &.
BACKGROUND MUSIC: in bar, restaurant.
LOCATION: seafront, 650 yds W of Hastings pier, free parking vouchers issued.
CHILDREN: not under 5.
DOGS: not allowed.
CREDIT CARDS: Amex, MasterCard, Visa.
PRICES: [2013] per person B&B £49.50–£123, D,B&B £89.50–£137.50. À la carte £30. 1-night bookings often refused Sat.

ST MARY'S Isles of Scilly

Map 1: inset C1

STAR CASTLE

🄲 *César award in 2009*

With views of the sea and isles in every direction, this star-shaped Tudor fortress owned by the Francis family has an 'enchanting' location. James Francis runs front-of-house with a long-serving staff, who create 'a very friendly atmosphere'. In keeping with the age of the building, bedrooms in the historic castle have dark furniture and deep colours; the more modern garden rooms (at times a 'blustery' walk from the main building) have nautical stripes or cheerful gingham prints. 'Our garden room had its own veranda with steamer chairs – perfect for enjoying the sunshine each afternoon and early evening.' In the beamed *Castle* restaurant and airy *Conservatory*, local produce shapes the menu: a kitchen garden provides many of the vegetables; lobsters and crabs are caught each morning in season by James's father, Robert, in the hotel's fishing boat. Chef Gareth Stafford's 'excellent, inventive' menus of English/French dishes change daily, and might include butter-roasted cod, champ potatoes, mussel and spinach bonne femme. At breakfast, Tim, the boatman, stops by guests' tables to help plan the day's itinerary. (*J and MB, and others*)

The Garrison, St Mary's
Isles of Scilly
Cornwall TR21 0JA

T: 01720-422317
F: 01720-422343
E: info@star-castle.co.uk
W: www.star-castle.co.uk

BEDROOMS: 38, 27 in 2 garden wings.
OPEN: 11 Feb–Nov, 23 Dec–2 Jan.
FACILITIES: lounge, bar, 2 restaurants, free Wi-Fi, civil wedding licence, 3-acre grounds (covered swimming pool, 12 by 3 metres, tennis), beach nearby, unsuitable for &.
BACKGROUND MUSIC: none.
LOCATION: ¼ mile from town centre, boat (2¾ hours)/helicopter (20 mins) from Penzance, air links.
CHILDREN: not under 5 in restaurants.
DOGS: not allowed in restaurants.
CREDIT CARDS: Amex, MasterCard, Visa.
PRICES: [2013] per person B&B £65–£184, D,B&B £88–£194. Set dinner £38.50–£42.50.

ST MAWES Cornwall

Map 1:E2

TRESANTON

🎖 *César award in 2009*

'A lovely hotel with spectacular views; the utterly brilliant staff are what makes it special.' Praise for Olga Polizzi's luxurious hotel, a cluster of restored houses (once a yacht club) on the edge of this fishing village. Federica Bertolini is the manager. Some of the bedrooms, which are spread over five buildings, are reached by flights of stairs through lush gardens; in some cases, 'quite a climb'. They have a 'simple, elegant' style, and are furnished with 'carefully selected' antiques and Cornish artwork; all have a view of the sea; some have a private terrace. The all-white restaurant has full-length doors opening on to a large terrace where guests may dine in fine weather. Paul Wadham, the chef, serves modern dishes with a Mediterranean influence, perhaps sardines, roast pepper; Red Ruby beef, rösti potato, spinach, artichokes. 'Great for those who like fresh fish,' says a visitor who would have liked more variety. Guests can take a trip on a racing yacht. Olga Polizzi also owns *Hotel Endsleigh*, Milton Abbot (see entry). (*JS-M, PO, and others*)

27 Lower Castle Road
St Mawes TR2 5DR

T: 01326-270055
F: 01326-270053
E: info@tresanton.com
W: www.tresanton.com

BEDROOMS: 30, in 5 houses.
OPEN: all year.
FACILITIES: 2 lounges, bar, restaurant, cinema, playroom, conference facilities, free Wi-Fi, civil wedding licence, terrace, ¼-acre garden, by sea (shingle beach, safe bathing, 15-metre yacht).
BACKGROUND MUSIC: none.
LOCATION: on seafront, valet parking (car park up hill).
CHILDREN: all ages welcomed, not under 6 in restaurant in evening.
DOGS: allowed in some bedrooms, not in public rooms.
CREDIT CARDS: Amex, MasterCard, Visa.
PRICES: [2013] per room B&B £190–£550. Set lunch £22–£28, à la carte £42. 1-night bookings refused weekends in high season.

SALCOMBE Devon

Map 1:E4

THE TIDES REACH

In a tree-fringed sandy cove on the Salcombe estuary, the Edwards family's hotel has a particular appeal to an older generation who 'enjoy the traditions', say *Guide* readers. Children under the age of eight are not accepted. The 1960s building has angular balconies and bright blue awnings: it stands in a big garden, with safe sea bathing and water sports opposite. Leisure activities centre on the indoor swimming pool, spa bath and sauna; treatments are offered in a small beauty spa. The sun lounge, where lunch can be taken, has a water feature and large picture windows facing the estuary; the cocktail bar has a sea aquarium. Many of the bedrooms have estuary views, some have a balcony. In the *Garden Room* restaurant, long-serving chef Finn Ibsen serves a daily-changing menu of dishes like Teign Estuary mussels cooked in cider; guineafowl breast, aronia berry and beetroot jam, mixed beans and smoked bacon. Snack lunches can be taken in the garden by a large duck pond or in the sun lounge. Cream teas are served in the garden in fine weather. Breakfast is a 'leisurely affair'.

South Sands
Salcombe TQ8 8LJ

T: 01548-843466
F: 01548-843954
E: enquire@tidesreach.com
W: www.tidesreach.com

BEDROOMS: 32.
OPEN: 13 Feb–30 Nov.
FACILITIES: lift, ramps, 3 lounges, 2 bars, restaurant, free Wi-Fi, leisure centre (indoor swimming pool, 13 by 6 metres, gym, games room, beauty treatments), ½-acre grounds (pond), sandy beach 10 yds, unsuitable for &.
BACKGROUND MUSIC: none.
LOCATION: on Salcombe estuary, 1 mile from town.
CHILDREN: not under 8.
DOGS: allowed in some bedrooms, 1 lounge.
CREDIT CARDS: Amex, MasterCard, Visa.
PRICES: [2013] per room B&B £130–£310, D,B&B £150–£350. Set dinner £36. 1-night bookings sometimes refused.

SEE ALSO SHORTLIST

SCOTBY Cumbria

WILLOWBECK LODGE

Guests receive 'a great welcome' from 'friendly, helpful' owners Liz and John McGrillis at this architect-designed guest house. It stands among mature weeping willows, and beech and oak trees. With views of the duck pond or gardens, the 'spacious, superbly furnished' bedrooms have 'a contemporary finish'; two dormer rooms have French windows and a Juliet balcony. 'Our room was very nice indeed: newly decorated, with comfortable chairs and plenty of space. The bathroom was bright and well appointed.' DVDs, board games and cards are available to borrow; the guest lounge has a wall of books and a common work station. The house is 'very modern; a wonderful galleried dining room has masses of windows allowing you to look at the stars through a powerful telescope'. Here, Liz McGrillis serves a fixed menu at 7.30 pm; her dinners (vegetarian options available) might include garlic king prawns; fish roasted Mediterranean style with tomatoes and olives. Breakfast, cooked to order, is 'something to behold'; there are home-made bread and jam, porridge served with brown sugar or Scotch whisky, 'an excellent full English'. (*Ken Sproston, SP*)

Lambley Bank
Scotby, nr Carlisle CA4 8BX

T: 01228-513607
F: 01228-501053
E: info@willowbeck-lodge.com
W: www.willowbeck-lodge.com

BEDROOMS: 6, 2 in cottage annexe.
OPEN: all year except 20–28 Dec, restaurant closed Sun.
FACILITIES: lounge, lounge/dining room, conference/function facilities, free Wi-Fi, civil wedding licence, 1½-acre garden (stream, pond), unsuitable for &.
BACKGROUND MUSIC: 'at owners' discretion'.
LOCATION: 2½ miles E of Carlisle.
CHILDREN: not under 12.
DOGS: not allowed.
CREDIT CARDS: MasterCard, Visa.
PRICES: [2013] per person B&B £55–£125. Set dinner £30.

SHAFTESBURY Dorset

Map 2:D1

LA FLEUR DE LYS

In a hilltop town surrounded by 'pretty countryside' – the 'Shaston' of Thomas Hardy's novels – this restaurant-with-rooms is liked for its 'wonderful' meals and 'hands-on' owners. It is run by David and Mary Griffin-Shepherd and Marc Preston in a former girls' boarding school. 'The staff are a credit; the owners are keen on encouraging and training local young people.' The ivy-clad stone building is 'clean, welcoming, comfortable'. In good weather, guests take afternoon tea and pre-dinner drinks in the courtyard garden. There are home-made biscuits and fresh milk in the 'well-kept' bedrooms; large superior rooms have a sofa and a laptop computer. In the dining room, the cooking of David Griffin-Shepherd and Marc Preston is 'excellent without being fussy'; their 'well-presented' dishes might include chargrilled veal, Somerset Brie, crispy prosciutto. Special diets can be catered for. Breakfast has fresh fruit and yogurt; a choice of cooked dishes. 'They seem to do or need little by way of direct advertising, relying on word of mouth to spread the news of this excellent example of a restaurant-with-rooms.' (*Kay and Peter Rogers, AB*)

Bleke Street
Shaftesbury SP7 8AW

T: 01747-853717
E: info@lafleurdelys.co.uk
W: www.lafleurdelys.co.uk

BEDROOMS: 8, 1 on ground floor.
OPEN: all year, restaurant closed Sun night, midday Mon and Tues.
FACILITIES: lounge, bar, dining room, conference room, free Wi-Fi, small courtyard.
BACKGROUND MUSIC: none.
LOCATION: edge of centre, car park.
CHILDREN: all ages welcomed.
DOGS: not allowed.
CREDIT CARDS: Amex, MasterCard, Visa.
PRICES: [2013] per room B&B single £85–£105, double £120–£170. D,B&B from £87.50 per person, set meals £27–£33, à la carte £33.

SHANKLIN Isle of Wight

RYLSTONE MANOR

There are 'wonderful sea views' from the garden of this small traditional hotel owned and run by Mike and Carole Hailston. In the centre of a small public park on a cliff-top above Sandown Bay, the house, built as a gentleman's residence in 1863, blends Gothic, Tudor and Georgian influences. There are 'wonderful decorative details'; heavy fabrics, books and ornaments in the green-walled lounge; basket chairs in a Victorian covered patio. Bedrooms, each named after an English tree, vary in size; they have antique furniture, chintz, striped wallpaper; beds are 'comfortable'. Ash is the lightest room, furnished in white; Elm has tulip wall coverings and fabrics, lead crystal and brass light fittings; Fir has William Morris wallpaper and hand-painted wooden furniture. In the dining room, with its ornate chandelier with matching wall lights, Mike Hailston serves a short menu of modern European dishes like scallops on a green salad, balsamic dressing; extra mature sirloin of beef, a red wine jus. *Rylstone Manor*'s secluded private garden is 'a pleasant place to sip wine on a summer afternoon'. (*DC, and others*)

25% DISCOUNT VOUCHERS

Rylstone Gardens
Popham Road, Shanklin
PO37 6RG

T/F: 01983-862806
E: rylstone.manor@btinternet.com
W: www.rylstone-manor.co.uk

BEDROOMS: 9.
OPEN: 10 Feb–20 Nov.
FACILITIES: drawing room, bar lounge, dining room, free Wi-Fi, terrace, 1-acre garden in 4-acre public gardens, direct access to sand/shingle beach, unsuitable for &.
BACKGROUND MUSIC: none.
LOCATION: Shanklin old village.
CHILDREN: not allowed.
DOGS: not allowed.
CREDIT CARDS: MasterCard, Visa.
PRICES: [2013] per person B&B £67.50–£82.50, D,B&B £96.50–£111.50. Set menu £29–£33. 1-night bookings refused June–Aug and bank holidays (unless space permits).

SHREWSBURY Shropshire

Map 3:B4

LION AND PHEASANT

By the English Bridge, the main crossing over the Severn into this 'lovely old town', this former coaching inn has been modernised with 'a simple but sure touch'. The bedrooms are 'well furnished and equipped'; the food is 'excellent'. It is 'a pleasant place to stay, handy for the town centre', say visitors this year. 'The receptionist who greeted us was good at her job, friendly but thoughtful.' The bar has oak floors, slatted benches, painted furniture. The focal point of the inner casual dining area is an inglenook fireplace; it has low beams, flagstone floors. Upstairs is a split-level dining area. The 'interesting' dishes of the chef, Matthew Strefford, might include seafood stew, spicy mussel and saffron sauce, sourdough and aïoli. A warren of beamed corridors with white walls, grey skirting boards and doors, leads to the bedrooms. 'Ear plugs by the bed were a nice touch in our corner room, which overlooked the bridge. We slept well despite the morning traffic noise (also dampened by double glazing); the compact modern bathroom was well lit.' Breakfast has a small buffet, 'good' cooked dishes. (*DB, FW*)

50 Wyle Cop
Shrewsbury SY1 1XJ

T: 01743-770345
F: 01743-770350
E: info@lionandpheasant.co.uk
W: www.lionandpheasant.co.uk

BEDROOMS: 22.
OPEN: all year except 25/26 Dec.
FACILITIES: restaurant, 3 bars, function room, free Wi-Fi, unsuitable for &.
BACKGROUND MUSIC: in public areas.
LOCATION: central, near English Bridge.
CHILDREN: all ages welcomed.
DOGS: not allowed.
CREDIT CARDS: MasterCard, Visa.
PRICES: [2013] per room B&B £99–£219. À la carte £30.

SEE ALSO SHORTLIST

SOAR MILL COVE Devon

Map 1:E4

SOAR MILL COVE HOTEL

'Friendly and welcoming; excellent service from all the staff.' Keith Makepeace's family-friendly hotel above a sandy cove on the south Devon coast continues to please readers. There has been considerable renovation this year. The heated indoor swimming pool has been enlarged as part of a new leisure suite, 'a spacious weatherproof environment where you can kick back and relax on a lounger'. New facilities include a spa tub, a sauna, a mini-gym, a treatment area and a café. The restaurant has been given a clean, modern look, with new tables, chairs, surfaces and carpets. The chef, Ian MacDonald, is praised for his 'high-quality and varied' menus: 'We were able to have a different dish every evening; the fish dishes were fantastic' (perhaps lobster and crab bisque; sea bass with Mediterranean ratatouille). All the bedrooms and family suites have French doors opening on to a private patio with loungers, chairs and a sun umbrella. Children of all ages will be kept occupied in the indoor and outdoor play areas; or they can stroll down to the beach. (*Jan Todd, Margaret H Box*)

Soar Mill Cove
nr Salcombe TQ7 3DS

T: 01548-561566
F: 01548-561223
E: info@soarmillcove.co.uk
W: www.soarmillcove.co.uk

BEDROOMS: 22, all on ground floor.
OPEN: all year, except Jan, 1–13 Feb.
FACILITIES: lounge, 2 bars, restaurant (pianist), coffee shop, free Wi-Fi in public areas, indoor swimming pool (10 by 7 metres), treatment room (hairdressing, reflexology, aromatherapy, etc), civil wedding licence, 10-acre grounds (tennis, children's play area), sandy beach, 600 yds.
BACKGROUND MUSIC: in restaurant and bar.
LOCATION: 3 miles SW of Salcombe.
CHILDREN: all ages welcomed.
DOGS: well-behaved small dogs allowed, but not in public rooms other than coffee shop.
CREDIT CARDS: MasterCard, Visa.
PRICES: [2013] per room B&B £150–£215, D,B&B £195–£255. À la carte £35.

SOMERTON Somerset

Map 1:C6

THE LYNCH COUNTRY HOUSE

'A delight', this Grade II listed Regency house is set 'in lovely grounds' yet is close to the centre of a small town on the edge of the River Cary. It is run as a B&B by Mike and Chris McKenzie, 'a friendly but not overbearing couple', for the owner, former jazz musician Roy Copeland. The house retains a 'homely' feel with family photographs and jazz memorabilia. The extensive grounds have a large lawned area, a topiary, and a lake with resident black swans. The largest of the 'nicely furnished and decorated' bedrooms are on the first floor of the main building; two rooms in the eaves, one of which has a 'campaign' couch for younger guests, have a starlight window. Four ground-floor rooms are in the coach house, which has its own private entrance, ideal for family groups. Breakfast, 'a great start to the day', is served between 8 and 10 am in the light and airy orangery: it has freshly squeezed orange juice; 'proper' dry-cured bacon and mixed sautéed mushrooms in the full English. Advice is given about local eating places. (*John Ford, and others*)

4 Behind Berry
Somerton TA11 7PD

T: 01458-272316
F: 01458-272590
E: enquiries@
   thelynchcountryhouse.co.uk
W: www.thelynchcountryhouse.co.uk

BEDROOMS: 9, 4, in coach house, on ground floor.
OPEN: all year (limited opening at Christmas/New Year).
FACILITIES: breakfast room, small sitting area, free Wi-Fi, 2½-acre grounds (lake), unsuitable for &.
BACKGROUND MUSIC: none.
LOCATION: N edge of village.
CHILDREN: all ages welcomed.
DOGS: allowed in coach house, not in public rooms.
CREDIT CARDS: Amex, MasterCard, Visa.
PRICES: per person B&B £40–£80. 1-night bookings sometimes refused.

SOUTHAMPTON Hampshire

Map 2:E2

THE PIG IN THE WALL NEW

Between two medieval gates in the city wall, this white-painted building (brightly lit at night) is an 'eye-opening treat', say *Guide* inspectors in 2013. It has been given the same 'shabby-chic' styling by Robin and Judy Hutson as its sister hotel, *The Pig*, Brockenhurst (see entry). Rachael Brazier is the 'friendly and efficient' manager. An open-plan public area has a mix of wooden tables, leather seating, armchairs, an open fire; a deli counter serves simple dishes (perhaps pepper and goat's cheese quiche) from noon until 7 pm. There are three sizes of bedroom: snug, comfy and spacious. 'Our spacious room had a beamed ceiling and original iron fireplace; a bath planked on a wooden board seemed a little unnecessary; two semi-tub chairs and a table; a huge, comfortable bed with crisp white linen. Everything worked well and was provided for in the bathroom, which had stunning coloured floor tiles.' Guests are given free transfers to *The Pig* for a 'tempting and delicious' dinner. 'What struck us was the way the efficient, mainly young staff were enthusiastic about the ethos of both places.'

8 Western Esplanade
Southampton SO14 2AZ

T: 02380-636900
E: reservations@
    thepiginthewall.com
W: www.thepighotel.com

BEDROOMS: 12, 2 on ground floor.
OPEN: all year.
FACILITIES: lounge, bar, deli counter, free Wi-Fi.
BACKGROUND MUSIC: in public areas.
LOCATION: central.
CHILDREN: all ages welcomed.
DOGS: not allowed.
CREDIT CARDS: all major cards.
PRICES: [2013] per room B&B £125–£185. Breakfast £10.

STAMFORD Lincolnshire

Map 2:B3

THE GEORGE

♨ *César award in 1986*

Kings used to stay at this 16th-century coaching inn on the old Great North Road; today, guests can still eat like royalty. 'An excellent dinner; and it was nice to see a carving trolley and a sweet trolley,' a visitor reported this year. 'We had a jolly good and very nourishing meal in the splendid *George* restaurant,' another said. 'The roast beef is excellent – one could be a real glutton.' In the stone-built town of Stamford, this inn, owned by Lawrence Hoskins, has 'a nice, old-fashioned atmosphere (nothing old-fashioned about the facilities, though)'. The service is roundly praised: 'Staff are wonderful without exception. I stayed at this hotel on my own but never felt neglected or discriminated against.' Bedrooms vary: a 'spacious' room overlooking the cobbled courtyard had a 'large, smart bathroom'; a suite on the main road was 'slightly noisy'. 'Having early-morning coffee and papers delivered to the bedroom was a bonus.' The oak-panelled *York Bar*, log fires burning, is popular with locals and visitors. At breakfast, hot chocolate is served with brandy or dark rum. (*David Craig, John Barnes, Helen Davies*)

71 St Martins
Stamford
PE9 2LB

T: 01780-750750
F: 01780-750701
E: reservations@
   georgehotelofstamford.com
W: www.georgehotelofstamford.com

BEDROOMS: 47.
OPEN: all year.
FACILITIES: ramps, 2 lounges, 2 bars, 2 restaurants, 4 private dining rooms, business centre, free Wi-Fi, civil wedding licence, 2-acre grounds (courtyard, gardens), only public areas suitable for ♿.
BACKGROUND MUSIC: none.
LOCATION: ½ mile from centre.
CHILDREN: all ages welcomed.
DOGS: allowed, but not unattended in bedrooms, only guide dogs in restaurants.
CREDIT CARDS: all major cards.
PRICES: [2013] per room B&B single £95–£150, double £150–£290. À la carte £44. 1-night bookings sometimes refused Sat.

SEE ALSO SHORTLIST

STANTON WICK Somerset

Map 1:B6

THE CARPENTER'S ARMS

Converted from a row of miners' cottages, this
'warm and welcoming' pub-with-rooms in a
Somerset hamlet is liked for its 'great location'
in the rural Chew valley south of Bristol. 'I
didn't believe it possible to find anywhere so
quiet, yet so close to an airport. It was lovely to
sit outside before dinner among the flowers
and shrubs.' Other praise: 'A good room, good
drinks and good food.' There's a range of cask
ales in the bar, which has a large open fire,
newspapers, wooden tables and sofas. In the two
dining areas, chef Chris Dando serves 'generous
portions' of 'unfussy but hearty' dishes on a
seasonally changing menu (fish from Cornwall,
West Country beef and game), perhaps asparagus,
pancetta and black pudding salad, poached egg;
steak and mushroom suet pudding, chips, peas
and red wine sauce. Bedrooms are decorated in
simple, unfussy style; all have flat-screen TV
with Freeview, tea- and coffee-making kit (with
fresh milk); 'not a cobweb in sight'. Bathrooms
are modern, with bath and shower, 'fluffy' towels.
Secure parking. (*JB, Irene and Anno Boon*)

Stanton Wick, nr Pensford
BS39 4BX

T: 01761-490202
F: 01761-490763
E: carpenters@buccaneer.co.uk
W: www.the-carpenters-arms.co.uk

BEDROOMS: 12.
OPEN: all year except 25/26 Dec,
1 Jan.
FACILITIES: bar, 2 restaurants,
function room, free Wi-Fi, patio,
unsuitable for &.
BACKGROUND MUSIC: none.
LOCATION: 8 miles S of Bristol,
8 miles W of Bath.
CHILDREN: all ages welcomed.
DOGS: allowed in bar only.
CREDIT CARDS: Amex, MasterCard,
Visa.
PRICES: [2013] per room B&B single
£72.50, double £105, D,B&B single
£90, double £137.50. À la carte
£27.85.

STEWTON Lincolnshire

THE OLD RECTORY AT STEWTON

 NEW

Down a quiet lane, this early Victorian former rectory stands in large grounds with mature trees and lawns in a hamlet near the Georgian market town of Louth. It is run as a B&B by the owners, Linda and Alan Palmer. 'It is delightfully quirky with rooms that aren't the usual boring rectangle,' says the nominator (a *Guide* hotelier). 'There is no canned music, no pretentious nonsense. The hosts are friendly in the relaxed and charming way that makes you think, "Yes, I like it here."' Guests have use of a large sitting room with a wood fire and a conservatory. 'The bedrooms have nooks and crannies; my friend's room had a cosy little lounge hidden away. The beds are comfortable; the linen is top quality; bathrooms are scrupulously clean; each room has a collection of art and artefacts.' Children are welcomed: 'The hosts have a rapport with younger guests that is easy and relaxed.' Dogs are also welcomed (£5 charge per visit). Breakfast has local free-range eggs, a full English, and three types of fish: smoked salmon, smoked haddock, kipper fillets; a vegetarian option. (*Wendy Charles-Warner*)

Stewton
Louth LN11 8SF

T: 01507-328063
E: alanjpalmer100@aol.com
W: www.louthbedandbreakfast.co.uk

BEDROOMS: 4.
OPEN: all year except Christmas/New Year.
FACILITIES: sitting room, breakfast room, free Wi-Fi, 3-acre garden, unsuitable for &.
BACKGROUND MUSIC: none.
LOCATION: in hamlet 2½ miles SE of Louth.
CHILDREN: all ages welcomed.
DOGS: allowed (£5 charge per visit), in public rooms 'depending on other guests'.
CREDIT CARDS: MasterCard, Visa.
PRICES: [2013] per room B&B single £45, double £65–£75.

STOCKBRIDGE Hampshire

Map 2:D2

THE GREYHOUND ON THE TEST

NEW

On the 'elegant' high street of a small town ('a Hampshire classic'), Lucy Townsend's old inn has fishing rights on the River Test, which flows at the bottom of the garden. 'We were immediately made welcome by the friendly young staff,' said a *Guide* inspector in 2013. 'The inviting low-ceilinged bar had a good buzz.' Work by local artists (for sale) is displayed in the public areas and the bedrooms. 'Personal touches, like the books on the bedside tables, made ours feel like a friend's comfortable guest bedroom. Decorated in muted colours, it had an excellent king-size bed with high-quality linen; the bathroom had an effective shower.' There's an honesty bar in the corridor outside the bedroom ('watch out for low beams'). In the restaurant (candles on wooden tables), the cooking of the chef, Alan Haughie, is judged 'very good'. There is a short daily-changing set menu and a longer carte with 'interesting' dishes like pressed lamb breast croquette, smoked eel; lemon-scented fish crumble, seasonal greens. Breakfast has 'excellent orange juice and coffee'; cooked dishes include 'delicious' roast smoked haddock, spinach, poached egg.

31 High Street
Stockbridge SO20 6EY

T: 01264-810833
E: info@thegreyhoundonthetest.co.uk
W: www.thegreyhoundonthetest.co.uk

BEDROOMS: 7.
OPEN: all year except 25/26 Dec.
FACILITIES: bar/lounge, restaurant, free Wi-Fi, garden, unsuitable for &.
BACKGROUND MUSIC: in public areas.
LOCATION: town centre.
CHILDREN: all ages welcomed.
DOGS: not allowed in restaurant.
CREDIT CARDS: all major cards.
PRICES: [2013] per room B&B single £70, double £100–£125. À la carte £25.

STRATFORD-UPON-AVON Warwickshire   Map 3:D6

CHERRY TREES

'A remarkably peaceful spot, and so handy for the theatre.' Royd Laidlow and Tony Godel's architect-designed house stands south of the River Avon near a footbridge to the theatre. 'Good location, lovely rooms, extremely spacious and exceptionally clean,' says a visitor this year. 'They are perfect hosts, welcoming us with tea and home-baked scones in our room,' is another comment. There are three ground-floor bedrooms. The 'huge' Garden room has a four-poster bed, a rain shower, a seating area with television, and a conservatory. The Terrace room, which has a king-size bed, also has a conservatory. The Art Nouveau-inspired Tiffany suite has a fireplace and a sitting room. 'Its round stained-glass window at night creates a pretty pattern of stars on the ceiling over the comfy king-size bed.' Breakfast, 'one of the best ever', includes home-made granola and breads; a choice of omelette; the usual cooked dishes. 'It was interesting to exchange opinions on the theatre productions with Tony, a former stage manager.' 'It is good to have parking within walking distance of the theatre.' (*John Saul, Christopher Lee*)

Swan's Nest Lane
Stratford-upon-Avon CV37 7LS

T: 01789-292989
E: cherrytreesstratforduponavon@
   gmail.com
W: www.cherrytrees-stratford.co.uk

BEDROOMS: 3, all on ground floor.
OPEN: Feb–Dec.
FACILITIES: breakfast room, free Wi-Fi, garden, unsuitable for &.
BACKGROUND MUSIC: none.
LOCATION: central, near river.
CHILDREN: not under 12.
DOGS: not allowed.
CREDIT CARDS: MasterCard, Visa.
PRICES: [2013] per room B&B £110–£125. 1-night bookings sometimes refused.

STRATFORD-UPON-AVON Warwickshire Map 3:D6

WHITE SAILS

'From the warmth of the reception to the comfort of the rooms, everything is first class.' Praise comes in 2013 for this upmarket B&B run by owners Phillip Manning and Chiung-Wen Liang. The suburban house might 'lack character', said inspectors, but 'the lovely young couple' more than compensate, delighting in 'having people to stay and keen to discuss the evening's theatre viewing'. Complimentary sherry is given in a small guest sitting room which has books, guides and local information. 'Standards are high' in the bedrooms. 'Our room was a decent size for a short stay; a large bed; red-patterned wallpaper.' Double glazing 'kept out noise efficiently'; air-conditioning units help control the temperature. A ground-floor room has an 'enticing' conservatory and a 'modern bathroom with stylish fittings'. Breakfast is 'nicely laid out', with 'beautiful buffet fruit choices' (perhaps spiced peaches), apple juices and marmalade from local suppliers, 'real bread toast'; a 'good' vegetarian option among the cooked dishes; the smoked haddock is 'recommended'. The town centre is 'quite a step away' but buses pass the door. (*Graham and Barbara Stradling, Ian Moor*)

85 Evesham Road
Stratford-upon-Avon CV37 9BE

T: 01789-550469
E: enquiries@white-sails.co.uk
W: www.white-sails.co.uk

BEDROOMS: 5, 1 on ground floor.
OPEN: all year.
FACILITIES: lounge, dining room, free Wi-Fi, garden (summer house).
BACKGROUND MUSIC: none.
LOCATION: 1 mile W of centre.
CHILDREN: not under 12.
DOGS: not allowed.
CREDIT CARDS: MasterCard, Visa.
PRICES: per room B&B £105–£132, 1-night bookings sometimes refused weekends.

STUCKTON Hampshire

Map 2:E2

THE THREE LIONS

On the edge of the New Forest national park, this restaurant-with-rooms has 'a very relaxed ambience', says a visitor this year. The owners, Jayne and Mike Womersley, are 'friendly and professional'. The former farmhouse and pub has a bar with a small lounge area, a 'pretty' dining room with flowers on the tables, and a conservatory. 'The decor is old-fashioned in the best sense (proud to be retro): cosy, warm and relaxed. We noticed a silvery mushroom on the sideboard and wooden ones behind the bar; Jayne told us these were gifts to acknowledge Mike's love of cooking the divine fungi.' The menu is chalked up on a portable blackboard: 'We shared a starter of wild mushrooms with asparagus; slow-cooked confit of duck was melt-in-your-mouth tender.' Four of the bedrooms are in a wooden single-storey chalet-style building in the garden; others are in the main house. 'Our bedroom and bathroom were spacious and well appointed in country living style.' At breakfast, the table 'was laid with a pretty cloth; a jug of orange juice, fresh fruit and home-made bread and pastries'. (*Penelope Visman*)

25% DISCOUNT VOUCHERS

Stuckton, nr Fordingbridge
SP6 2HF

T: 01425-652489
F: 01425-656144
E: the3lions@btinternet.com
W: www.thethreelionsrestaurant.
   co.uk

BEDROOMS: 7, 4 in courtyard block on ground floor.
OPEN: all year except last 2 weeks Feb, restaurant closed Sun night/Mon.
FACILITIES: ramps, conservatory, meeting/sitting room, public bar, restaurant, free Wi-Fi, 2½-acre garden (sauna, whirlpool).
BACKGROUND MUSIC: on request, in bar.
LOCATION: 1 mile E of Fordingbridge.
CHILDREN: all ages welcomed.
DOGS: allowed in bedrooms, conservatory.
CREDIT CARDS: MasterCard, Visa.
PRICES: per room B&B single £79–£125, double £125. À la carte £42.

STURMINSTER NEWTON Dorset

Map 2:E1

PLUMBER MANOR

♙ *César award in 1987*

'What a glorious place.' Deep in Thomas Hardy country, this restaurant-with-rooms is a Jacobean brick-and-stone manor house which has been the family home of the Prideaux-Brunes since it was built in the 1600s. Richard Prideaux-Brune 'runs the place superbly with evident enjoyment which clearly infects the rest of the staff'; his wife, Alison, is 'simply everywhere'; his brother, Brian, is the chef. The house stands in 'wonderful' gardens with manicured lawns, fine herbaceous borders and a stream. 'There were lovely flowers everywhere in the house.' The 'lived-in comfort' is liked. The bedrooms in the main house lead off a gallery hung with portraits; they overlook the gardens. Ten larger rooms are in a converted barn around a courtyard and have window seats facing the river and topiary garden. Dogs are allowed here in four rooms with direct access to the car park. The dining rooms are 'well appointed, with well-spaced tables'. A daily-changing menu of 'extremely good' English/French dishes might include potted shrimps, crab mousseline, lemon sole, supreme of chicken. 'Very reasonable' wine list. (*MM-D*)

Sturminster Newton DT10 2AF

T: 01258-472507
F: 01258-473370
E: book@plumbermanor.com
W: www.plumbermanor.com

BEDROOMS: 16, 10 on ground floor in courtyard.
OPEN: all year except Feb.
FACILITIES: lounge, bar, 3 dining rooms, gallery, free Wi-Fi, 20-acre grounds (garden, tennis, croquet, stream).
BACKGROUND MUSIC: none.
LOCATION: 2 miles SW of Sturminster Newton.
CHILDREN: all ages welcomed, by prior arrangement.
DOGS: allowed in 4 bedrooms, not in public rooms.
CREDIT CARDS: MasterCard, Visa.
PRICES: [2013] per room B&B single £115–£140, double £150–£230. Set dinner £29–£36.

SWAFFHAM Norfolk

Map 2:B5

STRATTONS

🌿 *César award in 2003*

'Memorable and enjoyable', this Grade II-listed Palladian villa stands in neatly planted gardens off the square of a small town. It was restored from a run-down state by Les and Vanessa Scott, who gave it an 'amazingly creative' decor. It is run by their daughter, Hannah, and her husband, Dominic Hughes, with a 'charming, young staff'. 'Eclectic may be an overused word but it certainly describes the interiors,' said an inspector. The entrance has 'bronze shabby-chic walls and lots of ornamentation'. The bedrooms are 'imaginatively designed': Boudoir is spacious and romantic; the enormous Red Room has a four-poster bed mounted on a dais; a small double room 'was beautifully arranged'. A strong environmental ethic is followed ('we feel we are the caretakers, rather than the owners, of this unique building,' say the Scotts). Guidance is given on getting around the area without a car. Whenever possible, the food for the kitchen comes from within a 20-mile radius. In the *Rustic* restaurant, chef Sam Bryant serves modern dishes like gluttony soup (glut of the harvest); skate wing, coronation butter sauce, roasted cauliflower, apricot purée.

4 Ash Close
Swaffham PE37 7NH

T: 01760-723845
F: 01760-720458
E: enquiries@strattonshotel.com
W: www.strattonshotel.com

BEDROOMS: 14, 7 in annexes, 1 on ground floor.
OPEN: all year except 1 week at Christmas.
FACILITIES: drawing room, reading room, restaurant, free Wi-Fi, terrace, 1½-acre garden.
BACKGROUND MUSIC: 'chill out/jazz' in lounges, restaurant.
LOCATION: central, parking.
CHILDREN: all ages welcomed.
DOGS: allowed in some bedrooms, lounges.
CREDIT CARDS: Amex, MasterCard, Visa.
PRICES: [2013] per room B&B £100–£230, D,B&B £187–£310. À la carte £40. 1-night bookings refused weekends.

SWINBROOK Oxfordshire

Map 3:D6

THE SWAN INN   NEW

By a bridge over the River Windrush in a 'delightful' rural village near Burford, this lovely old inn is owned by the Dowager Duchess of Devonshire (Debo Mitford), who was brought up in the village. She has leased the inn to Nicola and Archie Orr-Ewing (who own *The King's Head Inn*, Bledington, see entry). They have styled it 'beautifully', say *Guide* inspectors in 2013, 'in homage to the Mitford sisters, with large black-and-white pictures of the family and associated memorabilia'. The bar and restaurant are a series of interconnected rooms with 'mismatched wooden tables and chairs'. A recently added wood-and-glass extension opens on to the garden, where hens roam freely. 'The cooking is excellent for a pub: new season asparagus with Parma ham and a poached egg was delicious; our steaks were equally good; the waitresses were chatty and precise.' The bedrooms are in converted stables. 'Our delightful room was decorated in restrained modern style; limed beams, white walls; a table, two chairs; interesting books and pictures.' The owner occasionally stays in Debo's, the largest room. Work has begun on additional rooms in a cottage across the road.

Swinbrook
nr Burford OX18 4DY

T: 01993-823339
E: info@theswanswinbrook.co.uk
W: www.theswanswinbrook.co.uk

BEDROOMS: 6, 4 on ground floor.
OPEN: all year.
FACILITIES: bar, restaurant, free Wi-Fi, garden, orchard.
BACKGROUND MUSIC: in bar and restaurant.
LOCATION: in village 2 miles E of Burford.
CHILDREN: all ages welcomed.
DOGS: not allowed in bedrooms.
CREDIT CARDS: MasterCard, Visa.
PRICES: [2013] per room B&B single (Sun–Thurs) £80–£100, double £120–£180. À la carte £30. 1-night bookings refused weekends.

TALLAND-BY-LOOE Cornwall

Map 1:D3

TALLAND BAY HOTEL

'From the moment we were met in the car park on arrival to the time we left, everything was excellent,' says a visitor this year to Vanessa Rees's hotel in a quiet position on the south Cornwall coast. Stephen Waite is the new manager. The 400-year-old white-painted manor house stands in large subtropical gardens. An additional bedroom has been created this year, and there is a new conservatory. Dogs are welcomed in three cottages in the grounds (muted colours, French-style furnishings); one with two bedrooms is good for a family. The rooms in the main house vary in size and style: 'Our room was comfortable and spotless.' Three ground-floor rooms have direct access to the patio. The lounge has soft lighting, sofas with a startling zebra-print cover, and blue-grey high-backed chairs; some visitors may find the ornaments 'rather kitsch'. In the striking wood-panelled dining room, chef Daniel Watkins serves a daily-changing menu of modern dishes which might include ham hock terrine, brioche; assiette of rabbit, potato galette, carrot and parsley. 'The food is well presented and delicious.' Lighter meals can be taken in the bar. (*Colonel GM Chirnside*)

Porthallow, nr Looe
PL13 2JB

T: 01503-272667
F: 01503-272940
E: info@tallandbayhotel.co.uk
W: www.tallandbayhotel.co.uk

BEDROOMS: 22, 6 on ground floor.
OPEN: all year.
FACILITIES: lounge, bar, restaurant, free Wi-Fi, civil wedding licence, patio, 2-acre garden.
BACKGROUND MUSIC: 'easy listening' in lounge.
LOCATION: 2½ miles SW of Looe.
CHILDREN: all ages welcomed.
DOGS: not allowed in restaurant.
CREDIT CARDS: MasterCard, Visa.
PRICES: [2013] per room B&B £100–£245, D,B&B £190–£315. Set dinner £32–£38. 1-night bookings sometimes refused Sat, high season.

TARRANT LAUNCESTON Dorset

Map 2:E1

LAUNCESTON FARM

Guests are invited to 'soak up the sights, sounds and smells' of Sarah Worrall's working organic beef farm in a peaceful setting on the Dorset/Wiltshire border. Her son, Jimi, leads tours to give an insight into the life of the farm he manages. Accommodation is in the Grade II listed Georgian farmhouse, which has been renovated throughout. The six individually styled bedrooms are accessed by an original Victorian iron staircase; they have been furnished with a mix of auction-house finds (Persian rugs, carved wardrobes, silk hangings). Three bathrooms have a roll-top bath; all are supplied with Fairtrade teas and coffee, organic toiletries, a flat-screen TV. A self-catering cottage for two (*The Bothy*) is in the grounds. Bookings must be made in advance for the three-course evening meal, which is taken communally. Sarah Worrall sources free-range meats, vegetables and herbs from the plot, and trout from the River Tarrant. Breakfast, also taken communally at a pre-arranged time, has organic sausages and bacon from rare breed pigs, eggs from the orchard chickens, and home-made preserves. There are many pubs in the area. More reports, please.

Tarrant Launceston
nr Blandford Forum DT11 8BY

T: 01258-830528
E: info@launcestonfarm.co.uk
W: www.launcestonfarm.co.uk

BEDROOMS: 6.
OPEN: all year.
FACILITIES: 2 lounges, dining room, breakfast room, free Wi-Fi, terrace, 1-acre walled garden, unsuitable for &.
BACKGROUND MUSIC: classical during breakfast.
LOCATION: 5 miles NE of Blandford Forum.
CHILDREN: not under 12.
DOGS: only allowed in *The Bothy*.
CREDIT CARDS: MasterCard, Visa.
PRICES: per room B&B £90–£105. D,B&B £25 added per person.

TAUNTON Somerset

Map 1:C5

THE CASTLE AT TAUNTON

César award in 1987

Once a Norman fortress, this wisteria-covered, castellated hotel has been an inn since the 12th century. It is owned by Kit and Louise Chapman; Marc MacCloskey is the manager. The public rooms match the exterior: they have dark carved wood, tapestries, paintings, fresh flowers, the smell of polish. 'It is a pleasure to pass through the revolving door into the warm hotel lobby,' says a visitor on a wet winter's day. 'A friendly porter carried our bags and showed us to our room.' The bar is 'contemporary in style; comfortable seating around small tables, with recesses for guests seeking privacy'. There are two dining options. In *BRAZZ*, a 'vibrant modern' brasserie, bar and café, meals are served all day. In the *Grill*, a retro-chic restaurant which opened in 2012, dinner is served from Wednesday to Saturday; the chef, Liam Finnegan, uses West Country produce for his modern dishes which might include terrine of Quantock Hill rabbit; Lyme Bay brill, tempura oyster, lemon balm velouté. Louise Chapman designed the bedrooms, which are reached by a fine wrought iron staircase. (*TL*)

Castle Green
Taunton TA1 1NF

T: 01823-272671
F: 01823-336066
E: reception@the-castle-hotel.com
W: www.the-castle-hotel.com

BEDROOMS: 44.
OPEN: all year, *Grill* closed Sun eve/Mon/Tues.
FACILITIES: lift, ramps, lounge, bar, *BRAZZ*, *Grill*, private dining/meeting rooms, free Wi-Fi, billiard room, civil wedding licence, 1-acre garden, shop.
BACKGROUND MUSIC: in bar and brasserie.
LOCATION: central.
CHILDREN: all ages welcomed.
DOGS: not allowed in public rooms.
CREDIT CARDS: all major cards.
PRICES: [2013] per room B&B £94.50–£230, D,B&B £115–£300. Set menu (*Grill*) £27–£34, tasting menu (*Grill*) £52, à la carte (*BRAZZ*) £27.

TEFFONT EVIAS Wiltshire

Map 2:D1

HOWARD'S HOUSE

♀ *César award in 2010*

In an unspoilt village 'without an ugly building in sight', this 'beautiful' stone dower house stands in a 'peaceful' sloping garden with mown lawns and fruit trees. It is run as a small hotel by a partnership that includes the chef, Nick Wentworth. His mother-in-law, Noële Thompson, and Simon Greenwood are the managers. 'It is a splendid place to stay; we were made to feel most welcome,' says a visitor this year. All the bedrooms were refurbished in 2012. 'They are decorated in pale, restful colours and have pretty curtains.' A dissenter, who was unhappy about the state of a bathroom, found the staff 'friendly' and appreciated the turn-down service. The lounge has 'deep, comfortable' sofas, exposed beams, hunting prints, 'stunning flower arrangements'. Everyone agrees about the 'delicious' cooking in the restaurant. The 'varied' menu of seasonal, modern dishes might include Cornish mackerel pickled with apple juice, remoulade sauce; duo of Dorset lamb, sweet shallot purée, spinach, thyme jus. 'The service was excellent without being overdone.' Breakfast is 'good and tasty'. (*Joanna Russell, David Innes, and others*)

25% DISCOUNT VOUCHERS

Teffont Evias
nr Salisbury SP3 5RJ

T: 01722-716392
E: enq@howardshousehotel.co.uk
W: www.howardshousehotel.co.uk

BEDROOMS: 9.
OPEN: all year except 25/26 Dec (available for exclusive use).
FACILITIES: lounge, restaurant, free Wi-Fi, 2-acre grounds (croquet), river, fishing nearby, only restaurant suitable for &.
BACKGROUND MUSIC: 'easy listening', jazz.
LOCATION: 10 miles W of Salisbury.
CHILDREN: all ages welcomed.
DOGS: allowed (£11 surcharge in rooms).
CREDIT CARDS: Amex, MasterCard, Visa.
PRICES: per room B&B single £120, double £190–£210. D,B&B £29.50 added per person, à la carte £45.

TEIGNMOUTH Devon

Map 1:D5

THOMAS LUNY HOUSE

César award in 1995

Set back from the street and approached through an archway into a walled courtyard, this Georgian house is run as an upmarket B&B by John and Alison Allan. 'Standards are high' in the 'immaculate' house built by marine artist Thomas Luny in the town's heyday, when it was fashionable with admirals and sea captains. A spacious drawing room, furnished with antiques and comfortable sofas and chairs, stretches the length of the house. Arriving guests are offered tea or coffee with home-made cake by a log fire (they can also take it in their room or, in warm weather, in the south-facing walled garden). Three bedrooms are spacious, the fourth is small. The Chinese room has hand-painted oriental furniture and a canopy bed; the Luny room, which has a king-size bed which can be adapted to twin beds, is nautical; Clairmont has an Edwardian look; the smaller Bitton room is dominated by a four-poster bed. Breakfast had leaf tea, freshly squeezed orange juice, home-made fruit compote and preserves; an extensive choice for the full English or 'something lighter', perhaps melon with Parma ham.

Teign Street
Teignmouth TQ14 8EG

T: 01626-772976
E: alisonandjohn@
   thomas-luny-house.co.uk
W: www.thomas-luny-house.co.uk

BEDROOMS: 4.
OPEN: all year.
FACILITIES: 2 lounges, breakfast room, free Wi-Fi, small walled garden, sea (sandy beach 5 mins' walk), unsuitable for &.
BACKGROUND MUSIC: none.
LOCATION: town centre.
CHILDREN: not under 12.
DOGS: not allowed.
CREDIT CARDS: MasterCard, Visa.
PRICES: per person B&B £40–£75. 1-night bookings sometimes refused.

TEMPLE SOWERBY Cumbria

Map 4: inset C3

TEMPLE SOWERBY HOUSE

'As good as ever', this Grade II listed red brick mansion is run with 'palpable enthusiasm and professionalism' by the owners, Paul and Julie Evans. 'It exudes warmth, with open fires and cosy bedrooms in winter, and a lovely garden in summer,' say returning visitors this year. 'The staff are unfailingly kind and thoughtful.' The house stands within large walled gardens in a village of 18th- and 19th-century houses in the Eden valley. In the restaurant, which faces lawns and herbaceous borders, the long-serving chef, Ashley Whittaker, 'never runs out of creative ideas' for his contemporary menus. Typical dishes: Ash's corned beef, braised ox cheek, onion mousse; steamed sea bream, pak choi, jasmine rice. The 'honest' wine list 'does not break the bank'. The largest bedrooms are in the Georgian wing, which was added to the front of an older farmhouse. They have high ceilings and views of the village green; other rooms have original beams; all have a modern bathroom. Four rooms are in a coach house across the courtyard. No buffet at breakfast, which is served entirely at table. (*Simon and Mithra Tonking*)

25% DISCOUNT VOUCHERS

Temple Sowerby
Penrith CA10 1RZ

T: 017683-61578
F: 017683-61958
E: stay@templesowerby.com
W: www.templesowerby.com

BEDROOMS: 12, 2 on ground floor, 4 in coach house (20 yds).
OPEN: all year except 25/26 Dec.
FACILITIES: 2 lounges, bar, restaurant, conference/function facilities, free Wi-Fi, civil wedding licence, 2-acre garden (croquet).
BACKGROUND MUSIC: in restaurant at night.
LOCATION: village centre.
CHILDREN: not under 12.
DOGS: by prior arrangement in 2 bedrooms, not allowed in public rooms.
CREDIT CARDS: Amex, MasterCard, Visa.
PRICES: per room B&B £135–£160. D,B&B £85–£120 per person (min. 2 nights), set dinner £32.50–£41.50. 1-night bookings occasionally refused.

TETBURY Gloucestershire

Map 3:E5

CALCOT MANOR

♥ *César award in 2001*

'Child-friendly yet civilised for adults', this converted 14th-century farmhouse with surrounding outbuildings stands in extensive grounds in Cotswold countryside. Richard Ball is the managing director; his wife, Cathy, runs the spa. 'It was an inspired choice for our golden wedding celebration,' say visitors in 2013 in a three-generation party. 'We were given five rooms around a courtyard, close to the main house. All were extremely comfortable; we lacked for nothing. The staff were, without exception, friendly and helpful.' This year the *Conservatory* restaurant has been 'brought up to date' and given a 'relaxed' menu under the supervision of new executive chef Michael Stenekes. Dishes range from 'bite-size munchies' to 'ample and generous'. Alternative dining is in the *Gumstool Inn* which 'buzzes with activity'. 'Over three nights we dined in both restaurants and enjoyed everything we were given.' The youngest children have an Ofsted-registered *Playzone*; older ones have games consoles and computers in *The Mez*. 'We all enjoyed the spa.' *Barnsley House*, Barnsley (see entry), is under the same ownership. (*John and Jean Saul*)

nr Tetbury GL8 8YJ

T: 01666-890391
F: 01666-890394
E: frontdesk@calcotmanor.co.uk
W: www.calcotmanor.co.uk

BEDROOMS: 35, 10 (family) in cottage, 11 around courtyard, on ground floor.
OPEN: all year.
FACILITIES: ramps, lounge, 2 bars, 2 restaurants, private dining room, cinema, crèche, free Wi-Fi, civil wedding licence, 220-acre grounds (tennis, heated outdoor 8-metre swimming pool, children's play area, spa with 16-metre swimming pool).
BACKGROUND MUSIC: in restaurants.
LOCATION: 3 miles W of Tetbury.
CHILDREN: all ages welcomed.
DOGS: in courtyard bedrooms.
CREDIT CARDS: all major cards.
PRICES: [2013] per room B&B £280–£490, D,B&B (min. 2 nights midweek) £360–£580. À la carte £40. 1-night bookings usually refused weekends.

SEE ALSO SHORTLIST

THORPE MARKET Norfolk

Map 2:A5

THE GUNTON ARMS

On the edge of a deer park, this old inn (flint walls and red-painted gables) has been given a 'vibrant' interior by art dealer Ivor Braka and his artist wife, Sarah Graham. They have filled it with unusual pieces and artwork. 'A very relaxed place', it is run as a restaurant-with-rooms. The public areas have stone-flagged floors, roaring fires, mounted antlers on wood-panelled walls. The art ranges from Stubbs engravings to Tracey Emin neon signs. No expense has been spared on the bedrooms, which have handmade wallpaper, Turkish rugs, antique furniture; 'plenty of storage (free-range hangers) and the best lighting we've seen for ages'; 'a double washbasin and a huge retro bath in the bathroom'. No television; instead a Roberts radio 'in colours to match the decor'. There's help-yourself juices and tea/coffee in a downstairs pantry. Each of the two large lounges has a television. In a dining room 'like a medieval banqueting hall', the chef, Stuart Tattersall, cooks 'chunks of meat' (steaks, Barnsley chops, sausages, etc) and potatoes on a grill set over a huge open fire. Bread is fresh from the oven.

Cromer Road
Thorpe Market NR11 8TZ

T: 01263-832010
E: office@theguntonarms.co.uk
W: www.theguntonarms.co.uk

BEDROOMS: 8.
OPEN: all year except 25/26 Dec.
FACILITIES: 2 lounges, bar, restaurant, pantry, free Wi-Fi.
BACKGROUND MUSIC: in public areas.
LOCATION: 4 miles S of Cromer.
CHILDREN: all ages welcomed.
DOGS: allowed (£10 charge).
CREDIT CARDS: all major cards.
PRICES: [2013] per room B&B £95–£165. À la carte £35. 1-night bookings refused weekends.

TILLINGTON West Sussex

Map 2:E3

THE HORSE GUARDS INN **NEW**

'Everyone's idea of an English village pub', this 350-year-old inn stands opposite the church in a conservation village in the South Downs national park. It is owned and managed by Sam Beard and his partner, Michaela Hofirkova, whose 'can-do' attitude impressed *Guide* inspectors in 2013. On a cold, windy evening, 'our immediate impression was of warmth: from the log fires and in the greeting'. The bar has a sofa, wooden tables and chairs, stripped floorboards, a window seat. The adjoining dining room has low beams, a wood-burning stove. Mark Robinson is the chef. 'The food and drink are excellent: we declined Sussex snails with garlic butter, but enjoyed a feta cheese and spinach pastry; venison haslet from the daily-changing menu.' Two bedrooms are above the bar: 'Our room, up a steep flight of stairs, was surprisingly spacious. Simply decorated in shades of white and taupe, it had a beamed ceiling, a good wardrobe, a desk and a rocking chair; lights that were fit for purpose in the bathroom.' A third room is in a cottage next door. Breakfast has 'particularly good sausages'.

Upperton Road, Tillington
Petworth GU28 9AF

T: 01798-342332
E: info@thehorseguardsinn.co.uk
W: www.thehorseguardsinn.co.uk

BEDROOMS: 3, 1 in adjacent cottage.
OPEN: all year except 25 Dec.
FACILITIES: bar, dining room, free Wi-Fi, 1-acre garden, unsuitable for &.
BACKGROUND MUSIC: 'quiet' in pub.
LOCATION: 1 mile W of Petworth.
CHILDREN: all ages welcomed.
DOGS: allowed in 1 bedroom, public rooms.
CREDIT CARDS: MasterCard, Visa.
PRICES: [2013] per room B&B £85–£140. À la carte £25.

TITCHWELL Norfolk

Map 2:A5

TITCHWELL MANOR

In a pretty village overlooking barley fields and marshes, this stylish hotel/restaurant occupies a restored Victorian farmhouse with high ceilings, open fires ('kept going all day in winter') and views of the north Norfolk coastline. It is owned by Ian and Margaret Snaith; their son, Eric, is the chef. Visitors routinely praise the staff: 'Without exception, everyone is there to help and make guests feel relaxed, in an informal and unobtrusive way.' Varying in size and style, the 'well-equipped' bedrooms are spread between the manor house, the converted dairy, a modern building in the herb garden, and the Potting Shed (private entrance, roll-top bath, log burner). 'Traditional' rooms have muted colours; others in the main house have bold wallpaper and mismatched furniture. Eric Snaith's 'outstanding' dishes are served in the 'attractive' *Conservatory* restaurant, where a tasting menu might include mackerel cooked with a blowtorch, bergamot miso curd, cucumber. Informal, yet no less surprising, meals (parsnip crêpe, shiitake, truffle, thyme) are taken in the *Eating Rooms*, with its mermaid-print wallpaper and sea-facing terrace. (*Ann Williams, and others*)

Titchwell, nr Brancaster
PE31 8BB

T: 01485-210221
E: info@titchwellmanor.com
W: www.titchwellmanor.com

BEDROOMS: 27, 12 in herb garden, 4 in converted farm building, 1 in Potting Shed, 2 suitable for &.
OPEN: all year.
FACILITIES: 2 lounges, bar, 2 restaurants, free Wi-Fi, civil wedding licence, ⅓-acre garden (beaches, golf nearby).
BACKGROUND MUSIC: in public rooms.
LOCATION: on coast road, 6 miles E of Hunstanton.
CHILDREN: all ages welcomed.
DOGS: not allowed in main restaurant.
CREDIT CARDS: Amex, MasterCard, Visa.
PRICES: [2013] per room B&B £95–£250. D,B&B (min. 2 nights) £72.50–£127.50 per person, set menus £45–£60, à la carte £35. 1-night bookings sometimes refused weekends.

TITLEY Herefordshire

THE STAGG INN

🏆 *César award in 2013*

At the junction of two drovers' roads, this white-painted inn is an unusual combination of rustic pub (filled with locals) and *Michelin*-starred restaurant. It is run by Steve (the chef) Reynolds and his wife, Nicola. The three best bedrooms are in a part-Georgian, part-Victorian former vicarage 300 yards down the road (transport can be provided). In well-maintained gardens with a stream, it has 'handsome' bedrooms with a high ceiling, rugs on a wooden floor, fireplaces. Some guests found the road noisy; others 'were not bothered by the odd passing tractor'. 'The bedrooms above the bar have 'a comfortable bed, a spacious bathroom'. The 'understated' pub dining room (mismatched wooden tables, ochre walls) might lack the atmosphere of the bar but the cooking is admired. 'Steve uses great local ingredients, and knows what to do with them,' is this year's comment. 'The style is easy going,' according to an inspector. 'Starters and desserts stood out – cured salmon, avocado cream; three wonderful crèmes brûlées (a delicate lavender, coffee, and vanilla).' Breakfast, in the pub, has freshly squeezed orange juice, 'chunky' toast; 'excellent' cooked dishes.

Titley, nr Kington
HR5 3RL

T: 01544-230221
F: 01544-231390
E: reservations@thestagg.co.uk
W: www.thestagg.co.uk

BEDROOMS: 6, 3 at *Old Vicarage* (300 yds).
OPEN: all year except Sun night/Mon, 25/26 Dec, 1 Jan.
FACILITIES: (*Old Vicarage*) sitting room, free Wi-Fi, 1½-acre garden, (*Stagg Inn*) bar, restaurant areas, free Wi-Fi, small garden, unsuitable for &.
BACKGROUND MUSIC: none.
LOCATION: on B4355 between Kington (3½ miles) and Presteigne.
CHILDREN: all ages welcomed.
DOGS: only allowed in pub, some pub bedrooms.
CREDIT CARDS: all major cards.
PRICES: per room B&B £110–£140. À la carte £35. 1-night bookings sometimes refused.

TUDDENHAM Suffolk

Map 2:B5

TUDDENHAM MILL   NEW

On the Suffolk/Cambridgeshire border, this 18th-century mill (Grade II listed) has been given a modern make-over with bedrooms added in two wood-clad buildings. Owned by Agellus Hotels, a group of four hotels in East Anglia, it is managed by Lyndon Barrett-Scott. 'The style is luxurious, generous, thoughtful,' says the nominator. 'The mill has been nicely restored; open stonework, beams, the old mill race and grinding stones featured.' Her bedroom in one of the new buildings was 'light, modern; painted floorboards, crisp white linen, original art, minimal furniture; a really good bed; French windows opened on to a deck with seating'. The well-equipped bathroom had a 'powerful' walk-in shower; 'but nowhere to put storage bags'. The first-floor restaurant has outside decking overlooking the millpond. The chef, Paul Foster, serves 'interesting, delicious' dishes with 'delicate portions, well presented, if slightly samey. We enjoyed ray wing, vanilla-poached chicory; beef cheek and loin, artichoke purée, pickled turnip.' Breakfast has 'freshly squeezed orange juice, real butter, chunky marmalade, thick bread toast; good cooked dishes'. (*Carol Jackson*)

25% DISCOUNT VOUCHERS

High Street, Tuddenham
nr Newmarket IP28 6SQ

T: 01638-713552
E: info@tuddenhammill.co.uk
W: www.tuddenhammill.co.uk

BEDROOMS: 15, 12 in 2 separate buildings, 8 on ground floor, 1 suitable for &.
OPEN: all year.
FACILITIES: bar, restaurant, 2 function rooms, free Wi-Fi, 12-acre grounds.
BACKGROUND MUSIC: 'modern' in bar and restaurant.
LOCATION: in village, 8 miles NE of Newmarket.
CHILDREN: all ages welcomed.
DOGS: allowed (£15 a night).
CREDIT CARDS: MasterCard, Visa.
PRICES: [2013] per room B&B £185–£395. À la carte £38. 1-night bookings refused weekends.

TWO BRIDGES Devon

Map 1:D4

PRINCE HALL

NEW

In a 'glorious' position high on Dartmoor, with panoramic south-facing views, this small hotel is run by the owners, Fi and Chris Daly, who have 'a knack of making their guests feel special'. It is upgraded to a full entry after a positive report from a regular visitor (and *Guide* correspondent). 'It has improved beyond measure; service has become slicker, though it remains as friendly as ever to guests and their dogs.' Canine visitors, who stay free of charge, are given treats and can enjoy 'memorable walks' on the moor. The Dalys have 'redecorated inside and out, and refurnished to a high and agreeable standard'. The bedrooms have a country house style: the best (some with a sitting area) face the moors. Guests wanting to get away from it all can stay in a replica shepherd's hut in the grounds: it has an en suite bathroom with a limited supply of hot water. In the dining room, chef Richard Greenway uses local produce in his 'outstanding' daily-changing menu: the 'imaginative' modern dishes might include ballottine of pheasant, spiced potatoes, redcurrant jus; brill, pea and saffron risotto, pickled fennel. (*Paul Marland*)

Two Bridges
Dartmoor PL20 6SA

T: 01822-890403
E: info@princehall.co.uk
W: www.princehall.co.uk

BEDROOMS: 8, plus Shepherd's Hut in grounds.
OPEN: all year except 1st week Jan.
FACILITIES: 2 lounges, dining room, free Wi-Fi in bar/lounge, terrace, 5-acre grounds, only ground floor suitable for &.
BACKGROUND MUSIC: classical in early evening.
LOCATION: 1 mile E of Two Bridges.
CHILDREN: not under 10.
DOGS: allowed.
CREDIT CARDS: MasterCard, Visa.
PRICES: [2013] per room B&B £95–£180, D,B&B £165–£250. Set dinner £36.50–£42.50.

ULLSWATER Cumbria

Map 4: inset C2

HOWTOWN HOTEL

César award in 1991

Set back from the water on the quieter eastern shore on Lake Ullswater, the Baldry family's simple guest house 'evokes memories of times past'. The many repeat guests are attracted by the lack of mobile phone signal, Wi-Fi and the other essentials of modern life. The hotel doesn't have a computer, let alone an email address: bookings must be made by phone and confirmed in writing. There is only one television (in a lounge). Guests might choose not to watch it as they are encouraged to talk to each other. Newcomers who might be nervous of the house drills (a gong announces dinner at 7 pm and breakfast at 9 am) will be guided by returnees. Jacquie Baldry has been in charge for more than 50 years; she is assisted by her son, David. The bedrooms are simple (pink blankets) but there is turn-down in the evening. Most rooms have a lake view; four have a private bathroom across the corridor. A four-course dinner of traditional dishes is served six nights a week. Sunday has a cold supper. Breakfasts are generous. Superb walking from the door.

Ullswater, nr Penrith CA10 2ND

T: 01768-486514
W: www.howtown-hotel.com

BEDROOMS: 13, 4 in annexe, 4 self-catering cottages for weekly rent.
OPEN: Mar–1 Nov.
FACILITIES: 3 lounges, TV room, 2 bars, dining room, no Wi-Fi, 2-acre grounds, 200 yds from lake (private foreshore, fishing), walking, sailing, climbing, riding, golf nearby, unsuitable for &.
BACKGROUND MUSIC: none.
LOCATION: 4 miles S of Pooley Bridge, bus from Penrith station 9 miles.
CHILDREN: all ages welcomed (no special facilities).
DOGS: not allowed in public rooms.
CREDIT CARDS: none.
PRICES: [2013] per person D,B&B £89. Set dinner £25. 1-night bookings sometimes refused.

SEE ALSO SHORTLIST

ULVERSTON Cumbria

Map 4: inset C2

THE BAY HORSE

🐾 *César award in 2009*

'What a view to wake up to; we watched the sunrise from our balcony.' Robert Lyons and Lesley Wheeler's 17th-century former coaching inn has a 'serene setting' on the shore of the tidal Leven estuary, a birdwatchers' delight. 'Always reliable, and a real treat,' says a visitor in 2013. The bedrooms are small and bathrooms are simple; there is 'plenty of attention to detail in the housekeeping'. Visitors might find the decor 'somewhat retro', but all rooms are well equipped (a hospitality tray, magazines, board games, books). Best of all, six have French windows opening on to a terrace with seating. Robert Lyons is the chef in the 'excellent' conservatory restaurant (which has new chairs this year), where the evening meal is served at a single sitting at 8 pm ('We will be flexible about time whenever possible,' say the owners). 'He clearly loves cooking; my husband raved about his beef casserole.' The bar, which has new banquette seating, has a simpler menu. At the 'terrific' breakfast 'everything seemed to be home made or sourced locally'. 'Real value for money,' says a returning visitor. (*WK Wood, Lynn Wildgoose*)

Canal Foot
Ulverston
LA12 9EL

T: 01229-583972
F: 01229-580502
E: reservations@
thebayhorsehotel.co.uk
W: www.thebayhorsehotel.co.uk

BEDROOMS: 9.
OPEN: all year, restaurant closed Mon midday (light bar meals available).
FACILITIES: bar lounge, restaurant, free Wi-Fi, picnic area, unsuitable for ♿.
BACKGROUND MUSIC: mixed 'easy listening'.
LOCATION: 8 miles NE of Barrow-in-Furness.
CHILDREN: not under 9.
DOGS: not allowed in restaurant.
CREDIT CARDS: all major cards.
PRICES: per room B&B £95–£120. À la carte £30. 1-night bookings refused bank holidays.

UPPINGHAM Rutland

Map 2:B3

LAKE ISLE HOTEL & RESTAURANT

NEW

'A lovely place in the oldest part of a delightful town', Richard and Janine Burton's small hotel/ restaurant is named after the poem by WB Yeats. It is upgraded to a full entry thanks to an enthusiastic report by regular correspondents. 'It is very well run: the uniformly pleasant service (without effusiveness) was in keeping with the overall style.' In the restaurant, chef Stuart Mead cooks 'imaginative dishes in a contemporary British style without fuss or over-elaboration; all our choices over three nights were very good', perhaps shoulder of lamb, broad bean, mascarpone and pea risotto, glazed goat's cheese, courgette rösti. A bedroom in one of two attached cottages was 'carefully designed; immaculate and beautifully presented, nothing missed; good lighting and storage, a sitting area; everything we needed'. The rooms in the main house are individually designed; some have a whirlpool bath. 'Breakfast has a notably good choice with some original touches: compote of prunes and apricots in a light cinnamon and Earl Grey syrup; salmon and smoked haddock fishcakes. Good ingredients and flavours throughout.' (*Tony and Ginny Ayers*)

16 High Street East
Uppingham LE15 9PZ

T: 01572-822951
F: 01572-824400
E: info@lakeisle.co.uk
W: www.lakeisle.co.uk

BEDROOMS: 12, 2 in cottages.
OPEN: all year except bank holiday Mon, 1–3 Jan, restaurant closed Sun night, Mon lunch.
FACILITIES: lounge, bar, restaurant, free Wi-Fi, unsuitable for &.
BACKGROUND MUSIC: in restaurant.
LOCATION: town centre.
CHILDREN: all ages welcomed.
DOGS: allowed in bedrooms by arrangement, not in public areas.
CREDIT CARDS: Diners, MasterCard, Visa.
PRICES: per room B&B single £59.50–£69.50, double £80–£110, D,B&B single £89.50–£99.50, double £135–£165. À la carte £30.

VENTNOR Isle of Wight

Map 2:E2

HILLSIDE

The Danish owner (and 'wildlife enthusiast'), Gert Bach, is 'a most charming host' at this small hotel, in a thatched mellow stone villa overlooking the Victorian seaside town. 'He provided exceptional standards of service' to a visitor this year. 'All our needs were superbly catered for,' is another comment, from a guest whose allergies required a change to non-feather bedding. The Grade II listed Georgian house has a 'modern, fresh, Scandinavian decor' and 'superb views across the sea'; bedrooms are styled in shades of white with contrasting Welsh blankets. An 'excellent' dinner is served 'efficiently and with a smile' between 7 pm and 8 pm (meals must be ordered in advance); French-influenced menus include 'much local produce', perhaps a seasonal home-made terrine; pan-fried sea bass, Ventnor Bay crab and spring onion risotto. The wine list has 'reasonable prices'; many wines are offered by the glass. In Ventnor, the *Bistro*, under the same ownership, 'served up the same wonderful standards as the hotel'. 'Breakfast reflected the quality of dinner', with home-made muesli and preserves; cooked dishes have home-made sausages. (*Elaine and Frank Sandell, Bill Bennett*)

25% DISCOUNT VOUCHERS

151 Mitchell Avenue
Ventnor PO38 1DR

T: 01983-852271
E: mail@hillsideventnor.co.uk
W: www.hillsideventnor.co.uk

BEDROOMS: 12, plus 2 self-catering apartments.
OPEN: all year, restaurant closed Sun.
FACILITIES: bar, lounge, restaurant, conservatory, free Wi-Fi, terrace, 5-acre garden, unsuitable for &.
BACKGROUND MUSIC: in public areas.
LOCATION: Top of town, at foot of St Boniface Down.
CHILDREN: not under 12.
DOGS: not allowed.
CREDIT CARDS: MasterCard, Visa.
PRICES: per person B&B £75, D,B&B £99. Set meals £28. Min. 2-night stay.

SEE ALSO SHORTLIST

VERYAN-IN-ROSELAND Cornwall

Map 1:D2

THE NARE

🏆 *César award in 2003*

'Impossible to describe without running out of superlatives', Toby Ashworth's luxury hotel has a beautiful setting above Carne Beach on the Roseland peninsula. It may be old school in style ('a long-gone world') but it attracts many repeat visitors. 'Everything is so perfect that somehow the rather steep bill seems quite reasonable,' explains a *Guide* inspector. Guests are greeted by name and helped to unload their car which is then driven away. There are 'masses of current magazines, fresh flowers and wonderful log fires' in the public rooms. 'Best of all is the staff', who are 'attentive, highly efficient, cheerful'. The bedrooms have 'lovely antiques' and modern plumbing; a computerised heating system and a hot-water bottle left in the bed at turn-down. Sea-facing rooms are larger (and more expensive) than country-facing rooms. 'Although an informal atmosphere prevails at the *Nare* in the evening, most gentlemen prefer to wear a jacket and tie in the *Dining Room*,' says Toby Ashworth. Informal dining is available in the *Quarterdeck*. Wi-Fi is now without charge. (*Peter Govier, and others*)

Carne Beach
Veryan-in-Roseland
nr Truro TR2 5PF

T: 01872-501111
F: 01872-501856
E: stay@narehotel.co.uk
W: www.narehotel.co.uk

BEDROOMS: 37, some on ground floor, 1 in adjoining cottage, 5 suitable for ♿.
OPEN: all year.
FACILITIES: lift, ramps, lounge, drawing room, sun lounge, bar, billiard room, light lunch/supper room, 2 restaurants, conservatory, free Wi-Fi, indoor 10-metre swimming pool, gym, 2-acre grounds (heated 15-metre swimming pool, tennis, safe sandy beach), concessionary golf at Truro golf club.
BACKGROUND MUSIC: none.
LOCATION: S of Veryan, on coast.
CHILDREN: all ages welcomed.
DOGS: not allowed in public rooms.
CREDIT CARDS: Amex, MasterCard, Visa.
PRICES: [2013] per room B&B £270–£768. Set dinner £50, à la carte £60.

WADDESDON Buckinghamshire

Map 2:C3

THE FIVE ARROWS

On the site of an old coaching inn, this 'immaculate' small hotel at the gates of Waddesdon Manor was built in 1887 to house the architects and craftsmen working on the manor itself. Like the historic house, the hotel is run by the Rothschild family trust for the National Trust; the manager is Alex McEwen. It is 'a broadly comfortable environment with helpful, cheerful staff,' say visitors this year. The individually designed bedrooms have antiques from the manor; those overlooking the courtyard (rather than the busy road in front) are the most tranquil. 'Our room was quiet and comfortable; there was not enough light for reading.' The 'pleasant' dining room has 'well-spaced tables'; chef Karl Penny's modern European menu (changed weekly) has some 'interesting choices', perhaps slow-cooked pork belly, poached Granny Smith; pan-fried fillet of trout, marinated tomatoes, pea shoot salad. 'Breakfast was excellent, with a full range of main dishes served promptly.' Less liked is the 'limited lounge space'. National Trust members qualify for a ten per cent discount on B&B rates.

High Street
Waddesdon HP18 0JE

T: 01296-651727
F: 01296-658596
E: five.arrows@nationaltrust.org.uk
W: www.thefivearrows.co.uk

BEDROOMS: 11, 3, in courtyard, on ground floor.
OPEN: all year.
FACILITIES: bar, restaurant, free Wi-Fi, civil wedding licence, 1-acre garden.
BACKGROUND MUSIC: none.
LOCATION: in village.
CHILDREN: all ages welcomed.
DOGS: allowed in 1 bedroom, not in public rooms.
CREDIT CARDS: Amex, MasterCard, Visa.
PRICES: per person B&B £52.50–£117.50, D,B&B £80–£120. À la carte £28.

WAREHAM Dorset

Map 2:E1

THE PRIORY

🦋 *César award in 1996*

In a 'stunning' location by the River Frome, this old country hotel with its beautifully kept gardens has 'lots of character and charm'. A former 16th-century convent, it is owned by Anne Turner and her brother-in-law, Stuart. 'I was afraid it might be somewhat stuffy but not a bit of it,' said a trusted reporter. 'The atmosphere was relaxed, the well-heeled clientele (many making a return visit) were friendly, and the hosts were most welcoming.' The public rooms are 'full of antique (but comfortable) furniture'; in fine weather, alfresco lunches are taken on linen-covered tables on the terrace. In the main house and the converted boathouse on the riverbank, bedrooms have books, magazines and fresh fruit. 'Our first-floor room had a view over the garden and river; housekeeping was of a high standard.' After pre-dinner drinks and home-made canapés ('the jazz pianist in the drawing room was a lovely touch and not overwhelming'), guests dine in the *Abbot's Cellar*, where the tables are 'beautifully laid'; chef Stephan Guinebault's 'very good' meals might include line-caught cod, bouillabaisse risotto. (*Bill Bennett, and others*)

25% DISCOUNT VOUCHERS

Church Green
Wareham
BH20 4ND

T: 01929-551666
F: 01929-554519
E: reservations@theprioryhotel.co.uk
W: www.theprioryhotel.co.uk

BEDROOMS: 18, some on ground floor (in courtyard), 4 suites in Boathouse.
OPEN: all year.
FACILITIES: ramps, lounge, drawing room, bar, 2 dining rooms, free Wi-Fi, 4-acre gardens (croquet, river frontage, moorings, fishing), unsuitable for &.
BACKGROUND MUSIC: pianist in drawing room Sat night.
LOCATION: town centre.
CHILDREN: not under 14.
DOGS: not allowed.
CREDIT CARDS: all major cards.
PRICES: [2013] per room B&B £210–£370. D,B&B £132.50–£212.50 per person, set dinner £45. 1-night bookings sometimes refused.

WATERMILLOCK Cumbria

Map 4: inset C2

RAMPSBECK

'We received a warm welcome, with a brolly, in the rain and were given an upgrade to "make up for your horrid journey".' John Brooksbank's whitewashed 18th-century Lakeland country house stands in mature grounds with views over Ullswater and the Fells. There have been significant changes in personnel this year. Valentin Gadzhonov has joined as manager and Ian Jackson is now the chef. There are comfortable settees in the panelled hall, where a log fire burns in the winter; the drawing room has an ornate ceiling and a marble fireplace. Afternoon tea and light meals can be taken on a terrace in warmer months. Most bedrooms face the lake or garden: 'Ours was Martindale, a junior suite, which had lovely views through an enormous window. A very elegant room with sofa, chair and coffee table, a beautifully dressed bed and sumptuous curtains.' In the candlelit dining room, Ian Jackson's 'Taste Cumbria' menu might include caramelised scallops, apple purée, black pudding; Lowther Estate venison, artichoke gratin, baby vegetables. (*Barbara Watkinson, John Barnes, and others*)

Watermillock on Ullswater
nr Penrith CA11 0LP

T: 01768-486442
F: 01768-486688
E: enquiries@rampsbeck.co.uk
W: www.rampsbeck.co.uk

BEDROOMS: 19.
OPEN: all year.
FACILITIES: 3 lounges, bar, restaurant, free Wi-Fi, civil wedding licence, 18-acre grounds (croquet), lake frontage (fishing, sailing, windsurfing, etc).
BACKGROUND MUSIC: none.
LOCATION: 5½ miles SW of Penrith.
CHILDREN: children under 7 not allowed in restaurant at night.
DOGS: allowed in 3 bedrooms, hall lounge.
CREDIT CARDS: Diners, MasterCard, Visa.
PRICES: [2013] per person B&B £72.50–£150, D,B&B £120–£195. Set dinner £59.95. 1-night bookings occasionally refused.

WELLS Somerset

STOBERRY HOUSE

'It's like a home away from home but better.'
The view is 'stunning' from Frances and Tim
Young's converted coach house (dating back to
1745), and 'the hospitality is outstanding'. Praise
from a visitor this year to this elegant B&B
(Wolsey Lodge). 'Frances and her husband,
Tim, are a delightful couple and fantastic hosts;
they go above and beyond to help.' The house
stands in parkland with grazing sheep and a
formal garden – 'a vast and interesting area with
sculptures dotted about the grounds and ponds
stocked with sizeable fish providing hours of
diversion'. Visitors are welcomed with hot drinks
and home baking on arrival; guests staying in
the main house have access to a pantry for light
snacks. Bedrooms are individually styled; one
has a four-poster bed. Breakfast is 'copious and
delicious': 'There must have been four or five
home-made breads, plus home-made scones and
croissants.' Special diets are catered for. There
are many walks from the bottom of the grounds:
birdwatching kits and a comprehensive picnic
menu (salads, pork pies, pâtés, roulade) are
available. (*Lizzy Laczynska, and others*)

Stoberry Park
Wells BA5 3LD

T: 01749-672906
F: 01749-674175
E: stay@stoberry-park.co.uk
W: www.stoberry-park.co.uk

BEDROOMS: 5, 1 in studio cottage.
OPEN: all year except 15 Dec–5 Jan.
FACILITIES: sitting room, breakfast
room, free Wi-Fi, 6½-acre grounds,
unsuitable for &.
BACKGROUND MUSIC: none.
LOCATION: outskirts of Wells.
CHILDREN: all ages welcomed.
DOGS: not allowed.
CREDIT CARDS: Amex (*3%
surcharge*), MasterCard, Visa.
PRICES: per person B&B
(continental) £42.50–£80. Cooked
breakfast £5.50.

WEST HOATHLY West Sussex

Map 2:E4

❧ THE CAT INN

[NEW]

César award: newcomer of the year

Opposite the church in a pretty hilltop village in the Sussex Weald, this 16th-century inn has a 'welcoming atmosphere and interesting food' (says a *Guide* inspector). It is run by the 'helpful proprietor', Andrew Russell, who was formerly the respected manager of *Gravetye Manor*, East Grinstead (see entry). 'He welcomed us warmly and carried our bag to our first-floor room. Simply but pleasantly furnished, it was immaculate; a good king-size bed; oak chests, bedside tables with reading lamps; a proper mirror; a shower over the bath and decent towels and dressing gowns with an embroidered black cat.' The bar, which has a range of real ales and an 'excellent' wine list, opens on to two dining areas (with cosy nooks and crannies, one with an inglenook fireplace). Max Leonard is the chef. 'We enjoyed rare roast beef with a truffle oil salad; Rye Bay plaice with grey shrimps. The staff were full of enthusiasm and very efficient.' Breakfast, served by Andrew Russell, had 'cereals, fresh fruit; delicious bacon in the full English'. Maps are available for the 'numerous walks in the area'.

25% DISCOUNT VOUCHERS

North Lane
West Hoathly RH19 4PP

T: 01342-810369
E: thecatinn@googlemail.com
W: www.catinn.co.uk

BEDROOMS: 4.
OPEN: all year except 25 Dec, restaurant closed Sun evening.
FACILITIES: bar, 2 dining areas, free Wi-Fi, small terrace.
BACKGROUND MUSIC: none.
LOCATION: in village.
CHILDREN: not under 7.
DOGS: allowed.
CREDIT CARDS: MasterCard, Visa.
PRICES: [2013] per room B&B single £90–£130, double £110–£150. À la carte £25–£30.

WHASHTON North Yorkshire

Map 4:C3

THE HACK & SPADE   NEW

In a tiny hilltop village in the Swale valley, this old pub has been renovated by Jane and Andy Ratcliffe, who run it as an 'unpretentious' restaurant-with-rooms. 'Hospitable and enthusiastic hosts, they have created a quirky, interesting place,' say *Guide* inspectors, who had a 'most enjoyable stay' in 2013. 'The uncluttered bedrooms have a cool, contemporary feel. Our large room had an enormous bed with an upholstered headboard; two walls were painted off-white, two had striking tulip-design wallpaper; ample storage and free-range hangers in an oak wardrobe. A huge tiled bathroom added the wow factor.' A wood-burning stove separates a lounge from the restaurant, which has wooden tables, 'interesting' pictures and displays. Jane Ratcliffe is the chef: 'We had a very good twice-baked soufflé; tasty and well-cooked lemon sole fillets with brown shrimps; a large dish of vegetables (this is Yorkshire).' No menu at breakfast, just a question: 'What would you like?' 'We chose scrambled eggs on brown toast: we were asked whether we would like the toast buttered – extra brownie points. The eggs arrived hot and runny, the toast buttery; excellent.'

Whashton
Richmond DL11 7JL

T: 01748-823721
E: reservations@hackandspade.com
W: www.hackandspade.com

BEDROOMS: 5.
OPEN: all year except 2 weeks Jan.
FACILITIES: lounge, restaurant, free Wi-Fi, only restaurant suitable for &.
BACKGROUND MUSIC: none.
LOCATION: 4 miles NW of Richmond.
CHILDREN: not under 7.
DOGS: not allowed.
CREDIT CARDS: MasterCard, Visa.
PRICES: [2013] per room B&B £110–£130. À la carte £25.

WHITEWELL Lancashire

Map 4:D3

THE INN AT WHITEWELL

Above a river full of trout and salmon, this 14th-century manor house in the Forest of Bowland is run with good humour by Charles Bowman. In his absence, inspectors reported that 'whoever you ask for anything replies, "Of course." It is a busy place; the bars were humming on a sunny weekend.' A reader's comment (in 2013): 'Just perfect.' Most of the ground floor is occupied by the bar and restaurant: 'Nice old wooden tables and chairs of all shapes and sizes; some sofas, sporting and fashion prints on the walls; all great fun.' In the 'calm' dining room – with 'well-spaced tables and a carpet, so you can hear yourself talk' – the chef is Jamie Cadman: 'We enjoyed a good dinner: a vegetable ravioli; rack of lamb. No muzak, a joy.' The bedrooms are individually styled; the best have river views. 'Our huge room was one of the nicest we have stayed in; it had a good-sized bed, old-fashioned wardrobe, gas fire; a modern bathroom with an old marble floor. The bay windows looked over the river to ancient trees and cattle; we were provided with two pairs of binoculars.' (*John Butterfield, and others*)

Whitewell, Forest of Bowland
nr Clitheroe BB7 3AT

T: 01200-448222
F: 01200-448298
E: reception@innatwhitewell.com
W: www.innatwhitewell.com

BEDROOMS: 23, 4 (2 on ground floor) in coach house, 150 yds.
OPEN: all year.
FACILITIES: 2 bars, restaurant, boardroom, private dining room, free Wi-Fi, civil wedding licence, 5-acre garden, 7 miles fishing (ghillie available), unsuitable for &.
BACKGROUND MUSIC: none.
LOCATION: 6 miles NW of Clitheroe.
CHILDREN: all ages welcomed.
DOGS: not allowed in dining room.
CREDIT CARDS: MasterCard, Visa.
PRICES: [2013] per room B&B £88–£194. À la carte £35.

WILMINGTON East Sussex

Map 2:E4

CROSSWAYS HOTEL

'Having completed 25 years at *Crossways*, we are going into our second quarter-century with the same passion,' say David Stott and Clive James. Their restaurant-with-rooms at the foot of the South Downs national park attracts many returning visitors. 'A two-day Glyndebourne stay has become an annual ritual,' says a long-term fan. 'There was lots of badinage over dinner, which fits in with the place.' The modern bedrooms in the white-painted Georgian house are styled in neutral tones with brightly contrasting fabrics; one has a balcony overlooking the 'delightful' garden. The many extra touches are appreciated, eg, a slipcase full of Penguin classics. David Stott seeks local producers and suppliers for his four-course menus of modern English dishes. In the newly refurnished dining room, his meals may include wild mushroom éclair; guineafowl breast wrapped in bacon. Breakfast is served in a 'sunny, pleasing' room with an 'astonishing collection of covered cheese dishes'; cooked dishes use eggs laid just down the road. In fine weather, a recently erected gazebo provides a place for guests to lounge alfresco. (*Richard Parish*)

25% DISCOUNT VOUCHERS

Lewes Road
Wilmington
BN26 5SG

T: 01323-482455
F: 01323-487811
E: stay@crosswayshotel.co.uk
W: www.crosswayshotel.co.uk

BEDROOMS: 7, also self-catering cottage.
OPEN: all year except 22 Dec–22 Jan, restaurant closed Sun/Mon evening.
FACILITIES: breakfast room, restaurant, free Wi-Fi, 2-acre grounds (duck pond), unsuitable for &.
BACKGROUND MUSIC: quiet classical in restaurant.
LOCATION: 2 miles W of Polegate on A27.
CHILDREN: not under 12.
DOGS: not allowed.
CREDIT CARDS: Amex, MasterCard, Visa.
PRICES: per room B&B £135–£170. D,B&B £110–£120 per person, set dinner £40.

WINCHCOMBE Gloucestershire

Map 3:D5

THE LION INN

NEW

In the centre of a Saxon town, this 15th-century inn has been given a contemporary make-over by the owner, Annie Fox-Hamilton. 'She has done a fine job, creating a relaxed, modern air,' say *Guide* inspectors in 2013. The public areas have been decorated in Scandinavian style; a 'club room' has 'good seating, an open fire, lots of magazines, newspapers'. There are 'superb floral displays throughout'. Meals can be taken in the bar ('a buzzy, warm atmosphere') or in the restaurant with its well-spaced wooden tables. The chef, Martyn Pearn, describes his style as rustic. 'His cooking is excellent: a memorable starter, heritage tomato consommé, was bursting with flavour; lemon sole was stuffed with plump freshwater crayfish; a side dish of buttered vegetables. Alas, the background music became increasingly irksome.' The bedrooms are decorated in subdued colours: 'Our high-ceilinged room was painted in shades of grey; a vast chest of drawers, a built-in wardrobe with free-range hangers. No TV (a radio would have been nice); some noise from the courtyard.' Two rooms, reached by a courtyard staircase, were being amalgamated in late 2013.

37 North Street
Winchcombe GL54 5PS

T: 01242-603300
E: reception@thelionwinchcombe.co.uk
W: www.thelionwinchcombe.co.uk

BEDROOMS: 6, 2 accessed by external staircase.
OPEN: all year.
FACILITIES: club room, bar, restaurant, free Wi-Fi in bar, some bedrooms, courtyard garden, unsuitable for &.
BACKGROUND MUSIC: in bar and restaurant.
LOCATION: town centre.
CHILDREN: all ages welcomed.
DOGS: allowed in bedrooms (£15), bar.
CREDIT CARDS: MasterCard, Visa.
PRICES: per room B&B £110–£180, D,B&B £170–£240. À la carte £30.

WINDERMERE Cumbria

Map 4: inset C2

GILPIN HOTEL AND LAKE HOUSE

César award in 2000

'As always, a perfect stay: it might have become more glitzy as it has expanded, but it remains our favourite, a gold standard for small luxury hotels.' Praise from a trusted reporter this year, returning to the Cunliffe family's country house hotel (Relais & Châteaux). It is run by Barney and Zoë Cunliffe, and his parents, John and Christine. The Edwardian building has extensive grounds with terrace, pond, waterfall, croquet lawn. 'Our suite had a door to the garden, a nice sitting area; fresh milk in the fridge for the tea- and coffee-making facilities.' Another comment: 'Such luxury; our room was well furnished, with a large sofa, easy chairs and a dressing table; our only problem was the lack of storage, virtually no drawer space; an enormous bathroom.' There is a new chef this year, Dan Grigg. 'His dishes were quite rich but he would make alterations which was most helpful,' said a visitor in 2013. A typical dish: taste of Herdwick mutton (shoulder, rib, suet), tomato essence, swede. 'The young staff seemed to enjoy what they were doing.' Breakfast is 'excellent'. (*Wolfgang Stroebe, Sue Raymond*)

Crook Road
nr Windermere LA23 3NE

T: 015394-88818
F: 015394-88058
E: hotel@gilpinlodge.co.uk
W: www.gilpinlodge.co.uk

BEDROOMS: 26, 6 in orchard wing, 6 in *Lake House* (½ mile from main house).
OPEN: all year.
FACILITIES: ramps, bar, 2 lounges, 4 dining rooms, free Wi-Fi, 22-acre grounds (ponds, croquet), free access to nearby country club, golf course opposite, unsuitable for &.
BACKGROUND MUSIC: none.
LOCATION: on B5284, 2 miles SE of Windermere.
CHILDREN: not under 7.
DOGS: not allowed (kennels at nearby farm).
CREDIT CARDS: all major cards.
PRICES: [2013] per person B&B £128–£258, D,B&B £40 added. Set dinner £58.50. 1-night bookings refused Sat.

SEE ALSO SHORTLIST

WINDERMERE Cumbria

Map 4: inset C2

HOLBECK GHYLL

'A wonderful welcome and a proper
introduction to the hotel facilities,' was given to
a visitor in 2013 to this creeper-covered former
hunting lodge in large grounds overlooking
Lake Windermere. Owned by Stephen and Lisa
Leahy, it is managed by Andrew McPherson.
The Arts and Crafts-inspired house has been
restored with great attention to detail: fine
stained glass, wood carvings on the stair banister.
'A lovely fire greeted us in the hall, even in
June.' 'The resident dog, Daisy, will generously
allow you to tickle her ears.' Individually styled
bedrooms overlook the lake or the hills; the
Lodge, up 'a steep bit' from the hotel, has
'magnificent' views. A decanter of locally
distilled damson gin is left in the room. 'My wife
was impressed that a hot-water bottle had been
put in the bed.' In the restaurant, chef David
McLaughlin has a *Michelin* star for his modern
cooking (dishes like cèpe-scented pork fillet,
braised belly, black pudding beignet, cassoulet).
The hotel is 'ideally placed' for walking: 'a
superb cooked breakfast kept us going all day'.
(*Helen Hobson, Barbara Watkinson, and others*)

Holbeck Lane
Windermere LA23 1LU

T: 015394-32375
F: 015394-34743
E: stay@holbeckghyll.com
W: www.holbeckghyll.com

BEDROOMS: 25, 1 suitable for ♿, 6 in
lodge, 5 in cottages, 2 suites.
OPEN: all year.
FACILITIES: ramp, 2 lounges, bar,
restaurant, free Wi-Fi, function
facilities, civil wedding licence,
small spa, 17-acre grounds (tennis,
putting, croquet, jogging track).
BACKGROUND MUSIC: none.
LOCATION: 4 miles N of
Windermere.
CHILDREN: not under 8 in restaurant.
DOGS: allowed in lodge rooms;
welcome pack.
CREDIT CARDS: Amex, MasterCard,
Visa.
PRICES: per room B&B £190–£470,
D,B&B £310–£590. Set dinner £65
per person. 1-night bookings
sometimes refused Sat.

SEE ALSO SHORTLIST

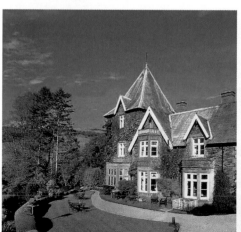

WOLD NEWTON East Yorkshire

Map 4:D5

THE WOLD COTTAGE

In landscaped grounds within a 300-acre farm, this red brick Georgian country house has a 'wonderful rural location'. It is run as a B&B (with evening meals by arrangement) by the owners, Katrina and Derek Gray. Four of the spacious bedrooms are in the main house; two are in a converted barn. A 'light and airy barn room was well appointed; plenty of hot water and toiletries'. There are two self-catering cottages in the grounds. Evening meals, cooked by Katrina Gray and served by her husband, are taken in the candlelit dining room. She places importance on the provenance of the produce; fruit and vegetables are grown in the garden, and local organic flour is used for making fresh bread every morning. The 'excellent' breakfast has locally smoked fish, cereals, fresh fruit, yogurt; full English. Jams are home made. Guests can explore the immediate area (don't miss the obelisk that marks the spot, 150 yards from the house, where a 56-pound meteorite landed in 1795). The Yorkshire Wolds landscape was the inspiration for David Hockney's *A Bigger Picture*. (*F and RB, and others*)

Wold Newton, nr Driffield
YO25 3HL

T/F: 01262-470696
E: katrina@woldcottage.com
W: www.woldcottage.com

BEDROOMS: 6, 2 in converted barn, 1 on ground floor.
OPEN: all year.
FACILITIES: lounge, dining room, free Wi-Fi, 3-acre grounds (croquet) in 300-acre farmland.
BACKGROUND MUSIC: at mealtimes, contemporary.
LOCATION: just outside village.
CHILDREN: all ages welcomed.
DOGS: not allowed.
CREDIT CARDS: MasterCard, Visa.
PRICES: [2013] per person B&B £50–£75, D,B&B £78–£103. Set dinner £28.

WOLTERTON Norfolk

Map 2:A5

THE SARACEN'S HEAD

In a 'lovely, quiet setting in the north Norfolk countryside', this creeper-clad Georgian building was designed (on an architect's whim) in the style of a Tuscan farmhouse. It is run as a rural inn by the owners, Tim and Janie Elwes, who say they seek 'to provide a relaxed home from home'. He is 'an informal host', said inspectors who found the inn 'an honest place, very laid-back'. The public areas have been decorated in traditional style, while the bedrooms have a more modern look. 'We slept really well in a large, firm bed; modern units in the bathroom, which had plenty of storage, nice toiletries.' The chef, Mark Sayers, serves a seasonal menu which may be taken in the 'homely' bar ('like a snug' with a wood-burning stove), or in the smarter parlour, which has an open fire. Typical dishes: Norfolk mussels, shallots, smoked bacon, tomatoes; chargrilled sirloin steak, sauté potatoes and peppercorn sauce. Children are welcomed and have their own menu. The small upstairs sitting room is supplied with guides, maps and books. Breakfast has 'delicious scrambled eggs with smoked salmon'.

Wall Road
Wolterton, nr Erpingham
NR11 7LZ

T: 01263-768909
F: 01263-768993
E: info@saracenshead-norfolk.co.uk
W: www.saracenshead-norfolk.co.uk

BEDROOMS: 6.

OPEN: all year except Christmas, restaurant closed Mon, Tues lunchtime except summer.

FACILITIES: lounge, bar, restaurant, free Wi-Fi, courtyard, 1-acre garden, accommodation unsuitable for &.

BACKGROUND MUSIC: 'when suitable' in bar and dining rooms.

LOCATION: 5 miles N of Aylsham.

CHILDREN: all ages welcomed.

DOGS: not allowed in restaurant.

CREDIT CARDS: MasterCard, Visa.

PRICES: [2013] per room B&B single £70, double £100. D,B&B £30 added per person, à la carte £30.

WOOLACOMBE Devon

Map 1:B4

WATERSMEET

In 'the most glorious' setting, on a cliff above Woolacombe Bay, Amanda James's traditional hotel does 'most things right'. 'The loveliness of the views is matched by the graciousness of the accommodation,' says a visitor in 2013. It is a 'welcoming' place; 'staff are polite, efficient and interested'. In the dining room, which has 90-degree views of the bay, the chef, John Prince, serves classic dishes, perhaps confit duck salad, honey and cider dressing; John Dory, tarragon sauce, peas, bacon and wild mushrooms. 'All nicely cooked, presented and served,' wrote a guest who was disappointed only with the desserts and the lack of variety in the menu. The background music in the public areas was 'low and non-repetitive' to one visitor, 'jarring' to another. Simpler meals 'for all ages' are available in the *Bistro*, which is open to non-residents. All but three of the bedrooms have a sea view; the best have a wooden balcony or a garden terrace. 'My spacious room had a seating area with a view of the cove; a comfortable bed, responsive heating; a beautiful, well-equipped bathroom.' (*Sara Hollowell, Robin Wright, and others*)

Mortehoe
Woolacombe EX34 7EB

T: 01271-870333
F: 01271-870890
E: info@watersmeethotel.co.uk
W: www.watersmeethotel.co.uk

BEDROOMS: 29, 3 on ground floor, 1 suitable for &.
OPEN: all year.
FACILITIES: lift, lounge, bar, restaurant, bistro, function room, free Wi-Fi, civil wedding licence, terrace, ½-acre gardens, heated indoor and outdoor swimming pools, sandy beach below.
BACKGROUND MUSIC: classical/modern.
LOCATION: by sea, 4 miles SW of Ilfracombe.
CHILDREN: all ages welcomed.
DOGS: not allowed.
CREDIT CARDS: MasterCard, Visa (*3% surcharge on credit cards*).
PRICES: [2013] per person B&B £67–£206, D,B&B £92–£231. À la carte (*Bistro*) £30.

YARM North Yorkshire

Map 4:C4

JUDGES

The 'care and attention to detail' are praised this year at this traditional hotel, a restored Victorian mansion in extensive grounds (that became a residence for circuit judges). Owned by the Downs family, it is managed by Tim Howard ('friendly and charming'). 'All is peaceful and quiet' in the extensive grounds, which have well-tended lawns, a kitchen garden; waterfalls and ornate bridges; natural woodland with pathways and shady seats. 'Charming' bedrooms have watercolours and prints in gilt frames, fresh flowers, a decanter of sherry and 'all the usual modern equipment'; three have a four-poster bed. 'A novelty was a goldfish, Finn, who we were asked to talk to and feed.' All the bathrooms have now been renovated, and work has begun on the bedrooms. The conservatory dining room is 'light and bright, with beautiful views over the gardens'; chef John Schwarz's 'excellent' modern dishes might include diver-caught scallop; caramelised foie gras, satay, radish, lime; English rose veal, wild mushrooms, sweetbread ragout. Breakfast has freshly squeezed orange juice, fresh fruits and 'plenty of cooked options'. Popular with wedding parties. (*RW, and others*)

25% DISCOUNT VOUCHERS

Kirklevington Hall
Yarm TS15 9LW

T: 01642-789000
F: 01642-782878
E: reservations@judgeshotel.co.uk
W: www.judgeshotel.co.uk

BEDROOMS: 21, some on ground floor.
OPEN: all year.
FACILITIES: ramps, lounge, bar, restaurant, private dining room, free Wi-Fi, function facilities, business centre, civil wedding licence, 36-acre grounds (paths, running routes), access to local spa and sports club.
BACKGROUND MUSIC: none.
LOCATION: 1½ miles S of centre.
CHILDREN: all ages welcomed.
DOGS: only guide dogs allowed.
CREDIT CARDS: all major cards.
PRICES: [2013] per person B&B £65–£110, D,B&B £97.50–£142.50. Set dinner £37.50, à la carte £55.

YORK North Yorkshire

MIDDLETHORPE HALL & SPA

'From the moment we arrived, we were surrounded by antiques, beautiful furnishings and friendly, attentive but discreet staff: we had entered a calmer world.' Praise for a 'very special place', a red brick William and Mary country mansion by the racecourse on the outskirts of York. Owned by the National Trust, it is managed by Lionel Chatard. It is 'a pleasure to stroll around the well-tended gardens', which have a lake, and many specimen trees which partly shield the noise of York's busy ring road. Public rooms, decorated in period style, have leather chesterfields, antiques, gilded mirrors and historic paintings. In the formal panelled dining room (smart casual dress required; white damask tablecloths and napkins), chef Nicholas Evans serves an 'excellent' modern British menu of dishes like roast king scallops, carrots, blood orange, gingerbread; slow-cooked neck of lamb, quinoa, broccoli, wild garlic. The 'attention to detail is exemplary' in the bedrooms. The best, in the main house, have a sitting room and a gas coal fire. A suite in the coach house was 'delightful in every way; a comfortable king-size bed; relaxing lounge; excellent bathroom'. (*JB*)

Bishopthorpe Road
York YO23 2GB

T: 01904-641241
F: 01904-620176
E: info@middlethorpe.com
W: www.middlethorpe.com

BEDROOMS: 29, 17 in courtyard, 2 in garden, 1 suitable for &.
OPEN: all year.
FACILITIES: drawing room, sitting rooms, library, bar, restaurant, free Wi-Fi, civil wedding licence, 20-acre grounds, spa (indoor swimming pool, 10 by 5 metres).
BACKGROUND MUSIC: none.
LOCATION: 1½ miles S of centre.
CHILDREN: not under 6.
DOGS: only in garden suites, not in public rooms.
CREDIT CARDS: Amex, MasterCard, Visa.
PRICES: [2013] per room B&B single £139–£179, double £199–£499. D,B&B from £129 per person, set dinner £43, à la carte £55. 1-night bookings refused weekends in summer.

SEE ALSO SHORTLIST

ZENNOR Cornwall

Map 1:D1

THE GURNARD'S HEAD

César award in 2009

In an isolated position 'in wildest Cornwall' near Land's End, this old yellow-painted inn 'oozes character and generosity', says a visitor in 2013. 'There is something homely and likeable about this place with its open fires, wooden floors and plenty of reading material.' The owners, brothers Charles and Edmund Inkin, have promoted Chris Curnow, a local, to manager. This year there has been more refurbishment of the bedrooms: a new shower room has been fitted in two rooms, a bigger bathroom in the largest. 'Our simple room was cosy and warm; we lacked for nothing. There is (mercifully) no TV, just a radio; fresh flowers gave it a lived-in atmosphere.' Chef Bruce Rennie's seasonal menu can be taken in the restaurant or the bar: 'It is well above average pub grub without the pretentions of a smart restaurant. Breakfast has honest fare: Cornish apple juice; home-made soda bread and jams; a large farmhouse loaf; a proper full English or a kipper from Tregida smokehouse.' The Inkin brothers also run *The Old Coastguard* in nearby Mousehole (see entry). (*John Rowlands*)

25% DISCOUNT VOUCHERS

Treen, nr Zennor
St Ives TR26 3DE

T: 01736-796928
E: enquiries@gurnardshead.co.uk
W: www.gurnardshead.co.uk

BEDROOMS: 7.
OPEN: all year except 24/25 Dec, 4 days in Dec.
FACILITIES: bar area (with free Wi-Fi), small connecting room with sofas, dining room, ½-acre garden, unsuitable for &.
BACKGROUND MUSIC: during service and at other times.
LOCATION: 6½ miles SW of St Ives, on B3306.
CHILDREN: all ages welcomed.
DOGS: not allowed in dining room.
CREDIT CARDS: MasterCard, Visa.
PRICES: [2013] per person B&B £50–£85, D,B&B £73.75–£108.75. À la carte £36. 1-night bookings occasionally refused.

SCOTLAND

Kilchurn Castle, Loch Awe

ARDUAINE Argyll and Bute

Map 5:D1

LOCH MELFORT HOTEL

In a 'peaceful setting', sheltered by woodland on Asknish Bay, Calum and Rachel Ross's country hotel is 'a very good place to stay'. He is 'very much present, well presented and charming'. Twenty of the bedrooms, each with a balcony or terrace, are in a timber-framed extension linked to the house by a partly open walkway. 'The view from our room was breathtaking: it was light, with plenty of storage, and a good-sized bathroom (though a feeble shower).' Children are welcomed: extra beds can be provided for two suites and certain bedrooms. There are Highland cattle, ducks and hens 'to keep little ones interested'; good walks in the grounds. In the summer, family-friendly meals are served in the *Chartroom II* bistro, which has a playground in front, and a box of toys and games. In the more formal *Asknish Bay* restaurant, chef Peter Carr's locally sourced menus might include dishes like sea bass, sweet potato, soured lime and curry spiced dressing. Guests can walk to a small beach; Arduaine Garden (National Trust for Scotland) adjoins the grounds. (*Margaret Wall, and others*)

25% DISCOUNT VOUCHERS

Arduaine
By Oban PA34 4XG

T: 01852-200233
F: 01852-200214
E: reception@lochmelfort.co.uk
W: www.lochmelfort.co.uk

BEDROOMS: 25, 20 in *Cedar Wing* annexe, 10 on ground floor.
OPEN: all year except 2 weeks Jan, and mid-week Nov–Mar.
FACILITIES: sitting room, library, bar, restaurant, wedding facilities, free Wi-Fi in public rooms and main house bedrooms, 17-acre grounds (including National Trust for Scotland's Arduaine Garden).
BACKGROUND MUSIC: modern Scottish in public areas.
LOCATION: 16 miles S of Oban.
CHILDREN: all ages welcomed, under-2s free.
DOGS: allowed in 6 bedrooms, not in public rooms.
CREDIT CARDS: MasterCard, Visa.
PRICES: [2013] per person B&B £74–£134, D,B&B £105–£153, £30 single supplement. Set menu £39.50, à la carte £45.

AUCHENCAIRN Dumfries and Galloway   Map 5:E2

BALCARY BAY HOTEL   **NEW**

In a 'beautiful' setting on the shore of the Solway
Firth, this 'charming', white-painted hotel is run
by the 'super-efficient' proprietor, Graeme Lamb;
Elaine Ness is the manager. 'Time for a promotion
to a full entry,' says a *Guide* correspondent
visiting in 2013. 'The delightful staff are so
helpful. A lounge where a log fire always burns
is cosy, and there is a fine residents' lounge with
up-to-date magazines and a lovely outlook.'
Another comment: 'Immaculate; an instantly
relaxing atmosphere.' The bedrooms vary in size
and aspect. Charlie, the resident pheasant, might
be seen from the windows of a garden-view
room; steps to some of the upper rooms might be
steep; each of three larger ground-floor sea-view
rooms has a private patio. In the dining room,
chef Craig McWilliam uses 'wonderful local
produce' for his much-praised cooking of modern
Scottish dishes 'with a European influence'.
'We enjoyed chicken parfait with truffle foam;
excellent beef and salmon fillets; beautifully
presented desserts.' Breakfast has a buffet with
fresh fruit salad and fruit compote; 'eggs with
deep orange yolks', smoked salmon and smoked
haddock in addition to the usual offerings.
(*E Aline Templeton, Richard Shaw, Robert Riding*)

Shore Road
Auchencairn
Castle Douglas DG7 1QZ

T: 01556-640217
F: 01556-640272
E: reservations@
   balcary-bay-hotel.co.uk
W: www.balcary-bay-hotel.co.uk

BEDROOMS: 20, 3 on ground floor.
OPEN: Feb–Nov.
FACILITIES: 2 lounges, bar,
conservatory, restaurant, free Wi-Fi,
3½-acre grounds.
BACKGROUND MUSIC: none.
LOCATION: on shore, 2 miles SW of
village.
CHILDREN: all ages welcomed.
DOGS: allowed.
CREDIT CARDS: MasterCard, Visa.
PRICES: per person B&B £75–£90,
D,B&B £87–£114. Set meals
£34–£50. 1-night bookings usually
refused weekends.

AULDEARN Highland

Map 5:C2

BOATH HOUSE

🏵 *César award in 2013*

'A lovely Regency house in large grounds with a lake and walled garden.' Wendy and Don Matheson, who rescued this fine mansion from Historic Scotland's 'endangered list', have restored it with style. Their son, Sam, is the manager. The lounges and library are 'full of interesting pictures and sculptures'. The bedrooms are individually decorated in country house fashion. A 'lovely, large' room had a four-poster bed, a day bed at the window. 'The bathroom was well furnished' with soft towels and gowns. Before dinner, guests gather in the candlelit drawing room for drinks and canapés. The cooking of the *Michelin*-starred chef, Charlie Lockley, is widely praised. He serves a daily-changing six-course set menu (dislikes discussed beforehand) in modern Scottish style 'with French influences'. 'Two of the best dishes I have ever tasted; foie gras on savoury meringue; and scallop on samphire,' said a reporter this year. A 'wonderful' breakfast is served at the table; 'lovely organic porridge with yogurt and apricots, duck eggs served with wild mushrooms or black pudding; toast made from home-made bread, and with home-made jam or marmalade'.

Auldearn
Nairn
IV12 5TE

T: 01667-454896
F: 01667-455469
E: info@boath-house.com
W: www.boath-house.com

BEDROOMS: 8, 1 in cottage (50 yds) suitable for ♿.
OPEN: all year.
FACILITIES: 2 lounges, library, orangery, restaurant, health/beauty spa, free Wi-Fi, wedding facilities, 20-acre grounds (woods, gardens, meadow, streams, trout lake).
BACKGROUND MUSIC: none.
LOCATION: 1½ miles E of Nairn.
CHILDREN: all ages welcomed.
DOGS: not in public rooms.
CREDIT CARDS: MasterCard, Visa.
PRICES: [2013] per room B&B single £190–£260, double £230–£335, D,B&B £345–£450. Set dinner £70.

BALLANTRAE South Ayrshire

Map 5:E1

COSSES COUNTRY HOUSE

'A really lovely place and very good value', Susan and Robin Crosthwaite's small guest house is 'a gem in a little hidden valley'. *Guide* inspectors were 'welcomed by Susan and her black Labrador, Monty, and were given tea with cake'. Two of the bedrooms, each with a private sitting room, are in a converted byre. 'Ours was lovingly furnished in blue and yellow; it had all kinds of pretty extras made by Susan and her mother, who lives next door. There was plenty of space to put your things, a large double bed and a single. Lots of hot water for the bath but a feeble electric shower.' In the evening, dinner is taken communally around a large table. 'Robin served us drinks in the lounge; he and Susan joined us and another couple for a glass of wine, which was a nice touch. She takes pride in the local, seasonal produce in her no-choice menus: we had Ballantrae prawns and locally smoked salmon; duck from a nearby farm, with home-grown vegetables. A delicious meal with good company.' Breakfast, in the kitchen, has 'everything you could wish for'.

Ballantrae
KA26 0LR

T: 01465-831363
F: 01465-831598
E: staying@cossescountryhouse.com
W: www.cossescountryhouse.com

BEDROOMS: 3, on ground floor, 2 across courtyard.
OPEN: 6 Jan–23 Dec, closed occasionally other times.
FACILITIES: drawing room, dining room, games room (table tennis, darts), free Wi-Fi, 12-acre grounds.
BACKGROUND MUSIC: none.
LOCATION: 2 miles E of Ballantrae.
CHILDREN: not under 12.
DOGS: allowed by arrangement in 1 suite, not in public rooms.
CREDIT CARDS: MasterCard, Visa.
PRICES: [2013] per person B&B £45–£75. Set dinner £35.

BALLANTRAE South Ayrshire

Map 5:E1

GLENAPP CASTLE

Up a 'lengthy, wooded driveway', this baronial castle was turned over six years by owners Fay and Graham Cowan into a country house hotel (Relais & Châteaux). The 'delightful gardens' are 'pretty with flowers', and there are views to the sea and Ailsa Craig. Despite the grandeur, 'it is a pleasant place with a relaxed ambience'. The castle has been furnished with fine paintings, Middle Eastern rugs, antiques. There is a 'good country house feel in the bright airy lounge with its squishy sofas'. Matt Worswick, formerly sous-chef at the two *Michelin*-starred *Champignon Sauvage* in Cheltenham, joined in 2013 as chef. He uses produce from the kitchen garden for his seasonal six-course menus with modern dishes like butter-poached lobster tail, wilted lettuce, eucalyptus foam; pavé of lamb, potato and haggis terrine, crisp shoulder, mint jus. The large bedrooms have swagged curtains and wide bed, spacious bathrooms (separate bath and shower) have a 'good supply of fluffy towels'. One visitor would return 'just for the autumn colours' in the extensive grounds. 'Not inexpensive, but in the main you get what you pay for.' (*ST*)

Ballantrae
KA26 0NZ

T: 01465-831212
F: 01465-831000
E: info@glenappcastle.com
W: www.glenappcastle.com

BEDROOMS: 17, 7 on ground floor.
OPEN: 27 Mar–3 Jan, except Christmas.
FACILITIES: ramp, lift, drawing room, library, 2 dining rooms, wedding facilities, free Wi-Fi, 36-acre gardens (tennis, croquet), fishing, golf nearby, access to spa.
BACKGROUND MUSIC: none.
LOCATION: 2 miles S of Ballantrae.
CHILDREN: no under-5s in dining room after 7 pm.
DOGS: allowed in certain bedrooms, not in public rooms, no charge.
CREDIT CARDS: Amex, MasterCard, Visa.
PRICES: [2013] per room B&B £370–£575, D,B&B £430–£635. Set dinner £65. 1-night bookings refused at bank holidays, New Year.

25% DISCOUNT VOUCHER

THE GOOD HOTEL GUIDE 2014

Use this voucher to claim a 25% discount off the normal price for bed and breakfast at hotels with a `25% DISCOUNT VOUCHERS` sign at the end of the entry. **You must request a voucher discount at the time of booking and present this voucher on arrival. Further details and conditions overleaf.** Valid to 7th October 2014.

25% DISCOUNT VOUCHER

THE GOOD HOTEL GUIDE 2014

Use this voucher to claim a 25% discount off the normal price for bed and breakfast at hotels with a `25% DISCOUNT VOUCHERS` sign at the end of the entry. **You must request a voucher discount at the time of booking and present this voucher on arrival. Further details and conditions overleaf.** Valid to 7th October 2014.

25% DISCOUNT VOUCHER

THE GOOD HOTEL GUIDE 2014

Use this voucher to claim a 25% discount off the normal price for bed and breakfast at hotels with a `25% DISCOUNT VOUCHERS` sign at the end of the entry. **You must request a voucher discount at the time of booking and present this voucher on arrival. Further details and conditions overleaf.** Valid to 7th October 2014.

25% DISCOUNT VOUCHER

THE GOOD HOTEL GUIDE 2014

Use this voucher to claim a 25% discount off the normal price for bed and breakfast at hotels with a `25% DISCOUNT VOUCHERS` sign at the end of the entry. **You must request a voucher discount at the time of booking and present this voucher on arrival. Further details and conditions overleaf.** Valid to 7th October 2014.

25% DISCOUNT VOUCHER

THE GOOD HOTEL GUIDE 2014

Use this voucher to claim a 25% discount off the normal price for bed and breakfast at hotels with a `25% DISCOUNT VOUCHERS` sign at the end of the entry. **You must request a voucher discount at the time of booking and present this voucher on arrival. Further details and conditions overleaf.** Valid to 7th October 2014.

25% DISCOUNT VOUCHER

THE GOOD HOTEL GUIDE 2014

Use this voucher to claim a 25% discount off the normal price for bed and breakfast at hotels with a `25% DISCOUNT VOUCHERS` sign at the end of the entry. **You must request a voucher discount at the time of booking and present this voucher on arrival. Further details and conditions overleaf.** Valid to 7th October 2014.

CONDITIONS

1. Hotels with a `25% DISCOUNT VOUCHERS` sign have agreed to give readers a discount of 25% off their normal bed-and-breakfast rate.
2. One voucher is good for the first night's stay only, at the discounted rate for yourself alone or for you and a partner sharing a double room.
3. Hotels may decline to accept a voucher reservation if they expect to be fully booked at the full room price.

CONDITIONS

1. Hotels with a `25% DISCOUNT VOUCHERS` sign have agreed to give readers a discount of 25% off their normal bed-and-breakfast rate.
2. One voucher is good for the first night's stay only, at the discounted rate for yourself alone or for you and a partner sharing a double room.
3. Hotels may decline to accept a voucher reservation if they expect to be fully booked at the full room price.

CONDITIONS

1. Hotels with a `25% DISCOUNT VOUCHERS` sign have agreed to give readers a discount of 25% off their normal bed-and-breakfast rate.
2. One voucher is good for the first night's stay only, at the discounted rate for yourself alone or for you and a partner sharing a double room.
3. Hotels may decline to accept a voucher reservation if they expect to be fully booked at the full room price.

CONDITIONS

1. Hotels with a `25% DISCOUNT VOUCHERS` sign have agreed to give readers a discount of 25% off their normal bed-and-breakfast rate.
2. One voucher is good for the first night's stay only, at the discounted rate for yourself alone or for you and a partner sharing a double room.
3. Hotels may decline to accept a voucher reservation if they expect to be fully booked at the full room price.

CONDITIONS

1. Hotels with a `25% DISCOUNT VOUCHERS` sign have agreed to give readers a discount of 25% off their normal bed-and-breakfast rate.
2. One voucher is good for the first night's stay only, at the discounted rate for yourself alone or for you and a partner sharing a double room.
3. Hotels may decline to accept a voucher reservation if they expect to be fully booked at the full room price.

CONDITIONS

1. Hotels with a `25% DISCOUNT VOUCHERS` sign have agreed to give readers a discount of 25% off their normal bed-and-breakfast rate.
2. One voucher is good for the first night's stay only, at the discounted rate for yourself alone or for you and a partner sharing a double room.
3. Hotels may decline to accept a voucher reservation if they expect to be fully booked at the full room price.

BALLATER Aberdeenshire

Map 5:C3

DEESIDE HOTEL

'Consistently excellent', Gordon Waddell and Penella Price's small hotel on the outskirts of a resort town on the River Dee is 'excellent value for money'. This year's praise (from annual visitors): 'The service, the rooms, and the quality of the food remain as good as ever.' The bedrooms, some with a king-size bed, vary in size; storage is good, and they are well supplied (the hospitality trays have Deeside mineral water, herbal teas, biscuits). Two rooms overlook the south-facing walled garden. The character of the Victorian house has been retained: a royal stag's head from the Glenlivet estate stands above the original pitch pine staircase. A log fire burns in the tartan-carpeted lounge and bar. Gordon Waddell's much-admired modern menus might include home-smoked Gressingham duck breast, citrus salad; roast loin of rabbit with red pepper and black olives wrapped in bacon. Much choice at breakfast: a Highland special has haggis, tattie scones, bacon and egg; other choices include French toast with bacon; or a sausage sandwich. Red squirrels can be seen in the 'pretty wooded garden'. (*Alan and Edwina Williams*)

45 Braemar Road
Ballater AB35 5RQ

T: 013397-55420
F: 0871 989 5933
E: mail@deesidehotel.co.uk
W: www.deesidehotel.co.uk

BEDROOMS: 9, 2 on ground floor.
OPEN: April–Dec, closed Christmas/New Year.
FACILITIES: ramp, library, lounge/bar, restaurant, free Wi-Fi, 1-acre garden.
BACKGROUND MUSIC: classical in bar and restaurant.
LOCATION: village outskirts.
CHILDREN: all ages welcomed.
DOGS: not allowed.
CREDIT CARDS: MasterCard, Visa.
PRICES: [2013] per person B&B £55–£65, D,B&B £83.50–£93.50. Set dinner £30. 1-night bookings sometimes refused Sat in season.

BLAIRGOWRIE Perth and Kinross

KINLOCH HOUSE

'Bravo: what a fantastic experience.' A regular *Guide* correspondent was 'blown away' this year by the Allen family's country house hotel (Relais & Châteaux). The early Victorian mansion (with a less appealing modern extension) has a 'magnificent' hillside setting. 'The welcoming, attentive staff create a relaxed atmosphere.' The spacious public rooms 'are beautifully furnished, comfortable sofas, a small log fire burning in August'. Tables are 'well laid' and well spaced in the formal dining room, where chef Steve MacCallum serves a short daily-changing menu. 'Each dish was perfectly balanced; I had a lovely hot quail salad with artichokes; sublime turbot with girolles, fresh peas, a delicious sauce; the cheese plate, with home-made oatmeal biscuits, was in perfect condition. A memorable meal.' The bedrooms are 'nicely decorated with traditional furniture; lots of cupboard space; a wonderfully comfortable bed made up with sheets and blankets; a huge bathroom'. A minor quibble: 'It is disappointing to be charged for early-morning tea in the bedroom.' Breakfast has a 'good selection of freshly baked breads, freshly squeezed orange juice; lovely cold ham with poached eggs'. (*Jim Grover*)

Dunkeld Road
by Blairgowrie PH10 6SG

T: 01250-884237
F: 01250-884333
E: reception@kinlochhouse.com
W: www.kinlochhouse.com

BEDROOMS: 15, 4 on ground floor.
OPEN: all year except 14–29 Dec.
FACILITIES: ramp, 5 public rooms, private dining room, free Wi-Fi, wedding facilities, 25-acre grounds.
BACKGROUND MUSIC: none.
LOCATION: 3 miles W of Blairgowrie.
CHILDREN: no under-6s in dining room at night.
DOGS: allowed by arrangement only.
CREDIT CARDS: MasterCard, Visa.
PRICES: [2013] per room B&B £215–£325. D,B&B £160–£215 per person, set dinner £53. 1-night bookings refused at New Year.

BROADFORD Highland

TIGH AN DOCHAIS

In a 'wonderful' position on Broadford Bay, this contemporary house was designed to give uninterrupted views of the sea and the mountains. It is run as a small B&B by Neil Hope and Lesley Unwin, 'delightful hosts'. The striking building is entered by a bridge to the upper floor, which houses the guest lounge and dining room. The lounge has a wood-burning stove, books to read, the view to enjoy from the 'huge picture windows'. There is solid oak flooring throughout; contemporary art. The spacious bedrooms, on the lower floor, have 'wonderful views across the bay'. They are equipped with 'everything you might need to pass the time in bad weather'. Guests can walk to local restaurants and bars; Neil Hope will cook an evening meal with advance notice (likes and dislikes will be discussed). He uses Skye produce for his menus, which might include fish landed that day (perhaps poached sea trout). Guests may bring their own wine. Breakfast, at a communal table, has a buffet of fruits, cereals, home-made bread and preserves, island cheeses, muffins and yogurt; cooked dishes include locally smoked haddock and kippers. (*MF, and others*)

13 Harrapool, Broadford
Isle of Skye IV49 9AQ

T: 01471-820022
E: hopeskye@btinternet.com
W: www.skyebedbreakfast.co.uk

BEDROOMS: 3, all on ground floor.
OPEN: Apr–Nov.
FACILITIES: lounge, dining area, free Wi-Fi, ½-acre garden, unsuitable for &.
BACKGROUND MUSIC: Celtic at breakfast.
LOCATION: 1 mile E of Broadford.
CHILDREN: all ages welcomed.
DOGS: not allowed.
CREDIT CARDS: Amex, MasterCard, Visa.
PRICES: per person B&B £42.50–£45. Set dinner £25. 1-night bookings sometimes refused.

BRODICK North Ayrshire

Map 5:E1

KILMICHAEL COUNTRY HOUSE

In grounds patrolled by peacocks and ducks, this white-painted 17th-century mansion has long been run as a small hotel by the owners, Geoffrey Botterill and Antony Butterworth. 'Much in evidence', they treat visitors as 'personal guests' in the atmosphere of a private house. The furniture, pictures and artefacts have been collected with care from around the world. Despite its 'proud history' (said to be the oldest building on the island), the house remains intimate. Guests have use of two first-floor lounges where pre-dinner drinks are served. Mr Butterworth cooks, by arrangement, a daily-changing set dinner. 'We take account of allergies and intolerances, but we are reluctant to modify our entire menu to suit those who were startled by a piece of broccoli as a child,' he says. The garden supplies fruit, salads and vegetables for the menu, which might include smoked salmon and prawn cheesecake, herbs and flowers; roast breast of Gressingham duck stuffed with wild rice, walnuts and raspberries. Five of the bedrooms are in the main house; three are in converted stables a short walk away. More reports, please.

Glen Cloy, by Brodick
Isle of Arran KA27 8BY

T: 01770-302219
F: 01770-302068
E: enquiries@kilmichael.com
W: www.kilmichael.com

BEDROOMS: 8, 3 in converted stables (20 yds), 7 on ground floor, 4 self-catering cottages.
OPEN: Easter–Oct, restaurant closed Mon and Tues.
FACILITIES: 2 drawing rooms, dining room, free Wi-Fi (in Yellow drawing room), 4½-acre grounds (burn).
BACKGROUND MUSIC: light classical during meals.
LOCATION: 1 mile SW of village.
CHILDREN: not under 12.
DOGS: not allowed in public rooms.
CREDIT CARDS: MasterCard, Visa.
PRICES: [2013] per room B&B single £78–£98, double £130–£205. Set dinner £45. 1-night bookings sometimes refused Sat.

SEE ALSO SHORTLIST

CARRADALE Argyll and Bute

Map 5:E1

DUNVALANREE IN CARRADALE

In an 'idyllic' setting, above the beach in a village on the Kintyre peninsula, Alan and Alyson Milstead's small hotel/restaurant is 'laid-back and homely'. He is a much-liked host 'with a dry sense of humour'; she is an accomplished cook. She turns to local fishermen and farmers for her daily-changing menu of dishes like smoked haddock and dill risotto; rack of Ifferdale lamb, garlic, rosemary, Marsala gravy. 'Beautiful ingredients, lovingly prepared; each evening we were given a tiny bowl of delicious soup as an amuse-bouche,' says one visitor. Alan Milstead, who serves, might pull up a chair at the table for a chat. The simple bedrooms have modern pine furniture, pale colours. 'Our compact room and bathroom were good, clean; comfortable beds, robes and a generous supply of good toiletries.' Some rooms overlook Carradale Bay, others Kilbrannan Sound; those at the back face the garden. At breakfast 'each person has an individual jug of freshly squeezed juice'; there is thick toast; 'fantastic' cooked dishes. The place has 'an old-fashioned air'; 'not for upwardly mobile 30-somethings, but many will love it'. (*CLH, and others*)

25% DISCOUNT VOUCHERS

Port Righ, Carradale
PA28 6SE

T: 01583-431226
E: book@dunvalanree.com
W: www.dunvalanree.com

BEDROOMS: 7, 1 on ground floor suitable for &.
OPEN: all year except Christmas.
FACILITIES: lounge, dining room, free Wi-Fi, ½-acre garden.
BACKGROUND MUSIC: jazz in dining room.
LOCATION: on edge of village 15 miles N of Campbeltown.
CHILDREN: all ages welcomed.
DOGS: allowed in bedrooms only.
CREDIT CARDS: MasterCard, Visa.
PRICES: [2013] per person B&B £35–£70, D,B&B £60–£90. Set meals £24.50–£28.

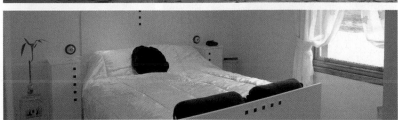

CHIRNSIDE Scottish Borders

CHIRNSIDE HALL   NEW

'We felt very much at home at this relaxed hotel,' says a regular correspondent, restoring to a full entry Tessa and Christian Korsten's late Georgian manor after a period without reports. 'Tessa is quite a character; a natural front-of-house, she is smoothly efficient and friendly.' Open fires burn in the two large lounges, which have 'lots of sofas piled high with cushions'. In the 'elegant' dining room, Tim Holmes is now the chef. 'His cooking is superb, modern Scottish with a touch of bistro. The four-course evening meals are always a treat: our favourites were home-smoked roe deer; squash, chilli and coconut milk soup; lamb with couscous salad; a good selection of local cheeses.' The bedrooms are well equipped. 'Our large room had far-reaching views of the Borders countryside; it had a sofa, a small dressing area, a hospitality tray; a large, modern tiled bathroom.' Breakfasts have fruit compotes, home-made muesli; 'a good selection of nicely cooked dishes' (perhaps local black pudding and haggis or Eyemouth kippers). *Chirnside Hall* is busy with sporting parties in the winter. 'Extremely good value.' (*GC*)

Chirnside, nr Duns
TD11 3LD

T: 01890-818219
F: 01890-818231
E: reception@chirnsidehallhotel.com
W: www.chirnsidehallhotel.com

BEDROOMS: 10.
OPEN: all year except Mar.
FACILITIES: 2 lounges, dining room, private dining room, free Wi-Fi, billiard room, fitness room, library/conference rooms, wedding facilities, 5-acre grounds, unsuitable for &.
BACKGROUND MUSIC: 'easy listening' and classical.
LOCATION: 1½ miles E of village, NE of Duns.
CHILDREN: all ages welcomed.
DOGS: not allowed in public rooms, unattended in bedrooms.
CREDIT CARDS: Amex, MasterCard, Visa.
PRICES: [2013] per person B&B £85–£95, D,B&B £110–£120. Set dinner £35.

COLONSAY Argyll and Bute

Map 5:D1

THE COLONSAY

'A wild and remote location; nice simple bedrooms, spacious and comfortable public rooms, plenty of attentive staff.' Jane and Alex Howard's renovated mid-18th-century inn, on a hill above the harbour, is 'just right for the setting' (say inspectors). A reader agreed: 'You have to make allowances for the remoteness and the fact that they have to be all things to all visitors; overall it is a good effort.' Irina and Ivan Lisovyy joined as managers in 2013. Some of the bedrooms have sea views; others look towards the hills or the church. They are simply furnished, with whites or pastel shades on the walls. The 'well-maintained' garden has outdoor seating areas; public rooms 'have good sofas and plenty of light; wood-burning stoves and open fires to give them a cosy feel'. There is locally brewed beer in the bar, which is popular with islanders and visiting sailors. In the dining room, head chef Robert Smyth's 'simply prepared but delicious' dishes are prepared with vegetables and herbs from the hotel's kitchen garden. There is a children's menu. The continental breakfast has home-made bread and jams; cooked dishes cost extra.

Isle of Colonsay
PA61 7YP

T: 01951-200316
F: 01951-200353
E: hotel@colonsayestate.co.uk
W: www.colonsayestate.co.uk

BEDROOMS: 9.
OPEN: Mar–Oct, Christmas, New Year, no check-in Mon and Sat.
FACILITIES: conservatory lounge, log room, bar, restaurant, free Wi-Fi, wedding facilities, accommodation unsuitable for &.
BACKGROUND MUSIC: 'easy listening' occasionally in bar.
LOCATION: 400 yds W of harbour.
CHILDREN: all ages welcomed.
DOGS: allowed in 2 bedrooms.
CREDIT CARDS: MasterCard, Visa.
PRICES: [2013] per room B&B £70–£145. D,B&B £30 per person added.

CONTIN Highland

Map 5:C2

COUL HOUSE

Dominated by its fine octagonal-bayed frontage, this stone-built Georgian hunting lodge is in 'beautiful country' down a long track by a Highland village. *Guide* regulars on a first visit 'thoroughly enjoyed our stay'. It is run by 'pleasant and helpful' Susannah and Stuart Macpherson. 'Proud owners', they continue with renovation: this year a biomass boiler was installed. 'Our bedroom was large and adequate,' says a guest, who agreed with the owners' assessment (on the website) that 'bathrooms are quite dated'. 'It deserves its place in the *Guide* because of its other attributes', such as the already renovated and 'beautifully proportioned' public rooms, including the 'stunning' octagonal dining room. Here guests enjoyed 'seriously good food' from the chef Garry Kenley, who serves dishes like duo of Highland game, chicory tarte Tatin: 'Tasty soups; vegetables cooked to perfection; yummy traditional puddings', eg, lemon curd tart, caramelised apple pie. Breakfast is taken in a 'handsome, high-ceilinged room', and has home-baked bread, home-made marmalade and 'good' coffee. Children and dogs are welcomed and there are 'attractive wooded grounds'. (*Val Ferguson*)

25% DISCOUNT VOUCHERS

Contin
by Strathpeffer
IV14 9ES

T: 01997-421487
F: 01997-421945
E: stay@coulhouse.com
W: www.coulhouse.com

BEDROOMS: 21, 4 on ground floor.
OPEN: all year except Christmas.
FACILITIES: ramp, bar, lounge, restaurant, conference/wedding facilities, 8-acre garden (children's play area, 9-hole pitch and putt).
BACKGROUND MUSIC: in lounge bar and restaurant.
LOCATION: 17 miles NW of Inverness.
CHILDREN: all ages welcomed, discounts up to age 15.
DOGS: allowed except in restaurant (£5 per day, less for longer).
CREDIT CARDS: MasterCard, Visa.
PRICES: per room B&B single £90–£99, double £165–£225. À la carte £32.50.

CRINAN Argyll and Bute

Map 5:D1

CRINAN HOTEL

'An art gallery with rooms', this 'eccentric and artistic' hotel is run by Frances Ryan (the painter Frances Macdonald) and her husband, Nick. Her seascapes and work by other Scottish artists (including her son, Ross) are displayed throughout. The white-painted building, a former drovers' inn in a village on the Crinan Canal basin, has views over the sea and distant hills to inspire any artist. The 'friendly informality' makes it 'a nice place to stay', says a fan. All the bedrooms, each named after a Scottish artist, have 'your own private view'; the best have a balcony. 'In the late afternoon, you see the langoustines being landed' at a quayside in front of the hotel. Chef Gregor Bara's menus specialise in seafood ('those who prefer meat are catered for'). Dishes in the *Westward* restaurant ('spanking white linen') might include risotto of Sound of Jura lobster, cream cheese and chives. Meals can also be taken in a seafood bar (popular with non-residents, including passing yachtsmen). *Lock 16*, a rooftop restaurant, reopened in 2013 on Friday and Saturday nights in high season. Breakfast is served entirely at table. (*ST*)

25% DISCOUNT VOUCHERS

Crinan
by Lochgilphead
PA31 8SR

T: 01546-830261
F: 01546-830292
E: reservations@crinanhotel.com
W: www.crinanhotel.com

BEDROOMS: 20.
OPEN: all year except Christmas, possibly New Year.
FACILITIES: lift, ramps, 2 lounges, gallery bar, seafood bar, 2 restaurants, coffee shop, free Wi-Fi, treatment room (health and beauty), wedding facilities, patio, ¼-acre garden.
BACKGROUND MUSIC: none.
LOCATION: village centre, waterfront.
CHILDREN: all ages welcomed.
DOGS: not allowed in restaurants.
CREDIT CARDS: MasterCard, Visa.
PRICES: [2013] per person B&B £65–£135, D,B&B £105–£175. Set dinner (restaurant and *Lock 16*) £45, à la carte (*Seafood Bar*) £21.50.

CUMNOCK East Ayrshire

Map 5:E2

DUMFRIES HOUSE LODGE NEW

The Prince of Wales led a consortium of heritage charities to save Dumfries House (built in the 1750s by Robert Adam for the Earl of Dumfries); a charitable trust now runs the former factor's lodge on the estate as an upmarket B&B. 'The highlight of our Scottish trip, and the best value,' say *Guide* inspectors in 2013. 'We were encouraged to treat the beautifully furnished house as our country home.' Many 'beautiful' pieces from the mansion have been incorporated in the renovation of the lodge, which has two 'pretty' drawing rooms and a kitchen where guests can prepare hot drinks and snacks. The bedrooms are individually styled: 'Our spacious room had a huge modern bed, an antique chest of drawers; tables and comfy chairs; state-of-the-art coffee-making; a huge bathroom with a powerful shower and big marble-topped bath.' Mark Robson, the 'friendly, efficient' manager, serves a 'good' breakfast (from 8 to 10 am): 'We enjoyed freshly baked croissants, eggs Benedict cooked to order.' From Thursday to Saturday, guests can dine in the 'handsome' library of the main house; 'everything was delicious'. House tours can be booked.

Dumfries House
Cumnock KA18 2NJ

T: 01290-429920
E: info@dumfrieshouselodge.com
W: www.dumfrieshouselodge.com

BEDROOMS: 5.
OPEN: all year.
FACILITIES: lounge, snug, dining room, free Wi-Fi, 2,000-acre estate, unsuitable for &.
BACKGROUND MUSIC: none.
LOCATION: 2 miles W of Cumnock.
CHILDREN: not under 10.
DOGS: not allowed.
CREDIT CARDS: MasterCard, Visa.
PRICES: [2013] per room B&B single £60, double £70–£125.

DERVAIG Argyll and Bute

Map 5:C1

KILLORAN HOUSE

On an island of 'dramatic landscapes and wonderful seascapes', Janette and Ian McKilligan's new-built small hotel stands on a hillside near Tobermory. 'Please call me Janette,' the hostess told inspectors before 'seizing our cases (unasked) to carry to our room'. The white-painted house is 'immaculate', its interior mostly in pale and neutral tones. A well-proportioned sitting room on the first floor, with full-height windows opening on to a balcony, has 'dramatic views of the sea loch and the high ground beyond'; binoculars are provided. 'Tea and very good cake' are served here when guests have settled in. Ian McKilligan is the chef, serving dinner at 7.30 pm. Menus have a choice of main course, eg, pan-fried fillet of sea bass with red onion, chorizo and cherry tomato. Bedrooms and bathrooms are 'cleaned and polished to perfection'. Furnished mainly in modern pine, they vary in size and view. There are power showers and 'plenty of hot water and fluffy towels'. Breakfast has a choice of cereals; stewed fruit; 'chunky home-made bread for toast'; 'delicious' cooked dishes. More reports, please.

Dervaig, Isle of Mull PA75 6QR

T: 01688-400362
E: enquiries@killoranmull.co.uk
W: www.killoranmull.co.uk

BEDROOMS: 6, 1 on ground floor suitable for &.
OPEN: all year except Christmas/New Year.
FACILITIES: sitting room, study, conservatory dining room, free Wi-Fi, 1¾-acre gardens.
BACKGROUND MUSIC: 'easy listening' in dining room.
LOCATION: 1½ miles SW of Dervaig.
CHILDREN: not under 13.
DOGS: not allowed in public rooms.
CREDIT CARDS: MasterCard, Visa.
PRICES: [2013] per person B&B (min. 2 nights) £62.50–£92 per person. Set dinner £25 (2 courses)–£36 (4 courses). Discount for returning guests.

DUNVEGAN Highland

Map 5:C1

THE THREE CHIMNEYS AND THE HOUSE OVER-BY

♥ *César award in 2001*

In the remote north-west corner of Skye, this restaurant-with-rooms has long been popular with gourmet travellers prepared to go the extra mile. 'An amazing couple of days: the welcome, service and hospitality were outstanding,' says a visitor this year, who endured a ten-hour drive. The founding owners, Shirley and Eddie Spear, have retired to North Berwick: the 'quirky, and absolutely convincing' cooking of the chef/ director, Michael Smith, continues to win plaudits. His tasting menu (Seven Courses of Skye) might include Colbost skink, Marag and Talisker crumb, croft egg yolk; saddle and slow-cooked haunch of Lochalsh venison, salsify, beetroot and blaeberries. 'The service is five star without pretension; there are no rules; staff are considerate and consistently knowledgeable.' The contemporary bedrooms, in *The House Over-By* next door, are 'large and comfortable'; they have a six-foot bed and a sofa. An 'excellent' breakfast, taken in the Morning Room, has freshly squeezed orange juice, porridge (made to order), a hot dish. 'We were made to feel special.' (*Hilary Vane*)

Colbost, Dunvegan
Isle of Skye IV55 8ZT

T: 01470-511258
F: 01470-511358
E: eatandstay@threechimneys.co.uk
W: www.threechimneys.co.uk

BEDROOMS: 6, all on ground floor in separate building, 1 suitable for &.
OPEN: all year except 1 Dec–23 Jan, restaurant closed for lunch Nov–Feb and Sun Oct–May.
FACILITIES: ramps, 3 public rooms, free Wi-Fi, garden on loch.
BACKGROUND MUSIC: in lounge in evenings.
LOCATION: 4 miles W of Dunvegan.
CHILDREN: no under-5s at lunch, no under-8s at dinner, tea at 5 pm.
DOGS: not allowed.
CREDIT CARDS: Amex, MasterCard, Visa.
PRICES: [2013] per room B&B £295, D,B&B (Oct–spring) £385. Set lunch £28.50–£37, set dinner £60–£110.

DUROR Argyll and Bute

BEALACH HOUSE

♀ *César award in 2009*

Visitors this year 'were entertained both by the peanut butter-eating pine martin on the terrace and the company of our fellow guests at the communal dinner and breakfast, which worked very well.' Jim and Hilary McFadyen's small guest house has a 'fabulous' location between Oban and Fort William. The former farmhouse, the only remaining building in the glen, is reached by a long forestry track. Its lounge has a wood-burning stove, books and games, jigsaw puzzles. Bedrooms, if not large, 'had everything we needed'. Each has a tea- and coffee-making kit. 'We particularly approved of the jugs of fresh milk in a fridge in the corridor, a thoughtful touch.' Bathrooms have a power shower (one also has a bath). The conservatory and patio have 'wonderful views', as do the eight-acre grounds. In the dining room, Hilary McFadyen serves a daily-changing 'modern British' menu (which always has one vegetarian option); her dishes might include baked haggis with creamy whisky and onion sauce; peppered venison steak, red onion marmalade. Breads, jams and chutneys are home made. (*Frances Thomas, and others*)

Salachan Glen
Duror PA38 4BW

T: 01631-740298
E: enquiries@bealachhouse.co.uk
W: www.bealachhouse.co.uk

BEDROOMS: 3.
OPEN: Feb–Nov, dining room closed Mon evening.
FACILITIES: lounge, conservatory, dining room, free Wi-Fi (limited), 8-acre grounds, unsuitable for &.
BACKGROUND MUSIC: none.
LOCATION: 2 miles S of Duror, off A828.
CHILDREN: not under 14.
DOGS: not allowed.
CREDIT CARDS: MasterCard, Visa.
PRICES: per room B&B £90–£110. Set dinner £30.

EDINBANE Highland

Map 5:C1

GRESHORNISH HOUSE

There are 'gorgeous' views of a sea loch from Neil and Rosemary Colquhoun's 'elegant' white-painted country house (Georgian with Victorian additions) in a 'tranquil' corner of Skye. Set in 'beautiful' grounds, it once belonged to the local laird. 'We felt like guests of friends at a grand estate.' The interiors are 'archetypal country house hotel', with 'squashy' sofas, log fires, a billiard room. There is no background music; no mobile phone signal in the house, but limited Wi-Fi is available in the bedrooms. These are named after Scottish islands: Islay, on the first floor with a loch view, was originally the Georgian drawing room; it has the original cornice and picture rails. Jura was once the laird's bedroom. All rooms have a kettle, snacks, books and magazines. There are 'heaps of fluffy white towels' in the bathrooms. In the dining room, chef Glyn Musker serves classic menus of seasonal local produce, perhaps seared Skye scallops, goat's cheese and artichoke mousse, Stornoway black pudding and parsnip velouté; loin of Lochaber venison, port and orange sauce, roasted pear. Lighter dinners are available by arrangement.

25% DISCOUNT VOUCHERS

Edinbane, by Portree
Isle of Skye IV51 9PN

T: 01470-582266
F: 01470-582345
E: info@greshornishhouse.com
W: www.greshornishhouse.com

BEDROOMS: 6, plus 2 attic rooms if booked with a double.
OPEN: mid-Mar–early Nov, dining room closed Mon.
FACILITIES: drawing room, bar, billiard room, dining room, conservatory, free Wi-Fi (limited), only public rooms accessible for &.
BACKGROUND MUSIC: none.
LOCATION: 17 miles NW of Portree.
CHILDREN: all ages welcomed.
DOGS: not allowed in public rooms, or unaccompanied in bedrooms.
CREDIT CARDS: MasterCard, Visa.
PRICES: [2013] per person B&B £65–£95. Light dinner from £30, set dinners £38–£45. 1-night bookings usually refused.

EDINBURGH

Map 5:D2

ARDMOR HOUSE

'Immaculate and welcoming', Robin Jack's 'boutique-style' B&B offers a refuge from the continuing 'traffic chaos in central Edinburgh' (due to endless work on the new tramlines), says a visitor this year. On Edinburgh's north-east side, on the border with Leith, it has free street parking ('a rarity in the city'); a bus gives direct access to the centre. The house is 'tastefully furnished' in modern style with 'Baroque touches'. 'Our large bedroom at the front had a sofa; a good tray of tea and coffee, and chocolate bars.' The rooms are well equipped: an iPod dock, a digital radio and a hairdryer are standard. 'Don't hesitate to ask' for other extras (an iron, ice, etc). 'There are daily papers in the morning in the breakfast room, which faces Pilrig Park. An extensive buffet has fresh fruit, home-made oatcakes, cereals and bread for do-it-yourself toasting. Cooked dishes include porridge ('for the authentic Scottish experience'); smoked bacon, potato waffles and maple syrup. Parts of the area may be 'looking tawdry' but there is 'excellent food' to be had in nearby Leith. (*Michael Brown, and others*)

74 Pilrig Street
Edinburgh EH6 5AS

T/F: 0131-554 4944
E: info@ardmorhouse.com
W: www.ardmorhouse.com

BEDROOMS: 5, 1 on ground floor.
OPEN: all year.
FACILITIES: breakfast room, free Wi-Fi.
BACKGROUND MUSIC: classical in breakfast room.
LOCATION: Leith, 1 mile NE of city centre.
CHILDREN: all ages welcomed.
DOGS: allowed by arrangement.
CREDIT CARDS: Diners, MasterCard, Visa.
PRICES: [2013] per room B&B £85–£145. 1-night bookings refused at weekends, busy times.

SEE ALSO SHORTLIST

EDINBURGH

THE BONHAM

Within walking distance of Princes Street 'but very quiet', Peter Taylor's 'relaxed' hotel is a conversion of three Victorian town houses in a West End square. Part of the small Town House Collection, it is managed by Johanne Falconer. The 'venerable' buildings have been filled with contemporary artwork and collages by thirty up-and-coming Scottish artists. New this year is the *Consulting Room* bar, whose name reflects the history of the buildings, one of which was a private clinic run by two Edinburgh surgeons. A bedroom with oak-panelled walls and a freestanding copper bath was the main consulting room. Another room has a 'quirky bath with integrated neo-Victorian shower'. All rooms are decorated in modern style with bold colours. In the oak-panelled dining room, Maciej Szymik has returned as the chef. His modern classic dishes might include pork rillettes, sourdough toast; Loch Duart salmon, cauliflower, fettuccine, brown shrimp dressing. High chairs are provided in the restaurant for visiting children ('the chef is happy to create something suitable for your little one'). A Doggy Dreams package includes an in-room meal, a dog bed, a welcome toy and treat. (*CB and RM*)

35 Drumsheugh Gardens
Edinburgh EH3 7RN

T: 0131-226 6050
F: 0131-226 6080
E: reception@thebonham.com
W: www.thebonham.com

BEDROOMS: 49, 1 suitable for &.
OPEN: all year.
FACILITIES: reception lounge, bar, restaurant, free Wi-Fi, wedding facilities.
BACKGROUND MUSIC: in public areas all day.
LOCATION: central, free parking.
CHILDREN: all ages welcomed.
DOGS: not allowed in public rooms, additional charge in bedrooms.
CREDIT CARDS: all major cards.
PRICES: [2013] per room B&B £100–£400. D,B&B £25 added per person, à la carte £30. 1-night bookings sometimes refused Sat, Christmas/New Year.

SEE ALSO SHORTLIST

EDINBURGH

Map 5:D2

THE HOWARD   `NEW`

In an elegant New Town street, this luxury hotel (part of the Edinburgh Collection) is liked for its intimacy (just 18 bedrooms): 'You feel as if you are in your own Georgian town house.' The service is 'exemplary', say visitors this year, 'friendly, thoughtful, attentive'. Butlers will unpack and press clothes, clean shoes, shop for guests. There is no tea tray in the bedrooms: a butler will bring complimentary 'proper loose-leaf tea and home-made shortbread biscuits'. The bedrooms, which vary in size and shape, have rich fabrics, period furnishings, fine art. 'Our large room at the back was very quiet and comfortable.' Bathroom lighting is 'particularly good', though bedside lamps were 'dim'. 'We liked the candles in the drawing room but did not appreciate the piped music.' Bookings are recommended for the *Atholl* restaurant, which seats only 14 people. The Scottish/French menu of the chef, William Poncelet, might include Jerusalem artichoke velouté; guineafowl supreme, wilted spinach, château potatoes. 'The prices are reasonable for the quality of the cooking.' The 'very good' breakfast has freshly squeezed orange juice, Arbroath smokies, 'and much else besides'. (*Robin Orme, and others*)

34 Great King Street
Edinburgh EH3 6QH

T: 0131-557 3500
F: 0131-557 6515
E: reserve@thehoward.com
W: www.thehoward.com

BEDROOMS: 18.
OPEN: all year.
FACILITIES: drawing room, restaurant, free Wi-Fi, wedding facilities, small garden.
BACKGROUND MUSIC: 'minimal' classical in drawing room, restaurant.
LOCATION: central.
CHILDREN: all ages welcomed.
DOGS: only guide dogs allowed.
CREDIT CARDS: all major cards.
PRICES: [2013] room from £130. Breakfast £18, set dinner £24.50 £32, à la carte £33. 1-night bookings refused weekends.

SEE ALSO SHORTLIST

EDINBURGH

Map 5:D2

MILLERS64

'Beautifully conceived and maintained', this Victorian town house off Leith Walk gives 'a good level of luxury and comfort at a reasonable price'. It is run as an upmarket B&B by widely travelled sisters Shona and Louise Clelland, who have retained original features in their restoration of the house, giving it a clean, modern look with Eastern influences. 'They are a joy to converse with, and are aware of the needs of their guests while being sensitive to giving them space,' say trusted reporters. Little touches, like a scented candle in the hall in the evening, 'made it a place you were keen to get back to'. The colour scheme 'makes it feel chic but not cold'. A front-facing bedroom was 'spacious with high ceiling, stunning Victorian detailing; a sofa by the bay window, lots of storage'. The 'huge, gorgeous' bathroom had 'a chandelier, silver basin, lovely toiletries'. 'Watch out for Louise's home-made specials' at breakfast, taken at a communal table in the front room, which has sofas, newspapers and magazines. Free on-street parking and a bus-stop outside. (*A and BB*)

64 Pilrig Street
Edinburgh EH6 5AS

T/F:0131-454 3666
E: reservations@millers64.com
W: www.millers64.com

BEDROOMS: 3.
OPEN: all year.
FACILITIES: dining room, patio, free Wi-Fi, unsuitable for &.
BACKGROUND MUSIC: none.
LOCATION: Leith.
CHILDREN: not under 12.
DOGS: not allowed.
CREDIT CARDS: none.
PRICES: per room B&B £95–£150. Min. 3-night stay 'in busy periods'.

SEE ALSO SHORTLIST

EDINBURGH

Map 5:D2

23 MAYFIELD

NEW

A 'strong recommendation' by *Guide* inspectors earns a full entry for Ross Birnie's B&B, a handsomely furnished Victorian house close to the city centre. 'He is a courteous and sympathetic host and was much in evidence during our stay.' He has redecorated the house, taking care to match the original Victorian features. A 'club room' has a library of rare books – and popular paperbacks, leather armchairs and sofas; an honesty bar, self-help tea and coffee. 'Our ground-floor bedroom was pleasantly warm; three walls were panelled in dark mahogany. The huge bed had an excellent mattress and quality bedlinen; a capacious wardrobe with free-range hangers; a superb sound system and a large TV; masses of hot water and a walk-in shower in the small bathroom. Heavy curtains and wooden shutters ensured that we heard no noise from the busy main road.' An award-winning breakfast is taken at tables with linen cloths and napkins in a well-proportioned dining room. 'Full marks for attentive service: we enjoyed outstanding scrambled eggs, bacon and sausage (locally supplied) from the comprehensive menu.' 'Superb value.'

23 Mayfield Gardens
Edinburgh EH9 2BX

T: 0131-667 5806
E: info@23mayfield.co.uk
W: www.23mayfield.co.uk

BEDROOMS: 8, 1 on ground floor.
OPEN: all year except Christmas.
FACILITIES: club room, dining room, free Wi-Fi, ½-acre garden, patio (hot tub), unsuitable for &.
BACKGROUND MUSIC: in club room, dining room.
LOCATION: 1 mile S of city centre.
CHILDREN: all ages welcomed.
DOGS: not allowed.
CREDIT CARDS: MasterCard, Visa.
PRICES: [2013] per room B&B single £65–£95, double £80–£160.

SEE ALSO SHORTLIST

EDNAM Scottish Borders

EDENWATER HOUSE

By a 17th-century kirk in a peaceful hamlet in
the Scottish Borders, this old stone manse with a
pretty garden is run by 'friendly' owners Jacqui
and Jeff Kelly. He looks after front-of-house and
she is the chef. Guests are greeted on arrival
with tea or coffee in front of a log fire in the cosy
lounge; it might come with Selkirk bannock.
The bedrooms are 'spacious, elegant', with
'everything you might need'. The Kellys tells
us they are upgrading the bedrooms and the
bathrooms; a ground-floor room has been
converted into a self-catering apartment with its
own private patio. In the dining room, Jacqui
Kelly serves a 'superb' no-choice three-course
menu which might include spider crab salad,
avocado cream, apple jelly, curried crème
fraîche; loin of Highland venison on parsnip and
carrot mash, macerated currants and cumin, red
wine sauce. Breakfast is 'substantial and varied',
with a 'good range' of fresh fruits, cereals,
yogurts and cooked dishes. There are gourmet
weekend breaks, and wine tastings with a light
supper are served in *The Wine Shed*, which
doubles as a games room during the day.

Ednam, nr Kelso
TD5 7QL

T: 01573-224070
E: winendine@
   edenwaterhouse.co.uk
W: www.edenwaterhouse.co.uk

BEDROOMS: 3, plus a self-catering
apartment.
OPEN: Mar–20 Dec, dining room
closed Sun.
FACILITIES: drawing room, TV
room, study, dining room, wine-
tasting room, free Wi-Fi, 5-acre
grounds, unsuitable for &.
BACKGROUND MUSIC: none.
LOCATION: 2 miles N of Kelso on
B6461.
CHILDREN: not under 12.
DOGS: not allowed.
CREDIT CARDS: MasterCard, Visa.
PRICES: per person B&B £45–£65,
D,B&B £85–£105. Set dinner £40.

ERISKA Argyll and Bute

ISLE OF ERISKA HOTEL, SPA AND ISLAND

🏵 *César award in 2007*

'A super hotel; expensive, but very, very good.' A visitor this year praises the Buchanan-Smith family's luxury hotel (Relais & Châteaux), a baronial mansion on a private island near Oban. Beppo Buchanan-Smith, whose parents bought the island 40 years ago, is a 'hands-on, efficient' host. 'There was a welcome letter for our dog, with dog biscuits; he agrees that this is a special place.' The 'well-furnished' bedrooms in the main house have a contemporary feel with traditional flourishes; each of the spa suites in the grounds has a private terrace with a spa tub. An open fire burns daily in the hall; the library has an Art Deco fireplace. In the dining room, chef Simon McKenzie serves an 'excellent' modern Scottish menu, using local produce, perhaps smoked West Coast mackerel, cucumber, oyster; loin of Highland venison, beetroot, cabbage, blackberries. *Eriska* is a resort as well as a hotel: it has a nine-hole golf course and a driving range, a sports hall with badminton and table tennis, and a spa with a swimming pool. Light meals are served on a veranda. (*David RW Jervois*)

Benderloch, Eriska
by Oban PA37 1SD

T: 01631-720371
F: 01631-720531
E: office@eriska-hotel.co.uk
W: www.eriska-hotel.co.uk

BEDROOMS: 23, including 5 spa suites and 2 garden cottages, some on ground floor.
OPEN: all year except 3–30 Jan.
FACILITIES: ramp, 5 public rooms, free Wi-Fi, leisure centre, swimming pool (17 by 6 metres), gym, sauna, treatments, wedding facilities, tennis, 350-acre grounds, 9-hole golf course.
BACKGROUND MUSIC: none.
LOCATION: 12 miles N of Oban.
CHILDREN: all ages welcomed, but no under-5s in leisure centre, and special evening meal arrangements.
DOGS: not allowed in public rooms or unattended in bedrooms.
CREDIT CARDS: Amex, MasterCard, Visa.
PRICES: [2013] per room B&B £360–£440. Set dinner £50. 2-night min. stay.

FORT AUGUSTUS Highland

Map 5:C2

THE LOVAT

On the southern shore of Loch Ness, this former railway hotel has been updated by the owner, Caroline Gregory, who runs it with an eco-conscious ethos. It is a 'comfortable, well-run place', says a *Guide* inspector, who found the ambience 'pleasing', and the staff 'willing'. The bedrooms, which vary in size and view, are 'well furnished and comfortable, decorated in modern big-hotel style; ours had attractive views over green lawns up to hills beyond; a good-sized bathroom'. Each of six studio rooms in an annexe has a private parking space. The lobby/sitting room has 'a big open fire and a grand piano'; the drawing room is 'nice and light'. There are two styles of dining. In the 'elegant' dining room, chef Sean Kelly serves a no-choice 'Scottish creative' menu of five 'delicious' courses, 'perfectly judged in size and variety'. Dishes might include ham hough and rabbit terrine; Wester Ross salmon, Shetland mussels, linguine and saffron. Simpler dishes are served in a smart conservatory brasserie. The 'very good' breakfast has a continental buffet which includes roast ham and cheese; smoked haddock and kippers are among the cooked choices.

Fort Augustus
PH32 4DU

T: 0845-4501100
F: 01320-366677
E: info@thelovat.com
W: www.thelovat.com

BEDROOMS: 28, 6 in annexe, 2 suitable for &.
OPEN: all year, restaurant closed Sun–Tues Nov–Mar.
FACILITIES: drawing room, dining room, brasserie, Reception, bar, free Wi-Fi, wedding facilities, 2-acre grounds.
BACKGROUND MUSIC: in bar.
LOCATION: in village SW of Inverness by A82.
CHILDREN: all ages welcomed.
DOGS: allowed in 1 bedroom only and bar.
CREDIT CARDS: Amex, MasterCard, Visa.
PRICES: [2013] per room B&B £70–£265, D,B&B £120–£355. Set menu £45, à la carte £30.

FORT WILLIAM Highland

Map 5:C1

THE GRANGE

'A gracious house in a delightful, well-maintained garden high above Loch Linnhe.' *Guide* inspectors were 'impressed' this year by John and Joan Campbell's B&B in a white-painted Victorian house. 'Joan Campbell gave us a warm welcome, carried our bags and explained the house rules over tea in the lounge.' There are three bedrooms: 'Everything in ours, Rob Roy, was immaculately presented, down to the tiniest details: binoculars, playing cards, clothes brush, iron and ironing board, sherry, apples and a teddy; no fewer than eleven cushions. The furnishings were of the highest quality, even the blinds were woven tweed to match the chairs, bedding, carpet, etc; plenty of drawer and wardrobe space. The ornamentation was slightly over the top, especially the tassels on the drawer handles. The bathroom had a large walk-in shower and a bath, a multitude of mirrors and vast displays of glassware, flowers, ornaments, candles.' Breakfast is ordered the evening before and is served no later than 9 am in a 'delightful dining room with beautiful furnishings'. The menu has 'interesting dishes' (like smoked haddock with cream sauce), 'an excellent fresh fruit platter'.

Grange Road
Fort William PH33 6JF

T: 01397-705516
E: joan@thegrange-scotland.co.uk
W: www.grangefortwilliam.com

BEDROOMS: 3.
OPEN: Mar–Oct.
FACILITIES: lounge, breakfast room, free Wi-Fi, 1-acre garden, unsuitable for &.
BACKGROUND MUSIC: none.
LOCATION: edge of town.
CHILDREN: not under 16.
DOGS: not allowed.
CREDIT CARDS: none.
PRICES: [2013] per person B&B £60–£65. 1-night bookings sometimes refused high season.

SEE ALSO SHORTLIST

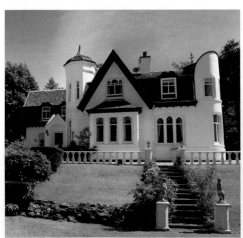

FORT WILLIAM Highland

Map 5:C1

INVERLOCHY CASTLE

A castle by a loch is the beau idéal of Scottish country house hotels. Queen Victoria certainly liked it when she visited this baronial mansion in the foothills of Ben Nevis in 1873 (not a hotel in those days): 'I never saw a lovelier or more romantic spot.' *Guide* regulars agreed. 'It was the absolute highlight of our holiday. Our Queen suite had a fantastic view.' Visitors are greeted at the door by 'friendly, courteous staff'. The 'stunning' double-height Great Hall has Venetian chandeliers and a decorative painted ceiling. Men are asked to wear a jacket and tie in the three dining rooms (it is said that when the rules were relaxed a guest dined in trainers with no socks). The chef, Philip Carnegie, has a *Michelin* star for his menus. 'The best dinner we enjoyed in Scotland: creative but never exaggerated', eg, braised halibut with watercress and caviar; hazelnut panna cotta, date cake and cassis figs. Bedrooms are 'light and spacious', as are the bathrooms, which have 'classy toiletries'. Good walking in the 'beautifully kept' grounds and walled garden. There is also fishing on the estate. (*CB and RM*)

Torlundy
Fort William PH33 6SN

T: 01397-702177
F: 01397-702953
E: info@inverlochy.co.uk
W: www.inverlochycastlehotel.com

BEDROOMS: 17, plus 2 in Gate Lodge.
OPEN: all year.
FACILITIES: Great Hall, drawing room, dining room, wedding facilities, free Wi-Fi, 600-acre estate (tennis), only restaurant suitable for ♿.
BACKGROUND MUSIC: pianist or harpist in Great Hall in evening.
LOCATION: 4 miles NE of Fort William.
CHILDREN: all ages welcomed, young children not allowed in public areas after 6 pm.
DOGS: not in public rooms.
CREDIT CARDS: Amex, MasterCard, Visa.
PRICES: [2013] per room B&B £320–£695. Set dinner £67, tasting menu £85.

SEE ALSO SHORTLIST

GLASGOW

Map 5:D2

GRASSHOPPERS

A 'modern city hotel with a twist', Barry Munn's conversion of the top floor of a Victorian railway company's headquarters is 'incredibly good value', said *Guide* inspectors. The 'unpromising' position (at the end of Union Street next to Central Station) is 'convenient', and the smart modern styling and 'friendly, willing' staff soon 'transform the experience'. Entry is by a lift that opens on to clean, Scandinavian interiors – light wooden flooring throughout. The bedrooms, decorated in a variety of (mainly light) colours, are 'stylish and spare', with big Victorian windows ('the kind you can open'). Each room has a desk; storage is limited. 'Our tiny bathroom was well designed and equipped'. Light suppers ('Nigel Slater-style') are served from Monday to Thursday in the 'bright and cheerful' *Kitchen*, which has handmade ash tables, panelled walls and variable lighting. Typical dishes: 'juicy, old-fashioned prawn cocktail'; smoked haddock with mustard gravy. Guests can take their meals to their bedroom ('the choice is yours'). Breakfast is a buffet, with do-it-yourself toast, cereals and fruit juices. Eggs are cooked to order. Porridge is on offer, and kedgeree may be available.

6th floor Caledonian Chambers
87 Union Street
Glasgow G1 3TA

T: 0141-222 2666
F: 0141-248 3641
E: info@grasshoppersglasgow.com
W: www.grasshoppersglasgow.com

BEDROOMS: 29.
OPEN: all year, restaurant closed Fri–Sun.
FACILITIES: breakfast/supper room, free Wi-Fi, unsuitable for &.
BACKGROUND MUSIC: none.
LOCATION: by Central Station.
CHILDREN: all ages welcomed.
DOGS: allowed.
CREDIT CARDS: all major cards.
PRICES: per room B&B £85–£115, D,B&B £95–£125. Set menus £13.75–£16.75.

SEE ALSO SHORTLIST

GLENFINNAN Highland

Map 5:C1

GLENFINNAN HOUSE HOTEL

A Victorian Scots take on a small French château, this 'comfortable, welcoming hotel' stands in 'an idyllic setting' between Loch Shiel and the mountains. 'Wonderful; the old building has been sympathetically furnished to maintain its character without compromising on comfort or quality,' say visitors this year. 'There are fresh flowers everywhere.' There are no keys to the bedrooms, which have Edwardian antiques and Regency-stripe bedcovers. They vary in size: a top-floor family suite was 'vast, with a huge bathroom and a very comfortable bed'. 'The view from our window was amazing, across the lawn to the lochside, where deer were grazing, and snow-capped Ben Nevis beyond. For our last night we were moved to a more compact room which was just as comfortable.' Guests can eat in the 'busy' bar or more formal dining room where the chef, Duncan Gibson, serves a 'very good' traditional Scottish menu, which might include roast monkfish with green pea and crayfish risotto. Breakfast has a buffet with 'delicious home-made jam and marmalade'; 'wonderful' cooked dishes. Packed lunches are available. Children are well catered for. (*Alan and Edwina Williams, and others*)

25% DISCOUNT VOUCHERS

Glenfinnan
by Fort William PH37 4LT

T: 01397-722235
F: 01397-722249
E: availability@glenfinnanhouse.com
W: www.glenfinnanhouse.com

BEDROOMS: 14.
OPEN: 20 Mar–2 Nov.
FACILITIES: ramps, drawing room, playroom, bar, restaurant, wedding facilities, free Wi-Fi, 1-acre grounds, playground, unsuitable for &.
BACKGROUND MUSIC: Scottish in bar and restaurant.
LOCATION: 15 miles NW of Fort William.
CHILDREN: all ages welcomed.
DOGS: not in restaurant.
CREDIT CARDS: Amex, MasterCard, Visa.
PRICES: [2013] per room B&B single £65–£75, double £130–£210. À la carte £25–£30.

GLENFINNAN Highland

Map 5:C1

THE PRINCE'S HOUSE

Built as a 'change house' to provide shelter and a change of horse for travellers on the road to the isles, this traditional white-painted coaching inn is run in an 'informal and relaxed manner' by owners Kieron and Ina Kelly. She is the attentive front-of-house; he is the chef. The bedrooms are on the first and second floors; best ones at the front. They are traditionally furnished (stripes and patterns abound): 'Ours was well appointed and comfortable.' The spacious bar, which serves local ales, has a huge vaulted pine ceiling. In the dining room, the host serves a daily-changing menu of locally sourced ingredients; foraged fruit and herbs, venison from the surrounding hills, fish and shellfish landed at Mallaig; fruit and vegetables from a local organic grower, meat from the West Highlands. Typical dishes: celeriac cream soup, crème fraîche and Lanark Blue cheese; baked fillet of Wester Ross salmon, braised lettuce and Loch Eil mussel broth. A blackboard menu is available in the bar (including home-made ice cream in 'unusual' flavours). Breakfast has freshly squeezed fruit juice, 'excellent' porridge. (*AJG*)

25% DISCOUNT VOUCHERS

Glenfinnan
by Fort William PH37 4LT

T: 01397-722246
E: princeshouse@glenfinnan.co.uk
W: www.glenfinnan.co.uk

BEDROOMS: 9.
OPEN: mid-Mar–early Nov, 27 Dec–2 Jan, restaurant open Easter–end Sept.
FACILITIES: lounge/bar, bar, dining room, free Wi-Fi, small front lawn, only bar suitable for &.
BACKGROUND MUSIC: classical in public areas.
LOCATION: 15 miles NW of Fort William.
CHILDREN: all ages welcomed.
DOGS: allowed in bar.
CREDIT CARDS: MasterCard, Visa.
PRICES: [2013] per person B&B £65–£90, D,B&B £95–£120. Set menu £30, à la carte £35–£40.

GRANTOWN-ON-SPEY Highland

Map 5:C2

CULDEARN HOUSE

A one-time home of the Earls of Seafield, this 'delightful' but 'unassuming' Victorian house was found by returning visitors 'just as good as before'. Set 'peacefully' beside woods on the edge of a pretty Speyside town, it is run by 'charming' William Marshall and his wife, Sonia, whose 'good, home-cooked food' was much enjoyed. There are 'lots of armchairs and sofas' in the lounge, which has a log fire, and where visitors are welcomed with tea. Bedrooms, decorated individually with a mix of antique and modern furniture and floral curtains and covers, vary in size. Spacious bath/shower rooms are 'immaculate'. This is whisky country and it is a subject on which Mr Marshall, with 50 on offer in the lounge, is 'very knowledgeable'. The four-course dinner menu changes daily and is served by candlelight. 'Beautifully cooked meat' might include medallions of pork with a lime and coriander sauce. Breakfast has 'outstanding' warm fruit compote and lots of cooked dishes. Outdoor activities abound and there are distilleries to visit. *Culdearn* 'provided just the right setting for our wedding reception' for one couple this year. (*Jill and Mike Bennett, and others*)

Woodlands Terrace
Grantown-on-Spey PH26 3JU

T: 01479-872106
F: 01479-873641
E: enquiries@culdearn.com
W: www.culdearn.com

BEDROOMS: 6, 1 on ground floor.
OPEN: all year.
FACILITIES: lounge, dining room, free Wi-Fi, ¾-acre garden.
BACKGROUND MUSIC: pre-dinner classical in lounge.
LOCATION: edge of town.
CHILDREN: not under 10.
DOGS: only guide dogs allowed.
CREDIT CARDS: Diners, MasterCard, Visa.
PRICES: [2013] per person B&B £69–£79, D,B&B £100–£140. À la carte £39.50.

SEE ALSO SHORTLIST

INVERNESS Highland

Map 5:C2

TRAFFORD BANK GUEST HOUSE

Once the home of the Bishop of Moray and Ross-shire, this bay-windowed, sandstone Victorian house has been renovated by interior designer Lorraine Pun. She has furnished it with a mix of antiques and contemporary pieces (some of which she designed herself); there is artwork everywhere (including interesting sculptures in the mature gardens). Most of the bedrooms are large; they are generously equipped with a hospitality tray, decanter of sherry, silent fridge, flat-screen TV, iPod docking; organic toiletries in the bathroom. The Floral Suite has a large, modern half-tester bed; a roll-top bath; the decor of the Tartan Room is self-evident; it has a Victorian-style roll-top bath in the bathroom, and a separate shower. The Trafford Suite has an extra single bed for family use. Visitors have commented on the quality of the welcome and the accommodation: 'The best we have found in Inverness.' Breakfast, ordered the evening before, is taken in a conservatory overlooking the garden. It 'hits all the right buttons': home-made scones and oat cakes, 'excellent choices, served piping hot'. The house is a short walk from the city centre. More reports, please.

96 Fairfield Road
Inverness IV3 5LL

T: 01463-241414
F: 01463-241421
E: enquiries@
traffordbankguesthouse.co.uk
W: www.traffordbankguesthouse.
co.uk

BEDROOMS: 5.
OPEN: all year except mid-Nov–mid-Dec.
FACILITIES: ramps, 2 lounges, conservatory, free Wi-Fi, garden, unsuitable for &.
BACKGROUND MUSIC: none.
LOCATION: 10 mins' walk from centre.
CHILDREN: all ages welcomed.
DOGS: only guide dogs allowed.
CREDIT CARDS: MasterCard, Visa.
PRICES: per room B&B £98–£128.

SEE ALSO SHORTLIST

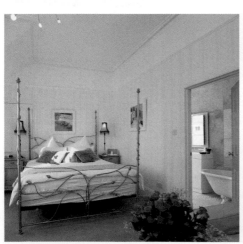

KILBERRY Argyll and Bute

Map 5:D1

KILBERRY INN

César award in 2010

'The *Kilberry Inn* has a "special atmosphere" and is still very worthy of its *César* award.' So say *Guide* regulars on their fifth annual visit to David Wilson and Clare Johnson's small red-roofed restaurant-with-rooms in a tiny hamlet 'sandwiched between the sea and rolling green hills' on the Argyll coast. The drive down 16 miles of single-track road is 'wild and magical'. David Wilson is a 'charming' and 'attentive' host, offering wit and a cocktail of the day in the 'unpretentious' bar. The 'simple, comfortable' guest rooms are set round the back in individual cottages; the largest is a suite, 'usually given to dog owners'. It has a walk-in shower. The real draw is Clare Johnson's short, seasonal menu, served in the beamed, stone-walled dining room. The food was found 'sublime' by inspectors and 'delightful and very moreish' and 'in a class of its own' by other visitors. 'Among our favourites were crab cakes with lime mayonnaise, lamb with coriander bulgar wheat, panna cotta with blackcurrants.' There are beaches, boat trips, golf and 'fantastic walks' to be enjoyed nearby. (*GC, and others*)

Kilberry, by Tarbert
PA29 6YD

T: 01880-770223
E: relax@kilberryinn.com
W: www.kilberryinn.com

BEDROOMS: 5, all on ground floor.
OPEN: Tues–Sun 15 March–end Oct, weekends only Nov and Dec, and New Year.
FACILITIES: bar/dining room, smaller dining room, no Wi-Fi (Kilberry is in a 'not spot').
BACKGROUND MUSIC: in larger dining room, lunch and dinner.
LOCATION: 16 miles NW of Tarbert, on B8024.
CHILDREN: no under-12s.
DOGS: only in one bedroom, not in public rooms.
CREDIT CARDS: MasterCard, Visa.
PRICES: [2013] per room D,B&B £210. À la carte £35. 1-night bookings sometimes refused weekends.

KILCHRENAN Argyll and Bute

Map 5:D1

ARDANAISEIG

'It must be the most peaceful hotel in Britain,' says a *Guide* regular who knew *Ardanaiseig* as a child in the 1930s. By the shores Loch Awe, this late Georgian baronial mansion lies in wooded grounds down more than ten miles of winding track. Another comment: 'Well worth the effort to get there.' The dramatic interior reflects the owner Bennie Gray's past as an antique dealer. 'Most unusual.' There are deep colours and gilt, Middle Eastern rugs on the floors, decorative objects everywhere. The bedrooms, mostly spacious and each with a Highland place name, are individually designed. Awe has a Gothic brass bed, Kilchurn a four-poster. Most bathrooms have a bath with shower over. A seven-course no-choice (allergies discussed) menu is served in the dining room overlooking the loch, by chef Gary Goldie. 'Fewer courses and more choice would have been welcome,' say some guests this year. Others found the food, eg, breast of duck, confit of leg pithivier, grelot onions, salsify, foie gras sauce, 'varied, inventive and delicious'. He forages in the woods for ingredients, and welcomes company on these trips. (*JBH, RC, CJM*)

Kilchrenan
by Taynuilt PA35 1HE

T: 01866-833333
F: 01866-833222
E: info@ardanaiseig.com
W: www.ardanaiseig.com

BEDROOMS: 18, some on ground floor, 1 in boatshed, 1 self-catering cottage.
OPEN: all year.
FACILITIES: drawing room, library/bar, games room, restaurant, free Wi-Fi, wedding facilities, 360-acre grounds on loch (open-air theatre, tennis, bathing, fishing).
BACKGROUND MUSIC: classical/jazz in restaurant during dinner.
LOCATION: 4 miles E of Kilchrenan.
CHILDREN: all ages welcomed, but no under-10s at dinner.
DOGS: not allowed in public rooms (£20 charge).
CREDIT CARDS: Amex, MasterCard, Visa.
PRICES: [2013] per room B&B £173–£363. Set dinner £50.

KILLIECRANKIE Perth and Kinross

Map 5:D2

KILLIECRANKIE HOTEL

❧ *César award in 2011*

Overlooking the River Garry on the Pass of Killiecrankie, this white house is run in hands-on style as a small hotel by Henrietta Fergusson. 'Everything about the hotel and the service continues to be outstanding,' say returning visitors this year. The young staff, smartly dressed in tartan trousers, are 'efficient and friendly'. Readers praise the 'open-heartedness' of the 'ubiquitous' hostess: 'If I owned a hotel, she would be my first choice to run it.' The bedrooms are a 'delight': 'Our refurbished room reflected the consistently high standard of elegance and comfort.' Extra touches include 'good coffee and shortbread biscuits' on the tea tray; luxurious toiletries in the bathroom; the hot-water bottle that appears at turn-down. The modern cooking of the chef, Mark Easton, is much admired: his table d'hôte menu might include crab, coriander and lime cake, chilli sauce; best end of Perthshire lamb, red onion marmalade mousse, carrot spaghetti, Madeira jus. Breakfast has 'a lavish selection of jams, honey, etc'. The house stands in large wooded grounds; there is much to see in the area. (*Alan and Edwina Williams*)

25% DISCOUNT VOUCHERS

Killiecrankie
by Pitlochry PH16 5LG

T: 01796-473220
F: 01796-472451
E: enquiries@killiecrankiehotel.co.uk
W: www.killiecrankiehotel.co.uk

BEDROOMS: 10, 2 on ground floor.
OPEN: 18 Mar–3 Jan.
FACILITIES: ramp, sitting room, bar with conservatory, dining room, breakfast conservatory, free Wi-Fi, 4½-acre grounds.
BACKGROUND MUSIC: none.
LOCATION: hamlet 3 miles W of Pitlochry.
CHILDREN: all ages welcomed.
DOGS: not allowed in eating areas, some bedrooms.
CREDIT CARDS: MasterCard, Visa.
PRICES: [2013] per person B&B £90–£100, D,B&B £115–£145. Set dinner £42. 1-night bookings sometimes refused weekends.

KILMARTIN Argyll and Bute

Map 5:D1

DUNCHRAIGAIG HOUSE

25% DISCOUNT VOUCHERS

Opposite a group of standing stones in an area rich in prehistoric sites, this 'excellent' B&B is run by Cameron Bruce and Lynn Jones, 'hands-on, and competent' hosts. The five bedrooms, decorated in 'relaxing' colours, have views of the stones or of woodland at the back (from which deer or the 'resident' pine martin may emerge). The Green Room has a double aspect and a shower room; the Blue Room overlooks the stones and the Isle of Jura beyond. The Lilac Room has a king-size bed; a corner bath and walk-in shower. Breakfast (taken communally or at separate tables) includes eggs from the resident hens, fruit from the garden, home-made jams. Each guest is given an individual fruit salad; muffins or rolls are baked daily. There is an extensive cooked menu and a dish of the day: a favourite was the 'orange-eggy bread with maple syrup; three rounds, wow'. 'Lynn has researched a huge amount of information on the area; walking and driving sheets are laminated for borrowing.' She will provide a 'generous' packed lunch. Nearby inns are recommended for eating out. More reports, please.

Kilmartin Glen
Lochgilphead PA31 8RG

T: 01546-510396
E: info@dunchraigaig.co.uk
W: www.dunchraigaig.co.uk

BEDROOMS: 5.
OPEN: Mar–Nov.
FACILITIES: lounge, dining room, free Wi-Fi, ½-acre garden, unsuitable for &.
BACKGROUND MUSIC: none.
LOCATION: 1 mile south of village, 7 miles N of Lochgilphead.
CHILDREN: not under 12.
DOGS: not allowed.
CREDIT CARDS: none.
PRICES: [2013] per person B&B £35–£50. 1-night bookings refused bank holiday weekends.

KINGUSSIE Highland

Map 5:C2

THE CROSS AT KINGUSSIE

On the leafy banks of the River Gynack, this converted tweed mill is run as a restaurant-with-rooms by new owners Derek and Celia Kitchingman. Their chef, Ross Sutherland, was named young Highland chef of the year in a competition run by Albert Roux. 'His five-course tasting menu is delicious and a real bargain at the price, showing intensity of flavour and first-class portion control,' says a *Guide* inspector. 'We particularly liked the spicy onion and squash soup; quail and mushroom ravioli; and apple tarte Tatin, pearl barley ice cream and cob nuts,' says a reader. 'Service was most efficient.' Five of the bathrooms have been upgraded. 'Our large room, with a view over the river, was warm and comfortable.' Books and magazines are available in an upstairs lounge, which has separate seating areas with armchairs and sofas. The white-walled dining room has 'striking' paintings in Gauguin style by an East Lothian artist; French doors open on to a riverside patio. A 'life-affirming' breakfast has 'scrambled eggs cooked to perfection, sweet bacon and black pudding and a full buffet selection including delicious freshly squeezed orange juice'. (*GC, and others*)

25% DISCOUNT VOUCHERS

Tweed Mill Brae, Ardbroilach Road
Kingussie PH21 1LB

T: 01540-661166
E: relax@thecross.co.uk
W: www.thecross.co.uk

BEDROOMS: 8.
OPEN: early Feb–early Jan except Christmas.
FACILITIES: 2 lounges, restaurant, free Wi-Fi in some areas, 4-acre grounds, only restaurant suitable for &.
BACKGROUND MUSIC: none.
LOCATION: 440 yds from village centre.
CHILDREN: all ages welcomed.
DOGS: allowed by arrangement, not in public rooms.
CREDIT CARDS: Amex, MasterCard, Visa.
PRICES: [2013] per room B&B £100–£140, D,B&B £200–£240. Set dinner £50.

KIRKBEAN Dumfries and Galloway

Map 5:E2

CAVENS

'Delightful; the peaceful location is perfect for a relaxing stay.' Praise this year from fellow *Guide* hoteliers for Angus and Jane Fordyce's small country hotel, a white-painted manor house near Dumfries. 'Angus runs a very good ship.' The bedrooms, 'immaculate and comfortable', vary in size and aspect. They are decorated in traditional country house style, with tea- and coffee-making kit, fruit, biscuits; a modern bathroom. The cottages have a simpler style. 'I had a large bedroom on the ground floor, with a well-equipped, cavernous bathroom.' Angus Fordyce, the chef, uses vegetables from the kitchen garden and seasonal produce for his 'tasty' dishes on an 'excellent-value' set menu (there is also à la carte). It is served in the 'impressive' dining room ('antique furniture, white tablecloths, beautiful glassware, silver cutlery'). Dishes might include salmon and dill tartlet; fillet of Galloway pork, wholegrain and cream sauce. There's a 'well-thought-out' wine list. Breakfast was 'spot on; the poached eggs and black pudding were the best we have eaten'. 'Angus gives great advice on local treasures. Would we return? Very soon.' (*Tim Culkin and Austin Lynch, David Craig*)

25% DISCOUNT VOUCHERS

Kirkbean
by Dumfries DG2 8AA

T: 01387-880234
F: 01387-880467
E: enquiries@cavens.com
W: www.cavens.com

BEDROOMS: 6, 1 on ground floor, also 2 self-catering cottages.
OPEN: Mar–Nov, New Year.
FACILITIES: sitting room, dining room, wedding/meeting facilities, free Wi-Fi, 20-acre grounds, unsuitable for &.
BACKGROUND MUSIC: light classical 'sometimes' in sitting room.
LOCATION: 13 miles S of Dumfries.
CHILDREN: all ages welcomed.
DOGS: allowed by arrangement, not in public rooms.
CREDIT CARDS: MasterCard, Visa.
PRICES: [2013] per room B&B £100–£200. Set dinner £25, à la carte £35. 1-night bookings refused Easter, bank holidays.

KIRKCUDBRIGHT Dumfries and Galloway Map 5:E2

GLENHOLME COUNTRY HOUSE

'A civilised place', this high Victorian mansion is run as an upmarket guest house by retired diplomat Laurence Bristow-Smith and his artist wife, Jennifer. 'An adaptable and hands-on host, he introduced himself by first name, showed us round and brought us tea,' said an inspector. The owners have given the house a 'cultivated feel'. The library is lined with bookshelves (books of the kind 'you want to read'); upstairs is a collection of 'well-thumbed Penguin paperbacks'. The bedrooms are named after Victorian politicians: Nicolson, decorated in soft greens, has a colonial four-poster bed with an antique Durham quilt. Lansdowne is a 'charming' room in white and pale grey; a huge antique mirror in the shower room. In the dining room, which overlooks the lawn and orchard, the host, an enthusiastic cook, serves a three-course, no-choice menu by arrangement with dishes like Stilton and leek risotto; chicken in filo pastry, lime and ginger sauce. Guests may bring their own wine. Breakfast, served until 10 am, has a buffet of fruit and cereal, freshly squeezed orange juice; chunky toast, 'delicious marmalade made by Jennifer'; 'all manner of cooked dishes'.

Tongland Road
Kirkcudbright DG6 4UU

T: 01557-339422
E: info@
   glenholmecountryhouse.com
W: www.glenholmecountryhouse.
   com

BEDROOMS: 4.
OPEN: all year.
FACILITIES: library, dining room, free Wi-Fi, 1½-acre garden, unsuitable for &.
BACKGROUND MUSIC: music system in library and dining room at guests' discretion.
LOCATION: 1 mile N of town.
CHILDREN: not under 12.
DOGS: not allowed.
CREDIT CARDS: MasterCard, Visa.
PRICES: [2013] per room B&B single £80–£95, double £95–£120. 1-night bookings sometimes refused weekends in high season.

KYLESKU Highland

❦ KYLESKU HOTEL

César award: Scottish hotel of the year

'Our first visit since the change of ownership and we were not disappointed.' *Guide* regulars enjoyed their return to this white-painted former coaching inn in an 'idyllic setting' by a sea loch on the remote north-west coast. New owners Tanja Lister, 'full of enthusiasm and energy', and Sonia Virechauveix, who oversees the kitchen, 'are chatty and hands-on'. Other *Guide* regulars 'were warmly greeted by well-trained young seasonal staff'. Bedrooms are not large, but all are now refurbished. 'New beds, improved lighting and a new bathroom. The views are majestic – particularly from the loo seat'. A common menu is served in the bar ('popular with locals') and dining room with a 'sweeping view', where 'residents can reserve a table of choice'. Service was 'prompt' and 'informal'. 'We enjoyed the freshest seafood, including Lochinver haddock and Achiltibuie kippers.' Breakfast was 'delicious and nicely presented'; it might be 'blueberry pancakes with maple syrup; creamy yogurt, smoked salmon, kippers'. 'Superb walks and drives' all around and 'Tanja can arrange boat trips'. (*Janet and Dennis Allom, Robert Gower, Jill and Mike Bennett*)

Kylesku
IV27 4HW

T: 01971-502231
E: info@kyleskuhotel.co.uk
W: www.kyleskuhotel.co.uk

BEDROOMS: 8, 1 in annexe.
OPEN: 1 Mar–4 Nov.
FACILITIES: lounge, bar, restaurant, free Wi-Fi in bar and lounge, small garden (tables for outside eating), unsuitable for ᕇ.
BACKGROUND MUSIC: in bar.
LOCATION: 10 miles S of Scourie, 30 miles north of Ullapool.
CHILDREN: all ages welcomed.
DOGS: allowed.
CREDIT CARDS: MasterCard, Visa.
PRICES: [2013] per room B&B £92.50–£115. À la carte £27.50.

LANARK South Lanarkshire

Map 5:E2

NEW LANARK MILL HOTEL

The New Lanark Trust has 'lovingly restored' this World Heritage Site, a converted 18th-century cotton mill in a steep valley of native woodland below the Falls of Clyde. Originally a manufacturing centre developed by the utopian social pioneer, Robert Owen, the 'fascinating' complex has a visitor centre, shops, self-catering accommodation, a youth hostel as well as a hotel which is managed by John Stirrat. It might not be a typical *Guide* hotel (not least because it is popular for weddings), but it is recommended for the wider interest and the 'good value' for the area. Most of the spacious, 'well-furnished and clean' bedrooms overlook the river. 'Nothing fancy, but comfortable.' A quieter alternative is the self-catering two-storey *Waterhouses* in a separate building. In the restaurant, head chef Linsey Scott serves contemporary dishes like aromatic duck fritter, chilli and soya dressing; slow-cooked Scottish beef cheeks, ham and chive-mashed potatoes, caramelised onion sauce. 'Pleasant' light meals are available in the bar. Breakfast has a buffet of hot dishes and cooked-to-order choices (preferred). Reader's hint: check about weddings when booking and avoid the fifth floor. (*DF, and others*)

25% DISCOUNT VOUCHERS

Mill One, New Lanark Mills
Lanark ML11 9DB

T: 01555-667200
F: 01555-667222
E: hotel@newlanark.org
W: www.newlanarkmillhotel.co.uk

BEDROOMS: 38, 4 suitable for &.
OPEN: all year.
FACILITIES: roof garden, lounge, bar, restaurant, free Wi-Fi, heated indoor swimming pool (16.5 by 4.5 metres), wedding facilities, conference centre.
BACKGROUND MUSIC: instrumental, in public areas.
LOCATION: 1 mile S of Lanark.
CHILDREN: all ages welcomed.
DOGS: only guide dogs in public rooms.
CREDIT CARDS: all major cards.
PRICES: per person B&B
£29.50–£59.50, D,B&B
£51.50–£81.50. À la carte £25.

LOCHEPORT Western Isles

LANGASS LODGE

On an island of 'wonderful beaches and glorious scenery', this former shooting lodge above a sea loch is owned and run by Niall and Amanda Leveson Gower. 'It is so relaxing with complete peace and quiet; we can't wait to go back,' says a visitor. 'The staff are charming and the food is wonderful.' Game from the North Uist estate and seafood appear in the menus of the chef, John Buchannan. In the two-tier conservatory restaurant, his dishes might include home-cured beetroot gravadlax, pickled fennel; baked whole Dover sole, Barra prawns, micro salad. Simpler meals are served in the bar (eg, battered fish of the day). The largest rooms are in a hillside wing (four have a door opening on to the garden, with loch views). Smaller and cheaper rooms are in the main house. Children are 'genuinely welcomed': a family room in the hillside wing has two extra beds. There is a children's special menu, and toys are in the lounge. A host of activities can be arranged: fishing, shooting, kayaking, boat trips. 'We walked at the nearby RSPB reserves and on the white-sand beaches.' (*MW*)

Locheport
Isle of North Uist
Western Isles HS6 5HA

T: 01876-580285
F: 01876-580385
E: langasslodge@btconnect.com
W: www.langasslodge.co.uk

BEDROOMS: 11, 1 suitable for &.
OPEN: all year except 24–26 Dec, 31 Dec/1 Jan.
FACILITIES: lounge, bar, restaurant, free Wi-Fi, wedding facilities, 11-acre garden.
BACKGROUND MUSIC: in bar.
LOCATION: 7½ miles S of Lochmaddy.
CHILDREN: all ages welcomed.
DOGS: allowed 'everywhere', £5 charge.
CREDIT CARDS: MasterCard, Visa.
PRICES: [2013] per room B&B single £65–£95, double £95–£145. Set dinner £30–£36, à la carte (bar) £27.

LOCHINVER Highland

THE ALBANNACH

'It is as superb as ever.' Visitor returning after ten years to Lesley Crosfield and Colin Craig's restaurant-with-rooms found the food still 'exquisite, beautifully served by the friendly staff'. The white-painted Victorian house has views over the sea loch to the Assynt mountains including the 'sugar-loaf' Suilven. The rooms are individually decorated: a 'surprisingly modern' penthouse suite has under-floor heating, a terrace with hot tub; a large bathroom with shower and a 'bath for two'. 'We awoke to see dawn breaking with a glorious display of colours over Suilven.' The Byre suite has its own terrace and hot tub looking across Wester Ross. There is a compact conservatory where pre-dinner drinks and home-baked afternoon tea (included in the price) are taken. In the more formal panelled dining room, the owners (joint chefs) serve a no-choice (preferences discussed) five-course dinner, giving 'a good variety, even over five days'. The hand-written menus feature dishes like roast wild turbot, charred fennel, white and green asparagus, garden burgundy potatoes. Herbs and vegetables are grown in the chefs' own polytunnel. (*Jill and Mike Bennett, Frances Thomas*)

Baddidarroch
Lochinver
Sutherland IV27 4LP

T: 01571-844407
E: info@thealbannach.co.uk
W: www.thealbannach.co.uk

BEDROOMS: 5, 1 in byre.
OPEN: mid-Mar–early Jan, closed Mon.
FACILITIES: ramp, snug, conservatory, dining room, free Wi-Fi, ½-acre garden, unsuitable for &.
BACKGROUND MUSIC: none.
LOCATION: ½ mile from village.
CHILDREN: not under 12.
DOGS: not allowed.
CREDIT CARDS: MasterCard, Visa.
PRICES: [2013] per room D,B&B £248–£375. Set dinner £65. 1-night bookings generally refused Sat.

SEE ALSO SHORTLIST

LOCHRANZA North Ayrshire

Map 5:D1

APPLE LODGE

❦ César award in 2000

The 'homely' atmosphere is liked by visitors to John and Jeannie Boyd's small guest house, a white-painted manse close to the ferry to the Kintyre peninsula. John Boyd greets guests, 'carrying bags and helping with parking'. 'They have certainly thought of everything; our room was comfortable,' said recent visitors. The decor may be 'slightly fussy': 'elaborate frills and lace trimmings, ornaments everywhere, dozens of knitted toys'. The four bedrooms, each named after an apple variety, have antique fireplace, embroidery, paintings, books and local information. Permain overlooks the hills and golf course; south-facing Russet catches the mountain views (watch out for wildlife); Apple Cottage, a self-contained suite with a sitting room and kitchen, has French doors opening on to the garden. Jeannie Boyd serves a three-course, no-choice dinner menu (not Tuesdays, or in July and August) at 7 pm, with dishes discussed beforehand. Locally sourced and garnished with herbs from the garden, they might include roast chicken, celery, almond and apple stuffing, creamy bread sauce. No licence; bring your own wine. Breakfasts are 'hearty'.

Lochranza
Isle of Arran KA27 8HJ

T/F: 01770-830229
E: applelodge@ymail.com
W: www.applelodgearran.co.uk

BEDROOMS: 4, 1 on ground floor.
OPEN: all year except mid-Dec–mid-Jan, dining room closed for dinner Tues and July/Aug.
FACILITIES: lounge, dining room, free Wi-Fi, ¼-acre garden, unsuitable for ⅚.
BACKGROUND MUSIC: none.
LOCATION: outside village on N side of island.
CHILDREN: not allowed.
DOGS: not allowed.
CREDIT CARDS: none.
PRICES: per person B&B £39, D,B&B £64, usually min. 3-night booking. Set dinner £25.

MUIR OF ORD Highland

Map 5:C2

THE DOWER HOUSE

🏵 *César award in 2008*

In a 'large, beautiful, wooded garden' bordered by the Beauly and Conon rivers, this single-storey Georgian cottage-orné is run as a small guest house by Robyn and Mena Aitchison. She is the 'charming' hostess; he is an 'excellent' cook. They have filled the house with antiques, Chinese vases; there are Persian rugs, chintzy wallpaper, flowery fabrics, potted plants and stacked bookcases. Some find that it creates a cluttered feel; others that it is like a 'treasure chest'. The host, a self-taught cook, uses local produce and home-grown herbs and vegetables for his no-choice menu (discussed in advance). Served in the elegant dining room, it might include tomato and lovage risotto; darn of sea bream, mint and noodles. The lounge has a log fire; a wide range of whiskies can be found in a self-service 'malt' cupboard. The bedrooms are individually decorated and have views over the grounds (which have monkey puzzle trees, shrubs and a miniature orchard). Some are small but all have a large bed and a well-equipped bathroom. Generous breakfasts include fresh fruit salad, free-range eggs, heather honey. Children are welcomed. (*EC, and others*)

Highfield
Muir of Ord IV6 7XN

T/F: 01463-870090
E: info@thedowerhouse.co.uk
W: www.thedowerhouse.co.uk

BEDROOMS: 4, all on ground floor.
OPEN: all year except Christmas/New Year.
FACILITIES: lounge, dining room, TV room, free Wi-Fi, wedding facilities, 4½-acre grounds, unsuitable for ♿.
BACKGROUND MUSIC: none.
LOCATION: 14 miles NW of Inverness.
CHILDREN: no under-5s at dinner (high tea at 5).
DOGS: not allowed in public rooms.
CREDIT CARDS: MasterCard, Visa.
PRICES: [2013] per room B&B single £90–£110, double £135–£155. Set dinner £38.

MUTHILL Perth and Kinross

Map 5:D2

BARLEY BREE

In a conservation village with an 11th-century bell tower, this former coaching inn is run as a restaurant-with-rooms by French chef Fabrice Bouteloup and his wife, Alison. 'The welcome is warm and helpful; our room was comfortable and the food was excellent,' says a regular correspondent. The candlelit restaurant, popular with locals, was 'buzzy on a Saturday evening, but the service was good', is another comment. The host promises to combine French skill with Scottish ingredients for his modern dishes, perhaps peat-smoked haddock and mussels, curry sauce; braised Aberdeen Angus ox cheek, barley, charred white cabbage. 'We had the "Sunday roast", best-ever beef carved so thin.' Bedrooms are individually decorated in 'classic contemporary style' with muted colours. 'We had a huge bedroom and bathroom which, despite being on the corner of a main road, was quiet on a Saturday night.' Families are encouraged to eat together: children have a short menu of their own ('but no chips, a ruling that also applies to adults'). There is a family bedroom, and a travel cot is available. (*JBH, Frances Thomas, WK Wood*)

6 Willoughby Street
Muthill PH5 2AB

T: 01764-681451
E: info@barleybree.com
W: www.barleybree.com

BEDROOMS: 6.
OPEN: all year except Christmas.
FACILITIES: lounge, restaurant, free Wi-Fi, small terrace, unsuitable for &.
BACKGROUND MUSIC: classical in lounge.
LOCATION: village centre.
CHILDREN: all ages welcomed.
DOGS: only guide dogs allowed.
CREDIT CARDS: MasterCard, Visa.
PRICES: [2013] per room B&B £105–£150. À la carte £32–£40.

NAIRN Highland

Map 5:C2

SUNNY BRAE HOTEL   NEW

Facing the green and promenade of a seaside town on the Moray Firth, this small hotel has been run by the Bochel family for 15 years. 'Good value for money,' says a *Guide* inspector who enjoyed a 'pleasing stay' this year. Ian Bochel is 'a civilised and natural host, conversational without intruding'; his wife, Sylvia, oversees the 'excellent' cooking. The 1960s building has been 'tastefully extended' to front and rear to provide a glass-fronted lounge which enjoys the 'panorama of the sea'. The 'well-lit' dining room has a large central table with a 'beautiful' flower arrangement. 'I enjoyed cream of yellow courgette soup; pink and irresistible venison with al dente vegetables.' There is an extensive wine list, with a good choice by the glass; the whisky selection is equally comprehensive. Four of the bedrooms face the sea; the others overlook the 'well-kept garden which has a hedged lawn and flowerbeds. 'My quiet room had comfortable bedding, slightly dated furnishings, a small fitted wardrobe.' Breakfast has freshly squeezed orange juice, 'good coffee, proper toast, conserve served in china vessels; moist Nairn black pudding, crispy bacon'.

Marine Road
Nairn IV12 4EA

T: 01667-452309
F: 01667-454860
E: reservations@sunnybraehotel.com
W: www.sunnybraehotel.com

BEDROOMS: 8, 1 suitable for &.
OPEN: Feb–Nov.
FACILITIES: lounge, dining room, free Wi-Fi, terrace, ½-acre garden.
BACKGROUND MUSIC: none.
LOCATION: on seafront.
CHILDREN: all ages welcomed.
DOGS: only guide dogs.
CREDIT CARDS: MasterCard, Visa.
PRICES: [2013] per person B&B single £75–£115, double £40–£85, D,B&B single £99–£143, double £68–£113. À la carte £35.

NEWTON STEWART Dumfries and Galloway   Map 5:E1

KIRROUGHTREE HOUSE

César award in 2003

In 'breathtaking' countryside in the Galloway national park, this imposing bow-windowed mansion (built in 1791, with Victorian additions) is managed by Jim Stirling for the small McMillan group. 'A superb country house', it has many fans who appreciate the 'friendly and attentive' service which reaches to the car park where guests are greeted. The 'relaxing and beautiful' public rooms are decorated in grand baronial style, with oak-panelled walls, opulent drapes in the lounge. In the high-ceilinged dining room, meals feel 'like a special occasion'. Chef Matt McWhir uses local produce in his daily-changing menus, which might include puff pastry case filled with wild mushrooms in a garlic and tarragon cream sauce; fillet of pork, grain mustard-mashed potatoes, sage cream sauce. Dietary preferences are accommodated – and remembered. Bedrooms, which have a traditional decor, are spacious (each has a sitting area); they contain fresh fruit, biscuits and a decanter of sherry. A 'well-furnished' second-floor room had 'marvellous views and a great bath'. A disabled guest praised the 'wonderful kindness' of the cleaners. (*MK, and others*)

Newton Stewart DG8 6AN

T: 01671-402141
F: 01671-402425
E: info@kirroughtreehouse.co.uk
W: www.kirroughtreehouse.co.uk

BEDROOMS: 17.
OPEN: Feb–2 Jan.
FACILITIES: lift, 2 lounges, 2 dining rooms, free Wi-Fi, 8-acre grounds (gardens, tennis, croquet, pitch and putt).
BACKGROUND MUSIC: none.
LOCATION: 1½ miles NE of Newton Stewart.
CHILDREN: not under 10.
DOGS: allowed in lower ground-floor bedrooms only, not in public rooms.
CREDIT CARDS: Amex, MasterCard, Visa.
PRICES: [2013] per person B&B £75–£131, D,B&B £95–£164. Set dinner £35. 1-night bookings sometimes refused.

OBAN Argyll and Bute

Map 5:D1

THE MANOR HOUSE

On a rocky headland, this listed Georgian stone mansion has 'beautiful views over Oban bay to the islands beyond'. Owned by Leslie and Margaret Crane, it is managed by Gregor MacKinnon. 'Quietly spoken but larger than life, he was friendly and professional,' said inspectors, who 'enjoyed the atmosphere'. Most of the 'pristine' bedrooms have the view of the harbour and the busy island ferries; binoculars are provided. 'We had a comfortable, quiet night in our small room; the bed, which had a soft springy mattress, was made up with sheets and blankets; plenty of shelf space in the efficient bathroom.' The entrance hall has mosaic tiles, a grand staircase; public rooms have rich colours, 'interesting books and pictures'. In the bar, which is popular with locals, 'the manager looked after everyone in an efficient but laid-back manner'. The dining room has mirrors on each side of alcoved windows and well-spaced tables. The cooking of the chef, Shaun Squire, is 'first class': his traditional menu might include crab salad, concasse of tomato and cucumber; roast rack of lamb, baby fondant, honey-glazed vegetables. (*AR, and others*)

Gallanach Road
Oban PA34 4LS

T: 01631-562087
F: 01631-563053
E: info@manorhouseoban.com
W: www.manorhouseoban.com

BEDROOMS: 11, 1 on ground floor.
OPEN: all year except Christmas.
FACILITIES: 2 lounges, bar, restaurant, free Wi-Fi, wedding facilities, 1½-acre grounds, unsuitable for &.
BACKGROUND MUSIC: traditional in bar and dining room.
LOCATION: ½ mile from centre.
CHILDREN: not under 12.
DOGS: by arrangement, not allowed in public rooms.
CREDIT CARDS: all major cards.
PRICES: per room B&B £105–£225, D,B&B £140–£295. Set dinner £39.

SEE ALSO SHORTLIST

PEAT INN Fife

Map 5:D3

THE PEAT INN

'A real treat worth saving for', this whitewashed 17th-century former coaching inn in a hamlet near St Andrews is a 'focus for foodies'. It is run as a restaurant-with-rooms by chef/patron Geoffrey Smeddle and his wife, Katherine. 'Great attention to detail is shown in the bedrooms', which are in an adjoining building (umbrellas provided); seven are split-level, with a gallery sitting room which has a table for breakfast. A large room had a good selection of magazines; 'there were thick, comfortable bathrobes in the well-appointed bathroom'. In the candlelit restaurant, Geoffrey Smeddle has a *Michelin* star for his 'imaginative' cooking of seasonal 'modern Scottish/French' dishes, perhaps a warm salad of soft-poached duck egg, young leeks, pickled girolles and lemon dressing; maple-glazed breast of Gartmorn duck, Savoyarde potatoes, broad beans, pickled peaches, Madeira jus. There is also a tasting menu for £65 and an extensive wine list. A continental breakfast is brought to the room: 'Two efficient ladies swept in and laid the table beautifully. A perfectly soft-boiled egg; wonderful home-made granola; an exotic fruit salad; Ayrshire ham.'

Peat Inn, by St Andrews
KY15 5LH

T: 01334-840206
F: 01334-840530
E: stay@thepeatinn.co.uk
W: www.thepeatinn.co.uk

BEDROOMS: 8 suites, all on ground floor in annexe, 7 split level.
OPEN: all year except Christmas, restaurant closed Sun/Mon.
FACILITIES: ramp, lounge, restaurant, free Wi-Fi, ½-acre garden.
BACKGROUND MUSIC: none.
LOCATION: 6 miles SW of St Andrews.
CHILDREN: all ages welcomed.
DOGS: only guide dogs allowed.
CREDIT CARDS: Amex, MasterCard, Visa.
PRICES: [2013] per room B&B £185–£195, D,B&B £230–£285. Set dinner £45, à la carte £58.

PITLOCHRY Perth and Kinross

Map 5:D2

CRAIGATIN HOUSE AND COURTYARD

'Warm and inviting', this Victorian house is run as a B&B by Martin and Andrea Anderson, 'charming hosts'. 'It could hardly be bettered,' say visitors in 2013. Stone-built, the house stands in wooded grounds near the centre of the resort town. The bedrooms are divided between the main house and a courtyard of converted stables behind. They have a modern decor with bright colours and feature wallpaper. All have a hospitality tray with mineral water, tea and coffee, and local biscuits. A striking Scandinavian-style extension with a vaulted ceiling and floor-to-ceiling windows houses a guest lounge and dining room. Breakfast is 'top class': a buffet table has porridge with whisky, compote of apricots, fresh fruit salad, yogurt and cereals. The cooked choices include a full Scottish; apple pancake with bacon and maple syrup (banana for vegetarians); French toast with mixed fruits; a 'divine' omelette Arnold Bennett. Visitors who arrived on a winter evening to find the trees draped with fairy lights 'woke refreshed to birdsong and views of misty mountains'. The Andersons will suggest nearby restaurants for dinner. (*John and Jean Saul, and others*)

25% DISCOUNT VOUCHERS

165 Atholl Road
Pitlochry PH16 5QL

T: 01796-472478
E: enquiries@craigatinhouse.co.uk
W: www.craigatinhouse.co.uk

BEDROOMS: 14, 7 in courtyard, 2 on ground floor, 1 suitable for &.
OPEN: Mar–Nov, New Year.
FACILITIES: lounge, 2 dining rooms, free Wi-Fi, 2-acre garden.
BACKGROUND MUSIC: light jazz.
LOCATION: central.
CHILDREN: not under 13.
DOGS: not allowed.
CREDIT CARDS: MasterCard, Visa.
PRICES: per room B&B £80–£116 (single prices by arrangement). 1-night bookings refused Sat.

SEE ALSO SHORTLIST

PITLOCHRY Perth and Kinross

Map 5:D2

DALSHIAN HOUSE

In woodland and well-tended gardens (with rhododendron bushes and shrubs) on the outskirts of Pitlochry, this 18th-century house is run as a B&B by Martin and Heather Walls. They have decorated it in small country house style 'with a hint of shabby chic'. The lounge has a wood-burning stove, sofas and armchairs in neutral colours. There are sitting areas in the garden; red squirrels and interesting birdlife in the woodland. Bedrooms are spacious, and individually decorated with a mix of traditional furnishings and more contemporary colours. There is a hairdryer and self-controlled heating in each. Two rooms on the top floor are available for a family. An 'exceptional' breakfast is served at well-spaced tables in an attractive dining room. The extensive buffet might include vanilla-scented pears, poached apple and sultanas with nutmeg, Earl Grey-infused figs. The cooked selection has full Scottish (with black pudding); eggs Benedict; French toast (perhaps with bacon), maple syrup. Visitors are encouraged to sit in the lounge, which has sofas and armchairs, an open fire. The hosts will advise on excursions and local restaurants for dinner. (*A and RM*)

Old Perth Road
Pitlochry PH16 5TD

T: 01796-472173
E: dalshian@btconnect.com
W: www.dalshian.co.uk

BEDROOMS: 7.
OPEN: all year except Christmas/New Year.
FACILITIES: lounge, dining room, free Wi-Fi, 1-acre garden, unsuitable for &.
BACKGROUND MUSIC: none.
LOCATION: 1 mile S of centre.
CHILDREN: all ages welcomed.
DOGS: allowed by arrangement, not in public rooms.
CREDIT CARDS: MasterCard, Visa.
PRICES: [2013] per person B&B £34.50–£40.

SEE ALSO SHORTLIST

PITLOCHRY Perth and Kinross

Map 5:D2

THE GREEN PARK

'The staff are clearly regarded by the owners as part of the family,' according to visitors to this traditional hotel in a prime position on the banks of Loch Faskally on the outskirts of the resort town. It is run by two generations of the McMenemie family, who have 'extended the facilities without allowing modernity to prejudice the elegance and charm'. There are two lifts and 16 ground-floor bedrooms (one has a fully equipped disabled bathroom). Guests 'tend towards the mature', say the family. New this year is a 'jigsaw area … it's in lieu of a gym', jokes Alistair McMenemie. There are also 3,000 books available to guests. The 'well-kept' three-acre grounds are overlooked by the lounge where 'special little extras' such as complimentary tea and cakes or 'a glass or two' of sherry before dinner are served. Staff are 'invariably thoughtful'. A daily-changing menu of Franco-Scottish dishes is served by chef Chris Tamblin and might include roast pheasant breast filled with haggis, with whisky cream sauce and toasted oats. Early meals are provided for guests going to the Festival Theatre. (*O and BM, GT*)

Clunie Bridge Road
Pitlochry PH16 5JY

T: 01796-473248
F: 01796-473520
E: bookings@thegreenpark.co.uk
W: www.thegreenpark.co.uk

BEDROOMS: 51, 16 on ground floor, 1 suitable for &.
OPEN: all year except Christmas.
FACILITIES: 2 lifts, 3 lounges, library, bar, restaurant, free Wi-Fi, 3-acre garden.
BACKGROUND MUSIC: none.
LOCATION: western edge of town.
CHILDREN: all ages welcomed.
DOGS: allowed, not in public rooms.
CREDIT CARDS: MasterCard, Visa.
PRICES: [2013] per person B&B £71–£83, D,B&B £82–£108. À la carte £25–£27.

SEE ALSO SHORTLIST

PORT APPIN Argyll and Bute

Map 5:D1

THE AIRDS HOTEL

Once a simple ferry inn, Shaun and Jenny McKivragan's 'excellent' luxury hotel (Relais & Châteaux) has a 'stunning location with views of the loch and mountains behind'. At the front is a conservatory where light lunches are served; there are two 'delightful' lounges (one refurbished this year). 'We spent a perfect afternoon sitting next to a log fire, reading after a long walk.' Guests are asked to reserve a time for dinner in the dining room where service is 'formal, attentive'. David Barnett, the chef, cooks modern French dishes 'with a hint of Scotland', perhaps Argyll pork, smoked ham haugh bon bon, garlic and shallot purée. 'Dinner was a highlight of our stay.' Bedrooms have a mix of plain and floral fabrics, flat-screen TV with DVD-player, fresh fruit and a decanter of Whisky Mac. Guests this year appreciated their 'soft bathrobes and upmarket toiletries'. Breakfast, served at the table, has 'good porridge', croissants and bannocks, freshly squeezed fruit juices and fruit salad; locally smoked kippers on an extensive and 'good' cooked menu. (*George Potter, and others*)

Port Appin PA38 4DF

T: 01631-730236
F: 01631-730535
E: airds@airds-hotel.com
W: www.airds-hotel.com

BEDROOMS: 11, 2 on ground floor, also self-catering cottage.
OPEN: all year except 2 days a week Nov, Dec, Jan.
FACILITIES: 2 lounges, conservatory, snug bar, restaurant, wedding facilities, free Wi-Fi, ¾-acre garden (croquet, putting), unsuitable for &.
BACKGROUND MUSIC: none.
LOCATION: 25 miles N of Oban.
CHILDREN: all ages welcomed, but no under-9s in dining room after 7.30 (high tea at 6.30).
DOGS: allowed by prior agreement, not in public rooms.
CREDIT CARDS: Amex, MasterCard, Visa.
PRICES: per room D,B&B £285–£505.

SEE ALSO SHORTLIST

PORTPATRICK Dumfries and Galloway

Map 5:E1

KNOCKINAAM LODGE

In a 'wonderful, secluded' position facing a small curved bay on the Irish Sea, this former hunting lodge has been given a 'country house feel' by the owners, Sian and David Ibbotson. *Guide* inspectors found 'much to recommend: a caring, well-trained staff, lovely grounds, an excellent "what to do in the area" booklet'. Churchill met Eisenhower secretly here during World War II: you can stay in his bedroom, the largest. It has a huge sleigh bed, a seating area with the original fireplace; in the bathroom is an enamelled concrete soaking bath. An 'attractive' first-floor room had a 'huge bathroom' with a window overlooking the pond and gardens. The 'welcoming' public rooms are filled with 'comfy' sofas, stags' heads and paintings of pastoral scenes. In the candlelit dining room, chef Tony Pierce has a *Michelin* star for his modern Scottish tasting menus (including, perhaps, grilled fillet of Luce Bay cod, a mussel, saffron and coriander emulsion; slow-roasted fillet of Speyside Angus beef, sweetheart cabbage and crispy shallot, a port and truffle reduction. Breakfast includes 'plenty for those who don't want a cooked affair; I had delicious compote of pears, prunes and pineapple'.

Portpatrick
DG9 9AD

T: 01776-810471
F: 01776-810435
E: reservations@
   knockinaamlodge.com
W: www.knockinaamlodge.com

BEDROOMS: 10.
OPEN: all year.
FACILITIES: 2 lounges, 1 bar, restaurant, free Wi-Fi, wedding facilities, 30-acre grounds, only restaurant suitable for &.
BACKGROUND MUSIC: classical in restaurant.
LOCATION: 3 miles S of Portpatrick.
CHILDREN: no under-12s in dining room after 7 pm (high tea at 6).
DOGS: allowed in some bedrooms, not in public rooms.
CREDIT CARDS: Amex, MasterCard, Visa.
PRICES: [2013] per room D,B&B £180–£440. Set dinner £60. 1-night bookings sometimes refused.

PORTREE Highland

Map 5:C1

VIEWFIELD HOUSE

César award in 1993

Hugh Macdonald's family have lived in this 'baronial pile' on the outskirts of Portree since the 1840s and he is the third generation of his family to run it as a 'homely, quirky' guest house. The 'elegant and historic' house is liked for its 'faded grandeur', 'value' and 'charming hosts'. 'Everything I'd wished for on Skye; a beautiful room, delicious meals, attentive staff,' says a visitor this year. It made a Dutch visitor last year 'feel like a Scottish king'. There are stags' heads in the hall, log fires, Persian rugs and relics of the family's colonial service in the drawing room. Supper is available by arrangement (check when you book), from a menu that might include fillet of sole, hazelnut and coriander butter; lemon polenta cake, fresh raspberries. Some bathrooms are vast, as are many bedrooms, with their pretty floral curtains and wallpapers, brass beds. There is a television in the morning room, but not in the bedrooms; Wi-Fi can be patchy. A 'very good', generous breakfast is served in the large dining room. (*Wendy Thwaites, ML*)

25% DISCOUNT VOUCHERS

Viewfield Road
Portree
Isle of Skye IV51 9EU

T: 01478-612217
F: 01478-613517
E: info@viewfieldhouse.com
W: www.viewfieldhouse.com

BEDROOMS: 11, 1, on ground floor, suitable for &.
OPEN: Easter–mid-Oct.
FACILITIES: ramp, drawing room, morning/TV room, dining room, 20-acre grounds (croquet, swings).
BACKGROUND MUSIC: none.
LOCATION: S side of Portree.
CHILDREN: all ages welcomed.
DOGS: not allowed in public rooms except with permission of other guests (except guide dogs).
CREDIT CARDS: MasterCard, Visa.
PRICES: per person B&B £58–£75. Set dinner £25.

SEE ALSO SHORTLIST

ST OLA Orkney Islands

FOVERAN

In an 'unassuming', modern, single-storey building overlooking Scapa Flow, the Doull family gives a 'warm welcome' at their restaurant-with-rooms. The views from the 'large and light' dining room and the lounge, where dinner orders are taken and drinks served by an open fire, are 'wonderful'. Paul Doull's menu, with daily specials, highlights local produce such as Grimbister cheese (which 'occasionally can be eaten in every course') and Highland Park whisky. Typical dishes: smoked haddock chowder, cream and parsley; Orkney saddleback pork, slow-roasted with rosemary and garlic, green beans, pear and wholegrain mustard sauce. Coffee comes with home-made Orkney tablet, 'a great treat'. A Highland coffee was 'generous' in its whisky measure. 'Relaxed and professional' service is by 'a splendid team of youngsters'. Some of the bedrooms (decorated in blond woods), which overlook the countryside not the water, may be small, but they are well equipped and 'comfortable'. Breakfast is thought 'excellent'. Kirkwall is three miles away and guests can walk to the beach where 'there is plenty of wildlife'. There are also important archaeological sites nearby. More reports, please.

St Ola
Kirkwall KW15 1SF

T: 01856-872389
F: 01856-876430
E: info@thefoveran.com
W: www.thefoveran.com

BEDROOMS: 8, all on ground floor.
OPEN: mid-Apr–early Oct, by arrangement at other times, only restaurant Christmas/New Year, restaurant closed Sun evening end Sept–early June.
FACILITIES: lounge, restaurant, free Wi-Fi, 12-acre grounds (private rock beach).
BACKGROUND MUSIC: Scottish, in evening, in restaurant.
LOCATION: 3 miles SW of Kirkwall.
CHILDREN: all ages welcomed.
DOGS: not allowed.
CREDIT CARDS: MasterCard, Visa.
PRICES: [2013] per person B&B £55–£78, D,B&B £80–£103. À la carte £27. 1-night bookings sometimes refused.

SCARISTA Western Isles

Map 5:B1

SCARISTA HOUSE

César award in 2012

In a 'wonderful' position, 'marooned on the western brink of Harris', this handsome white-painted manse is 'a special place'. It is run as a small hotel by the 'hospitable owners', Tim and Patricia Martin. 'The service is friendly, and the food excellent; a nice atmosphere altogether,' says a visitor this year. The house, which looks across fields to a white-sand beach, is 'every inch the Georgian manse, lined with bookshelves and Persian rugs'. It has a 'sociable, easy-going' air, as guests gather in the downstairs library (where they might be joined by Misty, the resident cat, or Maud, the pug) and first-floor drawing room (pet free), which have open fires. Three bedrooms are in the main house; the others are in a converted outbuilding, where a room with a separate sitting area had 'a lovely view' of the sea. The hosts share the cooking, which is served in two adjoining areas. 'Immediately available' produce is used for the set menu of dishes like Stornoway-landed halibut, champagne and chive sauce, garden vegetables. Bread and jams at breakfast are home made. (*David Craig, and others*)

Scarista
Isle of Harris HS3 3HX

T: 01859-550238
E: stay@scaristahouse.com
W: www.scaristahouse.com

BEDROOMS: 6, 3 in annexe.
OPEN: 1 Feb–21 Dec.
FACILITIES: drawing room, library, dining room, free Wi-Fi, 1-acre garden, unsuitable for &.
BACKGROUND MUSIC: none.
LOCATION: 15 miles SW of Tarbert.
CHILDREN: all ages welcomed.
DOGS: by arrangement in bedrooms, library.
CREDIT CARDS: Amex, MasterCard, Visa.
PRICES: [2013] per room B&B £210–£235. Set meals £43. 1-night bookings 'might be refused' in high season.

SKIRLING Scottish Borders

Map 5:E2

SKIRLING HOUSE

♥ *César award in 2004*

'A favourite over many years' for *Guide* readers, this 'fascinating' Arts and Crafts house is by the green of a tiny village in lovely Borders countryside. It is run as a guest house by Isobel and Bob Hunter, 'welcoming' hosts. Built in 1908 as the summer retreat of the art collector Sir Thomas Gibson-Carmichael, *Skirling House* has a 'stunning collection' of contemporary Scottish art. The drawing room has a 16th-century carved Florentine ceiling, full-height windows, and a baby grand piano. Guests 'are made to feel very much at home', say visitors this year. 'The bedrooms are thoughtfully fitted with books, games, DVDs, fresh fruit, tea, coffee and biscuits, fresh milk.' Before dinner, 'olives and savouries are served with drinks in a communal gathering around the sitting-room fire'. Bob Hunter cooks classic dishes, served at separate tables in a conservatory. Likes and dislikes are discussed for the no-choice menu: 'We always ask for his excellent rendition of guineafowl.' The 'delicious' breakfast has kippers, 'Bob's special soufflé omelette', a basket of small scones with seasonal fruit. (*P and MB*)

25% DISCOUNT VOUCHERS

Skirling, by Biggar ML12 6HD

T: 01899-860274
F: 01899-860255
E: enquiry@skirlinghouse.com
W: www.skirlinghouse.com

BEDROOMS: 5, plus 1 single available if let with a double, 1 on ground floor suitable for &.
OPEN: Mar–Dec.
FACILITIES: ramps, 4 public rooms, free Wi-Fi, 5-acre garden (tennis, croquet) in 100-acre estate with woodland.
BACKGROUND MUSIC: none.
LOCATION: 2 miles E of Biggar, by village green.
CHILDREN: all ages welcomed.
DOGS: allowed by arrangement, not in public rooms or unattended in bedrooms.
CREDIT CARDS: MasterCard, Visa.
PRICES: [2013] per person B&B £60–£90. Set dinner £30.

SLEAT Highland

Map 5:C1

TORAVAIG HOUSE

Renovated from the foundations to the roof by the owners, Anne Gracie and Kenneth Gunn, this handsome white-painted hotel has fine views across to Knoydart. 'It is smartly and stylishly furnished,' says a visitor in 2013. 'The lovely little drawing room has comfy sofas, an open fire, a baby grand piano.' Richard Massey has joined as the chef: 'His cooking is very good indeed; a procession of small portions of inventive dishes. Little carrot soufflés and deep-fried haggis balls were excellent tasters; Cullen skink velouté had lovely flavours; our scallops were ultra-fresh and perfectly cooked. The young woman who acted as manager and head waitress coped brilliantly with a power cut. We didn't like the soft background music which played all day.' An earlier visitor commented on the 'high standards of housekeeping'. A small side room had a 'pleasant hillside view; the bathroom was so small that it was impossible to dry yourself'. Breakfast, served until 10 am ('much appreciated'), has the 'best porridge'; 'delicious toast'; an extensive choice of cooked dishes. Nearby, *Duisdale House* (see Shortlist) is under the same ownership. (*SM, and others*)

Knock Bay, Sleat
Isle of Skye
IV44 8RE

T: 01471-820200
F: 01471-833404
E: info@skyehotel.co.uk
W: www.skyehotel.co.uk

BEDROOMS: 9.
OPEN: Apr–Oct, Christmas/New Year.
FACILITIES: lounge, dining room, free Wi-Fi, wedding facilities, 1-acre grounds, unsuitable for ♿.
BACKGROUND MUSIC: all day.
LOCATION: 7 miles S of Broadford.
CHILDREN: not under 5.
DOGS: not allowed.
CREDIT CARDS: MasterCard, Visa.
PRICES: per person B&B £65 £125, D,B&B £89–£172. Set dinner £48.

SEE ALSO SHORTLIST

STRATHYRE Perth and Kinross

Map 5:D2

CREAGAN HOUSE

In their 17th-century cream-painted farmhouse, this restaurant-with-rooms is personally run by the owners, Cherry and Gordon Gunn. She is a 'welcoming hostess, managing everything front-of-house with quiet efficiency'. He is the chef serving 'French dinners and Scottish breakfasts' in a 'bonkers' mock-baronial vaulted dining hall with stone walls and a vast open fireplace. 'I made the booking on the promise of good food and was not disappointed.' Vegetables from a polytunnel in the garden, eggs from the house's own hens, are used for dishes like supreme of guineafowl, crispy mushroom, apple and Serrano ham, black pudding purée, Calvados sauce. The wine list and cheese plate are also praised. 'Our bedroom was well appointed and presented; there were unusually good reading lights on the four-poster bedhead. Noise from the road might disturb some visitors (we live somewhere very quiet).' The complimentary afternoon tea with home-made shortbread was appreciated, as was the vacuum flask of milk in the bedrooms. *Creagan House* is in a 'stunning' part of the country, on the side of a sheltered valley at the head of Loch Lubnaig. (*Wendy Montague, and others*)

25% DISCOUNT VOUCHERS

Strathyre FK18 8ND

T: 01877-384638
F: 01877-384319
E: eatandstay@creaganhouse.co.uk
W: www.creaganhouse.co.uk

BEDROOMS: 5, 1 on ground floor.
OPEN: all year except Christmas, 14 Jan–14 Mar, 4–21 Nov, closed Wed/Thurs.
FACILITIES: lounge, restaurant, private dining room, free Wi-Fi, 1-acre grounds.
BACKGROUND MUSIC: none.
LOCATION: ¼ mile N of village.
CHILDREN: all ages welcomed.
DOGS: not allowed in public rooms.
CREDIT CARDS: MasterCard, Visa.
PRICES: per person B&B £65–£95, D,B&B £100–£130. Set dinner £35.

SEE ALSO SHORTLIST

STRONTIAN Highland

Map 5:C1

KILCAMB LODGE

Surrounded by woodland and hills on the shore of Loch Sunart in the remote Ardnamurchan peninsula ('which feels like another world'), this is one of the oldest stone houses in Scotland. It is run as a luxury hotel by the owners, Sally and David Ruthven-Fox; Steven Turton is the new manager this year. The seating in the public areas is 'nicely spread out to give a little privacy while retaining a homely feeling'. In the candlelit dining room, chef Gary Phillips serves a set menu of sophisticated dishes like braised Aberdeen Angus suet pudding, star anise jus; seared salmon, broad bean and smoked haddock risotto cake, sauce vierge. New in 2013 is the *Driftwood Brasserie*, where lighter lunches and evening meals can be taken. There are tartan throws and carpets in the bedrooms; 'everything was scrupulously clean in the bathroom'. Two rooms have been refurbished this year. Breakfast has 'delicious home-made bread and jams', home-made muesli, 'lovely' porridge; cooked dishes include kippers and haddock with poached egg. Dogs are welcomed; they will enjoy walks in the ancient forests and splashing in the loch (towels provided).

25% DISCOUNT VOUCHERS

Strontian
PH36 4HY

T: 01967-402257
F: 01967-402041
E: enquiries@kilcamblodge.co.uk
W: www.kilcamblodge.co.uk

BEDROOMS: 10.
OPEN: all year except Jan, closed Mon and Tues, Nov to Feb.
FACILITIES: drawing room, lounge bar, dining room, brasserie, free Wi-Fi, wedding facilities, 22-acre grounds, unsuitable for &.
BACKGROUND MUSIC: jazz/classical/guitar in dining room.
LOCATION: edge of village.
CHILDREN: not under 10.
DOGS: not allowed in public rooms.
CREDIT CARDS: Diners, MasterCard, Visa.
PRICES: per room D,B&B £220–£375. Set dinner (restaurant) £49.50, à la carte (*Driftwood Brasserie*) £32.

TARBERT Western Isles

CEOL NA MARA

Guests are offered a complimentary drink on arrival at John and Marlene Mitchell's B&B, a renovated stone house above a rocky tidal loch (the Gaelic name translates as 'music of the sea'). 'It's an old Scottish tradition and one we enjoy upholding; slàinte,' the hosts say. The bedrooms ('without a mark or blemish') all have the view; they are well equipped – flat-screen television, fridge, 'masses of storage'; a 'good shower room, not a bath'. There is free Wi-Fi ('so you can make your friends jealous by sending them pictures of Harris'). There are lounges on each of the upper floors, including a sun lounge with far-reaching views, and a decked terrace overlooking Loch Kindebig. Breakfast has the 'most generous choice ever': on a buffet table are prunes and fresh fruit, home-made yogurt, bread and rolls, cereals. Porridge can be made with water or milk and served with cream or honey; cooked choices include Granny's pancake surprise (haggis, pancake and bacon, with a herb mini-omelette). No evening meal: local restaurants include the *Pierhouse* at the nearby *Hotel Hebrides* (see Shortlist). More reports, please.

7 Direcleit, Tarbert
Isle of Harris HS3 3DP

T: 01859-502464
F: 01859-575707
E: midgie@madasafish.com
W: www.ceolnamara.com

BEDROOMS: 4.
OPEN: all year.
FACILITIES: 2 lounges, sun lounge, dining room, free Wi-Fi, unsuitable for &.
BACKGROUND MUSIC: soft Highland/Celtic at breakfast.
LOCATION: ½ mile S of Tarbert.
CHILDREN: all ages welcomed.
DOGS: not allowed.
CREDIT CARDS: Diners, MasterCard, Visa (*3% surcharge*).
PRICES: per room B&B £80–£100.

SEE ALSO SHORTLIST

THORNHILL Dumfries and Galloway

Map 5:E2

TRIGONY HOUSE

Surrounded by rolling hills, this small country hotel was built as a shooting lodge for Closeburn Castle. Adam and Jan Moore are the 'welcoming' owners; 'chatty and friendly', she is ready to advise on what to see and do in the area. The 'handsome' panelled hall has an elegant staircase leading to the bedrooms, which are traditionally furnished. 'Our large and comfortable room had a conservatory sitting room; a big bed; a well-equipped bathroom with a power shower and a lovely old-fashioned radio.' Home-made biscuits and sparkling water were appreciated. The public rooms are 'cosy', with roaring fires, board games, period furniture. The wood-floored dining room overlooks the pretty garden with a terrace for alfresco eating ('Scottish weather permitting'). In the light and airy restaurant, Adam Moore uses locally sourced meat, game and fish as well as vegetables from the hotel's walled garden. His dishes might include warm salad of wood pigeon breast, black pudding; beef braised in field mushrooms and red wine. Simpler dishes are available on a bar menu. Breakfast is, 'if anything, over-generous'. Good walking and fishing nearby. *Trigony* is 'extremely' dog-friendly.

25% DISCOUNT VOUCHERS

Closeburn
Thornhill DG3 5EZ

T: 01848-331211
F: 01848-331303
E: info@trigonyhotel.co.uk
W: www.
    countryhousehotelsscotland.com

BEDROOMS: 9, 1 on ground floor.
OPEN: all year except 24–26 Dec.
FACILITIES: lounge, bar, dining room, free Wi-Fi, wedding facilities, 4½-acre grounds.
BACKGROUND MUSIC: jazz in bar in evening.
LOCATION: 1 mile S of Thornhill.
CHILDREN: all ages welcomed.
DOGS: not allowed in dining room.
CREDIT CARDS: Amex, MasterCard, Visa.
PRICES: per room B&B £105–£150, D,B&B £165–£250. Set dinner £35. 1-night bookings refused Sat in high season.

THURSO Highland

Map 5:B2

FORSS HOUSE

`NEW`

In woodland below a waterfall on the River Forss, Sabine and Ian Richards's grand old Georgian mansion has been managed for 25 years by the 'welcoming' Anne Mackenzie. 'She is famous for her sharp wit, swift retorts and knowledge of every whisky on the bar,' say the owners. 'She looks after all of us – staff and guests.' The house, which was built in 1820, is entered through an 'odd-looking addition' at the front, erected as a trophy room by a previous owner, a Victorian adventurer. Inside are a wood-burning stove, newspapers on the tables. A whisky bar has almost 300 malts. In the dining room, which overlooks the garden and river, Paul Ruttledge (who joined as chef in 2013) serves a modern menu of dishes like lightly curried scallops, Aultbea black pudding; 'Tofts of Tain' lamb cooked three ways, red wine jus. The bedrooms ('nice and clean') are in the main house, the *River House* and the *Fishing Lodge*. The Forss is noted for its salmon fishing. Or you can take 'a lovely walk down the side of the river to the sea'. (*DF*)

`25% DISCOUNT VOUCHERS`

Forss
by Thurso KW14 7XY

T: 01847-861201
E: relax@forsshousehotel.co.uk
W: www.forsshousehotel.co.uk

BEDROOMS: 14, 3 in main house on ground floor, 4 in *River House*, 2 in *Fishing Lodge*.
OPEN: all year except 23 Dec–3 Jan.
FACILITIES: entrance lounge, bar, dining room, private dining room, free Wi-Fi, wedding facilities, 20-acre grounds.
BACKGROUND MUSIC: classical in dining room.
LOCATION: 5 miles W of Thurso.
CHILDREN: all ages welcomed.
DOGS: not allowed in main building.
CREDIT CARDS: all major cards.
PRICES: [2013] per room B&B single £97–£130, double £130–£185. D,B&B £35 per person added, à la carte £30–£40.

TIRORAN Argyll and Bute

Map 5:D1

TIRORAN HOUSE

'A delightful, wonderful place; we received the usual warm welcome.' This year's praise from returning visitors to Laurence and Katie Mackay's Victorian hunting lodge in 'beautiful' gardens on Loch Scridain. The Mackays tell us that they have redecorated the public rooms and all the bedrooms; bathrooms have been given a shower. The rooms vary in size. 'The large East Room has lovely views over the loch; double doors open on to a spacious bathroom. The Green Room is smaller but has a separate sitting room.' Visitors are asked to choose their dishes for dinner from the menu at 6.30 pm; they are 'encouraged' to come down before the meal 'to meet other guests in either of the two charming sitting rooms; great fun, we met some lovely people'. Craig Ferguson has joined as chef ('Katie now has time to tend her amazing kitchen garden'). He serves a short daily-changing menu of 'delicious' dishes, perhaps terrine of chicken and foie gras, Jerusalem artichoke purée; saddle of Forres lamb, a brioche herb crust, lamb sweetbreads. 'Laurence arranged a memorable trip to feed the sea eagles.' (*Barbara Watkinson*)

25% DISCOUNT VOUCHERS

Tiroran, Isle of Mull
PA69 6ES

T: 01681-705232
E: info@tiroran.com
W: www.tiroran.com

BEDROOMS: 10, 2 on ground floor, 4 in annexes.
OPEN: mid-Mar–Dec.
FACILITIES: 2 sitting rooms, dining room, conservatory, free Wi-Fi, 17½-acre grounds, beach with mooring.
BACKGROUND MUSIC: none.
LOCATION: N side of Loch Scridain.
CHILDREN: all ages welcomed.
DOGS: allowed in 4 bedrooms, not in public rooms.
CREDIT CARDS: MasterCard, Visa.
PRICES: [2013] per room B&B £165–£210. À la carte £44–£48.

TOBERMORY Argyll and Bute

HIGHLAND COTTAGE

On a street on a hill above the 'unbelievably pretty' harbour, this 'cosy' purpose-built small hotel is run by the owners, David and Josephine Currie. 'They are chatty, and helpful with ferry bookings and suggestions for walks,' say visitors in 2013. The bedrooms vary in size and decor. 'Our comfortable, light room had windows overlooking the Sound of Mull; it was newly furnished and had a good bed; the well-appointed bathroom had a large bath and fluffy towels.' There are two 'smallish' public rooms, which have a 'slightly cluttered feel, lots of knick-knacks'. A conservatory seating area off the dining room has sofas and chairs: pre-dinner drinks are taken here. The 'comfortable' first-floor lounge has an honesty bar. Josephine Currie uses island produce for her three-course menus: 'The pre-dinner nibbles (deep-fried smoked oyster, crab cakes) and a pre-starter Jerusalem artichoke soup were delicious. The main courses had large portions; tender scallops (too many) came with mountains of mash. A very good Hebridean blue cheese and Mull Cheddar. The background music was loud and unwelcome. Full Scottish breakfast was good and freshly cooked.'

Bredalbane Street
Tobermory
Isle of Mull PA75 6PD

T: 01688-302030
E: davidandjo@highlandcottage.co.uk
W: www.highlandcottage.co.uk

BEDROOMS: 6, 1 on ground floor.
OPEN: Easter–late Oct.
FACILITIES: 2 lounges, restaurant, free Wi-Fi.
BACKGROUND MUSIC: in 1 lounge, restaurant.
LOCATION: village centre.
CHILDREN: not under 10.
DOGS: not allowed in restaurant.
CREDIT CARDS: MasterCard, Visa.
PRICES: [2013] per room B&B £135–£165, D,B&B £198–£244. Set dinner £39.50, 1-night bookings refused Sat.

SEE ALSO SHORTLIST

TORRIDON Highland

THE TORRIDON

'Spectacular mountain views' are among the attractions of this grand former shooting lodge, now a luxury hotel run by owners Rohaise and Daniel Rose-Bristow. The wooded estate by the side of a vast sea loch is 'wildly beautiful'; the welcome in the hotel 'wonderful'. The reception rooms, which have big open fireplaces and leather sofas, are 'lovely'; the moulded plaster ceilings and panelling lending them 'a sense of Victorian grandeur'. The best bedrooms have views of the loch, the rest of the mountains or grounds. They vary in size, and from traditional to contemporary in style; beds are large; all rooms are 'well equipped, with everything from a shoehorn to a clothes brush'. The bar has 350 malts. Bruno Birkbeck, the chef, cooks a five-course seasonal Franco-Scottish menu with dishes like red mullet with fennel shavings, aubergine caviar, red pepper dressing; fillet of hake, smoked salmon, butter beans, confit onion. Also on the estate is the more informal, family-friendly *Torridon Inn*. There is a year-round calendar of complimentary activities from gorge scrambling and archery to guided walks at dawn and sunset. (*PH*)

Annat, by Achnasheen
IV22 2EY

T: 01445-791242
F: 01445-712253
E: info@thetorridon.com
W: www.thetorridon.com

BEDROOMS: 18, 1, on ground floor, suitable for &, 1 deluxe suite in adjacent cottage.
OPEN: all year except Jan, Mon–Wed Nov–Mar.
FACILITIES: ramp, lift, drawing room, library, whisky bar, dining room, wedding facilities, free Wi-Fi, 58-acre gardens.
BACKGROUND MUSIC: classical at night in dining room.
LOCATION: 10 miles SW of Kinlochewe.
CHILDREN: all ages welcomed.
DOGS: in cottage only.
CREDIT CARDS: Amex, MasterCard, Visa.
PRICES: [2013] per person B&B £115–£235, D,B&B £128–£290. Set dinner £55. 1-night bookings sometimes refused.

ULLAPOOL Highland

Map 5:B2

THE CEILIDH PLACE

In a pretty harbour town, this 'lovely, welcoming hotel' is formed from a collection of white-washed cottages. Run by the owner, Jean Urquhart, it also comprises a bookshop, arts centre, café and bar. *Guide* inspectors in 2013 were charmed: 'The public areas are spacious and light despite being a warren of rooms; the main area, mostly conservatory style, has wooden tables and mismatched chairs; a cosy corner bar. On one side is a bookshop (they take literature seriously). The service is informal but efficient: my soggy boots were whisked away.' In the white-walled dining room, the cooking of chef Scott Morrison is 'robust and flavourful: we enjoyed smoked haddock chowder; haggis-in-a-pot with whisky and cream (a good combination)'. The bedrooms are decorated in rustic country style: 'Our large room had an ultra-wide bed; good shelf space in a well-arranged small bathroom.' A guest lounge with windows on both sides is 'an unexpected bonus; a gorgeous, rambling place with hosts of comfy chairs; an eclectically stocked library; a little kitchen where you can help yourself to coffee and tea'.

25% DISCOUNT VOUCHERS

14 West Argyle Street
Ullapool IV26 2TY

T: 01854-612103
F: 01854-613773
E: stay@theceilidhplace.com
W: www.theceilidhplace.com

BEDROOMS: 13, 10 with facilities en suite, plus 11 in Clubhouse across road.
OPEN: all year except 14 Jan.
FACILITIES: bar, parlour, café/bistro, free Wi-Fi, restaurant, bookshop, conference/function/wedding facilities, 2-acre garden, only public areas suitable for &.
BACKGROUND MUSIC: 'variable' in public areas.
LOCATION: village centre, large car park.
CHILDREN: all ages welcomed.
DOGS: not allowed in public rooms.
CREDIT CARDS: MasterCard, Visa.
PRICES: per person B&B £57–£82. À la carte £24.

SEE ALSO SHORTLIST

WALKERBURN Scottish Borders

WINDLESTRAW LODGE

With views of the Elibank and Traquair forests and the River Tweed, this 'stunning' Edwardian house, built for a mill owner's bride, is a small hotel run by 'engaging and professional' owners, Alan and Julie Reid. 'They have put their stamp on the house, which is beautifully decorated with many original touches,' says a visitor in 2013. There are deep plaster friezes and decorative wood panelling in the dining room and open-plan public rooms. There are family photographs and objets d'art, open fires; six distinct sitting areas. Bedrooms, all recently upgraded, are 'smart and comfortable'; all have a bath and overhead or walk-in shower. 'Our delightful room had a lovely view of the hills.' Alan Reid serves a daily-changing menu using local meat and seafood. 'Delicious dishes include my favourite, expresso soup, which I've never found anywhere else.' An 'equally good' breakfast might include 'outstanding' pinhead oatmeal porridge, smoked haddock and poached egg. Orange juice is freshly squeezed. The Reids cater for small house parties and weddings. The Southern Upland Way is handy for walkers, as are the historic Borders towns.

Galashiels Road
Tweed Valley
Walkerburn EH43 6AA

T: 01896-870636
E: reception@windlestraw.co.uk
W: www.windlestraw.co.uk

BEDROOMS: 6, all on first floor.
OPEN: all year except Jan, Christmas/New Year.
FACILITIES: bar lounge, sun lounge, drawing room, dining room, free Wi-Fi, 1-acre grounds, unsuitable for &.
BACKGROUND MUSIC: none.
LOCATION: outskirts of village, 2 miles E of Innerleithen.
CHILDREN: not under 12 at dinner (high tea 5–6 pm).
DOGS: not allowed in some public rooms.
CREDIT CARDS: MasterCard, Visa.
PRICES: [2013] per person B&B £75–£97.50. Set dinner £46, 6-course tasting menu £61.

WALLS Shetland Islands

Map 5: inset B2

BURRASTOW HOUSE `NEW`

In a 'magnificent' setting on the western edge of the island, this small 'very comfortable' guest house is run in personal style by the owner, Pierre Dupont. Built in 1759 as a 'Haa' house for the local laird, it looks across a sandy-bottomed bay to the island of Vaila. Three bedrooms are in an extension. 'Guests are made to feel at home in the old house, which is open all day,' says the nominator. 'The main building, a maze of stairs and corridors, has a comprehensive library and a cosy lounge with an enormous wood-burning stove.' There is no bar: 'You record what you drink from a well-stocked cabinet and wine cellar. Pierre is the chef and creates each evening's meal according to what is available; he serves each course himself with a delightful explanation of what you are about to receive; over three nights I was never disappointed by my voyage into the unknown.' Typical dishes: asparagus risotto; sea bass with peppers and tomatoes. 'On two nights, my aperitif was accompanied by the sight of otters fishing in front of the house.' (*Ian Mylroi*)

Walls
Shetland ZE2 9PD

T: 01595-809307
E: info@burrastowhouse.co.uk
W: www.burrastowhouse.co.uk

BEDROOMS: 7, 3 in extension, 2 on ground floor.
OPEN: Apr–Oct.
FACILITIES: sitting room, library, dining room, free Wi-Fi, wedding facilities, unsuitable for &.
BACKGROUND MUSIC: none.
LOCATION: 27 miles NW of Lerwick.
CHILDREN: all ages welcomed.
DOGS: small dogs allowed by arrangement, in ground-floor rooms only.
CREDIT CARDS: MasterCard, Visa.
PRICES: [2013] per person B&B £50–£55, D,B&B £85–£90.

WALES

Pen y Fan, Brecon Beacons

ABERAERON Ceredigion

Map 3:C2

HARBOURMASTER HOTEL

♥César award in 2005

'Very lovely, very Welsh', this Grade II listed former harbourmaster's residence on the harbour of a Georgian town is today a 'buzzy' small hotel with 'delightful service'. Glyn and Menna Heulyn, the owners, are 'hard working and much in evidence': 'They ought to write a book for those who think it is a doddle to run a good hotel.' The bedrooms, 'comfortable, well equipped', are divided between the original building, a converted grain store next door, and a historic cottage two doors away. Each has bold colours, Welsh blankets and a cafetière with proper coffee; two have a terrace facing Cardigan Bay. There is 'good gastropub food' in the restaurant and 'chic' bar, where chefs Loudovic Dieumegard (who joined as executive chef in June 2013) and Kelly Thomas cook modern Welsh dishes. Their menu might include potted duck, cognac and onion marmalade, walnut toast; loin of Brecon venison, artichoke mash, game croquette. 'Excellent lobster is usually available.' 'Super' breakfasts have fresh croissants, 'unusual' juices and smoked salmon from Rhydlewis. The Ceredigion Coastal Path is nearby; bicycles are available to borrow. (*FT, LW, PA*)

Pen Cei, Aberaeron
SA46 0BT

T: 01545-570755
F: 01545-570762
E: info@harbour-master.com
W: www.harbour-master.com

BEDROOMS: 13, 2 in cottage, 1 suitable for ♿.
OPEN: all year except 25 Dec.
FACILITIES: bar, restaurant, free Wi-Fi (in bar and original bedrooms; broadband in warehouse rooms), pebble beach (safe bathing nearby).
BACKGROUND MUSIC: 'modern, relaxed'.
LOCATION: central, on harbour.
CHILDREN: under-5s in cottage only.
DOGS: not allowed.
CREDIT CARDS: MasterCard, Visa.
PRICES: [2013] per room B&B single £65, double £110–£250. D,B&B (min. 2 nights) £80–£150 per person, set dinner £25–£30, à la carte £30. 1-night bookings refused weekends.

ABERDYFI Gwynedd

Map 3:C3

TREFEDDIAN HOTEL

On a hillside above a championship golf course, the Cave family's hotel, a large white, much-balconied building, has 'glorious views' over Cardigan Bay. *Trefeddian* has two loyal constituencies. During school holidays, it is a magnet for families with children, who enjoy the games room, the play areas, and the outdoor life in the grounds and beyond. In quieter periods, 'many of our fellow guests are elderly like us, profiting from a special tariff'. Attractions include the 'freedom from piped music, a blessing'; the 8 am newspaper delivery which 'is welcome to people like us who stay indoors for a fair part of the day'; the car park, 'cunningly hidden' so as not to interrupt the views. The bedrooms, traditionally furnished, are thoughtfully equipped: a 'generous' hospitality tray; a 'comprehensive' information pack; good bedside lighting. In the formal dining room ('which runs like clockwork'), chef Tracy Sheen serves a traditional English/French menu on a daily-changing menu ('what a joy, so much better than a seasonal one'). Breakfast is 'better than most' with an 'impressive' buffet which has a wide choice of fresh fruit, cheeses; 'first-class' cooked dishes. (*Ken and Mildred Edwards, and others*)

Tywyn Road
Aberdyfi LL35 0SB

T: 01654-767213
F: 01654-767777
E: info@trefwales.com
W: www.trefwales.com

BEDROOMS: 59.
OPEN: Jan–Nov.
FACILITIES: lift, 3 lounges, bar lounge, restaurant, free Wi-Fi, fitness centre, indoor swimming pool (6 by 12 metres), beauty salon, 15-acre grounds (tennis, putting green).
BACKGROUND MUSIC: none.
LOCATION: ½ mile N of village.
CHILDREN: all ages welcomed.
DOGS: allowed in 1 lounge, some bedrooms.
CREDIT CARDS: MasterCard, Visa.
PRICES: [2013] per person B&B £45–£65, D,B&B £69–£110. Set dinner £29.50. 1-night bookings sometimes refused.

ABERGAVENNY Monmouthshire

THE ANGEL HOTEL

'The social and commercial hub of the market town', this 19th-century former coaching inn is owned by the Griffiths family; William Griffiths is the manager. 'The staff are unfailingly courteous; they went out of their way to speak to us and offer help,' says an inspector this year. 'The public areas are well done: the *Foxhunter* bar is popular with locals; award-winning afternoon teas in the delightful drawing room have become an institution in the area.' Restoration is a continuing process. The dining room has been given a clean new look, and renamed the *Oak Room*. Wesley Hammond, the chef, serves an extensive contemporary menu of dishes like cawl (Welsh lamb and vegetable broth); whole lemon sole, new potatoes, shrimp butter. Not all the bedrooms have been updated: 'Ask for a renovated room: our old-fashioned room at the side had a comfortable bed, good storage; we were woken by noise from the street.' Stylish refurbished rooms have cream walls, white bedcovers, quality brown furnishings. The Griffiths family also own an 'excellent' neighbouring art shop, and co-own with Shaun Hill the *Michelin*-starred *Walnut Tree* restaurant.

15 Cross Street
Abergavenny NP7 5EN

T: 01873-857121
F: 01873-858059
E: mail@angelabergavenny.com
W: www.angelabergavenny.com

BEDROOMS: 35, 2 in adjacent mews, plus 2 cottages.
OPEN: all year except 25 Dec.
FACILITIES: ramps, lift, lounge, bar, restaurant, private function rooms, free Wi-Fi, civil wedding licence, courtyard.
BACKGROUND MUSIC: during afternoon tea.
LOCATION: town centre.
CHILDREN: all ages welcomed.
DOGS: allowed in bedrooms (£10 charge), bar, not in restaurant.
CREDIT CARDS: Amex, MasterCard, Visa.
PRICES: [2013] per room B&B £89–£188. D,B&B from £80.50 per person, set dinner £25, à la carte £30.

ABERSOCH Gwynedd

Map 3:B2

PORTH TOCYN HOTEL

César award in 1984

'Spot on. We enjoyed yet another stay in the spring and no doubt will repeat it in a year,' say returning visitors to this country hotel with 'stupendous' views across Cardigan Bay and Snowdonia. Occupying a row of converted lead miners' cottages, the 'laid-back, homely' hotel has been run by the 'enthusiastic' Fletcher-Brewer family for three generations. Cosy sitting rooms have books, watercolours and fresh flowers; the garden hides quiet nooks for tea or coffee. Children are welcomed with a dedicated snug and a games conservatory. Most of the individually decorated bedrooms have a sea view; some have been upgraded with new beds this year. Over antique dining tables, 'memorable' modern British menus with intriguing ingredients (perhaps pickled mackerel, soused baby vegetables; Welsh lamb, watermelon gel, tomato soil) change daily. Simple suppers of soups, pastas and deli boards provide a lighter option. A casual, buzzy children's high tea is served at 5.30 pm; under-5s are not allowed in the restaurant for dinner. There are good walks from the door, including the Wales Coast Path. Picnic lunches are available. (*Derek Lambert*)

Bwlch Tocyn
Abersoch LL53 7BU

T: 01758-713303
F: 01758-713538
E: bookings@porthtocyn.fsnet.co.uk
W: www.porthtocynhotel.co.uk

BEDROOMS: 17, 3 on ground floor.
OPEN: week before Easter–end Nov.
FACILITIES: ramp, sitting rooms, children's rooms, cocktail bar, dining room, free Wi-Fi, 25-acre grounds (swimming pool, 10 by 6 metres, heated May–end Sept, tennis), telephone to discuss disabled access.
BACKGROUND MUSIC: none.
LOCATION: 2 miles outside village.
CHILDREN: High tea for under-5s; no babies or young children at dinner.
DOGS: by arrangement, not allowed in public rooms.
CREDIT CARDS: MasterCard, Visa.
PRICES: [2013] per room B&B single £75–£90, double £100–£180. Set dinner £37–£44. 1-night bookings occasionally refused.

ABERYSTWYTH Ceredigion

GWESTY CYMRU

In a white-painted listed house on the Victorian seafront promenade, Huw and Beth Roberts's smart restaurant-with-rooms takes the Welsh land and seascape as inspiration. Modern bedrooms, which have oak furniture handcrafted by a local artisan, are decorated in shades of the 'fresh green mountains of Ystwyth valley' or 'the foaming white surf of the sea on a stormy day'. Spacious front-facing rooms overlook Cardigan Bay; No. 6 has views from the bathtub. The bedrooms vary in size: one visitor said her ground-floor room at the back was 'small, but spotlessly clean and comfortable'. Some rooms can be interconnected to accommodate a family. There are 'generous' portions at dinner in the slate-floored restaurant, where chef Pawel Banaszynski ('Polish, with a Welsh soul,' says Huw Roberts) has an 'innovative take on local Welsh ingredients', perhaps Magic Welsh Rarebit (made with Tomos Watkin's Magic Lager); pan-fried haddock, lemon and caper cream, smoked haddock bonbon. Breakfast includes freshly squeezed orange juice and Welsh laver bread. The owners promise 'spectacular sunset views' from the restaurant's sea-facing terrace. (*AA, and others*)

19 Marine Terrace
Aberystwyth SY23 2AZ

T: 01970-612252
F: 01970-623348
E: info@gwestycymru.co.uk
W: www.gwestycymru.co.uk

BEDROOMS: 8, 2 on ground floor.
OPEN: all year except Christmas, restaurant closed for lunch Tues.
FACILITIES: bar, restaurant, terrace, free Wi-Fi, secure parking (book in advance), unsuitable for &.
BACKGROUND MUSIC: in Reception and restaurant.
LOCATION: central, on seafront.
CHILDREN: all ages welcomed at lunch, no under-5s to stay or in restaurant in evenings.
DOGS: not allowed.
CREDIT CARDS: MasterCard, Visa.
PRICES: [2013] per room B&B single £67–£80, double £87–£160, £10 supplement for twin beds, D,B&B (Nov–Mar, Sun–Thurs) single £85–£110, double £145. À la carte £30 per person.

BALA Gwynedd

Map 3:B3

♨ BRYNIAU GOLAU

César award: Welsh guest house of the year

'A real haven for those who love peace and quiet.' In a 'magical' setting on a secluded hillside overlooking Bala Lake, 'charming' hosts Katrina Le Saux and Peter Cottee welcome visitors to their 'beautiful' Victorian home with tea and home-made cake. 'It just gets better and better,' returning visitors said this year. 'This was our second visit; we were made to feel like friends,' other guests reported. The newly redecorated sitting room has a log fire and an honesty bar; 'breathtaking' sunsets over the Arenig Mountains can be watched from the terrace. The 'beautifully appointed' bedrooms have been recently refurbished; all have views of the lake. 'Our room was spotlessly clean; we even had electric blankets.' A home-cooked dinner, perhaps with mountain lamb or game in season, is served by arrangement (special diets can be catered for). 'Peter is a talented and creative cook.' The 'substantial' breakfast has home-made granola and *Bryniau Golau* honey from the house's own bees. Bala, a 14th-century town, is within walking distance. (*Linda Ferstendik, Susan Ashworth, Lynn and Ann Mainwaring*)

25% DISCOUNT VOUCHERS

Llangower, Bala
LL23 7BT

T: 01678-521782
E: katrinalesaux@hotmail.co.uk
W: www.bryniau-golau.co.uk

BEDROOMS: 3.
OPEN: Mar–end Oct.
FACILITIES: sitting room, dining room, free Wi-Fi, ½-acre garden, unsuitable for ♿.
BACKGROUND MUSIC: none.
LOCATION: 2 miles SE of Bala.
CHILDREN: not under 12.
DOGS: not allowed.
CREDIT CARDS: MasterCard, Visa.
PRICES: [2013] per room B&B £90–£100. Set dinner £20–£25, £4 corkage for BYOB. 1-night bookings refused weekends and peak times.

BARMOUTH Gwynedd

Map 3:B3

LLWYNDU FARMHOUSE

'A delightful place to relax and unwind.' With 'stunning' views from its hillside position overlooking Cardigan Bay, this restored 16th-century farmhouse (Grade II listed) is a 'comfortable and welcoming' hotel and restaurant, run by 'warm, engaging hosts' Peter and Paula Thompson. 'It is small enough to feel personal and intimate, yet spacious enough to feel like guest accommodation rather than someone's home.' There are exposed oak beams, inglenook fireplaces and a stone spiral staircase; characterful bedrooms have quirks such as a sink fitted to a door, or a latrine converted into a walk-in wardrobe. Three large, high-ceilinged rooms in the former granary lead straight into the garden; these are good for a family. In the candlelit restaurant, Peter Thompson's 'skilfully home-cooked' menus have a Mediterranean influence; typical dishes include lentil-stuffed peppers; baked hake with king prawns. The wine list has 'sensible prices'. There are freshly grilled Manx kippers and a full Welsh at breakfast; vegetarian options are available. 'The personal touches (like Welsh cakes and a pot of tea when we arrived) make all the difference.' (*PJ, and others*)

Llanaber
Barmouth LL42 1RR

T: 01341-280144
E: intouch@
llwyndu-farmhouse.co.uk
W: www.llwyndu-farmhouse.co.uk

BEDROOMS: 6, 3 in granary, 1 on ground floor.
OPEN: all year except 25/26 Dec, restaurant closed Sun evening.
FACILITIES: lounge, restaurant, free Wi-Fi, 4-acre garden, unsuitable for &.
BACKGROUND MUSIC: occasionally 'depending on the guests'.
LOCATION: 2 miles N of Barmouth.
CHILDREN: all ages welcomed.
DOGS: allowed in some bedrooms, not in public rooms.
CREDIT CARDS: MasterCard, Visa.
PRICES: per person B&B £55–£65, D,B&B £88–£99. Set dinner £24.50–£28, à la carte £35–£45. 1-night bookings refused peak weekends.

BEAUMARIS Isle of Anglesey

Map 3:A3

YE OLDE BULLS HEAD

'One of our favourites: we are always impressed by the friendly young staff.' Praise from returning visitors this year to this 500-year-old inn, which was once the staging post for coaches coming to the town for the ferries to Ireland. It is owned by David Robertson (the manager) and Keith Rothwell. The oldest part of the building has ancient beams and creaking staircases: there is a well-furnished lounge, and an atmospheric bar with log fires. The bedrooms are split between the main building and *The Townhouse*, a contemporary renovation of a 16th-century building 100 yards away. 'Our *Townhouse* room was modern and well equipped; the bed was comfortable.' Guests appreciate a choice of restaurants: in the *Loft*, Hefin Roberts has a fine-dining menu of dishes like peppered beef, curried oyster, watercress purée; wild sea bass, spiced crab bonbon, Anna potato, wild garlic oil. Bistro-style dishes are served in the 'buzzy' brasserie in converted stables with stone walls and slate floors. 'We ate well in both.' Breakfast is 'excellent, especially the fruit compote and yogurt, and the locally sourced cooked food'.
(*Robert and Shirley Lyne*)

Castle Street
Beaumaris, Isle of Anglesey
LL58 8AP

T: 01248-810329
F: 01248-811294
E: info@bullsheadinn.co.uk
W: www.bullsheadinn.co.uk

BEDROOMS: 26, 2 on ground floor, 1 in courtyard, 13 in *Townhouse* adjacent, 1 suitable for &.
OPEN: all year, except 25/26 Dec, *Loft* restaurant closed lunch, Sun/Mon nights.
FACILITIES: lift (in *Townhouse*), lounge, bar, brasserie, restaurant, free Wi-Fi, sea 200 yds, only brasserie and *Townhouse* suitable for &.
BACKGROUND MUSIC: in brasserie.
LOCATION: central.
CHILDREN: no under-7s in restaurant or bedroom suites.
DOGS: only assistance dogs allowed.
CREDIT CARDS: Amex, MasterCard, Visa.
PRICES: [2013] per room B&B single £82.50–£87.50, double £105–£125. Set dinner (restaurant) £42.50, à la carte (brasserie) £26–£28.

BRECHFA Carmarthenshire

Map 3:D2

TŶ MAWR

🏅*César award in 2011*

'Outstanding value with welcoming hosts and
a friendly atmosphere.' On the edge of the
Brechfa forest, Annabel and Stephen Thomas's
'comfortable' 16th-century country house is
surrounded by a large garden – populated by
finches, robins and woodpeckers. 'On arrival, we
were greeted by Annabel Thomas and offered
tea in the pleasant garden, before being shown
to our room.' Bedrooms, simply decorated with
pine furniture, have dressing gowns and tea-
and coffee-making facilities. 'Our spacious room
had a huge bed; plenty of hot water in the
shower.' At dinner, Stephen Thomas cooks a
daily-changing menu of 'excellent' food using
Welsh produce; the organic lamb and Welsh
Black beef are from a farm two miles away.
'We chose our dinner over a drink in the very
pleasant bar. After our first meal, we asked if
our vegetables could be cooked a little more
in future – and they were.' A help-yourself
breakfast bar has fresh fruit salad and organic
Welsh yogurt; cooked dishes include free-range
eggs, local bacon and home-made bread.
'Breakfast was a feast.' (*John and Eileen Avison,
PW Taylor*)

25% DISCOUNT VOUCHERS

Brechfa SA32 7RA

T: 01267-202332
E: info@wales-country-hotel.co.uk
W: www.wales-country-hotel.co.uk

BEDROOMS: 6, 2 on ground floor.
OPEN: all year.
FACILITIES: sitting room, bar,
breakfast room, restaurant, free
Wi-Fi, 1-acre grounds, unsuitable
for ♿.
BACKGROUND MUSIC: classical in
restaurant.
LOCATION: village centre.
CHILDREN: not under 12.
DOGS: by arrangement (no charge),
not allowed in breakfast room,
restaurant.
CREDIT CARDS: Amex, MasterCard,
Visa.
PRICES: [2013] per room B&B double
£113–£130, D,B&B £155–£175. Set
dinner £24–£29 per person, à la
carte £29.

BRECON Powys

CANTRE SELYF

Close to the church in this historic market town, Helen and Nigel Roberts's 'delightful as ever' 17th-century town house (Grade II listed) retains many original features: moulded ceilings, elegant fireplaces and oak beams. It has a cosy sitting room with a log-burning fireplace, books and board games; the well-kept walled garden has nooks and benches, an impressive magnolia tree. Up an old wooden staircase ('the creaks and squeaks are authentic,' the Robertses say), the bedrooms have a 'comfortable' brass bed and a hospitality tray with biscuits. The rooms vary in size: Selyf, a large double, overlooks the garden; Tewdos, a smaller double room, has moulded ceilings. There is a good choice at breakfast, with fresh fruit, yogurt and home-made scones and soda bread; cooked dishes include French toast and a full Welsh breakfast. Special diets can be catered for. A short walk from the River Usk, the B&B is well placed for exploring the town (there are guidebooks and maps to borrow); Brecon Beacons national park is 15 minutes' drive away. Popular during the town's various music festivals. (*Jill and Mike Bennett*)

5 Lion Street
Brecon LD3 7AU

T: 01874-622904
E: enquiries@cantreselyf.co.uk
W: www.cantreselyf.co.uk

BEDROOMS: 3.
OPEN: closed Dec/Jan.
FACILITIES: sitting room, dining room, free Wi-Fi, 1-acre walled garden, unsuitable for &.
BACKGROUND MUSIC: none.
LOCATION: central.
CHILDREN: all ages welcomed.
DOGS: not allowed.
CREDIT CARDS: MasterCard, Visa.
PRICES: [2013] per room B&B single £62, double £82–£92.

BROAD HAVEN Pembrokeshire

Map 3:D1

THE DRUIDSTONE

On a cliff-top above a sandy beach, this idiosyncratic 'family holiday centre' is favoured by those who prefer informality and 'the feeling of total freedom'. We are sad to report the death of the founder, Jane Bell, whose aim was to 'revive the work worn' and create a beacon of the arts. Her son, Angus, and his partner, Beth Wilshaw, are 'much to the fore' in a place whose 'style doesn't change'. A fan revisiting in 2013 says: 'It doesn't suit everyone; shabby chic isn't a bad description though others might say homely and welcoming. The pluses are the location and the space to wander or just sit.' The accommodation is simple: the best rooms, on the second floor, have an en suite bathroom and a shared balcony. Six other bedrooms share three bathrooms 'in the style of a family holiday house'. The public rooms, which have books, maps and local information, open on to terraces overlooking the sea. Children (and pets) are welcomed: they have early suppers in the farmhouse kitchen. 'International' meals are served in the bar and restaurant; Italian and Spanish 'feast nights' are held.

nr Broad Haven
Haverfordwest SA62 3NE

T: 01437-781221
E: enquiries@druidstone.co.uk
W: www.druidstone.co.uk

BEDROOMS: 11, also 5 holiday cottages.
OPEN: all year.
FACILITIES: sitting room, TV room, bar (occasional live music), farmhouse kitchen, restaurant, small conference/function facilities, free Wi-Fi, civil wedding licence, 22-acre grounds, sandy beach, safe bathing 200 yds.
BACKGROUND MUSIC: in bar and on feast nights.
LOCATION: 7 miles W of Haverfordwest.
CHILDREN: all ages welcomed.
DOGS: not allowed in restaurant.
CREDIT CARDS: Amex, MasterCard, Visa.
PRICES: [2013] per person B&B £50–£90. À la carte £30. 1-night bookings usually refused Sat mid-season.

CAERNARFON Gwynedd

Map 3:A2

PLAS DINAS COUNTRY HOUSE

'Fascinating' history blooms along with springtime bluebells and daffodils at this 17th-century gentleman's residence, once the country home of the Armstrong-Jones family. The owners, Andy and Julian Banner-Price, are 'kind and attentive without being overpowering', says a visitor in 2013, who enjoyed the 'relaxed' atmosphere. They have filled the Grade II listed building with original antiques and royal memorabilia. Bedrooms mix 400-year-old features with modern design; several have statement wallpaper and an original fireplace. The Judges Room, with its sloping floor, has been redecorated this year. 'The rooms are well presented; beds are luxurious; nice touches include fresh milk for the tea tray, complimentary mineral water by the bed.' Guests take pre-dinner drinks on the terrace in warm weather, or in front of the drawing-room fire. In the candlelit dining room, Andy Banner-Price's 'excellent' dinners of traditional recipes (prepared by arrangement) might include fish pie with a cheesy mash; a bramble bombe of summer fruit. 'The lovely breakfast has a wide range of cereals and a fabulous full Welsh.'
(*Luke Barnett, James Rushby*)

25% DISCOUNT VOUCHERS

Bontnewydd
Caernarfon LL54 7YF

T: 01286-830214
E: info@plasdinas.co.uk
W: www.plasdinas.co.uk

BEDROOMS: 9, 1 on ground floor.
OPEN: all year except Christmas/New Year, restaurant closed Sun/Mon.
FACILITIES: drawing room, dining room, gun room, free Wi-Fi, civil wedding licence, 15-acre grounds.
BACKGROUND MUSIC: in dining room.
LOCATION: 2 miles S of Caernarfon.
CHILDREN: not under 12.
DOGS: small dogs welcomed (£10 charge).
CREDIT CARDS: Amex, MasterCard, Visa.
PRICES: [2013] per person B&B £64.50–£137.50, D,B&B £90.50–£167.50. Set dinner £26–£30, à la carte £40.

CRICKHOWELL Powys

Map 3:D4

GLANGRWYNEY COURT

On the edge of the Brecon Beacons national park, this 'opulent' Palladian house (Grade II listed) is the family home of Christina and Warwick Jackson. Readers like the 'very personal touch' and the 'wonderful ambience'. 'It lived up to its reputation.' The house stands in large grounds with parkland and formal gardens. Guests, who are welcomed on a B&B basis, are encouraged to enjoy the lounge, with its log fires, comfortable seating areas with period furnishings. There's an honesty bar in the library, a large collection of books. Summer drinks can be taken on a patio; there are 'secret sitting areas' in the garden. A cantilevered staircase leads to the eight spacious bedrooms in the main house, which are individually decorated in country house style. They have antique furniture; pretty porcelain, interesting artwork. 'We had a large, light, attractive room and found no fault with anything.' One room has a private bathroom across the landing (bathrobes provided). A ground-floor room is in the garden courtyard. A converted barn is used for weddings, functions and courses. (*Teresa Biggs, and others*)

Glangrwyney, Crickhowell
NP8 1ES

T: 01873-811288
F: 01873-810317
E: info@glancourt.co.uk
W: www.glancourt.co.uk

BEDROOMS: 9, 1, on ground floor, in courtyard, 4 cottages in grounds.
OPEN: all year.
FACILITIES: sitting room, library/honesty bar, dining room, free Wi-Fi, civil wedding licence, 4-acre garden (croquet, boules, tennis) in 33-acre parkland, unsuitable for &.
BACKGROUND MUSIC: on request.
LOCATION: 2 miles SE of Crickhowell, off A40.
CHILDREN: all ages welcomed.
DOGS: allowed in cottages only.
CREDIT CARDS: MasterCard, Visa.
PRICES: [2013] per room B&B £105–£135. 1-night bookings sometimes refused weekends.

SEE ALSO SHORTLIST

CRICKHOWELL Powys

Map 3:D4

GLIFFAES

❧César award in 2009

In a 'beautiful' setting on the River Usk, this 'lovely' family-run hotel is in the Brecon Beacons national park. The comfortable, elegant 19th-century Italianate building has remained in the same ownership for more than 60 years. Today, 'very hands-on' owners Peta Brabner and James and Susie Suter are in charge. A visitor with three young children found staff 'helpful and tolerant'. Individually decorated bedrooms have views of the river or the expansive garden. Beyond the manicured lawns and collection of specimen trees, foraging sessions take guests among the hedgerows and wild plants; fishing courses are held on the hotel's private stretch of the river. A tandem bicycle can be borrowed. Under chef Karl Cheetham, the kitchen has a commitment to regional food and local producers; daily-changing modern British menus might include 'delightfully pink Welsh lamb, the best ever'. An 'excellent' breakfast, with home-made muesli and local maple-cured bacon, may be taken in bed. 'Definitely one to return to soon.' (*Brian and Gwen Thomas, and others*)

Crickhowell
NP8 1RH

T: 01874-730371
F: 01874-730463
E: calls@gliffaeshotel.com
W: www.gliffaeshotel.com

BEDROOMS: 23, 4 in annexe, 1 on ground floor.
OPEN: all year except Jan.
FACILITIES: ramp, 2 sitting rooms, conservatory, bar, dining room, free Wi-Fi, civil wedding licence, 33-acre garden (tennis, croquet, fishing).
BACKGROUND MUSIC: in bar in evening.
LOCATION: 3 miles W of Crickhowell.
CHILDREN: all ages welcomed, £23 B&B on a camp bed in parents' room.
DOGS: not allowed indoors.
CREDIT CARDS: all major cards.
PRICES: per room B&B £100–£265, D,B&B £184–£349. Set dinner £42. 1-night bookings refused weekends.

SEE ALSO SHORTLIST

DOLFOR Powys

THE OLD VICARAGE

Chickens roam the gardens at this Victorian former vicarage which is now an intimate guest house run by 'friendly and accommodating' owners Helen and Tim Withers. There are log fires, locally hand-made blankets and 'glorious' views over the Montgomeryshire countryside; 'a special pleasure was tea and cake on arrival'. The individually styled bedrooms vary in size: one visitor liked her 'large, high-ceilinged' room; another wrote of his too-small space. Guests have 'drinks and nibbles' before dinner; in the restaurant, Tim Withers's Aga-cooked meals focus on organic food, typically a 'glorious' twice-baked cheese soufflé; 'first-rate' lemon and raspberry posset. (One visitor minded the lack of choice of a main course.) Herbs and vegetables come from the garden; 'Tim is also magic with seafood.' 'Flexible hosts, Tim and Helen laid on an early dinner as we had booked a couple of evening concerts at the nearby Gregynog Festival.' Breakfast in the sunlit dining room has just-laid eggs and 'excellent' fruit salad. Guests arriving by public transport, on foot, by bicycle or electric car are given a ten per cent discount. (*Bryan Glastonbury, and others*)

Dolfor, nr Newtown
SY16 4BN

T: 01686-629051
F: 01686-207629
E: tim@theoldvicaragedolfor.co.uk
W: www.theoldvicaragedolfor.co.uk

BEDROOMS: 4.
OPEN: all year except Christmas/ New Year.
FACILITIES: drawing room, dining room, free Wi-Fi, 2-acre garden, unsuitable for &.
BACKGROUND MUSIC: none.
LOCATION: 3 miles S of Newtown.
CHILDREN: all ages welcomed.
DOGS: not allowed.
CREDIT CARDS: Amex, MasterCard, Visa.
PRICES: [2013] per person B&B £47.50–£75, D,B&B £72.50–£110. Set dinner £25–£35, à la carte £30.

DOLGELLAU Gwynedd

Map 3:B3

BRYN MAIR HOUSE [NEW]

On an incline in a market town in Snowdonia national park, this three-storey former Georgian rectory (Grade II listed) is run as a B&B by owners Jan and Peter Ashley. 'They are extremely welcoming, and have furnished the house simply and elegantly,' says the nominator. Guests can enjoy 'magnificent' views of the town and the mountains beyond from the lounge, which has a telescope; there is a library of books to borrow in the dining room. 'Our double-aspect bedroom was beautifully furnished and well equipped; there was an iPod docking system, satellite television, a tea/coffee tray with fresh milk and shortbread biscuits; the bed was comfortable; the small wet room had recently been renovated.' A fridge, within a 'beautiful cabinet', has bottled water for visitors. The 'delicious' breakfast includes fruit juices, home-made granola, yogurt and fresh fruit on the sideboard. 'I couldn't believe how yellow my scrambled eggs were; apparently, the hens roam freely in a wood.' Below Cadair Idris, the house has a large walled garden in which guests are encouraged to 'unwind'. Walking, climbing and mountain biking are among the many activities in the area. (*Lizzy Laczynska*)

Love Lane, Dolgellau
LL40 1SR

T: 01341-422640
E: jan@janashley.wanadoo.co.uk
W: www.brynmairbedandbreakfast.co.uk

BEDROOMS: 3.
OPEN: all year except Christmas.
FACILITIES: lounge, dining room, free Wi-Fi, 1-acre garden, unsuitable for &.
BACKGROUND MUSIC: none.
LOCATION: central.
CHILDREN: not under 14.
DOGS: not allowed.
CREDIT CARDS: MasterCard, Visa.
PRICES: [2013] per room B&B single £75–£85, double £95–£105. 1-night bookings refused Apr–Oct.

SEE ALSO SHORTLIST

DOLYDD Gwynedd

Y GOEDEN EIRIN

❦ *César award in 2008*

Paintings, ceramics, well-read books and
scattered objets d'art make this informal, stone-
built guest house on the edge of the Snowdonia
national park a personal place. 'Engaging hosts'
Eluned and John Rowlands, retired academics,
welcome visitors with sherry, fresh fruit or
home-made biscuits. Occupying renovated farm
outbuildings surrounded by pastureland, this
small guest house has views of mountains and
sea: nature is the main attraction. Indoors,
'everything about our room showed care and
attention to the needs of the guest', with 'good-
sized bathrooms', Welsh blankets and
under-floor heating. While the Rowlandses have
'no pretensions to haute cuisine', no-choice, Aga-
cooked dinner menus (guests are consulted
beforehand) showcase 'enjoyable home cooking'
using home-grown and local ingredients –
perhaps braised leeks, Pantsygawn goat's cheese;
Welsh lamb stew. Cooked breakfasts have
freshly squeezed fruit juice and home-made
brown bread. The bilingual hosts like to share
Welsh culture with their guests: they are
seriously green but not in 'any oppressive way'.
(*HR, and others*)

25% DISCOUNT VOUCHERS

Dolydd, Caernarfon
LL54 7EF

T: 01286-830942
E: john_rowlands@tiscali.co.uk
W: www.ygoedeneirin.co.uk

BEDROOMS: 3, 2 in annexe.
OPEN: all year except
Christmas/New Year, dining room
occasionally closed.
FACILITIES: dining room (occasional
live piano music), lounge by
arrangement, free Wi-Fi, 20-acre
pastureland, unsuitable for &.
BACKGROUND MUSIC: none.
LOCATION: 3 miles S of Caernarfon.
CHILDREN: not under 12.
DOGS: not allowed.
CREDIT CARDS: none, cash or cheque
payment requested on arrival.
PRICES: per room B&B single
£45–£65, double £80–£90. Set dinner
£28. 1-night bookings sometimes
refused weekends.

EGLWYSFACH Powys

Map 3:C3

YNYSHIR HALL

Backed by ancient trees, this white manor house (Relais & Châteaux) stands in 'large and lovely' grounds in the foothills of the Cambrian Mountains. It once belonged to Queen Victoria. Joan and Rob Reen, who are the owners with John and Jenny Talbot, have made a fresh start after buying back the hotel from the collapsed von Essen group. Renovation continues apace: they have created two garden suites overlooking the lawns; one has a conservatory sitting room. Two smaller bedrooms have been turned into a suite; new bathrooms have been fitted in two rooms. The exterior and interior have been painted, and the lounge bar refurbished. The boldly coloured bedrooms, named after famous artists, are 'fun if sometimes opulent'. 'Our room, Matisse, was very pink, but had a sitting area and a large, comfortable bed.' A kitchen garden supplies the produce for the restaurant, where chef Paul Croasdale cooks elaborate modern dishes on a short carte and a tasting menu, perhaps roast scallops, earth-baked celeriac, muscatels; Borth Bay lobster tail, kohlrabi, sweetcorn. A 'leisurely' breakfast, served at table was thought 'good: lovely, flaky croissants; nothing packaged'.

25% DISCOUNT VOUCHERS

Eglwysfach
nr Machynlleth SY20 8TA

T: 01654-781209
F: 01654-781366
E: info@ynyshirhall.co.uk
W: www.ynyshirhall.co.uk

BEDROOMS: 10, 2 garden suites, 1 in studio annexe, 1 on ground floor.
OPEN: all year except Jan.
FACILITIES: drawing room, bar lounge, breakfast room, restaurant, free Wi-Fi, civil wedding licence, 14-acre gardens in 1,000-acre bird reserve.
BACKGROUND MUSIC: classical in bar, restaurant.
LOCATION: 6 miles SW of Machynlleth.
CHILDREN: not under 9 in evening in restaurant.
DOGS: allowed in some bedrooms, not in public rooms.
CREDIT CARDS: Amex, MasterCard, Visa.
PRICES: [2013] per room B&B single £150–£495, double £205–£550. D,B&B £175–£347.50 per person, set dinner £75–£90.

EGLWYSWRW Pembrokeshire

Map 3:D2

AEL Y BRYN

NEW

'A remarkable place where every detail has been thought about, every need addressed.' *Guide* inspectors were 'bowled over' by this unusual B&B, an 'immaculate' conversion of a former prisoner-of-war camp in farmland outside a Pembrokeshire village. The hosts, Robert Smith and Arwel Hughes, have reclaimed the single-storey buildings with 'flair and imagination'. The 'striking' entrance has a patio and pond; there is a music room with a piano, an organ, and a wood-burning stove. This leads to a conservatory with comfortable seats, exotic plants, a telescope. 'The furniture and hangings are smart traditional; there are interesting paintings throughout.' The bedrooms are well equipped ('good books, guides, generous facilities for hot drinks; a cornucopia of extras in the bathroom, which had an exceptional shower'). The hosts share the cooking for dinner, taken in a baronial-style hall with a 'spectacular' chandelier. 'We enjoyed a pleasant leek and hard-boiled egg quiche; a wonderful breadcrumb-crusted chicken breast; four oven dishes of vegetables.' Guests bring their own wine. Breakfast, also 'beautifully laid out', was also 'excellent'.

Crymych SA41 3UL

T: 01239-891411
E: stay@aelybrynpembrokeshire.
co.uk
W: www.aelybrynpembrokeshire.
co.uk

BEDROOMS: 4, all on ground floor.
OPEN: all year except Christmas/
New Year.
FACILITIES: library, music room,
dining room, conservatory, free
Wi-Fi, courtyard, garden (wildlife
pond, stream, bowls court).
BACKGROUND MUSIC: 'easy
listening'/classical.
LOCATION: ½ mile N of village.
CHILDREN: not under 14.
DOGS: not allowed.
CREDIT CARDS: MasterCard, Visa.
PRICES: [2013] per room B&B single
£65–£80, double £88–£100. Set
dinner £23–£27.

FELIN FACH Powys

Map 3:D4

THE FELIN FACH GRIFFIN

❧ *César award in 2013*

On the edge of a village on the busy road between the Brecon Beacons and the Black Mountains, this country coaching inn is a 'ridiculously welcoming place'. Managed by Julie Bell for brothers Charles and Edmund Inkin, it has 'friendly, capable staff' and a laid-back ambience. Downstairs is a network of linked rooms: an open fire connects the library and bar; meals are served in a tack room, which has a fire, and the Aga room, which has doors on to the terrace and garden. The chef, Ross Bruce, turns to the kitchen gardener, Joe Hand, for vegetables, herbs and soft fruit. Typical dishes: cured pork belly with Joe's beetroot; loin of Welsh lamb, garlic pomme purée, Kelvedon Wonder peas, thyme sauce. The small bedrooms are decorated in country style, with checked curtains, Welsh wool blankets. They have fresh flowers, books, a Roberts radio (a TV can be provided if you ask). Children are welcomed, as are dogs. The brothers also own *The Gurnard's Head*, Zennor (see entry) and *The Old Coastguard*, Mousehole (see entry). (*SH, and others*)

Felin Fach, nr Brecon
LD3 0UB

T: 01874-620111
E: enquiries@felinfachgriffin.co.uk
W: www.felinfachgriffin.co.uk

BEDROOMS: 7.
OPEN: all year except 24/25 Dec.
FACILITIES: bar area, dining room, breakfast room, private dining room, free Wi-Fi, 1-acre garden (stream, kitchen garden), only bar/dining room suitable for &.
BACKGROUND MUSIC: Radio 4 at breakfast, 'carefully considered music at other times'.
LOCATION: 4½ miles NE of Brecon, in village on A470.
CHILDREN: all ages welcomed.
DOGS: allowed in bedrooms, at some tables in bar.
CREDIT CARDS: MasterCard, Visa.
PRICES: [2013] per room B&B £115–£165, D,B&B £145–£215. Set menus £23–£28.50, à la carte £38.50. 1-night bookings occasionally refused.

FISHGUARD Pembrokeshire

THE MANOR TOWN HOUSE

'Delightful – it gets better and better.' Praise this year from a regular visitor to this stylish, sky blue-painted B&B in the centre of the harbour town. Run by 'friendly' owners Helen and Chris Sheldon, the Grade II listed Georgian house has 'wonderful views' over the working port and across the water to Dinas Head. Guests are greeted with freshly baked Welsh cakes and bara brith, taken in front of the wood-burning stove in the lounge or, in warm weather, on a terrace facing the sea. Individually decorated with antique furniture, many of the 'warm, accommodating' bedrooms overlook the sea. An Edwardian-inspired room has an ornate mirror and a vintage fireplace; another room, painted a warm grey, was redecorated in 2013 and given walnut Art Deco-style furniture. There is much to choose from at breakfast: smoked salmon and scrambled eggs, a full Welsh with laver bread; waffles with fresh fruit and Greek yogurt – Helen Sheldon's speciality. The Pembrokeshire Coastal Path is accessed through the woods below the garden; packed lunches can be arranged. Popular with passengers taking the ferries to Ireland. (*David Humphreys, and others*)

11 Main Street
Fishguard SA65 9HG

T: 01348-873260
E: enquiries@manortownhouse.com
W: www.manortownhouse.com

BEDROOMS: 6.
OPEN: all year except Christmas.
FACILITIES: 2 lounges, breakfast room, free Wi-Fi, small walled garden, unsuitable for &.
BACKGROUND MUSIC: classical at breakfast.
LOCATION: central.
CHILDREN: all ages welcomed.
DOGS: not allowed.
CREDIT CARDS: MasterCard, Visa.
PRICES: [2013] per room B&B single £65–£85, double £85–£105. 1-night bookings sometimes refused weekends.

GLYNARTHEN Ceredigion

Map 3:D2

PENBONTBREN

♔ *César award in 2012*

'A very happy atmosphere.' Richard Morgan-Price and Huw Thomas have converted a 19th-century livestock farm into an 'attractive' B&B with 'beautiful, spacious' suites. 'The attention to detail throughout is amazing,' said one guest. Each bedroom – in the former stable or granary, the old mill or threshing barn – has a sitting room and private terrace; one, with a separate single bedroom and a wet room, is suitable for families and wheelchair-users. 'Richard and Huw are great hosts – able and friendly owners. And our two King Charles spaniels were welcomed by Richard and Huw's dogs.' There are 'excellent' nearby eateries for dinner: 'Richard recommended a lovely pub that serves really fresh fish.' Alternatively, a farm shop caters for guests wishing to eat in. 'Our kitchenette had everything necessary and a fridge filled with wine.' 'Varied, generous' breakfasts have linen table napkins, eggs from the house's own hens, and smoked fish from neighbouring Rhydlewis. *Penbontbren* is surrounded by 'delightful countryside' with views towards the Preseli Mountains. (*Simon Rodway, HW*)

25% DISCOUNT VOUCHERS

Glynarthen
Llandysul SA44 6PE

T: 01239-810248
F: 01239-811129
E: contact@penbontbren.com
W: www.penbontbren.com

BEDROOMS: 5 in annexe, 3 on ground floor, 1 suitable for &.
OPEN: all year except Christmas.
FACILITIES: breakfast room, free Wi-Fi, 32-acre grounds.
BACKGROUND MUSIC: none.
LOCATION: 5 miles N of Newcastle Emlyn.
CHILDREN: all ages welcomed.
DOGS: not allowed in breakfast room, most bedrooms.
CREDIT CARDS: MasterCard, Visa.
PRICES: per room B&B single £80, double £105. 1-night bookings sometimes refused peak weekends.

HARLECH Gwynedd

Map 3:B3

CASTLE COTTAGE

NEW

Near the castle in the historic coastal town, this restored 17th-century coaching inn is run as a restaurant-with-rooms in personal style by Glyn (the owner/chef) and Jacqueline Roberts. 'We were impressed: the setting, on the steep slope above the river estuary, is amazing; the food is excellent,' say visitors this year, restoring *Castle Cottage* to a full entry. The public areas have a contemporary look: white and cream linen on Welsh oak tables; black leather armchairs. Canapés are served in a bar area while dinner is ordered. 'The food was delicious with imaginative combinations such as melon and smoked salmon starter, a tarragon crème brûlée dessert. With large portions and chef's appetisers, you feel you have eaten well by the end.' The beamed bedrooms are in the main building and a Grade II listed stone cottage next door: 'Our enormous superior room was beautifully decorated in modern style; under-floor heating in the tiled bathroom.' Breakfast has freshly squeezed orange juice, fruit compotes and cereals, yogurt with Welsh honey; laver bread (seaweed) is among the cooked choices. 'Definitely a place to return to.' (*Alan and Edwina Williams*)

25% DISCOUNT VOUCHERS

Y Llech, Harlech
LL46 2YL

T: 01766-780479
E: glyn@castlecottageharlech.co.uk
W: www.castlecottageharlech.co.uk

BEDROOMS: 7, 4 in annexe, 2 on ground floor.
OPEN: all year except Christmas and 3 weeks Nov.
FACILITIES: bar/lounge, restaurant, free Wi-Fi.
BACKGROUND MUSIC: in bar/dining room.
LOCATION: town centre.
CHILDREN: all ages welcomed.
DOGS: not allowed.
CREDIT CARDS: MasterCard, Visa.
PRICES: [2013] per person B&B £65–£125, D,B&B £100–£160. 1-night bookings refused bank holidays.

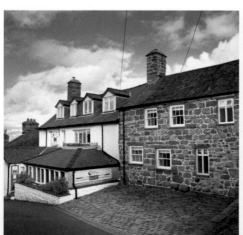

KNIGHTON Powys

Map 3:C4

MILEBROOK HOUSE

In a 'wonderful setting', this mellow stone house (once the home of explorer Sir Wilfred Thesiger) is a 'delightful small country hotel', run by long-time resident owners, Beryl and Rodney Marsden. 'We wished we had discovered it years ago,' says a visitor in 2013. 'Mrs Marsden is a constant presence, a very good hostess.' 'Relaxed, peaceful, welcoming,' said an earlier guest. 'Tea and scones, yes with cream and jam, were served in the prettily furnished parlour, where a cat snoozed by an open fire.' The 'accommodation is excellent': 'Our good-sized room looked out over the garden; the bathroom was clean and well equipped.' Rear rooms are the quietest (the road at the front can be busy). The chef, Chris Lovell, serves meals in the 'intimate' bar and the restaurant. 'Delicious haddock risotto with green peas; excellent John Dory; a choice of four desserts or cheese (no supplement, a minor miracle). The wine list was sensible, no showing off.' Breakfast is 'of the same high standard'. 'An ideal base for walking, as well as exploring the bookshops in Hay-on-Wye.' (*Clive T Blackburn, and others*)

Milebrook
Knighton
Powys LD7 1LT

T: 01547-528632
F: 01547-529490
E: hotel@milebrookhouse.co.uk
W: www.milebrookhouse.co.uk

BEDROOMS: 10, 2 on ground floor.
OPEN: all year, restaurant closed Mon lunch.
FACILITIES: lounge, bar, 2 dining rooms, free Wi-Fi, 4-acre grounds on river (terraces, pond, croquet, fishing).
BACKGROUND MUSIC: classical in bar and restaurant.
LOCATION: on A4113, 2 miles E of Knighton.
CHILDREN: not under 8.
DOGS: not allowed.
CREDIT CARDS: MasterCard, Visa.
PRICES: [2013] per room B&B £136, D,B&B £190. À la carte £33.

LAMPETER Ceredigion

THE FALCONDALE

NEW

In 'handsome' landscaped gardens on a south-facing promontory, Chris and Lisa Hutton's Italianate hotel has 'magnificent views' over the Teifi valley. 'We really enjoyed staying here,' said *Guide* inspectors in 2013. 'It is run in good traditional taste, without any pretention. We were given a cheerful welcome and presented with a complimentary glass of Prosecco; our luggage was taken to our room.' The public rooms are 'spacious, and pleasingly decorated; interesting pictures everywhere'; a grand piano in the lounge. A 'gorgeous' atrium has 'deep seats, lots of glossy magazines'. The bedrooms vary in size: 'Our enormous room had a sitting area, a giant bed, classical furnishings; "his and hers" bathrooms – a shower in his, a deep, long bath in hers. Every detail had been thought of.' Mike Green is the chef. Dinner, in an elegant dining room, was 'extremely good: just-right grilled scallops with crispy Italian bacon; tender duck rare (as requested) with fondant potatoes, shredded red cabbage, celeriac chips'. Breakfast is 'all it should be; a comprehensive buffet; home-made jams; locally sourced cooked ingredients'. 'Very dog-friendly.'

25% DISCOUNT VOUCHERS

Falcondale Drive
Lampeter SA48 7RX

T: 01570-422910
E: info@thefalcondale.co.uk
W: www.thefalcondale.co.uk

BEDROOMS: 19.
OPEN: all year.
FACILITIES: lift, bar, lounge, conservatory, restaurant, free Wi-Fi, civil wedding licence, terrace, 14-acre gardens.
BACKGROUND MUSIC: in public areas.
LOCATION: 1 mile N of Lampeter.
CHILDREN: all ages welcomed.
DOGS: not allowed in restaurant.
CREDIT CARDS: MasterCard, Visa.
PRICES: [2013] per room B&B single £100–£150, double £140–£190. Set dinner £40.

SEE ALSO SHORTLIST

LLANARMON DYFFRYN CEIRIOG Denbighshire Map 3:B4

THE HAND AT LLANARMON

At the crossroads of two old drovers' roads, this 500-year-old inn is a 'laid-back country hotel' run by owners Gaynor and Martin De Luchi, helped by 'friendly' staff. Locals and guests gather in the beamed bar for meals and drinks. In the restaurant, with its wood-burning stove, chef Grant Mulholland's dishes are 'well cooked and plentiful', perhaps venison terrine, basil jam; ox cheek bourguignon, Guinness gravy, creamed potatoes. Bedrooms are in the original farmhouse, overlooking the village, or in converted stables and barns, with views of 'rolling, sheep-grazed hills'. 'Our room in the country wing was not large, but adequate for a short stay. The bathroom appeared to be quite newly fitted (pity about the hot-water pressure).' A ground-floor room has been fully adapted for wheelchair-users; disabled visitors have found access 'excellent'. There is a good choice at breakfast, with organic yogurt, home-made marmalade, and sausages and bacon from a local butcher. In 'outstandingly beautiful' surroundings in the Ceiriog valley, the inn is well placed for walkers; the hosts can provide a book of walks from the door. (*R and JG, and others*)

Llanarmon Dyffryn Ceiriog
Ceiriog Valley
LL20 7LD

T: 01691-600666
F: 01691-600262
E: reception@thehandhotel.co.uk
W: www.thehandhotel.co.uk

BEDROOMS: 13, 4 on ground floor, 1 suitable for &.
OPEN: all year, accommodation closed at Christmas.
FACILITIES: ramp, lounge, bar, restaurant, games/TV room, free Wi-Fi (in public rooms), terrace, ¾-acre grounds.
BACKGROUND MUSIC: none.
LOCATION: 10 miles W of Oswestry.
CHILDREN: all ages welcomed.
DOGS: not allowed in some bedrooms.
CREDIT CARDS: MasterCard, Visa.
PRICES: per room B&B single £55–£74, double £90–£127.50. À la carte £29–£36. 1-night bookings sometimes refused.

LLANDRILLO Denbighshire

Map 3:B4

TYDDYN LLAN

♥César award in 2006

'Superb food, comfortable rooms, great service from the efficient young staff.' There is much praise this year for Bryan and Susan Webb's restaurant-with-rooms. Their pretty Georgian country house stands amid lawns and gardens with views of the mountains to the north. Its shaded veranda on two sides makes 'a nice place to have tea or just read on a warm day'. There is a small bar, 'comfortable, clubbish' lounges. One of the two dining rooms is 'grand, in keeping with the era of the house'; the other has 'a New England feel'. Bryan Webb has a *Michelin* star for his 'excellent' cooking: a reader warns against eating too many of the 'best-ever' canapés before the meal. The seasonal Welsh dishes might include loin of venison, savoy cabbage, goat's cheese gnocchi, port sauce. Bedrooms have a mix of styles. One visitor found a modern room (black curtains and headboard, black leather armchairs) 'too trendy for my taste'. Other rooms have lighter decor (all can be viewed on the website). 'Breakfast is substantial and varied.' (*Peter Anderson, Zara Elliott, and others*)

25% DISCOUNT VOUCHERS

Llandrillo
nr Corwen LL21 0ST

T: 01490-440264
F: 01490-440414
E: info@tyddynllan.co.uk
W: www.tyddynllan.co.uk

BEDROOMS: 13, 1, on ground floor, suitable for ♿.
OPEN: all year, except last two weeks Jan.
FACILITIES: ramp, 2 lounges, bar, 2 dining rooms, free Wi-Fi, civil wedding licence, 3-acre garden.
BACKGROUND MUSIC: none.
LOCATION: 5 miles SW of Corwen.
CHILDREN: all ages welcomed.
DOGS: allowed in some bedrooms, not in public rooms.
CREDIT CARDS: MasterCard, Visa.
PRICES: [2013] per room B&B £160–£300, D,B&B £250–£390. Set dinner £45–£85.

LLANDUDNO Conwy

Map 3:A3

BODYSGALLEN HALL AND SPA

♥*César award in 1988*

'What a beautiful old house which, with its gardens, is so well maintained.' This 17th-century mansion stands in extensive wooded parkland and formal gardens overlooking Conwy Castle and Snowdonia. It is run by Historic House Hotels for the National Trust. The Grade I listed building has original oak panelling, stone mullioned windows; there are log fires and antique furniture in the entrance hall and drawing room. Staff are 'friendly and efficient'. 'We were upgraded to a large and well-appointed room; the bathroom was down a short flight of stairs,' say visitors this year. Some rooms are in stone cottages in the gardens, suitable for families. There is plenty to occupy guests in the grounds: woodland walks, lily pad ponds, follies. In the restaurant overlooking the lawns, chef Michael Cheetham cooks an imaginative modern menu that might include seared mackerel fillet, Szechuan ice cream; roast pumpkin cream, coriander and pumpkin risotto, pumpkin crisps. More casual meals are available in *1620 Bistro*, in the converted coach house. 'We enjoyed our cream tea on the lawn in the sunshine.' (*Robert and Shirley Lyne*)

Llandudno LL30 1RS

T: 01492-584466
F: 01492-582519
E: info@bodysgallen.com
W: www.bodysgallen.com

BEDROOMS: 31, 16 in cottages, 1 suitable for &.
OPEN: all year, restaurant closed Mon.
FACILITIES: hall, drawing room, library, bar, dining room, bistro, free Wi-Fi, civil wedding licence, 220-acre park (gardens, tennis, croquet), spa (16-metre swimming pool).
BACKGROUND MUSIC: none.
LOCATION: 2 miles S of Llandudno.
CHILDREN: no children under 6 in hotel, under 8 in spa.
DOGS: allowed in some cottages.
CREDIT CARDS: Amex, MasterCard, Visa.
PRICES: per person B&B (continental) £84.50–£212.50, D,B&B £132.50–£245. 1-night bookings sometimes refused.

SEE ALSO SHORTLIST

LLANDUDNO Conwy

Map 3:A3

OSBORNE HOUSE [NEW]

'An interesting, unusual and exciting place; altogether a happy experience.' Praise from a regular *Guide* correspondent brings an upgrade to a full entry for this small hotel on Llandudno's promenade. It is a sister to the larger *Empire Hotel*, 200 yards away. Elyse Waddy is the manager; Michael Waddy the chef. Each of the six bedrooms has a separate sitting room. 'Our gorgeous second-floor suite was furnished with original Victorian pieces. The sitting room had a large, squashy sofa and coffee table in front of a gas fire. There was a breakfast table in the window; original wood floor covered with large rugs; beautiful silk curtains. The bedroom had an extremely comfortable, ornate brass bed. A separate dressing area had a hanging cupboard; the marble bathroom a roll-top bath and a separate walk-in shower.' Downstairs has a 'theatrical' lounge, a bar and a café which serves 'good gastropub standard' food all day. A continental breakfast is brought to the bedroom; a cooked option is available at the *Empire* for no extra charge; guests can also use the pool and spa at the sister hotel. (*Barbara Watkinson*)

17 North Parade
Llandudno, LL30 2LP

T: 01492-860330
F: 01492-860791
E: sales@osbornehouse.co.uk
W: www.osbornehouse.co.uk

BEDROOMS: 6.
OPEN: all year, except Christmas.
FACILITIES: sitting room, bar, café/bistro, free Wi-Fi, unsuitable for &.
BACKGROUND MUSIC: 'varied' in café/bistro.
LOCATION: on promenade.
CHILDREN: not under 16.
DOGS: not allowed.
CREDIT CARDS: all major cards.
PRICES: per room B&B £125–£175, D,B&B £155–£205. Set menu £20.95. 1-night bookings refused Sat.

SEE ALSO SHORTLIST

LLANDUDNO Conwy

Map 3:A3

ST TUDNO HOTEL

❦ *César award in 1987*

Despite a near fiasco with the dining-room chairs the day the hotel opened in 1972, owner Martin Bland today confidently seats and welcomes visitors to this traditional seaside hotel, in a Grade II listed building steps from the sandy beach. Returning visitors like the friendly atmosphere: 'Mr Bland is an excellent host, and the staff are always helpful.' Opposite the Victorian pier and gardens, the hotel has sea views from its richly wallpapered sitting rooms; upstairs, bedrooms overlooking Llandudno Bay are sought after: 'We love the Rhoda Suite with its panoramic view.' The Italianate dining room has a floral chandelier and a mural of Lake Como; here, chef Andrew Foster's 'excellent' modern classics might include char-cured mackerel fillet, pickled beetroot, horseradish; duo of Welsh lamb, dauphinoise potato, Madeira jus. In good weather, guests may take lunch and afternoon tea – with buttered Welsh cakes and bara brith – on the patio facing the sea. 'Everything was brought to the table' at breakfast: kippers and smoked haddock, bread baked on the premises, sausages from a butcher in nearby Conwy. (*MS, BE*)

North Parade, Promenade
Llandudno LL30 2LP

T: 01492-874411
F: 01492-860407
E: sttudnohotel@btinternet.com
W: www.st-tudno.co.uk

BEDROOMS: 18.
OPEN: all year.
FACILITIES: lift, three lounges, restaurant, free Wi-Fi, indoor heated swimming pool (8 by 4 metres), civil wedding licence, patio, 'secret garden', unsuitable for &.
BACKGROUND MUSIC: occasionally when quiet.
LOCATION: on promenade opposite pier, parking.
CHILDREN: all ages welcomed, under-5s have early supper.
DOGS: by arrangement (£10 per night), only in coffee lounge, not unattended in bedrooms.
CREDIT CARDS: all major cards.
PRICES: [2013] per person B&B single from £75, double £49–£110, D,B&B £79–£140. Set meals £22.50–£27.50, à la carte £35.

SEE ALSO SHORTLIST

LLANGAMMARCH WELLS Powys

Map 3:D3

THE LAKE

❦ *César award in 1992*

Built as a hunting lodge, later remodelled as a barium resort (the only one outside Germany), this half-timbered building stands in extensive parkland with a lake by the River Irfon. It is run by the owner, Jean-Pierre Mifsud, as a country house and spa retreat. He is 'very much in evidence in the drawing room and dining room in the evening', says a visitor this year, who 'warmed to the experience'. The decor and manner of service is traditional: there are three lounges, with antiques and paintings, sofas and armchairs. 'We enjoyed pre-dinner drinks in a very pleasant sitting room, which had interesting furniture.' The chef, Russell Stach, cooks modern British dishes, perhaps potted brown shrimp and Aberaeron white crab, caper mayonnaise; casserole of Brecon venison, rustic Swedish mash, game chips. 'Dinner could not be faulted.' The bedrooms in the main house have a country house decor ('but no hospitality tray or fruit – and only one armchair by the television'). Twelve more contemporary suites are in an adjacent lodge; they have an open-plan sitting room. (*BW, and others*)

25% DISCOUNT VOUCHERS

Llangammarch Wells
LD4 4BS

T: 01591-620202
F: 01591-620457
E: info@lakecountryhouse.co.uk
W: www.lakecountryhouse.co.uk

BEDROOMS: 30, 12 suites in adjacent lodge, 7 on ground floor, 1 suitable for ♿.
OPEN: all year.
FACILITIES: ramps, 3 lounges, orangery, restaurant, free Wi-Fi, spa (15-metre swimming pool), civil wedding licence, 50-acre grounds (tennis).
BACKGROUND MUSIC: none.
LOCATION: 8 miles SW of Builth Wells.
CHILDREN: all ages welcomed.
DOGS: allowed (£10 charge), not in public rooms.
CREDIT CARDS: Amex, MasterCard, Visa.
PRICES: per room B&B £195–£260, D,B&B £245–£310. Set dinner £38.50.

LLANIDLOES Powys

Map 3:C3

LLOYDS

Coins were supplied free of charge to operate the house's electric heaters when Tom Lines and Roy Hayter first opened their B&B in this medieval market town on the River Severn. After 21 years of 'refreshment and renewal', they continue to give 'as warm a welcome as ever, both personally and practically'. It remains 'excellent and, if anything, has improved', say visitors returning after a two-year break. The 'comfortable' sitting room has newspapers and books for browsing; up a steep flight of narrow stairs (the owners help with luggage), the homely bedrooms have original art. 'Our room was nicely decorated, well equipped, satisfyingly modern and of a good size.' The owners tell us that from 2014 they will be simplifying their popular dinners; a three-course menu will replace the five-course version, which will be confined to special occasions. 'Tom presents the menu, while Roy cooks.' His 'imaginative' dishes might include Gruyère and Emmental soufflé, tomato tarte Tatin, parsnip crisps; wild trout fishcakes, glazed pears, samphire. There is 'plenty of choice' at breakfast, with cooked-to-order local bacon and sausages, and eggs from free-range hens. (*Stephen and Pauline Glover*)

25% DISCOUNT VOUCHERS

6 Cambrian Place
Llanidloes SY18 6BX

T: 01686-412284
E: lloyds@dircon.co.uk
W: www.lloydshotel.co.uk

BEDROOMS: 7.
OPEN: mid-Mar–early Jan, closed Christmas.
FACILITIES: sitting room, breakfast room, restaurant, free Wi-Fi, unsuitable for &.
BACKGROUND MUSIC: none.
LOCATION: near the town centre.
CHILDREN: all ages welcomed.
DOGS: not allowed.
CREDIT CARDS: MasterCard, Visa.
PRICES: [2013] per person B&B £42–£69, D,B&B (min. 2 nights) £78–£82.50. Set dinner £44.

LLANWRTYD WELLS Powys

Map 3:D3

CARLTON RIVERSIDE

🏵 *César award in 1998*

In an 'attractive position' by a bridge on the River Irfon, this old stone house, said to be the second oldest in town, has windows framed in bright blue. Inside, 'warm, welcoming hosts' Mary Ann and Alan Gilchrist are the long-time owners of this small restaurant-with-rooms. The house is neat, homely, 'comfortable'; there are armchairs by shelves filled with books, and a slate-floored basement bar with sofas and home-made pizzas. In the modern restaurant overlooking the stone bridge, Mrs Gilchrist's 'excellent' dinners, served at a leisurely pace, might include pea mousse, Carmarthen ham, pea and shallot salad; beef bourguignon, smoked bacon, creamy mash. Special diets can be catered for by arrangement. Bedrooms vary in size and aspect: the Bridge room has views of the chapel and the river; the small Chapel room, looking towards the valley, has tables and cabinets in Venetian glass. 'Our room was big, quiet and comfortable; the noisy toilet was unfortunate.' In the morning, a 'satisfactory' breakfast has 'very good scrambled eggs'; a dissenter would have liked 'more choice beyond the cereal and full fry-up'. 'An eccentric place.'

25% DISCOUNT VOUCHERS

Irfon Crescent
Llanwrtyd Wells LD5 4ST

T: 01591-610248
E: carltonriverside@hotmail.co.uk
W: www.carltonriverside.com

BEDROOMS: 5.
OPEN: all year except 22–31 Dec, restaurant closed Sun.
FACILITIES: Reception, bar/lounge, restaurant, free Wi-Fi, unsuitable for ♿.
BACKGROUND MUSIC: classical piano in lounge.
LOCATION: town centre, no private parking.
CHILDREN: all ages welcomed.
DOGS: not allowed in public rooms.
CREDIT CARDS: MasterCard, Visa.
PRICES: [2013] per person B&B £37.50–£50, D,B&B £70. À la carte £25–£40. 1-night bookings sometimes refused Sat, bank holidays.

SEE ALSO SHORTLIST

LLYSWEN Powys

LLANGOED HALL

'Serenely sitting in large grounds with the River Wye flowing through', this lovely 17th-century mansion (redesigned by Sir Clough Williams-Ellis) was for many years run as a smart hotel by the late Sir Bernard Ashley, later by the von Essen group. It is restored to the *Guide* under new private ownership; Calum Milne, a former manager, has returned as managing director. More than £2 million has been spent on renovation; work in the grounds has been completed; soft furnishings in the public rooms have been reupholstered and a new carpet laid; work on the bedrooms is continuing. 'Talk about the good old days,' says a visitor (a hotelier). 'We were greeted by the charismatic Calum, luggage was wrestled from us and tea flawlessly served in the drawing room, which had a roaring fire and no annoying music.' Nick Brodie is the chef: his modern cooking, 'immaculately presented on lovely china', is 'an absolute pleasure' with dishes like cannelloni of crab, lemon grass and ginger; duck breast, confit leg, salt-baked beetroot, Alsace cabbage. Service is 'silky smooth' at the à la carte breakfast. (*Richard Morgan-Price, and others*)

Llyswen
Brecon LD3 0YP

T: 01874-754525
F: 01874-754545
E: enquiries@llangoedhall.com
W: www.llangoedhall.co.uk

BEDROOMS: 23.
OPEN: all year.
FACILITIES: morning room, drawing room, billiard room, function rooms, free Wi-Fi, 17-acre gardens.
BACKGROUND MUSIC: pianist in morning room at weekends.
LOCATION: 1 mile N of Llyswen.
CHILDREN: all ages welcomed, over-5s only in restaurant.
DOGS: allowed, not in restaurant (heated kennels).
CREDIT CARDS: MasterCard, Visa.
PRICES: per room B&B £150–£400. Set dinner £55.

NANT GWYNANT Gwynedd

Map 3:A3

PEN-Y-GWRYD HOTEL

♧ *César award in 1995*

'It is a remarkable establishment that preserves some of the best facets of the hotels we knew in our youth.' The Pullee family's historic hotel (the training base for the climbers who conquered Everest in 1953) is a converted 19th-century farmhouse in the foothills of Snowdon. The service is 'cheerful, friendly and informal'. Brothers Nick and Rupert are the 'self-effacing' hosts, 'helping out at breakfast and in the bar'. The food is 'good, honest fare, locally sourced and always fresh'. A gong summons guests to dinner which, contrary to previous reports in the *Guide*, is not a communal affair (except when groups choose to dine together): 'You keep your own table for the whole of your stay; it is set with white linen, good silver, bone-handled knives and one's own silver napkin ring.' Nor is the atmosphere like a 'house party': 'Everyone greets you and asks about your day, but if you prefer to be alone, there is every opportunity to do so.' The bedrooms are small and simple. Only five have a private bathroom. (*Robert Turner*)

Nant Gwynant
LL55 4NT

T: 01286-870211
E: escape@pyg.co.uk
W: www.pyg.co.uk

BEDROOMS: 16, 1 on ground floor, garden suite in annexe.
OPEN: Mar–Nov, New Year, weekends Jan/Feb.
FACILITIES: lounge, bar, games room, dining room, Wi-Fi (£2 charge), chapel, 1-acre grounds (natural unheated 60-metre swimming pool, sauna).
BACKGROUND MUSIC: none.
LOCATION: between Beddgelert and Capel Curig.
CHILDREN: all ages welcomed.
DOGS: allowed (£2 charge), not in some public rooms.
CREDIT CARDS: Amex, MasterCard, Visa.
PRICES: [2013] per person B&B £42–£52. Set dinner £25–£30. 1-night bookings often refused weekends.

NARBERTH Pembrokeshire

Map 3:D2

THE GROVE

The roof was leaking and the windows were rotten when Neil Kedward and Zoë Agar bought this 18th-century mansion facing the Preseli hills. Six years of restoration work culminated this year with the opening of a new wing, which has added eight bedrooms and an expanded restaurant. *Guide* readers like the 'wonderfully relaxed atmosphere' and the service by a 'polite, helpful' staff. Duncan Barham, the chef, serves 'excellent' modern dishes in the restaurant, perhaps line-caught mackerel, beetroot, watercress, horseradish; Nant Ddu pork, parsnip, red cabbage, chanterelle ravioli. The bedrooms are in the main house, the new wing, a coach house and an adjacent 15th-century longhouse. Those in the eaves and the longhouse have the most character. A spacious room in the main house overlooking the 'beautiful' formal gardens was enjoyed; the decor of a darker room was less liked. The house has a 'curious mix' of neo-Gothic Arts and Crafts design (added during 19th-century renovations) and Jacobean styling. There are original fireplaces, cosy wood-panelled nooks. The work of contemporary Welsh artists is displayed throughout. (*Zara Elliott, and others*)

25% DISCOUNT VOUCHERS

Molleston
Narberth SA67 8BX

T: 01834-860915
F: 01834-861000
E: info@thegrove-narberth.co.uk
W: www.thegrove-narberth.co.uk

BEDROOMS: 20, 2 in coach house (1 on ground floor), 4 in longhouse, plus 4 self-catering cottages.
OPEN: all year.
FACILITIES: 4 lounges, library, restaurant, breakfast room, free Wi-Fi, civil wedding licence, 26-acre grounds.
BACKGROUND MUSIC: jazz, 'easy listening' in public areas.
LOCATION: 1 mile S of village.
CHILDREN: all ages welcomed.
DOGS: allowed in public areas.
CREDIT CARDS: Amex, MasterCard, Visa.
PRICES: [2013] per room B&B £150–£320, D,B&B £248–£418. Tasting menus £64–£78, à la carte £49.

SEE ALSO SHORTLIST

NEWPORT Pembrokeshire

CNAPAN

In the centre of a medieval town between the Preseli hills and the Pembrokeshire coast, this pink-painted restaurant-with-rooms has been run by three generations of the Lloyd and Cooper families since 1984. 'Lovely, caring owners' Judith and Michael Cooper are helped by their son, Oliver, who has taken a prominent role in running the family business. The listed Georgian town house is also their family home; decorated with personal knick-knacks, it has a 'comfortable', lived-in feel. Pretty, simply styled bedrooms have pictures and books to borrow, including local maps and guides. The bedrooms are fitted with a shower: a shared bathroom is available for guests who prefer a bath. The family room, which sleeps three, was refurbished in 2013. Non-residents and staying guests alike praise Mrs Cooper's 'high-quality', 'splendid' dinners, which use local ingredients, perhaps wild mushroom and egg gratin, Perl Las cheese and thyme scone; Preseli lamb cutlets, minted pea purée, salsa verde. A small garden is a pleasant place to sit in on a sunny day. 'One of the friendliest places we have ever stayed in.' *(AL, MK, DL)*

25% DISCOUNT VOUCHERS

East Street, Newport
nr Fishguard SA42 0SY

T: 01239-820575
F: 01239-820878
E: enquiry@cnapan.co.uk
W: www.cnapan.co.uk

BEDROOMS: 5, plus a self-catering cottage.
OPEN: Mar–early Jan, closed Christmas, restaurant closed Tues.
FACILITIES: lounge, bar, restaurant, free Wi-Fi, small garden, unsuitable for &.
BACKGROUND MUSIC: jazz/Latin in evenings in dining room.
LOCATION: town centre.
CHILDREN: all ages welcomed (£15 for B&B in triple room, half price in other rooms).
DOGS: only guide dogs allowed.
CREDIT CARDS: MasterCard, Visa.
PRICES: [2013] per person B&B £45–£60, D,B&B £75. À la carte £25–£30. 1-night bookings sometimes refused during peak season and on Saturdays.

SEE ALSO SHORTLIST

NEWPORT Pembrokeshire

Map 3:D1

LLYS MEDDYG

Between the beach and the Preseli hills, Ed and Lou Sykes's smart restaurant-with-rooms is in a Grade II listed Georgian coaching inn in this pretty estuary town. 'Everyone was exceptionally friendly.' 'Stylish' modern bedrooms have confident colours, hand-spun Welsh blankets and a minibar with fresh local milk; some rooms have a sofa bed to accommodate a family. A 'spacious' attic room is 'a place you could enjoy spending time in'. Fresh wild flowers brighten up the rustic dining room, where chef Daniel Jones's menu highlights local ingredients, perhaps Welsh mussels, roasted garlic soup; Preseli lamb rump, root vegetables. (During a half-day foraging course, guests sweep the countryside for chanterelles and scour the shoreline for seaweed and shellfish.) Simple, child-friendly dishes are available by arrangement. Downstairs, locals gather at the flagstoned cellar bar for drinks or an informal supper. The family-friendly kitchen garden, open for meals in the summer, has toddler bikes, massive beanbags and garden games. There are freshly squeezed orange juice, fresh fruit pancakes and house-smoked salmon at breakfast – 'great fuel for a day's walking'.

East Street, Newport
nr Fishguard SA42 0SY

T: 01239-820008
E: info@llysmeddyg.com
W: www.llysmeddyg.com

BEDROOMS: 8, 1 on ground floor, 3 in annexe, plus a cottage.
OPEN: all year.
FACILITIES: bar, restaurant, sitting room, free Wi-Fi, civil wedding licence, garden.
BACKGROUND MUSIC: in bar and restaurant.
LOCATION: central.
CHILDREN: all ages welcomed.
DOGS: allowed in 3 bedrooms, cellar bar.
CREDIT CARDS: MasterCard, Visa.
PRICES: per person B&B £50–£90, D,B&B £80–£120. Set dinner £29.50–£35, à la carte £40. 1-night bookings sometimes refused weekends.

SEE ALSO SHORTLIST

PENMYNYDD Isle of Anglesey

Map 3:A3

NEUADD LWYD

♥ *César award in 2010*

'Everything is first class' at this 'lovely' grey-stoned Victorian rectory, run by owners Susannah and Peter Woods as a rural guest house. There are large sofas and an open fire in the sitting room, and views of the Anglesey countryside and Snowdonia beyond. Individually styled, the pretty bedrooms have upholstered armchairs, wool blankets, fresh flowers; one, Edmwnd, has a claw-footed slipper bath painted aubergine. Books, magazines and DVDs are available to borrow. In the dining room looking towards the peaks of Snowdonia, 'you cannot fault Susannah's fantastic cooking'. *Ballymaloe*-trained, she supports the Anglesey food producers' network and favours organic ingredients; her daily-changing, no-choice menu might include potted hot smoked salmon, capers; slow-roasted Anglesey duck, melted leeks, Aga-roasted potatoes. (Vegetarians are catered for by arrangement.) On balmy evenings, guests are encouraged to step through the French windows and dine alfresco. There are home-made preserves, home-baked bread and a selection of local honey at breakfast. (*GF*)

Penmynydd
nr Llanfairpwllgwyngyll
Isle of Anglesey LL61 5BX

T/F: 01248-715005
E: post@neuaddlwyd.co.uk
W: www.neuaddlwyd.co.uk

BEDROOMS: 4.
OPEN: Mar–Oct, closed Sun–Tues except bank holidays.
FACILITIES: drawing room, lounge, dining room, 6-acre grounds, only dining room suitable for &.
BACKGROUND MUSIC: none.
LOCATION: 3 miles W of Menai Bridge.
CHILDREN: not under 16.
DOGS: only guide dogs allowed.
CREDIT CARDS: MasterCard, Visa.
PRICES: per room B&B single £130–£180, double £150–£200, D,B&B single £140–£200, double £190–£250. Set dinner £42.

PENTREFOELAS Denbighshire

Map 3:A3

HAFOD ELWY HALL

Lost in the rolling heather moor and deep forest of the Hiraethog region, this 'characterful' B&B is on a working farm in the Denbighshire mountains. It is run by the owners, Roger and Wendy Charles-Warner, who have won awards for sustainability. In a low, grey farmhouse dating back to medieval times ('hafod' is Welsh for 'summer dwelling'), many historic features remain. There are slate floors, stone walls, a bread oven and 'lots of odd knick-knackery'. Two bedrooms have a four-poster bed; for larger groups, a suite has two double bedrooms and a single, sharing a large Edwardian bathroom. In the evenings, the 'always attentive' hosts prepare country-style dinners (special diets catered for by arrangement), perhaps home-made pâté; locally caught grey mullet; a tart of sweetened quinces. Meals are accompanied by just-picked vegetables from the farm. (No licence; bring your own wine.) Breakfast is abundant, with sausages, eggs and bacon from the farm's 'happy, free-range animals'. There are good walks from the front door; guests may also fish on the Alwen reservoir using the house's fishing rights. More reports, please.

Hiraethog, nr Pentrefoelas
LL16 5SP

T: 01690-770345
F: 01690-770266
E: enquiries@hafodelwyhall.co.uk
W: www.hafodelwyhall.co.uk

BEDROOMS: 3, 1 on ground floor suitable for &.
OPEN: all year.
FACILITIES: lounge, sun room, gun room, dining room, free Wi-Fi (limited), 60-acre grounds (private fishing).
BACKGROUND MUSIC: none.
LOCATION: 12 miles SE of Betws-y-Coed, 11 miles SW of Denbigh, 6½ miles N of Pentrefoelas off A543.
CHILDREN: not under 16.
DOGS: allowed in sun room and lounge 'if clean and well behaved', not in bedrooms.
CREDIT CARDS: MasterCard, Visa.
PRICES: per room B&B single £55–£85, double £75–£120. Set dinner £20. 1-night bookings refused high-season weekends.

PORTMEIRION Gwynedd

HOTEL PORTMEIRION

💫 *César award in 1990*

'Staying in Portmeirion is like living in a giant theatre set with hidden delights.' In woodlands on a Snowdonia peninsula, this 'quirky' resort has subtropical gardens, a beach, a stone boat, a shell grotto, a bell tower, a dog cemetery and a pan-tiled temple housing a golden statue of Buddha. 'Children particularly adore the fairy-tale aspect of the village.' Created in 1926 by the architect Sir Clough Williams-Ellis – who famously said, 'I would rather be vulgar than boring' – the village now welcomes 250,000 visitors a year (many just for the day). Overnight guests stay in the main hotel; the Victorian castellated mansion, *Castell Deudraeth*, or rooms, suites and curious, colourful cottages around the estate. Two new family suites were being created as the *Guide* went to press. Around the village, guests eat in a brasserie, an Italian-style trattoria or a self-service restaurant; in the hotel's main dining room overlooking the estuary, Mark Threadgill's modern menu might include sautéed langoustine tails, smoked apple purée; wild sea bass, crab tortellini, pak choi. 'Breakfast, cooked to order, was very good.' (*AT, and others*)

Minffordd
Penrhyndeudraeth LL48 6ER

T: 01766-770000
E: stay@portmeirion-village.com
W: www.portmeirion-village.com

BEDROOMS: 55, 14 in hotel, some on ground floor, 1 suitable for ♿; 11 in *Castell Deudraeth*, 30 in village.
OPEN: all year.
FACILITIES: hall, lift, 3 lounges, bar, restaurant, brasserie in *Castell*, children's supper room, function room, beauty salon, free Wi-Fi, civil wedding licence, 170-acre grounds (garden), heated swimming pool (8 by 15 metres, May–Sept).
BACKGROUND MUSIC: harpist Fri and Sat nights, Sun lunch during peak season.
LOCATION: 2 miles SE of Porthmadog.
CHILDREN: all ages welcomed.
DOGS: only guide dogs allowed.
CREDIT CARDS: all major cards.
PRICES: [2013] per person B&B £54.50–£119, D,B&B £79–£144.50. Set meals £39, à la carte £50. 1-night bookings sometimes refused.

PWLLHELI Gwynedd

Map 3:B2

THE OLD RECTORY

'A memorable stay.' In three acres of 'cared-for' gardens and paddocks, 'helpful and friendly hosts' Gary and Lindsay Ashcroft run a B&B in this Georgian former rectory near the village church. 'We were given the warmest of welcomes. Tea was offered in the sitting room as soon as we had settled in.' Bedrooms have complimentary sherry or sloe gin, and views of the grounds. 'Everything – from the furniture to the pictures to the pretty cups on the tea tray in the bedroom – has been chosen with care.' A 'cosy' twin room had 'comfortable' beds, an armchair and 'a light and airy feel'; a large bathroom was 'spotless' and had 'plenty of towels'. No evening meal is offered, but the Ashcrofts happily suggest nearby options. Guests sit together at a large table for breakfast, with help-yourself juices, cereals and yogurts, and 'delicious Aga-cooked local sausages and bacon'. Dogs are welcomed in a 'clean, well-built and sheltered kennel'; the house's Labradors are 'obedient' and discreet. This is a 'stunning' location ideal for 'enjoying the local beauty spots'. 'We felt that we had been truly spoilt.' (*Lynn and Ian James, and others*)

Boduan
nr Pwllheli LL53 6DT

T: 01758-721519
E: theashcrofts@theoldrectory.net
W: www.theoldrectory.net

BEDROOMS: 3, also self-catering cottage.
OPEN: all year except Christmas.
FACILITIES: drawing room, dining room, free Wi-Fi, 3½-acre grounds, walking, riding, sailing.
BACKGROUND MUSIC: none.
LOCATION: 4 miles NW of Pwllheli.
CHILDREN: all ages welcomed.
DOGS: not allowed in house (kennel and run available).
CREDIT CARDS: MasterCard, Visa.
PRICES: [2013] per room B&B £75–£105. 1-night bookings sometimes refused high season and bank holidays.

PWLLHELI Gwynedd

PLAS BODEGROES

♧César award in 1992

'The warmth of the welcome and the relaxing ambience ensure our repeated visits to this romantic retreat.' Praise in 2013 for Chris and Gunna Chown's restaurant-with-rooms, in a Georgian house on the remote Lleyn peninsula. The Grade II listed building is approached down an avenue of 200-year-old beeches; inside, 'caring staff' and 'excellent, imaginative cooking' create an 'outstanding' experience. In a dining room decorated with modern Welsh paintings, Chris Chown and Hugh Bracegirdle prepare 'beautifully presented' modern interpretations of traditional dishes. These might include Arbroath smokie tart, watercress salad, saffron crème fraîche; bara brith and butter pudding, Welsh whisky ice cream. Painted in muted heritage shades, the Scandinavian-style bedrooms overlook the 'exceptionally attractive' gardens; two bathrooms have recently been refurbished. Guests may request morning tea and coffee in their room; afternoon tea is taken on the rose- and wisteria-covered veranda. There is an 'excellent selection' at breakfast. (*Wendy Andrews, and others*)

Nefyn Road
Efailnewydd
Pwllheli LL53 5TH

T: 01758-612363
F: 01758-701247
E: gunna@bodegroes.co.uk
W: www.bodegroes.co.uk

BEDROOMS: 10, 2 in courtyard cottage.
OPEN: Mar–Nov, closed Sun and Mon except bank holidays.
FACILITIES: lounge, bar, breakfast room, restaurant, free Wi-Fi, 5-acre grounds, unsuitable for &.
BACKGROUND MUSIC: none.
LOCATION: 1 mile W of Pwllheli.
CHILDREN: all ages welcomed, but no under-5s in restaurant.
DOGS: not allowed in public rooms, 1 bedroom.
CREDIT CARDS: MasterCard, Visa.
PRICES: [2013] per room B&B £130–£180. D,B&B (2 nights) £195–£245 per person, set dinner £45. 1-night bookings sometimes refused.

REYNOLDSTON Swansea

Map 3:E2

FAIRYHILL

Standing in extensive grounds in the unspoilt
Gower peninsula, this small country hotel, in an
18th-century Georgian mansion, has picture
windows, an open fire in the bar, and 'friendly,
attentive' staff. It is owned by Andrew
Hetherington and Paul Davies. It is well liked
for its restaurant, where guests will find
'exemplary service and an excellent meal', a
visitor said this year. Neil Hollis, the chef, bases
his menus on local produce, perhaps Welsh
Cheddar and red onion soufflé, beetroot salad;
sea bream, pak choi, laverbread butter sauce.
The hotel's walled garden provides fruit,
vegetables and herbs. 'We sat outside on the
lawn in the sunshine, having drinks before
dinner. Amuse-gueule (delicious) were brought
to the table; we had terrine followed by hake,
both of the highest standard.' The 'well-
equipped' bedrooms are individually styled:
some have tartan armchairs, others painted
beams, still others boldly striped wallpaper. The
surrounding grounds have an ornamental lake
and ancient orchard, with woodlands beyond;
closer to home base, guests play croquet on the
front lawn. Holistic therapy treatments can be
booked in advance. (*AR*)

Reynoldston, Gower
nr Swansea SA3 1BS

T: 01792-390139
F: 01792-391358
E: postbox@fairyhill.net
W: www.fairyhill.net

BEDROOMS: 8.
OPEN: all year except 24–26 Dec,
first 3 weeks in Jan.
FACILITIES: lounge, bar, 3 dining
rooms, meeting room, free Wi-Fi,
civil wedding licence, spa treatment
room, 24-acre grounds, unsuitable
for &.
BACKGROUND MUSIC: jazz/classical/
pop in lounge, bar, dining room at
mealtimes.
LOCATION: 11 miles W of Swansea.
CHILDREN: not under 8.
DOGS: 'well-behaved' dogs allowed
in bedrooms, no dogs in public
rooms.
CREDIT CARDS: MasterCard, Visa.
PRICES: [2013] per room B&B single
£160–£260, double £180–£280.
D,B&B £115–£185 per person, set
lunch £20–£25, set dinner £35–£45.
1-night bookings refused Sat.

ST DAVID'S Pembrokeshire

CRUG-GLAS

On an 'immaculate' working farm in open countryside, this restaurant-with-rooms is run by owners Perkin and Janet Evans. 'They were as welcoming as ever,' says a returning visitor this year. 'Her cooking is exceptional.' Another comment: 'A most unusual place, with friendly service and attractive grounds.' The Georgian house has a 'comfortable and relaxing' drawing room, which has a 'lovely' grandfather clock, ornaments, paintings and family photographs, games, books and magazines. Pre-dinner drinks are taken from an honesty bar 'with a reasonable selection of beers, wines and spirits'. Guests are asked to choose in advance from a menu 'with wide choice' for dinner in a smartly furnished room with a 'happy atmosphere'. Typical dishes: Abercastle crab cake; monkfish tails, spinach, blue cheese sauce. Side dishes of vegetables and potatoes show 'no signs of portion control'. The bedrooms vary in size: 'Our well-appointed and -furnished room had an interesting tin bath in the corner.' A room at the top of the house was 'as big as a London flat'. Breakfast has 'the widest choice of fresh fruits seen anywhere'. (*Peter Adam, David RW Jervois*)

25% DISCOUNT VOUCHERS

nr Abereiddy, St David's
Haverfordwest SA62 6XX

T: 01348-831302
E: janet@crugglas.plus.com
W: www.crug-glas.co.uk

BEDROOMS: 7, 2 in coach house, 1 on ground floor.
OPEN: all year except 22–28 Dec.
FACILITIES: drawing room, dining room, free Wi-Fi, civil wedding licence, 1-acre garden on 600-acre farm.
BACKGROUND MUSIC: classical in restaurant.
LOCATION: 3½ miles NE of St David's.
CHILDREN: not under 12.
DOGS: allowed in one suite only, not in public rooms.
CREDIT CARDS: Amex, MasterCard, Visa.
PRICES: per room B&B £115–£170. À la carte £32.

SKENFRITH Monmouthshire

Map 3:D4

THE BELL AT SKENFRITH

By a bridge over the River Monnow, this refurbished 17th-century coaching inn is run 'smoothly and precisely' by owners Janet and William Hutchings. 'Nothing here is out of place.' Named after brown trout fishing flies – a guest called this 'a fisherman's hotel' in a 'masculine' style – bedrooms have freshly ground coffee, fresh milk and home-made shortbread biscuits. There are Welsh blankets on the beds; attic suites have exposed oak beams. 'The view from our room, Wickham's Fancy, was of cultivated fields and undulating hills.' There is an 'interesting' wine list in the 'elegant, well-run' dining room, where chef Kieran Gough's modern dishes use local produce, heritage vegetables from the large kitchen garden, and hams and sausages from *The Bell*'s own pigs. 'The food is well worth coming here for. We enjoyed our dinner and its ambition.' Guests staying for three nights would have preferred more daily changes on the menu. There are good walks from the front door, with detailed maps leading guests across farmland and along river banks; a children's detective trail introduces young sleuths to the medieval Skenfrith Castle. (*David Berry, and others*)

25% DISCOUNT VOUCHERS

Skenfrith NP7 8UH

T: 01600-750235
F: 01600-750525
E: enquiries@skenfrith.co.uk
W: www.skenfrith.co.uk

BEDROOMS: 11.
OPEN: all year except Tues Nov–Mar (not Christmas fortnight).
FACILITIES: open sitting area, bar, restaurant, private dining room, free Wi-Fi, 1-acre grounds, only restaurant suitable for &.
BACKGROUND MUSIC: none.
LOCATION: 9 miles W of Ross-on-Wye.
CHILDREN: all ages welcomed, organic menu at children's high tea, no under-8s in restaurant in the evening.
DOGS: not unattended in bedrooms, not allowed in restaurant.
CREDIT CARDS: MasterCard, Visa.
PRICES: [2013] per person B&B single (Sun–Thurs) £75–£120, double £55–£110. À la carte £30. 1-night bookings refused Sat, bank holidays.

TALSARNAU Gwynedd

Map 3:B3

MAES-Y-NEUADD

❦ *César award in 2003*

There are nooks and crannies aplenty in this 14th-century slate- and granite-built manor house on a wooded hillside between Snowdon and the sea. A 'laid-back place' in 'a wonderful, peaceful location', it is run as a small hotel by Lynn Jackson and her brother-in-law, Peter Payne. There are thick stone walls and oak beams; a newly refurbished bar has leather chesterfields; home-made biscuits with morning coffee. 'Service, atmosphere and food are all spot on.' In the main building and converted coach house, bedrooms vary considerably in style: some have a four-poster bed, others 16th-century beams and a log-burning stove. Most have views of the mountains or the coastline of Cardigan Bay; all have a plate of fresh fruit and a decanter of home-made sloe gin. Two restored walled gardens provide herbs, vegetables and fruit for the restaurant, where chef John Owen Jones cooks 'a fusion of modern Welsh, traditional English and classic French' dishes, perhaps duck, pork and pistachio pâté, whisky and orange confit; redcurrant and port-marinated Welsh lamb steak, rosemary potatoes. (*GH*)

25% DISCOUNT VOUCHERS

Talsarnau LL47 6YA

T: 01766-780200
F: 01766-780211
E: maes@neuadd.com
W: www.neuadd.com

BEDROOMS: 15, 4 in coach house, 3 on ground floor.
OPEN: all year.
FACILITIES: lift, ramps, lounge, bar, conservatory, family dining room, main dining room, free Wi-Fi (in conservatory only), civil wedding licence, terrace, 20-acre grounds.
BACKGROUND MUSIC: traditional music during special breaks.
LOCATION: 3 miles NE of Harlech.
CHILDREN: all ages welcomed but no under-8s in main dining room at night.
DOGS: allowed in 2 bedrooms only.
CREDIT CARDS: MasterCard, Visa.
PRICES: [2013] per person B&B £54–£108, D,B&B £93–£148. Set dinner £30–£35, à la carte £44.

TYWYN Gwynedd

Map 3:B3

DOLFFANOG FAWR

In good walking country with magnificent driving scenery ('for those less active'), this small guest house is 'professionally run' by the owners Alex Yorke and Lorraine Hinkins. 'They like to chat and give advice on potential routes for ramblers and climbers,' say the nominators. There are no house rules (except for the times of the meals). Guests take a three-course no-choice dinner communally. 'We had been asked for our likes and dislikes when booking. Other guests regaled us with the delights to come, and we were indeed impressed.' Service in the 'attractive' dining room was 'perfect'. A typical menu: home-made fishcakes; Arthog pork fillet, Puy lentils, Dijonnaise sauce, sautéed potatoes, cauliflower; yogurt panna cotta, rhubarb compote. The extensive wine list 'reflects Alex's hobby and travels'. 'We were nervous of the communal aspect but the conversations were interesting and informative.' Three of the bedrooms in the restored 18th-century farmhouse have a large window seat from which to admire the view of Lake Talyllyn. A small well-appointed room had 'good lighting and storage, a sparkling bathroom'. Breakfast is 'generous, especially at this price'. (*D and JA*)

Talyllyn
Tywyn LL36 9AJ

T: 01654-761247
E: info@dolffanogfawr.co.uk
W: www.dolffanogfawr.co.uk

BEDROOMS: 4.
OPEN: mid-Mar–Oct, dining room closed Sun/Mon except bank holidays.
FACILITIES: lounge, dining room, free Wi-Fi, 1-acre garden, unsuitable for &.
BACKGROUND MUSIC: varied.
LOCATION: by lake 10 miles E of Tywyn.
CHILDREN: not under 7.
DOGS: allowed in bedrooms and lounge.
CREDIT CARDS: MasterCard, Visa.
PRICES: [2013] per person B&B £50. Set menu £25. 1-night bookings sometimes refused.

CHANNEL ISLANDS

St Peter Port, Guernsey

HERM

Map 1: inset D6

THE WHITE HOUSE

César award in 1987

There are no televisions, clocks or telephones in the bedrooms of the only hotel on this small, car-free island. Asked if there is background music in the restaurants, the manager, Siôn Dobson Jones, writes NO (underlined). 'The only sounds might be the occasional tractor or the piping of oystercatchers,' wrote returning fans, who report this year that 'everything is as good as ever'. Tradition is 'cherished': guests are asked to dress up for dinner (jacket and tie for men) in the conservatory restaurant where the chef, Nigel Waylen, uses locally caught fish and shellfish for his daily-changing menus. Younger diners are given high tea; baby-listening is available. All ages can eat together informally at the *Ship Inn* brasserie. There is good storage in the 'light and airy' bedrooms, which are decorated in neutral colours; the bathrooms are well equipped. In the hotel grounds are tennis, croquet and a solar-heated swimming pool. It might take only a morning to walk around the island, but there is much to see: six white sand beaches, cliff-path walks with wild flowers, wildlife (puffins in season). (*Nigel and Jennifer Jee*)

Herm, via Guernsey GY1 3HR

T: 01481-750075
F: 01481-710066
E: hotel@herm.com
W: www.herm.com

BEDROOMS: 40, 18 in cottages, some on ground floor.
OPEN: 28 Mar–5 Oct.
FACILITIES: 3 lounges, 2 bars, 2 restaurants, conference room, wedding facilities, free Wi-Fi, 1-acre garden (tennis, croquet, 7-metre solar-heated swimming pool), beach 200 yds, Herm unsuitable for &.
BACKGROUND MUSIC: none.
LOCATION: by harbour, air/sea to Guernsey, then ferry from Guernsey (20 mins).
CHILDREN: all ages welcomed.
DOGS: allowed in 1 room, not allowed in public rooms.
CREDIT CARDS: MasterCard, Visa.
PRICES: [2013] per person D,B&B £95–£150. Set dinner £27.50. 1-night bookings refused Sat.

ST BRELADE Jersey

Map 1: inset E6

THE ATLANTIC HOTEL

In a 'wonderful, quiet location', this luxury hotel stands like an ocean liner above the five-mile beach at St Ouen's Bay. 'A modern hotel but with character', it was opened in 1970 by Henry Burke, and is now run by his son, Patrick. Mark Yates is the manager. The 'very comfortable' bedrooms are well equipped: they are decorated in muted colours; there are large beds, good lighting, rugs on wooden floors; marble bathrooms. Some rooms have a full-length, sliding window and a terrace or a Juliet balcony. The 'pleasant' public rooms have antique terracotta flagstones, a wrought iron staircase, rich carpeting, urns, fountains, antiques, specially designed furniture. The *Ocean* restaurant, in blue, white and beige, reflects the coastal setting. Here, head chef Mark Jordan has a *Michelin* star for his sophisticated cooking. Local ingredients are used whenever possible for his daily-changing set menu, which might include butter-poached lobster surprise; pot-roast squab pigeon with pear and blue cheese risotto. The large grounds, surrounded by pine and palm trees, have well-tended flowerbeds, and lawns which slope down to a swimming pool. More reports, please.

Le Mont de la Pulente
St Brelade JE3 8HE

T: 01534-744101
F: 01534-744102
E: info@theatlantichotel.com
W: www.theatlantichotel.com

BEDROOMS: 50, some on ground floor.
OPEN: 1 Feb–2 Jan.
FACILITIES: lift, lounge, library, cocktail bar, restaurant, private dining room, fitness centre (swimming pool, sauna, mini-gym), free Wi-Fi, wedding facilities, 6-acre garden (tennis, indoor and outdoor heated swimming pools, 10 by 5 metres), unsuitable for &.
BACKGROUND MUSIC: in restaurant.
LOCATION: 5 miles W of St Helier.
CHILDREN: all ages welcomed.
DOGS: not allowed.
CREDIT CARDS: all major cards.
PRICES: [2013] per room B&B £150–£350, D,B&B £250–£450. Set dinner £55, à la carte £65.

SEE ALSO SHORTLIST

ST SAVIOUR Jersey

Map 1: inset E6

LONGUEVILLE MANOR

'Extremely well run', this extended 14th-century manor house has been run as a luxurious hotel (Relais & Châteaux) by the Lewis family for six decades. Today Malcolm Lewis, his wife, Patricia, and her brother-in-law, Pedro Bento, are in charge. Patricia Lewis oversaw the renovation of the public rooms to incorporate contemporary elements while retaining the feel of a Jersey manor house. They are furnished with antiques, original paintings, bold floral decorations. Afternoon tea is an event: 'real leaf tea, poured for you'. Bedrooms are spacious, blending modern fabrics with traditional textiles. Even a standard room has a sitting area with soft chairs; 'the bed was comfortable; copious cushions were removed at turn-down'; there are local toiletries in the bathroom. An 'immaculate' kitchen garden in the grounds supplies vegetables and herbs for the cooking of chef Andrew Baird. His modern menu might include roast saddle of rabbit wrapped in Parma ham, cannelloni, carrot and cumin. Breakfast has a buffet with champagne alongside the fruit juices; cheeses, ham on the bone; the usual range of cooked dishes. More reports, please.

Longueville Road
St Saviour JE2 7WF

T: 01534-725501
F: 01534-731613
E: info@longuevillemanor.com
W: www.longuevillemanor.com

BEDROOMS: 31, 8 on ground floor, 2 in cottage.
OPEN: all year.
FACILITIES: lift, ramp, 2 lounges, cocktail bar, 2 dining rooms, free Wi-Fi, function/conference/wedding facilities, 15-acre grounds (croquet, tennis, heated swimming pool, woodland), sea 1 mile.
BACKGROUND MUSIC: in restaurant.
LOCATION: 1½ miles E of St Helier.
CHILDREN: all ages welcomed.
DOGS: not allowed in public rooms.
CREDIT CARDS: all major cards.
PRICES: [2013] per room B&B £175–£570, D,B&B £250–£645. Set dinner £57.50, à la carte £80.

SARK

Map 1: inset E6

LA SABLONNERIE

'As wonderful as ever; eating lunch in the garden is the nearest thing I know to paradise.' Renewed praise this year comes from a returning visitor to Elizabeth Perrée's whitewashed 16th-century farmhouse on a charming car-free island noted for its abundant flora and fauna. Ms Perrée, whose parents transformed a tumbledown building into this small hotel 65 years ago, is ever present, on friendly terms with her guests. 'Not only does she greet returning visitors by name; on departure one gets kisses plus a bottle of wine.' The most spacious bedrooms are in small buildings in the garden. Beds, with sheets and blankets, are comfortable and, at night, all is quiet; there is no light pollution: Sark is the first designated 'dark sky' island. 'Our favourite room over the bar has lovely views; we have never found it noisy.' The dining room (free of background music) has formal place settings: chef Colin Day's daily-changing menu might include baby courgette flowers filled with lobster mousse; caramelised Barbary duck, sarladaise potato, green peppercorn and sage jus. A pony and trap transports visitors from the ferry. (*John Barnes*)

Little Sark
Sark, via Guernsey GY10 1SD

T: 01481-832061
F: 01481-832408
E: reservations@sablonneriesark.com
W: www.sablonneriesark.com

BEDROOMS: 22, also accommodation in nearby cottages.
OPEN: Easter–Oct.
FACILITIES: 3 lounges, 2 bars, restaurant, Wi-Fi not available, wedding facilities, 1-acre garden (tea garden/bar, croquet), Sark unsuitable for &.
BACKGROUND MUSIC: classical/piano in bar.
LOCATION: S part of island, boat from Guernsey (hotel will meet).
CHILDREN: all ages welcomed.
DOGS: allowed at hotel's discretion, but not in public rooms.
CREDIT CARDS: MasterCard, Visa.
PRICES: per person B&B £40–£97.50, D,B&B £69.50–£165. Set meal £29.50, à la carte £49.50 (*excluding 10% service charge*).

IRELAND

Kinsale, Co. Cork

BAGENALSTOWN Co. Carlow

Map 6:C6

⚜ LORUM OLD RECTORY

César award: Irish guest house of the year

'A charming house in a scenic landscape; a wonderful host and a most pleasant atmosphere.' 'A perfect short stay; Bobbie Smith's hospitality is warm in her beautiful and comfortable home.' This year's praise for this ever-popular guest house, a Victorian rectory in the 'picturesque' Barrow valley. A member of Euro-Toques, dedicated to using local and organic produce, Bobbie Smith serves an 'excellent' five-course dinner. 'I plan what I am going to cook and discuss it with the people staying,' she says. Dinner is served communally around a large mahogany table in the red dining room. Tea and home-baked scones, and after-dinner port, may be taken by a log fire in the drawing room with its books, family photographs and memorabilia. 'The house is furnished and decorated with obvious passion for detail.' The spacious, high-ceilinged bedrooms have 'perfect proportions'; some have a four-poster bed; all have good views. The 'wonderful', leisurely breakfast has fresh orange juice, a good full Irish, home-baked breads, much fruit. (*Mavis and Neil Crump, and others*)

Kilgreaney, Bagenalstown

T: 00 353 59-977 5282
F: 00 353 59-977 5455
E: bobbie@lorum.com
W: www.lorum.com

BEDROOMS: 4.
OPEN: Feb–Nov.
FACILITIES: drawing room, study, dining room, free Wi-Fi, wedding facilities, 1-acre garden (croquet), 18-acre grounds, unsuitable for ♿.
BACKGROUND MUSIC: none.
LOCATION: 4 miles S of Bagenalstown.
CHILDREN: all ages welcomed.
DOGS: allowed by arrangement.
CREDIT CARDS: MasterCard, Visa.
PRICES: per person B&B €75. Set dinner €45.

BALLINGARRY Co. Limerick

Map 6:D5

THE MUSTARD SEED AT ECHO LODGE

'Peaceful, elegant and charming', this Victorian lodge in 'interesting' gardens near the village of Adare is run in personal style by the owner, Daniel Mullane. 'He welcomed us as if we were family,' say visitors this year. 'He took us to the library where we chatted about our journey. Tea, scones, soda bread and Alpine strawberry jam (all home-made) appeared effortlessly.' The house has a 'quirky' decor: 'Unusual paintings and artefacts cover every wall and surface; porcelain elephants, lovely china and glassware, books galore.' The large gardens ('worth exploring') supply much of the produce for the restaurant (popular locally). Angel Pirev's 'excellent' menus might include baked turbot, pearl barley and smoked salmon risotto; assiette of rabbit, shiitake mushrooms, potato farl, parsley cream. Dishes are 'beautifully presented'; a vegetarian was 'well catered for'. The bedrooms have a mix of styles: 'Our room was elegant; the bathroom was old-fashioned in the best sense.' Breakfast has eggs from hens in the grounds, porridge with a shot of Irish whiskey. 'Not cheap, but special and personal.' (*Dr Helena Shaw, Mamie Atkins, John Lawrie*)

Ballingarry

T: 00 353 69-68508
F: 00 353 69-68511
E: mustard@indigo.ie
W: www.mustardseed.ie

BEDROOMS: 15, 1, on ground floor, suitable for &.
OPEN: all year except 24–26 Dec, mid-Jan–1 Feb.
FACILITIES: lounge, library, dining room, free Wi-Fi (in public areas, some bedrooms), wedding facilities, 12-acre grounds.
BACKGROUND MUSIC: in restaurant.
LOCATION: in village, 18 miles SW of Limerick.
CHILDREN: all ages welcomed.
DOGS: not allowed in public rooms.
CREDIT CARDS: Amex, MasterCard, Visa.
PRICES: [2013] per person B&B €65–€165, D,B&B €99–€170. Set menus €42–€60.

BALLYLICKEY Co. Cork

SEAVIEW HOUSE

In large grounds above Bantry Bay, this extended, white, bay-windowed Victorian building was the family home of Kathleen O'Sullivan. 'Kindly and thoughtful', she has run it, in hands-on fashion, as a small hotel for more than 30 years. The atmosphere is traditional ('perhaps in a time warp,' said a visitor this year). There is a library with books in mahogany cases, and a lounge filled with antiques, flowers, a 'vast collection' of paintings, ornaments. Conversation not background music can be heard in the bar, which is often busy with locals. The chef, Eleanor O'Donovan, serves generous portions of country house dishes on an extensive menu in the conservatory restaurant. 'Our meal was good: decent home-made bread; rack of lamb cooked exactly as requested and served with a fine selection of vegetables. It was fair value, as was the wine list.' Bedrooms, which vary in size, are in the old house and in an extension. Those at the front of the house have sea views (through the mature trees in the grounds). A 'good' breakfast has a large buffet; interesting cooked dishes. (*EC, and others*)

25% DISCOUNT VOUCHERS

Ballylickey, Bantry Bay

T: 00 353 27-50073
F: 00 353 27-51555
E: info@seaviewhousehotel.com
W: www.seaviewhousehotel.com

BEDROOMS: 25, 2, on ground floor, suitable for &.
OPEN: mid-Mar–mid-Nov.
FACILITIES: bar, library, 2 lounges, restaurant/conservatory, free Wi-Fi, wedding facilities, 3-acre grounds on waterfront (fishing, boating), riding, golf nearby.
BACKGROUND MUSIC: none.
LOCATION: 3 miles N of Bantry.
CHILDREN: all ages welcomed, special menus and babysitting available.
DOGS: not allowed in public rooms.
CREDIT CARDS: Amex, MasterCard, Visa.
PRICES: per person B&B €60–€85, D,B&B €95–€105. Set dinner €35–€45.

BALLYMOTE Co. Sligo

Map 6:B5

TEMPLE HOUSE `NEW`

On an estate that has been home to the Perceval family since 1665, this Georgian mansion (remodelled in 1864) is surrounded by parkland with a lake and the ruin of a Knights Templar castle. 'We are not a boutique hotel but a historic home,' say Roderick and Helena Perceval, the current custodians, who welcome guests 'with a warm handshake'. 'Highly recommended' by a *Guide* inspector in 2013, the house 'retains a lived-in feel (with the odd paintwork scuffs), despite considerable recent renovation'. The entrance vestibule has stags' heads, a collection of fossils, boots for guests; a sweeping staircase leads to the bedrooms. 'They have high ceiling, big windows, heavy curtains, country prints; our room, painted in deep lavender, had a huge wardrobe, dressing table and boudoir seat; a modern bathroom.' Guests gather for pre-dinner drinks in a drawing room with French windows overlooking the terraced garden. A set meal (dislikes discussed) is taken communally at a large mahogany table dressed with family silver. 'We enjoyed generous portions of salmon terrine (delicious home-made bread); lamb cutlets with a tomato and rosemary jus; a decent Irish cheeseboard.'

Ballinacarrow
nr Ballymote

T: 00 353 71-918 3329
E: stay@templehouse.ie
W: www.templehouse.ie

BEDROOMS: 7.
OPEN: Apr–Nov, dining room closed Sun eve.
FACILITIES: drawing room, snooker room, dining room, free Wi-Fi in some bedrooms, 1½-acre garden, 1,000-acre estate, unsuitable for &.
BACKGROUND MUSIC: none.
LOCATION: 12 miles S of Sligo.
CHILDREN: all ages welcomed.
DOGS: not allowed in house.
CREDIT CARDS: MasterCard, Visa.
PRICES: per person B&B €80–€95. Set dinner €47.

BANGOR Co. Down

Map 6:B6

CAIRN BAY LODGE

On the outskirts of a resort town on the Belfast
Lough, this white, pebble-dashed seaside villa
is run as a B&B by the 'delightful, attentive'
owners, Chris and Jenny Mullen. 'They were
most accommodating when we needed to check
in early,' says a visitor this year. Two oak-
panelled lounges at the front of the house have
a 'beautiful view' of Ballyholme Bay: they are
furnished with antiques, 'quirky finds', 'lots of
books and magazines'. The bedrooms are well
equipped, with 'thoughtful touches' including a
tea/coffee tray with snacks; rooms at the front
have views across a west-facing beach. 'Our
bright and spacious room had a comfortable bed
and a balcony.' Guests appreciate the fresh milk
and home-baked cake left on a dresser on the
landing. Breakfast has a buffet of fruit juices
and cereals. Chris Mullen's interesting cooked
dishes include smoked salmon omelette, rocket
and dill, lemon crème fraîche; Copeland Island
crab with scrambled eggs and chilli jam. Jenny
Mullen, a beauty therapist, offers treatments in a
salon; there is a small gift shop. (*Mrs E Davison,
Heather Armond, and others*)

25% DISCOUNT VOUCHERS

278 Seacliff Road
Ballyholme, Bangor
BT20 5HS

T: 028-9146 7636
F: 028-9145 7728
E: info@cairnbaylodge.com
W: www.cairnbaylodge.com

BEDROOMS: 7, plus 2 self-catering
villas each sleeping 8.
OPEN: Feb–Dec.
FACILITIES: 2 lounges, dining room,
free Wi-Fi, beauty salon, small
shop, ½-acre garden, unsuitable
for &.
BACKGROUND MUSIC: in dining
room during breakfast.
LOCATION: ¼ mile E of centre.
CHILDREN: all ages welcomed.
DOGS: not allowed.
CREDIT CARDS: MasterCard, Visa.
PRICES: per person B&B £45–£50.
1-night bookings refused weekends
in high season.

CAPPOQUIN Co. Waterford

Map 6:D5

RICHMOND HOUSE

In the Blackwater valley, 'an attractive area off the main tourist routes', this 'charming' country house is run in 'relaxed' style as a small hotel and restaurant by the owners, Paul and Claire Deevy. Built for the Earl of Cork in 1704, the house is decorated with hunting and fishing trophies. It has a homely feel; many of the long-serving staff are local. The public rooms have been furnished with 'appropriate' antiques and have flowers, chintz and floral wallpaper. The bedrooms vary considerably in size: they are decorated in country house style, and have period pieces. Food is an 'important attraction': Paul Deevy supports local producers for the ingredients for his seasonal menus (with daily changes); vegetables and herbs come from the garden. The portions are generous in dishes like chorizo risotto, steamed mussels, light butter sauce; seared breast of duckling, confit of duck leg, braised red cabbage. Background music might be 'intrusive' in the dining room. Muffins and scones come straight from the oven at breakfast which has 'lots of fresh fruit including pineapple and raspberries'. The hot dishes have 'excellent' ingredients.

Cappoquin

T: 00 353 58-54278
F: 00 353 58-54988
E: info@richmondhouse.net
W: www.richmondhouse.net

BEDROOMS: 10.
OPEN: 15 Jan–23 Dec, restaurant normally closed Sun/Mon except July and Aug.
FACILITIES: lounge, restaurant, free Wi-Fi, 12-acre grounds, fishing, golf, pony trekking nearby, unsuitable for &.
BACKGROUND MUSIC: 'easy listening' in restaurant.
LOCATION: ½ mile E of Cappoquin.
CHILDREN: all ages welcomed.
DOGS: not allowed.
CREDIT CARDS: all major cards.
PRICES: [2013] per person B&B €60–€70. Early bird dinner €28–€33, set dinner €55.

CARAGH LAKE Co. Kerry

Map 6:D4

CARRIG COUNTRY HOUSE

'If you were looking for a room with a view, this is a candidate,' said an inspector visiting Frank and Mary Slattery's country hotel on the wooded shore of Caragh Lake. The welcome, on first-name terms, is 'warm'. Visitors arriving early after a dawn flight were ushered into the dining room for a late breakfast and given immediate access to their bedroom. Rooms are decorated in period style ('old-fashioned and appealing'), with antiques, matching dark wood furniture, flowered fabrics. The best rooms have a view of the lake, across to the hills opposite; others look out over the big gardens. Soft classical background music plays in the 'pleasant' drawing room; another smaller lounge, a snug and the library are quiet. The candlelit restaurant is open to non-residents. The chef, Patricia Teahan, cooks modern Irish and international dishes, perhaps sautéed chicken livers, pancetta, garlic crostini and rocket; seared John Dory, caramelised artichoke, basil sauce, crispy squid. Breakfast has a generous buffet table with compotes, cereals, yogurts and jam; delicious breads; 'good' scrambled eggs. 'I often feel short-changed as a non-cooked-breakfast eater; not here.'

25% DISCOUNT VOUCHERS

Caragh Lake
Killorglin

T: 00 353 66-976 9100
E: info@carrighouse.com
W: www.carrighouse.com

BEDROOMS: 17, some on ground floor.
OPEN: Mar–Nov, restaurant open only at weekends Mar/Apr.
FACILITIES: 2 lounges, snug, library, TV room, dining room, free Wi-Fi, wedding facilities, 4-acre garden on lake.
BACKGROUND MUSIC: classical in lounge and restaurant.
LOCATION: 22 miles W of Killarney.
CHILDREN: not under 8 (except infants under 12 months).
DOGS: not allowed in house (kennel available).
CREDIT CARDS: MasterCard, Visa.
PRICES: [2013] per person B&B €75–€155, D,B&B from €99. Set dinner €45, à la carte €42.

CASHEL BAY Co. Galway

Map 6:C4

CASHEL HOUSE

'The highlight of our Irish trip; a very pleasant staff and good all-round service.' Praise this year for the McEvilly family's 19th-century mansion which they have run as a country house hotel for over 40 years. The family matriarch, Kay McEvilly, remains a dominant presence and might be found working in the 'lovely' gardens. 'We were given immediate help with our luggage and offered tea in one of the excellent lounges. The decor is slightly old-fashioned, rather chintzy, but none the worse for that.' The bedrooms vary in size and aspect; 'Our first room seemed fine, but we were spontaneously offered a bigger ground-floor room that had a magnificent window looking on to the garden.' In the conservatory restaurant, chef John O'Toole serves an Irish country house menu of dishes like steamed Killary mussels in chilli, coconut and lemongrass cream; rack and braised shoulder of lamb in Guinness, honey and sweet shallot sauce. 'The set menu had too many courses for us; we preferred dining à la carte for an enjoyable, if not gourmet, meal.' (*Jeremy Christie-Brown*)

Cashel Bay

T: 00 353 95-31001
F: 00 353 95-31077
E: res@cashel-house-hotel.com
W: www.cashel-house-hotel.com

BEDROOMS: 29.
OPEN: all year except Jan.
FACILITIES: ramps, 2 lounges, bar, library, dining room/conservatory, free Wi-Fi, wedding facilities, 50-acre grounds (tennis, riding, small private beach).
BACKGROUND MUSIC: harpist plays occasionally at dinner.
LOCATION: 42 miles NW of Galway.
CHILDREN: all ages welcomed.
DOGS: not allowed in public rooms.
CREDIT CARDS: Amex, MasterCard, Visa.
PRICES: [2013] (*10% service charge added*) per room B&B single €95–€190, double €170–€315. D,B&B €50 per person added. Set dinner €58.

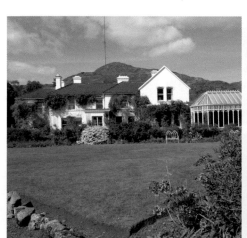

CASTLEHILL Co. Mayo

Map 6:B4

ENNISCOE HOUSE

Described as the last great house in north Mayo, this handsome Georgian mansion has been the home of the Kellett family for centuries. Susan Kellett, of the thirteenth generation, runs it as a private hotel with her son, always known as DJ. 'The sort of place the *Guide* is all about', the place has a relaxed grandeur. A massive front door opens on to a high-ceilinged hall. Through another door is an 'extraordinary' elliptical staircase: 'It's not the drink, the treads really do slope towards the centre of the curve.' This leads to the three front bedrooms which face the lough. Other staircases lead to further bedrooms. The Rose Room has a canopy bed, wardrobe and dressing table; two armchairs and an upholstered window seat with the view. 'Susan and DJ are happy to explain the antiques and family memorabilia' in the two vast sitting rooms. In the dining room, the 'lovely' wooden tables are well spaced. The menu has two choices for each course. Typical dishes: smoked mackerel pâté on sour bread toast; roast fillet of lamb with anchovy and mint. (*Esler Crawford, and others*)

Castlehill, Ballina

T: 00 353 96-31112
F: 00 353 96-31773
E: mail@enniscoe.com
W: www.enniscoe.com

BEDROOMS: 6, plus self-catering units behind house.
OPEN: Apr–Oct, groups only at New Year.
FACILITIES: 2 sitting rooms, dining room, free Wi-Fi, wedding facilities, 150-acre estate (garden, tea room, farm, heritage centre, conference centre, forge, fishing), unsuitable for &.
BACKGROUND MUSIC: none.
LOCATION: 2 miles S of Crossmolina.
CHILDREN: all ages welcomed.
DOGS: not allowed in public rooms, some bedrooms.
CREDIT CARDS: MasterCard, Visa.
PRICES: per person B&B €98–€130, D,B&B €146–€178. Set menus €30–€50.

CASTLELYONS Co. Cork

Map 6:D5

BALLYVOLANE HOUSE

❦ *César award in 2009*

In their family home, a fine Georgian house, Justin and Jenny Green entertain guests in relaxed house-party style. There are no keys for the 'lovely old' bedrooms, which are furnished in informal country house style. There are big beds, and all the necessary facilities – a radio as well as television, tea- and coffee-making kit, home-made blackcurrant cordial and a jar of freshly baked cookies. Visitors seeking greater informality can choose a 'glamping' option in the summer, sleeping in bell tents in the grounds. They have proper beds, a tea-light chandelier; 'luxurious loos' are in an adjacent wash house. Glamping guests can take the full Irish breakfast, which is served in the house until noon. All breads, pastries, jams and marmalade are made in the kitchen. House guests take drinks from an honesty bar in the drawing room before a communal dinner at a mahogany table. The vegetables for Teena Mahon's country house meals may have been picked that afternoon from the walled garden, tended by Justin Green's father, Jeremy. The Greens have four beats on the River Blackwater.

25% DISCOUNT VOUCHERS

Castlelyons, Fermoy

T: 00 353 25-36349
F: 00 353 25-36781
E: info@ballyvolanehouse.ie
W: www.ballyvolanehouse.ie

BEDROOMS: 6.
OPEN: all year except Christmas/New Year, closed Mon–Wed in winter.
FACILITIES: hall, drawing room, honesty bar, dining room, free Wi-Fi, wedding facilities, 80-acre grounds (15-acre garden, croquet, 3 trout lakes), unsuitable for &.
BACKGROUND MUSIC: no.
LOCATION: 22 miles NE of Cork.
CHILDREN: all ages welcomed.
DOGS: allowed.
CREDIT CARDS: MasterCard, Visa.
PRICES: per person B&B €95–€115. Set dinner €55.

CLIFDEN Co. Galway

Map 6:C4

THE QUAY HOUSE

❧ César award in 2003

Liked for the 'lovable eccentricity' and the 'friendly professionalism' of the owners, Paddy and Julia Foyle's quirky B&B is spread across three buildings on the waterfront of this small Connemara town. Visitors are impressed by the 'adaptable, not at all pushy' hospitality. The public rooms are furnished with gilt-framed family photos, 'wonderful' original Irish artwork, antiques and Napoleonic mementos; the spacious drawing room has an open fire. Most bedrooms overlook the tidal harbour – one of the buildings was the former harbourmaster's house; six have a balcony, two have garden views. They are individually decorated and some are themed: the Mirror has a gilded antique mirror behind the bed; the Parrot Room is 'popular with bird lovers'; the Napoleon Bonaparte Room has appropriate artefacts. All bathrooms have a large tub and a shower; six of the studios have a kitchenette. Breakfast, served in the conservatory, includes freshly squeezed orange juice, home-made compotes, fresh seafood; farm cheese; brown bread and fruit brack are baked in the Aga. The Foyles will recommend restaurants for dinner in the town.

Beach Road
Clifden

T: 00 353 95-21369
F: 00 353 95-21608
E: thequay@iol.ie
W: www.thequayhouse.com

BEDROOMS: 14, 2 on ground floor, 1 suitable for ♿, 7 studios (6 with kitchenette) in annexe.
OPEN: end Mar–end Oct.
FACILITIES: 2 sitting rooms, breakfast conservatory, free Wi-Fi, ½-acre garden, fishing, sailing, golf, riding nearby.
BACKGROUND MUSIC: none.
LOCATION: harbour, 8 mins' walk from centre.
CHILDREN: all ages welcomed.
DOGS: not allowed.
CREDIT CARDS: MasterCard, Visa.
PRICES: per person B&B €60–€80. 1-night bookings refused bank holiday weekends.

CLIFDEN Co. Galway

Map 6:C4

SEA MIST HOUSE

Restored throughout and 'beautifully maintained', this 1820s town house is one of the oldest in the largest town in Connemara. It is run today as a B&B by Sheila Griffin, whose family has owned the house for more than a century. Her grandfather was an auctioneer; the house is furnished with unusual pieces (and well-chosen artwork). This year two of the bedrooms have been renovated. They vary in size (and price): a light room was 'decorated in relaxing colours'; the divide to make the bathroom was well done with cornicing; the L-shape was used with good effect to include a single as well as a decent double bed; good mirrors.' No TV in the bedrooms ('in keeping with the style of the house'); there is free Wi-Fi throughout and the lounge has a television set with a supply of DVDs. Breakfast, in a conservatory overlooking the garden, has a 'good' buffet of juices, fresh and stewed fruit; an extensive choice of hot dishes includes 'a traditional fry, American pancakes, scrambled eggs (with smoked salmon or feta cheese)'. Close to restaurants and pubs. 'Very good value.'

Seaview
Clifden

T: 00 353 95-21441
E: sheila@seamisthouse.com
W: www.seamisthouse.com

BEDROOMS: 4.
OPEN: Mar–Oct.
FACILITIES: 2 sitting rooms, conservatory dining room, free Wi-Fi, ¾-acre garden, unsuitable for &.
BACKGROUND MUSIC: none.
LOCATION: central.
CHILDREN: not under 4.
DOGS: not allowed.
CREDIT CARDS: Amex, MasterCard, Visa.
PRICES: per person B&B €40–€60.

CLONES Co. Monaghan

Map 6:B6

HILTON PARK

'Make no mistake, *Hilton Park* is not a hotel, it is a family home. It is a place I have loved since my first visit in the mid-1980s.' An American visitor 'always juggles her Irish itineraries' to stay at the Madden family's grand country house. 'I was sad to leave,' concurs an inspector. The home of the Madden family since 1734, it is run in house-party style by Fred and Joanna (he's the ninth generation); he is helped in the kitchen by his mother, Lucy. His father, Johnny, 'entertains guests with stories about the house'. Bedrooms are spacious. 'My four-poster was extremely comfortable.' In the imposing dining room, guests can dine communally at a large mahogany table or separately at smaller tables. The food is 'fresh, creatively served'; dishes might include lovage soup, pike quenelle; pork fillet wrapped in chard and pancetta. Breakfast, 'a banquet', has eggs from the family chickens and 'tasty' black pudding. 'You get value for every penny spent.' The constantly changing light over the grounds gives 'a peek at pure tranquillity'. (*Susan Canning Stochl, and others*)

Clones

T: 00 353 47-56007
F: 00 353 47-56033
E: mail@hiltonpark.ie
W: www.hiltonpark.ie

BEDROOMS: 4.
OPEN: Apr–Sept, groups only Oct–Mar.
FACILITIES: drawing room, sitting room, TV room, breakfast room, dining room, free Wi-Fi, 400-acre grounds (3 lakes, golf course, croquet), unsuitable for &.
BACKGROUND MUSIC: none.
LOCATION: 3 miles S of Clones.
CHILDREN: not under 8.
DOGS: not allowed in bedrooms, public areas.
CREDIT CARDS: MasterCard, Visa.
PRICES: per person B&B €85–€135. Set dinner €55.

CONG Co. Mayo

Map 6:C4

BALLYWARREN HOUSE

In farming country on the edge of Connemara, David and Diane Skelton provide 'peaceful, elegant and warm hospitality' at their creeper-covered family home built in Georgian style. 'We really love looking after people and we hope it shows,' they say. Visitors are greeted with tea, home-baked 'goodies' and a chat in a cosy sitting room. He is a 'perfect' host; she asks guests in advance about their likes and dislikes before posting her no-choice menu on a blackboard. Meals are taken in a 'lovely' dining room overlooking the garden. Many of the dishes are slow-cooked in the Aga, perhaps cream of asparagus soup; Connemara lamb shanks with vermouth, tomatoes and garlic. All bread, cakes, preserves and ice cream are made on the premises. Coffee is served in the 'cosy' drawing room, which has a fire burning peat and logs. The 'light, airy' bedrooms have 'wonderful views': they are furnished with antiques and supplied with magazines, chocolates and sherry. Breakfast has an extensive buffet; a choice of six cooked dishes with eggs from hens that roam the garden; 'excellent' coffee. (CL)

Cross, Cong

T/F: 00 353 9495-46989
E: ballywarrenhouse@gmail.com
W: www.ballywarrenhouse.com

BEDROOMS: 3.
OPEN: all year.
FACILITIES: reception hall, sitting room, 2 dining rooms, free Wi-Fi, 1-acre garden in 6-acre grounds (lake, fishing nearby), unsuitable for &.
BACKGROUND MUSIC: none.
LOCATION: 2 miles E of Cong.
CHILDREN: not under 14, except babies.
DOGS: not allowed in house.
CREDIT CARDS: Amex, MasterCard, Visa.
PRICES: per person B&B €68–€80. Set dinner €48. 1-night bookings occasionally refused.

SEE ALSO SHORTLIST

DUBLIN

Map 6:C6

ARIEL HOUSE

In leafy Ballsbridge, this extended Victorian town house (built for a wealthy merchant in 1850) has been renovated by the McKeown family, who run it as a B&B hotel. Managed by Deirdre McDonald, it has 'a personal feel'. Victorian features (stained glass, iron railings, Flemish brick bonding) have been retained. The bedrooms in the main building have 'been furnished correctly for its age' with antiques; many have a high ceiling, an original fireplace and plasterwork; some have a four-poster bed. 'Our large and airy bathroom had high-quality fittings.' Eight smaller bedrooms in a recently added extension at the back have large windows facing the private garden. Breakfast is served by a 'well-groomed young staff' in a split-level dining room (until 11 am at weekends). There are Irish cheeses, home-baked breads, fresh fruits and home-made granola on a buffet table. 'Starters' include a grilled fruit brochette, two kinds of porridge and forest berry crunch. Eggs Florentine and a potato cake with smoked salmon are among the cooked options. *Ariel House* is close to the Aviva stadium and the RDS showgrounds. (*K and CB*)

50–54 Lansdowne Road
Ballsbridge, Dublin 4

T: 00 353 1-668 5512
F: 00 353 1-668 5845
E: reservations@ariel-house.net
W: www.ariel-house.net

BEDROOMS: 37, 8 in garden mews.
OPEN: all year except 22–28 Dec.
FACILITIES: Drawing room, dining room, free Wi-Fi, garden.
BACKGROUND MUSIC: classical, jazz.
LOCATION: Ballsbridge.
CHILDREN: all ages welcomed.
DOGS: not allowed.
CREDIT CARDS: Amex, MasterCard, Visa.
PRICES: per room B&B €79–€199.

SEE ALSO SHORTLIST

DUNGARVAN Co. Waterford

Map 6:D5

THE TANNERY RESTAURANT & TOWNHOUSE

Founded as a restaurant in 1997 by chef/patron Paul Flynn, whose wife Máire runs front-of-house, *The Tannery* is located in a former leather factory in the small seaside resort and harbour town of Dungarvan. He also runs a cookery school on the premises, and they provide accommodation in a Georgian town house around the corner. Paul Flynn, who is well known in Ireland as a television chef, can be seen cooking in the ground-floor kitchen of the two-floor restaurant, which is bright and airy and retains some of its industrial history in the decor, such as cast-iron beams. His modern dishes might include crab crème brûlée; glazed pork belly, apple sauce and celeriac cream. Bedrooms in the *Townhouse* have high ceilings and a large bed; cool colours on the walls give them a Scandinavian feel, bed throws and cushions add a touch of brightness. A light continental breakfast is left in the bedroom (there are no communal spaces); fridges in each room are stocked with milk, fruit juice and yogurt; a bag with fresh bread and pastries is hung on the door overnight.

10 Quay Street
Dungarvan

T: 00 353 58-45420
E: info@tannery.ie
W: www.tannery.ie

BEDROOMS: 14, 2 on ground floor.
OPEN: all year except Christmas, 2 weeks in Jan, restaurant closed Sun evening, Mon.
FACILITIES: restaurant, private dining room, free Wi-Fi.
BACKGROUND MUSIC: light jazz.
LOCATION: town centre.
CHILDREN: all ages welcomed.
DOGS: not allowed.
CREDIT CARDS: Amex, MasterCard, Visa.
PRICES: [2013] per person B&B €55–€65. 'Easy evening' menu €30, à la carte €48–€50, tasting menu €65.

SEE ALSO SHORTLIST

DUNLAVIN Co. Wicklow

Map 6:C6

RATHSALLAGH HOUSE NEW

In horse-racing territory, this conversion of Queen Anne stables is run as a country hotel by the O'Flynn family, 'lovely people who make you feel so welcome'. 'It is my favourite place, totally spoiling, and the best breakfast in Ireland,' says a visitor in 2013. The family run the house in a low-key style ('we are not a hotel,' they insist). It stands in extensive parkland with a championship golf course and a walled garden. Turf and log fires burn in the bar and drawing rooms which are decorated in country house style. The bedrooms vary considerably in size: some are spacious with garden views; there are simple rooms in the stable yard; other rooms in a more recent extension are large. In the dining room, the chef, Nico Krumbholz, serves a modern menu of dishes like sandwich of house-smoked salmon tartare, crostini, horseradish jelly; beef medallions, mushroom duxelles, crispy onions, sage and Merlot jus. An Edwardian breakfast buffet has a sideboard with home-baked bread, and home-made jams, ham on the bone, Irish cheeses, smoked salmon; cooked dishes include devilled kidneys. (*Dede Gold*)

Dunlavin

T: 00 353 45-403112
F: 00 353 45-403343
E: info@rathsallagh.com
W: www.rathsallagh.com

BEDROOMS: 29, 20 in courtyard.
OPEN: all year except 23–27 Dec.
FACILITIES: 2 drawing rooms, bar, dining room, snooker room, free Wi-Fi, wedding facilities, 500-acre grounds (golf course, tennis).
BACKGROUND MUSIC: in dining room.
LOCATION: 2 miles SW of village.
CHILDREN: not under 6.
DOGS: allowed (heated kennels).
CREDIT CARDS: all major cards.
PRICES: [2013] per room B&B €159–€190. À la carte €45.

ENNISCORTHY Co. Wexford

Map 6:D6

BALLINKEELE HOUSE

🏵 *César award in 2012*

'The house and grounds are lovely, and the interiors magnificent,' say visitors to this Georgian Italianate mansion, which was built for the Maher family in 1840. In December 2012, Margaret Maher handed over the running of the house to her son, Val, and his wife, Laura. Despite the formality of the building (porticoes of Wicklow granite adorn the entrance), visitors are welcomed on first-name terms to the home of the fifth and sixth generations of the family. The bedrooms, individually decorated in country house style, are spacious and airy; there are large beds, big windows, original antique furniture, pictures, period details. Guests take pre- and after-dinner drinks in the 'lovely' drawing rooms; they dine around the family's original large mahogany table. A separate table can be laid for those who prefer to eat independently. The no-choice 'home-style' menu, using game from the estate and seasonal fruit and vegetables from the walled garden, might include chicken liver and sherry pâté; pheasant breast braised in cider. There are lovely walks in the parkland and woodland.
(*Jeremy Christie-Brown*)

Ballymurn
Enniscorthy

T: 00 353 53-913 8105
E: info@ballinkeele.ie
W: www.ballinkeele.ie

BEDROOMS: 5.
OPEN: 1 Feb–30 Nov.
FACILITIES: 2 drawing rooms, dining room, free Wi-Fi, 6-acre gardens in 350-acre estate, lakes, ponds, unsuitable for ♿.
BACKGROUND MUSIC: none.
LOCATION: 6 miles SE of Enniscorthy.
CHILDREN: all ages welcomed.
DOGS: not allowed.
CREDIT CARDS: Amex, MasterCard, Visa.
PRICES: per person B&B €75–€105. Set dinner €35.

ENNISCORTHY Co. Wexford

Map 6:D6

SALVILLE HOUSE

César award in 2013

'About as far as you can get from the anonymity of a plastic chain hotel', Gordon and Jane Parker's 'atmospheric' Victorian country house stands in wooded grounds on a quiet hilltop. 'It's a handsome place, with high ceilings, creaking floorboards and the heady air of faded glamour that clings to the old houses of Ireland,' says a reporter this year. 'If you haven't tried Gordon's cooking, you need to,' says a fan. 'We had succulent asparagus in a crisp coating of pine nuts; grilled aubergine with mozzarella, baba ganoush and Provençal vegetables.' Guests are encouraged to bring their own wine. Bedrooms at the front of house overlook the Slaney valley. 'Our large, airy room was decorated in shades of pink, apple green, white and touches of cerise; it had a wooden floor with rugs, a selection of well-chosen books on the mantelpiece, lots of well-thought-out detail.' Two rooms in a self-catering apartment at the back overlook the garden. The 'excellent' breakfast has freshly squeezed juice, stewed plums, home-made jams and bread. Close to the Wexford opera festival and the Rosslare ferries. (*Jeanette Bloor, and others*)

Salville
Enniscorthy

T/F: 00 353 53-923 5252
E: info@salvillehouse.com
W: www.salvillehouse.com

BEDROOMS: 5, 2 in apartment at rear.
OPEN: all year except Christmas/New Year.
FACILITIES: drawing room, dining room, free Wi-Fi, 5-acre grounds ('rough' tennis, badminton, croquet), golf nearby, beach, bird sanctuary 10 miles, unsuitable for &.
BACKGROUND MUSIC: none.
LOCATION: 2 miles S of town.
CHILDREN: all ages welcomed.
DOGS: allowed by arrangement.
CREDIT CARDS: none.
PRICES: [2013] per person B&B €55. Set dinner €40.

GOREY Co. Wexford

MARLFIELD HOUSE

On a large estate with a lake, wildlife reserve and formal gardens, this handsome Regency house is run as a luxury country house hotel (Relais & Châteaux) by sisters Margaret and Laura Bowe. The family shows 'faultless care and attention', say recent visitors. Entered through an imposing set of gates, the former residence of the earls of Courtown is furnished in grand style: it has a marble hall, a lounge with an open fire, antiques, period paintings, spectacular flower displays. In the formal restaurant, with its frescoed walls and domed conservatory, Sebastien Geber is now the chef, serving classically based dishes, perhaps ballottine of organic salmon, horseradish cream, beetroot salad; roasted rump of Slaney Valley lamb, fondant potato, sherry jus. The kitchen garden supplies vegetables, fruit and herbs. The best bedrooms have antiques, dramatic wallpaper and curtains, a marble bathroom. Children are welcomed; under-eights have their own high tea menu; babysitting can be arranged. There is much for guests to do within the grounds: tennis, croquet, woodland walks. Many famous gardens to visit nearby. (*P and PB*)

Courtown Road
Gorey

T: 00 353 53-942 1124
F: 00 353 53-942 1572
E: info@marlfieldhouse.ie
W: www.marlfieldhouse.com

BEDROOMS: 19, 8 on ground floor.
OPEN: Mar–Dec except Christmas, restaurant closed Mon/Tues in Mar/Apr, Oct–Dec.
FACILITIES: reception hall, drawing room, library/bar, restaurant with conservatory, free Wi-Fi, wedding facilities, 36-acre grounds (gardens, tennis, croquet, wildfowl reserve, lake).
BACKGROUND MUSIC: classical in library.
LOCATION: 1 mile E of Gorey.
CHILDREN: no under-8s at dinner, high tea provided, babysitting available.
DOGS: not allowed in public rooms.
CREDIT CARDS: all major cards.
PRICES: per person B&B €75–€300, D,B&B €140–€360. Set dinner €64. 1-night bookings sometimes refused Sat.

HOLYWOOD Co. Down

RAYANNE HOUSE

In large gardens in a town on the Belfast Lough, this Victorian merchant's mansion has been given an 'ambience of cheerful, comfortable luxury' by the owners, Conor and Bernadette McClelland. They have filled the house with 'charming' ornamentation on an Art Deco theme. A sweeping staircase leads to the 'pretty' bedrooms, which have many thoughtful touches: a hospitality tray with Jaffa cakes and chocolate bars; 'the pièce de résistance was an electric blanket that had been switched on'. A ground-floor bedroom is fully equipped for disabled visitors. In the bathroom is 'everything extra you can think of – tissues, cotton wool, deodorant (male and female)'. Conor McClelland is an accomplished cook: breakfast has an 'amazing menu'. The choice (made the evening before) is 'really hard'. There are seven starters, from cereals to unusual dishes like prune soufflé on a purée of green figs. A dozen main courses might include crock-baked Irish ham and eggs, Italian tomato sauce, crusty bread. Children are welcomed: games, bath toys, books, and discounts at family-friendly restaurants are available. In warm weather, drinks can be taken in a decked area.

60 Demesne Road
Holywood BT18 9EX

T/F: 028-9042 5859
E: info@rayannehouse.com
W: www.rayannehouse.com

BEDROOMS: 10, 1, on ground floor, suitable for &.
OPEN: all year.
FACILITIES: 2 lounges, dining room, free Wi-Fi, conference facilities, 1-acre grounds.
BACKGROUND MUSIC: light jazz in dining room.
LOCATION: ½ mile from town centre, 6 miles E of Belfast.
CHILDREN: all ages welcomed.
DOGS: not allowed.
CREDIT CARDS: Amex, MasterCard, Visa.
PRICES: [2013] per person B&B £75–£85. Set menus £49–£69, à la carte £49.

INIS MEÁIN Co. Galway

Map 6:C4

INIS MEÁIN RESTAURANT AND SUITES

On the remotest of the three Aran Islands (population 160), this 'stunning' stone-and-glass building is run as a restaurant-with-rooms by returning islander Ruairí de Blacam with his wife, Marie Thérèse. The building is designed to blend into the terraced stone fields of the island; from the bedrooms and the restaurant there are panoramic views to Galway Bay and the mountains of Connemara. The welcome is 'gentle and warm'. The main ingredients for the host's menus come from the islanders: the 'unparalleled' lobster and crab are caught by fishermen from traditional currachs; vegetables are grown in the shelter of stone walls ('the most delicious potatoes'). Typical dishes: cured wild salmon, cucumber, dill and mustard sauce; lobster, asparagus, chilli, coriander and garlic butter. The five suites, which have wooden floors and modern furnishings, are decorated in muted colours. Each has a large bed, a living area, an outside sitting area. Guests are provided with bicycles, fishing rods and swimming towels. A breakfast tray is delivered to the suite. The island is a stronghold of Irish culture.

Inis Meáin, Aran Islands
Galway

T: 00 353 86-826 6026
E: post@inismeain.com
W: www.inismeain.com

BEDROOMS: 5.
OPEN: Apr–Sept, hotel and restaurant closed Sun–Tues.
FACILITIES: restaurant, free Wi-Fi, 3-acre grounds, unsuitable for &.
BACKGROUND MUSIC: Irish music in evening.
LOCATION: on island, 15 miles off Galway coast (45-minute ferry from Ros a' Mhíl, flights from Connemara airport).
CHILDREN: all ages welcomed.
DOGS: not allowed.
CREDIT CARDS: MasterCard, Visa.
PRICES: [2013] per room (min. stay 2 nights) B&B €237–€400. À la carte €50.

KENMARE Co. Kerry

Map 6:D4

SHELBURNE LODGE

'Full of the personality of the owners', this handsome 18th-century farmhouse is run as a B&B by the Foley family. 'Any minor imperfections like a temperamental shower are completely outweighed by the cheery, helpful charm of Maura and Tom,' says a trusted correspondent. The house has a 'peaceful setting' yet is just a short walk from the 'buzzing' town and the 'excellent' restaurants 'either owned or recommended by the Foleys. Try the ever-popular bar/restaurant *Packie's*, noted for its fish. Eight of the bedrooms are in the main house: they have antiques, rugs on polished wooden floors. The house is handsomely presented with plants and flowers, much artwork, bold colours. Home-made cake and tea is given to arriving guests in an elegant drawing room. Tom Foley is responsible for the 'splendid' breakfast which has Irish pancakes, home-made bread, freshly squeezed orange juice; the cooked items include fish of the day landed in small boats at Castletownbere (perhaps John Dory). 'The remarkable wide-ranging selection of guests are all very happy. Everyone is a friend from the moment of arrival.' (*ES*)

Cork Road
Kenmare

T: 00 353 64-664 1013
F: 00 353 64-664 2135
E: shelburnekenmare@eircom.net
W: www.shelburnelodge.com

BEDROOMS: 8, plus 2 in coach house.
OPEN: mid-Mar–mid-Nov.
FACILITIES: drawing room, library, lounge in annexe, breakfast room, free Wi-Fi, 3-acre garden (tennis), golf adjacent, unsuitable for &.
BACKGROUND MUSIC: none.
LOCATION: on R569 to Cork, ⅛ mile E of centre.
CHILDREN: all ages welcomed.
DOGS: not allowed.
CREDIT CARDS: MasterCard, Visa.
PRICES: per person B&B €50–€95.

SEE ALSO SHORTLIST

KENMARE Co. Kerry

VIRGINIA'S GUESTHOUSE

In the centre of a popular little resort town on the Ring of Kerry, this unpretentious guest house is on the first and second floors above a restaurant. It has long been liked by *Guide* readers for the 'engaging charm' of the owners, Neil and Noreen Harrington. 'Our house is designed for down-to-earth and friendly people,' they say. He talks to guests at breakfast, to help them with 'their plans for the day' (in season, the scenic drive around the ring requires careful navigation). 'He gave us all the information we could wish for,' said a guest. The 'homely, cheerful' bedrooms are 'bright and spotless'; earplugs are provided for light sleepers in rooms at the front: the street can be noisy when the pubs are closing. The guest sitting room has tea- and coffee-making facilities. A time for breakfast is agreed when it is ordered the evening before. Noreen Harrington produces 'delicious' cooked dishes from a tiny galley: everything is home made and organic, from the porridge, bread and preserves to the eggs, bacon, mushrooms, cheese and rhubarb. Orange juice 'comes from real oranges squeezed every morning'. (*VD, and others*)

36 Henry Street
Kenmare

T: 00 353 86-372 0625
E: virginias.guesthouse@gmail.com
W: www.virginias-kenmare.com

BEDROOMS: 8.
OPEN: all year except 20–27 Dec.
FACILITIES: library, breakfast room, free Wi-Fi, unsuitable for &.
BACKGROUND MUSIC: classical, in breakfast room.
LOCATION: central.
CHILDREN: not under 12.
DOGS: not allowed.
CREDIT CARDS: MasterCard, Visa.
PRICES: per person B&B €32.50–€45. 1-night bookings refused bank holidays.

SEE ALSO SHORTLIST

LETTERFRACK Co. Galway

Map 6:C4

ROSLEAGUE MANOR

♥César award in 2010

Looking out across gardens to sea and mountains
on the shores of Ballinakill Bay, this Georgian
manor house is owned by Mark Foyle and his
father, Edmund. 'Mark is regularly in attendance;
he is assisted by long-serving locals augmented
by students who are friendly and capable.' Praise
this year from a long-term fan who acknowledges:
'It suits me perfectly, but I feel sure that even a
more objective judge would find plenty to
enjoy.' Recent first-time visitors were 'very
pleased with our experience'. The 'elegant'
lounges have 'deep sofas, a log and turf fire';
huge flower arrangements. In the 'stately' dining
room, the chef, Emmanuel Neu, 'treats good
local ingredients in a straightforward way, with
the occasional Mediterranean and north African
influence; portions are sensible'. Bedrooms range
'from large to enormous'. 'A ground-floor
suite has two small anterooms leading into the
bedroom, a bathroom to the side. The main
space has a large bed, a sitting area and plenty
of furniture without feeling cluttered.'
Breakfast has an extensive buffet; home-baked
bread and scones; freshly cooked hot dishes.
(*Ann Walden, CA*)

Letterfrack

T: 00 353 95-41101
F: 00 353 95-41168
E: info@rosleague.com
W: www.rosleague.com

BEDROOMS: 20, 2 on ground floor.
OPEN: mid-Mar–mid-Nov.
FACILITIES: 2 drawing rooms,
conservatory/bar, dining room,
wedding facilities, 25-acre grounds
(tennis), unsuitable for &.
BACKGROUND MUSIC: none.
LOCATION: 7 miles NE of Clifden.
CHILDREN: all ages welcomed.
DOGS: 'well-behaved dogs' allowed
in bar, with own bedding in 2
bedrooms.
CREDIT CARDS: MasterCard, Visa.
PRICES: [2013] per person B&B
€65–€105, D,B&B €95–€135. Set
dinner €46. 1-night bookings
refused bank holiday Sat.

LIMERICK Co. Limerick

Map 6:D5

NO. 1 PERY SQUARE

'Highly recommended' again this year, Patricia Roberts's small hotel, a conversion of two fine Georgian town houses, is thought 'one of the nicest places in Ireland'. Opposite the People's Park, the building has been restored throughout. The largest bedrooms, in the oldest part, are decorated in period style. Named after former residents of the house, they overlook the park or the terrace/garden. 'Club' bedrooms in a newer wing are smaller: they are 'well furnished' with a large bed; a monsoon shower in the bathroom. Some face the terrace, others overlook the city. A suite on the top floor has its own bar and dining area. A turf fire burns in the elegant drawing room, where afternoon tea can be taken. In *Brasserie One*, the chef, Christian Baldenecker, serves a modern menu of Irish and French dishes like smoked trout mousse, sea salt crostini, horseradish cream, pickled cucumber; pan-fried pork fillet, prune confit, potato gratin and thyme jus. 'There is a more than usually interesting wine list at very realistic prices.' Limerick is Ireland's first national city of culture in 2014. (*David Carment, and others*)

Georgian Quarter
1 Pery Square
Limerick

T: 00 353 61-402402
F: 00 353 61-313060
E: info@oneperysquare.com
W: www.oneperysquare.com

BEDROOMS: 20, 2 suitable for ♿.
OPEN: all year except 24–29 Dec, restaurant closed Mon.
FACILITIES: lounge, drawing room, bar, restaurant, private dining room, free Wi-Fi, wedding facilities, terrace, basement spa.
BACKGROUND MUSIC: 'easy listening' in public areas.
LOCATION: central.
CHILDREN: all ages welcomed.
DOGS: only guide dogs allowed.
CREDIT CARDS: all major cards.
PRICES: per person B&B €67.50–€125, D,B&B €30 added. Set menus €25–€29, à la carte €50.

LISDOONVARNA Co. Clare

SHEEDY'S

In a village famed for its annual matchmaking festival, John and Martina Sheedy's small hotel/restaurant is much liked for a welcome that is 'open and warm'. 'Ever present', she 'leads by example'; he is the 'assured' chef. The bar and library (good seating, books and local information) are 'cosy' rooms. 'We preferred to take pre-dinner drinks in the reception area, which has a turf fire and long windows overlooking the garden.' In the smartly laid restaurant, which is open to non-residents, John Sheedy uses locally sourced produce for his dishes which might include Liscannor Bay crab claws in garlic cream; roast rack of Burren lamb, slow-braised shoulder, roast red peppers. The portions are 'extremely generous'; the vegetables are 'perfectly cooked'. There are 'pleasingly old-fashioned touches': beds made with blankets and sheets; leaf tea; a buffet-free breakfast (which has 'imaginative' options – apricots poached in Cointreau; crepes with fresh fruit; banana bread is a house speciality. The bedrooms have a traditional decor; Regency stripes, curtains with tie-backs. 'An excellent small hotel in a wonderful location on the edge of the Burren.' (*F and RB, and others*)

Lisdoonvarna

T: 00 353 65-707 4026
F: 00 353 65-707 4555
E: info@sheedys.com
W: www.sheedys.com

BEDROOMS: 11, some on ground floor, 1 suitable for &.
OPEN: Apr–early Oct.
FACILITIES: ramp, sitting room/library, sun lounge, bar, restaurant, free Wi-Fi, ¼-acre garden (rose garden).
BACKGROUND MUSIC: light jazz at dinner.
LOCATION: 20 miles SW of Galway.
CHILDREN: all ages welcomed.
DOGS: not allowed.
CREDIT CARDS: MasterCard, Visa.
PRICES: [2013] per room B&B €99–€160. D,B&B €100–€120 per person, à la carte €40.

MAGHERALIN Co. Armagh

Map 6:B6

NEWFORGE HOUSE

In large and well-kept grounds on the edge of a village, this fine Georgian country house has been owned by the Mathers family for six generations. Today it is the home of John and Louise Mathers, who have sympathetically converted it as a guest house. 'A dream; we'd love to come again for the hospitality, the meals, the rooms,' says a visitor this year. John Mathers is a 'regular presence', greeting guests on first-name terms and 'offering advice on outings, and tea when we returned from them'. In a light dining room, overlooking the garden, he serves a daily-changing menu of 'simple and seasonal' dishes like king scallops, cauliflower purée, watercress salad; rib-eye of shorthorn beef, smoked garlic butter. 'Food of the highest order,' is a recent comment. The sitting room and dining room have open log fires, antiques, good artwork, up-to-date magazines; 'good-quality fabrics with muted tones'. The spacious bedrooms have good storage, fruit and flowers, tea-making facilities with fresh milk. The 'delicious' breakfast includes fresh, stewed and dried fruit, a 'fine' grill, 'delectable' scrambled eggs (from the Matherses' hens). (*Yolanda Burrows-Hueppi*)

25% DISCOUNT VOUCHERS

58 Newforge Road
Magheralin
Craigavon BT67 0QL

T: 028-9261 1255
F: 028-9261 2823
E: enquiries@newforgehouse.com
W: www.newforgehouse.com

BEDROOMS: 6.
OPEN: all year except 21 Dec–31 Jan.
FACILITIES: drawing room, dining room, free Wi-Fi, civil wedding licence, 4-acre gardens (vegetable garden, orchard), unsuitable for &.
BACKGROUND MUSIC: mixed in dining room.
LOCATION: edge of village, 3 miles E of Craigavon.
CHILDREN: not under 10 (except for under-1s).
DOGS: not allowed.
CREDIT CARDS: Diners, MasterCard, Visa.
PRICES: [2013] per room B&B single £80–£110, double £120–£170. Set dinner £38.

MOUNTRATH Co. Laois

Map 6:C5

ROUNDWOOD HOUSE

🏵 *César award in 1990*

'This is a house and a home, not an immaculate hotel. You can feel the history all around you.' Guests are received in relaxed style at Paddy and Hannah Flynn's Palladian villa, which has been a restoration project for her family for more than 30 years. It has a 'lived-in feel' but 'everything is spotlessly clean', says a trusted reporter. 'He moved his mower so we could sit at a wrought iron table on his freshly cut lawn; she brought us glasses of wine as we chatted about the flowers and plants.' The main hall has creaking floorboards, an eclectic collection of books, furniture and ornaments. The drawing room feels intimate despite its size, thanks to small groupings of sofas and chairs. Bedrooms in the house are spacious, and have many original features; deep colours on the walls. Smaller rooms in the *Yellow House* face a walled garden. Guests eat communally in the dining room, where Paddy Flynn serves an 'excellent' five-course no-choice dinner five nights a week (a shorter supper on other evenings). Don't miss the home-made ice cream. (*JB*)

Mountrath

T: 00 353 57-873 2120
F: 00 353 57-873 2711
E: info@roundwoodhouse.com
W: www.roundwoodhouse.com

BEDROOMS: 10, 4 in garden building.
OPEN: all year except Christmas.
FACILITIES: drawing room, study/library, dining room, playroom, table tennis room, free Wi-Fi, wedding facilities, 20-acre grounds (garden, woodland), golf, walking, river fishing nearby, unsuitable for &.
BACKGROUND MUSIC: none.
LOCATION: 3 miles N of village.
CHILDREN: all ages welcomed.
DOGS: not allowed indoors.
CREDIT CARDS: all major cards.
PRICES: [2013] per person B&B €60–€85. Supper €35 (Sun/Mon), set dinner (Tues–Sat) €50.

MULTYFARNHAM Co. Westmeath

Map 6:C5

MORNINGTON HOUSE

In extensive parkland with ancient trees near Lough Derravaragh, this 'rather grand' old country house is a 'great find' (said *Guide* inspectors). The owners, Warwick and Anne O'Hara, welcome guests on house-party lines to their 'gracious country home' (his family have lived in the house for 150 years). It remains much as it has been since it was remodelled in 1896, with original furniture, and family portraits on the colourful walls. The bedrooms vary in style: 'Our room was spacious and comfortable; the big bathroom was well laid out.' Guests gather for dinner in the drawing room, where drinks are laid out on a tray. Meals are 'relaxed and informal': Warwick O'Hara assigns places at a large table with 'good-quality cutlery and napery'. Anne O'Hara is a 'great cook': her four-course set menu allows for dietary preferences. Vegetarian visitors enjoyed carrot and orange soup; stuffed mushrooms and a baked tomato with herbs and pine nuts; individual dishes of vegetables. Breakfast has freshly squeezed orange juice, seasonal fruits from the garden; hot dishes cooked to order. (*F and AR, and others*)

Multyfarnham

T: 00 353 44-937 2191
F: 00 353 44-937 2338
E: stay@mornington.ie
W: www.mornington.ie

BEDROOMS: 4.
OPEN: Apr–Oct.
FACILITIES: drawing room, dining room, 5-acre garden, 50-acre grounds (croquet, bicycle hire), unsuitable for &.
BACKGROUND MUSIC: none.
LOCATION: 9 miles NW of Mullingar.
CHILDREN: all ages welcomed.
DOGS: not allowed in house.
CREDIT CARDS: all major cards.
PRICES: per person B&B €75, D,B&B €120. Set dinner €45.

OUGHTERARD Co. Galway

Map 6:C4

CURRAREVAGH HOUSE

🦋 *César award in 1992*

'The sort of hotel one hopes will never change. We enjoyed our second visit even more than our first, because we knew what to anticipate: peace, changing views of Loch Corrib, and delicious meals.' A visitor articulates this year why *Currarevagh House* is one of only four hotels to have had an entry in every edition of the *Guide*. 'Henry Hodgson and his mother, June, make guests feel comfortable in their family home.' Dinner, cooked by Henry's wife, Lucy, 'goes from strength to strength' (says an annual visitor). She serves a no-choice four-course menu ('you can ask for a change'). 'She made gorgeous vegetarian dishes for our son; plates are garnished with petals from the garden, and seconds are always offered: who could resist a second slice of roast goose?' Breakfast, laid out on a sideboard, has baked ham, smoked salmon; bacon, sausages and eggs. 'You eat so much that you aren't hungry until the cakes, baked by Henry, appear at 4 pm.' The bedrooms 'are comfortable, with a good bathroom; Wi-Fi seems to have spread further through the house'. (*Mamie Atkins, Richard Parish*)

Oughterard

T: 00 353 91-552312
F: 00 353 91-552731
E: info@currarevagh.com
W: www.currarevagh.com

BEDROOMS: 12.
OPEN: 28 Mar–27 Oct.
FACILITIES: sitting room/hall, drawing room, library/bar with TV, dining room, free Wi-Fi, 180-acre grounds (lake, fishing, ghillies available, boating, swimming, tennis, croquet), golf, riding nearby, unsuitable for ♿.
BACKGROUND MUSIC: none.
LOCATION: 4 miles NW of Oughterard.
CHILDREN: all ages welcomed.
DOGS: allowed.
CREDIT CARDS: Amex, MasterCard, Visa.
PRICES: per person B&B €75–€85, D,B&B €110–€130. Set dinner €47.50.

OUGHTERARD Co. Galway

Map 6:C4

ROSS LAKE HOUSE

In 'idyllic and quiet surroundings' deep in the Connemara countryside, this fine Georgian house is run as an intimate hotel by Henry and Elaine Reid. 'They are a lovely couple who look after their clients well. We already look forward to our next time there,' say visitors from Switzerland. The house stands among rambling woods and rolling lawns close to Lough Corrib, popular with fisher folk. Visitors like the lack of 'notices of dos and don'ts; whatever we needed was provided without hesitation'. The spacious bedrooms are 'furnished and decorated with lots of taste'; the largest rooms have a sitting area. The lounge and bar have warm period furnishings, plenty of comfortable seating. In the softly lit dining room, Elaine Reid's daily-changing menus have 'outstanding, hearty' traditional dishes, perhaps chicken liver pâté with Cumberland sauce; rack of Connemara lamb. 'The head waiter seemed like an old friend,' say recent visitors. There are extensive walks within the grounds as well as a tennis court; good golfing, horse riding and fishing nearby. (*C and LW, and others*)

Rosscahill
Oughterard

T: 00 353 91-550109
F: 00 353 91-550184
E: rosslake@iol.ie
W: www.rosslakehotel.com

BEDROOMS: 13.
OPEN: 15 Mar–1 Nov.
FACILITIES: drawing room, library bar, restaurant, free Wi-Fi, 7-acre grounds (tennis), unsuitable for &.
BACKGROUND MUSIC: classical in bar and restaurant.
LOCATION: 14 miles NW of Galway city.
CHILDREN: all ages welcomed.
DOGS: not allowed.
CREDIT CARDS: Amex, MasterCard, Visa.
PRICES: per person B&B €67–€95, D,B&B €110–€135. Set dinner €43.

RATHMULLAN Co. Donegal

Map 6:B5

RATHMULLAN HOUSE

In well-tended gardens on a two-mile sandy beach on Lough Swilly (an inlet of the sea), this Georgian mansion is owned and managed by Mark Wheeler. 'We loved the superb location and helpful staff,' says a visitor this year. Another comment: 'An enjoyable stay: there was a good mix of ages among the staff, all were friendly and helpful.' The elegant sitting rooms have ornate plasterwork, marble fireplaces, picture windows, comfortable sofas; children are welcomed, but one lounge is designated child-free. In the *Weeping Elm* restaurant, the chef, Kelan McMichael, uses Donegal meat and fish in his dishes, perhaps Lough Swilly salmon and haddock fishcake, lemon butter sauce; dry-aged sirloin of beef, girolles, caramelised shallots, red wine jus. 'My only gripe was that the same vegetables were served every night.' Simpler meals are available in *Batt's Bar* and the *Cellar Bar*. The style of the bedrooms in the main house is traditional; rooms in an extension are contemporary; each of the ground-floor rooms has a door that leads to an outside sitting area. The 'excellent' breakfast can be taken until 11 am. (*Kate MacMaster, Yolanda Burrows-Hueppi*)

Rathmullan

T: 00 353 74-915 8188
F: 00 353 74-915 8200
E: info@rathmullanhouse.com
W: www.rathmullanhouse.com

BEDROOMS: 32, some on ground floor, 2 suitable for &.
OPEN: mid-Feb–6 Jan, closed midweek Nov/Dec, Christmas.
FACILITIES: ramps, 4 sitting rooms, library, TV room, cellar bar/bistro, restaurant, free Wi-Fi in lounges, 15-metre indoor swimming pool, wedding facilities, 7-acre grounds (tennis, croquet).
BACKGROUND MUSIC: none.
LOCATION: ½ mile N of village.
CHILDREN: all ages welcomed.
DOGS: allowed in 1 bedroom, but not in public rooms.
CREDIT CARDS: Amex, MasterCard, Visa.
PRICES: [2013] per person B&B €70–€125, D,B&B €115–€170. Set dinner €45/€55. 1-night bookings refused bank holiday Sat.

RIVERSTOWN Co. Sligo

Map 6:B5

COOPERSHILL

🏆 *César award in 1987*

'An unforgettable experience', is an inspector's comment on this imposing Palladian mansion in a sizeable, 'luxuriant' estate with woodland and a deer farm. This year a reader agreed: 'Very special; back to bygone times.' The mansion is run on house-party lines by Simon O'Hara (his family have owned the house for eight generations); his partner, Christina McCauley, is the *Ballymaloe*-trained chef. They follow a green ethos; public rooms are heated with windblown wood from the estate, electricity comes from renewable sources, while rainwater is mixed with spring water and filtered for use. There are no locks on the doors of the spacious bedrooms, which are furnished with original antiques; each has a modern en suite bathroom. A room at the top of the staircase had 'a wonderful view of greenery and distant hills'. Dinner is taken at separate tables in the 'gracious' dining room. The 'wonderful' meal might include Ummera organic salmon, sweet cucumber pickle; rack of Riverstown lamb with redcurrants. 'The attention to detail in the house is of the highest standards.' (*Yolanda Burrows-Hueppi, and others*)

Riverstown

T: 00 353 71-916 5108
E: ohara@coopershill.com
W: www.coopershill.com

BEDROOMS: 8.
OPEN: Apr–Oct, off-season house parties by arrangement.
FACILITIES: 2 halls, drawing room, dining room, snooker room, free Wi-Fi, wedding facilities, 500-acre estate (garden, tennis, croquet, woods, farmland, river with trout fishing), unsuitable for &.
BACKGROUND MUSIC: none.
LOCATION: 11 miles SE of Sligo.
CHILDREN: by arrangement.
DOGS: by arrangement.
CREDIT CARDS: MasterCard, Visa.
PRICES: [2013] per person B&B single €134–€157, double €99–€122. Set dinner €49.

SCHULL Co. Cork

Map 6:D4

GROVE HOUSE

Built as a hotel in 1880 above the harbour of this pretty village, this unusual building is an informal guest house run by the 'charming' Swedish owner, Katarina Runske, and her son, Nico, who is the chef. On view in the library is the original guest book, signed by George Bernard Shaw and Jack B Yeats, the artist. 'We continue as an artistic hub,' says Katarina Runske, who organises musical gigs and recitals, exhibitions and writers' retreats. Artwork (much of it for sale) is displayed throughout the house, which is liked for the 'well-used feel – a fair share of clutter'. In the dining room, which has a conservatory extension, Nico Runske uses produce from the kitchen garden (enhanced this year by new polytunnels) for his daily-changing three-course menus of simple dishes like squid with chilli sauce; rack of lamb Provençal. 'Great pride' is taken in the wine list. The nicely proportioned bedrooms, named after the writers who have stayed in the house, vary in aspect; they overlook either the harbour or nearby Mount Gabriel. Original fireplaces have been retained. (*EC*)

Colla Road
Schull

T: 00 353 28-28067
F: 00 353 28-28069
E: info@grovehouseschull.com
W: www.grovehouseschull.com

BEDROOMS: 5.
OPEN: all year except Christmas.
FACILITIES: bar, sitting room, dining room, free Wi-Fi, wedding facilities, terrace, 1-acre garden, only dining room suitable for &.
BACKGROUND MUSIC: classical in dining room.
LOCATION: outskirts of village.
CHILDREN: all ages welcomed.
DOGS: allowed in bedrooms.
CREDIT CARDS: Amex, MasterCard, Visa.
PRICES: [2013] per room B&B single €40–€50, double €70–€80. Set dinner €25.

SHANAGARRY Co. Cork

Map 6:D5

BALLYMALOE HOUSE

❧ *César award in 1984*

'The epitome of Irish country house hospitality', the Allen family's renowned ivy-covered Georgian mansion wins a 'strong endorsement' this year from a visitor returning after many years. A 'true family affair', *Ballymaloe* was founded by Myrtle Allen; the hotel/restaurant is managed by her daughter-in-law, Hazel; another daughter-in-law, Darina, runs the famous cookery school. 'They are still very much in evidence.' The large number of staff are 'infallibly helpful and relaxed'. Bedrooms, individually decorated, vary in size and view: a 'cosy' room had two deep armchairs, a large wardrobe, good lighting; a smallish bathroom. Public rooms are 'varied and comfortable'. In the dining room (where the mood is 'cheerful, with lots of chatter'), head chef Jason Fahey serves a 'delicious' five-course menu ('quantities are well judged'): 'Every ingredient was locally sourced or home made; we enjoyed excellent soups, lovely bread; rare slices of sirloin and duck.' Breakfast, served until 10.30 am, has fruit compotes, home-made preserves, delicious breads, 'all the usual things attractively presented'. (*Richard Parish, and others*)

25% DISCOUNT VOUCHERS

Shanagarry

T: 00 353 21-465 2531
F: 00 353 21-465 2021
E: res@ballymaloe.ie
W: www.ballymaloe.ie

BEDROOMS: 29, 7 in adjacent building, 4 on ground floor, 5 self-catering cottages suitable for &.
OPEN: all year except 23–26 Dec, 2 weeks in Jan.
FACILITIES: drawing room, 2 small sitting rooms, conservatory, 7 dining rooms, free Wi-Fi, wedding and conference facilities, 6-acre gardens, 400-acre grounds (tennis, swimming pool, 10 by 4 metres), cookery school nearby.
BACKGROUND MUSIC: none.
LOCATION: 20 miles E of Cork.
CHILDREN: all ages welcomed.
DOGS: allowed in courtyard rooms, not in house.
CREDIT CARDS: all major cards.
PRICES: [2013] per person B&B €90–€135, D,B&B €160–€205. Set dinner €70.

UPPERLANDS Co. Londonderry

Map 6:B6

ARDTARA COUNTRY HOUSE NEW

Built by the linen magnate Harry Jackson Clark, this Victorian mansion with bow-fronted windows is run as a country hotel. It is owned by Dr Alistair Hanna; Valerie Ferson is the manager. 'The domestic atmosphere and consistently friendly service are a joy,' says a trusted correspondent, restoring *Ardtara* to a full entry after a long period without reports. It stands in 'extensive and beautifully kept' grounds with fine mature trees and well-cut lawns. A small formal lounge has comfortable seating, views of the garden; original fireplaces have been retained (with gas imitation fires). In the dining room (slightly dark with an oriel window on the north wall), Julian Davidson serves a short menu of 'well-cooked' dishes, perhaps goat's cheese galette, walnuts and red pepper salad; French trimmed pork rack, bacon dust, date-crushed potatoes. 'My large bedroom overlooked the front of the house: full-length turquoise curtain and green-striped wallpaper; a comfortable king-size bed; a Victorian dresser with mirror and wardrobe; a high-ceilinged bathroom with a tub bath and a walk-in shower.' Breakfast had 'excellent spiced black pudding'; packaged juice. (*Robert Gower*)

8 Gorteade Road
Upperlands BT46 5SA

T: 028-7964 4490
F: 028-7964 5080
E: Valerie_ferson@ardtara.com
W: www.ardtara.com

BEDROOMS: 9, 1 on ground floor suitable for ♿.
OPEN: all year except 25/26 Dec.
FACILITIES: 2 lounges, sun room, bar, dining room, free Wi-Fi, civil wedding licence, 8-acre grounds, tennis.
BACKGROUND MUSIC: none.
LOCATION: outskirts of village, 3 miles NE of Maghera.
CHILDREN: all ages welcome.
DOGS: not allowed.
CREDIT CARDS: Amex, MasterCard, Visa.
PRICES: [2013] per room B&B £100–£120, D,B&B £155–£190. À la carte £30.

SHORTLIST

The Shortlist complements our main section by including potential but untested new entries and appropriate places in areas where we have limited choice. It also has some hotels that have been full entries in the *Guide*, but have not attracted feedback from our readers.

Losehill House, Hope

LONDON

Map 2:D4

THE ALMA, 499 Old York Road, SW18 1TF. Tel 020-8870 2537, www.thealma.co.uk. Behind a popular Victorian pub, this modern hotel (Young's Hotels) is a conversion of a former metal works. It is run on green lines: solar panels provide energy for hot water and electricity; lights and electrical appliances are programmed to work only when guests are indoors. The entrance to the brick-and-glass building is down a cobbled alley; spacious bedrooms have bold wallpaper and bespoke furniture. The dining room at the back of the busy bar serves typical gastropub fare; on weekends, breakfast is served until 11 am. Bar, restaurant, function room. Free Wi-Fi. Background music. Civil wedding licence. Use of local Virgin Spa and Gym. Children welcomed. 23 bedrooms (2 on ground floor suitable for &). Per room B&B £129–£159. (Wandsworth Town railway station; 15 mins to Waterloo)

THE AMPERSAND, 10 Harrington Road, SW7 3ER. Tel 020-7589 5895, www.ampersandhotel.com. Taking inspiration from neighbouring museums and the Royal Albert Hall nearby, this large, informal hotel in a renovated Victorian building is decorated with references to botany, music, geometry, ornithology and astronomy. Staff are 'laid back'. The modern bedrooms have a high ceiling, an oversized bedhead; free soft drinks from the minibar. Mediterranean dishes are served in the white-tiled basement restaurant, *Apero*; the *Drawing Rooms* have light meals and afternoon tea.

Drawing room, library, bar, restaurant, private dining room; games room (table tennis); gym; running maps and information on activities in Hyde Park (horse riding, in-line skating) available. Free Wi-Fi. Children welcomed. Public parking nearby (reservation required). 111 bedrooms and suites. Room only from £182. À la carte breakfast from £5. (Underground: South Kensington)

AVO HOTEL, 82 Dalston Lane, Hackney, E8 3AH. Tel 020-3490 5061, www.avohotel.com. Amiable owners Narendra Kotecha and family run this small hotel in a former post office and newsagent's shop in lively Dalston. Snug black-and-white bedrooms have an iPod docking station and a memory-foam mattress; the smart bathrooms have dressing gowns. The in-house Vinvixen 'liquor store and lounge' sells wine and food of 'exceptional interest or artisanal character'. At breakfast, special diets can be catered for. Lounge, bar. Free Wi-Fi. DVD library; mobile phone loans for overseas visitors. Occasional background music. Children welcomed. 6 bedrooms. Per room B&B (continental) from £79. (Overground: Dalston Junction)

B+B BELGRAVIA, 64–66 Ebury Street, SW1W 9QD. Tel 020-7259 8570, www.bb-belgravia.com. With 'excellently appointed' bedrooms, this 'modern' B&B, in an elegant Grade II listed Georgian town house, offers 'a great price for a London hotel'. Some rooms have views over the garden; larger studios are well equipped for eating in. A 'sumptuous' breakfast has croissants, cereals, toast and fruit; 'bacon and eggs so good I had them twice'. Lounge (fireplace, complimentary tea/coffee/hot chocolate and biscuits, DVDs, library), open-plan kitchen/ breakfast room (organic breakfasts), small garden. Free Wi-Fi and bicycles. No background music. Children and dogs welcomed. 17 bedrooms (2 family; 1 suitable for ♿), plus 9 studios close by. Per room B&B £89–£225. (Underground: Victoria)

BASE2STAY, 25 Courtfield Gardens, SW5 0PG. Tel 020-7244 2255, www.base2stay.com. A short walk from the museums and Kensington Gardens, this neat, modern hotel occupies a white stucco town house in a quiet square. It is managed by Sandra Anido for the small Nadler Hotels group, whose goal is no-frills 'affordable luxury' (see also Liverpool). Each bedroom has a mini-kitchen (microwave, fridge, sink); larger rooms also have a Nespresso coffee machine. There is no restaurant or bar, but guests receive discounts at local eating spots. Reception lobby (background music). Free Wi-Fi, music library, games. Children welcomed. 67 bedrooms (some with bunk beds; 1 suitable for ♿). Room only £120–£220. (Underground: Earls Court, Gloucester Road)

BERMONDSEY SQUARE HOTEL, Bermondsey Square, Tower Bridge Road, SE1 3UN. Tel 020-7378 2450, www.bermondseysquarehotel.co.uk. With weekend markets on its doorstep (antiques on Friday, produce on Saturday) and an art-house cinema across the square, this contemporary hotel gives guests a taste of local life in a vibrant area. Stylish bedrooms have an Apple iMac, and a wet room with a drench shower; *Gregg's Bar & Grill* (by

MasterChef judge Gregg Wallace) serves 'uncomplicated' British food. Well placed for Borough Market and walks across Tower Bridge. Background music. Business facilities. Lift. Free Wi-Fi. Children and dogs welcomed (boutique dog beds). 80 bedrooms (5 suites; some suitable for ♿). Room only from £120. À la carte breakfast from £3. (Underground: Bermondsey, Tower Hill)

CHARLOTTE STREET HOTEL, 15–17 Charlotte Street, W1T 1RJ. Tel 020-7806 2000, www.charlottestreet hotel.com. Inspired by the Bloomsbury Set, this luxury hotel just north of Soho displays original work by Vanessa Bell, Duncan Grant and Roger Fry, as well as other British artists of the period. It is managed by Anna Jackson for Tim and Kit Kemp's Firmdale group. Bedrooms are boldly decorated; bathrooms are of solid granite, most with a walk-in shower and double basins. Drawing room, library, *Oscar* bar, open-plan restaurant (run by chef Robin Read). 3 private dining/meeting rooms, 75-seat screening room, gym. Free Wi-Fi. No background music. Children welcomed (cots; babysitting). 52 bedrooms. Room only from £300. Breakfast £18–£20. (Underground: Goodge Street, Tottenham Court Road)

COUNTY HALL PREMIER INN, Belvedere Road, SE1 7PB. Tel 0871-527 8648, www.premierinn.com. On the banks of the Thames, this busy hotel (owned by Whitbread) occupies part of the historic Portland stone County Hall building along with restaurants and tourist attractions such as the SEA LIFE London Aquarium and the London Dungeon. The functional, simply furnished bedrooms have double-glazed windows; some have views of the London Eye and the river. Self-service check-in. Lobby, bar, *Thyme* restaurant; lift. Conference facilities. Wi-Fi (first half-hour free; subsequently £3 per 24 hours or £10 per 7 days). Background music. Children welcomed. 314 bedrooms (some suitable for &). Room only from £189. Meal deal (dinner and breakfast) £22.99 per person. (Underground: Waterloo)

COVENT GARDEN HOTEL, 10 Monmouth Street, WC2H 9HB. Tel 020-7806 1000, www.firmdalehotels.com. Liked for its 'superb comfort and fantastic service', this 'distinctively decorated' hotel is part of Tim and Kit Kemp's small Firmdale group. A stone staircase leads from the lobby to the wood-panelled drawing room, an opulent space with vivid upholstery and a French stone fireplace; the adjoining library has an honesty bar. Furnished with leather seats, the basement screening room hosts Saturday movie nights. In *Brasserie Max*, 'excellent' meals (also available on room service) have 'a light European touch'; pre- and post-performance suppers are ideal for theatre-going guests. Breakfasts (extra charge) have a vast choice. Drawing room, library (honesty bar), restaurant. Meeting room, screening room; gym. Free Wi-Fi. No background music. Children welcomed. 58 bedrooms. Room only £315–£2,210. Breakfast £18–£26. (Underground: Covent Garden, Leicester Square)

DORSET SQUARE HOTEL, 39–40 Dorset Square, Marylebone, NW1 6QN. Tel 020-7723 7874, www.firmdalehotels.com.

On a quiet garden square in Marylebone, this small hotel in a Regency town house is vibrantly decorated with a loud and lively mixture of colours, patterns and textiles. It is part of the Firmdale Hotels group owned by Kit and Tim Kemp. The contemporary English-style bedrooms can be small, but many have views of the leafy square. Children have their own menu and toiletries. Drawing room (fireplace, honesty bar), *The Potting Shed* brasserie. Free Wi-Fi. No background music. Room service. DVD library. 38 bedrooms. Room only from £195. Breakfast from £14.50. (Underground: Marylebone)

THE EGERTON HOUSE HOTEL, 17–19 Egerton Terrace, SW3 2BX. Tel 020-7589 2412, www.egertonhousehotel.com. Sumptuously decorated with prints and paintings, richly patterned wallpaper and antique furniture, this luxury town house hotel (Red Carnation group) is steps away from Harrods and the V&A Museum. The well-equipped bedrooms (iPod docking station, flat-screen TV, etc) have fresh fruit and magazines; children are welcomed with books, games, their own bathrobe and slippers. Guests have use of a gym and pool at a local club. Drawing room, bar (classical background music), breakfast room. Lift. Free Wi-Fi. 24-hour butler service. Children welcomed. Valet parking. 30 bedrooms (some on ground floor). Room only £432–£516. Breakfast £21–£29.50. (Underground: Knightsbridge, South Kensington)

FLEET RIVER ROOMS, 71 Lincoln's Inn Fields, WC2A 3JF. Tel 020-7691 1457, www.fleetriverbakery.com. Surrounded by freshly baked muffins, cheesecakes, tarts and biscuits, guests at this bakery-with-rooms check in through the popular café on a quiet corner of a public square. Upstairs, the simple, modern studio apartments have a polished wood floor, sash windows, a sitting area and a white-tiled kitchen (fridge, oven, microwave, washing machine). Some rooms have a sofa bed to accommodate a large group. No dinner is served, but guests who want to eat out have the restaurants of Covent Garden and Bloomsbury on their doorstep. Breakfast in the bakery has scrambled eggs, sourdough toast, fruit salad, yogurt; generous portions. Free Wi-Fi. Children welcomed. 4 bedrooms. Per room B&B £84–£115. (Underground: Holborn)

41, 41 Buckingham Palace Road, SW1W 0PS. Tel 020-7300 0041, www.41hotel.com. On a site by turns home to a coach builder, a linen emporium and a ballroom for debutante dances, this historic building today houses two Red Carnation hotels: *The Rubens* and, on its fifth floor, *41*. An intimate space with mahogany panelling and polished brass, *41* has the atmosphere of a private club – albeit one where guests are invited to 'plunder the pantry' and help themselves to complimentary snacks each evening. Decorated to a black-and-white theme, the modern bedrooms have state-of-the-art technology, a selection of magazines and books, and season-appropriate bathrobes. Close to Buckingham Palace and St James's Park. Room, and butler service. Background music. Free Wi-Fi. Business facilities. Complimentary pass to nearby fitness club (swimming pool, sauna, spa). Children and dogs welcomed. 30 bedrooms and suites. Room only £443–£467. Breakfast £19.50–£25. (Underground: Victoria)

GRIM'S DYKE HOTEL, Old Redding, Harrow Weald, HA3 6SH. Tel 020-8385 3100, www.grimsdyke.com. 'A good base with a country house atmosphere', this hotel is in a restored house designed by Richard Norman Shaw. The former country residence of Sir William Gilbert, it has become a shrine for Gilbert and Sullivan enthusiasts. Many original features have been retained: flamboyant stone carvings, an inglenook fireplace, shelves reputed to have held some 400 volumes (now filled with wines, liqueurs and more than 40 single malts in the bar). It stands in extensive gardens and woodlands; Victorian greenhouses and beehives supply fruit, vegetables and honey to the restaurant, where head chef Daren Mason serves 'reasonably priced' menus and afternoon teas. Comfortable rooms, furnished in traditional style, are housed in the main building or in modern lodges; some have a balcony. *Library* bar, *Gilbert's* restaurant; terrace; garden (open to the public); croquet. Free Wi-Fi. Children welcomed. Parking. 46 bedrooms (9 in main house; 2 with easy access in lodges). Room only £75–£115. (Station: Harrow & Wealdstone, Stanmore, Harrow-On-The Hill; 10 mins by train to Euston, 30 mins by tube to Baker Street)

THE HALKIN BY COMO, 5 Halkin Street, SW1X 7DJ. Tel 020-7333 1000, www.halkin.como.bz. Among the embassies and grand residences in this elegant, Georgian-style neighbourhood, this tranquil, contemporary hotel blends Asian and Italian design. Bedrooms have neutral interiors and a marble bathroom; some overlook the garden. *Ametsa with Arzak Instruction*, a Basque restaurant run by *Michelin*-starred daughter-and-father team Elena and Juan Mari Arzak, opened in March 2013. Light lunches and afternoon tea are taken in the more casual *Halkin Bar*. There is background music in the bar and restaurant. Guests have access to the Shambhala Urban Escape spa in sister hotel *Metropolitan* on Park Lane. Bar, restaurant. Gym (trainer and yoga teacher available). Free Wi-Fi. Children welcomed. 41 bedrooms. Room only from £288. (Underground: Hyde Park Corner)

HAYMARKET HOTEL, 1 Suffolk Place, SW1Y 4HX. Tel 020-7470 4000, www.haymarkethotel.com. 'Beautifully furnished' in contemporary style by Kit Kemp, this hotel occupies three John Nash-designed buildings in the heart of London's theatre district. It is managed by Lisa Brooklyn, with 'the nicest and most helpful staff', for Firmdale Hotels. Families are welcomed: young guests are provided with books, DVDs and popcorn, Nintendo Wii, and their own bathrobes and toiletries. Lift, conservatory, library, bar, *Brumus* restaurant. 'Stunning' indoor swimming pool, gym. Background music. Free Wi-Fi. Civil wedding licence. 50 bedrooms (2 suites; 5-bedroom town house). Room only from £325. Breakfast from £18. (Underground: Green Park, Piccadilly)

HOTEL 55, 55 Hanger Lane, W5 3HL. Tel 020-8991 4450, www.hotel55-london.com. The red light in the porch of this privately owned hotel in the west London suburbs serves as a cheeky wink at the building's colourful past: No. 55 was the local brothel. Today, it has been restored by the Tohani family, who have given it a modern interior enlivened by original abstract art. Bedrooms are compact; garden rooms are the quietest. The conservatory dining room houses a Japanese restaurant popular with locals; a decked walkway leads to the landscaped garden. 24-hour lounge bar (background music), *Momo* restaurant. Free Wi-Fi. Children welcomed. 30 mins from Heathrow and central London by tube. Limited free parking. 26 bedrooms (some suitable for &). Per room B&B (continental) £85–£129. Dinner from £35. (Underground: North Ealing)

THE HOXTON, 81 Great Eastern Street, EC2A 3HU. Tel 020-7550 1000, www.hoxtonhotels.com. With a 'buzzy' bar and brasserie and 'helpful young staff', this lively east London hotel is at once 'intensely stylish' and 'curiously comforting'. 'Well-equipped' bedrooms have a 'good' tea and coffee tray, fresh milk in the fridge and an 'excellent' rain shower; seven individually styled 'concept' rooms take inspiration from the neighbourhood and have exposed brick walls, street art or a bed made from reclaimed floorboards. The room rate includes a breakfast bag (yogurt, granola, banana, orange juice) delivered to the room each morning. Lounge (background music) and outdoor space (interior courtyard). Lift. Meeting rooms; shop. Free Wi-Fi. Children welcomed. 208 rooms. Per room B&B £69–£179. (Underground: Old Street)

H10 LONDON WATERLOO, 284–302 Waterloo Road, SE1 8RQ. Tel 020-7928 4062, www.hotelh10londonwaterloo. com. Handy for the South Bank, this good-value Spanish chain hotel has attentive staff and 'high standards'. Occupying a purpose-built, 11-storey building, it has a sleek, contemporary interior. The bright, compact bedrooms have large windows; some have impressive views of the London Eye and the city skyline. 'A breakfast buffet of considerable size.' On a busy road south of Waterloo station (some traffic noise). Lounge, bar, *Three O Two* restaurant. Leisure centre (gym, sauna, hydromassage shower; treatments); meeting rooms. Free Wi-Fi. 177 bedrooms. Room only £155–£228. Dinner £30. (Underground: Waterloo)

INDIGO, 16 London Street, W2 1HL. Tel 020-7706 4444, www.hipaddington. com. Conveniently located for Paddington station and the London–Heathrow Express, this modern hotel (part of the InterContinental Hotels group) has artful views of the local area: bedrooms are decorated with photographic murals of nearby Hyde Park and Little Venice. Simply furnished in contemporary style, the rooms (some can be small) have a hardwood floor, spa-inspired shower, bright colours on a neutral background. Lounge/lobby, bar, brasserie; terrace. Fitness studio. Background music. Free Wi-Fi. Children welcomed. 64 bedrooms (some with private balcony or terrace; 2 suitable for &). Per room B&B £183–£303. (Underground: Paddington)

KNIGHTSBRIDGE HOTEL, 10 Beaufort Gardens, SW3 1PT. Tel 020-7584 6300, www.knightsbridgehotel.com. Decorated with flair, this white-pillared town house hotel (Firmdale Hotels) stands in a peaceful, tree-lined cul-de-sac, close to designer stores and museums. Managed by Fiona Milne, it has an intimate feel: cosy sitting areas have open fires and interesting 20th-century British art. In modern English style, the colourful bedrooms have a writing desk and a bathroom of granite and oak; most rooms have views of Beaufort Gardens or across Harrods and the city skyline. Afternoon tea is also available to non-residents. Drawing room, library, bar. Free Wi-Fi. Room service; in-room beauty treatments by arrangement. No background music. Children welcomed. 44 bedrooms. Room only from £235. Breakfast from £18. (Underground: Knightsbridge)

THE MAIN HOUSE, 6 Colville Road, Notting Hill, W11 2BP. Tel 020-7221 9691, www.themainhouse.co.uk. The antithesis of a large chain hotel, this 'elegant home from home' is on a quiet street off Portobello Road. Each suite occupies an entire floor and has period features, antique furnishings, modern technology and an airy, uncluttered look. A complimentary newspaper and morning coffee or tea are brought to the room or served on the balcony (organic continental or full English breakfast also available). Guests receive special day rates at the nearby BodyWorksWest health club, and discounts at several smart delis and an artisan baker nearby. Roof terrace. Free Wi-Fi. No background music. Mobile phones available to borrow; DVD library. Children welcomed. Reasonable rates for chauffeur service to airports.

4 bedrooms. Room only from £110 (min. 3-night stay). (Underground: Notting Hill Gate)

THE ORANGE, 37 Pimlico Road, SW1W 8NE. Tel 020-7881 9844, www.theorange.co.uk. 'Much enjoyed', this smart pub-with-rooms occupies an impressive white-painted building dating back to 1846. Renovated in chic-rustic style, it is part of the Cubitt House group (see also *The Grazing Goat*, Marble Arch, London, main entry). The ground-floor pub is popular with well-heeled locals; in the restaurant on the first floor, the wood-fired pizzas are 'a highlight'. Up the narrow stairs, the bedrooms are 'well designed, simple, yet very smart and comfortable'; they have limewashed walls, a king-size bed, a marble bathroom. Bar, dining room. Background music (soul, jazz). Free Wi-Fi. Children welcomed. 4 bedrooms. Room only £195–£225. À la carte breakfast from £3.50; dinner from £32. (Underground: Sloane Square, Victoria)

THE ROOKERY, 12 Peter's Lane, Cowcross Street, EC1M 6DS. Tel 020-7336 0931, www.rookeryhotel.com. In a lively neighbourhood once infamous for footpads and cutpurses, this small luxury hotel occupies three Georgian houses painstakingly refurbished by owners Peter McKay and Douglas Blain (who also own *Hazlitt's*, Soho, London, see main entry). The public rooms have polished wood panelling, flagstone floors, open fires; the atmosphere of a private club. Furnished with pictures and antiques, the bedrooms have a 17th-century carved oak or Georgian four-poster bed. The remarkable Rook's Nest penthouse suite overlooks St Paul's

Cathedral and the Old Bailey. Drawing room, library, conservatory; meeting rooms. Free Wi-Fi. Courtyard garden. No restaurant, but a limited room-service menu is available. No background music. Children welcomed. 33 bedrooms. Room only £222–£660. Continental breakfast £11.95. (Underground: Farringdon, Barbican)

ST JAMES'S HOTEL AND CLUB, 7–8 Park Place, SW1A 1LS. Tel 020-7316 1600, www.stjameshotelandclub.com. In a quiet cul-de-sac, this luxury town house hotel (Althoff Hotel & Gourmet Collection) has been opulently renovated: there are marble pillars; Murano glass chandeliers; silk, velvet and cashmere fabrics, and original artwork including a collection of portraits from the 1920s to the 1940s. Henrik Muehle is the manager. The restful bedrooms have a glamorous bathroom; some rooms have their own balcony. In the dramatically designed restaurant (striking wallpaper; bold mixtures of patterns and rich colours), chef William Drabble has a *Michelin* star for his French-inspired cooking. Lounge, bar, *William's* bar and bistro, *Seven Park Place* (closed Sun, Mon). Background music. 4 meeting rooms. Free Wi-Fi. Children welcomed (dedicated kids' concierge). 60 bedrooms (10 suites; 2 on ground floor). Room only from £260; suite from £440. Breakfast £16–£22. (Underground: Green Park)

SANCTUARY HOUSE HOTEL, 33 Tothill Street, SW1H 9LA. Tel 020-7799 4044, www.sanctuaryhousehotel.co.uk. On one of the oldest streets in Westminster, there are good-value rooms upstairs and home-made pies downstairs in this updated Victorian ale-and-pie house (part of Fuller's Hotels and Inns). Decorated in neutral shades, the modern bedrooms above the popular pub are 'very comfortable' (some can be snug). Minutes from Westminster Abbey, the Houses of Parliament and St James's Park. Bar, restaurant. Free Wi-Fi. Background music. Lift. Room service. Children welcomed. 34 bedrooms (some suitable for ᵫ). Room only £150–£190. Breakfast £9.25–£12.95. (Underground: St James's Park)

Sloane Square Hotel, 7–12 Sloane Square, SW1W 8EG. Tel 020-7896 9988, www.sloanesquarehotel.co.uk. The 'clever design', 'smart interiors' and 'nice, helpful staff' stand out at this 'very pleasant' hotel on a fashionable square. 'Our modern room was very small, but brilliantly fitted out, with an extremely comfortable bed, desk/dressing table with coffee-maker; minibar filled with things you might actually want.' Breakfast has 'good cooked dishes', fresh fruit and patisseries from the buffet. *Chelsea* brasserie (background music), bar. Free Wi-Fi, and local and national phone calls. Lift. Parking (charge). Children welcomed. 102 bedrooms. Room only £170–£260. Continental buffet breakfast £12.95. (Underground: Sloane Square)

The Soho Hotel, 4 Richmond Mews, off Dean Street, W1D 3DH. Tel 020-7559 3000, www.sohohotel.com. A ten-foot-high Botero bronze cat welcomes guests to this glamorous hotel (part of Tim and Kit Kemp's Firmdale group) on a quiet side street in an animated neighbourhood. Among Kit

Kemp's design touches are elegant bedrooms with floor-to-ceiling windows, imaginative mixes of colours and patterns, luxurious bathrooms in dark woods and marble. Families are welcomed (children's menu, books, Sony PlayStation, Nintendo Wii, DVDs and popcorn). Drawing room, library, bar, *Refuel* restaurant, 4 private dining rooms. Gym, beauty treatment rooms. 2 screening rooms; DVD library. Background music. Free Wi-Fi. Lift. Civil wedding licence. 91 bedrooms and suites (some suitable for ᵫ). Also 4 apartments. Room only £295–£4,140. Full English breakfast £21.50. (Underground: Leicester Square)

South Place Hotel, 3 South Place, EC2M 2AF. Tel 020-3503 0000, www.southplacehotel.com. Sophisticated and lively, with Conran-designed interiors and contemporary art by London-based artists, this purpose-built hotel was opened by restaurant group D&D London in September 2012. The bedrooms (four categories) are simply styled in a modern palette of greys and white; they have a built-in oak wardrobe and a marble bathroom. The top-floor *Angler* restaurant (closed Sat lunch, and Sun) has a mirrored ceiling and floor-to-ceiling windows with views across the City; head chef Tony Fleming features British seafood dishes. Bistro food is available all day at *3 South Place* bar and grill (DJ most nights). 3 bars, 2 restaurants, *Le Chiffre* residents' lounge and games room (books, magazines, games, turntable, cocktails); roof terrace; 'secret' garden. Gym; treatment room. Private dining, meeting rooms. Free Wi-Fi. Background music. Children welcomed (cots; interconnecting rooms).

80 bedrooms, studios and suites (4 suitable for &). Room only £185–£480. Breakfast £16.50. (Underground: Moorgate, Liverpool Street)

SYDNEY HOUSE CHELSEA, 9–11 Sydney Street, SW3 6PU. Tel 020-7376 7711, www.sydneyhousechelsea.com. Lavender bushes flank the entrance of this Georgian town house hotel (part of Brownsword Hotels' Baby ABode collection) on a residential street minutes from the King's Road. Styled in biscuit shades, the neat, modern bedrooms have quality linens and Scottish lambswool throws; the Room at the Top has a private roof garden with terracotta pots and teak chairs. Drawing room, bar, restaurant (open to non-residents for breakfast), room service (light snacks); roof terrace; boardroom. Free Wi-Fi. Background music in lobby. Children welcomed. 21 bedrooms. Room only £125–£280. À la carte breakfast from £5.95. (Underground: South Kensington)

TEN MANCHESTER STREET, Marylebone, W1U 4DG. Tel 020-7317 5900, www.tenmanchesterstreethotel. com. On a residential street in fashionable Marylebone, this discreet, designer-furnished hotel (Bespoke Hotels) is in a red brick Edwardian town house. Bedrooms are individually styled; four open on to a private terrace with seating, music and heaters. Italian food features on the lunch and dinner set menus; snacks are available all day in the cosy, L-shaped *Ten Lounge Bar*. Cigar smokers have a humidor and large cigar menu, and an all-weather smoking terrace. Lounge/bar (background music). Free Wi-Fi. 24-

hour room service; chauffeur service. 45 bedrooms (9 suites). Room only £152–£400. Breakfast £15.95–£17.95. (Underground: Bond Street)

THREADNEEDLES, 5 Threadneedle Street, EC2R 8AY. Tel 020-7657 8080, www.hotelthreadneedles.co.uk. An impressive hand-painted stained-glass dome curves over the reception lounge of this City hotel (Eton Collection), formerly a Victorian banking hall. Beyond the walnut-panelled walls and grand marble floors, the modern bedrooms are decorated with photographs and abstract art; a shoe-shine service and daily newspaper are included in the room rate. Background music. Bar, *Bonds* restaurant (modern British cuisine; Stephen Smith is chef; closed at weekends). Lift. 3 meeting rooms; conference facilities. Free Wi-Fi. 74 bedrooms (1 suitable for &). Room only £135–£445. Breakfast £15. (Underground: Bank)

TOWN HALL HOTEL & APARTMENTS, Patriot Square, E2 9NF. Tel 020-7871 0460, www.townhallhotel.com. Once Bethnal Green town hall, this refurbished Grade II listed Edwardian building in east London is now a striking modern hotel with 'friendly, helpful staff'. Many original features have been restored: ornate moulded ceilings, marble pillars, a green stone lobby. The spacious, individually styled bedrooms have vintage furniture, sheepskin rugs, handmade chocolates. 'Our large, airy apartment had an excellent, stylish kitchen; a modern bathroom with lots of storage space; large, opening windows.' Downstairs, *Viajante* restaurant is run by Portuguese chef Nuno Mendes, who has a *Michelin* star for his experimental fusion food. Parking can be difficult. Bar, 2 restaurants. 'Gorgeous' indoor pool, gym (open 6 am to midnight). Free Wi-Fi. Background music. Civil wedding licence/function facilities. Lift. Children welcomed. 98 bedrooms and studios (with kitchen). Room only from £174. Breakfast from £15. (Underground: Bethnal Green)

ENGLAND

ALFRISTON East Sussex
Map 2:E4
WINGROVE HOUSE, High Street, BN26 5TD. Tel 01323-870276, www. wingrovehousealfriston.com. In a village close to the River Cuckmere, Nick Denyer's restaurant-with-rooms occupies a 19th-century colonial-style house with a charming veranda. 'We were welcomed with tea in front of the fire in the lounge.' The stylish bedrooms have seagrass flooring, a bespoke chandelier and an oversized bedhead; 'perfection'. Each has views of the village and surrounding countryside. 'Top-quality' modern British dinners have 'lots of good choices': locally reared meat and game; fish and organic produce sourced from nearby suppliers. Background music. Lounge/bar, brasserie (closed Mon–Fri lunchtime). Free Wi-Fi. Children welcomed. 5 bedrooms (2 with access to balcony). Per room B&B £100–£175. Dinner £30.

AMBLESIDE Cumbria
Map 4: inset C2
NANNY BROW, Clappersgate, LA22 9NF. Tel 015394-33232, www.nannybrow.co.uk. 'Could not be

faulted, and we can be quite fussy.' Sue and Peter Robinson have devoted 'a lot of thought' to the restoration of their Arts and Crafts house; eco-efficient improvements include a biomass boiler, insulation and thermal blackout blinds. Up a steep drive, the bright white guest house sits in a prominent position above Brathay village, with a 'most attractive' view of a winding river below and the fells beyond. In neutral colours, the large rooms are decorated with modern fabrics and antiques. 'We were made very welcome.' Lakeland breakfasts. Lounge, bar, dining room. Free Wi-Fi. 'Easy listening' background music. Parking. 6 acres of formal garden and woodlands; 1½ miles W of town. Resident dog and cat. 10 bedrooms (2 in an adjacent annexe, ideal for a family). Per room B&B £120–£270. 2-night min. stay at weekends.
25% DISCOUNT VOUCHERS

ARNSIDE Cumbria
Map 4: inset C2
NUMBER 43, The Promenade, LA5 0AA. Tel 01524-762761, www.no43.org.uk. Guests enthuse about the views from Lesley Hornsby's modern B&B, in a row of Victorian hillside villas on the promenade. With vistas across the Kent estuary, the front terrace is ideal for breakfast or languid pre-dinner drinks; in the summer months, there are barbecues on the working Victorian fireplace on the secluded terrace at the back. Decorated in light, fresh tones, bedrooms have home-made biscuits, freshly ground coffee, a jug of fresh milk; one suite has a bay window and binoculars for birdwatching. Traditional Cumbrian breakfasts; Buck's Fizz on Sunday mornings. Light suppers (meat,

cheese and smoked fish platters) available; summer barbecue packs by arrangement. Lounge (books, magazines, CDs), dining room (honesty bar); garden; front and rear terrace. Free Wi-Fi. Children over 5 allowed. 6 bedrooms (some with estuary views). Per room B&B £120–£185.

BARNSLEY Gloucestershire
Map 3:E6

THE VILLAGE PUB, Barnsley, GL7 5EF. Tel 01285-740421, www.thevillagepub.co.uk. There are 'excellent' dinners and smart country-style bedrooms at this refurbished pub-with-rooms in a pretty Cotswold village. It is under the same ownership as *Calcot Manor*, Tetbury, and *Barnsley House*, up the street (see main entries); pub guests have free access to the famous gardens at *Barnsley House*. In shades of cream, bedrooms have a separate entrance from the pub; some have exposed beams, others a four-poster bed. (Some rooms face the road and may have traffic noise.) 'Busy, though not rowdy – and without muzak', the welcoming dining room is 'quite upmarket for a pub': chef Graham Grafton's modern dishes use locally sourced produce and fruit and vegetables from *Barnsley House*'s kitchen garden. English farmhouse breakfasts; home-made jams and home-baked bread. Free Wi-Fi. 6 bedrooms. Per room B&B from £100–£150.

BATH Somerset
Map 2:D1

ABBEY HOTEL, 1 North Parade, BA1 1LF. Tel 01225-461603, www.abbeyhotelbath.co.uk. A handsome stone building close to the Abbey, this Best Western hotel has been given a makeover by experienced hoteliers Christa and Ian Taylor. The bedrooms, which have a modern decor, have good storage; they range from small doubles to large rooms suitable for a family. Under head chef Chris Staines, the all-day eaterie, *Allium Brasserie* (oak flooring, plush purple seating, modern art), serves 'excellent if pricey' food, with some Asian influences; bread is home-made. Outside, on the wide pavement with huge umbrellas, lunches, teas and light snacks can be taken in the *Terrace* café. Lounge, bar, restaurant. Lift. Background music. Free Wi-Fi. Children and dogs (£10 per day charge) welcomed. 60 bedrooms (7 family rooms; 1 suitable for &). Per person B&B £60–£100, D,B&B £90–£160.

AQUAE SULIS, 174–176 Newbridge Road, BA1 3LE. Tel 01225-420061, www.aquaesulishotel.co.uk. A pleasant 30-minute stroll along the river leads guests from the town centre to David and Jane Carnegie's traditional guest house, in an Edwardian building in the suburbs. (A short bus ride is an alternative.) The simply furnished, well-equipped bedrooms (hospitality tray, writing facilities, iPod docking station) are named after personalities associated with Bath, and have a modern bathroom. French and Spanish are spoken. Lounge bar, dining room (evening snack menu), computer lounge; patio/garden. Free Wi-Fi. Background music. Courtesy car to and from Bath Spa railway and bus station. Private parking, and unrestricted parking on street. Children welcomed; dogs by arrangement. 14 bedrooms (some on ground floor; 2 with private bathroom). Per room B&B single £59–£99, double £69–£130. 2-night min. stay at weekends.

BRINDLEYS, 14 Pulteney Gardens, BA2 4HG. Tel 01225-310444, www.brindleysbath.co.uk. White-painted furniture, pretty fabrics and fresh flowers give a contemporary French ambience to this 'attractive' Victorian villa. The 'very smart and bright' breakfast room overlooks the 'well-kept' front garden; it has comfortable chairs and is decorated with interesting culinary ornaments and pictures. Owned by Michael and Sarah Jones, and run with great enthusiasm by James Grundy and his wife, Ancl, the B&B is in a quiet residential area south of the city (a ten-minute walk to the centre). Lounge, breakfast room (soft background music); small garden. Free Wi-Fi. Complimentary on-street parking permits. 6 bedrooms (some are small). Per room B&B £90–£185. 2-night min. stay at weekends preferred.

DORIAN HOUSE, 1 Upper Oldfield Park, BA2 3JX. Tel 01225-426336, www.dorianhouse.co.uk. In a quiet neighbourhood within walking distance of the Roman Baths, this B&B in a Victorian stone house is imbued with a musical atmosphere. 'Friendly, chatty' owners Tim (a cellist) and Kathryn Hugh have refurbished it with style, from the striking black-and-white-tiled foyer to the modern art hung throughout the building. Named after musicians, the bedrooms have 'fabulous' views over the Royal Crescent or gardens; one, Slava, has a modern four-poster bed and a slipper bath. Robert and Lize Briers are the managers.

Lounge (open fire), conservatory breakfast room/music library; classical background music. Free Wi-Fi. 'Immaculate, vertiginous' small garden. Parking. Children welcomed. 13 bedrooms (1 on ground floor). Per room B&B £80–£165.

HARINGTON'S HOTEL, 8–10 Queen Street, BA1 1HE. Tel 01225-461728, www.haringtonshotel.co.uk. In a 'blissful' location on a quiet, cobbled side street, Melissa and Peter O'Sullivan's small, modern hotel (managed by Julian Mather) is formed from three Georgian town houses. Jewel-toned cushions and feature wallpaper enrich the otherwise neutral bedrooms. Chef Steph Box serves light meals and snacks in the café/bar until 9 pm; staff are happy to recommend local restaurants. Breakfasts cooked to order; gluten-free meals available. Lounge, café/bar ('easy listening' background music); small conference room. Free Wi-Fi. Small courtyard; outdoor hot tub (£7.50 per hour). Secure reserved parking nearby (£11 for 24 hrs). Children welcomed. 13 bedrooms, plus 2 self-catering apartments. Per room B&B £89–£168. 2-night min. stay at weekends preferred.

THE KENNARD, 11 Henrietta Street, BA2 6LL. Tel 01225-310472, www.kennard.co.uk. 'Helpful' owners Mary and Giovanni Baiano have brought an ornate Italian feel to their Georgian town house B&B, with Venetian chandeliers, elegant seating, and a golden urn set on a Corinthian column. Some superior rooms have a high ceiling, fine plasterwork and a canopied bed; most smaller rooms have views over the garden. Breakfast, served on tables set with fine linen and china, is 'excellent'. The 'well-kept, carefully designed' small garden is inspired by Jane Austen. Conveniently situated just over Pulteney Bridge. 'We were impressed.' No background music. 2 sitting areas, breakfast room; courtyard. Free Wi-Fi. Children over 8 allowed. Drivers are given a free parking permit. 12 bedrooms (2 on ground floor; 2 share a bathroom. 6 flights of stairs). Per person B&B £55–£80. 2-night min. stay at weekends preferred.

THREE ABBEY GREEN, 3 Abbey Green, BA1 1NW. Tel 01225-428558, www.threeabbeygreen.com. On a quiet square in the centre of Bath, 'friendly' mother-and-daughter team Sue Wright and Nici Jones run their 'very comfortable' B&B with great efficiency. Handsome bedrooms in the Grade II listed town house retain original features such as wood panelling and a fireplace; they are furnished with antiques. There is 'a good choice at breakfast, all freshly cooked and served promptly'. The hosts offer visitors plenty of helpful information about the city. Close to the Abbey, Roman Baths and Pump Rooms. Dining room (background radio). Free Wi-Fi (computer available). Children welcomed. 10 bedrooms (3 in adjoining building; 2 mobility-friendly on ground floor). Per person B&B £45–£90. 2-night min. stay at weekends.

BELFORD Northumberland
Map 4:A3
WAREN HOUSE, Waren Mill, NE70 7EE. Tel 01668-214581, www.warenhousehotel.co.uk. 'In a lovely spot' with views of Holy Island, Anita and Peter Laverack's Georgian country house overlooks the natural bird sanctuary of Budle Bay. They have filled it with family treasures. Given a 'thumbs-up' by a reader, it is liked for the 'tranquil surroundings', the 'comfortable and spacious room' and the 'superb' food: head chef Steven Owens's modern Northumberland dishes are 'beautifully cooked and presented'. Steve's wife, Lynne, manages the hotel. Drawing room; *Grays* restaurant (open to non-residents). Free Wi-Fi. No background music. Formal garden in 7-acre grounds; secure parking. Children not allowed. Dogs welcomed (in 2 rooms). 6 miles from Bamburgh. 15 bedrooms (3 suites; 4 rooms in courtyard; 2 suitable for &). Per person B&B £75–£100, D,B&B £75–£180.
25% DISCOUNT VOUCHERS

BELPER Derbyshire
Map 2:A2
DANNAH FARM, Bowmans Lane, Shottle, DE56 2DR. Tel 01773-550273, www.dannah.co.uk. Joan and Martin Slack's country B&B is on a working farm on a ridge in the Derbyshire Dales. Bedrooms have views over the garden and surrounding farmland; many of the indulgent bathrooms have a spa bath. A spa cabin (available for exclusive use) houses a Finnish sauna and a double steam shower; an outdoor hot tub sits on a large secluded terrace. Cooked farmhouse breakfasts include award-winning black pudding and home-made bread (vegetarians catered for); supper platters are available. 2 sitting rooms, dining room; meeting room. Free Wi-Fi. Licensed. No background music. Large walled garden; arbour; medieval moat. Parking. Children welcomed.

8 bedrooms (4 in courtyard; 3 on ground floor). Per room B&B £165–£295. Supper platter £16.95.

BERWICK East Sussex
Map 2:E4

GREEN OAK BARN, Alfriston Road, BN26 5QS. Tel 01323-870164, www.englishwine.co.uk. Oenophiles will appreciate the choice of more than 100 varieties of English wine at Christine and Colin Munday's English Wine Centre in landscaped gardens on the South Downs. A modern barn has 'smart and comfortable' bedrooms above a large communal space with a bar, sofas, baby grand piano and convincing book wallpaper. In the thatched *Flint Barn* next door, chefs Mark Goodwin and Tony Rutland serve a 'short, interesting' seasonal menu, accompanied by unusual wines by the glass. Dinner and breakfast are 'excellent'. Bar/ lounge, restaurant (no background music; closed Mon; dinner Fri/Sat only); wedding facilities (civil wedding licence). Free Wi-Fi. Garden with water features. Wine shop; tutored wine tastings. Children welcomed. 5 bedrooms. Per room B&B £135–£175, D,B&B £215–£255. 2-night min. stay at weekends preferred.

BEXHILL-ON-SEA East Sussex
Map 2:E4

COAST, 58 Sea Road, TN40 1JP. Tel 01424-225260, www.coastbexhill.co.uk. In an elegant Edwardian villa, this small B&B is close to the seafront, and convenient for local shops, restaurants and the station. Friendly and informative, owners Linda and Chris Wain pay great attention to detail; the bright, modern rooms (Teal, Sage and Crimson) have a large bed, sparkling bathroom and every comfort. Varied breakfasts include vegetarian options. Breakfast room. No background music. Free Wi-Fi. Children over 5 allowed. 3 bedrooms. Per person B&B £35–£45.

BIBURY Gloucestershire
Map 3:E6

BIBURY COURT, GL7 5NT. Tel 01285-740337, www.biburycourt.com. In a village named by William Morris as 'the most beautiful in England', this renovated Grade I listed Jacobean mansion by the River Coln has a 'magical' setting. It is owned by John Lister (of Shipton Mill organic flour) and managed by the chef, Adam Montgomery. The 'wonderful' old hall has polished stone floors; there is a 'beautiful' high-ceilinged lounge, and a bar with 1920s panelling and a striking chandelier. Bedrooms vary in size and style; some have been recently refurbished. Dining is in an informal conservatory or a 'luxurious' dining room. With a menu based on seasonal ingredients, Adam Montgomery serves 'sophisticated dishes with rich flavours'. Drawing room, bar. Free Wi-Fi (second-floor bedrooms have a weak signal). Background music. In-room treatments. Civil wedding licence. Children (£25 charge), and dogs (in some rooms; £15 charge) welcomed. 7 miles from Cirencester. 18 bedrooms. Per room B&B from £145, D,B&B from £215.

THE SWAN, GL7 5NW. Tel 01285-740695, www.cotswold-inns-hotels. co.uk. On the banks of the River Coln, this 17th-century former coaching inn (part of the small Cotswold Inns and Hotels group) has been refurbished in

English country house style by owners Pamela and Michael Horton. Most bedrooms overlook the river; one superior room has a four-poster bed and a large dressing area. Modern European cuisine is served in the new brasserie, which is decorated with oil paintings, a highly patterned floor and a log wall; in summer months, it opens on to a courtyard for alfresco dining. Background music. Lounge, bar (wood-burning stove), brasserie. Free Wi-Fi. Lift. 14-acre garden. Civil wedding licence; function facilities. Children, and dogs (in some bedrooms) welcomed. Trout fishing can be arranged. 22 bedrooms (4 in garden cottages, 1 with hot tub). Per person B&B £85–£185, D,B&B £114.50–£214.50.
25% DISCOUNT VOUCHERS

BIRKENHEAD Merseyside
Map 4:E2
THE RIVERHILL HOTEL, Talbot Road, Oxton, CH43 2HJ. Tel 0151-653 3773, www.theriverhill.co.uk. In a residential area on the Wirral peninsula, this small hotel is set back from the road in landscaped gardens. It is owned and run by Nick and Michele Burn, with 'friendly, welcoming' staff. Traditionally furnished bedrooms are large, with plenty of storage space. 'Good' breakfasts have a well-stocked buffet; there is a range of options for dinner (modern English food cooked by Claire Lara). The Birkenhead tunnel and the Woodside ferry to Liverpool are five minutes' drive away. Lounge, bar, *Bay Tree* restaurant (open to non-residents; background music). Free Wi-Fi. Civil wedding licence; business facilities. Parking. 15 bedrooms. Per room B&B from £70. Dinner from £16.95.

BISHOP'S TACHBROOK
Warwickshire
Map 2:B2
MALLORY COURT, Harbury Lane, CV33 9QB. Tel 01926-330214, www.mallory.co.uk. 'Elegant and calm', this 'timeless' manor house (Relais & Châteaux) has been extended to provide extra accommodation, meeting facilities and a 'bright, modern' brasserie. Sarah Baker is the long-serving manager. Bedrooms in the main house are traditional; some bathrooms have original Art Deco fittings. In the adjacent Knights Suite annexe, rooms are simply decorated in a more modern style. The 'beautiful' garden, arranged in six distinct areas, has a formal Old English rose garden; a pond garden with its original stone paths, mature trees and shrubs; herbaceous borders; manicured lawns; and a kitchen garden, where herbs, vegetables and soft fruits are grown year-round for use in the restaurants. 2 lounges, brasserie, restaurant (*Michelin* star; Simon Haigh is chef). Background music. Free Wi-Fi. Terrace (alfresco snacks). Outdoor pool, tennis court, croquet. Civil wedding licence; function facilities. 31 bedrooms (11 in new wing). Per room B&B £135–£485. Dinner £45–£59.50.

BLACKBURN Lancashire
Map 4:D3
MILLSTONE AT MELLOR, Church Lane, Mellor, BB2 7JR. Tel 01254-813333, www.millstonehotel.co.uk. At his stone-built former coaching inn (part of Thwaites Inns of Character) in the Ribble valley, Anson Bolton cooks award-winning seasonal Lancashire dishes that support local producers. 'We had a very good lunch, served by the

chef/patron in a most pleasant, spacious, wood-panelled room.' Comfortable, country-style bedrooms have fluffy bathrobes, home-made biscuits and lavender pouches. Breakfasts are hearty. Residents' lounge (log fire; views over village Remembrance Park), bar, restaurant (open to non-residents); new terrace (alfresco dining); background radio at breakfast. Free Wi-Fi. Parking. Children welcomed. 23 bedrooms (6 in courtyard; 2 suitable for &). Per person B&B from £45, D,B&B from £75.

STANLEY HOUSE, Mellor, BB2 7NP. Tel 01254-769200, www.stanleyhouse.co.uk. In an elevated position at the end of a long drive, this glamorous hotel 'in marvellous surroundings' is managed by Philip Wharton. It was extended in 2012; accommodation is now spread between the Grade II listed 17th-century manor house and the spacious Woodland Rooms (equipped with media hub, in-safe laptop-charging facility, etc) in a separate courtyard building. A luxury spa was also added (gym, thermal suite, hydro pool; treatments). An adjoining, sympathetically converted barn houses the reception area, with its large inglenook fireplace and wood-burning stove, and two restaurants (one for formal dining). Lounge, bar, *Mr Fred's* brasserie, *Grill on the Hill* restaurant (Stephen Williams is the new chef; closed Sun eve, Mon). Free Wi-Fi. Background music. 53-acre grounds. Civil wedding licence; function facilities. Parking. Children welcomed. 3 miles from Blackburn. 30 bedrooms (18 in a separate building; some suitable for &). Per room B&B £185–£285.

BLACKPOOL Lancashire
Map 4:D2

NUMBER ONE ST LUKE'S, 1 St Luke's Road, South Shore, FY4 2EL. Tel 01253-343901, www.numberoneblack pool.com. Mark and Claire Smith's stylish B&B is in a detached 1930s Art Deco house in the residential South Shore area. Well-equipped rooms are imaginatively decorated and have a king-size bed; state-of-the-art gadgetry includes a large plasma TV screen, DVD- and CD-player, whirlpool bath and remote lighting. Conservatory; garden (hot tub), water feature; putting green. Background music. Free Wi-Fi. Parking. Children over 3 allowed. 3 bedrooms. Per person B&B £50–£110.

NUMBER ONE SOUTH BEACH, 4 Harrowside West, FY4 1NW. Tel 01253-343900, www.numberonesouth beach.com. With sea views over South Beach Promenade, this low-carbon-footprint boutique hotel has a welcoming atmosphere and a lively modern interior. It is owned by Janet and Graham Oxley, with Claire and Mark Smith (see *Number One St Luke's*, above). Colourful bedrooms are thoughtfully equipped; some have a four-poster bed, balcony and whirlpool bath. Lounge, bar, restaurant; background music; pool table; meeting/conference facilities. Free Wi-Fi. Lift. Garden with putting green. Parking. 14 bedrooms (disabled facilities). Per room B&B single £78–£130, double £120–£150. Dinner £30. 2-night min. stay at weekends in high season.

RAFFLES HOTEL & TEA ROOM, 73–77 Hornby Rd, FY1 4QJ. Tel 01253-294713, www.raffleshotelblackpool.co.uk. In their flowery, bay-fronted house close to the Winter Gardens and Promenade, Graham Poole and Ian Balmforth run an impeccably kept small hotel and traditional English tea room (closed Mon). Home-made cakes and light snacks are served at teatime; good-value three-course set dinners are also available. There is an extensive choice at breakfast. Classical background music. Lounge, bar, breakfast room, tea room. Free Wi-Fi. Parking. Children welcomed; dogs by arrangement. 17 bedrooms, plus 4 apartment suites. Per person B&B £36–£40. Dinner (set menu) from £8.95.

BORROWDALE Cumbria
Map 4: inset C2

LEATHES HEAD HOTEL, CA12 5UY. Tel 017687-77247, www.leatheshead.co.uk. Popular with regular guests, this country hotel in an Edwardian house has 'magnificent' views across the valley, and easy access to Keswick. Jamie Adamson and Jane Cleary are the 'enthusiastic, helpful, caring' managers. Bedrooms are a blend of old-style elegance and modern comforts; some bathrooms have a whirlpool spa bath and walk-in monsoon shower. 'Still producing good food', the long-serving chef, David Jackson, serves local British cuisine on his monthly menus, which have a daily special. 'Can't wait to return.' Background music. Lounge, bar; conservatory. Free Wi-Fi. Dogs allowed in 2 rooms (£7.50 per day). 11 bedrooms. Per room B&B £148–£188, D,B&B £178–£243. Closed end Dec–Feb.
25% DISCOUNT VOUCHERS

BOURNEMOUTH Dorset
Map 2:E2

URBAN BEACH, 23 Argyll Road, BH5 1EB. Tel 01202-301509, www.urbanbeachhotel.co.uk. A short walk from Boscombe beach, this small, contemporary hotel has a laid-back vibe. It is owned by Mark Cribb, who runs it with new manager Helen McCombie and friendly staff. A large outdoor deck area was recently added. Individually decorated rooms have luxury bedding and toiletries, and are equipped with a plasma TV and DVD-player. The bar has a large cocktail list; the lively bistro serves local, seasonal produce and home-baked bread. Hotel guests have priority booking at *Urban Reef*, the sister restaurant on the beach. Bar, bistro; background music; seating deck. Free Wi-Fi. DVD, iTunes library. Wellies, umbrellas provided. Complimentary use of local gym. Children welcomed. 12 bedrooms. Per room B&B single £72, double £97–£180. Dinner from £28. 2-night min. stay at weekends.

BOWNESS-ON-WINDERMERE Cumbria
Map 4: inset C2

LINDETH HOWE, Lindeth Drive, Longtail Hill, LA23 3JF. Tel 015394-45759, www.lindeth-howe.co.uk. In magnificent countryside a mile from the village, this traditional country house overlooks the lake. It is where Beatrix Potter spent family holidays, and completed *The Tale of Timmy Tiptoes* and *The Tale of Pigling Bland*. The hotel, jointly managed by Alison Magee-Barker and Tony Holden, has cosy lounges with books and board games. Pretty bedrooms have views of the lake, gardens or woodland and beyond; family rooms are available. Chef Marc Guibert's five-course seasonal dinners and taster menus are served in a candlelit dining room. Lounge, library,

bar, restaurant. Free Wi-Fi. Background music. Sun terrace; indoor swimming pool, sauna, fitness room. 6-acre grounds. Children welcomed (no under-7s in the restaurant at night; children's high tea, babysitting available). 34 bedrooms (some on ground floor). Per room B&B £170–£360. Dinner from £44.50. Closed 2–16 Jan.
25% DISCOUNT VOUCHERS

BRANSCOMBE Devon
Map 1:C5
THE MASON'S ARMS, EX12 3DJ. Tel 01297-680300, www.masonsarms.co.uk. Ten minutes from the beach, this creeper-covered 14th-century inn is 'a lovely, relaxing place in a sleepy village'. Seven bedrooms are in the main building; the others are in thatched cottages on the hillside, with views over the valley or out to sea. With slate floors, stone walls, log fireplace and real ales, the bar is popular with village locals. The restaurant serves 'excellent food' using locally grown, reared or caught produce; lobster and crab landed on Branscombe beach. Lounge, restaurant, bar; garden with outdoor seating. Free Wi-Fi (in main bar only). No background music. Children, and dogs (in some cottages) welcomed. 21 bedrooms (14 in cottages). Per room B&B £80–£180. Dinner £35.

BRIDPORT Dorset
Map 1:C6
THE BULL HOTEL, 34 East Street, DT6 3LF. Tel 01308-422878, www.thebullhotel.co.uk. In the centre of a busy market town, owners Nikki and Richard Cooper, with 'young, very friendly and helpful' staff, welcome guests to this former coaching inn (Grade II listed), today painted a handsome blue. 'Quirky, spacious' bedrooms have striking wallpaper and imaginatively mismatched furniture; some have a bay window, others a vintage roll-top bath, yet others a four-poster bed. Chef George Marsh serves locally sourced food in the restaurant and *Venner* bar, where Friday-night canapés are a local tradition. 2 bars (background music), restaurant, *The Stable* cider house; ballroom; private dining room; sunny courtyard. Free Wi-Fi. Civil wedding licence; function facilities. Children welcomed (toys, DVDs, organic nappies; babysitting; children's tea by arrangement). 19 bedrooms (3 accessed via courtyard). Per room B&B £85–£210.

BRIGHTON East Sussex
Map 2:E4
DRAKES, 43/44 Marine Parade, BN2 1PE. Tel 01273-696934, www.drakesofbrighton.com. Within walking distance of The Lanes, this conversion of two white stucco Regency town houses (owned by Andy Shearer, managed by Richard Hayes) has a striking modern interior. 'The staff are courteous and helpful; standards are high.' Some sea-facing bedrooms have a bath by the window overlooking the pier. Many rooms have a wet room ('it lives up to its name, soaking everything in sight'). In the basement restaurant, which has subtle lighting and exposed brickwork, chef Andrew MacKenzie serves 'seriously good' food. Breakfast is 'also excellent'. Lounge/bar (light background music), restaurant. Free Wi-Fi. 20 bedrooms. Room only £115–£345. Breakfast £6–£12.50, dinner £39.95.

Five, 5 New Steine, BN2 1PB. Tel 01273-686547, www.fivehotel.com. A stone's throw from the beach and pier, and a short walk to shops and restaurants, Caroline and Simon Heath's friendly B&B is in a Georgian town house in a lovely Regency square. Modern bedrooms are bright and well equipped; many face the sea. Continental breakfast hampers with local treats (and 'surprises') are delivered to the room at a time to suit guests. 2 public rooms. Free Wi-Fi. No background music. DVD library. Children over 5 allowed. 9 bedrooms (some with sea views). Per person B&B £50–£65.

Paskins, 18–19 Charlotte Street, BN2 1AG. Tel 01273-601203, www.paskins.co.uk. 'Met my needs perfectly.' Near the seafront, Susan and Roger Marlowe's environmentally friendly B&B occupies two Grade II listed 19th-century houses in Kemp Town. Bedrooms are immaculate and 'comfortable', though small. In the Art Deco breakfast room, Roger Marlowe serves 'delicious' organic breakfasts: 'I loved the anchovies with scrambled eggs on toast.' Vegetarian and vegan guests are well catered for. Lounge, dining room. Free Wi-Fi. No background music. Children and dogs welcomed. 19 bedrooms (some with sea views). Per person B&B £50–£75.

A Room with a View, 41 Marine Parade, BN2 1PE. Tel 01273-682885, www.aroomwithaviewbrighton.com. Close to all Brighton's attractions, this stylish new Kemp Town guest house is in a Grade II listed building on the seafront. There are sea views from every room. Modern, unfussy bedrooms have wooden flooring and soft neutral tones; a room at the top has a staircase up to a roof terrace with panoramic views of the water. Some rooms have a stylish bathroom with roll-top bath, others have a walk-in power shower wet room; bathrobes are provided. Some steep stairs. Lounge, dining room. Free Wi-Fi. Parking (for 6 cars). 9 bedrooms. Per room B&B £80–£190.

BROADSTAIRS Kent
Map 2:D6
Burrow House, Granville Road, CT10 1QD. Tel 01843-601817, www.burrowhouse.com. Gavin Cox runs his tastefully furnished B&B in a spacious Victorian house close to the golden sands of Viking Bay. Guests are welcomed with light refreshments in the comfortable, chandeliered drawing room. Bedrooms have a French antique or rococo-style bed and a modern bathroom; two have a bath. Organic breakfasts include local produce. Complimentary newspaper. Drawing room, dining room. Licensed. Free Wi-Fi. Children over 4 allowed. Parking. 4 bedrooms. Gourmet weekends with 5-course menus. Per room B&B £95–£165. 2-night min. stay at weekends.

Royal Albion Hotel, 6–12 Albion Street, CT10 1AN. Tel 01843-868071, www.albionbroadstairs.co.uk. Once a residence of Charles Dickens, this Georgian hotel is on the seafront at Viking Bay. Some superior rooms have a sea-facing balcony. Drinks and meals can be taken on the popular terrace and in the garden overlooking the bay. Managed by Shane and Marie Godwin for the brewers Shepherd Neame, it is a focal point of the town's annual Dickens celebrations, and a music venue for the folk festival. Coffee lounge, bar, restaurant (seafood specialities; sea views). Free Wi-Fi. Garden; terrace. Parking permits available. 21 bedrooms. Per room B&B from £85.

BUCKFASTLEIGH Devon
Map 1:D4

KILBURY MANOR, Colston Road, TQ11 0LN. Tel 01364-644079, www. kilburymanor.co.uk. In impressive four-acre grounds, Julia and Martin Blundell's renovated 17th-century longhouse overlooks the River Dart; a private island is a short walk down the fields. Rooms are spacious and 'tastefully furnished', with a spick-and-span bathroom; breakfasts are extensive (special dietary needs catered for). The garden and courtyard are peaceful places in which to sit. The Blundells are 'outstandingly kind' hosts, and offer helpful advice on local eating places. One mile from town; the South Devon Railway is close by. Breakfast room (wood-burning stove). No background music. Free Wi-Fi. Bicycle and canoe storage. Resident dogs, Dillon and Buster. 4 bedrooms (2 in converted stone barn; plus one 1-bedroom cottage). Per room B&B single £65–£79, double £75–£89.

BUDLEIGH SALTERTON Devon
Map 1:D5

ROSEHILL ROOMS AND COOKERY, 30 West Hill, EX9 6BU. Tel 01395-444031, www.rosehillroomsandcookery.co.uk. Food enthusiasts are well catered for at Willi and Sharon Rehbock's B&B in a Grade II listed Victorian house close to the centre of town. A professional chef, Willi Rehbock hosts cookery classes and demonstrations on bread-making,

seafood, Mediterranean cuisine, etc. Sleek bedrooms have large windows, a sofa, home-made cakes or biscuits; communal breakfasts are plentiful. A large veranda overlooks the garden, with distant views to the sea. Close to the beach and Coastal Path. Dining room. Free Wi-Fi. 4 bedrooms (3 en suite, 1 with private bathroom). Per room B&B £95–£125 (2-night min. stay).

BUNGAY Suffolk
Map 2:B6

EARSHAM PARK FARM, Old Railway Road, Earsham, NR35 2AQ. Tel 01986-892180, www.earsham-parkfarm.co.uk. Set in well-tended gardens, Bobbie and Simon Watchorn's elegant, homely Victorian farmhouse is part of a 600-acre working arable farm. Country-style bedrooms have antique furniture and views over the fields and the Waveney valley. Served around a communal table, breakfast has sausages and bacon from the farm; home-made breads and jam; eggs from local free-range hens. Guests are welcome to visit the Watchorns' herd of free-range pigs. No background music. Lounge, dining room. Free Wi-Fi. Garden. Farm walks; birdwatching. Parking. 2 miles from Bungay. Children, dogs and horses (by arrangement) welcomed. 4 bedrooms. Per person B&B single £50–£62, double £82–£102. 2-night min. stay on bank holiday weekends.

BURFORD Oxfordshire
Map 2:C2

BAY TREE HOTEL, Sheep Street, OX18 4LW. Tel 01993-822791, www.cotswold-inns-hotels.co.uk. Blue wisteria climbs up the honey-coloured limestone facade of this 'lovely old building' near the high street, which has been welcoming visitors for more than 400 years. It is part of Michael and Pamela Horton's small Cotswold Inns and Hotels group, which also owns the nearby *Lamb Inn* and *The Broadway Hotel* in Broadway (see main entries). The hotel has a galleried staircase, oak-panelled rooms, an inglenook fireplace, tapestries and flagstone floors. Chef Brian Andrews serves modern British food in the elegant restaurant overlooking the patio and garden. Library, *Woolsack* bar (background music); patio (alfresco dining). Free Wi-Fi. Walled garden; croquet. Civil wedding licence; function facilities. Children and dogs welcomed. 21 bedrooms (2 on ground floor in outbuilding). Per person B&B £90–£135, D,B&B £117.50–£162.50.

BURY ST EDMUNDS Suffolk
Map 2:B5
THE ANGEL HOTEL, 3 Angel Hill, IP33 1LT. Tel 01284-714000, www.theangel. co.uk. Vintage furniture and modern art come together at this historic, ivy-covered coaching inn opposite the cathedral and Abbey Gardens. It has been run by the Gough family since 1973; Lynn Cowan is the manager. Popular with locals, the restaurant serves bistro food 'cooked well'; in a 12th-century vault under the hotel, *Wingspan* bar is furnished with a mix of curiosities. Lounge (log fire), bar, restaurant (Simon Barker is chef); background music. Free Wi-Fi. Function facilities. Children welcomed; dogs by arrangement (£5 charge). Limited parking. 80 bedrooms (some on ground floor). Per room B&B £110–£340. Dinner £40.
25% DISCOUNT VOUCHERS

OAK FARM BARN, Moat Lane, Rougham, IP30 9JU. Tel 01359-270014, www.oakfarmbarn.co.uk. In a 'magnificent' 19th-century timber-framed barn down a quiet country lane, Rachel and Ray Balmer give B&B guests a 'warm welcome' with tea and cake. The homely, 'well-appointed' rooms have 'luxurious' beds, hot-water bottles and original oak beams; public rooms have full-length windows. There are plenty of thoughtful extras: maps of walks, boots to borrow, books, DVDs. 'Breakfast, cooked to order, was a real treat, with eggs from the hosts' own chickens.' Lounge, seating area overlooking patio. Free Wi-Fi. Background music. Garden with outdoor seating. Parking. 3 bedrooms (2 on ground floor; 1 suitable for &.). Per room B&B £80.

OUNCE HOUSE, Northgate Street, IP33 1HP. Tel 01284-761779, www.ouncehouse.co.uk. In a spacious Victorian merchant's house on a residential street, this B&B is within easy walking distance of shops, restaurants and tourist sites. Owners Simon and Jenny Pott have furnished it in traditional style with antiques and period furniture, photographs and ornaments. Well-equipped bedrooms have a flat-screen TV, DVD- and CD-player, and fresh flowers. Communal breakfasts. Drawing room (honesty bar), snug/bar/library, dining room. Free Wi-Fi. No background music. Parking. Children welcomed. 5 bedrooms (quietest 2 face the ⅓-acre walled garden). Per room B&B single £90–£95, double £130–£140.

CAMBRIDGE Cambridgeshire
Map 2:B4

HOTEL DU VIN CAMBRIDGE, 15–19
Trumpington Street, CB2 1QA. Tel
01223-227330, www.hotelduvin.com.
Quirky architectural features have been
retained in this 'rambling' modern
conversion of five town houses dating,
in parts, to medieval times. The hotel
has exposed brickwork, reconditioned
fireplaces, a 'very nice' upstairs lounge,
and a vaulted cellar with a well-stocked
bar, sitting areas and a wine shop – 'all
very charming'. The informal bistro has
French-influenced home-grown and
local dishes, cooked by Jonathan Dean
in an open-view kitchen. Staff are 'very
obliging'. Library, bar, bistro, wine-
tasting room; terrace. Free Wi-Fi.
Background music. Civil wedding
licence; function facilities. Children
welcomed. 41 bedrooms (some on
ground floor, with private terrace).
Room only from £229. Breakfast
£12.95–£14.50, dinner £34.

DUKE HOUSE, 1 Victoria Street, CB1 1JP.
Tel 01223-314773, www.dukehouse
cambridge.co.uk. Close to the city's
historic colleges, Liz and Rob
Cameron's B&B is run along sustainable
lines. The home of the Duke of
Gloucester between 1967 and 1969,
when he studied architecture at the
university, the Victorian house 'still
carries his stamp'; original features such
as wooden shutters, brass fittings and a
marble surround have been retained.
Bedrooms, decorated in muted shades,
are named after famous dukes;
breakfast has a buffet of organic muesli
and granola, fresh fruit, yogurts and
cheeses, and a weekly cooked special.
Sitting room, breakfast room; balcony,

courtyard with mural. Free Wi-Fi.
Occasional background music. Parking,
by prior arrangement. Babies, and
children over 10 welcomed. 4 bedrooms.
Per room B&B £95–£195.

HOTEL FELIX, Whitehouse Lane,
Huntingdon Road, CB3 0LX. Tel
01223-277977, www.hotelfelix.co.uk.
In extensive landscaped gardens on the
edge of the city, this large hotel occupies
a late Victorian yellowbrick mansion
with modern extensions. Shara Ross is
the manager. The simple, sleek interior
is enlivened with striking contemporary
art; Mediterranean-influenced dishes are
served in the restaurant overlooking the
terrace and garden. Small lounge, bar,
Graffiti restaurant; conservatory. Free
Wi-Fi. Background music. Civil
wedding licence; function facilities. 4-
acre garden, terrace (alfresco dining),
gazebo. Parking. Children welcomed.
52 bedrooms (4 suitable for &). Per
person B&B (continental) £102.50–£150,
D,B&B £107.50–£155. Full English
breakfast £7.99.
25% DISCOUNT VOUCHERS

THE VARSITY HOTEL & SPA,
Thompson's Lane, off Bridge Street,
CB5 8AQ. Tel 01223-306030,
www.thevarsityhotel.co.uk. Ideally
placed, this recently built, minimalist
hotel overlooks the river near
Magdalene Bridge, and has panoramic
views from its rooftop terrace. Loft-style
rooms have floor-to-ceiling windows,
air conditioning, under-floor heating
and up-to-date technology (LCD TV,
DVD library, iPod docking station).
Nintendo Wii and an iPad are available
on request. Bathrooms (some small)
have a monsoon shower. *The River Bar*

steakhouse and grill, set on two levels in a restored 17th-century warehouse on the quayside, is next door (background music). Roof terrace; *Glassworks* health club and spa (spa bath overlooking the River Cam); lift; gym. Free Wi-Fi. Civil wedding licence; conference facilities. Valet parking service (parking charge); local car parks. Children welcomed. 48 bedrooms (3 suitable for &). Per room B&B (continental) £195–£695.

CANTERBURY Kent
Map 2:D5
MAGNOLIA HOUSE, 36 St Dunstan's Terrace, CT2 8AX. Tel 01227-765121, www.magnoliahousecanterbury.co.uk. In a peaceful conservation area close to Westgate, Isobelle Leggett's comfortable Georgian guest house has well-equipped bedrooms with complimentary wine, and fresh milk for coffee and tea; books, magazines and board games are available to borrow. The considerate hostess gives helpful recommendations on local places to eat and visit. There is lots of choice at breakfast, including home-made jam and marmalade. Dinner is served by arrangement in winter (Nov–Feb); no licence – bring your own bottle. Cutlery and crockery can be provided for picnics in the walled garden. Sitting room, dining room (background music). Free Wi-Fi. Parking. Children over 12 welcomed. 6 bedrooms (some with a four-poster bed). Per person B&B £49.50–£125. Dinner £35.

CHADDESLEY CORBETT
Worcestershire
Map 3:C5
BROCKENCOTE HALL, DY10 4PY. Tel 01562-777876, www.brockencotehall.com. Extensively refurbished 'to a high standard', this country house hotel (Eden Hotel Collection) is in a Victorian building in the style of a French château. It stands in 'lovely' parkland with a 'serene' lake and grazing sheep. Comfortable bedrooms are spacious, with a modern bathroom and views of the estate. In the *Chaddesley* restaurant (open to non-residents), accomplished chef Adam Brown serves 'very good' dinners; 'charming, excellent service'. Bar, lounge, restaurant, 2 private dining rooms. Free Wi-Fi. Light jazz background music. 70-acre grounds; 3 miles SE of Kidderminster. Children welcomed. 21 bedrooms (some suitable for &). Per room B&B single from £95, double from £120.

CHAGFORD Devon
Map 1:C4
MILL END HOTEL, Sandy Park, TQ13 8JN. Tel 01647-432282, www.millendhotel.com. In a 'beautiful' riverbank setting by a bridge on the River Teign, this small hotel is in a former 15th-century corn mill, with an 18-foot working waterwheel. It is owned by Sue and Peter Davies. Country house-style rooms have views of the gardens; some have a balcony or private patio. A flexible dining menu has been introduced in the evenings; Chris Billingsley is the chef. Within Dartmoor national park, with river path walks to Fingle Bridge and Castle Drogo. Packed lunches available. 3 lounges (log fires), bar, restaurant. Free Wi-Fi. 15-acre grounds: river, fishing, bathing. Background music (classical in the hall, restaurant and one lounge). Children (high teas; under-12s not allowed in restaurant in evening) and dogs welcomed. 15 bedrooms (3 on

ground floor). Per room B&B single £75–£165, double £90–£180. Dinner £22–£40.

CHARMOUTH Dorset
Map 1:C6

THE ABBOTS HOUSE, The Street, DT6 6QF. Tel 01297-560339, www. abbotshouse.co.uk. 'The attention to detail was amazing.' Sheila and Nick Gilbey provide lots of home-made treats and comforts at their small B&B in a carefully updated house with 16th-century origins. Daintily decorated rooms have oak-panelled walls, a flagstone floor and an ornate beamed ceiling; bathrooms have a double-ended bath and flat-screen TV. Mrs Gilbey's breakfasts are 'a delight'; her home-made jams and marmalade, and home-baked bread, are available for purchase. Close to the centre, and a five-minute walk from the beach. Lounge, garden room, garden (model railway). Background music at breakfast. Free Wi-Fi. 4 bedrooms (plus 1-bedroom self-contained cottage in the garden). Per room B&B £120–£140 (2-night min. stay). Closed 16 Dec–10 Jan.

CHATTON Northumberland
Map 4:A3

CHATTON PARK HOUSE, Alnwick, NE66 5RA. Tel 01668-215507, www.chattonpark.com. 'We spent a great week there.' Paul and Michelle Mattinson are the 'welcoming' hosts at this B&B in an imposing Georgian house on the edge of Northumberland national park. Well-equipped bedrooms, named after local towns or villages, are furnished in period style; 'superlative' breakfasts have much local produce. Packed lunches and a luggage

drop-off and pick-up service for walkers and cyclists. 'Huge' sitting room, cosy bar, breakfast room; no background music. Free Wi-Fi; weak mobile phone signal. 6-acre grounds; grass tennis courts (Apr–Oct). ½ mile from Chatton; Alnwick, Bamburgh and Holy Island are close by. 4 bedrooms (plus 2-bedroom self-catering stone lodge with private garden). Per room B&B £99–£180. Closed Jan.
25% DISCOUNT VOUCHERS

CHELTENHAM Gloucestershire
Map 3:D5

BEAUMONT HOUSE, 56 Shurdington Road, GL53 0JE. Tel 01242-223311, www.bhhotel.co.uk. Built for a wealthy Victorian merchant, Fan and Alan Bishop's modernised, cream-painted B&B stands in large gardens one mile out of the city. The large lounge has an honesty bar and complimentary hot drinks and biscuits; a limited room-service menu is available in the evenings (Mon–Thurs). Two bedrooms (Out of Asia and Out of Africa) are themed and have a whirlpool bath. Breakfast is taken in the dining room overlooking the flower garden; breakfast in bed can be arranged. Lounge, conservatory, dining room (background music). Free Wi-Fi. Parking. Children welcomed. 16 bedrooms. Per room B&B £69–£190.

BUTLERS, Western Road, GL50 3RN. Tel 01242-570771, www.butlers-hotel. co.uk. Robert Davies and Guy Hunter run their butler-themed B&B in this former gentleman's residence on a quiet street within walking distance of the centre. Bedrooms are named after well-known butlers from literature and film (Jeeves, Hudson, etc). Breakfast is taken in a spick-and-span room overlooking the walled garden. Ten minutes' walk to the bus and railway stations. Lounge, dining room (quiet radio in the mornings); garden. Free Wi-Fi. Parking. Children over 5 welcomed. 7 bedrooms (self-catering rooms available for longer stays). Per room B&B single £60–£75, double £85–£120.

THE CHELTENHAM TOWNHOUSE, 12–14 Pittville Lawn, GL52 2BD. Tel 01242-221922, www.cheltenhamtownhouse. com. Complimentary bicycles and helmets are available at Adam and Jayne Lillywhite's B&B in a leafy location well situated for both town and racecourse. The grand Regency building has been renovated in fresh, contemporary style with airy bedrooms; four self-contained apartments with a kitchen are located nearby. The Lillywhites are happy to recommend local restaurants and places to visit. Lounge (honesty bar; help-yourself fruit bowl), breakfast room (background music); sun deck. DVD library. Free Wi-Fi. Lift. Parking. Children welcomed (family rooms). 21 bedrooms (1 with private bathroom), 5 studio apartments (4 in nearby annexe), 1 two-bed suite. Per room B&B single £58–£93, double £68–£108.

HANOVER HOUSE, 65 St George's Road, GL50 3DU. Tel 01242-541297, www. hanoverhouse.org. Guests enjoy a decanter of sherry in their spacious, colourful bedroom at Veronica and James McIntosh-Ritchie's B&B (Wolsey Lodges) close to the centre. 'Charming' hosts, they have filled their 'beautiful' Italianate home with 'interesting objects' and a 'splendidly varied selection of books'. Breakfast has home-made bread and preserves, and locally sourced produce. Drawing room (open fire in winter), breakfast room; walled garden. Free Wi-Fi. Classical background music. 3 bedrooms. Per person B&B £50–£70.

MONTPELLIER CHAPTER, Bayshill Road, GL50 3AS. Tel 01242-527788, www.themontpellierchapterhotel.com. 'The staff smiled and went out of their way to help at all times.' In the fashionable Montpellier district, this hotel in a handsome Regency building has been given a sleek make-over by the Hong Kong-based Swire group. Interesting works of contemporary art hang in the corridors and bedrooms. Well-equipped rooms have a Nespresso machine and a complimentary minibar (replenished daily). Dinner can be taken in the modern, glass-veiled courtyard at the back, or in the main restaurant, with its open kitchen and wood oven. Guests have access to the pool, and squash and tennis courts at Cheltenham Ladies' College, 5 mins' walk away. Lounge, library, bar, restaurant; conservatory, garden room; terrace. Background music in public areas. Free Wi-Fi. Spa (steam room, treatments). Children welcomed; dogs allowed by arrangement. Parking. 60 bedrooms (3 on ground floor, suitable for &). Per room (*excluding VAT*) B&B £140–£200. **25% DISCOUNT VOUCHERS**

CHESTER Cheshire
Map 3:A4
THE CHESTER GROSVENOR, Eastgate, CH1 1LT. Tel 01244-324024, www. chestergrosvenor.com. In centre of the city, this Grade II listed large, luxurious hotel, gabled and half-timbered, is close

to the cathedral and the ancient city walls. It is owned by the Duke of Westminster. The interior has grand chandeliers and elegant, traditionally styled bedrooms. There are three dining options: light meals are served in the *Arkle* bar and lounge; the informal *Brasserie* has barbecued meats cooked on a wood-burning grill; the Michelin-starred restaurant, *Simon Radley at The Chester Grosvenor*, is 'an experience not to be missed'. Drawing room. Free Wi-Fi. Background music. Civil wedding licence; function facilities. Spa (crystal steam room, herb sauna, themed shower, ice fountain; 5 treatment rooms). Children welcomed (interconnecting family rooms). 80 bedrooms and suites. Room only from £230 (*excluding VAT*). Dinner £50–£100 (*plus 12½% discretionary service charge*).

GREEN BOUGH HOTEL, 60–62 Hoole Road, CH2 3NL. Tel 01244-326241, www.greenbough.co.uk. Occupying two Victorian town houses (on a busy road, one mile east of the town), this popular hotel is owned by Janice and Philip Martin, and run with 'helpful, friendly' staff. Bedrooms are decorated in lavish, traditional style; each has a teddy bear on the bed. In the *Olive Tree* restaurant, guests have a choice of menus based on regional produce, including a 'free-from' menu incorporating vegetarian, and lactose- and gluten-free dishes. Philip Martin runs one- and two-day courses at Cheshire Cooks cookery school, 15 miles away in Tarporley. Background music (classical, jazz). Lounge, bar, restaurant. Free Wi-Fi. Function/conference facilities. Rooftop garden with seating and water feature. Off-street parking. 15 bedrooms (8 in lodge, linked by feature bridge; some suitable for &.). Per room B&B from £175.
25% DISCOUNT VOUCHERS

CHEWTON MENDIP Somerset
Map 2:D1
THE POST HOUSE, Bathway, BA3 4NS. Tel 01761-241704, www.theposthouse bandb.co.uk. Karen Price has 'beautifully' renovated this Grade II listed former post office and village bakery. Immaculate rooms are decorated in rustic French style with white-painted furniture, and lime-washed walls in muted colours; one room has an unusual square bath. Breakfast is 'delicious'. *The Old Bakery* ('a luxurious space') is equipped for self-catering; it has a stone fireplace and its own secluded courtyard. The lovely Mendip village is 5 miles N of Wells. Sitting room, dining room (no background music); Mediterranean-style courtyard; small garden. Free Wi-Fi. Parking. Children welcomed. Resident dog, Monty. 2 bedrooms (plus 1 self-catering cottage). Per room B&B £80–£120 (2-night min. stay at weekends).

CHICHESTER West Sussex
Map 2:E3
CROUCHERS, Birdham Road, PO20 7EH. Tel 01243-784995, www.croucherscountryhotel.com. With patios overlooking farmland and 'refreshing' greenery, there is 'plenty of scope for relaxing alfresco' at this hotel and restaurant close to the harbour and West Wittering beach. Lloyd van Rooyen is the owner. Bedrooms are decorated in neutral tones; some have a four-poster bed. In the oak-beamed restaurant overlooking green fields, chef Nick Markey's dishes, using lots of local

produce, are 'impeccable'. 3 miles S of the town centre. Lounge, bar, restaurant (classical background music; open to non-residents); courtyard; 2-acre garden. Free Wi-Fi. Civil wedding licence; function facilities. Children welcomed (family rooms). 26 bedrooms (23 in coach house, barn and stables; 10 with a patio; 2 suitable for ♿). Per room B&B £105–£165, D,B&B £162–£214.

CHIDDINGFOLD Surrey
Map 2:D3
THE CROWN INN, The Green, Petworth Road, GU8 4TX. Tel 01428-682255, www.thecrownchiddingfold.com. 'Exactly what we expected: very good.' A quintessentially English country pub on the edge of the village green, this cream-painted 14th-century inn owned by Daniel and Hannah Hall has retained a welcoming, old-fashioned atmosphere. There are dark oak beams, sloping floors, 'passageways a bit like a rabbit warren', and stained-glass windows; modern comforts in the rooms include a hand-made bed, flat-screen TV and DVD library. 2 bars (*Crown* and *Half Crown* with open fire), 'superb' oak-panelled restaurant (Kevin Stuart is chef; background music/radio); small courtyard for alfresco dining; private dining room. Free Wi-Fi. Children welcomed. 8 bedrooms (front ones hear traffic). Per room B&B £100–£200. Dinner £25–£30.

CHRISTCHURCH Dorset
Map 2:E2
CHRISTCHURCH HARBOUR HOTEL, 95 Mudeford, BH23 3NT. Tel 01202-483434, www.christchurch-harbour-hotel.co.uk. In a 'fabulous' situation, this sympathetically restored and extended

hotel overlooks the quay. Part of the small, privately owned Harbour Hotels group, it has a luxury spa and simple, stylish bedrooms, many with sea views. Perched on the water's edge, the modern restaurant, *The Jetty*, serves fresh fish, local oysters and lobsters; it is headed by *Michelin*-starred chef Alex Aitken. 'Quick and simple' meals are taken early till late in the *Upper Deck* bar and restaurant, with harbour views from the terrace. Extra accommodation has been created in a new wing. 2 restaurants, terrace (alfresco dining). Cinema room (Nintendo Wii); spa (sauna, steam room, salt grotto, hydrotherapy pool). Background music. Free Wi-Fi. Civil wedding licence; function facilities. Children welcomed. 60 bedrooms. Per room B&B £160–£285, D,B&B £215–£340.

THE KINGS ARMS, 18 Castle Street, BH23 1DT. Tel 01202-588933, www.thekings-christchurch.co.uk. In a smart Georgian building in the centre of town, this small hotel (Harbour Hotels) overlooks a manicured bowling green. Modern bedrooms are elegantly styled; the best have full-length French windows with views of the green and the ruins of an ancient priory. Early evenings mark Gin O'Clock in the bar, when jazz music plays, and classic cocktails are both shaken and stirred; in the restaurant, chef Alex Aitken's 15 Mile Menu showcases locally sourced food from Dorset and the New Forest. Sister to the *Christchurch Harbour Hotel* (see above). Lounge, bar, restaurant; sun terrace (alfresco dining). Free Wi-Fi. Background music. Lift. Civil wedding licence; function facilities. Children welcomed. 20 bedrooms. Per room B&B

£95–£175; D,B&B £125–£205 (2-night min. stay at weekends).

CLEY-NEXT-THE-SEA Norfolk
Map 2:A5

CLEY WINDMILL, The Quay, NR25 7RP. Tel 01263-740209, www.cleywindmill. co.uk. By an old quay on the north Norfolk coast, this 18th-century grinding mill has been converted into a characterful small B&B by Julian and Carolyn Godlee. It is managed by Charlotte Martin and Simon Whatling. The circular sitting room at the base of the mill has an open fire and a beamed ceiling; upstairs, the bedrooms and galleries have far-reaching views across the salt marshes and the sea. Accessed via a steep ladder, the top-floor Wheel Room has a four-poster bed and four windows, each with a different panoramic view. A daily-changing, three-course menu is served in the cosy, candlelit dining room in the original granary (background jazz). Free Wi-Fi (in dining room, some bedrooms). Sitting room, restaurant (open to non-residents); garden. Civil wedding licence. Children welcomed in some rooms (early suppers by arrangement). 9 bedrooms (3 in converted boathouse and granary). Per room B&B £99–£199 (2-night min. stay on Fri and Sat nights). Dinner £32.50.

COMBE HAY Somerset
Map 2:D1

THE WHEATSHEAF, BA2 7EG, Tel 01225-833504, www.wheatsheafcombe hay.co.uk. In large gardens, surrounded by beautiful countryside, this white-painted 18th-century inn overlooks a village five miles from Bath. Run by Ian Barton and his son, James, it has been refurbished in contemporary rustic style. At its heart is the restaurant, where chef Eddy Rains, cooks with local ingredients (honey and eggs from the inn's own bees, chickens and ducks; vegetables and fruit from the kitchen garden). Menus include a seven-course 'Taste of the West Country'. A wide selection of ales and wines (the Bartons are wine buffs) can be taken beside the fire, or on the terrace. Soothing bedrooms have modern furniture and luxurious extras, such as fine-quality bedlinen and a 'tuck box' of Italian coffee and biscuits; *The Barn Room*, in a separate riverside building nearby, has soaring beams and vintage decoration. Sitting room, bar, restaurant, terrace. Background music. Free Wi-Fi (in main building). 'Polite' dogs welcomed; resident dogs, Milo and Brie. 4 bedrooms. Per room B&B £120–£150.

COVENTRY Warwickshire
Map 2:B2

BARNACLE HALL, Shilton Lane, Shilton, CV7 9LH. Tel 02476-612629, www.barnaclehall.co.uk. In a rural location five miles NE of the city centre, Rose Grindal's welcoming, small B&B is in a Grade II listed 16th-century farmhouse with an 18th-century limestone facade. Full of nooks and crannies, it has oak beams, polished wood and an inglenook fireplace with a wood-burning stove. Large, comfortable bedrooms are furnished in period style. Sitting room, dining room. No background music. Free Wi-Fi (in some rooms). Garden, patio. Children welcomed. 3 bedrooms (1 with private bathroom). Per person B&B single £40–£50, double £70–£80.

COVERACK Cornwall
Map 1:E2

THE BAY HOTEL, North Corner, nr Helston, TR12 6TF. Tel 01326-280464, www.thebayhotel.co.uk. In a peaceful village on the coast, this white-painted hotel is owned and managed by Ric and Gina House and their daughter, Zoë. Decorated in coastal shades, the pleasant lounge and many of the comfortable bedrooms have panoramic views across the water. In the candlelit restaurant, Ric House uses Cornish produce, and fresh fish landed in the bay for his cooking. Full Cornish breakfasts. Lounge, bar/restaurant, terrace; garden. Free Wi-Fi; no mobile phone signal; no telephone in the rooms. Background music (between 7 pm and 9 pm). Children over 8 welcomed. 15 bedrooms (1 on ground floor suitable for &). Per person D,B&B £59–£130. Closed mid-Nov–23 Mar.

CRAYKE North Yorkshire
Map 4:D4

THE DURHAM OX, Westway, YO61 4TE. Tel 01347-821506, www.thedurhamox.com. There are stunning views over the Vale of York from Mike and Sasha Ibbotson's characterful 300-year-old pub-with-rooms. A fire crackles in the wood-burning stove in winter; elsewhere, there are exposed beams, tiled floors, carved wood panelling and an inglenook fireplace. Unpretentious food, cooked by chef Peter Harrison, is served in three areas: the flagstone-floored dining room, a traditional bar or the *Burns Bar*, a glassed, all-weather garden room. Specialities include Crayke game, local meats, fresh fish and seafood dishes. An events and functions barn was added in 2013. 3 bars, restaurant, private dining room. Free Wi-Fi. Background music. Function facilities. Convenient for Park and Ride into York. Children and dogs welcomed. 6 bedrooms (1 suite, accessed via external stairs; others in converted farm cottages; 2 on ground floor). Per person B&B £50–£75. Dinner £28.

CROSTHWAITE Cumbria
Map 4: inset C2

THE PUNCH BOWL INN, Lyth Valley, Kendal, LA8 8HR. Tel 01539-568237, www.the-punchbowl.co.uk. Standing beside a handsome parish church, this popular 300-year-old inn in the picturesque Lyth valley also doubles as the village post office. Owned by Richard Rose, it retains the feel of a local pub. Individually styled, the beamed bedrooms are 'big and comfortable'; dinner is taken in the busy traditional bar, or in the 'pleasant' L-shaped dining room with its polished floorboards, leather chairs and a stone fireplace. The 'excellent' meals have 'interesting flavour combinations' and are 'very nicely presented, without too much fussiness'; 'good portions keep even the most assiduous walkers well fed'. Complimentary tea and scones are offered every afternoon. 2 bars, restaurant (background jazz); 2 terraces. Free Wi-Fi (in bar only). Parking. Civil wedding licence; conference facilities. Children welcomed. 9 bedrooms. Per room B&B £165–£305.

CUCKFIELD West Sussex
Map 2:E4

OCKENDEN MANOR, Ockenden Lane, nr Haywards Heath, RH17 5LD. Tel 01444-416111, www.hshotels.co.uk. Standing in nine acres of 'well-maintained' gardens and parkland, this peaceful Elizabethan manor house (with Victorian additions) has views across the South Downs. It is managed by Adam Smith for the Historic Sussex Hotels group. There is an open fire in the elegant drawing room and a wood-burning stove in the oak-panelled bar; a 'fantastic' new spa is in a purpose-built structure in the walled garden, which also houses six modern bedrooms (those in the main house are traditionally furnished). In the 'light and airy' *Michelin*-starred restaurant overlooking the gardens, head chef Stephen Crane serves a choice of fixed-price menus. Drawing room, bar, restaurant. No background music. Free Wi-Fi. Spa (heated indoor and outdoor linked pool fed by natural spring water, hot tub, sauna steam room, relaxation room, gym, fitness studio, flotation tank). Civil wedding licence; conference facilities. 20 mins' drive from Gatwick airport. 28 bedrooms (some with four-poster; 6 in spa building). Per room B&B £190–£350.

DARLINGTON Co. Durham
Map 4:C4

HEADLAM HALL, nr Gainford, DL2 3HA. Tel 01325-730238, www.headlamhall.co.uk. Surrounded by rolling farmland, the Robinson family's handsome 17th-century country house has a Jacobean hall, stone walls, huge fireplaces and traditional furnishing. Modern British and continental cuisine is served in the intimate, panelled dining room, the fresh, airy *Orangery* and the spa brasserie. Private dining is also available. 3 lounges, drawing room, bar, restaurant (classical/jazz background music). Free Wi-Fi. Lift. Spa (outdoor

hydrotherapy pool, sauna, gym; treatment rooms). Terraces. 4-acre walled garden: lake, ornamental canal; tennis, 9-hole golf course, croquet. Children and dogs welcomed. 40 bedrooms (6 in mews, 9 in coach house, 7 in spa; 2 suitable for &). Per room B&B £125–£185. D,B&B £90–£124 per person.

DARTMOUTH Devon
Map 1:D4

BROWNS HOTEL, 27–29 Victoria Road, TQ6 9RT. Tel 01803-832572, www.brownshoteldartmouth.co.uk. Attentive hosts Clare and James Brown run their informal hotel in a 200-year-old town house up a side street. It has been given a contemporary interior. Brightly decorated bedrooms have space to sit; there are squashy sofas in the large, open-plan wine bar. Jamie Smith's Mediterranean dishes use home-smoked food from Devon producers. Lounge, bar (complimentary tapas on Fri eve), restaurant (closed Sun–Tues). Free Wi-Fi. Modern/jazz background music. Parking permits supplied. Children welcomed. 8 bedrooms. Per room B&B £90–£185. Dinner from £20.

STOKE LODGE, Cinders Lane, Stoke Fleming, TQ6 0RA. Tel 01803-770523, www.stokelodge.co.uk. On the south Devon coast, Christine and Steven Mayer's traditionally furnished country hotel has a friendly, relaxing atmosphere. Dating from the 17th century, it has been extended to provide many facilities for families: a games room (table tennis) and snooker room, indoor and outdoor heated swimming pools, an all-weather tennis court, a putting green, and a giant chess set. In the *Garden* restaurant, chef Paul

Howard serves an extensive, daily-changing menu. 2 miles W of Stoke Fleming. 2 lounges, bar, restaurant; terrace; sauna, whirlpool. Free Wi-Fi. Background music. 3-acre grounds; duck pond. Children and dogs (the latter not in public rooms) welcomed. 25 bedrooms. Per person B&B £49.50–£73, D,B&B £73.50–£93.50.
25% DISCOUNT VOUCHERS

STRETE BARTON HOUSE, Totnes Road, Strete, TQ6 0RU. Tel 01803-770364, www.stretebarton.co.uk. Stuart Litster and Kevin Hooper's 16th-century manor house has a contemporary interior with an eastern flavour; bedrooms have silks, Buddha carvings and bold prints. Guests enjoy tea and home-made cake beside a roaring fire in winter; on warmer days, they sit on the terrace with panoramic views across Start Bay, from Start Point lighthouse to the mouth of the River Dart. Seasonal fruit and local farm yogurts are served at breakfast. Close to the South West Coast Path, 5 miles SW of Dartmouth. Sitting room, breakfast room (classical/ 'easy listening' background music); garden. Free Wi-Fi. In-room massages/ spa treatments, by arrangement. Children over 8 welcomed. 6 bedrooms (1 in cottage; dogs allowed). Per room B&B £105–£195 (2-night min. stay at weekends and in peak season).

DITTISHAM Devon
Map 1:D4
FINGALS, Old Coombe, Dartmouth, TQ6 0JA. Tel 01803-722398, www.fingals.co.uk. 'We loved every moment of it.' Staying at Richard and Sheila Johnston's extended old farmhouse near Dartmouth is 'rather like visiting a relaxed country house'. 'Quirky, comfortable and original', public rooms have inglenook fireplaces and oak beams. 'Delicious' dinners are cooked (by arrangement) by Ben Chambers; they can be served communally, at a long table in the oak-panelled dining room, or at separate tables in a smaller room. 'Breakfasts were wonderful.' Lounge, TV room, 2 dining rooms, honesty bar, library. Free Wi-Fi. Background music in bar. Indoor heated pool with partly removable roof, spa bath, sauna; orangery, summer house; grass tennis court, croquet lawn; games room; art gallery. Children, and dogs (in some rooms) welcomed. Resident dogs. 8 bedrooms (2 in separate buildings beside a stream). Per room B&B £95–£190. Dinner £36. Closed Jan–Easter.

DOUGLAS Isle of Man
Map 4: inset D1
INGLEWOOD, 26 Palace Terrace, Queens Promenade, IM2 4NF. Tel 01624-674734, www.inglewoodhotel-isleofman.com. 'We were made very welcome.' At this modern guest house on a peaceful section of the promenade, Pip and Andy Cross are praised for their excellent hospitality: they help plan days out, provide picnic lunches, and will book restaurants and taxis. Bright, spacious bedrooms have a memory foam mattress and comfortable seating; those at the front have sea views. 'The extra touches made all the difference.' A coffee and cake shop serves home-made food throughout the day. Bar/lounge, dining room. No background music; occasional radio at breakfast. Free Wi-Fi. Steep stairs. 20 mins' walk from

the ferry terminal. 16 bedrooms. Per person B&B from £42.50.

DOVER Kent
Map 2:D5

LODDINGTON HOUSE, 14 East Cliff, CT16 1LX. Tel 01304-201947, www. loddingtonhousehotel.co.uk. Close to the ferry and cruise terminals, Robert Cupper's elegant Grade II listed Regency house has views over the harbour and the White Cliffs. The comfortable bedrooms are traditionally furnished; some have views of the harbour and the English Channel. Three-course evening meals can be arranged (Oct–May); afternoon teas in summer. Lounge (balcony with sea view), dining room. Free Wi-Fi. No background music. Small garden. Parking. 6 bedrooms (en suite or private facilities). Per room B&B single £40–£55, double £55–£75. Dinner from £25.

WALLETT'S COURT, Westcliffe, St Margaret's-at-Cliffe, CT15 6EW. Tel 01304-852424, www.wallettscourt hotelspa.com. 'There is something for everyone here.' Opposite the Norman church, in a pretty hamlet ten minutes' drive from the port, this white-painted Jacobean manor house is run as a small hotel by the owners, Christopher and Leonora Oakley. Rooms in the old building and restored barns are decorated in country house style. 'A building of great character, an excellent dinner and a very comfy bed.' There are luxury tipis for glamping in the seven-acre landscaped gardens. Lounge, bar, library, conservatory, restaurant (David Hoseason is chef; background music; open to non-residents). Free Wi-Fi. 12-metre indoor pool with Endless Pools

swim trainer and hydrotherapy massage, sauna, steam room, fitness studio, indoor hot tub, treatment cabins, relaxation room; tennis courts, croquet lawn, boules court; sun terraces. Civil wedding licence; function facilities. Children welcomed (baby-listening; high teas). 17 bedrooms (plus 2 tipis and 2 huts in grounds). Per room B&B £140–£210, D,B&B £220–£290.
25% DISCOUNT VOUCHERS

DRIFFIELD East Yorkshire
Map 4:D5

KILHAM HALL, Driffield Road, YO25 4SP. Tel 01262-420466, www. kilhamhall co.uk. 'A delightful place.' Joanne Long and David Berry greet guests with tea and home-made scones at their elegant home; in the large, landscaped gardens, butterflies, bees, hedgehogs and barn owls find a similarly warm welcome. With velvet, silks and faux fur, and mood lighting, bedrooms are 'sheer luxury'; bathrooms have an oversized bath and under-floor heating. There is an 'enormous' choice at breakfast: Aga-cooked eggs, local honey, home-made bread and jams. Picnic hampers available. Drawing room, dining room (background music), conservatory. Free Wi-Fi. In-room spa treatments. 1½-acre garden: outdoor heated pool (May–mid-Sept), all-weather tennis court, croquet. Drying room; bike storage. 3 bedrooms. Per room B&B £130–£170. Closed Nov–early Feb.

DULVERTON Somerset
Map 1:B5

THREE ACRES COUNTRY HOUSE, Brushford, TA22 9AR. Tel 01398-323730, www.threeacresexmoor.co.uk. Ideally placed for country walks, Julie

and Edward Christian's secluded B&B is set in mature grounds on the edge of Exmoor. Overlooking a peaceful village, it has stunning hillside views. The 1930s house is thoughtfully equipped; bedrooms have a large bed, a fridge, a silent-tick alarm clock. Breakfasts include a daily special, and home-made fruit compotes using berries from the garden. Light suppers (soups, pâtés, sandwiches, puddings) can be arranged. Picnic hampers available. Bar, sitting room with log fire, dining room; sun terrace. Free Wi-Fi. No background music. 2 miles S of Dulverton. Country pursuits arranged. Children welcomed. The house is also available for exclusive use. 6 bedrooms (1 on ground floor). Per person B&B £45–£60 (£15 single person supplement).
25% DISCOUNT VOUCHERS

DUNWICH Suffolk
Map 2:B6
THE SHIP AT DUNWICH, St James Street, IP17 3DT. Tel 01728-648219, www.shipatdunwich.co.uk. In cold weather, a wood-burning stove provides a 'welcoming atmosphere' at this old inn close to the beach. Owned by Agellus Hotels and managed by Matt Goodwin, the inn is in a peaceful village that was once the capital of East Anglia, before the sea destroyed the port. 'Exceptionally clean', the warren-like interior is full of character; the original stone and wood floors have been retained. 'Good' and 'Best' bedrooms are quirky, though 'space can be rather tight'; some are accessed via an outside staircase. 'Breakfast was very good.' Opposite a bird sanctuary and nature reserve. Bar, dining room, conservatory, courtyard; large garden. Free Wi-Fi.

No background music. Children and dogs welcomed. 15 bedrooms (4 on ground floor in converted stables; 1 suitable for ⅃). Per room B&B £95–£135. Dinner £22.
25% DISCOUNT VOUCHERS

DURHAM Co. Durham
Map 4:B4
CATHEDRAL VIEW, 212 Gilesgate, DH1 1QN. Tel 0191-386 9566, www.cathedralview.co.uk. 'We enjoyed our short stay here.' In a refurbished Georgian merchant's house with a view of the cathedral, 'very welcoming' hosts Jim and Karen Garfitt provide B&B accommodation. 'Very clean, with good decoration and fittings', it has comfortable, well-equipped rooms, and a relaxing lounge with complimentary sherry. Home-baked bread at breakfast. No background music. Lounge (communal guests' netbook with access to a printer), breakfast room. Free Wi-Fi. Garden, with decking, seating and fish ponds. 10 mins' walk to cathedral; near a main road. Parking (permits supplied). 5 bedrooms. Per room B&B £85–£150.

GADDS TOWN HOUSE, 34 Old Elvet, DH1 3HN. Tel 0191-384 1037, www.gaddstownhouse.com. 'A good city-centre hotel', this Grade II listed Georgian house (formerly *The Fallen Angel*) is owned by Deborah and Nigel Gadd. Individually styled, the themed bedrooms – one is inspired by a luxury cruise liner, another by an Edwardian steam train – have been refurbished with lavish fabrics and wall coverings. Some rooms have views of the cathedral, castle or river; three garden rooms have a private hot tub. Under chef Kevin

Dunn, the restaurant is 'excellent, to such an extent that we dined there two nights running'. A small terrace overlooks the river. Cocktail bar, restaurant (soft jazz background music; closed Sun evenings). Free Wi-Fi. Lift. Children welcomed. 11 bedrooms (1 suitable for ♿). Per room B&B £99–£250. Dinner £33.

EASTBOURNE East Sussex
Map 2:E4
GRAND HOTEL, King Edwards Parade, BN21 4EQ. Tel 01323-412345, www.grandeastbourne.com. Guests love the 'wonderful service' at this charmingly 'old-fashioned' Victorian hotel on the seafront – 'an excellent example of its type'. 'The whole atmosphere here is lovely.' Traditionally furnished rooms are 'sumptuous'; many have sea views. There has long been a live band at weekends; the monthly gathering of the Palm Court quartet at teatime is 'an event worth going to'. 2 lounges, bar, *Mirabelle* (closed Sun, Mon) and *Garden* restaurants (both with background music); 'nice' terrace. Free Wi-Fi. Civil wedding licence; conference/function facilities. Health spa; 'lovely' heated indoor and outdoor swimming pools; 2-acre garden: putting, etc. Children welcomed (Junior Crew club, family dining, crèche). Parking. 152 bedrooms (1 suitable for ♿). Per room B&B £230–£380.

OCKLYNGE MANOR, Mill Road, BN21 2PG. Tel 01323-734121, www.ocklyngemanor.co.uk. One of Eastbourne's oldest houses, Wendy and David Dugdill's pink Georgian mansion is built on a site once occupied by the Knights of St John of Jerusalem; it also bears a blue plaque dedicated to *Peter Pan* illustrator Mabel Lucie Attwell, who lived here in the 1930s. Comfortable country-style bedrooms overlook beautiful grounds; part of the National Gardens Scheme, they include a ¾-acre walled garden, well, 18th-century gazebo and 150-year-old manna ash. Organic breakfasts (home-made bread and marmalade). Bread-making courses (Nov–Mar). Free Wi-Fi. No background music. DVD-players. Garden. 1¼ miles from seafront. Parking. 3 bedrooms. Per person B&B single £45–£60, double £50–£60 (2-night min. stay at weekends preferred).

EVERSHOT Dorset
Map 1:C6
THE ACORN INN, 28 Fore Street, DT2 0JW. Tel 01935-83228, www.acorn-inn.co.uk. In a pretty Dorset village, this 16th-century stone inn (believed to have featured in Thomas Hardy's novels) 'manages the impossible – a blend of local pub for faithful regulars, and sophisticated place in which someone from Sloane Square would feel at home'. It is run in a relaxed way by Jack and Alex Mackenzie for the Red Carnation Hotel Collection; sister property *Summer Lodge* (see main entry) is across the street. The inn has beams, oak panelling, stone floors and log fires; traditional bedrooms have quirky touches. Guests may use *Summer Lodge*'s spa swimming pool, sauna and gym (£15 charge), and book treatments there. In the bars and smart restaurant, local, sustainably sourced produce is cooked by Chris Schacht. Lounge, 2 bars (skittle alley), restaurant with sitting area; small beer garden. Occasional background music. Free Wi-Fi

(in public areas only). Children and dogs welcomed. 10 bedrooms. Per room B&B £99–£200, D,B&B £159–£260.

EXETER Devon
Map 1:C5

THE MAGDALEN CHAPTER, Magdalen Street, EX2 4HY. Tel 01392-281000, www.themagdalenchapter.com. Substantial renovation in 2012 transformed the former West of England Eye Hospital into a sophisticated hotel that retains remnants of its heritage in original marble floors and old, gold-lettered visitor notices. Fiona Moores is the manager. Handsome, modern bedrooms have an iPad, Nespresso coffee machine and complimentary minibar. With a striking sloping ceiling like a circus tent, the bright restaurant has an open kitchen, where chef Ben Bulger cooks seasonal, daily-changing dishes. It opens on to the terrace and garden. Background music. Lounge, bar, library, dining room (Simon Hopkinson is culinary consultant). Free Wi-Fi. Walled garden; indoor-outdoor pool with wood-burning stove. Spa; treatments (open to non-residents); gym. Children and dogs welcomed. 59 bedrooms. Per room B&B from £150.

FALMOUTH Cornwall
Map 1:E2

THE ROSEMARY, 22 Gyllyngvase Terrace, TR11 4DL. Tel 01326-314669, www.therosemary.co.uk. 'Very welcoming owners' Lynda and Malcolm Cook provide tea and home-made cake to B&B guests staying at their 'comfortable, beautifully furnished' Edwardian house. The large drawing room and most of the bedrooms have

'gorgeous' sea views; well-presented Cornish breakfasts are 'superb'. Close to the town centre and a two-minute stroll to the beach. Bar, lounge, dining room (no background music); south-facing garden, sun deck. Free Wi-Fi. Children and dogs (the latter not in high season) welcomed. 8 bedrooms (two 2-bedroom suites, ideal for a family). Per room B&B single £48–£61, double £77–£105. Closed end Nov–Feb.

FOLKESTONE Kent
Map 2:E5

THE RELISH, 4 Augusta Gardens, CT20 2RR. Tel 01303-850952, www.hotelrelish.co.uk. Guests are welcomed with a glass of wine or beer at Sarah and Chris van Dyke's relaxed B&B; complimentary coffee, tea, soft drinks and home-made cake are available throughout the day. The grand, cream-painted 1850s merchant's house is furnished in a clean-lined, contemporary style. It has direct access to the private, four-acre Augusta Gardens; the town and Leas Cliff Hall are close by. Lounge (with open fire), breakfast room (Radio 2 played). Free Wi-Fi. Small terrace. On-street parking. Children welcomed. 10 bedrooms. Per room B&B single £75–£140, double £98–£150 (2-night min. stay Jul–Sept).

ROCKSALT, 4–5 Fish Market, CT19 6AA. Tel 01303-212070, www.rocksaltfolkestone.co.uk. Cantilevered over Folkestone's fishing harbour, chef Mark Sargeant's stylish restaurant is in a curved, dark-timber-and-glass building with a stunning contemporary interior. There are lime-washed oak flooring, curved benches, designer chairs, elegant lighting, and floor-to-ceiling windows looking over a terrace and out to sea. Kentish produce and locally caught fish are cooked simply and well. 'Exemplary service.' A lively bar above serves cocktails and light bites. Across a cobbled street, accommodation is in a converted old building on a narrow passageway; snug rooms have exposed brick walls, an antique bed and a wet room. Breakfast hampers ('meagre' continental) are delivered to the room. Bar, restaurant, terrace. Free Wi-Fi. No background music. Children welcomed. On-street parking. 4 bedrooms. Per room B&B £85–£100.

FROGGATT EDGE Derbyshire
Map 3:A6
THE CHEQUERS INN, Hope Valley, S32 3ZJ. Tel 01433-630231, www. chequers-froggatt.com. On the edge of the village, this Grade II listed 16th-century roadside inn is owned by Jonathan and Joanne Tindall and managed by Debbie Robinson. Graham Mitchell cooks pub-style food with European flourishes, served in two cosy eating areas or alfresco in the elevated garden. Home-made preserves and chutneys are available to buy. The inn is in 'a lovely area for walks'; a leaflet suggests a variety of hikes from the front door. Restaurant, garden. 'Discreet' classical background music; radio at breakfast. Free Wi-Fi. Children welcomed. 6 bedrooms. Per room B&B £85–£115. Dinner from £25.
25% DISCOUNT VOUCHERS

GATWICK West Sussex
Map 2:D4
LANGSHOTT MANOR, Ladbroke Road, Langshott, Horley, RH6 9LN. Tel 01293-786680, www.langshottmanor. com. In an Elizabethan timber-framed manor house close to Gatwick airport, this luxury hotel combines exposed beams, oak panels and feature fireplaces with elegant, individually designed bedrooms. Chef Phil Dixon adds an inventive slant to 'excellent' classic European dishes, served in the *Mulberry* restaurant; tasting menus include a vegetarian option. Katie Savage is the manager. 2 lounges (background music), bar, restaurant, terrace (alfresco dining). Free Wi-Fi. Civil wedding licence; conference facilities. 3-acre garden; medieval moat. Children welcomed. 22 bedrooms (7 in main house, some with four-poster bed; 15 across garden). Room only £199–£309. Breakfast £12.50–£16.95, dinner from £45.

GILSLAND Cumbria
Map 4:B3
HILL ON THE WALL, Brampton, CA8 7DA. Tel 01697-747214, www. hillonthewall.co.uk. On a hillside, this Grade II listed 16th-century fortified farmhouse (a cunningly christened 'bastle') is a mere 300 yards from Hadrian's Wall and has 'stunning' views over the Irthing valley. Elaine Packer welcomes guests to her 'beautifully furnished' B&B with tea and home-made cake in the 'magnificent' drawing room; locally sourced breakfasts, ordered the night before, are 'delicious'. Walkers and cyclists are welcomed; packed lunches available (£6). Lounge (library, wood-burning stove), breakfast room; terrace. No background music. Free Wi-Fi. 1-acre garden. Parking; secure cycle storage. Near Hadrian's Wall at Birdoswald. 3 bedrooms. Per person B&B £42.50–£62.50. Closed Dec–Feb.

WILLOWFORD FARM, CA8 7AA. Tel 01697-747962, www.willowford.co.uk. Liam McNulty and Lauren Harrison's B&B on a 100-acre working farm lies on one of the longest unbroken stretches of Hadrian's Wall. Along the National Trail between Gilsland village and Birdoswald Roman Fort, it has the remains of a bridge and two turrets. A former milking parlour, cart house and grain store have been converted into homely, energy-efficient bedrooms with exposed wooden beams, slate floors and antique furniture; bathrooms have under-floor heating and handmade organic soaps. Pre-booked three-course evening meals are accompanied by local Geltsdale ale or wines from small, family-run vineyards. Packed lunches available. Lounge, dining room. Free Wi-Fi. No background music. Children welcomed (family rooms); dogs by arrangement. Resident dogs. 5 bedrooms (all on ground floor). Per room B&B £75–£80. Dinner £18. Closed Dec–Mar.

GRAFFHAM West Sussex
Map 2:E3
WILLOW BARNS, nr Petworth, GU28 0NU. Tel 01798-867493, www. willowbarns.co.uk. Newly built using traditional methods in flint and brick, the serene rooms of Amanda Godman and Wendy Judd's B&B are set around a pretty courtyard. Each has its own front door, 'gorgeous' bathroom and wonderful views of the countryside. On the edge of a village, the B&B is within easy walking distance of two 'friendly' pubs; there are numerous footpaths and bridleways nearby. Home-cooked breakfasts, taken communally at the long dining-room table or in the courtyard on sunny mornings, are 'a feast'. Dining room; courtyard garden. Free Wi-Fi. No background music. Parking. Cyclists and riders welcomed; stabling, by arrangement, for visiting horses (or turnout in adjacent field). Clay-pigeon shooting can be organised. 5 bedrooms (all on ground floor). Per room B&B £100 (2-night min. stay at peak weekends).
25% DISCOUNT VOUCHERS

GRANGE-OVER-SANDS Cumbria
Map 4: inset C2
CLARE HOUSE, Park Road, LA11 7HQ. Tel 015395-33026, www.clarehousehotel. co.uk. 'There is much to appreciate' at this Victorian hotel run by the Read family. With a 'good combination of comfy – even homely – bedrooms, a great welcome and excellent food', it represents 'the very best of the traditional'. Andrew Read and Mark Johnston cook 'imaginative, beautifully presented' dinners featuring local produce, also available to non-residents. 'Wonderful' views over the garden to Morecambe Bay. 2 lounges, dining room. Free Wi-Fi. No background music. ½-acre grounds. Mile-long promenade at bottom of garden (bowling green, tennis courts, putting green; easy access to Ornamental Gardens). Parking. Children welcomed. 18 bedrooms (1 on ground floor suitable for &). Per person B&B £68–£73, D,B&B £88–£93. Closed mid-Dec–end Mar.
25% DISCOUNT VOUCHERS

GRASMERE Cumbria
Map 4: inset C2
WHITE MOSS HOUSE, Rydal Water, LA22 9SE. Tel 015394-35295, www. whitemoss.com. Bought in 1827 by William Wordsworth for his son, this

grey stone, creeper-clad house at the northern end of Rydal Water was occupied by the Wordsworth family until the 1930s. Today, it is a homely B&B owned by Sue and Peter Dixon, who offer guests complimentary afternoon tea on arrival and helpful recommendations on restaurants and local events. There is an oak-panelled lounge with comfy sofas, a wood-burning fire, flowers, books, games and a piano. Mr Dixon occasionally cooks for private house parties (five-course gourmet menus). Packed lunches available. No background music. Lounge, dining room. Free Wi-Fi. 2-acre garden/woodland (lake views); outdoor seating on a flowery terrace. Fishing permits. Free membership at local leisure club. Parking. Children welcomed. 1 mile from Grasmere. 5 bedrooms. Per person B&B £49–£59. Closed Dec–Mar.

GRASSINGTON North Yorkshire
Map 4:D3

GRASSINGTON HOUSE, 5 The Square, nr Skipton, BD23 5AQ. Tel 01756-752406, www.grassingtonhousehotel.co.uk. 'We were pleased with it in every way.' In a popular market town on the Dales Way trail, this refurbished hotel occupies a limestone Georgian house overlooking a cobbled square. It is run by chef/patron John Rudden and his wife, Sue, who has decorated the interior in a dramatic, contemporary style. The host cooks 'very enjoyable' classic English food with interesting flourishes, served in the smart restaurant or fireside bar, or on the terrace. The house's hand-reared rare-breed pigs provide the restaurant with bacon, sausages and pork (with plenty of crackling). Lounge, bar, *No.5*

restaurant. Free Wi-Fi. Background music. Children welcomed. Cookery master classes. Tracking and foraging days in the Dales. Civil wedding licence; function facilities. Parking. 8 bedrooms. Per room B&B £110–£130, D,B&B £190–£200.
25% DISCOUNT VOUCHERS

GREAT LANGDALE Cumbria
Map 4: inset C2

THE OLD DUNGEON GHYLL, LA22 9JY. Tel 015394-37272, www.odg.co.uk. In the Great Langdale valley, this extended inn has welcomed fell walkers and climbers for more than 300 years. Run by Jane and Neil Walmsley for the National Trust, it has comfortable, country-style bedrooms, open fires; no television. The lively *Hikers' Bar*, open to non-residents, has real ales and occasional open-mic nights. Packed lunches available. Residents' bar and lounge, dining room, public *Hikers' Bar* (old cow stalls); live music on first Wed of every month. No background music. Free Wi-Fi in public areas. Drying room. 1-acre garden. 12 bedrooms (6 with private facilities). Per person B&B £58, D,B&B £78 (2-night min. stay at weekends).

GURNARD Isle of Wight
Map 2:E2

THE LITTLE GLOSTER, 31 Marsh Road, PO31 8JQ. Tel 01983-200299, www. thelittlegloster.com. By the water's edge, on a little bay just west of Cowes, this laid-back restaurant-with-rooms occupies a low-built building with Scandinavian appeal. It is run by chef Ben Cooke with his wife, Holly, and support from family members; his Danish grandmother ensures that the minimalist restaurant is supplied with fresh flowers. Blue-and-white rooms have a nautical simplicity; two have wonderful sea views (binoculars supplied). The balcony suite has an enclosed terrace with a table, deckchairs and views across the Solent. Served in an airy dining room with huge picture windows looking out to sea, uncomplicated dishes focus on fresh, local food with Nordic influences. Bar, restaurant (closed Mon, and Tues in winter). Free Wi-Fi. Background music. Garden; croquet lawn. Function facilities. Children welcomed. 5 mins' drive from Cowes. 3 bedrooms (in adjoining building). Per room B&B £80–£145. Dinner £35. Closed Jan–mid-Feb.

HALIFAX West Yorkshire
Map 4:D3

SHIBDEN MILL INN, Shibden Mill Fold, HX3 7UL. Tel 01422-365840, www.shibdenmillinn.com. In a 'lovely' streamside setting in a wooded valley, Simon and Caitlin Heaton's 'very attractive' 17th-century country inn has oak beams, rafters and sloping ceilings. Glen Pearson is the manager. Bedrooms have recently been redesigned and modernised. The 'bustling' bar is popular with locals and visitors (ales include *Shibden Mill*'s own brew). Chef Darren Parkinson uses seasonal, locally sourced produce in his modern British dishes. Two miles NE of Halifax. Bar, restaurant; private dining room; patio (alfresco dining). Free Wi-Fi. Background music. Small conference facilities. Parking. Children welcomed (special menu). 11 bedrooms. Per room B&B single £90–£119, double £111–£139, double D,B&B £195–£260.

HARROGATE North Yorkshire
Map 4:D4

THE BIJOU, 17 Ripon Road, HG1 2JL. Tel 01423-567974, www.thebijou.co.uk. Stephen and Gill Watson's good-value B&B is in a Victorian villa, a five-minute walk from the town centre. It has contemporary furnishing and artwork, original wood and tiled floors, and a wood-burning stove in the sitting room. Modern bedrooms have up-to-date magazines and a hospitality tray with Jelly Tots and biscuits. Some steep stairs; the coach house behind the main building is ideal for a family. Lounge (afternoon teas; honesty bar; computer), breakfast room. Free Wi-Fi. Background music. Small front garden. Parking. Children welcomed. 10 bedrooms (2 in coach house; 1 on ground floor). Per room B&B single £64–£104, double £84–£114.

RUDDING PARK, Follifoot, HG3 1JH. Tel 01423-871350, www.ruddingpark. com. Daffodils, rhododendrons and azaleas bloom in the extensive grounds of this large hotel standing in parkland originally laid out by landscape designer Humphry Repton. The Grade I listed Regency mansion, with luxury spa and 18-hole golf course, is owned by Simon Mackaness and his family. Individually designed, the smart bedrooms are in two wings; some have a private terrace or balcony. The award-winning *Clocktower* restaurant, with its pink glass chandelier, has seasonal menus based on locally sourced ingredients; chefs forage in the grounds for wild garlic and herbs to use in the kitchen. Yorkshire breakfasts; complimentary newspapers. 2½ miles S of town. Bar, restaurant (background music), conservatory; terrace (alfresco dining); cinema. Free Wi-Fi. Spa (hammam, steam rooms, treatments); gym; off-road driving, falconry. Civil wedding licence; conference facilities. Children welcomed. 90 bedrooms (8 suites, 4 spa rooms, 1 family room; 3 suitable for &; plus 5 self-catering luxury lodges). Per room B&B from £144, D,B&B from £189.

25% DISCOUNT VOUCHERS

HARTINGTON Derbyshire
Map 3:A6

HARTINGTON HALL, Hall Bank, SK17 0AT. Tel 01298-84223, www.yha.org.uk/ hostel/hartington. A 'lovely old building in very good shape', this 17th-century manor house in 'immaculate' grounds is run as an upmarket youth hostel by the YHA. Period features (mullioned windows, oak panelling, log fires) make a handsome backdrop for basic accommodation in the main house; more rooms available in the coach house and the barn. 'Amazing value.' Walks and cycle routes from the front door; packed lunches available. Lounge, bar, restaurant (home-cooked English fare, local ingredients); background music. Games room; self-catering kitchen; drying room; meeting rooms. Free Wi-Fi (in public rooms only). Extensive grounds: beer garden, adventure playground, pet area. Civil wedding licence. Children and dogs welcomed. 35 bedrooms (19 en suite; 10 in barn annexe, 5 in coach house; 1 suitable for &). Room only from £20. Breakfast £4.99.

HATCH BEAUCHAMP Somerset
Map 1:C6

FARTHINGS, nr Taunton, TA3 6SG. Tel 01823-480664, www.farthingshotel.co.uk. In large, well-tended grounds, this 200-year-old white-painted house is run as a small hotel/restaurant by owner John Seeger. With curved bays and shuttered windows, it has many original features. The comfortable lounge has crackling log fires in winter; the 'intimate' dining room has subdued lighting and a large bay window overlooking the garden. Extensive orchards in the grounds provide figs, cherries, medlars and sweet chestnuts for chef Vincent Adeline's traditional menus; home-reared pigs provide bacon, sausages and pork joints. Background music in restaurant. Lounge, bar, 3 dining rooms; 3-acre grounds (orchards, roses; chickens, pigs). Wi-Fi (£5 per 24 hours). Civil wedding licence. Children, and well-behaved dogs (£8 charge) welcomed. Resident dogs. 11 bedrooms (2 on ground floor), plus 1-bed cottage. Per room B&B single £110–£155, double £130–£175. D,B&B from £75 per person.

25% DISCOUNT VOUCHERS

HAWORTH West Yorkshire
Map 4:D3

ASHMOUNT COUNTRY HOUSE, Mytholmes Lane, BD22 8EZ. Tel 01535-645726, www.ashmounthaworth.co.uk. In Brontë country, Ray and Gill Capeling's stone-built guest house was once the home of Dr Amos Ingham, physician to the Brontë sisters. It is a short stroll from the Brontë Parsonage Museum. Wayne and Claire Saud are the managers. Bedrooms are romantic; some have a private patio and hot tub, sauna cabin and whirlpool bath, music and mood lighting. In the restaurant overlooking the garden and the countryside beyond, chef Sara Knighton cooks modern dishes; vegetarian menus are available. Yorkshire breakfasts.

Lounge, morning room, *The Drawing Room* restaurant (open to non-residents; closed Mon, Tues). Free Wi-Fi. 'Easy listening' background music. Mature ¾-acre garden; picnics available. Civil wedding licence; function facilities. Ample private parking. Children over 10 welcomed. 12 bedrooms (4 in former chauffeur and gardener's cottage, across the street). Per room B&B £95–£225, D,B&B £155–£285 (2-night min. stay at weekends).

25% DISCOUNT VOUCHERS

HAY-ON-WYE Herefordshire
Map 3:D4
TINTO HOUSE, 13 Broad Street, HR3 5DB. Tel 01497-821556, www. tinto-house.co.uk. By the clock tower in the town centre, artist John Clare and his wife, Karen, run this small B&B in their handsomely furnished listed Georgian house. The country-style interior is decorated with original paintings, drawings and wooden sculptures; breakfast has home-made jams and compotes, and fruit from the garden. Bounded by the River Wye, and with distant views of the hills above Clyro, the garden is home to regular sculpture installations; the converted stable block contains an art gallery. Offa's Dyke is close by. Dining room, library. Free Wi-Fi. No background music. 1-acre garden. Children welcomed. 4 bedrooms. Per room B&B £60–£95. Closed for 4 weeks over Christmas/New Year.

HELMSLEY North Yorkshire
Map 4:C4
No54, 54 Bondgate, YO62 5EZ. Tel 01439-771533, www.no54.co.uk. Lizzie Would's welcoming B&B is in a house

formed from two cottages in a York stone terrace, half a mile from the market square. Tea and home-baked cake are served on arrival. The main building has flagstone floors and real fires; pretty bedrooms are set around a sunny, flowery courtyard. Breakfast, served at a communal table, includes locally smoked kippers and eggs from free-range hens just down the road. Sitting room. Free Wi-Fi. No background music. Garden. Near the North York Moors national park; picnics available. 3 bedrooms in courtyard. Per person B&B £50–£70.

HENLEY-ON-THAMES Buckinghamshire
Map 2:D3
FALAISE HOUSE, 37 Market Place, RG9 2AA. Tel 01491-573388, www.falaisehouse.com. Opposite the town hall, this well-located B&B is in a Grade II listed Georgian building with an entrance through a secluded cobbled courtyard. It is run by friendly owners, Jane and Richard Morgan. Furnished in a mix of period and modern styles, 'enchanting' rooms are decorated in soft colours and attractively patterned fabrics; immaculate shower rooms are compact, and have softened water and luxurious bathrobes. Breakfast, with hot chocolate and freshly squeezed orange juice, is 'perfect'. Breakfast room ('light' background music). Free Wi-Fi. Free overnight parking in Greys Road public car park, close by. 6 bedrooms. Per room B&B from £85.

HEREFORD Herefordshire
Map 3:D4
CASTLE HOUSE, Castle Street, HR1 2NW. Tel 01432-356321,

www.castlehse.co.uk. By the castle moat, just yards away from the cathedral, this handsome hotel is owned by David Watkins, a local farmer whose pedigree Hereford herd and other produce supply the restaurant menu. Accommodation is spread between the comfortable, traditionally furnished rooms in the main building (two converted Grade II listed houses) and the stylish, modern rooms in *Number 25*, a discreet town house down the street. 'Our well-appointed junior suite had good-quality furniture, excellent lighting, comfortable seating, a walk-in wardrobe; a marble bathroom.' Housekeeping is efficient and 'unobtrusive'; the staff are 'very helpful and friendly'. In the restaurant, dinner ('small portions') is cooked by Claire Nicholls; dishes have 'a smear of this, an artfully arranged that'. Lounge, *Bertie's* bar, restaurant, bistro; light jazz/classical background music. Free Wi-Fi. Lift. Garden, terrace (alfresco dining). Limited parking. Children welcomed. 24 bedrooms (8 in *Number 25*, available for exclusive use; 1 suitable for &). Per room B&B single £130, double £150–£190.

HERTFORD Hertfordshire
Map 2:C4
NUMBER ONE PORT HILL, 1 Port Hill, SG14 1PJ. Tel 01992-587350, www.numberoneporthill.co.uk. A short stroll from town, Annie Rowley's B&B, a Grade II listed Georgian town house, is mentioned in the Pevsner architectural guide to Hertfordshire. It has chandeliers, huge mirrors, vintage glassware, sculptures, candles and fresh flowers. Elegant bedrooms are on the top floor; the drawing room has an original corniced ceiling and roaring fire. An accommodating hostess, Annie Rowley serves a wide breakfast selection, taken at a communal table; home-cooked dinners are available on request. Drawing room; walled courtyard garden. Free Wi-Fi. No background music. Resident dog, Presley. Limited street parking. 3 bedrooms (1 with private bathroom). Per room B&B £95–£130. Dinner £30.

HEXHAM Northumberland
Map 4:B3
BARRASFORD ARMS, Barrasford, NE48 4AA. Tel 01434-681237, www.barrasfordarms.co.uk. 'A good bolthole.' In a small village close to Hadrian's Wall, this stone-built 1870s country pub-with-rooms offers 'a high standard of comfort, without any unnecessary flourishes'. Locals and visitors come for the hand-drawn real ales, and for chef/patron Tony Binks's traditional English dishes, cooked with a French twist. Bedrooms are smart and understated. Quoits tournaments, hunt meets, darts finals and vegetable competitions are regularly hosted here. Bar, 2 dining rooms; private dining. Background music in bar and restaurant. Free Wi-Fi. Parking. Children welcomed (family rooms). 7 bedrooms. Per room B&B £67–£87. Dinner from £25.

THE HERMITAGE, Swinburne, NE48 4DG. Tel 01434-681248, email katie.stewart@themeet.co.uk. 'A perfect bed and breakfast,' say two experienced hoteliers about Katie and Simon Stewart's stone-built house, which is approached through a grand arch and up a long drive. 'Traditional, but just lovely', the home has a 'true country house atmosphere'. Katie Stewart serves a welcoming tea in front of a roaring log fire, helps with restaurant bookings, and suggests circular walks on Hadrian's Wall nearby. Drawing rooms, breakfast room; 4-acre grounds: terrace, tennis. Free Wi-Fi. No background music. Children over 7 welcomed. Resident dogs. 7 miles N of Corbridge (ask for directions). 3 bedrooms. Per room B&B single £55, double £90. Closed Nov–Mar.

HOARWITHY Herefordshire
Map 3:D4

ASPEN HOUSE, HR2 6QP. Tel 01432-840353, www.aspenhouse.net. In a tranquil Wye valley village, enthusiastic hosts Sally Dean and Rob Elliott run Real Food Discovery weekends at their environmentally friendly B&B. Rooms in the 18th-century red sandstone farmhouse are simply furnished and comfortable; organic breakfasts have eggs from local farms, bacon from rare-breed pigs, and home-made bread and muesli. There is good walking from the front door (maps and drying facilities provided). Lounge (opening on to a decked area overlooking the ½-acre garden). Free Wi-Fi. No background music. 4 miles from Ross-on-Wye. 3 bedrooms (plus self-catering cottage). Per room B&B £45–£78.

HOPE Derbyshire
Map 3:A6

LOSEHILL HOUSE, Losehill Lane, Edale Road, S33 6AF. Tel 01433-621219, www.losehillhouse.co.uk. In a 'magnificent setting', Paul and Kathryn Roden's secluded spa hotel is in a white-painted Arts and Crafts house on a hillside, with footpath access to the Peak District national park. Refurbished modern bedrooms are decorated in neutral tones; a complimentary newspaper is provided. The outdoor hot tub has 'amazing' views over the Hope valley. Drawing room, bar, *Orangery* restaurant (chef Darren Goodwin cooks modern British food); lift. Free Wi-Fi. Background music. 1-acre garden; terrace. Spa: indoor swimming pool; hot tub; treatment rooms (open to non-residents). Civil wedding licence; function/conference facilities. Children, and dogs (in 2 rooms) welcomed. Parking. 23 bedrooms (4 with external entrance). Per room B&B £160–£250, D,B&B £200–£320.
25% DISCOUNT VOUCHERS

HUDDERSFIELD West Yorkshire
Map 4:E3

THE THREE ACRES INN & RESTAURANT, Roydhouse, Shelley, HD8 8LR. Tel 01484-602606, www.3acres.com. In rolling Pennine countryside, this characterful old roadside drovers' inn has been transformed over three decades by Brian Orme and Neil Truelove. It has a traditional bar, a popular restaurant serving traditional English food, and a new grill and rotisserie featuring locally sourced fish and shellfish cooked by chef Tom Davies. Bedrooms are comfortable and modern. 5 miles from the town centre (busy morning traffic). Bar, restaurant; ramp. Free Wi-Fi. Background music. Terraced garden; decked dining terrace. Civil wedding licence; small function/private dining facilities. Children, and dogs (in 1 room) welcomed. 17 bedrooms (1 suitable for ♿; 6 in adjacent cottages). Per room B&B £75–£125. Dinner from £45.

ILMINGTON Warwickshire
Map 3:D6

THE HOWARD ARMS, Lower Green, nr
Stratford-upon-Avon, CV36 4LT. Tel
01608-682226, www.howardarms.com.
Arched windows, beamed ceilings,
flagstone floors and a mix of old
furniture give character to this 400-year-
old Cotswold stone inn on the village
green; log fires are cheering on a cold
day. 'Fantastic, with impeccable service.'
Bedrooms vary in size and decor: they
may have a country-style painted wood
headboard or striking feature wallpaper.
The popular restaurant is praised for its
comforting cooking using produce from
local suppliers; a quiet garden (alfresco
dining) has plenty of space for exuberant
children. Snug, bar, dining room ('easy
listening' background music); patio/
garden. Free Wi-Fi. Parking. Children
welcomed. 8 bedrooms (5 through
separate door under covered walkway).
Per room B&B £95–£145.

ILSINGTON Devon
Map 1:D4

ILSINGTON COUNTRY HOUSE, nr
Newton Abbot, TQ13 9RR. Tel 01364-
661452, www.ilsington.co.uk. In
Dartmoor national park, with lovely
moorland views all around, the Hassell
family's traditional hotel is in an
'attractive' white-painted house
standing in ten acres of well-tended
grounds. 'Staff, without exception, were
welcoming and helpful.' Rooms on the
second floor have been refurbished; a
biomass wood-fuelled boiler was
installed in 2013. Chef Mike
O'Donnell's modern European menus
focus on local produce; they are served
in the dining room overlooking the
Devon countryside. 'We enjoyed quite

the best dinner for some time.' Bistro
food and snacks are taken in the *Blue
Tiger Inn*. An 'excellent' leisure centre
has a swimming pool, spa, sauna and
well-equipped gym (open to non-
residents). 2 lounges, bar, restaurant,
pub, conservatory; leisure complex;
croquet. Free Wi-Fi. Background
music. Lift. Civil wedding licence;
conference facilities. Children, and dogs
(in ground-floor rooms, conservatory;
£8 per night) welcomed. 25 bedrooms
(8 on ground floor). Per room B&B
£100–£200, D,B&B £156–£256.
25% DISCOUNT VOUCHERS

IPSWICH Suffolk
Map 2:C5

SALTHOUSE HARBOUR HOTEL,
1 Neptune Quay, IP4 1AX. Tel 01473-
226789, www.salthouseharbour.co.uk.
On the waterfront at Neptune Marina,
Robert Gough's 'cool, hip' converted
Victorian warehouse has 'splendid views
over the quay'. The stylish interior has
exposed brickwork, industrial pillars
and funky decoration; 'pleasant' public
areas are filled with quirky art, designer
rugs and modern sculpture. Bedrooms
are spacious; some have a free-standing
copper bath, others a balcony with a
harbour view. The popular *Eaterie*
serves all-day modern menus based
on ingredients from local suppliers
(background music). Lounge, bar,
brasserie. Free Wi-Fi. Conference
rooms. Children and dogs welcomed.
Limited parking. 70 bedrooms (4
suitable for &). Per room B&B £150–£350.

IRONBRIDGE Shropshire
Map 2:A1

THE LIBRARY HOUSE, Severn Bank,
TF8 7AN. Tel 01952-432299,

www.libraryhouse.com. In the centre of the town, well placed for the museums, this Grade II listed Georgian guest house by the River Severn is owned by Lizzie Steel, an 'immensely thoughtful and welcoming' hostess. Once the village library, the 'beautifully decorated' home is in a peaceful courtyard. The pretty bedrooms are well equipped: they have a hospitality tray, flat-screen TV and DVD-player, cotton waffle dressing gowns. Breakfast is 'superb'; cooked dishes are prepared to order and 'immaculately served' on tables with fresh flowers. Sitting room, dining room. Free Wi-Fi. No background music. Resident terrier, Fizz. Courtyard garden. Parking passes supplied for local car parks. Restaurants nearby. 4 bedrooms (1 with private terrace). Per room B&B from £80.

KESWICK Cumbria
Map 4: inset C2

DALEGARTH HOUSE, Portinscale, CA12 5RQ. Tel 017687-72817, www.dalegarth-house.co.uk. In an 'idyllic' situation above Derwentwater, with glorious fell and lake views, this spacious, traditionally furnished Edwardian house is owned by welcoming hosts Craig and Clare Dalton. Her home-cooked dinners ('a taste of the Lakes') are served at 7 pm, or earlier for guests attending the Theatre by the Lake. Cumbrian breakfasts. In a village 1 mile from Keswick. Background radio at breakfast; classical/'easy listening' music at dinner. Lounge, bar, restaurant. Free Wi-Fi. Garden. Parking. 10 bedrooms (2 in annexe). Per person B&B £44–£55, D,B&B £64–£75. Closed 8 Dec–mid-Feb.

LYZZICK HALL, Underskiddaw, CA12 4PY. Tel 017687-72277, www.lyzzickhall.co.uk. On the lower slopes of Skiddaw amid the 'stunning' scenery of the Borrowdale valley and Catbells, this hotel is owned by the Fernandez and Lake families. Most bedrooms have views towards the Lakeland fells. Lounges have comfortable seating and log fires; a spacious, sunny orangery has steps leading straight to the garden. Chef Ian Mackay's traditional and contemporary British cuisine, sourced from local suppliers, is served at elegantly set tables in the dining room; wine is mainly from the Iberian peninsula. 2 lounges, orangery, bar, restaurant (open to non-residents). Free Wi-Fi. Background music. Indoor pool, sauna, whirlpool bath. 4-acre landscaped grounds. Children welcomed. 30 bedrooms (1 on ground floor). Per person B&B £75–£121, D,B&B £97–£143.

KINGHAM Oxfordshire
Map 3:D6

THE KINGHAM PLOUGH, The Green, nr Chipping Norton, OX7 6YD. Tel 01608-658327, www.thekinghamplough.co.uk. Chef/patron Emily Watkins cooks 'inventive and flavourful food' at her pub-with-rooms in a 'charming' Cotswolds village. Working with Ben Dulley, she serves daily changing menus which have local game and produce, foraged fungi and sea vegetables. Pretty bedrooms have freshly baked biscuits and a DVD library; some are small. 4 miles SW of Chipping Norton. Bar, restaurant (background music); terrace; garden. Free Wi-Fi. Discount at *Daylesford Organic* spa, ½ mile away. Children, and dogs (annexe only; £10)

welcomed. 7 bedrooms (3 in annexe).
Per room B&B £95–£145. Dinner £30.

KINGSBRIDGE Devon
Map 1:D4
THURLESTONE HOTEL, Thurlestone,
TQ7 3NN. Tel 01548-560382, www.
thurlestone.co.uk. Close to the sea
and sandy beaches, this large, family-
friendly hotel stands in extensive
subtropical grounds. It has been owned
by the Grose family since 1896. There
is plenty to occupy guests: a heated
outdoor pool, a recently refurbished
spa, terraces for alfresco dining, a 16th-
century bar with real ales; during the
school holidays, there are films and
magicians for children. 'We all came
away feeling we had been spoilt.'
Lounges, bar, *Margaret Amelia*
restaurant (open to non-residents; Hugh
Miller cooks); lift. Outdoor Rock Pool
eating area (teas, lunches, snacks,
dinners); terrace; *The Village Inn* pub.
Spa (indoor swimming pool, laconium,
fitness studio, speciality showers,
treatments); outdoor heated swimming
pool (May–Sept); tennis, squash,
badminton, croquet, 9-hole golf course;
children's club in school holidays. Free
Wi-Fi. No background music. Civil
wedding licence; function facilities.
Children, and dogs (in some rooms only;
£8 per night charge) welcomed. 4 miles
SW of Kingsbridge. 65 bedrooms
(2 suitable for &; some with balcony,
sea views). Per room B&B £230–£450,
D,B&B £280–£500 (2-night min. stay).

KNUTSFORD Cheshire
Map 4:E3
BELLE EPOQUE, 60 King Street,
WA16 6DT. Tel 01565-633060, www.
thebelleepoque.com. Opulence abounds

in this theatrically decorated restaurant-
with-rooms in the town centre. It has
been owned by the Mooney family for
more than three decades; Richard
Walker is the manager. The interior is
an eclectic mix of Venetian glass mosaic
floor, marble pillars, oak beams, Art
Nouveau fireplaces, and life-sized
figurines; overlooking the roof garden
and walled courtyard, bedrooms and
bathrooms have a contemporary feel. In
the restaurant, chef Gareth Chappell
uses local produce in his modern, French-
influenced cooking (farmers and suppliers
are credited on the menu). Lounge/bar,
restaurant (closed Sun), private dining
rooms. Free Wi-Fi. Background jazz.
Roof garden (alfresco dining). 7
bedrooms. Per room B&B single £95,
double £110–£115. Dinner £30.

LANCASTER Lancashire
Map 4:D2
THE ASHTON, Well House, Wyresdale
Road, LA1 3JJ. Tel 01524-68460,
www.theashtonlancaster.com. In large
grounds, James Gray's sandstone
Georgian house lies on the outskirts
of the city, near Williamson Park and
the university. A former TV and film
set designer, James Gray has created a
contemporary B&B with elegant
bedrooms and indulgent bathrooms.
There is tea and home-made cake in
the afternoon; simple meals ('food for
friends') are served on weekday
evenings, by arrangement (from Fri–
Sun, platters of meat, fish and cheese
with salad, chutneys and home-baked
bread can be taken in the dining room
or in the bedroom). Breakfast, served
until 10 am, has eggs from the free
range hens that roam the garden.
Lounge, dining room (occasional

background music); 1-acre garden. Free Wi-Fi. Parking. Children welcomed (no under-8s on Sat eve). 5 bedrooms (1 on ground floor; some overlook the garden and park). Per room B&B £95–£175. Dinner £25.

LAVENHAM Suffolk
Map 2:C5

THE SWAN, High Street, CO10 9QA. Tel 01787-247477, www.theswanatlavenham. co.uk. Three timber-framed 15th-century buildings in the centre of a medieval village form this revitalised hotel. It has a bright, modern brasserie and an impressive medieval dining room with a high, timbered ceiling and minstrels' gallery; a snug bar is filled with memorabilia of US Air Force men stationed in the area during the Second World War. Characterful bedrooms, furnished in country house style, have oak beams; some have a four-poster bed and inglenook fireplace. Part of the Tim Rowan-Robinson's TA Hotel Collection, a small, Suffolk-based group, it is managed by Ingo Wiangke. Lounge, *Airmen's* bar, brasserie, *Gallery* restaurant (Justin Kett cooks classic British dishes using local, seasonal ingredients). Free Wi-Fi. Occasional background music. Garden. Civil wedding licence; private dining/function facilities. Children (early suppers), and dogs (in some rooms) welcomed. 45 bedrooms (some with facilities for &). Per room B&B £195–£290, D,B&B £245–£340.

LEEK Staffordshire
Map 2:A2

THE THREE HORSESHOES, Buxton Road, Blackshaw Moor, ST13 8TW. Tel 01538-300296, www.3shoesinn.co.uk. 'We really enjoyed our stay.' Beneath the gritstone outcrops of the Roaches, on the edge of the Peak District national park, this old stone inn is owned by the Kirk family. Period charm (beamed ceilings and dark oak furnishings) is retained. It has been extended to provide a range of accommodation and a number of dining options. Bedrooms are variously decorated in country-cottage style or with a smart, modern look; some superior rooms have a four-poster bed. Steve Kirk cooks modern British food with a Thai influence in an open kitchen in the modern brasserie; traditional pub dishes and popular carvery food can be taken in the original part of the inn. Background music. Bar, 2 restaurants, 7 dining areas; patio (alfresco dining); garden. Free Wi-Fi. Lift. Civil wedding licence; conference facilities; themed events in *Kirk's Restaurant*. Beauty treatments. Parking. Children welcomed (outdoor play area). 5 miles outside the town. 26 bedrooms. Per room B&B single £79.25–£116, double £88.50–£162. D,B&B from £69.25 per person.

LEICESTER Leicestershire
Map 2:B3

THE BELMONT, De Montfort Street, LE1 7GR. Tel 0116-254 4773, www.belmonthotel.co.uk. 'In a brilliant location' on leafy New Walk, within easy reach of the city, this hotel is formed from a row of Victorian residences. It has been owned by the Bowie family for four generations. Spacious bedrooms (some small) are 'modernised in an impeccable and stylish way'; the elegant, contemporary bars and restaurant have recently been refurbished (and renamed) and are popular with locals. Chef Alex Ballard cooks seasonal modern European food. Lounge/bar, bar/conservatory, *Windows on New Walk* restaurant (closed Sat lunch, Sun eve), conservatory. Wi-Fi (free for first 2 hours). Lift. Background music. Civil wedding licence; function facilities. Parking. Children, and dogs (by arrangement) welcomed. 75 bedrooms (3 family rooms; 1 suitable for &). Per room B&B £69–£149. Dinner £28–£35.

HOTEL MAIYANGO, 13–21 St Nicholas Place, LE1 4LD. Tel 0116-251 8898, www.maiyango.com. There are panoramic views across the city from the third-floor terrace bar of this chic hotel owned by Aatin Anadkat. In a 150-year-old former shoe factory near the centre, the refurbished hotel has handmade bespoke wood furnishings and commissioned artwork. The informal restaurant is decorated with coloured lanterns, cushions and curious booths made of uneven wooden slats; chef Phillip Sharpe cooks seasonal modern European dishes. The *Maiyango Kitchen Deli* around the corner serves 'convenience restaurant food' (available to take away). Bar, cocktail lounge, restaurant (closed lunchtime Sun–Tues); terrace. Free Wi-Fi. Lift. Background music in lobby/reception area. Function facilities. Cooking and cocktail classes. 14 bedrooms. Per room B&B £90–£105, D,B&B £140–£155.
25% DISCOUNT VOUCHERS

LEWDOWN Devon
Map 1:C3
LEWTRENCHARD MANOR, nr Okehampton, EX20 4PN. Tel 01566-783222, www.lewtrenchard.co.uk. Set among streams and ponds, fountains and statuary, this 'impressive' Jacobean stone manor house stands in extensive parkland. The ancestral home of the Reverend Sabine Baring-Gould, who wrote 'Onward, Christian Soldiers', it has ornate ceilings, stained-glass windows and ornamental carving. It is run as a small hotel by the Murray family, who bought it back in 2012 from the von Essen receivers. Matthew Peryer is the new chef; a recently restored walled garden provides fresh produce for his modern menus. Lounge, bar, 2 restaurants (open to non-residents; background music), ballroom. Free Wi-Fi. In-room beauty treatments. Croquet. Fishing, clay-pigeon shooting; falconry can be arranged. Children and dogs welcomed. 14 bedrooms (4 in courtyard annexe; bridal suite in 2-storey folly; 1 suitable for &). Per room B&B £155–£235, D,B&B £245–£325 (2-night min. stay at weekends Apr–Sept).
25% DISCOUNT VOUCHERS

LINCOLN Lincolnshire
Map 4:E5
THE CASTLE, Westgate, LN1 3AS. Tel 01522-538801, www.castlehotel.net. In the historic Bailgate area, this recently refurbished Grade II listed house is built on the site of the old Roman Forum; guests can reach out and touch the second-century Mint Wall – the outer wall of the old basilica. Most of the 'smart, slightly angular' bedrooms have views of the castle walls or the cathedral. Chef Mark Cheseldine's innovative European cuisine is served in the 'charming' panelled restaurant: 'We had an excellent meal, elegantly presented.' Breakfast has freshly squeezed juice, home-made muesli, eggs cooked any way. 2 small lounges, bar

(a popular local), *Reform* restaurant (evenings only; background music). Free Wi-Fi. Massage and beauty treatments. Wedding/function facilities. Parking. Children welcomed. 18 bedrooms (some in attic, some in courtyard; 1 suitable for &); plus 1 apartment. Per room B&B £110–£130, D,B&B £170–£190.

LIVERPOOL Merseyside
Map 4:E2

BASE2STAY LIVERPOOL, 29 Seel Street, L1 4AU. Tel 0151-705 2626, www. base2stay.com. Ideal for a 'fine, simple, short city stay', this 'practical and efficient hotel' (sister to *base2stay*, London – see Shortlist), is in a converted industrial building in the Rope Walks area. The lounge has black leather chairs, and art and music books; exposed brick walls display bright, modern art. The black-and-white bedrooms range from large singles to double-height gallery studios; all have a mini-kitchen with a microwave, fridge and sink, plus HDTV, music and games. There is no bar or dining room, but breakfast boxes (cornflakes, fresh milk, organic juice, yogurt, pastry) can be ordered in advance; discounts at local restaurants, bars and clubs are available. Free local and national landline calls for 30 minutes per day. Lounge, meeting room. Free Wi-Fi. Background music. Lift. Vending machines. Parking discounts. Children welcomed. 106 bedrooms (some suitable for &). Room only from £49. Breakfast £6–£8.50.

HARD DAYS NIGHT, Central Buildings, North John Street, L2 6RR. Tel 0151-236 1964, www.harddaysnighthotel.com. A minute from the Cavern Club, where Liverpool's most famous quartet performed in the early 1960s, this Beatles-themed hotel is in a grand, Grade II listed building fronted by marble columns. It is decorated with original artwork and photographs of the famous four. Modern rooms are individually designed, with a monsoon shower in the bathroom. Michael Dewey is the manager for the Classic British Hotels group. Lounge (live music on Fri and Sat nights), *Bar Four* cocktail bar, brasserie, *Blakes* restaurant (open to non-residents; closed Sun, Mon; 2- and 3-course menus; Paul Feery is chef); art gallery. Free Wi-Fi. Background music. Civil wedding licence; function facilities. Beatles tours can be arranged. 110 bedrooms. Room only from £95. Breakfast £15.95, dinner £11.95–£14.95.

HEYWOOD HOUSE, 11 Fenwick Street, L2 7LS. Tel 0151-224 1444, www. heywoodhousehotel.co.uk. Once the oldest bank building in the city (built in 1799), this hotel has 'a most pleasing and relaxing ambience', good-value accommodation, and an adjoining bar and brasserie. Period features have been retained. Bedrooms ('Comfy' or 'Plush') are decorated in rich colours; four have a balcony. There is a large continental buffet selection at breakfast. Laura Smith is the manager. Free Wi-Fi. Lift. Wedding/function facilities. Discounts for nearby parking. Children welcomed. 35 bedrooms. Per room B&B £79–£160.

HOPE STREET HOTEL, 40 Hope Street, L1 9DA. Tel 0151-709 3000, www. hopestreethotel.co.uk. David Brewitt's 'tastefully decorated' contemporary hotel is spread over two buildings opposite the Philharmonic Hall, in the city's cultural quarter. Minimalist bedrooms have a wooden floor, under-floor heating and a DVD- and CD-player (with extensive library); some have a huge picture window or skylight. 'Our room had a fantastic view of the cathedral and the Three Graces at the docks. We could even see the ferry on the Mersey going to Belfast.' Cast iron pillars and exposed brickwork are reminders of the building's former life as a 19th-century coach factory. *The London Carriage Works* restaurant serves modern international dishes. 'We enjoyed everything enormously.' Reading room (cocktails), bar, restaurant; lift; gym, treatment rooms. Background music. Free Wi-Fi. Parking nearby (£10 charge). Civil wedding licence; function facilities. Children, and dogs (£30 charge) welcomed. 89 bedrooms (some suitable for &). Room only £190–£240; penthouse suite £680.

LOOE Cornwall
Map 1:D3
BARCLAY HOUSE, St Martins Road, PL13 1LP. Tel 01503-262929, www.barclayhouse.co.uk. In extensive garden and woodland, this white-painted Victorian villa on a hillside, with glorious views over the East Looe river, is owned by the Brooks family; Graham Brooks is the manager. Locally caught fish is the mainstay of the 'modern coastal' cooking of the chef, Joe Sardari; his four-course table d'hôte and six-course taster menus are served in an airy dining room or alfresco on the terrace. Full Cornish breakfasts. Sitting room, bar, restaurant (background jazz; radio at breakfast; closed Sun); terrace (alfresco dining). Free Wi-Fi (in

reception and bar only). Gym, sauna; outdoor heated swimming pool. 6-acre gardens and woodland paths; some steep. Civil wedding licence. Children welcomed (family suite). 12 bedrooms (1 suitable for &), plus 8 self-catering cottages. Per room B&B £125–£195, D,B&B £185–£255.
25% DISCOUNT VOUCHERS

TRELASKE HOTEL & RESTAURANT, Polperro Road, PL13 2JS. Tel 01503-262159, www.trelaske.co.uk. 'A very enjoyable stay.' In a peaceful location, with 'excellent' views over the gardens and moorland beyond, Hazel Billington and Ross Lewin's hotel has 'good food, good facilities, and clean, spacious rooms'. The modern bedrooms have built-in storage and space to sit; each has a balcony or patio. 'Friendly and always smiling', Hazel Billington is a welcoming host; Ross Lewin's award-winning, daily-changing menus, using fruit, vegetables and herbs from the hotel's polytunnels, are 'a revelation – no complication, and real taste'. In 4-acre grounds, 2 miles outside town. 2 lounges, bar/conservatory (background music); terrace (summer barbecues). Free Wi-Fi (in main house only). Wedding/function facilities. Children welcomed (no under-4s in restaurant). Dogs allowed in 2 bedrooms (£6.50 per night). 7 bedrooms (4 in building adjacent to main house). Per room B&B £75–£110, D,B&B £120–£170.

LUDLOW Shropshire
Map 3:C4
HOPTON HOUSE, Hopton Heath Road, SY7 0QD. Tel 01547-530885, www.shropshirebreakfast.co.uk. In a lovely rural location ten miles west of

Ludlow, this former granary has been transformed by the owner, Karen Thorne, into a charming B&B with a modern rustic interior. Fully equipped, large bedrooms have a big bed, comfortable seating, double- or triple-aspect windows, and home-made cake and shortbread. The Paddock room has a balcony. Hens, which roam in the gardens, supply eggs for Karen Thorne's extensive breakfasts (ordered the night before). Supper platters (local cheese, smoked salmon, deli food; £7.50) can be requested; BYO wine (glasses and corkscrews supplied). Free Wi-Fi. Dogs (in 1 room only) welcomed, by arrangement; 2 resident dogs. Lounge, dining room (background music). 1¾-acre garden. 3 bedrooms (2 in separate building). Per room B&B £110– £120. **25% DISCOUNT VOUCHERS**

LUPTON Cumbria
Map 4: inset C2

THE PLOUGH, Cow Brow, LA6 1PJ. Tel 015395-67700, www.theploughatlupton. co.uk. With oak beams, antique furniture and wood-burning stoves, this painstakingly refurbished 18th-century coaching inn is 'an attractive (and dog-friendly) place to eat and stay'. 'The sense of quality is tangible.' It is owned by Richard Rose, proprietor of *The Punch Bowl Inn* at Crosthwaite (see Shortlist); attentive manager Abi Lloyd runs both inns. 'Our large, light bedroom had a comfortable, iron-framed bed, French rococo-style bedside tables and wardrobe, and an adjoining sitting room. The large bathroom had under-floor heating.' Adjoining the bar, with its striking slate-topped counter, the restaurant serves British dishes and a selection of sharing platters (Fisherman's,

Ploughman's and Gardener's). Bar, lounge, restaurant. Free Wi-Fi. Terrace; garden. Background music. Civil wedding licence. Children and dogs welcomed. 5 bedrooms. Per room B&B £115–£195.

LYME REGIS Dorset
Map 1:C6

1 LYME TOWNHOUSE, 1 Pound Street, DT7 3HZ. Tel 01297-442499, www. 1lymetownhouse.co.uk. Experienced hosts, Terrie and Brian Covington run their contemporary B&B in a three-storey, Grade II listed Georgian town house. On a hill above Lyme Bay, it is within easy reach of the town and harbour. Bedrooms have feature wallpaper, a quirky metalwork bed, a fridge and ironing facilities; some have views towards the sea. A daily-changing breakfast hamper (fresh juice, yogurt, fruits, home-made pastries and tarts) is delivered to the room each morning. Free Wi-Fi. No background music. Paid parking up the street. Special deals (Tues–Fri) are available for dining at Mark Hix's *Oyster & Fish House*. 7 bedrooms. Per room B&B £95–£110.

LYNMOUTH Devon
Map 1:B4

SHELLEY'S, 8 Watersmeet Road, EX35 6EP. Tel 01598-753219, www.shelleyshotel.co.uk. In the summer of 1812, when this 18th-century house was a more humble cottage, Percy Bysshe Shelley came here with his 16-year-old bride, Harriet, for their honeymoon. Today, Jane Becker and Richard Briden welcome guests. A short walk from the harbour, the small hotel looks out over Lynmouth Bay; most of the light, airy bedrooms have sea views.

Lounge, bar, conservatory breakfast room. Free Wi-Fi. No background music. 11 bedrooms (1 on ground floor). Per room B&B £79–£119. Closed Nov–Easter.

LYTHAM Lancashire
Map 4:D2

THE ROOMS, 35 Church Road, FY8 5LL. Tel 01253-736000, www.theroomslytham.com. 'Very centrally placed, within close walking distance of shops, restaurants and the sea', this smart, stylish B&B is owned by Jackie and Andy Baker. 'A helpful host', Mr Baker suggests restaurants and sites to visit, and offers help with luggage. Bedrooms (some with noise from the street) have a king-size bed and up-to-date technology (flat-screen TV, DVD-player, DAB radio, iPod docking station); bathrooms and wet rooms come with under-floor heating and bathrobes. 'Our modern room was beautifully fitted, with excellent lighting and very good tea and coffee provisions.' Breakfast, served in the walled garden in good weather, has 'a large choice' (one guest found portions 'a little controlled'); there are locally produced jams, home-made smoothies, 'good bacon, excellent coffee'. Breakfast room (background TV). Free Wi-Fi. No background music. Children welcomed. 5 bedrooms ('lots of stairs'), plus 2-bed serviced apartment. Per room B&B single £95–£125, double £125–£160.

MALVERN Worcestershire
Map 3:D5

THE OLD RECTORY, Cradley, WR13 5LQ. Tel 01886-880109, www.oldrectorycradley.com. 'A special place.' Beside the Church of St James the Great, in a pretty village four miles from Malvern, this fine Georgian house has elegant rooms, original art and 'wonderful cooking'. Claire and John Dawkins, who welcome B&B guests, serve a monthly-changing dinner menu, using ingredients from local suppliers, and produce from their own vegetable and herb gardens. 'We were made to feel welcome, whether we were having tea in the drawing room or relaxing in our huge and comfy room.' Good walks from the door; lifts are offered to and from the Malvern hills. Packed lunches available. Drawing room (open fire), library, morning room, dining room. Free Wi-Fi. 1-acre garden; croquet, boules. No background music. Parking. Well-behaved children and dogs welcomed. 4 bedrooms. Per room B&B £100–£150, D,B&B £137.50–£187.50.

MANCHESTER
Map 4:E3

DIDSBURY HOUSE, Didsbury Park, Didsbury Village, M20 5LJ. Tel 0161-448 2200, www.didsburyhouse.co.uk. 'Very nice staff, pleasant rooms, great breakfast – in fact, just the job.' Large Italian parasols shade guests from the sun on the pretty terrace of this chic contemporary hotel; inside, stylish decoration includes velvet armchairs, trompe l'oeil wallpaper and cheeky antiques (such as an old steamer trunk serving as a coffee table). A 'friendly' place, it is part of the Eclectic Hotel Collection (see *Eleven Didsbury Park*, below). 'Comfortable' bedrooms are individually styled; some have a freestanding roll-top bath in the room. In a leafy suburb reached by a 'quick train' from East Didsbury; otherwise, 'a cab ride from the centre late at night'.

'Pleasant walks' in the botanical gardens, nearby. 2 lounges, bar, breakfast room; meeting room; spa; gym; walled terrace with water feature. Free Wi-Fi. 'Chill-out' background music. Exclusive use for weddings/ functions. Children welcomed. 27 bedrooms. Room only £150–£220. Breakfast £13.50–£15.50.

ELEVEN DIDSBURY PARK, 11 Didsbury Park, Didsbury Village, M20 5LH. Tel 0161-448 7711, www.elevendidsburypark. com. Peacefully located in a leafy urban village 15 minutes from the city centre, this stylish modern hotel (Eclectic Hotel Collection) occupies a Victorian town house with a charming walled garden; loungers, a hammock and a croquet set decorate the lawn. Smart bedrooms (some are compact) have a CD- and DVD-player, and a complimentary butler tray with fresh milk; one large room has a private canopied terrace with an outdoor cast iron bathtub. A gentleman's afternoon tea has home-made Scotch eggs and Jack Daniels ice cream. Convenient for the airport (ten minutes' drive). 2 lounge/bars (background music), veranda. Free Wi-Fi. Gym; treatment room. Conference facilities. Large walled garden. Parking. Children and dogs welcomed. 20 bedrooms (1, on ground floor, suitable for &). Room only £150–£264. Breakfast £13.50–£15.50.

VELVET, 2 Canal Street, M1 3HE. Tel 0161-236 9003, www.velvetmanchester. com. Hedonistic in style, this hotel has a lively bar and decadently furnished bedrooms decorated with artwork and murals (some erotic). Indulgent, modern bathrooms have bathrobes and slippers,

steam-free mirrors, automatic lighting; some have a double bath and walk-in shower. An all-day menu in the basement restaurant has British comfort food, pizzas and snacks. Bar (DJs on Fri and Sat nights; noise may affect some rooms), restaurant (alfresco dining on front terrace; background music). Free Wi-Fi. Lift. Children welcomed. Within easy reach of the city centre and railway station. Discounted car park. 19 bedrooms. Room only £75–£245. Breakfast £9.50–£13.50, dinner £25.

MARCHAM Oxfordshire
Map 2:C2
B&B RAFTERS, Abingdon Road, OX13 6NU. Tel 01865-391298, www.bnb-rafters.co.uk. Friendly hosts Sigrid and Arne Grawert run this good-value B&B in their half-timbered house on the edge of a village eight miles south of Oxford. Bedrooms are decorated in muted tones, with feature wallpaper and colourful cushions; they have fresh flowers, a DVD-player, DAB radio, iPod docking station and speakers. A single room has a waterbed. Whisky porridge is a speciality at breakfast; other, organic options include home-baked bread, and home-made jams and marmalade. Vegetarian and special diets catered for. Lounge, breakfast room; garden. Free Wi-Fi. No background music. Parking. Children welcomed. 4 bedrooms. Per person B&B £50–£89.

MARGATE Kent
Map 2:D5
THE READING ROOMS, 31 Hawley Square, CT9 1PH. Tel 01843-225166, www.thereadingroomsmargate.co.uk. Handy for the Turner Contemporary art gallery and the beach, this

unconventional B&B stands out as a beacon of style and comfort. On a Georgian square, the town house has been painstakingly renovated in 'dilapidated grandeur' by owners Louise Oldfield and Liam Nabb. Intricate plasterwork has been revealed, a mantelpiece or mirror leans artfully; there are distressed walls, wooden floors, original shutters and carefully chosen antiques. Each white-painted bedroom takes up an entire floor and has crisp linen on a large bed; bathrooms are 'stunning – the size of a bedroom', with a roll-top bath, walk-in shower, luxury toiletries and bathrobes. Breakfast from an extensive choice is brought to the room and 'beautifully' served: 'As good as any I have eaten.' No background music. Free Wi-Fi. 3 bedrooms. Per room B&B £160–£180.

MATLOCK Derbyshire
Map 3:A6
MANOR FARM, Dethick, DE4 5GG. Tel 01629-534302, www.manorfarmdethick.co.uk. Once the home of Sir Anthony Babington, who in 1586 conspired to assassinate Queen Elizabeth, this historic Grade II* listed stone house is today an 'excellent' B&B. Run by 'welcoming and friendly' hosts Gilly and Simon Groom, it is on an attractive, 'user-friendly' farm in beautiful countryside. Country-style bedrooms have beams, old stonework or buttresses and corbels; the best are in the hayloft. Organic breakfasts are served on a large refectory table in the original Tudor kitchen (all diets catered for). Sitting rooms (TV, games), breakfast room. Free Wi-Fi. No background music. Drying facilities. Parking; bike/motorcycle storage. 2½ miles E of Matlock; collection from railway/bus station can be arranged. Children over 6 welcomed. 4 bedrooms (1 on ground floor). Per room B&B from £85 (2-night min. stay on Sat, Apr–Oct).

MELLS Somerset
Map 2:D1
THE TALBOT INN, Selwood Street, Mells, nr Frome, BA11 3PN. Tel 01373 812254. www.talbotinn.com. In a pretty hamlet, this old coaching inn (parts date to the 15th century) has been remodelled by the owners, Charlie Luxton, Dan Brod and Matt Greenless (the manager), who also have the *Beckford Arms*, Tisbury (see below). 'It is furnished in a similar style – *Country Living* with a touch of the Great Gatsby.' The bedrooms have sisal carpets, mirrored bedside tables, coat hangers with pegs in place of a wardrobe; larger rooms have a sofa. Chef Pravin Nayar serves 'satisfying' modern dishes in the dining room, a series of inter-connecting stone-flagged rooms with wooden tables and chairs. At weekends, fish and meats are grilled on an open fire in the *Coach House Grill Room* and served at long shared tables. Bar, restaurant. Snug, map room, sitting room, grill. Courtyard and garden. Free Wi-Fi. Background music. Unsuitable for ♿. Children welcomed, dogs allowed (in one bedroom). 8 bedrooms. Per room £95–£150. Dinner £30. Closed 25 Dec.

MELTON MOWBRAY Leicestershire
Map 2:A3
SYSONBY KNOLL, Asfordby Road, LE13 0HP. Tel 01664-563563, www.sysonby.com. Overlooking a quiet garden and the River Eye, this extended hotel and restaurant have been owned

and run by the same family since 1965. 'Friendly and flexible' hosts Jenny and Gavin Howling are currently at the helm, with Vicky Wilkin as manager. The brick-built Edwardian house is traditionally furnished; its restaurant has fine views across the Wreake valley. Good walks nearby. Complimentary fishing for guests (tackle available to borrow). Lounge, bar, restaurant. Free Wi-Fi. Background music. 4½-acre gardens and meadow (honey from hives overwintered in the gardens is available to buy). Parking. Children and dogs welcomed (resident dog). 30 bedrooms (some on ground floor; some in neighbouring annexe; ramp). Per room B&B £78–£135, D,B&B £90–£170.
25% DISCOUNT VOUCHERS

MEVAGISSEY Cornwall
Map 1:D2
TREVALSA COURT, School Hill, PL26 6TH. Tel 01726-842468, www. trevalsa-hotel.co.uk. 'Relaxing and slightly quirky.' On a cliff-top, this 'attractive' Arts and Crafts house is owned by Susan and John Gladwin, who run it as a small hotel with 'pleasant, helpful' staff. Landscaped subtropical gardens (with a summer house) lead to the Coastal Path; a steep staircase takes guests to a secluded sandy beach. Most of the individually styled bedrooms have 'great' sea views; there are books and games in the sitting room, and a roaring fire in cold weather. Drinks can be taken on a terrace overlooking the sea. Lounge, bar, restaurant (Adam Cawood is chef; light jazz background music). Free Wi-Fi. 2-acre garden. Children welcomed, dogs by arrangement. 14 bedrooms (3 on ground floor; family suite accessed from outside). Per room

B&B single £70–£105, double £90–£245. Dinner £30. Closed Dec–Feb.
25% DISCOUNT VOUCHERS

MIDHURST West Sussex
Map 2:E3
THE ANGEL, North Street, GU29 9DN. Tel 01730-812421, www.theangelmidhurst.co.uk. On the high street of a historic market town, this refurbished former coaching inn retains some traditional features, including 17th-century oak beams and a Victorian fireplace. Country house-style bedrooms have modern touches, such as an oversized headboard and a flat-screen TV; junior suites have a four-poster bed. In *Bentley's* restaurant (open to non-residents), chef Richard Cook's fixed-price menus feature traditional English dishes. Lounge, bar, café, restaurant (closed Sun eve and Mon); courtyard. Free Wi-Fi. Background music. Parking. Civil wedding licence; function facilities. Children, and dogs (in 4 rooms) welcomed. 15 bedrooms (4 in cottage; 1 suitable for &). Per room B&B £130–£215; D,B&B £180–£265.

MILLOM Cumbria
Map 4: inset C2
BROADGATE HOUSE, Broadgate, Thwaites, LA18 5JZ. Tel 01229-716295, www.broadgate-house.co.uk. Within the Lake District national park, this fine Georgian house has panoramic views across the Duddon estuary. Diana Lewthwaite, whose family has owned it for almost 200 years, provides country guest house accommodation. The house is decorated in period style; spacious bedrooms have antique furniture, vibrant fabrics and an original fireplace. The two-acre grounds are designed as a

series of 'garden rooms', with a walled garden, terraces, a croquet lawn and an 'oasis' with a palm tree. Drawing room, cosy sitting room (wood-burning stove), dining room, breakfast room. No background music. Free Wi-Fi. 3 miles W of Broughton-in-Furness. 5 bedrooms (private bathroom with throne loo, freestanding bath). Per person B&B £45–£55. Dinner (by arrangement) £30.

MISTLEY Essex
Map 2:C5
THE MISTLEY THORN, High Street, CO11 1HE. Tel 01206-392821, www.mistleythorn.co.uk. 'Worth a detour just for the food.' In an 'interesting' coastal village on the River Stour, this yellow-painted 18th-century coaching inn is run as a restaurant-with-rooms by chef/proprietor Sherri Singleton. Soothing, coastal-style bedrooms have a DVD-player and iPod dock; four overlook the estuary. The busy restaurant has an informal feel. 'The meal was exceptionally good, with lots of fresh fish.' Breakfast, ordered the evening before, has smoked salmon and scrambled eggs. A busy road runs through the village (quiet at night); a colony of swans lives on the river. Sherri Singleton runs cookery workshops. Small sitting area, bar, restaurant (background music); ramp. Free Wi-Fi. Children, and 'well-mannered' dogs (£5 per night charge) welcomed. 7 bedrooms. Per room B&B £75–£120, D,B&B £125–£180.

MONKTON COMBE Somerset
Map 2:D1
WHEELWRIGHTS ARMS, Church Lane, BA2 7HB. Tel 01225-722287, www. wheelwrightsarms.co.uk. In a peaceful hamlet in undulating countryside, three miles from Bath, this informal restaurant-with-rooms in a mellow stone 18th-century inn is owned by David Munn. Unfussy modern bedrooms are in a converted carpenter's workshop opposite; one has a sloping ceiling and its own entrance to the garden. There is an open fire in the cosy dining area; here, Dean Toon, who recently joined as head chef, serves a frequently changing dinner menu. Light lunches, bar snacks, and coffee and cake are also available. Tickets can be arranged for Bath Rugby home games. Bar, restaurant. Free Wi-Fi. Background music (optional). Outdoor seating (alfresco dining). Parking (narrow entrance). Children welcomed. Bus service into Bath. 7 bedrooms (some suitable for &). Per room B&B £95–£145. Dinner £26.50.

MORETON-IN-MARSH
Gloucestershire
Map 3:D6
THE OLD SCHOOL, Little Compton, GL56 0SL. Tel 01608-674588, www.theoldschoolbedandbreakfast.com. A monkey puzzle tree is a towering landmark in the front garden of Wendy Veale's converted Victorian stone-built schoolhouse, four miles from Moreton-in-Marsh. The bedrooms are named after local schools; each has fresh flowers, bathrobes, a fridge and a flat-screen TV with integral DVD-player. Guests may take drinks in the cosy, beamed sitting room, a handsome space with a striking church-style window. Wendy Veale, a food writer and stylist, prepares picnic hampers, supper trays and light meals; dinners are available on request (locally sourced food; BYO

bottle). Home-made cakes, cookies and preserves. Breakfast is served at a long oak table. Vaulted drawing room, dining room; boot room. Free Wi-Fi (computer available). No background music. Garden (pergolas, patios, fish pond, orchard; bantam hens; pet rabbits, cat). 4 bedrooms (1 on ground floor). Per person B&B £60–£150 (2-night min. stay at weekends). Dinner £32.

MULLION Cornwall
Map 1:E2
POLURRIAN BAY HOTEL, Helston, TR12 7EN. Tel 01326-240421, www.polurrianhotel.com. A recent extension at this imposing white Edwardian house has 180-degree views of the coastline from a glass-fronted lounge. 'Glorious sunsets.' Perched on cliffs above a sandy bay on the Lizard peninsula, the hotel (part of Nigel Chapman's Luxury Family Hotels group) has plenty to occupy children and their parents. There are books and board games, cream teas and cocktails, age-appropriate games rooms and a cinema. The 12 acres of landscaped gardens have plenty of space for younger guests, with an indoor and a (seasonal) outdoor pool, a hot tub, gym and spa (treatments); tennis courts, a sports field; an adventure playground and more. 6 lounges, dining room (background music), cinema; terrace. The Den (nursery for children 3 months–8 years old); The Blue Room (older children; video games, pool, table football). Free Wi-Fi. Civil wedding licence; function facilities. Children (baby equipment), and dogs (£10 per night charge) welcomed. 41 bedrooms (some on ground floor). Per room B&B

from £99, D,B&B from £159 (2-night min. stay in peak season).

NEWBY BRIDGE Cumbria
Map 4: inset C2
THE SWAN HOTEL & SPA, LA12 8NB. Tel 015395-31681, www.swanhotel.com. Family-focused, and with indulgent spa facilities for grown-ups, this whitewashed 17th-century coaching inn has been renovated with modern comforts by the Bardsley family, who have retained many original features. The hotel stands by a five-arch bridge on the banks of the River Leven, on the southern tip of Lake Windermere; it is popular with boating visitors. Sarah Gibbs is the manager. Pretty, modern bedrooms have feature wallpaper, and garden or river views. Sitting room, library (children's games and books), bar, *River Room* restaurant, breakfast room; terrace. Free Wi-Fi. Background music. Spa (treatments), indoor pool, hot tub, sauna, steam room; gym. Civil wedding licence; function facilities. Parking; mooring. Children welcomed (complimentary milk and biscuits before bedtime; adventure playground; nature trail). 51 bedrooms. Per room B&B £99–£209. Dinner £30.

NEWCASTLE UPON TYNE Tyne and Wear
Map 4:B4
HOTEL DU VIN, Allan House, City Road, NE1 2BE. Tel 0191-229 2200, www.hotelduvin.com. In the former home of the Tyne Tees Steam Shipping Company, this stylish, modern hotel (part of the Hotel du Vin group) is on the banks of the River Tyne – good views of the Millennium Bridge and the Quayside. The imposing red brick

building has been 'attractively converted'; there are exposed brick walls, leather club chairs, dark-stained floorboards and restored fireplaces. Teatime is taken seriously, with a tea sommelier and the chance for a 'G & Tea' (finger sandwiches, tea loaf, scones; gin and tonic in a china cup). Bistro (food is 'good'), *Bubble* bar, wine-tasting room, 2 private dining rooms; courtyard (alfresco dining). Free Wi-Fi. Background music. Humidor. Civil wedding licence; function facilities. Parking. 42 bedrooms (some with private terrace). Room only from £135. Breakfast from £11.95; dinner £35.

THE TOWNHOUSE, 1 West Avenue, Gosforth, NE3 4ES. Tel 0191-285 6812, www.thetownhousehotel.co.uk. 'Well ahead of the average B&B.' Cathy Knox has created 'an oasis of civilisation' at her elegant Victorian town house in a leafy suburb, a short metro ride from the centre. Bedrooms and bathrooms are decorated 'with flair'; breakfasts are 'generous and varied'. The café, which has a frequently changing blackboard menu of 'straightforward' home-cooked food, is popular locally. Background music. Breakfast room (morning TV; good supply of newspapers), café (afternoon teas with home-made scones and cakes; open until 6 pm; 4 pm on Sun). Free Wi-Fi. Parking permits provided. Children welcomed. 10 bedrooms. Per person B&B £47.50–£140. Dinner £12.95–£18.95.

NEWENT Gloucestershire
Map 3:D5
THREE CHOIRS VINEYARDS, Newent GL18 1LS. Tel 01531-890223, www. three-choirs-vineyards.co.uk. On the crest of a hill in attractive countryside, this restaurant-with-rooms is on an award-winning vineyard (one of the largest in Britain). Eight of the bedrooms are in a single-storey block beside the restaurant; each has a French door opening on to a small private patio. Three rooms are in a lodge among the vines. In the restaurant, which looks down on the vine-clad valley, chef Darren Leonard serves a modern European menu. Guests can join a tour of the vineyard. Lounge, restaurant (occasional background music), wine shop. Free Wi-Fi. 11 bedrooms (all on ground floor), 1 suitable for &. Per room B&B £90–£185. Dinner £35.

NEWQUAY Cornwall
Map 1:D2
THE HEADLAND HOTEL, Headland Road, TR7 1EW. Tel 01637-872212, www.headlandhotel.co.uk. On a jutting headland, this imposing red brick Victorian hotel has dramatic views of the Atlantic. Continual improvements have been made by the Armstrong family, who have owned it for three decades. A new wellness area was recently added (spa pool, sauna, Cornish salt steam room, aromatherapy showers); further spa facilities are planned. Darryl Redburn is the manager. Bedrooms are decorated in a mix of traditional and contemporary styles; many have sea views. Lounges, bar, 2 restaurants; *The Terrace* (background music; alfresco dining; Jan Wilhelm is chef); veranda. Free Wi-Fi. 10-acre grounds. Table tennis; 2 heated swimming pools (indoor and outdoor); croquet; 3 tennis courts; putting, boules; on-site surf school. Civil wedding licence; conference/event facilities.

Children welcomed (bunk beds; entertainment). Dogs welcomed (£15 per night). 96 bedrooms (12 suites; 1 room suitable for &; plus 40 self-catering cottages in the grounds). Per room B&B £79–£389, D,B&B £129–£439.
25% DISCOUNT VOUCHERS

NORWICH Norfolk
Map 2:B5
NORFOLK MEAD, Church Loke, Coltishall, NR12 7DN. Tel 01603-737531, www.norfolkmead.co.uk. Transformed by new owners James Holliday and Anna Duttson, this hotel in a Georgian merchant's house has a sleek, modern design. It is in a 'near-perfect' position with eight-acre grounds running down to the river. Light and bright bedrooms are individually styled; Sloe has a cedar-wood sleigh bed and elevated views over the lawns; Hawthorn has bay windows and French doors leading to a private terrace. Anna Duttson cooks modern British menus with Asian influences, inspired by locally sourced produce. Lounge, bar, snug, restaurant; background music. Free Wi-Fi. Private dining. Walled garden; fishing lake; off-river mooring. Small conference/wedding facilities. 7 miles NE of Norwich. Children, and dogs (in some rooms; £15 per night charge) welcomed. 13 bedrooms (some in cottage and summer house). Per room B&B £125–£175. Dinner £30.

OAKHILL Somerset
Map 2:D1
THE OAKHILL INN, Fosse Road, nr Radstock, BA3 5HU. Tel 01749-840442, www.theoakhillinn.com. In a pretty village with a long-standing history of brewing, there are real ales and log fires at this unpretentious, family-friendly pub-with-rooms owned by Charlie and Amanda Digney. Modern rustic rooms have bold colours and local art; two have a bathtub. Head chef Neil Creese cooks seasonal menus using local meat and produce; seafood is delivered daily from the Cornish coast. Breakfast, ordered the night before, has home-made Old Spot sausages and freshly baked pastries. 3 miles N of Shepton Mallet. 2 bars, restaurant; garden. Low-level background music. Free Wi-Fi. Parking. Children welcomed (family suite). 5 bedrooms. Per room B&B from £90.

OUNDLE Northamptonshire
Map 2:B3
LOWER FARM, Main Street, Barnwell, PE8 5PU. Tel 01832-273220, www.lower-farm.co.uk. On the edge of a pretty village three miles from Oundle, the old stables and milking parlour of a small arable farm have been converted into 'really nice', modern rooms, arranged around a central courtyard. A green philosophy has been followed: there are air source heat pumps, photovoltaic panels, under-floor heating, low-energy lighting and rainwater harvesting. Caroline Marriott, 'a friendly and accommodating hostess', looks after the B&B guests; her copious farmhouse breakfasts include a steak-and-eggs special. Husband John and his brother manage the farm, which has been in the Marriott family since the 1920s. Plenty of footpaths and cycleways in the area. Breakfast room (background music); courtyard garden with seating. Free Wi-Fi; no mobile phone signal. Children and dogs welcomed in some

rooms. Parking. 10 bedrooms (on ground floor; family rooms; 1 suitable for &). Per person B&B from £40.

OXFORD Oxfordshire
Map 2:C2

THE BELL, 11 Oxford Road, Hampton Poyle, OX5 2QD. Tel 01865-376242, www.thebelloxford.co.uk. In a small village four miles north of Oxford, this roadside pub owned by George Dailey has cosy snugs, flagstone floors, beams, leather seating and a large log fire. Light-filled bedrooms are decorated in soft tones, with pale wood furnishing. Chef Nick Anderson cooks pizzas, seafood and locally sourced meats in a wood-burning oven in the open-view kitchen. 2 bars (background music), library (for private parties), restaurant; terrace. Free Wi-Fi. Wedding facilities. Parking. Children, and dogs (in 1 bedroom) welcomed. 9 bedrooms (1 on ground floor). Per room B&B (continental) single £96–£125, double £120–£145. Dinner £30.

BURLINGTON HOUSE, 374 Banbury Road, OX2 7PP. Tel 01865-513513, www.burlington-hotel-oxford.co.uk. North of Summertown, this handsome Victorian merchant's house has been sympathetically modernised to form a 'cheerfully' decorated B&B. Snug bedrooms have striking wallpaper, coordinating fabrics and triple-glazed windows; Nes Saini is the 'extremely' efficient manager. In a suburb 10 minutes outside the city; there are frequent buses, nearby, into the centre. Sitting room, breakfast room. Free Wi-Fi. Small Japanese garden. No background music. Limited parking. 12 bedrooms (4 on ground floor; 2 in courtyard). Per room B&B single £66–£80, double £86–£112.

MACDONALD RANDOLPH HOTEL, Beaumont Street, OX1 2LN. Tel 0844 879 9132, www.macdonaldhotels.co.uk/randolph. Opposite the Ashmolean Museum, this elegant hotel in the heart of town (part of the Macdonald Hotels group) holds fast to tradition. It has impressive public rooms: the baronial-style restaurant has full-length windows looking on to the lively street; the panelled *Morse Bar* was frequented by the fictional detective. Smartly decorated bedrooms (some are small) have views of the city; some have a seating area with armchairs. In the restaurant, smoked salmon and roast beef are carved at the table; a flambé trolley might be wheeled out. Wood-panelled bar (open fire), restaurant, drawing room (pianist on Sat). Free Wi-Fi. Background music. Spa (steam rooms, saunas, plunge pool); gym. Civil wedding licence; conference facilities. Children and dogs welcomed. 151 bedrooms (1 suitable for &). Per room B&B £240–£360, D,B&B £290–£410.

VANBRUGH HOUSE HOTEL, 20–24 St Michael's Street, OX1 2EB. Tel 01865-44622, www.vanbrughhousehotel.co.uk. On a quiet side street near the Oxford Union, this new, impeccably designed hotel (Sojourn Hotels) has been formed from two centuries-old buildings. The handsome bedrooms are individually styled along three themes – Georgian, Eclectic, and Arts and Crafts; each has a fireplace, hand-crafted furniture and a media hub. The Vicarage Suite and Nicholas Hawksmoor Room have a private garden and terrace area. Lunch, dinner and pre-theatre brasserie menus are served in *Vanbrugh Vaults*, where remains of the old city walls can be seen; afternoon tea, canapés and aperitifs are taken in the elegant drawing room or on the sunken terrace with its 'secret' garden. Drawing room, bar, restaurant. No background music. Free Wi-Fi. Park and Ride recommended. 22 bedrooms. Per room B&B single £99, double £121–£189. Dinner from £30.

PENRITH Cumbria
Map 4: inset C2
WESTMORLAND HOTEL, nr Orton, CA10 3SB. Tel 01539-624351, www.westmorlandhotel.com. 'Excellent – exceeded our expectations.' Surrounded by open fell, this secluded, modern hotel, 'so quiet and peaceful', is a 'lovely' stop-over for trips to and from Scotland, or as a base for touring that side of the Lakes. It is located off the M6, between junctions 38 and 39, part of the Tebay Motorway Services site owned by the Dunning family. Contemporary interiors mix with traditional materials; bedrooms have locally made organic toiletries. Ken Kerr is the new manager. The restaurant serves 'well-cooked' rustic British dishes, particularly beef and lamb from the Dunnings' farm, less than a mile away. 'A real find.' Lounge, bar (log fires), dining room. 'Unobtrusive' background music. Free Wi-Fi. Civil wedding licence; function/conference facilities. Children and dogs welcomed. 51 bedrooms (some family rooms; 1 suitable for &). Per room B&B single £60–£90, double £65–£110. Dinner £27.
25% DISCOUNT VOUCHERS

PRESTON Lancashire
Map 4:D2
BARTON GRANGE HOTEL, 746–768 Garstang Road, Barton, PR3 5AA. Tel 01772-862551, www.bartongrangehotel.co.uk. Built in 1900 as the country home of a cotton mill owner, this old manor house is today a much-expanded, modernised hotel that has been run by the Topping family for more than 60 years. Ian Topping is in charge, with 'highly competent and charming' staff. Modern bedrooms are decorated with vivid colours; each is equipped with a minibar and a tea and coffee tray. On the site of the original kitchen garden, the *Walled Garden* bistro serves dishes cooked with locally sourced produce. A few minutes' drive from the M6. Lounge, bistro/wine bar. Free Wi-Fi. Background music. Leisure centre (indoor pool, sauna; gym). Pool/bar billiards. Private dining. Civil wedding licence; conference facilities. 51 bedrooms (8 in cottage in the grounds; 1 suitable for &). Per room B&B from £60. Dinner £25.

ROECLIFFE North Yorkshire
Map 4:D4
THE CROWN INN, Boroughbridge, YO51 9LY. Tel 01423-322300, www.crowninnroecliffe.com. Facing the village green, this 16th-century coaching inn has flagstone floors, oak beams and crackling log fires. Owned by the Mainey family, it is managed by Karl Mainey. Elegant, country-style bedrooms are decorated in soft tones; bathrooms have a freestanding bath. Chef Darryn Asher's creative modern British cooking features daily chalkboard specials, 'impeccably cooked and generous in portion size'. Eight miles from Ripon and within easy reach of the Yorkshire Dales and North

York Moors national parks. Bar, restaurant (background music), 3 dining areas. Free Wi-Fi. Garden. Civil wedding licence. Function facilities in converted medieval cow barn. Children welcomed. 4 bedrooms. Per room (including complimentary newspaper) B&B £80–£120, D,B&B £130–£170 (based on 2 people sharing).

ROMSEY Hampshire
Map 2:E2

THE WHITE HORSE, Market Place, SO51 8ZJ. Tel 01794-512431, www.thewhitehorseromsey.co.uk. In the centre of the market town, this 'smartly' refurbished medieval coaching inn has an equine theme: there is hunting scene wallpaper in the reception area; bedrooms are named after well-known racehorses. It is managed by Paul and Sarah Bingham. With exposed timbers and leather seating, the Tudor Lounge has a clubby atmosphere, a stove in the hearth; board games and newspapers. Chef Chris Rock's 'nicely presented' modern British dishes are served in the brasserie, 'a lovely place to eat – restful but interesting'. There is plenty of space to sit outside in good weather. 2 sitting rooms, *Silks* bar and brasserie; courtyard. Wedding/function facilities. Background music. Free Wi-Fi. Pay-and-display parking. Children and dogs welcomed. 31 bedrooms (5 in Coach House across the courtyard). Room only £95–£135. Breakfast £7.50–£14.50, dinner from £16.50.

ROSS-ON-WYE Herefordshire
Map 3:D5

THE HILL HOUSE, Howle Hill, HR9 5ST. Tel 01989-562033, www.thehowlinghillhouse.com. Duncan and Alex Stayton are the owners of this rambling 17th-century home, set in four acres of private woodlands with spectacular views of the Forest of Dean and the Wye valley. Quirky and full of character, the B&B is run in a laid-back manner: guests are invited to sip champagne in the seven-seater outdoor hot tub, relax in the oak-lined bar, and write on the 'Wisdom and Poetry' wall. Solar panels and a biomass boiler heat the water. Rooms are traditional, with Gothic elements; Old Mrs Thomas's Room has a Japanese bathtub for up-to-the-neck bathing. Aga-cooked organic suppers. Packed lunch/evening meal by arrangement. Vegetarians are catered for. Morning room, lounge, bar (background music: morning Radio 4), restaurant. Free Wi-Fi. Hot tub; sauna (£4–£6); cinema (DVD film library). Garden. Children, and dogs (by arrangement) welcomed. Resident dog, cats, pigs and chickens. 5 bedrooms. Per person B&B £34–£39. Supper £21.

ROWSLEY Derbyshire
Map 3:A6

THE PEACOCK AT ROWSLEY, Bakewell Road, DE4 2EB. Tel 01629-733518, www.thepeacockatrowsley.co.uk. On the edge of a Peak District village, this charming old inn by a bridge is owned by Lord Edward Manners, of nearby Haddon Hall. It is managed by Ian and Jenni MacKenzie, with 'very jolly' staff. Popular with fishermen, it was once a dower house: there are mullioned windows, leaded lights, and log fires in stone fireplaces. Soft furnishings in the 'cosy' bar have been updated in apple green and purple velvets. The quietest bedrooms overlook the gardens that run down to the River Derwent; those facing the busy road have double-glazed windows. Dan Smith cooks ambitious modern British dishes ('delicious bread; good, strong, local cheese'). No background music. Discounts for Haddon Hall and Chatsworth House. Lounge, bar, dining room. Free Wi-Fi. Civil wedding licence. Conference rooms. ½-acre garden on river (fishing Apr–Oct). Children (no under-10s Fri/Sat nights) and dogs welcomed. 15 bedrooms. Per room B&B £155–£450, D,B&B £215–£515. Closed end Dec and 2 weeks in Jan. **25% DISCOUNT VOUCHERS**

RYE East Sussex
Map 2:E5

THE HOPE ANCHOR, Watchbell Street, TN31 7HA. Tel 01797-222216, www.thehopeanchor.co.uk. In a 'lovely location' on a grassy square at the end of a cobbled street, this white-painted, family-owned hotel dates back to the 18th century, when it was a watering hole for sailors and shipbuilders. More recently, it featured in EF Benson's Mapp and Lucia novels. The spacious, modern dining room has views over the marshes; chef Kevin Sawyer serves dishes using fish, meat and produce from Rye and the surrounding area. Bedrooms are decorated in 'appealing' country style. Lounge, bar (snack menu), dining room. Free Wi-Fi. Background music. Room service. Wedding facilities. Children (cots, baby-listening devices, high chairs) and dogs welcomed. 16 bedrooms (1 in roof annexe; 2 apartments; cottage). Per room B&B £95–£180, D,B&B £110–£220.

THE SHIP INN, The Strand, TN31 7DB. Tel 01797-222233, www.theshipinnrye.co.uk. 'In a good position', this cosy inn with simple, seaside-themed bedrooms

was, in the 16th century, a warehouse used to store contraband seized from smugglers. Owned by Karen Northcote, it is managed by Theo Bekker. Uneven wooden floors and exposed beams (some low) are matched by retro decoration. There is bread from an artisan baker at breakfast; 'usually good' lunches and dinners, cooked by Ronny Balle, focus on seasonal, local ingredients, and fish from Rye Bay. Close to Rye Harbour Nature Reserve and Camber Sands. Lounge, bar, restaurant; terrace. Background music. Free Wi-Fi. Children and dogs welcomed. 10 bedrooms. Per room B&B £70–£120 (2-night min. stay on Sat). Dinner £24.

ST IVES Cornwall
Map 1:D1

BLUE HAYES, Trelyon Avenue, TR26 2AD. Tel 01736-797129, www.bluehayes.co.uk. Perched on Porthminster Point, Malcolm Herring's immaculate small hotel, a 1920s house, is decorated in chic coastal style; Nicola Martin is the manager. There are stunning views of the harbour and bay from the white balustraded terrace; a gate from the small garden leads directly to the beach (five minutes) or to the harbour (ten minutes). Bedrooms have sea views; some have a balcony, roof terrace or patio. 2 lounges, bar, dining room (light, Mediterranean-style suppers); terrace. Free Wi-Fi. No background music. Small function facilities. Parking. Children over 10 welcomed. 6 bedrooms. Per room B&B single £100–£110, double £170–£240. Supper from £18. Closed Nov–Mar.

NO1 ST IVES, 1 Fern Glen, TR26 1QP. Tel 01736-799047, www.no1stives.co.uk.

Within an easy downhill walk of the town and the Tate gallery, this small B&B is run by 'attentive' hosts Anna Bray and Simon Talbot. Their stone-built house is light and contemporary inside. Well-equipped bedrooms have hot drinks and biscuits (replenished daily), an iPod docking station, TV with Freeview and a DVD/CD-player; two have distant ocean views towards Godrevy Lighthouse. There is an extensive choice at breakfast, including much local produce. Sitting room, dining room (background jazz). Small back garden; terrace. Free Wi-Fi. Parking close by. Children over 7 welcomed. 4 bedrooms. Per room B&B £90–£135.

PRIMROSE VALLEY HOTEL,
Porthminster Beach, TR26 2ED. Tel 01736-794939, www.primroseonline. co.uk. In an 'attractive' seaside villa in a terrace of Edwardian houses, this small hotel, seconds from the beach, is run along environmentally friendly lines by owners Andrew and Sue Biss. Bedrooms, some with sea views, are snug; one has French doors opening on to a private terrace. Organic breakfasts. Close to town; reached via a steep, narrow road. Lounge, café/bar (Cornish platters; cream teas), breakfast room; small terrace overlooking sea. Free Wi-Fi. Background music. Parking. Children over 8 welcomed. 10 bedrooms. Per room B&B £75–£170 (2-night min. stay preferred at weekends and in high season).
25% DISCOUNT VOUCHERS

ST IVES HARBOUR HOTEL, The Terrace, TR26 2BN. Tel 01736-795221, www.stives-harbour-hotel.co.uk. Overlooking Godrevy Lighthouse, this grand Victorian building (formerly *The Porthminster*) above Porthminster Beach has undergone considerable restoration. It is now managed by Peter Holgate for Harbour Hotels. There are views over the bay from the restaurant and new terrace; menus feature Cornwall produce and fish landed daily at the harbour. Lounge, bar, cocktail bar, restaurant with terrace. Free Wi-Fi (in some rooms). Background music. Lift; ramps. Spa with heated indoor swimming pool and swimming jet areas; hydrotherapy pool, sauna, crystal steam room, fitness suite; treatment rooms. Civil wedding licence; function facilities. Children, and dogs (in some bedrooms) welcomed. 46 bedrooms (some family; some with balcony; 1 suitable for &). Per person B&B £60–£159.50, D,B&B £72.50–£179.50.

SALCOMBE Devon
Map 1:E4
SOUTH SANDS, Bolt Head, TQ8 8LL. Tel 01548-859000, www.southsands. com. 'Casual, without any stuffy formalities whatsoever', this family-friendly hotel by the Salcombe ferry is practically on the beach. The 'no-nonsense' interior ('not designer, just contemporary good taste') is decked out in maritime style. 'Our large bedroom (No. 20) was superb, with two big double windows and a wonderful view.' Some rooms have twin roll-top baths. The light, airy beachside restaurant has painted wicker chairs and wooden floors (it can be noisy); chef Stuart Downie cooks a seafood-focused menu. Bar, restaurant (background music); terrace. Free Wi-Fi. Civil wedding licence. Parking. Children, and dogs (in some bedrooms) welcomed.

27 bedrooms (5 beach suites). Per room B&B £150–£435 (2-night min. stay on Fri, Sat). Dinner £30.

SALISBURY Wiltshire
Map 2:D2

LEENA'S GUEST HOUSE, 50 Castle Road, SP1 3RL. Tel 01722-335419, www.leenasguesthouse.co.uk. A short riverside walk from the city centre and cathedral, this Edwardian guest house is run by Leena and Malcolm Street and their son, Gary. Good-value B&B accommodation is in traditionally furnished bedrooms; a family room sleeps three. The Streets are liked for the friendly welcome they extend to guests; 'excellent' breakfasts have fresh fruit, and hot dishes cooked to order. Lounge, breakfast room. Free Wi-Fi. No background music. Garden. Parking. Children welcomed. 6 bedrooms (1 on ground floor). Per room B&B single £37–£45, double £67–£69.

QUIDHAMPTON MILL, Netherhampton Road, SP2 9BB. Tel 01722-741171, www.quidhamptonmill.co.uk. Guests are welcomed with lemonade or a cream tea at Lesa and Martin Drewett's New Hampshire-style B&B overlooking water meadows and the River Wylye. The modern, dark-clapboard building has a light interior; simple, thoughtfully furnished bedrooms (including a 'just in case' tin with plasters and toothpaste) are in a separate building. Breakfasts have been praised: besides the full English, there are blueberry pancakes, pastries, fresh fruit salad. Picnic hampers available; dinner by arrangement. A classic Jaguar is available for hire. On the A3094; 10 mins' drive to Salisbury; bus stop at the

end of the street. No background music. Free Wi-Fi (iPad for guests). Garden. Parking. Children welcomed. 3 bedrooms. Per person B&B from £42.50. Dinner £20–£25.

SPIRE HOUSE, 84 Exeter Street, SP1 2SE. Tel 01722-339213, www.salisbury-bedandbreakfast.com. 'Really convenient', this small B&B in an 18th-century Grade II listed town house is close to the cathedral. Owners Lois and John Faulkner provide 'a very pleasant welcome' and useful advice about the city; 'They made our brief stay in Salisbury really good.' The 'nicely decorated' bedrooms ('no chintz!') are 'pleasant to be in'; two overlook the quiet walled garden. 'Tasty' breakfasts have lots of choice. Breakfast room. Free Wi-Fi. No background music. Garden. Parking opposite. 4 bedrooms. Room only £60–£80. Breakfast £5. Closed late Dec–Feb.

SAWLEY Lancashire
Map 4:D3

THE SPREAD EAGLE INN, nr Clitheroe, BB7 4NH. Tel 01200-441202, www.spreadeaglesawley.co.uk. There are many scenic walks to be taken from the doorstep of this stone-built pub-with-rooms (Individual Inns) beside the River Ribble. The smartly refurbished interior has flagstone floors and oak-beamed ceilings; 'comfortable', handsomely furnished bedrooms are individually styled. The informal eating areas (wooden tables, mismatched seating) have pub classics and sharing platters; special diets are catered for. Guided walks (with a bacon sandwich) regularly organised. Bar, dining room. Free Wi-Fi. Background music. Wedding/

function facilities. Parking. Children welcomed. 7 bedrooms. Per room B&B single £69–£90, double £85–£135.

SCARBOROUGH North Yorkshire
Map 4:C5

PHOENIX COURT, 8–9 Rutland Terrace, YO12 7JB. Tel 01723-501150, www. hotel-phoenix.co.uk. Formed from two Victorian houses overlooking North Bay and the beach, Alison and Bryan Edwards's environmentally friendly guest house welcomes walkers: packed lunches, route information and drying facilities are provided. Breakfasts, with home-baked fruit bread, showcase Yorkshire produce, including locally smoked kippers and sausages from local farms; a continental breakfast may be taken in the room. 10 mins' walk from the town centre. Lounge, bar area, dining room (background music). Free Wi-Fi. Parking. Children welcomed. 14 bedrooms (9 with sea views; 1 on ground floor; 2 family rooms). Per room B&B single £36–£40, double £50–£60. Closed Jan.
25% DISCOUNT VOUCHERS

SEAHOUSES Northumberland
Map 4:A4

ST CUTHBERT'S HOUSE, 192 Main Street, NE68 7UB. Tel 01665-720456, www.stcuthbertshouse.com. Musicians Jill and Jeff Sutheran have transformed a former Presbyterian church (built in 1810) into a characterful B&B that preserves the building's original features. The former sanctuary is today the guest lounge, the pulpit is now a balcony viewing area; elegant wooden pillars and the communion table remain. Traditional Northumbrian breakfasts include honey from the hosts'

own beehives. The Sutherans live in the former manse, next door. On a quiet road, ½ mile inland from the village and harbour. Monthly house concerts (acoustic roots, folk and Americana music). Lounge, breakfast room (occasional instrumental background music). Free Wi-Fi. Small garden. Small function facilities. Off-road parking. 6 bedrooms (1 suitable for &). Per room B&B single £70–£90, double £95–£110.

SHEFFIELD South Yorkshire
Map 4:E4

LEOPOLD HOTEL, 2 Leopold Street, Leopold Square, S1 2GZ. Tel 08450-780067, www.leopoldhotelsheffield.com. Arched doorways, panelled walls, school photos and ranks of coat pegs are part of the historic character of this former boys' grammar school, today a Grade II listed, quirkily converted hotel (part of Small Luxury Hotels of the World) in the city centre. Guests are given a choice of bedding in the modern bedrooms. Breakfast can be taken until 10.30 am at weekends; there are plenty of restaurants and cafés in Leopold Square. Lounge bar (afternoon teas, bar snacks), dining room; terrace. Free Wi-Fi. Background music. 24-hour room service; private dining rooms. Civil wedding licence; conference/function facilities. Parking discounts in public car park nearby. Children welcomed. 90 bedrooms (6 suitable for &). Room only £80–£110. Breakfast £7.95–£8.95.

SHERBORNE Somerset
Map 2:E1

THE KINGS ARMS, North Street, Charlton Horethorne, DT9 4NL. Tel 01963-220281, www.thekingsarms. co.uk. In the centre of a pretty village on the Somerset/Dorset border, this stately Edwardian building has been transformed by Anthony and Sarah Lethbridge into a modern pub and restaurant, with rooms above. Colourful, individually styled bedrooms have a marble wet room; some have views of the croquet lawn. Downstairs, a log-burning stove separates a cosy seating area from the slate- and wood-floored bar; chef Sarah Lethbridge's British dishes are served in the elegant restaurant. There are displays of local art and sculptures throughout. Lounge, snug, bar, restaurant. Free Wi-Fi. No background music. Terrace; garden; croquet. Function/small business facilities; shooting parties. Free use of sports centre in Sherborne (4 miles); discounts at Sherborne Golf Club; clay-pigeon shooting can be arranged. Lift. Parking. Children welcomed (special menu). 10 bedrooms (1 suitable for &; 3 accessible by lift). Per room B&B £125, interconnecting family room £200. Dinner £35.

SHREWSBURY Shropshire
Map 3:B4
CHATFORD HOUSE, Bayston Hill, Chatford, SY3 0AY. Tel 01743-718301, www.chatfordhouse.co.uk. Pretty, cottage-style bedrooms and Aga-cooked breakfasts are part of the rural experience at Christine and Rupert Farmer's B&B, in a handsome 18th-century Grade II listed farmhouse close to the Shropshire Way. Surrounded by organic farmland, the Farmers' smallholding is home to hens, ducks, geese, sheep and cattle; guests are welcome to visit the animals, and explore the pretty garden and orchard. There are tea and home-made cakes on arrival; home-made jams and compotes from orchard fruit at breakfast. 5 miles south of Shrewsbury; within walking distance of Lyth Hill. Sitting room, breakfast room (open fire; background piano, CDs). Free Wi-Fi. Garden; orchard. Children welcomed. 3 bedrooms. Per room B&B single from £50, double from £70.
25% DISCOUNT VOUCHERS (stays of 3 nights or more)

THE GOLDEN CROSS HOTEL, 14 Princess Street, SY1 1LP. Tel 01743-362507, www.goldencrosshotel.co.uk. Reputed to have served as an inn since 1428, this old building in the historic town centre has been owned and managed by Gareth and Theresa Reece for more than a decade. They have added contemporary comforts to its medieval structure, including, most recently, a courtyard garden. Bedrooms have antique furnishings and a flat-screen TV; one has a four-poster bed. Traditional home-made dishes have a rustic French influence; lighter meals are available in the bar. Shropshire breakfasts. 2 bars, restaurant (background music); private dining; courtyard garden. Free Wi-Fi. Children welcomed. Metered street parking (free from 6 pm and on Sundays) or long-term car park nearby. 4 bedrooms (1 suite suitable for a family). Per room B&B £75–£150. Dinner from £27.50.

GROVE FARM HOUSE, Condover, SY5 7BH. Tel 01743-718544, www.grovefarmhouse.com. In a peaceful country setting six miles south of the town, Liz Farrow welcomes B&B guests to her three-storey Georgian house. Cheerful bedrooms have home-made biscuits, and flowers from the garden; local maps and guides are available to borrow. Walks can be taken around the farm or through beautiful parkland and wooded areas. Breakfast has locally produced meat, eggs from home-reared chickens and home-made blueberry muffins. Afternoon tea is available, by arrangement; Ms Farrow makes recommendations for dinner at local restaurants. Lounge, dining room. Free Wi-Fi. No background music. 1½-acre garden. Children welcomed. 4 bedrooms (plus 2 self-catering suites with log burner and private courtyard). Per room B&B £60–£90 (2-night min. stay May–Sept).

THE INN AT GRINSHILL, High Street, Grinshill, SY4 3BL. Tel 01939-220410, www.theinnatgrinshill.co.uk. 'Excellent hosts', Victoria and Kevin Brazier, own and manage this country inn in a renovated Grade II listed Georgian building in the lee of Grinshill, a site of special scientific interest and an area of outstanding natural beauty. Understated bedrooms are decorated in soft hues, with modern rugs on wood flooring; they have a concealed Freeview TV and a stylish bathroom. Chef Chris Condé cooks 'delicious' gourmet dinners in the restaurant and conservatory; bistro meals are served in the cosy, wood-panelled bar, with books, games, comfy sofas and an open fire. 7 miles N of Shrewsbury. 2 bars (*The Elephant and Castle* and *Bubbles*), restaurant (closed Sun eve, Mon and Tues; background music). Free Wi-Fi. Rose garden with fountain. Function facilities. Parking. Children welcomed. 6 bedrooms. Per room B&B single £90–£100, double £120–£140. D,B&B £79.50–£89.50 per person (based on 2 people sharing). **25% DISCOUNT VOUCHERS** (Nov–Mar for guests who dine in)

THE SILVERTON, 9–10 Frankwell, SY3 8JY. Tel 01743-248000, www.thesilverton.co.uk. In a former dairy, this modern restaurant-with-rooms is just across the Welsh Bridge, and an easy walk to the riverside and town centre. It is managed by Tim Moody. Decorated in cream, brown and green, bedrooms are named after Shropshire hills; rooms at the back are quietest. Chef Michael Jordan cooks contemporary British dishes, and sources ingredients from local suppliers for 'excellent' breakfasts, lazy lunches, afternoon teas and dinner. Bar, restaurant; lift; terrace. Free Wi-Fi. Background music. Valet parking. Children welcomed. 7 bedrooms (1 suitable for &). Per room B&B £75–£135. Dinner £30. **25% DISCOUNT VOUCHERS**

SIDLESHAM West Sussex
Map 2:E3

THE CRAB & LOBSTER, Mill Lane, PO20 7NB. Tel 01243-641233, www.crab-lobster.co.uk. Peacefully located, this 350-year-old inn is on the banks of Pagham Harbour nature reserve in an area of outstanding natural beauty and special scientific interest. (Binoculars and a telescope are provided in some deluxe bedrooms.) The inn has been renovated in spare, modern style by structural engineer-turned-hotelier Sam Bakose and his wife, Janet. Fresh local fish, crab and lobster feature regularly in chef Malcolm Goble's dishes, cooked to a 'high standard' and served in a smart dining room; there is local honey at breakfast. Bar, restaurant (background jazz); terrace; garden. Free Wi-Fi. Children welcomed. 6 bedrooms (2 in adjoining cottage). Per person B&B £72.50–£92.50 (2-night min. stay on Fri, Sat). Dinner £40.

SIDMOUTH Devon
Map 1:D5

HOTEL RIVIERA, The Esplanade, EX10 8AY. Tel 01395-515201, www. hotelriviera.co.uk. 'With great dedication and charm', the Wharton family have run this traditional hotel, in a fine Regency terrace on the esplanade overlooking Lyme Bay, for more than 40 years. Staff are 'quite outstanding'. 'Good-quality, plentiful' English dishes and local seafood are served in the smart dining room (also open to non-residents); Matthew Weaver is the long-serving chef. Lounge, cocktail bar (live piano music), restaurant; ballroom; terrace. Free Wi-Fi. Lift; entrance ramp. 2 minutes from the town centre. Golf nearby; pheasant and duck shooting can be arranged. Children and dogs welcomed. 26 bedrooms (some suitable for &; many with sea views). Per person B&B £109–£179, D,B&B £129–£199.

VICTORIA HOTEL, The Esplanade, EX10 8RY. Tel 01395-512651, www. victoriahotel.co.uk. A 'favourite bolt hole' for many returning visitors, this large traditional hotel (part of Brend Hotels) stands in five acres of landscaped grounds overlooking the bay. It was recently lavishly refurbished. 'The three spacious lounges make it a very relaxing place in which to stay.' Most of the bedrooms are south facing; many have a balcony. Men are asked to wear a jacket and tie for dinner in the *Jubilee* restaurant, which has live musical

accompaniment, and dinner dances on Saturday nights. Background music. Free Wi-Fi. Sun lounge, lounge bar; outdoor and indoor swimming pools; tennis court, snooker, putting. Spa, sauna, treatments. Lift. Room service. Gift shop. Parking. Children welcomed. 61 bedrooms (3 poolside suites). Room only £185–£310. Breakfast £18. D,B&B (2-night min. stay) £125–£215 per person.

SISSINGHURST Kent
Map 2:D5

SISSINGHURST CASTLE FARMHOUSE, nr Cranbrook, TN17 2AB. Tel 01580-720992, www.sissinghurstcastlefarm house.com. On the Sissinghurst estate, Sue and Frazer Thompson's farmhouse B&B was painstakingly restored by the National Trust to preserve its Victorian quirkiness. It is elegantly furnished throughout, and has stunning views – of ancient woodland, fields, gardens or the castle's Elizabethan tower – from all rooms. Tea and cake are offered on arrival; bedrooms have up-to-date technology (digital TV, radio, iPod docking station) and a modern bathroom. Near the entrance to Sissinghurst Castle Garden; guests have access to the estate grounds. Sitting room, dining room. Free Wi-Fi. No background music. Lift. Meeting room; small functions. Resident dog. 7 bedrooms (easy access). Per room B&B £130–£175 (2-night min. stay on Fri, Sat, May–Sept). Closed Jan–Mar.

SKIPTON North Yorkshire
Map 4:D3

HELLIFIELD PEEL CASTLE, Peel Green, Hellifield, BD23 4LD. Tel 01729-850248, www.peelcastle.co.uk. 'Restoring a castle in the dales; total ruin; previous owner hung, drawn and quartered. Are you interested?' With these words, Francis and Karen Shaw found themselves featured on Channel 4's *Grand Designs* programme, which traced the restoration of their ancient, ruined tower house (parts dating from the 13th century), and its transformation into a beautifully designed home. Today, B&B guests relax by a wood-burning stove in the cosy, red-painted lounge, or luxuriate in spacious bedrooms that have an ornately carved tester or four-poster bed, fresh flowers, and lots of thoughtful touches, including hand-made chocolates and cakes. Each room is different: the Old Room has a log fire; the modern Attic Apartment has self-catering facilities and a private roof terrace. 'Warmly welcoming', Mrs Shaw cooks 'wonderful' breakfasts, with home-baked bread; vegetarian options are available. In parkland, ½ mile from village. No background music. Sitting room, breakfast room. Free Wi-Fi. 2-acre garden. Parking. Children over 8 welcomed. 5 bedrooms. Per room B&B single £135–£190, double £165–£220.

SOUTHPORT Merseyside
Map 4:E2

THE VINCENT, 98 Lord Street, PR8 1JR. Tel 01704-883800, www.thevincenthotel. com. Local restaurateur Paul Adams has transformed a former cinema near the train station into this large, fashionable hotel with a striking glass facade, and a lively bar and restaurant within. Alan Richmond is the manager. Decorated in restful tones, bedrooms vary in size: some are small, while others have an adjoining lounge and balcony. The *V-Cafe & Sushi Bar* is open early until late (outdoor seating; Andrew Carter is the chef).

Members' bar; background music. Free Wi-Fi. Spa; gym; beauty treatments. Civil wedding licence; function facilities. Valet parking. Children welcomed. 60 bedrooms (3 suitable for &). Per room B&B from £98. Dinner from £14.95.

SOUTHWOLD Suffolk
Map 2:B6

THE SWAN, Market Place, IP18 6EG. Tel 01502-722186, www.adnams.co.uk. Overlooking the market square, and a short walk from the sea, this hotel in a 300-year-old building is managed by Martin Edwards for the Adnams Brewery. Bedrooms in the main house are traditionally furnished; those in the wildlife-friendly garden are more modern, with a breezy, coastal feel and views of the lighthouse. Breakfasts 'deserve a special mention'. Drawing room, bar, reading room, restaurant (Rory Whelan is chef); private dining room. Free Wi-Fi (in public areas only). No background music. Lift. Garden. Civil wedding licence; function facilities. Beauty and natural healing treatments. Parking. Beach 200 yds. Children, and dogs (in Lighthouse rooms, which have their own patio), welcomed. 42 bedrooms (some in annexe in garden; 1 suitable for &). Per room B&B single £115–£125, double £185–£255. D,B&B £117–£157.50 per person.
25% DISCOUNT VOUCHERS

STAMFORD Lincolnshire
Map 2:B3

THE BULL AND SWAN AT BURGHLEY, High Street, St Martins, PE9 2LJ. Tel 08442-491114, www.thebullandswan. co.uk. Once used as a staging post for coaches on the Great North Road, this ancient stone building was also the alleged venue of The Honourable Order of Little Bedlam, a riotous gentlemen's drinking club founded in 1684. It has been updated by Hillbrooke Hotels and is managed by James Chadwick. Quirky bedrooms, given the pseudonyms of Little Bedlam members, are furnished with carved dark wood furniture, crisp linen and smart fabrics; one room has a freestanding bath. Chef Phil Kent serves British bistro food using produce from local suppliers, rounded off with a 'very good' crème brûlée of the day. 'Excellent' breakfasts include yogurt, fresh berries and eggs Benedict and Royale. The town is a short stroll across the river; Burghley House can be reached via a cross-country walk. Background music. Free Wi-Fi. Courtyard garden. Parking (narrow entrance). Children, and dogs (in 1 room) welcomed. 7 bedrooms. Per person B&B £45–£100, D,B&B from £70.

STOWMARKET Suffolk
Map 2:C5

BAYS FARM, Earl Stonham, IP14 5HU. Tel 01449-711286, www.baysfarmsuffolk. co.uk. In beautiful gardens on the outskirts of a peaceful village, this 'attractive, tastefully modernised' 17th-century farmhouse is run as a B&B by Stephanie and Richard Challinor. Overlooking the gardens, the 'charming' bedrooms have a large bed and lots of little extras (fresh flowers, coffee machine, DVD-player); the Hayloft suite is in a separate, converted building with a balcony. A communal breakfast is served in the former dairy, the oldest part of the house, at a time to suit guests; bread and preserves are home made. A supper menu and snacks are available. The four-acre grounds (included in the National Gardens Scheme) have an orchard, a wildflower garden, and vegetable and fruit gardens; guests may relax in the pavilion, which has its own heating, lighting and iPod docking station. Drawing room (open fire); dining room. Free Wi-Fi. Background music. Garden. 3 bedrooms. Per room B&B £75–£110.

SWINDON Wiltshire
Map 2:C2

CHISELDON HOUSE, New Road, Chiseldon, SN4 0NE. Tel 01793-741010, www.chiseldonhousehotel.co.uk. In a tranquil village in the Marlborough Downs, this Grade II listed Georgian country house is set in beautiful grounds. Owned by the Pennells brothers, it is managed by Sue Higgs. The comfortable bedrooms are traditionally styled; several have a balcony overlooking the garden. Served in the drawing room, a gin and tonic-laced afternoon tea is a twist on the original. Bar, drawing room (traditional fireplace), *Orangery* restaurant (Robert Harwood cooks modern British food); terrace. Free Wi-Fi. 'Mellow' background jazz. 3-acre gardens with seating. Open to non-residents. Civil wedding licence; conference facilities. Easy access to the M4. 5 miles from Swindon. Children welcomed (some restrictions in restaurant). 21 bedrooms. Per person B&B £57.50–£95, D,B&B £77.50–£115. **25% DISCOUNT VOUCHERS**

TAPLOW Berkshire
Map 2:D3

CLIVEDEN HOUSE, SL6 0JF. Tel 01628-668561, www.clivedenhouse.co.uk.

'Very much enjoyed' by a reader, this magnificent stately home stands in 'glorious' National Trust grounds by the Thames. Between April and October, guests can book a cruise, with champagne and a picnic lunch, on one of the hotel's vintage launches. Royalty and politicians have been among *Cliveden*'s many illustrious visitors; it was also the venue for John Profumo's first meeting with Christine Keeler. Elaborately decorated public rooms have interesting artworks; bedrooms (some have a fireplace or terrace) are furnished with antiques. Sue Williams is the manager; see main entry for sister hotel, *Chewton Glen*, New Milton. Background music; live pianist on Fri, Sat. Lounge, library, south-facing *Terrace* restaurant (Carlos Martinez cooks 'excellent' classic French food with a modern twist); private dining rooms; snooker room. Free Wi-Fi. Spa (outdoor and indoor pools, hot tubs, steam rooms, sauna; treatments; sun terrace); tennis courts. Ramp. Children welcomed (interconnecting bedrooms). Dogs welcomed in some rooms (doggie treats, basket, information on walks; dog-sitting and -walking service). 39 bedrooms (plus 'idyllic' Spring Cottage). Room only £252–£1572. À la carte breakfast from £5.50, dinner £60.

TELFORD Shropshire
Map 2:A1
CHURCH FARM GUEST HOUSE, Wrockwardine Village, TF6 5DG. Tel 01952-251927, www.churchfarm-shropshire.co.uk. In a pretty village three miles west of Telford, Melanie and Martin Board run their 'spotless and inviting' Georgian farmhouse (exposed brickwork, beams and open fires) as a guest house. Rooms are comfortable and well equipped. In *Basil's* restaurant, the host serves 'amazing' regional British dishes; 'Breakfast was in a class of its own, freshly made and delicious.' 'A perfect base for exploring the county', the guest house has facilities for cyclists and walkers, such as a drying room, maps and a puncture repair kit; packed lunches and baggage transfer by arrangement. Lounge, restaurant (open to non-residents; BYO wine); garden. Free Wi-Fi. No background music. Cookery courses. Children welcomed (toys, DVDs, books; outdoor games). Dogs welcomed in 1 annexe room. Resident dog, Basil. 5 bedrooms (1 with private bathroom). Per person B&B £40–£60, D,B&B £65–£70.
25% DISCOUNT VOUCHERS

TETBURY Gloucestershire
Map 3:E5
OAK HOUSE NO.1, The Chipping, GL8 8EU. Tel 01666-505741, www. oakhouseno1.com. An eclectic mix of rich fabrics, designer furniture, antiques, contemporary art and artefacts fill this Georgian house in the centre of the market town. It is owned by interior designer and art collector Gary Kennedy, who runs it as a luxurious B&B with Nicola MacWilliam. Elegantly furnished bedrooms and suites come with home-baked cakes and scones, and a gift; bathrooms are contemporary and luxurious. Sitting room, dining room. Free Wi-Fi. Background jazz music. Walled garden (complimentary afternoon tea). Luxury picnic hampers. Beauty treatments. Wellingtons and thick socks supplied for walkers wanting to explore the countryside. Babies, and children

over 11, welcomed. 4 bedrooms. Per
room B&B £175–£275.

THURNHAM Kent
Map 2:D4

THURNHAM KEEP, Castle Hill,
ME14 3LE. Tel 01622-734149,
www.thurnhamkeep.co.uk. A long
drive leads up to this 'very impressive'
Edwardian house in large grounds, with
views over the Weald of Kent. The
childhood home of owner Amanda
Lane, it has 'beautiful', traditionally
furnished rooms; two have a huge
Edwardian bath. B&B guests are
welcomed with freshly made scones
and tea; the communal breakfast
has 'everything you could wish for',
including home-made jams, honey from
the house's bees, and eggs from resident
free-range hens. Supper is available, by
arrangement; plenty of pubs nearby.
Oak-panelled sitting room (wood-
burning stove), conservatory, dining
room; terrace (alfresco breakfasts);
snooker room (in the old chapel). Free
Wi-Fi. Background music (weekend
eve only; 'easy listening'/classical/jazz).
7-acre terraced garden: heated outdoor
swimming pool (June–early Sept); pond;
kitchen garden, dovecote; summer
house; tennis, croquet. Parking.
3 bedrooms. Per room B&B single
£115–£145, double £130–£160.

TISBURY Wiltshire
Map 2:D1

THE BECKFORD ARMS, Fonthill Gifford,
SP3 6PX. Tel 01747-870385, www.
beckfordarms.com. An excellent base
for walkers, this unpretentious ivy-
covered gastropub-with-rooms lies on
the edge of the rolling parkland of the
Fonthill estate. It has been renovated

throughout in sophisticated style by
owners Dan Brod and Charlie Luxton.
The sitting room has comfy seating, an
open fire, newspapers, books and games,
and a projector for screening classic
movies on Sunday nights. Imaginative
seasonal menus are served in the award-
winning restaurant or alfresco on the
terrace; there are cocktails and snacks in
the bar. Light background jazz. Free
Wi-Fi. Bar, restaurant, sitting room;
private dining room. Function facilities.
1-acre garden: hammocks, boules.
In-room massages by arrangement.
Children, and dogs (1 room only)
welcomed. Resident dog, Elsa. 2 lodges
(each with a sitting room) added in
the grounds (hamper provided for
breakfast). 8 bedrooms (family room,
plus 2 self-catering lodges nearby). Per
room B&B £95–£120. Dinner from £30.

THE COMPASSES INN, Lower
Chicksgrove, SP3 6NB. Tel 01722-
714318, www.thecompassesinn.com.
There are low ceilings, huge beams, a
crackling log fire and plenty of nooks
and crannies in the cosy bar of Susie and
Alan Stoneham's thatched 14th-century
inn. In an area of outstanding natural
beauty, it is a good base for country
walks and visits to Longleat,
Stonehenge and Wilton House. Chef
Dave Cousin serves interesting dishes
alongside traditional 'pub grub', chalked
on blackboards. All vegetables are from
a local farm; there is an extensive wine
list. Guests reach their simple, light
rooms through a separate entrance.
Bar, dining room. Free Wi-Fi. No
background music. 2 gardens. Small
function facilities. Children (baby
monitor, babysitting, baby food) and
dogs welcomed. 4 bedrooms (plus

adjacent 2-bed cottage). Per room B&B £65–£85 (2-night min. stay on summer bank holiday weekends). Dinner from £24.

TOTNES Devon
Map 1:D4

ROYAL SEVEN STARS, The Plains, TQ9 5DD. Tel 01803-862125, www.royalsevenstars.co.uk. In the centre of the Bohemian town, this 17th-century coaching inn, owned by Anne and Nigel Way, has an imposing original facade and a bright, modern interior. Margaret Stone is the manager. The hotel has a lively atmosphere: it is a popular events venue, and its restaurant and bars are well patronised by local residents. Light bar meals are available all day; in the old stables at the end of the courtyard, chef John Gallagher's brasserie menus are served in the evening ('easy listening' background music). Lounge, 2 bars (log fires in winter), *TQ9* brasserie and grill, champagne bar; terrace (alfresco dining); balcony. Free Wi-Fi. Civil wedding licence; business facilities; ballroom. Parking. Children and dogs welcomed. 21 bedrooms (quietest at back). Per room B&B single £85–£115, double £119–£149. Dinner from £18.95.

TROUTBECK Cumbria
Map 4: inset C2

BROADOAKS, Bridge Lane, LA23 1LA. Tel 015394-45566, www.broadoaks countryhouse.co.uk. 'We had the warmest welcome from all the lovely staff.' Tracey Robinson's 'stunning' 19th-century house in traditional stone and slate is approached by a sweeping drive through extensive grounds. Richly decorated bedrooms are named after Lake District trees; garden suites near the river are colonial in style. Andrea Carter is the manager; Sharon Elders is the new head chef. Popular as a wedding venue; 'gorgeous'. Music room (vintage Bechstein piano; log fire), bar, *Oaks* restaurant. Free Wi-Fi. Background music. 7-acre grounds; stream. Civil wedding licence. Free membership at nearby spa. 19 bedrooms (some on ground floor; 5 in coach house; 3 detached garden suites, 5 mins' walk from house). Children, and dogs (in some rooms) welcomed. Resident cockapoo, Molly. Per person B&B £50–£130, D,B&B £75–£160.
25% DISCOUNT VOUCHERS

TUNBRIDGE WELLS Kent
Map 2:D4

HOTEL DU VIN TUNBRIDGE WELLS, 13 Crescent Road, TN1 2LY. Tel 08447-489266, www.hotelduvin.com. 'It suited us well.' This outpost of the du Vin group, an 18th-century Grade II listed sandstone mansion, faces Calverley Park. Philip Archer manages, with a team of 'friendly' staff. Bedrooms are handsomely decorated; some have a roll-top bath in the bathroom. The informal bistro has dark-stained floorboards, restored fireplaces, pictures and paintings; chef Daniel McGarey uses locally sourced and organic ingredients in his adaptation of French bistro classics. Bar, bistro, tea lounge; private dining room. Free Wi-Fi. No background music. Function facilities. 1-acre garden: terrace (alfresco dining); vineyard; boules. Close to the station. Limited parking. Children and dogs welcomed. 34 bedrooms (4 in annexe). Per room B&B £135–£350, D,B&B £185–£400.

ULLSWATER Cumbria
Map 4: inset C2

INN ON THE LAKE, Glenridding, Penrith, CA11 0PE. Tel 01768-482444, www.lakedistricthotels.net. In a spectacular location at the foot of the Helvellyn range, this 'wonderful' hotel stands in extensive grounds on the shores of Lake Ullswater. It is managed by Gary Wilson with staff who 'could not have been nicer or more helpful'. There are 'fabulous' lake and mountain views from bedrooms decorated in a mix of traditional and glamorous modern style; the lounge has large bay windows overlooking the landscaped gardens. Chef Fraser Souta creates 'superb' modern European dishes for the *Lake View* restaurant; the *Ramblers Bar* in the grounds has traditional pub food, local real ales, hot drinks, and a plasma TV for sports programmes. Lounge, bar, restaurant, orangery; lakeside terrace (alfresco dining). Free Wi-Fi. Gym, spa bath, sauna; 15-acre grounds: pitch and putt, croquet, 9-hole golf course; children's outdoor play area; private jetties. Civil wedding licence; conference facilities. Background music. Dogs welcomed in some rooms. 47 bedrooms. Per person B&B from £90, D,B&B from £122.

VENTNOR Isle of Wight
Map 2:E2

OCEAN VIEW HOUSE, 46 Zig Zag Road, PO38 1DD. Tel 01983-852729, www.oceanviewhouse.co.uk. Visitors in search of 'privacy and relaxation' are well catered for at Sarah Smith's B&B in this Victorian seaside town. Guests have a separate entrance, and can come and go as they please; a full breakfast is served in the room ('No more staring at strangers over breakfast!'). Two of the neat, modern bedrooms have a balcony with panoramic sea views; the terraced garden has hammocks and decked areas with sunshades and cushions. From Nov–Mar, a home-cooked dinner is available, by arrangement (from £8.95). There are takeaway menus, and tableware for picnics in a small dining area; fresh milk is stored in a communal fridge. The B&B is at the top of a steep hill overlooking Ventnor; the town and beach are a short stroll away (guests returning on foot catch their breath on a bench halfway, or take a bus or taxi back up). Picnic hampers are available (from £8). In-room massage treatments can be arranged. Free Wi-Fi. Garden. 1 mile N of town centre. 4 bedrooms. Per person B&B £70–£95. Closed mid-Dec–mid-Jan.

THE ROYAL HOTEL, Belgrave Road, PO38 1JJ. Tel 01983-852186, www.royalhoteliow.co.uk. A five-minute walk to the seafront and town centre, this traditional seaside hotel is liked for its 'olde-worlde charm'. It is owned by William Bailey, and managed by Philip Wilson, Paul Taylor and Maria Cirrone. Bedrooms are decorated in country house style, with silks, rich velvets and toile de Jouy fabrics. 'Our room looked south, and was very bright and cheerful.' The restaurant's menus include seafood landed on the beach below; lunch and afternoon tea can be taken on the geranium terrace. 'We were not disappointed.' Lounge, bar with terrace, *Appuldurcombe* restaurant, *Riviera* terrace (alfresco dining); conservatory. Lift to some rooms. Free Wi-Fi. Background music; resident

pianist during peak season weekends. Civil wedding licence; function rooms. 2-acre subtropical grounds: heated outdoor swimming pool (Apr–Sept), children's play area. In-room massages and beauty treatments. Sandy beach nearby (hilly walk). Picnic hampers available. Parking. Children welcomed (baby-listening facilities; children's high tea). Dogs welcomed (charge). 53 bedrooms (1 suitable for &). Per room B&B £175–£275, D,B&B £255–£355 (2-night min. stay at peak weekends). Closed 2 weeks in Jan.
25% DISCOUNT VOUCHERS

WALLINGTON Northumberland
Map 4:B3
SHIELDHALL, Morpeth, NE61 4AQ. Tel 01830-540387, www.shieldhallguest house.co.uk. Once owned by the family of Capability Brown, this stone house, which overlooks the National Trust's Wallington estate, stands amid gardens and parkland with a stream, woodland and natural meadow. It is run as a B&B by welcoming owners Stephen and Celia Gay, who converted the farmstead and decorated it with antiques, original art, and handcrafted furniture made by Stephen and his sons. Bedrooms (named after the wood used for their furniture and fittings) open on to a central courtyard; Oak has a panelled four-poster bed. Celia serves traditional Aga-cooked meals, using home-grown vegetables and fresh eggs from her own hens; 4-course dinners are served by arrangement. Daughter Sarah manages. Library, 'secret' bar, dining room. Free Wi-Fi. No background music. 4 bedrooms (all on ground floor). Per person B&B £48–£68. Dinner £28. Closed Dec–Jan.

WARMINSTER Wiltshire
Map 2:D1
CROCKERTON HOUSE, Crockerton Green, BA12 8AY. Tel 01985-216331, www.crockertonhouse.co.uk. In 'beautiful' gardens overlooking the Wylye valley, Enid and Christopher Richmond's meticulously restored, white-painted Georgian house (Grade II listed) is handsomely furnished with antiques. It has original features in the hall and lounge, and spacious bedrooms upstairs. Enid Richmond cooks two-course candlelit suppers (by arrangement) on the Aga, using fruit and vegetables from the garden; guests may bring their own wine. Afternoon tea with home-made cake is served in the drawing room beside the fire, or in the garden. No background music. Drawing room, dining room. Free Wi-Fi. 1½-acre garden (unsuitable for &). Parking. 1½ miles S of Warminster. 3 bedrooms (1 with private bathroom; plus self-catering cottage). Per room B&B £85–£139 (2-night min. stay on Sat). Supper £20.

WARTLING East Sussex
Map 2:E4
WARTLING PLACE, Herstmonceux, nr Hailsham, BN27 1RY. Tel 01323-832590, www.wartlingplace.co.uk. 'We were well looked after; all in all, a very pleasant stay.' Opposite a lovely church and a pub, Rowena and Barry Gittoes's tastefully furnished B&B is in a Grade II listed former rectory in a tiny village mentioned in the Domesday Book. The Georgian building stands in 'delightful' landscaped gardens on the edge of the Pevensey Levels nature reserve. Inside, there are interesting prints and pictures on the walls, and comfortable seating in

the large lounge. Copious breakfasts are served at a long mahogany table or can be taken in the room. An evening meal or late supper is available, by arrangement. No background music. Drawing room, dining room (honesty bar, CD-player). Free Wi-Fi. 3-acre garden. Parking. Children welcomed; dogs allowed in cottage suite. 4 bedrooms (plus 2-bedroom self-catering cottage; suitable for &). Per room B&B single £85–£95, double £125–£165.

WATERGATE BAY Cornwall
Map 1:D2

WATERGATE BAY, On the beach, TR8 4AA. Tel 01637-860543, www. watergatebay.co.uk. On a surfing beach, this large, extended hotel has plenty for families and those seeking outdoor activities. Mark Williams is the manager. There are organised games, evening supervision and entertainment for young guests; for the adventurous, the on-site Extreme Academy has courses ranging from waterskiing to power kiting. The leisure complex, Swim Club, has a 25-metre ocean-view infinity pool, fitness studio and treatment rooms (open to day members); a boardwalk leads to the beach. Inspired by the coast, bedrooms have dark wood flooring, bright colours and stripy fabrics; many face the sea. Chef Neil Haydock cooks European dishes in the dining room; less formal eating is in *The Living Space* with stunning coast views, or down at *The Beach Hut*. Children (special meals), and dogs (£15 per night charge) welcomed. Lounge, 3 restaurants; terrace, sun deck. Background music in restaurants. Free Wi-Fi. Indoor/outdoor pool. 69 bedrooms (family suites; 2 suitable

for &). Per room B&B £125–£285, D,B&B £160–£320.

WEDMORE Somerset
Map 1:B6

THE SWAN, Cheddar Road, BS28 4EQ. Tel 01934-710337, www.theswan wedmore.com. There are mismatched stools, 'eye-catching' design touches and neat, modern rooms at this 'smart', stylishly refurbished 18th-century beer house, today a popular village pub-with-rooms owned by the Draco Pub Company. It is managed by Natalie Patrick with 'welcoming, friendly staff'. Rooms are chicly decorated in soft neutrals and slate greys, with the latest gadgetry and 'super' organic toiletries; the bustling restaurant overlooks the sun terrace and the garden beyond. Chef Tom Blake (from the *River Cottage*) produces 'very good' food using Somerset produce and locally reared meat; breads and ice cream are home made. Bar (wood-burning stove), restaurant (closed Sun eve). Free Wi-Fi. Terrace; garden (wood-fired oven and barbecue). Function facilities. 'Eclectic' background music. Parking. Children welcomed. 6 bedrooms. Per room B&B £85–£120. Dinner from £28.

WEST LULWORTH Dorset
Map 2:E1

BINDON BOTTOM, Main Road, Lulworth Cove, BH20 5RL. Tel 01929-400256, www.bindonbottom.com. At the bottom of Bindon Hill, this stone-built Victorian country house (formerly *Graybank B&B*) has been completely revamped by owners Lisa and Clive Orchard. Cottage-style bedrooms have views over the garden, or across Hambury Tout and farmland hills;

there are many extras (suntan lotion, spare toothbrushes, a torch), along with local biscuits and snacks. Organic breakfasts, cooked by Clive Orchard, are ordered the night before; vegetarians and vegans are well catered for. Good walks in the area; walking guidebooks are available to borrow. No background music. Free Wi-Fi. DVD library. 5 bedrooms. Per room B&B £85–£105 (2-night stays preferred).

WESTON-SUPER-MARE Somerset
Map 1:B6

BEACHLANDS HOTEL, 17 Uphill Road North, BS23 4NG. Tel 01934-621401, www.beachlandshotel.com. At the southern end of Weston Bay, this recently refurbished hotel overlooks sand dunes and an 18-hole golf course. The beach and promenade are nearby. It is run in a cheerful fashion by owners Charles and Beverly Porter, with manager Stuart Merrick. Tranquil bedrooms are simply decorated; some have a veranda opening on to the secluded garden. Chef Matt Price's four-course, daily-changing menus are served in the dining room overlooking the garden. 4 lounges, bar, restaurant; private dining; background music. Free Wi-Fi. 10-metre indoor swimming pool, sauna. Garden. Civil wedding licence; function/conference facilities. Parking. Children welcomed (baby-listening service; high tea; swimming lessons by arrangement). 20 bedrooms (some on ground floor; some family rooms; 1 suitable for &). Per room B&B £92–£144.25, D,B&B £113.50–£182.75.

CHURCH HOUSE, 27 Kewstoke Road, BS22 9YD. Tel 01934-633185, www. churchhousekewstoke.co.uk. There are stunning views across the Bristol Channel and South Wales from this Georgian house by the village church. The former residence of Kewstoke vicars, it is now a friendly B&B run by Jane and Tony Chapman. Bedrooms are elegantly furnished, some in Provençal style. Home-made breakfasts have freshly baked bread, granola, farm eggs and Gloucester Old Spot sausages. Within walking distance of Sand Bay, a quiet, unspoilt beach; 2½ miles from Weston-super-Mare. Lounge, conservatory, breakfast room. Free Wi-Fi. Small garden. Dogs welcomed (£5 per day charge; not to be left unattended). 5 bedrooms. Per room B&B single £70, double £85.

WHEATHILL Shropshire
Map 3:C5

THE OLD RECTORY, Bridgnorth, WV16 6QT. Tel 01746-787209, www.theoldrectorywheathill.com. Guests are invited to bring their horses to Izzy Barnard's B&B, in a handsome Georgian house on a bridleway amid acres of riding country. Comfortable rooms (for humans) have hot-water bottles, bathrobes, sherry and a choice of bedding; afternoon tea with home-made scones and cake is offered on arrival. There are eggs from free-range hens at breakfast, along with jams and compotes made from garden fruit. A candlelit three-course dinner or light supper is available on request (BYO bottle). 7 miles E of Ludlow. Drawing room, dining room; sauna (in the cellar). Free Wi-Fi. Boot room. Loose boxes; tack room. No background music. Children, and dogs (£10 charge) by arrangement; horses welcomed (£15 charge; riding route maps). Resident dogs. 7-acre gardens (hens, ducks; ancient cedar tree). 3 bedrooms (1 with private bathroom). Per room B&B single £65–£105, double £80–£120. Dinner £30.

WHITSTABLE Kent
Map 2:D5

THE FRONT ROOMS, 9 Tower Parade, CT5 2BJ. Tel 01227-282132, www. thefrontrooms.co.uk. A modern photography gallery is an added attraction at Julie Thorne and Tom Sutherland's stylish B&B, in a restored Victorian town house a short stroll from the harbour. Painted in heritage whites, the airy rooms have a Victorian cast iron bed and complimentary minibar; Room 3 has a balcony. A continental breakfast (special diets catered for) is served in the gallery. Books, magazines, DVDs and board games are available to borrow; the hosts are happy to make recommendations for restaurants, walks and places to visit. Lounge/breakfast room/gallery. Background music. Free Wi-Fi. A short walk into town; bicycles for hire. 3 bedrooms (1 with private bathroom). Per room B&B £110–£140 (2-night min. stay at weekends).

WIGMORE Herefordshire
Map 3:C4

PEAR TREE FARM, HR6 9UR. Tel 01568-770140, www.peartree-farm.co.uk. On the outskirts of a small village with castle ruins, seven miles from Ludlow, Jill Fieldhouse and Steve Dawson's 17th-century stone-built farmhouse has charming bedrooms and romantic bathrooms with candles, bath oils and fluffy bathrobes. The hosts provide home-cooked dinners on Friday and Saturday evenings by arrangement, using local and free-range produce.

They offer a selection of wines, but guests may bring their own bottle (£6 corkage). Breakfast includes freshly squeezed orange juice, fruits from the garden, local yogurt and Steve's organic, home-baked bread. An early-morning tea or coffee tray is delivered to the room. Good walks from the doorstep. Sitting room (log fire, books and music), dining room. Free Wi-Fi. No background music. 2-acre garden. 2 resident dogs, 1 cat. 3 bedrooms (1 on ground floor). Per person B&B £52.50, D,B&B £90 (2-night min. stay). Closed Jan–Apr, except for house parties.

WILMSLOW Cheshire
Map 4:E3

KINGSLEY LODGE, 10 Hough Lane, SK9 2LQ. Tel 01625-441794, www. kingsleylodge.com. In a tranquil residential area, this 1950s Arts and Crafts house has been enlarged and remodelled into a luxurious B&B by Jeremy Levy and Cliff Thomson. It has been styled with flair: handcrafted antiques sit comfortably with more modern pieces; immaculate bedrooms have fresh flowers, scented candles and original works of art. There are a formal parterre, ponds, a pine wood and a seating deck with a water cascade in the large landscaped gardens. Lounge, breakfast room; patio. No background music. Free Wi-Fi (in public areas). Parking. Close to Manchester airport. 6 bedrooms. Per room B&B £110–£330.

WINCANTON Somerset
Map 2:D1

HOLBROOK HOUSE, BA9 8BS. Tel. 01963 824466, www.holbrookhouse.co.uk. An ancient cedar stands in the extensive grounds of this creeper-covered

Georgian country house and spa in the heart of the Wessex countryside. The historic building, once a gentleman's residence, is owned by John and Pat McGinley; son Darren manages. Large bedrooms are traditionally furnished with rich fabrics; all have views of the surrounding woodlands and pastures. Wincanton racecourse is nearby. British dishes are served in the *Cedar* restaurant; the bar overlooking the garden has light lunches. Popular with summer weddings. Lounges, bar, restaurant (closed lunch Mon–Thurs, dinner Sun). Background music in public areas. Free Wi-Fi. Private dining rooms. Civil wedding licence; business/function facilities. 20-acre grounds: lawns, streams, grass tennis court. Spa (indoor swimming pool, hot tub, sauna, steam room); treatment rooms; nail bar; health club (exercise classes). Children welcomed. 21 bedrooms (some in walled garden). Per room B&B £150–£220, D,B&B £230–£300.

WINCHESTER Hampshire
Map 2:D2
THE OLD VINE, 8 Great Minster Street, SO23 9HA. Tel 01962-854616, www.oldvinewinchester.com. There are elegant, well-furnished bedrooms at this small, design-conscious hotel in a Grade II listed 18th-century inn opposite the cathedral green. It is owned by Ashton Gray. Rooms have a mix of antique and modern furniture; there is a Nespresso coffee machine, and a fridge with fresh milk and complimentary soft drinks. Earplugs are supplied, 'but we were unaware of any bell noise [from the cathedral] within the hotel'. Hampshire produce is showcased in the oak-beamed restaurant, where an open fire burns in cool weather; the bar has real ales, a flower-filled patio and a bright conservatory. Bar ('easy listening' background music), restaurant, small patio. Free Wi-Fi. Children welcomed (no under-6s in restaurant and bar). Parking permits supplied for on-street parking. 5 bedrooms. Per person B&B £52.50–£155, D,B&B from £72.50.

THE WYKEHAM ARMS, 75 Kingsgate Street, SO23 9PE. Tel 01962-853834, www.wykehamarmswinchester.co.uk. Between the college and the cathedral, this 18th-century former coaching inn is managed by Jon and Monica Howard for Fullers Brewery. The characterful interior, much embellished with pictures, ale mugs and memorabilia, has cosy alcoves. Some bedrooms are above the pub, reached via a narrow staircase; others are in a 16th-century building opposite. Classic and modern pub dishes are served in the wood-panelled restaurant, which has old school desks as dining tables. 2 bars (local ales), 2 dining rooms, function room; small garden. Background music at breakfast. Free Wi-Fi (in public areas). Children over 12 welcomed. Parking. 14 bedrooms (7 in annexe). Per room B&B single £72, double £164–£184.

WINDERMERE Cumbria
Map 4: inset C2
CEDAR MANOR, Ambleside Road, LA23 1AX. Tel 015394-43192, www.cedarmanor.co.uk. Within easy walking distance of the lake and the village, Caroline and Jonathan Kaye's 19th-century hotel takes its name from the 200-year-old cedar tree in the walled gardens. The award-winning interior

has designer fabrics and handmade furniture. Some bedrooms have original arched windows, others a canopy or four-poster bed; a romantic, eco-friendly suite in the coach house has a lounge with a Juliet balcony, a full entertainment system and a luxurious bathroom. The restaurant focuses on seasonal, locally sourced produce; menus include a list of local suppliers. Lounge, dining room (light background music during meals). Free Wi-Fi. Small weddings. Children welcomed. 10 bedrooms (1 suite in coach house). Per room B&B £100–£350, D,B&B £179–£429 (2-night min. stay at weekends). Closed 6–23 Jan, 15–26 Dec.
25% DISCOUNT VOUCHERS

1 PARK ROAD, 1 Park Road, LA23 2AW. Tel 015394-42107, www.1parkroad.com. Hospitably run by Mary and Philip Burton, this small B&B, in a quiet area close to the centre of town, makes 'a great base'. It is a short walk from the lake. Formerly a gentleman's residence, it has retained the original stained-glass windows and staircase. Bedrooms have a DVD/CD-player and iPod docking station, a cafetière and fresh milk; the family room has a travel cot, books, crayons and pencils. Dinner is served on Friday and Saturday evenings; savoury platters (cheeses, cold meats, pâté, samosas) and home-made pies, served with wine or beer, are available throughout the week. Locally sourced Lake District produce at breakfast. Lounge (grand piano), dining room. Free Wi-Fi. Background music at breakfast. Picnic hampers/packed lunches, rucksacks available. Children and well-behaved dogs welcomed. Resident dog, Maggie. Parking.

6 bedrooms. Per room B&B £80–£110, D,B&B from £130 (2-night min. stay at weekends and bank holidays).
25% DISCOUNT VOUCHERS

WOODBRIDGE Suffolk
Map 2:C5

THE CROWN, The Thoroughfare, IP12 1AD. Tel 01394-384242, www.thecrownatwoodbridge.co.uk. A popular drop-in place for locals, this white-painted, 16th-century coaching inn (decorated with Nantucket overtones) is in the centre of a thriving market town near the Deben estuary. It is run by chef/patron Stephen David for the Suffolk-based TA Hotel Collection. Suspended from the ceiling, a wooden sailing skiff makes a striking feature over the chic, glass-roofed bar which has black granite and seasoned oak. Bright bedrooms are styled in neutral tones and shades of grey; modern lighting is 'excellent throughout'. Stephen David shares the modern European, brasserie-style cooking with Luke Bailey; meals are served in two informal dining rooms, at a communal table in the bar, or on sofas in front of the fire. Prosecco is available on draught alongside Suffolk brews. Fixed-price dinners available. Background music; monthly jazz evenings. Bars, 4 dining areas; courtyard garden. Free Wi-Fi. Private dining. Children welcomed. Parking. 10 bedrooms. Per room B&B £120–£180, D,B&B from £170.

WOODSTOCK Oxfordshire
Map 2:C2

THE FEATHERS, 16–20 Market Street, OX20 1SX. Tel 01993-812291, www.feathers.co.uk. 'Greatly enjoyed – the bedrooms were comfortable, the

food was excellent and, above all, the service was impeccable.' Occupying a row of buildings in a peaceful Cotswolds village near Blenheim Palace, this town house hotel dates in part from the 17th century. It was variously a sanatorium, a draper's, a butcher's and a number of cottages. Today, traditional features are offset with vibrant colours and bold wallpapers. Chef Kevin Barrett's English dishes ('rich and robust in winter, light and fresh in summer') are served in the wood-panelled dining room; light suppers and snacks are taken in the informal bar, which holds the Guinness World Record for having the largest number of varieties of gin (174 and growing). Breakfasts are 'excellent'. Pete Saunders is the manager. Study, *Courtyard* gin bar, restaurant. Jazz/'easy listening' background music. Free Wi-Fi. Function facilities. Picnic hampers. Children and dogs welcomed. 21 bedrooms (5 in adjacent town house; 1 suitable for &; 1 suite has private steam room). Per room B&B single (Mon–Thurs) £129–£159, double £199–£319. D,B&B from £207.
25% DISCOUNT VOUCHERS

WORCESTER Worcestershire
Map 3:C5
THE MANOR COACH HOUSE, Hindlip Lane, Hindlip, WR3 8SJ. Tel 01905-456457, www.manorcoachhouse.co.uk. In a semi-rural location two miles out of the city centre, Terry and Sylvia Smith's fine 1780s house sits in attractive gardens ('a bird lover's paradise'), where breakfast and tea can be enjoyed in fine weather. It has been recommended as a place to stay when walking the Worcester and Birmingham canal.

Simply furnished bedrooms are in a renovated outbuilding next to the main house. They are well equipped; one room has kitchenette facilities. Breakfast room. 1-acre garden. Free Wi-Fi. No background music. Parking. Children welcomed, by arrangement. 5 bedrooms (private courtyard; 2 family rooms; 1 suitable for &). Per person B&B single £55, double £40.

WROXTON Oxfordshire
Map 2:C2
WROXTON HOUSE HOTEL, Silver Street, OX15 6QB. Tel 01295-730777, www.bw-wroxtonhousehotel.co.uk. 'We were welcomed with strawberries and cream and Buck's Fizz – a nice touch.' On the edge of a picturesque village three miles west of Banbury, this 'exquisite' thatched-roof manor house, dating back to 1649, is ably run as a Best Western hotel by the Smith family. Sean Wilson is the manager. It has many original features (inglenook fireplace, oak beams) and characterful bedrooms; those in the new wing are more modern. Chef Steve Mason-Tocker's daily-changing modern British menus are praised. 'Good value.' 2 lounges (background music in one), bar, *1649* restaurant; terrace. Free Wi-Fi. 2 private function rooms. Civil wedding licence. Parking. Children welcomed. 32 bedrooms (7 on ground floor; 3 in adjoining cottage). Per room B&B £99–£132, D,B&B £151–£165 (2-night min. stay at weekends).

WYE Kent
Map 2:D5
THE WIFE OF BATH, 4 Upper Bridge Street, TN25 5AF. Tel 01233-812232, www.thewifeofbath.com. On the

edge of a pretty medieval village, this Victorian, bay-fronted roadside property houses a restaurant-with-rooms run by Mark Rankin and Vicky Hawkins. 'Well-appointed, immaculately clean' bedrooms have been smartly renovated; they retain original features such as wooden beams and a fireplace. Chef Robert Hymers serves interesting dishes in a pleasant dining room; breakfasts feature Kentish apple juice, local eggs, home-made granola, Greek yogurt and fresh berries. Traditional Sunday lunch (a whole joint is brought to the table for sharing); afternoon tea. Lounge, restaurant (closed Mon). Parking. Children welcomed. 5 bedrooms (2 in garden annexe). Per room B&B £75–£115. Dinner from £27.50.
25% DISCOUNT VOUCHERS

YORK North Yorkshire
Map 4:D4
BAR CONVENT, 17 Blossom Street, YO24 1AQ. Tel 01904-643238, www.bar-convent.org.uk. England's oldest active convent, this Grade I listed Georgian building has a 'magnificent' glass-roofed entrance hall. The simply decorated bedrooms have 'wickedly' comfortable beds; there is a library full of fascinating antique Catholic texts. 'Unlike any other hotel in which I have stayed.' By the historic city walls at Micklegate Bar, a five-minute walk to the centre. Communal self-catering facilities. Sitting rooms (on each floor, with TV), games room (small snooker table, board games); licensed café. Free Wi-Fi. Meeting rooms; museum; shop; 18th-century domed chapel (Catholic weddings); function facilities. Lift to 1st and 2nd floors. No background music. ½-acre garden. 19 bedrooms (14 with

nearby bathroom facilities; some suitable for &). Per room B&B (continental) single £36–£66, double £68–£94. 'Good-value' full English breakfast £4.50. Closed Sun; Easter; 18 Dec–18 Jan.

THE BLOOMSBURY, 127 Clifton, YO30 6BL. Tel 01904-634031, www.bloomsburyhotel.co.uk. Steve and Tricia Townsley are the 'courteous, very helpful' hosts at this B&B in a leafy neighbourhood close to Clifton Green; the Victorian house has recently been refurbished in traditional style. Bedrooms are 'fresh' and 'very quiet', with good lighting; 'excellent' breakfasts have fresh local produce and home-made preserves. On a bus route and within a mile of the city; guests can also reach the centre via a scenic river walk. Sitting room, dining room (optional background music); terrace. Free Wi-Fi. Flowery courtyard; 'secret garden'. Parking. Children welcomed. Resident dog. 6 bedrooms (1 on ground floor). Per person B&B £36.50–£50 (2-night min. stay on Sat). Closed 20 Dec–mid-Feb.
25% DISCOUNT VOUCHERS

DEAN COURT, Duncombe Place, YO1 7EF. Tel 01904-625082, www.deancourt-york.co.uk. In the city centre, this Best Western hotel is in a building constructed to house the clergy of the Minster. 'The pleasures are the friendliness and helpfulness of the staff, the bells ringing on one side from York Minster and the other from the Roman Catholic church, generally comfortable rooms, and good breakfasts.' The 'attractive' dining room has 'splendid' views over the west end of the Minster; *The Court* café/bistro, which has light meals and snacks, frequently has live

entertainment. Iain Weston is the new chef. 2 lounges, bar, *D.C.H.* restaurant (closed for lunch Mon–Fri), café/bistro. Free Wi-Fi. Background music. Civil wedding licence; conference facilities. Children welcomed (special menu). 37 bedrooms (3 suitable for ⅋). Per room B&B £115–£245; D,B&B £145–£305 (2-night min. stay).
25% DISCOUNT VOUCHERS

THE GRANGE, 1 Clifton, YO30 6AA. Tel 01904-644744, www.grangehotel. co.uk. Jeremy and Vivien Cassel's traditional hotel is in a Grade II listed Regency town house just outside the city walls. 'The service was excellent.' It has classically furnished bedrooms (some small), and two modern restaurants – *The Ivy* and the informal *Brasserie* – open to non-residents. Steven Hodgkinson is the manager; Mark Branklin recently joined as chef. Yorkshire breakfasts are 'very good, with a wide variety'. Lounge, 2 bars, *The Ivy* restaurant (dinners only Mon–Sat; Sun lunch; closed Sun eve), *Brasserie* (closed Sun lunch). Free Wi-Fi. Background music. Ramps. Civil wedding licence; function facilities. Limited parking on busy road. Children, and dogs (charge) welcomed. 36 bedrooms (some on ground floor). Per room B&B single from £79, double £140–£292. D,B&B from £109 per person.

SCOTLAND

ABERDEEN
Map 5:C3
ATHOLL HOTEL, 54 King's Gate, AB15 4YN. Tel 01224-323505, www.atholl-aberdeen.co.uk. In a residential area in the west of the city, this privately owned baronial-style hotel is popular with locals who pop in for drinks and snacks. Gordon Sinclair is now the manager. Simply furnished bedrooms have tartan blankets; some rooms are large enough to accommodate a family. The restaurant serves traditional Scottish fare cooked by Scott Craig (vegetarian options available); coffee and cake may be taken in front of an open fire in the lounge. A frequent bus goes to and from the city centre. Lounge, bar, restaurant; patio. No background music. Free Wi-Fi. Wedding/function facilities. Parking. Children welcomed. 34 bedrooms (some suitable for ⅋). Per room B&B £65–£155. Dinner £25.

ACHILTIBUIE Highland
Map 5:B1
SUMMER ISLES, by Ullapool, IV26 2YG. Tel 01854-622282, www.summerisles hotel.com. Reached by a single-track road north of Ullapool, this small hotel and restaurant is owned and managed by Terry and Irina Mackay (who also own *Castlebay Hotel*, Isle of Barra, below). A former fishing inn, it has spectacular views to the Summer Isles and the Hebrides; the 'pleasant, light and comfortable' lounge overlooks the sea. Accommodation is spread across the hotel and converted outbuildings; a three-bedroom cottage on the hillside is available out of season for self-catering. Alan White is the new chef this year: his modern Scottish dishes are served at 7.30 pm in the candlelit restaurant; the bar, popular with locals, has informal meals and a good selection of whiskies. The hotel has its own herd of Highland cattle and a fold of rare breed sheep. Bar (occasional live music), lounge

(pre-dinner canapés), restaurant, library. Free Wi-Fi. Children, and dogs (not in dining room or lounge) welcomed. 13 bedrooms (10 in annexe and cottage; 1 suitable for &). Per room B&B £155–£310, D,B&B £220–£320. Closed Nov–Apr.

25% DISCOUNT VOUCHERS

ARINAGOUR Argyll and Bute
Map 5:C1

COLL HOTEL, Isle of Coll, PA78 6SZ. Tel 01879-230334, www.collhotel.com. On a small Hebridean island, Kevin and Julie Oliphant's white-painted house stands in large gardens with views across a lovely bay to Staffa, Iona, Jura and the Treshnish Isles. The hotel is a lively hub for locals and visitors, who are drawn to the cosy bars, with their open fires in winter, and to the *Gannet* restaurant, where Julie Oliphant and chef Graham Griffiths use local fish and lobsters and island produce in their cooking. Guests are welcomed with tea or coffee and home-made shortbread on arrival; simply furnished bedrooms (four with sea views) have home-made biscuits, a book on birds and a glow-in-the-dark skyscope. No light pollution; astronomy workshops in the autumn and winter months. Complimentary pick-up from and return to the ferry pier. Lounge, 2 bars (darts, pool table), 2 restaurants. Free Wi-Fi. No background music. Garden (decking, plenty of seating; pétanque). Bicycles available to borrow (BYO helmet). Helipad. Children welcomed (special menu). 6 bedrooms. Per room B&B single £55–£65, double £100–£125. Dinner £20–£30 (house parties only at Christmas and New Year).

25% DISCOUNT VOUCHERS (Oct–Mar)

BALLYGRANT Argyll and Bute
Map 5:D1

KILMENY COUNTRY HOUSE, Isle of Islay, PA45 7QW. Tel 01496-840668, www.kilmeny.co.uk. On a working farm, this 19th-century house in an elevated position has 'spectacular views' over the Islay countryside. It is 'beautifully furnished and has a warm and homely feel'. 'Excellent' hosts Margaret and Blair Rozga offer tea and home-baked cakes, and 'make guests feel relaxed from the minute they arrive'. The 'exceptionally high-quality' dinners (Tues and Thurs only, by arrangement; BYO wine) include drinks and canapés before, and petits fours afterwards. Sitting room, sun room; garden. Free Wi-Fi. No background music. On the edge of a village, 4 miles from the ferry terminal at Port Askaig. Children over 6 welcomed. 5 bedrooms (2 on ground floor, with walk-in shower). Per room B&B £125–£155. Closed Nov–Mar.

BALQUHIDDER Stirling
Map 5:D2

MONACHYLE MHOR, Lochearnhead, FK19 8PQ. Tel 01877-384622, www.mhor.net. A four-mile track skirting Loch Voil in the Trossachs national park leads to this pink-painted 18th-century stone farmstead, where siblings Tom, Dick and Melanie Lewis run their restaurant-with-rooms. Handsomely decorated, bedrooms are furnished with a mix of antiques and modern furnishings and artwork; one room has twin slipper baths, another an Italian stone tub. Tom Lewis, the chef, serves a five-course table d'hôte menu. Freshly baked scones are available throughout the day. Sitting room, bar, conservatory restaurant (background music). Free Wi-Fi (in public areas only). Terrace, garden; pétanque; loch fishing. Wedding facilities. Children welcomed, dogs allowed (in 2 bedrooms; resident dog). 14 bedrooms (9 in courtyard buildings; some rooms are small). Per room B&B £195–£265, D,B&B £295–£365.

BOWMORE Argyll and Bute
Map 5:D1

HARBOUR INN AND RESTAURANT, The Square, Isle of Islay, PA43 7JR. Tel 01496-810330, www.harbour-inn.com. Refurbished by the Scott family, this old whitewashed inn by the harbour has been brought up to date with stylish bedrooms and a conservatory with views across Loch Indaal towards Jura. A peaceful lounge upstairs has books and games. Alex Moss cooks a seafood-strong menu; local beef, lamb and game are also available. Conservatory lounge (Hebridean afternoon tea), *Schooner* bar, restaurant (subdued background music); terrace, small garden. Free Wi-Fi. Complimentary use of nearby leisure centre with gym, pool and spa. Birdwatching tours arranged. Children over 10 welcomed. 7 bedrooms (plus 4 rooms in *The Inns Over-by*, a 'pebble's throw' from the main building). Per room B&B £135–£160, D,B&B £210–£235.

BRAE Shetland
Map 5: inset A2

BUSTA HOUSE, ZE2 9QN. Tel 01806-522506, www.bustahouse.com. In an idyllic setting on the shores of Busta Voe, this grand country house was built as a family home in 1588. Its long, curious history links a shipwreck, an illegitimate child, a ghost and a gallery

of gargoyles; it is today a busy, small hotel owned and run by Joe and Veronica Rocks. The house has a quirky layout, with lots of stairs. Bedrooms (slightly old-fashioned) are named after islands around the coast of mainland Shetland. A large lounge has a fire and a useful supply of guidebooks; the bar has local beers and around 160 malt whiskies. Chef Daniel Okroj's 'excellent' dishes, from a wide-ranging selection, are hearty in size. 2 lounges, bar/dining area, *Pitcairn* restaurant (background music). Free Wi-Fi; computer available. Garden. Children welcomed. Wedding facilities. 22 bedrooms. Per room B&B £115–£160. Dinner £21–£35.

BRODICK North Ayrshire
Map 5:E1

AUCHRANNIE HOUSE HOTEL, Isle of Arran, KA27 8BZ. Tel 01770-302234, www.auchrannie.co.uk. 'Everything you would expect in a country house.' In 'lovely' landscaped gardens, the Johnston family's child-friendly island enterprise includes a resort with two leisure clubs and two hotels. Throughout, 'everyone, from the owner to the staff, is on hand with a smile'. The original house (built in 1869) has modern bedrooms and 'plush lounges to relax in'. A complimentary bus service operates between the resort and the ferry terminal. Bar, 3 restaurants; spa (indoor pool, steam room, spa bath; gym). Free Wi-Fi. Background music. Parking. Children (play barn, external play and picnic area, library), and dogs welcomed. 28 bedrooms (plus accommodation in the modern spa resort, also 30 self-catering lodges). Per room B&B £169–£398. D,B&B £20 added per person.

CASTLEBAY Western Isles
Map 5: inset A1

CASTLEBAY HOTEL, Isle of Barra,
HS9 5XD. Tel 01871-810223, www.
castlebayhotel.com. On the most
southerly inhabited island in the Outer
Hebrides, this 'excellent' small hotel
perches above the village, and has
panoramic views of Castlebay, the
harbour and Kisimul Castle. It is well
located for the ferry from Oban. Terry
and Irina Mackay are the owners; the
hotel, managed by John Campbell, has
a friendly, relaxed ambience. Neatly
furnished rooms have tartan fabrics;
the sun lounge has a telescope for long-
distance views. In the restaurant, chef
Slawomir Pilarski's menus focus on
freshly landed fish and seafood. The
Mackays also own *Summer Isles*,
Achiltibuie (see above). Lounge, bar,
restaurant, conservatory/sun porch. Free
Wi-Fi. Background music; live music.
¼-acre garden. Children and dogs
welcomed. 15 bedrooms (4 family
rooms; 1 suitable for &). Per room B&B
£49–£170, D,B&B £74–£200 (2-night
min. stay at weekends).

CRAIGARD HOTEL, Isle of Barra,
HS9 5XD. Tel 01871-810200, www.
craigardhotel.co.uk. On a hillside
overlooking the bay, Julian Capewell
and Della Laflin's small hotel is in a
peaceful location with 'breathtaking
views' over Castlebay to Kisimul Castle,
Vatersay and the islands beyond. The
comfortable lounge has leather seating
and a TV; several of the snug, pretty
bedrooms have panoramic sea views.
Home-cooked food (specialities are
cockles, scallops and freshly landed fish)
is served in the popular restaurant.
Lounge, 2 bars (pool table; background

music), restaurant; terrace (panoramic
views). Free Wi-Fi; computer for guests'
use. Background TV/radio. Beach
airport 6 miles; town and ferry terminal
close by. Parking. Children welcomed
(not in public bar). 7 bedrooms. Per
person B&B £55–£120. Dinner £22.50.

DALKEITH Midlothian
Map 5:D2

THE SUN INN, Lothianbridge,
EH22 4TR. Tel 0131-663 2456,
www.thesuninnedinburgh.co.uk. Close
to the banks of the River Esk, this
gastropub-with-rooms is in a former
coaching inn, surrounded by five acres
of wooded grounds. It is run by
chef/proprietor Ian Minto with son
Craig, and other family members. The
charming public areas have hunting-
scene wallpaper, exposed stone walls
and log fires. Furnished with pieces
by local craftspeople, stylish, modern
bedrooms have DVDs, a Roberts radio
and home-made biscuits. The popular,
award-winning restaurant champions
local producers and brewers in its classic
pub fare; the covered courtyard has
barbecues and spritzers in the summer.
Edinburgh city centre is 20 mins'
drive away. Bar, restaurant (modern
background music); garden. Free Wi-Fi.
Parking. 5 bedrooms (1 suite with
copper bath). Per room B&B single
£70–£100, double £85–£150. Dinner
from £28. Closed 26 Dec and 1 Jan.

DORNOCH Highland
Map 5:B2

2 QUAIL, Castle Street, IV25 3SN.
Tel 01862-811811, www.2quail.com.
On a street of mellow stone houses, this
licensed B&B is run by golf enthusiasts
Michael and Kerensa Carr. It is within

easy reach of Royal Dornoch Golf Club, where Michael Carr, who trained at *The Ritz*, is executive chef. The family home is traditionally decorated with inherited furniture and antiques; bedrooms have a wood or iron bedstead. Breakfast is served in the tartan-carpeted dining room at an agreed time from 7 am ('for those with early tee times'). The beautiful stretch of sandy Dornoch beach is a short distance away. Lounge/library, dining room. Occasional background music. Free Wi-Fi. 'Babes in arms' and children over 10 welcomed. 3 bedrooms. Per room B&B from £80.

DUNDEE
Map 5:D3

DUNTRUNE HOUSE, Main Wing, Duntrune, DD4 0PJ. Tel 01382-350239, www.duntrunehouse.co.uk. Olwyn and Barrie Jack run their peaceful B&B in a restored 19th-century manor house surrounded by extensive garden and woodland, five miles north-east of Dundee. There are antiques, a stone staircase and, on colder evenings, a log fire in the sitting room; each of the elegant bedrooms has views over the gardens to Fife and beyond. Breakfast, taken communally at a large table, includes organic fruit and vegetables in season, grown in the grounds. Family history enthusiasts, the Jacks will help guests trace their ancestry in the local area. Sitting room, dining room. Free Wi-Fi. 8-acre garden. No background music. Parking. Children welcomed. Activity courses (painting, yoga, Bellyfit; sauna and beauty treatments) nearby. 3 bedrooms (1 on ground floor; plus a self-catering flat). Per person B&B £45–£50. Closed Nov–Mar.

EDINBURGH
Map 5:D2

THE BALMORAL, 1 Princes Street, EH2 2EQ. Tel 0131-556 2414, www.thebalmoralhotel.com. Next to Waverley station, this luxury hotel (Rocco Forte Hotels) is a grand Victorian edifice with a majestic clock tower. It is managed by Franck X Arnold. Rooms are decorated in a palette inspired by the Scottish moors, mists and heather; many of the understated modern bedrooms have views of the castle, the Scott monument and bustling Princes Street. In the sophisticated, *Michelin*-starred *number one* restaurant, chef Jeff Bland serves a six-course tasting menu; informal *Hadrian's*, which has an Art Deco-influenced interior, has brasserie dishes. Drawing room, bar, restaurant, brasserie. Wi-Fi (£15 charge; free if room is booked via the hotel's website). Background music. 15-metre indoor pool. Spa (treatment rooms, sauna, gym, exercise studio). Room service; 24-hour concierge. Wedding/conference facilities. Valet parking. Children welcomed. 188 bedrooms (3 suitable for &). Per room B&B £226–£425. Dinner £25–£28.

BROOKS HOTEL EDINBURGH, 70–72 Grove Street, EH3 8AP. Tel 0131-228 2323, www.brooksedinburgh.com. Andrew and Carla Brooks's latest venture (see *Brooks Guesthouse*, Bristol, main entry) is in a refurbished 1840s stone building close to the Edinburgh International Conference Centre, in the west end of the city. Contemporary, half-panelled bedrooms are simply decorated in pastel shades and a mix of modern and antique furniture; the lounge has an open fire and vintage leather seating. Weekly specials are available at breakfast, along with haggis and tattie scones. No evening meals. Susie Farley is the manager. Lounge (honesty bar), breakfast room; private dining room. Free Wi-Fi. Background music. Courtyard garden. Small conference facilities. Discounted parking nearby. Children welcomed. 46 bedrooms (some in annexe; 1 suitable for &). Per person B&B £55–£145.

94DR, 94 Dalkeith Road, EH16 5AF. Tel 0131-662 9265, www.94dr.com. Paul Lightfoot and John MacEwan have restored their Victorian town house B&B with verve. Contemporary rooms (Couture, Bespoke or Tailored) are decorated in muted greys with splashes of colour, and have panoramic views of the Salisbury Crags and Arthur's Seat, or over the walled gardens towards the Pentland hills. Home-made breakfasts, taken in the orangery, use organic local produce. Ten minutes by bus from the centre; bicycles are available to borrow. Lounge, drawing room, breakfast room (classical/jazz/'easy listening' background music). Free Wi-Fi. Walled garden. Children welcomed (books, DVDs, games, Xbox). Resident labradoodle, Molli. 6 bedrooms. Per person B&B £45–£80. 2-night min. stay on Sat in high season. Closed 5–20 Jan.

ONE ROYAL CIRCUS, EH3 6TL. Tel 0131-625 6669, www.oneroyalcircus. com. On a World Heritage-listed crescent in the heart of the elegant New Town, this chic, modern B&B is owned by Susan and Mike Gordon. The discreet entrance of the Georgian town house opens on to spacious, stylishly furnished public rooms; there are antique and modern pieces, vintage posters, a disco ball, a baby grand piano and, in the salon, original ceiling frescos dating from the 1820s. The best bedrooms overlook the private gardens; breakfast, in a diner-style kitchen, is cooked to order. Kitchen/breakfast room, lounge, drawing room (baby grand piano). Free Wi-Fi. Pool room (with Bonzini Babyfoot table), gym; key access to private gardens. Wedding facilities. Children welcomed (books, games; babysitting by arrangement). 5 bedrooms (plus a 1-bedroom apartment). Per room B&B from £178.

PRESTONFIELD, Priestfield Road, EH16 5UT. Tel 0131-225 7800, www.prestonfield.com. More is more at this extravagant hotel, in a grand Baroque home standing in 20 acres of private grounds by the Royal Holyrood Park. There are leather-panelled rooms, log fires, gilded furniture, a velvet-walled salon and black-kilted staff; seductive bedrooms, each with views over the parkland, have antiques, remarkable beds, and a bottle of chilled champagne on arrival. Visitors to *Rhubarb* restaurant called it 'an orgy for the eyes and senses; excellent food'. It is owned by James Thomson, who also owns *The Witchery by the Castle*, Edinburgh (see below). Restaurant, 2 drawing rooms, salon, whisky bar; 4 private dining rooms; background music. Free Wi-Fi. Terraces, 'Gothic' tea house. Lift. Parking. Wedding/ function facilities. Children and dogs welcomed. 23 bedrooms (5 suites; 1 suitable for &). Per room B&B £295– £375, D,B&B from £360.

THE SCOTSMAN, 20 North Bridge, EH1 1TR. Tel 0131-556 5565, www.thescotsmanhotel.co.uk. Occupying the former offices of the *Scotsman* newspaper, this luxury hotel has 'stylish accommodation and excellent staff'. Many features of the spectacular 1905 building have been preserved, such as oak panelling, ornate ceilings and an impressive Italian marble staircase. Well-equipped bedrooms have an Edinburgh Monopoly board game, *Scotsman* newspaper, Scottish shortbread and complimentary shoe-shine service; some superior rooms are 'enormous' and have an ornamental fireplace or a roll-top bath in a turret. Family rooms are available; children receive a welcome pack. Drawing room, breakfast room, bar/brasserie; lift, ramps. Free Wi-Fi. Background music. Cinema; health spa (16-metre swimming pool, sauna, gym, treatment rooms; juice bar, café). Wedding/conference facilities. 69 bedrooms (2 suitable for ♿). Per room B&B £175–£408.

SOUTHSIDE GUEST HOUSE, 8 Newington Road, EH9 1QS. Tel 0131-668 4422, www.southsideguesthouse.co.uk. In a terrace of Victorian houses, Franco and Lynne Galgani's 'friendly' B&B is near the Meadows and Holyrood Park, and has lovely views over Edinburgh. It is within easy walking distance of restaurants, pubs and shops; a bus-stop is nearby. Colourful, modern bedrooms have comfortable seating; one, with a four-poster bed, also has a fireplace and its own terrace. Breakfast includes vegetarian options, a daily special and Buck's Fizz. Breakfast room (light classical background music). Free Wi-Fi.

Limited parking. Children over 8 welcomed. 8 bedrooms. Per room B&B single from £65, double from £80.
25% DISCOUNT VOUCHERS

TIGERLILY, 125 George Street, EH2 4JN. Tel 0131-225 5005, www.tigerlilyedinburgh.co.uk. There are exuberant prints, beaded curtains and chic modern fireplaces in this stylish hotel, in a Georgian town house on a street popular for shopping and nights out. Bedrooms have organic fruit and fresh flowers; breakfast can be taken in the room. Downstairs, the lively bars have booths, revolving glitter balls and chandeliers; a cocktail trolley comes round to guests' tables. An international menu is served, day and night, in two glass-ceilinged courtyards. 2 bars (resident DJs), restaurant (background music); lift. Free Wi-Fi. Complimentary access to gym and pool, opposite. Children welcomed (cots; babysitting by arrangement). 33 bedrooms (some smoking). Per room B&B £210–£295.

20 ALBANY STREET, 20 Albany Street, EH1 3QB. Tel 0131-478 5386, www.20albanystreet.co.uk. In the heart of the city, Denise Walker welcomes guests to her elegantly furnished Georgian town house with tea, home-made cake and a wee dram of Highland malt whisky. Period bedrooms are spacious, with a large bed and bathroom; one has a freestanding roll-top bath. Served at a time to suit guests, sumptuous breakfasts have a seasonal fruit salad, freshly baked croissants, a full Scottish and a daily fish dish. Drawing room, dining room. Free Wi-Fi. Background music at breakfast.

Parking available (charge). Resident dog, Rolo. 3 bedrooms. Per room B&B £129–£179.

21212, 3 Royal Terrace, EH7 5AB. Tel 0845 22 21212, www.21212restaurant. co.uk. 'Practical for exploring the city', Paul Kitching and Katie O'Brien's award-winning restaurant-with-rooms is in a restored Grade A listed town house, at the end of a Georgian terrace. The glamorous drawing room has oversized windows and textured walls; on the upper floors, large, sleek bedrooms have an ample seating area, and views of the rear gardens or the city. Paul Kitching has a *Michelin* star for his modern French menus; in the restaurant, diners can watch him and his team of seven chefs at work in the open kitchen. Drawing room, restaurant (closed Sun, Mon); private dining rooms. Free Wi-Fi. Children over 5 welcomed. 4 bedrooms. Per room B&B £95–£325. Dinner from £48–£68. Closed 10 days in Jan; 10 days in summer.

THE WITCHERY BY THE CASTLE, Castlehill, EH1 2NF. Tel 0131-225 5613, www.thewitchery.com. At the gates of Edinburgh Castle, there are nooks and crannies, candlelit rooms and secret doors at this theatrical restaurant-with-suites in a collection of historic buildings dating to 1595. It is owned by James Thomson (see *Prestonfield*, above). Lavishly decorated with tapestries, antique velvet drapes and gold-laced brocade, Gothic-style accommodation is in two 16th- and 17th-century buildings overlooking the Royal Mile. A bottle of champagne is presented on arrival; in the morning, a breakfast hamper is delivered to the room. 2 restaurants:

The Witchery and *The Secret Garden* (Douglas Roberts is the chef; background music); terrace. 8 suites. Per room B&B £325–£350. Dinner £33.

ELGIN Moray
Map 5:C2
MANSION HOUSE HOTEL & COUNTRY CLUB, The Haugh, IV30 1AW. Tel 01343-548811, www.mansionhousehotel. co.uk. Along the Grampian Highland whisky trail, this country hotel in a 19th-century baronial mansion stands in extensive grounds on the banks of the River Lossie. Bedrooms have a large sleigh bed or four-poster. Chefs Barry Milne and Craig Keny use the hotel's home-grown organic fruit and vegetables in their modern dishes and Scottish favourites, served in the smart restaurant or in the less formal bistro. Piano lounge, bar, restaurant, bistro. Free Wi-Fi. Background music. Leisure club (indoor swimming pool, sauna, steam room; treatments; gym, snooker room). Room service. Wedding/function facilities. Parking. 23 bedrooms (some interconnecting). Per room B&B £154–£202, D,B&B £201–£246.

FORT WILLIAM Highland
Map 5:C1
THE LIME TREE, The Old Manse, Achintore Road, PH33 6RQ. Tel 01397-701806, www.limetreefortwilliam.co.uk. Near the town centre, this former manse has lovely views of Loch Linnhe and the hills beyond. It has been 'imaginatively' converted into an 'excellent' small hotel, restaurant and regional art gallery hosting exhibitions from touring national collections. The owner, David Wilson, is an artist; his 'exciting' work is displayed in both hotel

and gallery. Most of the modern rustic bedrooms have loch views; the cosy lounges have open fires. William MacDonald is the new chef in the award-winning restaurant, serving modern European food with a Scottish slant. 3 lounges ('books and guides to help guests plan their journeys'), restaurant (background music); gallery; garden with seating area. Free Wi-Fi. Drying room; bike storage. Children, and dogs (£5 charge) welcomed. 9 bedrooms (in main house and extension). Per room B&B £80–£120. Dinner £29.95.

GATESIDE Fife
Map 5:D2

EDENSHEAD STABLES, By Falkland, Cupar, KY14 7ST. Tel 01337-868500, www.edensheadstables.com. Gill and John Donald's restored pink-stone stable building sits in wooded grounds that lead down to the River Eden. B&B accommodation is in comfortable, traditionally furnished bedrooms; the sitting room has French doors that open on to a patio. Scottish breakfasts are taken communally around a large table. Lounge (magazines, guidebooks), dining room. No background music. Free Wi-Fi. 3-acre grounds. Golf, and cycle routes nearby; safe storage for equipment. Resident dogs. 3 bedrooms (all on ground floor). Per person B&B £48–£60 (2-night min. stay in summer). Dinner £30 (by arrangement, for groups of 4–6; BYO wine). Closed Dec–Mar.

GLASGOW
Map 5:D2

BLYTHSWOOD SQUARE HOTEL, 11 Blythswood Square, G2 4AD. Tel 0141-248 8888, www.blythswoodsquare.com.

'This place has style and class.' On a lovely garden square, this sleek, modern hotel (part of the Town House Collection) is in a Victorian building, the former clubhouse of the Royal Scottish Automobile Club. Thoughtfully decorated bedrooms ('contemporary, rich and stylish') have a marble bathroom; some superior rooms are large enough to accommodate a family. There are champagne afternoon teas in the salon; the vast ballroom is now an informal restaurant and lively cocktail bar. 'Great' breakfasts (lavish buffet; all hot dishes cooked to order). Salon, 3 bars, restaurant, private screening room. Free Wi-Fi. Background music. Lift. Spa (2 relaxation pools, treatment rooms, rasul mud chamber, relaxing lounge, café). Children (special menu), and dogs (in some bedrooms; £30 charge) welcomed. 100 bedrooms (some suitable for &). Per room £120–£300, D,B&B £149–£350.

15 GLASGOW, 15 Woodside Place, G3 7QL. Tel 0141-332 1263, www. 15glasgow.com. Warm, welcoming hosts Shane and Laura McKenzie have won a design award for their modern B&B in a restored Victorian town house. Original fireplaces, intricate cornicing, working wooden shutters, stained glass and oak panelling have been retained. Pared-down bedrooms, decorated in cool shades of silver, grey and caramel, are spacious and comfortable, with tall windows, high ceilings and mood lighting; Tunnock's teacakes are a welcome gesture. Breakfast is brought to the room at an arranged time. A short walk from the city centre; the University of Glasgow and museums are close by. Lounge (classical radio background music); garden. Free Wi-Fi. Parking. Children welcomed. 5 bedrooms. Per person B&B £50–£85 (min. 3-night stay for advance bookings).

GLENDEVON Perth and Kinross
Map 5:D2

THE TORMAUKIN HOTEL, FK14 7JY. Tel 01259-781252, www.tormaukin hotel.co.uk. In the Perthshire countryside, Dave and Lesley Morby have remodelled this 18th-century drovers' inn into a comfortable small hotel with characterful beamed rooms, wood and flagstone floors, and open fires. Run by friendly staff, the hotel has a relaxed atmosphere. Locally reared beef and lamb, and locally sourced fish and game feature on head chef Martin Cowan's menus. Lounge, bar, restaurant, conservatory; patio. Free Wi-Fi. Background music. Parking. Children welcomed; dogs by arrangement. 11 bedrooms (some on ground floor; 4 in adjoining stables block). Per person B&B £50–£80. Dinner £23.

GRANTOWN-ON-SPEY Highland
Map 5:C2

THE DULAIG, Seafield Avenue, PH26 3JF. Tel 01479-872065, www.thedulaig.com. 'It was so much fun!' 'Wonderful hosts' Carol and Gordon Bulloch run 'an utterly luxurious' B&B in their Edwardian house. It is in a rural position, a ten-minute walk from town. The Bullochs pay 'great attention to detail' and provide lots of 'small and thoughtful' touches; freshly baked treats are left daily by the 'cake fairy' in the spacious, elegant bedrooms. Extensive, 'top-of-the-line' breakfasts use home-grown produce and eggs from the Bullochs' flock of free-range Black Rock

hens. Packed lunches available. Drawing room (with Arts and Crafts furniture), dining room (quiet, contemporary Scottish background music), veranda; secluded garden (wildlife pond, summer house). Free Wi-Fi; computer available. Parking (garage for motorbikes and cycles). 3 bedrooms. Per person B&B £75–£120.

GULLANE East Lothian
Map 5:D3

GREYWALLS, Muirfield, EH31 2EG. Tel 01620-842144, www.greywalls.co.uk. 'Like a very elegant home', this hotel, in a crescent-shaped stone house designed by Sir Edwin Lutyens, has interiors faithful to the Edwardian period. A golfer's paradise, it overlooks the ninth and 18th holes of Muirfield golf course, and has 'spectacular' views to the Firth of Forth. *Chez Roux* chef Derek Johnstone cooks 'delicious, intensely flavoured' dishes mixing classic French techniques with Scottish produce; lighter meals are taken in the lounge or, in mild weather, on the terrace overlooking the garden. Bar/lounge, drawing room, library, *Chez Roux* restaurant (open to non-residents). No background music. Free Wi-Fi. Walled garden (hard and grass tennis courts, croquet lawn, putting green). Wedding/function facilities. Children, and dogs (in cottages only) welcomed. 23 bedrooms (some in cottage nearby). Per room B&B £85–£335. Dinner £29.50–£41. **25% DISCOUNT VOUCHERS**

INNERLEITHEN Scottish Borders
Map 5:E2

CADDON VIEW, 14 Pirn Road, EH44 6HH. Tel 01896-830208, www.caddonview.co.uk. In a handsome

Victorian house set in mature grounds, this comfortable guest house and licensed restaurant is run by Stephen and Lisa Davies, who provide tea and home-baked cake to arriving guests. With a country house atmosphere, the cosy drawing room has a log fire, books, maps, magazines and games. Some bedrooms have pretty floral wallpaper; others are more simply decorated. Stephen Davies's two- and three-course Scottish menus are served in the candlelit dining room (closed for dinner on Sun, Mon; room snacks available). Drawing room, dining room (background music). Free Wi-Fi (signal strength varies). Parking. Children, and dogs (in 1 bedroom; £5 per night charge) welcomed. Picnics available. Storage for bikes and fishing gear. 8 bedrooms (1 with private bathroom). Per room B&B £55–£110, D,B&B £75–£160.
25% DISCOUNT VOUCHERS

INVERKEILOR Angus
Map 5:D3

GORDON'S RESTAURANT WITH ROOMS, Main Street, by Arbroath, DD11 5RN. Tel 01241-830364, www.gordons restaurant.co.uk. 'A thoroughly enjoyable stay.' Gordon and Maria Watson's 1800s terraced house has been repainted in smart grey and white outside; the restaurant has been transformed with a light, modern look. 'First-rate' modern British dishes are cooked by Mr Watson and son Garry (the double-baked cheese soufflé is a highly praised favourite); Maria Watson is front-of-house. Between Montrose and Arbroath. Free Wi-Fi. No background music. Garden. Parking. Children welcomed (no under-9s at dinner). 5 bedrooms (1 in courtyard).

Per room B&B single £55–£85, double £110–£130. Dinner £48. Closed 2 weeks in Jan.

INVERNESS Highland
Map 5:C2

MOYNESS HOUSE, 6 Bruce Gardens, IV3 5EN. Tel 01463-233836, www. moyness.co.uk. 'Very handy for the town centre.' Jenny and Richard Jones run this comfortable B&B in their restored Victorian villa close to the River Ness. Formerly the home of Scottish Renaissance author Neil M Gunn, it has individually styled bedrooms named after Gunn's works. 'Good' breakfasts include Speyside haggis and whole kippers. The hands-on hosts are happy to advise on restaurants and things to do in the area. Sitting room, dining room; ⅓-acre garden. No background music. Free Wi-Fi. Parking. Children over 5 welcomed. 6 bedrooms (1 family room). Per room B&B £69–£110.

ROCPOOL RESERVE, 14 Culduthel Road, IV2 4AG. Tel 01463-240089, www. rocpool.com. In the city centre, this chic hotel has modern bedrooms, a cocktail bar and a light-filled restaurant serving 'honest country cooking'. Sleek rooms have a large bed, flat-screen TV, and Tassimo drinks machine for coffees and hot chocolates; some have a private balcony or outdoor hot tub. Norbert Lieder is the manager; sister hotels include *Inverlochy Castle*, Fort William (see main entry), and *Greywalls*, Gullane (see above). Children are well provided for with lots of activities: quad biking, go-carting, archery, ice skating and riding, all by arrangement. Lounge, r bar, *Chez Roux* restaurant; terrace.

In-room massages and treatments can be arranged. Background music. Free Wi-Fi. Wedding/conference facilities. Parking. Children welcomed (Xbox, board games, DVDs; kids' menu). 11 bedrooms (plus 3 serviced apartments in the West End). Per room B&B £185–£395, D,B&B £240–£450.

IONA Argyll and Bute
Map 5:D1

ARGYLL HOTEL, PA76 6SJ. Tel 01681-700334, www.argyllhoteliona.co.uk. In a 'lovely location', this hotel and restaurant, once a modest croft house, has been welcoming visitors for nearly 150 years. Today, it is owned and run in an 'unpretentious and laid-back' manner by two couples, Wendy and Rob MacManaway, and Katy and Dafydd Russon. There are fires in the lounge and the 'convivial' dining room, and books in public areas. 'Really delicious' seasonal meals are cooked by Richard Shwe on the 1920s Aga; marmalades, chutneys, scones, shortbreads and brownies are all home made (special diets catered for). 3 lounges, television room, dining room ('easy listening' background music; open to non-residents). No TV or phone in rooms. Free Wi-Fi (in dining room and sun lounge only). Organic kitchen garden. Children and dogs welcomed. 16 bedrooms (7 in annexe). Per room B&B (continental) £72–£201. Closed Nov–late Mar, except Dec when open on a B&B basis with a restricted menu.

KELSO Scottish Borders
Map 5:E3

THE CROSS KEYS, 36–37 The Square, TD5 7HL. Tel 01573-223303, www. cross-keys-hotel.co.uk. The 'delightful' Becattelli family have run this hotel, on a picturesque cobbled square in a historic Borders town, for more than 30 years. Bedrooms in the 18th-century coaching inn vary in size and shape; interconnecting family rooms, with a shared bathroom, are available. The *Oak Room* restaurant serves 'hearty' modern Scottish and continental dishes cooked by head chef Brian Crawford; good vegetarian choices. Popular with groups. Lounge, *No. 36* bar, restaurant, ballroom. Free Wi-Fi. Background music. Lift. Wedding/function/ conference facilities. Children welcomed. Parking. 26 bedrooms. Per person B&B £40–£75, D,B&B £55–£92.50.

KILLIN Perth and Kinross
Map 5:D2

ARDEONAIG HOTEL, South Loch Tay Side, FK21 8SU. Tel 01567-820400, www.ardeonaighotel.co.uk. Reached by a single-track road, this former drovers' inn on the shores of Loch Tay is today a comfortable, small hotel (now owned by Adamo Hotels) surrounded by farmland. Bedrooms, in a mix of modern and period design, are decorated in muted natural tones, with a large bed and luxurious linen. Some have views towards Loch Tay and Ben Lawers, others have a double-height ceiling and a peat-burning stove. In the grounds are cottage suites and round, heather-roofed shieling lodges with a large bed and freestanding bath. Chef David Maskell serves impressive six-course tasting menus. Rodney Doig is the manager. 7 miles E of Killin. Lounge, restaurant (closed Mon, Tues), bar/snug, library. Free Wi-Fi. Background music. Wine cellar. Terrace; gardens. Wedding/

function facilities. Children welcomed;
dogs by arrangement in some rooms.
No TV in the rooms. 17 bedrooms
(5 shieling lodges, 2 cottage suites). Per
person B&B £100–£250. Dinner £55.
Closed 5–24 Jan.

KINCLAVEN Perth and Kinross
Map 5:D2

BALLATHIE HOUSE, Stanley, nr Perth,
PH41 4QN. Tel 01250-883268,
www.ballathiehousehotel.com. 'Heartily
recommended', this 'impressive' 19th-
century house on the west bank of the
River Tay is owned by the Mulligan
family. It has long been associated with
salmon fishing; display cabinets in the
public rooms showcase 'monster' fishing
trophies. Public areas have old-style
grandeur, sporting prints and open fires;
country house-style bedrooms have
period features and views of the river
or surrounding countryside. Head chef
Scott Scorer's menus have trout and
salmon from local rivers, and home-
grown herbs; 'the dishes – especially the
desserts – were a work of art'. Jody
Marshall is the manager. Drawing
room, bar, restaurant; private dining
rooms. Free Wi-Fi. No background
music. Wedding/function facilities.
Children, and dogs (£20 charge)
welcomed. Golf, fishing, shooting,
sled-dog racing by arrangement.
53 bedrooms (16 in riverside building
reached via a lit garden pathway, 12 in
Sportsman's Lodge). Per person B&B
£110–£170, D,B&B from £150.

LOCHINVER Highland
Map 5:B1

INVER LODGE, Iolaire Road, IV27 4LU.
Tel 01571-844496, www.inverlodge.com.
Overlooking a quiet fishing village, this
purpose-built hotel on a hillside is
owned by Robin Vestey. It is managed
'with careful attention' by Nicholas
Gorton. Decorated in shades of heather,
bedrooms are named after nearby
mountains and lochs, and have
spectacular views; bathrooms have been
recently refurbished. The foyer lounge
has comfortable sofas, an open fire and
picture windows. In the *Chez Roux*
restaurant, chef Lee Pattie cooks French
country dishes with Scottish produce;
at breakfast, porridge may be served
with a dram of whisky. Lounge, bar,
restaurant. Free Wi-Fi. No background
music. Snooker table; sauna; massages
and treatments available. ½-acre
grounds (salmon and trout fishing).
Children and dogs welcomed. 21
bedrooms (some on ground floor). Per
room B&B £215–£320; D,B&B £290–
£390. Closed Nov–Mar.
25% DISCOUNT VOUCHER

LOCKERBIE Dumfries and Galloway
Map 5:E2

THE DRYFESDALE, Dryfebridge,
DG11 2SF. Tel 01576-202427, www.
dryfesdalehotel.co.uk. At the end of a
long drive bordered by beech trees, there
are 130 malt whiskies to be enjoyed in
front of a log fire at this Best Western
hotel. The 18th-century manse is
surrounded by acres of elevated
parkland; every bedroom has views of
the hotel grounds and surrounding
countryside. Lounge, bar, restaurant.
Free Wi-Fi. Background music.
Wedding/function/conference facilities.
5-acre grounds (9-hole putting green).
Children welcomed; dogs by
arrangement. 29 bedrooms (some in
garden suites, with French windows
opening on to a private patio; some

suitable for &). Per room B&B £125–£145, D,B&B £175–£190. Closed Christmas.

MELROSE Scottish Borders
Map 5:E3

BURT'S, Market Square, TD6 9PL. Tel 01896-822285, www.burtshotel.co.uk. 'An excellent, small, family-run hotel.' In a pretty market town on the banks of the River Tweed, the Henderson family's hotel, a listed 18th-century building, attracts anglers and other outdoorsy guests keen on the many rural pastimes – walking, cycling, stalking, game shooting – available on the doorstep. The restaurant specialises in local game and fish; the bar has a dedicated whisky menu and 'good' beer. 'Excellent mains and superb desserts.' 'Immaculate' bedrooms (some may be small) are decorated with tartan cushions and blankets. 2 lounges, bistro bar, restaurant (closed for lunch Mon–Fri); ¼-acre garden. Background music. Free Wi-Fi. Parking. Wedding/function facilities. Children welcomed (no under-8s in restaurant). Dogs by arrangement. 20 bedrooms (some recently refurbished). Per person B&B £65–£72, D,B&B from £90. Closed 6–13 Jan.

THE TOWNHOUSE, Market Square, TD6 9PQ. Tel 01896-822645, www. thetownhousemelrose.co.uk. 'It had no fault.' Across the town square from *Burt's* (see entry, above), this modern hotel is also owned by the Henderson family, who run it with 'extremely pleasant and helpful staff'. Individually designed bedrooms have striking wallpaper; new chef Phil White cooks Scottish fusion dishes in the brasserie or more formal restaurant. 'The food was

divine: the most tender venison, and sticky toffee pudding to die for!' Good walking nearby. Brasserie (background music), restaurant (table d'hôte menus), conservatory, patio/decked area; ramps. Free Wi-Fi. Wedding/function facilities. Children welcomed. 11 bedrooms (1 family room). Per room B&B single from £95, double £128–£145. D,B&B from £88 per person. Closed for 1 week mid-Jan.

MOFFAT Dumfries and Galloway
Map 5:E2

HARTFELL HOUSE & THE LIMETREE RESTAURANT, Hartfell Crescent, DG10 9AL. Tel 01683-220153, www. hartfellhouse.co.uk. On the edge of town, this listed Victorian home, built of local stone, is in a rural setting overlooking the surrounding hills. It is run as a guest house and restaurant by Robert Ash. Traditionally decorated rooms retain some original features, including ornate cornices and woodwork; bedrooms have a memory foam mattress, Freeview TV and Scottish biscuits. Chef Matt Seddon serves modern British dishes in the restaurant, which is popular with locals. There is home-baked bread at breakfast. Lounge, dining room (classical background music); garden. Free Wi-Fi (in public areas); computer available. Parking. Secure bike storage. Children welcomed. 7 bedrooms. Per person B&B £32.50–£37.50, D,B&B £55–£62.50. Closed 14–25 Oct, Christmas. Restaurant closed Sun, Mon.

OBAN Argyll and Bute
Map 5:D1

ALT NA CRAIG HOUSE, Glenmore Road, PA34 4PG. Tel 01631-564524, www.guesthouseinoban.com. In an elevated position with seascape views across Oban Bay to the isles of Mull, Kerrera and Lismore, this stone-built, turreted Victorian home is run as a B&B by Ina and Sandy MacArthur. Some of the attractive modern bedrooms have sea views; breakfast has plenty of Scottish options, including locally smoked haddock and Stornoway black pudding. 10 mins' walk into town. Breakfast room. No background music. Free Wi-Fi. 3-acre wooded grounds. Parking. 6 bedrooms. Per room B&B from £120.

PEEBLES Scottish Borders
Map 5:E2

CRINGLETIE HOUSE, off Edinburgh Road, EH45 8PL. Tel 01721-725750, www.cringletie.com. There is charm here in spades, from the service bells in each public room, to the house's own tartan, displayed in the hall and staircase, to the 400-year-old yew hedge, reputed to be the oldest in Scotland. Standing in extensive grounds with well-tended lawns, mature woodland, grazing sheep and a walled garden, this hotel, in a turreted, pink-stone Victorian baronial mansion, is owned by Jacob and Johanna van Houdt. Vivienne Bardoulet is the manager. Her husband, chef Patrick Bardoulet, serves two tasting menus under the frescoed ceiling in the *Sutherland* restaurant; log fires burn in the lounge, where afternoon tea can be taken. Individually decorated bedrooms have views of the hills beyond. In-room spa and beauty treatments are available. 2 sitting rooms, library, bar, restaurant (background music). Free Wi-Fi. Lift. 28-acre grounds: river, waterfall, dovecote, sculptures; vegetable patch, orchard; outdoor chess, pétanque, pitch and putt;

fishing. Wedding/conference facilities. Children and dogs welcomed. 13 bedrooms (1 suitable for &). Per room B&B from £99, D,B&B from £159.
25% DISCOUNT VOUCHERS

PERTH Perth and Kinross
Map 5:D2

THE PARKLANDS, 2 St Leonard's Bank, PH2 8EB. Tel 01738-622451, www.theparklandshotel.com. Overlooking South Inch Park, and convenient for the station and town, this hotel, in a Victorian stone-built house, has been run for ten years by Penny and Scott Edwards. At its heart are its two restaurants, *63@Parklands* and the informal *No. 1 The Bank Bistro*, both focused on seasonal Perthshire produce. Contemporary interiors have abstract art, feature wallpaper and brightly upholstered armchairs; simple bedrooms are enlivened by colourful fabrics. Lounge, bar, 2 restaurants (overseen by executive chef Graeme Pallister), private dining room; light background music. Free Wi-Fi. Terrace (alfresco dining); garden leading to park. Wedding/ function facilities. Parking. Dogs welcomed. 15 bedrooms (4 on ground floor). Per person B&B £54.50–£89.50, D,B&B £65.50–£97.50.
25% DISCOUNT VOUCHERS

SUNBANK HOUSE, 50 Dundee Road, PH2 7BA. Tel 01738-624882, www.sunbankhouse.com. Georgina and Remo Zane's traditionally furnished Victorian house is set in large landscaped gardens overlooking the River Tay and the city. Mr Zane cooks uncomplicated à la carte dinners, often with an Italian influence (bookings advised); sandwiches and snacks are served till late in the lounge. Packed lunches and picnics are available on request. A short walk from the centre. Lounge/bar, restaurant (light background music); terrace; garden. Free Wi-Fi. Parking. Wedding/ function facilities. Children welcomed. 9 bedrooms (some on ground floor; 2 suitable for ♿). Per person B&B £45–£79, D,B&B £70–£99.

PITLOCHRY Perth and Kinross
Map 5:D2

EAST HAUGH HOUSE, by Pitlochry, PH16 5TE. Tel 01796-473121, www.easthaugh.co.uk. Outdoor types have plenty to occupy them at the McGown family's small hotel, a turreted stone house set in two acres of gardens in highland Perthshire. There are salmon and trout fly-fishing on the River Tay (the fishing lodge has a barbecue and cooking facilities); stalking and shooting on nearby estates is regularly arranged. In the style of a modern sporting lodge, charming bedrooms are decorated in tartan and toile de Jouy; one has a fireplace. Chef/proprietor Neil McGown's menus feature fish and game in season (often caught by McGown himself). Lounge, bar, restaurant (background jazz); patio; ramps. Free Wi-Fi. 2-acre grounds; river beat. Wedding/business facilities. Parking. Children welcomed; dogs by arrangement. 13 bedrooms (2 suitable for ♿; 5 in a converted 'bothy' beside the hotel), plus 2 self-catering cottages. Per room B&B £118–£238; D,B&B £148–£268. Closed Christmas.

PINE TREES, Strathview Terrace, PH16 5QR. Tel 01796-472121, www. pinetreeshotel.co.uk. 'We thoroughly enjoyed our stay.' Valerie and Robert Kerr's Victorian mansion on a hill is set in peaceful woodland, with roe deer and red squirrels amid pine trees. It is within walking distance of the town. Public areas have cosy seating areas, half-panelled walls and an open log fire; comfortable bedrooms are traditionally furnished. 2 lounges, bar, restaurant (Cristian Cojocaru's cooking has a Scottish influence; soft background music). Free Wi-Fi (in lounge only). 7-acre grounds. Parking. ¼ mile N of town. 23 bedrooms (3 in annexe). Dogs welcomed (charge). Per room B&B from £126, D,B&B from £166.

TORRDARACH HOUSE, Golf Course Road, PH16 5AU. Tel 01796-472136, www.torrdarach.co.uk. 'Super friendly and extremely helpful', Louise and Struan Lothian run their 'charming' B&B in a raspberry-red house built in 1901. A stream runs through the wooded grounds thick with beech, Noble fir and Scots pine trees; views over the gardens and the Perthshire Highlands are 'astounding'. Immaculately decorated rooms have a blend of modern furniture and antiques, with original contemporary art on the walls; a new bedroom and conservatory breakfast room were recently added. A pre-loaded iPad for guests' use has subscriptions to *The Times* and *The Sunday Times*. 'Excellent' breakfasts include home-made marmalade, fruit compotes and granola; porridge with a dash of whisky; and home-smoked salmon. Sitting room, breakfast room; comprehensive bar service. Free Wi-Fi. No background music. 1-acre garden. Parking, bicycle storage. Children welcomed. 7 bedrooms (1 in 'bothy' behind the house). Per room B&B £88–£98. 2-night min. stay on Sat. Closed Nov–Mar.

PORT APPIN Argyll and Bute
Map 5:D1

THE PIERHOUSE, PA38 4DE. Tel 01631-730302, www.pierhousehotel.co.uk. On the shores of Loch Linnhe, this squat, curving structure, the 19th-century pier master's residence, has been converted into a relaxed hotel and restaurant run by Nick and Nikki Horne. Contemporary rooms, decorated in neutral tones, are in a modern, purpose-built block; several have views of the islands of Lismore and Shuna, and the Morvern peninsula beyond. The restaurant overlooks the original pier (the Lismore ferry still makes regular trips); menus feature seafood, game and meat, all locally sourced. *Ferry* bar, snug, restaurant (Tim Morris is chef); terrace. Free Wi-Fi. Celtic and 'easy listening' background music. Sauna; treatments available. Children (special menu), and dogs welcomed. Parking. Visitor moorings. Wedding facilities. 12 bedrooms. Per room B&B £105–£165, D,B&B £175–£235.

PORTREE Highland
Map 5:C1

CUILLIN HILLS HOTEL, Isle of Skye, IV51 9QU. Tel 01478-612003, www.cuillinhills-hotel-skye.co.uk. Standing in 15 acres of mature grounds, this privately owned hotel, in a Victorian hunting lodge, has views over Portree Bay, the Sound of Raasay and the Cuillin Mountain range. It is a ten-minute walk into town. Contemporary bedrooms have shortbread and fresh fruit; front-facing rooms have sea views. *The View* restaurant serves modern dishes, including much seafood; the malt bar

has more than 130 malt whiskies. Drawing room, restaurant, bar; background music. Free Wi-Fi. Parking. Wedding facilities. Children welcomed. 29 bedrooms (3 on ground floor; 7 in annexe; 1 suitable for ♿). Per room B&B £210–£310, D,B&B £280–£380.

ST ANDREWS Fife
Map 5:D3

RUFFLETS, Strathkinness Low Road, KY16 9TX. Tel 01334-472594, www.rufflets.co.uk. Originally built for the widow of a Dundee jute baron, this creeper-covered 1920s turreted mansion is now a 'beautifully furnished' hotel owned by Ann Murray-Smith. Stephen Owen is the manager. Rooms are decorated in a mix of antiques with contemporary fabrics and wallpaper; there are roaring fires in the drawing room and lounge. Chef David Kinnes offers a daily changing table d'hôte menu in the elegant *Terrace* restaurant, with plenty of choice; pastas, ice creams and sorbets are all made in house. Drawing room, library, music room bar, restaurant (background music). Free Wi-Fi. 10-acre gardens. 1 mile from the centre. Wedding/function facilities. Children and dogs welcomed. 24 bedrooms (3 in Gatehouse; 2 in Lodge; 1 suitable for ♿), plus 3 self-catering cottages. Per room B&B £150–£350, D,B&B £210–£410.

SANQUHAR Dumfries and Galloway
Map 5:E2

BLACKADDIE HOUSE, Blackaddie Road, DG4 6JJ. Tel 01659-50270, www.blackaddiehotel.co.uk. The River Nith runs past the end of the large garden of Jane and Ian McAndrew's traditionally furnished 16th-century manse, in a 'picturesque' setting on the edge of a village. Mr McAndrew serves 'very good food' in the award-winning restaurant; his daily changing modern menus use Scottish produce wherever possible. Bar, library, conservatory. Free Wi-Fi (on ground floor only). 'Easy listening' background music. 2-acre garden. Parking. Wedding/function facilities. Cookery school. Fishing and photography breaks. Children and dogs welcomed. On the Southern Upland Way; good riverbank walks. 8 bedrooms (plus 3 adjacent self-catering stone lodges). Per room B&B single £70–£75, double £100–£190. D,B&B £89–£147 per person. **25% DISCOUNT VOUCHERS**

SCOURIE Highland
Map 5:B2

EDDRACHILLES HOTEL, Badcall Bay, IV27 4TH. Tel 01971-502080, www. eddrachilles.com. At the head of Badcall Bay, Isabelle and Richard Flannery's relaxing hotel is in a refurbished 18th-century manse, in 'lovely, extensive grounds along the seashore'. 'Well-equipped' bedrooms are traditionally furnished. There are good views from the conservatory restaurant, where Isabelle Flannery cooks seafood from the bay with a French touch; a smokehouse in the grounds provides the restaurant with smoked fish and meats. Vegetarian visitors were 'impressed with the food, specially prepared for us'. Reception, breakfast room, restaurant (extensive wine list), bar (over 100 single malt whiskies); classical background music. Free Wi-Fi; computer available. 4-acre garden. Parking. Children welcomed (high tea for under-6s). 11 bedrooms. Per person B&B £52–£55, D,B&B £70–£73. Closed Oct–Mar.

SKEABOST BRIDGE Highland
Map 5:C1

THE SPOONS, 75 Aird Bernisdale, Isle of Skye, IV51 9NU. Tel 01470-532217, www.thespoonsonskye.com. 'Our fourth visit and we love it.' On a working croft overlooking Loch Snizort, 'perfect hosts' Marie and Ian Lewis have decorated their stylish B&B in muted earth tones and with original works by local artists; bedrooms have cashmere and sheepskin throws, a DVD/CD-player and a Nespresso coffee machine. 'Delicious', lavish breakfasts, taken communally, include home-baked bread, home-made granola, locally smoked fish, and freshly laid eggs from the house's own hens. Afternoon tea has home-baked treats. Good walks from the door. Sitting room (wood-burning stove), dining room. Free Wi-Fi. 8-acre grounds. Children over 10 welcomed. 3 bedrooms (1 on ground floor). Per person B&B £70–£80.

SLEAT Highland
Map 5:C1

DUISDALE HOUSE, Isle of Skye, IV43 8QW. Tel 01471-833202, www. duisdale.com. Decorated with bold prints and deep colours, this small hotel occupies a Victorian building in extensive gardens and woodland. It is owned by Anne Gracie and Ken Gunn, proprietors of nearby *Toravaig House* (see main entry). Stylish, modern bedrooms (several with a four-poster bed) have garden or sea views. Head chef David Allan uses local produce from Skye and the Highlands in his seasonal menus; afternoon tea is taken in front of the open fire in the lounge. Guests may book days out on the hotel's luxury yacht, with lunch and champagne included (whales, dolphins, seals and seabirds optional). Lounge, bar, restaurant, conservatory. Background music. Free Wi-Fi. 35-acre grounds (10-person garden hot tub). Wedding facilities. Children welcomed. 18 bedrooms (2 family rooms; 1 garden suite suitable for ♿). Per person B&B £65–£160, D,B&B £89–£205.

SPEAN BRIDGE Highland
Map 5:C2
SMIDDY HOUSE, Roy Bridge Road, PH34 4EU. Tel 01397-712335, www.smiddyhouse.com. 'A very special treat.' Robert Bryson and Glen Russell's 'immaculate and beautifully decorated' restaurant-with-rooms is in a village along the scenic West Highland rail route. 'Imaginative and delicious' dinners use much Scottish produce, including scallops from the Island of Mull, salmon from Wester Ross and Highland game; there are 'excellent' vegetarian options. Guests are welcomed with afternoon tea in the garden room, or sherry and home-made shortbread later in the evening. Scottish breakfasts. Golf, mountain bike trails nearby. Garden room, *Russell's* restaurant (booking essential; closed some days Nov–Mar). Free Wi-Fi. Classical background music. Parking. 4 bedrooms (plus self-catering accommodation in adjacent building, *The Old Smiddy*). Per room B&B £85–£115, D,B&B £150–£175.

STIRLING
Map 5:D2
POWIS HOUSE, FK9 5PS. Tel 01786-460231, www.powishouse.co.uk. Beneath the Ochil Hills, this 18th-century mansion set in mature ten-acre grounds has been restored by owners Jane and Colin Kilgour. Neat bedrooms have a Georgian fireplace, polished flooring and handmade Harris Tweed curtains and bed throws; home-made Florentines are an extra treat. Colin Kilgour's four-course dinners (cooked by arrangement) are taken communally in an elegant dining room; they may include home-reared lamb, garden vegetables and venison from locally stalked deer. Breakfast has eggs from the Kilgours' own hens. 4 miles NE of town. Sitting room (open fire, board games, DVDs), dining room. Free Wi-Fi. No background music. Terrace; garden (ha-ha; listed shafted stone sundial). Parking. Children welcomed. 3 bedrooms (plus 2 gypsy caravans and a shepherd's hut in the grounds). Per room B&B £90–£100, D,B&B £140–£150.

STRACHUR Argyll and Bute
Map 5:D1
THE CREGGANS INN, PA27 8BX. Tel 01369-860279, www.creggans-inn.co.uk. 'Lovely place, lovely people.' In a 'fantastic location' on the shores of Loch Fyne, this white-painted inn, run by Gill and Archie MacLellan, has simply decorated, pretty bedrooms with garden or loch views. The 'deservedly popular' bistro and restaurant provide 'excellent' food. Books and binoculars are available to borrow in the lounge, and there is a handsome rocking horse for younger visitors. Two moorings are available to guests arriving by boat. 2 lounges, bar/bistro ('easy listening' background music), restaurant; 2-acre garden. Free Wi-Fi. Wedding/function facilities. Children and dogs welcomed. Resident dog, Hector. 14 bedrooms. Per person B&B £50–£110, D,B&B £80–£140.
25% DISCOUNT VOUCHERS

STRATHYRE Perth and Kinross
Map 5:D2

AIRLIE HOUSE, Main Street, nr
Callendar, FK18 8NA. Tel 01877-
384247, www.airliehouse.co.uk. In the
Trossachs and Breadalbane area of
Scotland's first national park, where the
Highlands and Lowlands meet, Jacquie
and Ray Hill run this small B&B in
their early 1900s Scottish villa. It is
surrounded by countryside and hills;
most bedrooms have views of Ben
Sheann or the hillside beyond the
river. The Rob Roy Way is nearby.
Sitting room (log fires in winter), dining
room, drying room. Free Wi-Fi.
Background music. Parking. Children
welcomed; 'well-behaved' dogs by
arrangement. Resident dog, Poppy.
4 bedrooms (3 with views; 1 wheelchair-
friendly). Per room B&B single £45,
double from £68.

TARBERT Western Isles
Map 5:B1

HOTEL HEBRIDES, Pier Road,
HS3 3DG. Tel 01859-502364, www.
hotel-hebrides.com. By a pier in a small
ferry port, this modern hotel has bright,
well-equipped rooms and a lively bar.
It is run by owners Angus and Chirsty
Macleod. 'Light and airy', the *Pierhouse*
restaurant has an informal atmosphere.
The hotel is near the white sandy beach
at Luskentyre Bay and is well placed for
touring the Western Isles; boat trips can
be taken to St Kilda and other islands.
Mote bar (open for lunch and dinner),
restaurant (background music; closed
Oct–Mar). Free Wi-Fi. Small
conference facilities. Parking. Children
welcomed (special menu). 21 bedrooms
(some small). Per person B&B single
£50–£75, double £65–£80. Dinner £40.

TAYNUILT Argyll and Bute
Map 5:D1

ROINEABHAL COUNTRY HOUSE,
Kilchrenan, PA35 1HD. Tel 01866-
833207, www.roineabhal.com. Roger
and Maria Soep run this remote,
thoughtfully decorated country guest
house in the wild glens of Argyll, close
to Loch Awe. It is well placed for visits
to Inveraray, Glencoe, Fort William and
Kintyre; from the nearby port of Oban,
ferries offer transport to Skye, Mull,
Iona and the outer islands. Tranquil,
individually styled bedrooms, all with
good views, have fresh flowers and
home-made shortbread. Breakfast
includes locally smoked kippers,
porridge and home-made bread; light
supper platters of Scottish produce are
available, by arrangement. Lounge,
dining room, covered veranda; 2-acre
garden. Free Wi-Fi. No background
music. Ramp. Children and pets
welcomed. 18 miles E of Oban. 3
bedrooms (1 on ground floor suitable
for &). Per person B&B £50–£75. Closed
Nov–Easter.

TOBERMORY Argyll and Bute
Map 5:D1

THE TOBERMORY HOTEL, Main Street,
PA75 6NT. Tel 01688-302091, www.
thetobermoryhotel.com. In a row of
colourful converted fishermen's cottages
on the harbour front, Ian and Andi
Stevens run a small hotel with
comfortable lounges and simple, cosy
bedrooms (some with a window seat for
gazing over the bay). There is home-
made granola and local smoked fish at
breakfast; dinner, cooked by Mull native
Helen Swinbanks, is made with island
produce. Packed lunches are available
(home-made brownies tied with a tartan

ribbon make for a nice touch). 2 lounges, bar, restaurant (closed Mon). Free Wi-Fi. Background music. Maps, guide books and field guides; drying facilities. Wedding/conference facilities. Children and dogs welcomed. 16 bedrooms (most with sea view; 1 suitable for ♿). Per room B&B single £40–£65, double £70–£128. Dinner £29.50. Closed 7 Nov–25 Mar.

TONGUE Highland
Map 5:B2

THE TONGUE HOTEL, IV27 4XD. Tel 01847-611206, www.tonguehotel.co.uk. A former Victorian sporting lodge, this small hotel, in a sleepy coastal village beneath Ben Loyal, is run by Lorraine and David Hook with a team of local staff. It has original wood panelling, antique furniture, paintings, and views over the Kyle of Tongue. With seascape and landscape views, bedrooms have fruits, sweets and a decanter of sherry; many also retain an old fireplace or marble washstand. Simple Scottish fare is served in the restaurant, beside a cosy fire; breakfast has home-made compotes, granola and muesli, and porridge with cream and heather honey. Bar, restaurant; therapy room. Free Wi-Fi (in public areas only). Background music. Wedding facilities. Children welcomed. 19 bedrooms. Per person B&B £45–£140; D,B&B £82–£157.50.

UIG Western Isles
Map 5:B1

AUBERGE CARNISH, 5 Carnish, HS2 9EX. Tel 01851-672459, www. aubergecarnish.co.uk. The cheery turquoise door of Richard and Jo-Ann Leparoux's purpose-built beachside guest house matches the colour of the ocean. It is on a working croft perched above Uig Sands; views follow the water and sandy beach towards the hills. Modern bedrooms are styled in calming natural shades and have original local artwork; the residents' lounge has a wood-burning stove. In a restaurant filled with natural light, Mr Leparoux serves 'Franco-Hebridean' dishes that feature local ingredients in season (dietary requirements may be catered for). Breakfast has home-baked bread and home-made marmalade; guests may take their morning coffee on the decked terrace. Trips and day cruises to St Kilda. Dining room (open to non-residents), lounge (jazz/classical background music); patio. Free Wi-Fi. 4 bedrooms (1 suitable for ♿; plus 1-bedroom self-catering cottage). Per person B&B £65–£75, D,B&B £100–£110. Closed Dec–Jan.

ULLAPOOL Highland
Map 5:B2

RIVERVIEW, 2 Castle Terrace, IV26 2XD. Tel 01854-612019, www.riverviewullapool.co.uk. Nadine Farquhar's small, good-value B&B is in a modern house in a quiet residential area close to the harbour, shops, pubs and restaurants. There are DVDs and board games in the lounge, and a chocolate on the pillow at night; breakfast is a hearty affair served at a time to suit each visitor (vegetarians catered for). A microwave, crockery and cutlery are made available to guests; packed lunches on request. Open-plan lounge/dining room/library. Free Wi-Fi. Drying facilities. Complimentary use of leisure centre with pool. Off-street parking. 3 bedrooms. Per person B&B £35. Closed Nov–Jan and for Loopallu (Sept).

THE SHEILING, Garve Road, IV26 2SX. Tel 01854-612947, www.thesheiling ullapool.co.uk. On the edge of the village, Iain and Lesley MacDonald's comfortable, modern B&B has lawns sweeping down to Loch Broom. 'Spacious' bedrooms have complimentary sherry and sweets; an open fire burns in the lounge, where guests are provided with books, games, magazines, newspapers and a computer. Breakfast, served in a bright room overlooking the loch and the mountains beyond, has local sausages, and porridge with honey and cream. The town centre is ten mins' walk away; five mins to the ferry for the Hebrides. Sitting room, dining room; Sportsman's Lodge (guest laundry, drying room; sauna, shower, bike store). No background music. Free Wi-Fi (computer available). 1-acre garden; patio; fishing permits. Parking. Children, and dogs (by arrangement) welcomed. 6 bedrooms (2 on ground floor). Per person B&B £30–£42.50.

WALES

ABERGELE Conwy
Map 3:A3
THE KINMEL ARMS, St George, LL22 9BP. Tel 01745-832207, www. thekinmelarms.co.uk. 'A delightful hideaway.' In the Elwy valley, Lynn and Tim Watson run their Victorian inn on the edge of the Kinmel estate with 'an eye to detail and individuality'. Lofty rooms have an oak or maple super-king-size bed, paintings inspired by the North Wales landscape, a balcony or patio, and a limestone bathroom. A continental breakfast is served in the room. At the heart of the inn is a busy restaurant with à la carte evening menus

devised by Wesley Oakley; lunches are informal, brasserie-style. Background music. Bar (real ales, wood-burning stove), restaurant (closed Sun, Mon). Free Wi-Fi. Small garden. Parking. 4 bedrooms. Per room B&B £115–£175. Dinner from £35.

CARDIFF Cardiff
Map 3:E4
HOTEL ONE HUNDRED, 100 Newport Road, CF24 1DG. Tel 07916-888423, www.hotelonehundred.com. Close to the city centre, with shops, pubs and good eating places just around the corner, this small budget hotel in a renovated Victorian town house is run by brother-and-sister team Charlie and Abi Prothero. There are newspapers, games, books and a flat-screen TV in the lounge; minimalist bedrooms have an iPod docking system and a hospitality tray. Pre-dinner drinks may be taken on the decked terrace; a help-yourself breakfast buffet has Welsh cakes, yogurts, pastries and freshly ground coffee (special diets catered for). Breakfast room (background music), lounge (honesty bar); decked terrace. Free Wi-Fi. DVD library. Some self-catering facilities (guest fridge, microwave, plates, cutlery, glasses). Access to nearby fitness and leisure club (£7). Limited on-site parking. Children welcomed. 7 bedrooms (1 on ground floor). Per room B&B (continental) £50–£80. Cooked breakfast £5.

JOLYON'S AT NO. 10, 10 Cathedral Road, CF11 9LJ. Tel 029-2009 1900, www.jolyons10.com. The lively *Cwtch Mawr* bar is a popular local venue – the name is Welsh for 'big cuddle' – at Jolyon Joseph's small hotel, which has a youthful, 'laid-back vibe'. Richly coloured bedrooms are lavishly styled; there are velvet headboards, gold-painted armchairs, grand walnut wardrobes and tasselled four-poster beds; the suites have a chesterfield-style sofa bed to accommodate larger parties. Breakfast, with Glamorgan sausages, is served in a whitewashed room until 10 am (later at weekends). Opposite the Millennium Centre. Lounge, bar (occasional live music); terrace. Free Wi-Fi. Background music. Conference/function facilities. Parking. 7 bedrooms (1 on ground floor). Per room B&B £74–£114.

COLWYN BAY Conwy
Map 3:A3

ELLINGHAM HOUSE, 1 Woodland Park West, LL29 7DR. Tel 01492-533345, www.ellinghamhouse.com. 'Peacefully' situated in a leafy conservation area, this late Victorian villa has 'welcoming' owners (Ian Davies and Chris Jennings), whose attention to detail is praised. Rooms are elegantly furnished. Bedrooms have a DVD-player, bathrobes and a 'wonderful' bathroom; most are light and spacious. Wholesome breakfasts. A short walk to the sea and town. Lounge (DVD library). Free Wi-Fi. No background music. Parking. Children welcomed; dogs by arrangement (£5 per night). 5 bedrooms (1 with separate shower room). Per room B&B £78–£105. Closed Jan.
25% DISCOUNT VOUCHERS

CONWY Conwy
Map 3:A3

CASTLE HOTEL, High Street, LL32 8DB. Tel 01492-582800, www.castlewales.co.uk. On the site of a Cistercian abbey, this centrally located old coaching inn has an attractive Victorian-era facade of local granite and Ruabon brick; parts of the building, once two hostelries, date back to the 1400s. Today, it is run by the Lavin family as a hotel and restaurant. Quirky inside, with characterful nooks, crannies and creaky floors, public rooms are furnished with antiques and paintings by Victorian artist John Dawson Watson. Bedrooms vary in size; some have castle views. In the restaurant, head chef Andrew Nelson promotes Welsh produce from artisan suppliers; the blackboard menu features local seafood and a fish of the day. Bar, lounge, *Dawsons* restaurant. Free Wi-Fi. Background music. Courtyard garden (alfresco dining). Parking (narrow entrance). Children, and dogs (charge) welcomed. 28 bedrooms (1 with 16th-century four-poster bed; some on ground floor). Per person B&B £70–£95. Dinner £30–£40.

COWBRIDGE Vale of Glamorgan
Map 3:E3

THE BEAR, 63 High Street, CF71 7AF. Tel 01446-774814, www.bearhotel.com. 'A popular place with friendly staff', this quaint coaching inn dating back to the 12th century is in a pretty market town, 15 minutes' drive from Cardiff city centre. Bedrooms are 'bright and airy'; some have a beamed ceiling, four-poster bed or chandelier. Chef Richard Bowles's daily blackboard specials are served in the *Cellars* restaurant, with its stone-vaulted ceiling; in *Teddies Grill* bar; in the lounge by a fire; and alfresco in the courtyard. Breakfast, lunch and light snacks are available for non residents. Lounge, 2 bars, restaurant. Free Wi-Fi. Background music. Civil wedding licence; conference facilities. Parking. 33 bedrooms (plus 1- and 2-bedroom apartments a short walk away). Per person B&B £51–£82.

CRICKHOWELL Powys
Map 3:D4

THE MANOR, Brecon Road, NP8 1SE. Tel 01873-810212, www.manorhotel. co.uk. In 'an excellent location' in the Brecon Beacons national park, this white-painted 18th-century manor house is 'very comfortable, with good facilities'. The birthplace of Sir George Everest in 1790, it is now owned by Glyn and Jess Bridgeman and Sean Gerrard; Catherine Lloyd is the manager. The bistro has views over a valley and the River Usk; chef Andre Kerin cooks British dishes using locally reared, organic meat and poultry, mainly from the family farm, seven miles away. Lounge, bar, bistro (background music). Free Wi-Fi. Leisure suite (10-metre indoor swimming pool, sauna, steam room, whirlpool, gym). Civil wedding licence; conference facilities. Children and dogs welcomed. ¼ mile from town. 22 bedrooms. Per person B&B £37.50–£90, D,B&B £67.50–£120.
25% DISCOUNT VOUCHERS

DOLGELLAU Gwynedd
Map 3:B3

FFYNNON, Love Lane, LL40 1RR. Tel 01341-421774, www.ffynnontownhouse. com. At the foot of Cadair Idris, this former Victorian rectory is today a guest house owned by Debra Harris and Steven Holt. Period features, such as the Adam fireplace and stained-glass windows, have been retained; the stylish modern bedrooms have a walk-in drench shower or spa bath, flat-screen TV, DVD-player and iPod docking station. Lounge (background music), dining room, butler's pantry (honesty bar; room-service menu). Free Wi-Fi. ½-acre garden: patio; hot tub; outdoor play area. Small function facilities. Parking. Children welcomed (high tea, baby-listening; PlayStation). Steps and level changes. 3 mins' walk to town. 6 bedrooms. Per person B&B £72.50–£100 (2-night min. stay at weekends).
25% DISCOUNT VOUCHERS

LAMPETER Ceredigion
Map 3:D3

TŶ MAWR MANSION, Cilcennin, SA48 8DB. Tel 01570-470033, www. tymawrmansion.co.uk. 'Fantastic room, food and owners; we were given a brilliant welcome.' Four miles from Cardigan Bay and the picturesque village of Aberaeron, this Grade II listed country house in 'beautiful' grounds is owned by Catherine and Martin McAlpine. They have updated the building combining luxury modern touches and high-tech gadgetry (including a 27-seat cinema), while retaining its Georgian features. In the elegant, slate-blue restaurant, chef Geraint Morgan's modern Welsh dishes use much produce sourced from within a ten-mile radius of the hotel. Good walking, cycling and fishing, and plenty of local attractions nearby. 3 lounges, restaurant (open to non-residents; closed Sun); cinema. Free Wi-Fi. 'Easy listening' background music. Ramps. 'Well-behaved' children accepted. 12-acre grounds. 9 bedrooms (3 suites, 1 on ground floor in annexe). Per room B&B £95–£240, D,B&B £159–£299. Closed Christmas.
25% DISCOUNT VOUCHERS

LAUGHARNE Carmarthenshire
Map 3:D2

BROWNS HOTEL, King Street, SA33 4RY. Tel 01994-427688, www.browns-hotel.co.uk. A favourite watering hole of Dylan Thomas, this 18th-century inn was rescued from near ruin and transformed into a small modern hotel in 2012. A library of Thomas-related reading material helps keep the memory of the poet alive. Individually styled bedrooms mix period features (exposed stonework or beams here, a fireplace there) with modern facilities (HDTV, digital radio, iPod docking system); some are decorated with photographic wall murals and handsome 1950s furnishings. Light bites and snacks are available in the bar; *The New Three Mariners* pub-with-rooms next door, under the same management, has real ales and stone-baked pizzas. Charlie Dyer is the manager. Reading room, bar (traditional Welsh ales). 'Gentle' background music. Free Wi-Fi. Parking. 14 bedrooms. Per room B&B single £70–£80, double £80–£130.

LLANDDEINIOLEN Gwynedd
Map 3:A3

TY'N RHOS, Seion, LL55 3AE. Tel 01248-670489, www.tynrhos.co.uk. Splendid countryside surrounds Stephen and Hilary Murphy's secluded, creeper-covered hotel: sheep and cattle graze in the fields beyond the gardens, while families of ducks, coots and moorhens paddle on two small lakes. Bedrooms are named after wild flowers; some have patio doors opening on to the garden and ornamental pond. Two new rooms have been added this year, along with a new reception and bar area. The large conservatory has views across open countryside to Anglesey. In the restaurant, Stephen Murphy's dishes use local ingredients, and vegetables and herbs from the garden. Lounge (wood-burning fire; board games), *Garden View* restaurant (open to non-residents), conservatory. Free Wi-Fi (in public areas and some rooms only). Background music. 4 miles from Bangor and Caernarfon. Children welcomed; dogs in some rooms, by arrangement. Parking. 19 bedrooms (7 in 2 annexes; 1 family suite). Per room B&B £85–£165. Dinner £37.50 (2-night min. stay at peak weekends).
25% DISCOUNT VOUCHERS

LLANDEILO Carmarthenshire
Map 3:D3

FRONLAS, 7 Thomas Street, SA19 6LB. Tel 01558-824733, www.fronlas.com. Eva and Owain Huw run their stylish, modern B&B on eco-friendly principles (solar-assisted hot water and under-floor heating; organic mattresses and bedding; composting and recycling); guests arriving by train receive a complimentary box of chocolates from the town's chocolatier. The Edwardian town house, on a quiet street close to the centre, has 'striking, well-kept' bedrooms with bold wallpaper and a fluffy throw; bathrooms, with organic-cotton towels and bathrobes, are clad in natural stone. Lounge (wood-burning stove, honesty bar), breakfast room (background music). Free Wi-Fi. DVD library. Garden. Children over 3 welcomed. 4 bedrooms (2 with views of Tywi valley towards the Brecon Beacons). Per room B&B single £50–£100, double £60–£120. Closed Sun.

LLANDUDNO Conwy
Map 3:A3

ESCAPE, 48 Church Walks, LL30 2HL. Tel 01492-877776, www.escapebandb. co.uk. Sam Nayar's traditional white-stucco Victorian villa hides a hip, urban interior. The stylish B&B has contemporary and retro furnishings and fabrics against a backdrop of oak panelling, stained glass and period fireplaces; one bedroom has a floating bed. Up-to-date technology includes flat-screen TVs, Blu-ray players and iPod docking stations; guests may borrow from a DVD library. Josh Simonds is the manager. Lounge, breakfast room. Free Wi-Fi. Background music. Honesty bar. Children over 10 welcomed. 9 bedrooms. Per room B&B £89–£140.

LLANDYRNOG Denbighshire
Map 3:A4

PENTRE MAWR, LL16 4LA. Tel 01824-790732, www.pentremawrcountryhouse. co.uk. 'I would not hesitate to stay here again.' Graham and Bre Carrington-Sykes have created a 'homely, welcoming atmosphere' at their 'excellent' guest house, in a 400-year-old farmstead. Accommodation is spread between country house-style bedrooms in the main house; two cottage suites next door; and luxury canvas lodges in the grounds, each with an outdoor hot tub on a private terrace. Home-cooked dinners are 'great'; bread, cakes and other treats are baked daily. Sitting rooms, gallery, café, restaurant. Free Wi-Fi. No background music. 2-acre grounds: walled garden; solar-heated saltwater swimming pool. Dogs welcomed. 11 bedrooms (3 in main house; 2 suites in cottage; 6 lodges).

Per person B&B £75–£115, D,B&B £100–£140.

LLANGOLLEN Denbighshire
Map 3:B4

GALES, 18 Bridge Street, LL20 8PF. Tel 01978-860089, www.galesofllangollen. co.uk. On one of the oldest streets in Llangollen, this hotel in an 18th-century building has a restaurant at its centre; it is run by wine buff Richard Gale and his family. Simple, home-cooked menus, prepared by chef Daniel Gaskin, change daily; there are also an informal wood-panelled wine bar and a wine and gift shop. Comfortable accommodation is available in bedrooms above the wine bar and in a much older, timber-framed building opposite. Bar/restaurant (extensive wine list; closed Sun); small courtyard. Free Wi-Fi. Background music. Conference facilities. Children welcomed. Parking. 15 bedrooms (1 suitable for &). Per room B&B (continental) single £60, double £80. Cooked breakfast £5, dinner £24.

MANORHAUS LLANGOLLEN, Hill Street, LL20 8EU. Tel 01978-860775, www. manorhausllangollen.com. In a black-and-white Victorian town house with a striking red door, this smart restaurant-with-rooms is under the same ownership as *Manorhaus*, Ruthin (see below). Remodelled in 2012, contemporary bedrooms are handsomely decorated with fabrics from the Melin Tregwynt wool mill; many have a lounge with views of the Dinas Brân castle and hills. Modern Welsh dishes are served in the informal restaurant; a pre-dinner glass of Prosecco may be taken in the rooftop hot tub. Bar, restaurant; hot tub. Free Wi-Fi.

Background music. Parking permits supplied. 6 bedrooms. Per room B&B from £115, D,B&B from £170.

LLANWRTYD WELLS Powys
Map 3:D3
LASSWADE COUNTRY HOUSE, Station Road, LD5 4RW. Tel 01591-610515, www.lasswadehotel.co.uk. On the outskirts of the UK's smallest town, Roger and Emma Stevens's traditional Edwardian house offers 'superb' views of the Cambrian mountains, Mynydd Epynt and the Brecon Beacons. The helpful owners follow a green agenda; discounts are offered to guests using public transport. Roger Stevens uses mainly organic ingredients from local farms for his daily-changing menus; special diets are catered for. Breakfast is served in the conservatory with views over the River Irfon. Drawing room (log fire), restaurant; conservatory; function room. Free Wi-Fi. No background music. Garden. Parking. Children (no under-8s in restaurant), and dogs (in kennels provided) welcomed. 7 bedrooms. Per room B&B £85–£120. Dinner £35.
25% DISCOUNT VOUCHERS

MONTGOMERY Powys
Map 3:C4
THE CHECKERS, Broad Street, SY15 6PN. Tel 01686-669822, www.thecheckers montgomery.co.uk. On the town square, this 'charming' restaurant-with-rooms is in an old coaching inn 'brought tastefully up to date' by sisters Kathryn and Sarah Francis, and Sarah's husband, Stéphane Borie. He has a *Michelin* star for his seasonal menus of classic French dishes. Bedrooms (some low ceilings and doors) are cosy, and equipped with a

large bed, home-made biscuits and the latest gadgetry (flat-screen TV, DVD-player, iPod docking station); some bathrooms have a freestanding bath. There are local sausages and bacon at breakfast, and home-made brioche toast. Lounge, restaurant (6- or 9-course tasting menus; children over 8 in the evening); small terrace. Free Wi-Fi. No background music. Chef's masterclasses. Children welcomed (childminding by arrangement). 5 bedrooms (1 accessed via the roof terrace). Per room B&B £125–£170, D,B&B £235–£250 (mid-week). Closed 2 weeks in Jan.

MUMBLES Swansea
Map 3:E3
PATRICKS WITH ROOMS, 638 Mumbles Road, SA3 4EA. Tel 01792-360199, www.patrickswithrooms.com. On the promenade, this family-friendly restaurant-with-rooms is owned and run by two husband-and-wife teams, Catherine and Patrick Walsh, and Sally and Dean Fuller. The husbands are the chefs in the well-regarded restaurant, where foraged sloe berries and laver bread may appear on the seasonal menus. Bright, simply decorated bedrooms face the sea; breakfast can be served in the bedroom. Lounge/bar, restaurant. Free Wi-Fi. Background music. Gym. Greenhouse. Civil wedding licence; meeting room. Children welcomed (cots, high chairs, baby monitors, DVDs; playground across the road). 16 bedrooms. Per room B&B £115–£175.

NARBERTH Pembrokeshire
Map 3:D2
CANASTON OAKS, Canaston, SA67 8DE. Tel 01437-541254, www. canastonoaks.co.uk. David and Eleanor

Lewis run their relaxed B&B in converted farm buildings with modern additions designed and built by Pembrokeshire craftsmen. Homely bedrooms have views of the countryside; some have their own patio or sitting room. Good walks from the front door; a stroll through the extensive grounds leads to the river. 2½ miles from Narberth. Free Wi-Fi. Parking. Children welcomed. 7 bedrooms (all on ground floor; 2 suitable for &; 1 family room). Per room B&B £110–£150.

NEWPORT Pembrokeshire
Map 3:D1

Y GARTH, Cae Tabor, Dinas Cross, SA42 0XR. Tel 01348-811777, www. bedandbreakfast-pembrokeshire.co.uk. Midway between Newport and Fishguard, this B&B is within easy walking distance of the Pembrokeshire Coast national park. It is owned by Joyce Evans. The house is decorated with rich fabrics and bold contemporary wallpapers; bedrooms have distant views of the sea or open countryside. Extensive Pembrokeshire breakfasts use many locally sourced ingredients. Convenient for the ferry to Rosslare. Lounge, dining room (background music); patio with seating. Free Wi-Fi. Parking. 3 bedrooms (1 with private bathroom). Per person B&B £45–£55.

NEWTOWN Powys
Map 3:C4

THE FOREST COUNTRY GUEST HOUSE, Gilfach Lane, Kerry, SY16 4DW. Tel 01686-621821, www.bedandbreakfast newtown.co.uk. In a tranquil spot in the Vale of Kerry, this family-friendly B&B is owned by Paul and Michelle Martin. Run on eco-conscious lines, the Victorian

country house has solar panels for heating water, and photovoltaic cells for generating electricity. Rooms have views of the surrounding countryside or the large garden; breakfasts include locally sourced, organic produce, and eggs from the Martins' free-range hens. The B&B is a five-minute drive from Newtown, and well located for exploring the Marches area of Mid Wales. Drawing room, dining room; kitchenette. Free Wi-Fi. No background music. Games room (pool, table football, table tennis); toy box; DVDs. 4-acre garden; play area with forest fort; tennis. 3 miles SE of Newtown (train and bus stations). Children, and dogs (kennels £5 per night) welcomed; stabling available. Resident dog and cat; chickens and sheep. Secure bicycle storage. 5 bedrooms (plus 4 holiday cottages in outbuildings). Per person B&B £37.50–£75.

RUTHIN Denbighshire
Map 3:A4

MANORHAUS, Well Street, LL15 1AH. Tel 01824-704830, www.manorhaus. com. 'A most interesting and unusual place to stay.' Off the main square, Gavin Harris and Christopher Frost's 'stylish' restaurant-with-rooms is in a Grade II listed Georgian building. The restaurant and lounge serve as a gallery space to display work by contemporary Welsh artists; each bedroom has been designed and decorated around the artwork on the walls. The modern restaurant has home-cooked regional dishes including salt marsh lamb, Welsh Black beef, Menai mussels, and local honey and dairy products. Lounge, bar, restaurant, library. Free Wi-Fi. Jazz/world background music. Cinema;

Wii games console; fitness room, sauna, steam room. Seminar/meeting facilities. Parking nearby. 8 bedrooms. Per room B&B £115–£145, D,B&B £170–£200.

TAL-Y-LLYN Gwynedd
Map 3:B3
THE OLD RECTORY ON THE LAKE, LL36 9AJ. Tel 01654-782225, www.rectoryonthelake.co.uk. Binoculars are supplied for birdwatching at this peaceful stone-built house on the slopes of Cadair Idris in southern Snowdonia. The homely guest house has modern bedrooms and sumptuous baths; there are stunning views of the lake from every window. Daily-changing four-course dinners are cooked by Ricky Francis, who owns the guest house with John Caine. *Orangery* dining room (no dinners on Wed). No background music. Free Wi-Fi. Outdoor hot tub overlooking the lake. 1½-acre grounds. Bicycles available. 3 bedrooms (1 on ground floor; plus self-catering apartment, *The Rectory Retreat*, also available as B&B). Per person B&B £60, D,B&B £90 (2-night min. stay at weekends).
25% DISCOUNT VOUCHERS

CHANNEL ISLANDS

KINGS MILLS Guernsey
Map 1: inset D5
FLEUR DU JARDIN, Grand Moulins, Castel, GY5 7JT. Tel 01481-257996, www.fleurdujardin.com. In a pleasant village setting on the west side of the island, this pub and restaurant-with-rooms was once an old farmstead. Roaring fires, bleached timber walls and quaint coastal features give it an airy seaside feel. It is owned by Ian and Amanda Walker, and run by Sandra Le Scanff, with friendly staff. Cosy rooms are simply furnished and have a sandstone bathroom; gastropub food is served in the bar and restaurant. It is a 20-minute bus ride into town; 20 minutes' walk to the beach. Bar, restaurant (background music). Free Wi-Fi (in public areas). Health suite (beauty treatments, relaxation rooms). 2-acre garden: heated swimming pool, sunny terrace. Children welcomed. 19 bedrooms (2 garden suites; rooms at the back are quieter). Per room B&B £92–£142. Dinner from £22.

ST BRELADE Jersey
Map 1: inset E6
ST BRELADE'S BAY HOTEL, La Route de la Baie, JE3 8EF. Tel 01534-746141, www.stbreladesbayhotel.com. 'Warm and welcoming', this large hotel in lush subtropical gardens overlooks a 'magnificent' bay; private steps lead down to the sandy beach. It is owned by David Whelan (who also owns Wigan Athletic football club); Tony Jones is the manager. 'Stylishly refurbished' bedrooms are 'comfortable and spacious'; most sea-facing rooms have a balcony. 'Dinner is a major event', with locally caught seafood cooked by chef Franz Hacker; the *Petit Port Café* has less formal alfresco dining. The buffet breakfast has 'a wide range of cooked dishes'. There are excellent facilities for children, including a play area and a kids' swimming pool. Lounge, cocktail bar (background music), café, *The Bay* restaurant. Free Wi-Fi. Health club (indoor swimming pool and spa). Games room, snooker room; toddlers' room. Function room. Sun lounge; outdoor pool; tennis court. Lift. Civil wedding

licence; function facilities. Children welcomed (cots, high chairs; high tea). 77 bedrooms. Per room B&B £140–£240. Dinner £38.

ST MARTIN Guernsey
Map 1: inset E5
BELLA LUCE HOTEL, La Fosse, GY4 6EB. Tel 01481-238764, www.bellalucehotel.com. In the south of the island, this luxurious manor house with 12th-century origins is owned by Luke Wheadon. Michael McBride is the manager. Stylish bedrooms (some small) are tastefully decorated, and have magazines, bathrobes and slippers; some have a modern four-poster bed. Overlooking the courtyard garden, the rustic restaurant has candles and roaring log fires at night; in summer, French windows open on to a sunny terrace for alfresco dining. Bistro food is served in the intimate bar. Lounge, bar, *Garden* restaurant, cellar lounge (extensive wine list; background music). Free Wi-Fi. Garden (alfresco dining); courtyard. Swimming pool (heated in summer), spa, treatment rooms. Civil wedding licence; function facilities. 2 miles to St Peter Port; rock beach 5 mins' walk. Parking. Children welcomed. 25 bedrooms (2 on ground floor; some family). Per person B&B £109–£198. Dinner from £24.95. Closed 2 weeks in Jan.

ST PETER PORT Guernsey
Map 1: inset E5
THE CLUBHOUSE @ LA COLLINETTE, St Jacques, GY1 1SN. Tel 01481-710331, www.lacollinette.com. Colourful window boxes adorn the front of this family-friendly hotel run by the Chambers family for almost 50 years. It is close to the seafront and centre; the picturesque harbour nearby has access to the surrounding islands (and tax-free shopping). Rooms are bright and modern; lounges open on to the lawns, pool terrace or balcony. A small museum is housed in a former German naval signals bunker. Bar, restaurant (brasserie menu; seafood and local produce); background music. Free Wi-Fi. DVD library. Conference facilities. Garden; heated swimming pool; gym; massages. Children welcomed (teddy bear gift; children's pool; play area). 30 bedrooms (plus 15 self-catering cottages and apartments). Per person B&B £60–£78. Dinner from £20.

THE DUKE OF RICHMOND, Cambridge Park, Les Cotils, GY1 1UY. Tel 01481-726221, www.dukeofrichmond.com. Overlooking a quiet park, this large hotel (Red Carnation Hotels) has fine views over the town and harbour to the neighbouring islands of Herm and Sark beyond. Andrew Chantrell is the manager. Lavishly refurbished bedrooms have elegant fabrics, prints and decorative mirrors; some superior rooms have enough space to accommodate a family. Children are well provided for with DVDs, toy baskets, board and card games, bathtime treats and robes; dogs have their own treats, too. The *Leopard* bar and lounge is decorated in funky animal prints. Dining options range from formal to relaxed alfresco. Stamatis Loumousiotis is chef. Lounge, bar, restaurant, conservatory; terrace. Background music. Free Wi-Fi. Outdoor heated pool. Wedding/function facilities. Children and dogs welcomed. 73 bedrooms. Per room B&B £130–£330, D,B&B £185–£385.

La Frégate, Beauregard Lane, Les Cotils, GY1 1UT. Tel 01481-724624, www.lafregatehotel.com. In terraced gardens high above the town, this 18th-century manor house has 'fantastic' views over the harbour, the neighbouring islands and, on a clear day, the coast of France. Simon Dufty is the manager. Most of the simply styled bedrooms have a balcony or terrace; the restaurant, decorated in blue and white, has a fresh, coastal look, and fine views over St Peter Port harbour. Chef Neil Maginnis's menus are strong on local fish, shellfish and home-grown vegetables and herbs. Lounge/bar (light background music), restaurant; terrace; *The Boardroom* and *The Orangery* (function/conference facilities). Free Wi-Fi. Terraced garden. 2 mins' walk from centre. Children welcomed. 22 bedrooms (all with sea views; some with balcony). Per person B&B from £90. Dinner £37.50.

IRELAND

BALLINTOY Co. Antrim
Map 6:A6

WHITEPARK HOUSE, 150 Whitepark Road, BT54 6NH. Tel 028-2073 1482, www.whiteparkhouse.com. Four miles east of the Giant's Causeway, this crenellated 18th-century house sits above the spectacular sandy beach of Whitepark Bay. It is run as a cosy B&B by Bob and Siobhan Isles, who have decorated their home with art, artefacts and souvenirs from their travels around the world. Guests are welcomed with a cup of tea on arrival; the hosts are happy to advise on restaurants and places to visit. Bedrooms, with bathrobes and a hot-water bottle, have views of the garden or the sea; bathrooms are large.

Irish breakfasts (vegetarians catered for). Sitting room (peat fire), conservatory. No background music. Free Wi-Fi. 3 bedrooms. Per room B&B £80–£120.

BALLYCASTLE Co. Mayo
Map 6:B4

STELLA MARIS. Tel 00 353 96-43322, www.stellamarisireland.com. In a beautiful setting on Bunatrahir Bay, this small hotel is in a white-painted building that has, in former times, been a Coast Guard regional headquarters and, latterly, a convent. Restored and refurbished by Frances Kelly and her husband, Terence McSweeney (a keen golfer and sportswriter), it has simply furnished rooms named after famous golf courses; most look out to the Atlantic Ocean. The 'lovely' bar has fireplaces, old prints and golf memorabilia; in the restaurant, Frances Kelly ('a superb chef') serves a daily-changing menu of modern dishes. Breakfast has potato cakes and Irish bacon; bread is home made. Lounge, bar, restaurant, conservatory. Free Wi-Fi (in public areas only). Quiet background music. Ramp. Wedding facilities; 3-acre grounds. Children welcomed, by arrangement. Parking. 1½ miles W of Ballycastle. Sandy beach nearby. 12 bedrooms (1 on ground floor, suitable for &). Per person B&B €75, D,B&B €125. Closed Oct–20 Apr.

BALLYDAVID Co. Kerry
Map 6:D4

GORMAN'S CLIFFTOP HOUSE, Glashabeg. Tel 00-353 66-915-5162, www.gormans-clifftophouse.com. 'We would certainly want to go again.' In a 'splendid location' on the Dingle peninsula, seven generations of the

Gorman family have fished and farmed this area, where Síle and Vincent Gorman now run their guest house and restaurant. The purpose-built home has spacious modern bedrooms with sea or mountain views; there are open fires and board games in the lounge. Many of the ingredients for Vincent Gorman's 'very good' cooking are freshly picked from the large garden and polytunnel. Síle, with help from daughter Ciara, bakes breads and cakes; desserts, jams and vegetarian food are all home made. Lounge, library, restaurant (closed Sun; lighter meals available for staying guests). Free Wi-Fi. Classical and traditional Irish background music. Children welcomed. 4-acre garden, bogland and cliff. 8 bedrooms (1 family room). Resident dog, Molly. Per room B&B €110–€150, D,B&B €90–€120 per person. Closed Nov–Mar.

BALLYVAUGHAN Co. Clare
Map 6:C4
GREGANS CASTLE HOTEL. Tel 00 353 65-707 7005, www.gregans.ie. Donkeys, ducks and a pony roam the extensive grounds surrounding Simon Haden and Frederieke McMurray's 'magical' 18th-century country house overlooking Galway Bay. Public rooms have antiques, 'gorgeous, squashy sofas', and jugs of garden flowers; elegant bedrooms are decorated in sage and grey. David Hurley is chef, serving 'creative' modern Irish dishes. An early dinner for children is available by arrangement. 'We would go back tomorrow.' Drawing room, *Corkscrew* bar (background jazz), restaurant (closed Sun). Free Wi-Fi. 15-acre grounds: ornamental pool; croquet. No TV. Wedding facilities. Children welcomed (no under-6s in dining room at night). Dogs welcomed (in 2 bedrooms). 21 bedrooms (some on ground floor). Per room B&B €205–€245, D,B&B €315–€360. Closed mid-Nov–early Feb.

BELFAST
Map 6:B6
THE OLD RECTORY, 148 Malone Road, BT9 5LH. Tel 028-9066 7882, www.anoldrectory.co.uk. Guests are offered a hot whiskey on cool evenings at Mary Callan's homely guest house, in a leafy residential suburb close to the centre. The 19th-century rectory retains many original features, including stained-glass windows and fireplaces; bedrooms have books, magazines and biscuits. Award-winning breakfasts have plenty of choice and vegetarian options; raspberry jam, whiskey marmalade and soda bread are all home made. A small supper menu is available Mon to Fri. 10 mins' walk to Lagan Meadows (river walks). Drawing room. Garden. Free Wi-Fi. No background music. Parking. Children welcomed. 5 bedrooms (1 on ground floor). Per room B&B single £45–£55, double £84–£86. Closed Christmas.

RAVENHILL HOUSE, 690 Ravenhill Road, BT6 0BZ. Tel 028-9020 7444, www.ravenhillhouse.com. In this restored Victorian house two miles from the city centre, Roger and Olive Nicholson welcome B&B guests with tea, coffee and biscuits on arrival. Bedrooms have locally handcrafted furniture; the sitting room has a computer for guests' use and a library of local-interest books. There are freshly baked Irish wheaten bread and home-made granola and muesli at breakfast (plus good vegetarian options); the

Nicholsons share helpful tips about the city. Shops, pubs, restaurants and a park within walking distance. Sitting room, dining room; small garden. Free Wi-Fi. Occasional background music; Radio 3 at breakfast. Parking. Children welcomed. 5 bedrooms (1 on ground floor). Per room B&B single £55–£60, double £75–£85. Closed 15 Dec–Feb.

BUSHMILLS Co. Antrim
Map 6:A6

BUSHMILLS INN, 9 Dunluce Road, BT57 8QG. Tel 028-2073 3000, www.bushmillsinn.com. There is an easy-going atmosphere at this quirky old coaching inn and adjoining mill house, parts of which date back to the 17th century. It is run by Alan Dunlop, with friendly staff. Characterful features include a grand staircase, a 'secret' library, and a web of interconnecting cosy snugs with turf fires, oil lamps and ancient wooden booths. Traditional Irish music is performed in the *Gas* bar, lit by original gas lights; movies are screened on Thursday nights. Drawing room, gallery, oak-beamed loft; patio. The restaurant (modern cuisine) overlooks the garden courtyard. Free Wi-Fi. Conference facilities, 30-seat cinema, treatment room; 3-acre garden. Parking. Children welcomed (family rooms). 2 miles from the Giant's Causeway. 41 bedrooms (some on ground floor; spacious ones in mill house, smaller ones in inn). Per room B&B £148–£398. Dinner £40–£45.

CALLAN Co. Kilkenny
Map 6:D5

BALLAGHTOBIN COUNTRY HOUSE. Tel 00 353 56-772 5227, www.ballaghtobin.com. Fourteen generations of the Gabbett family have lived on the site of this 18th-century ancestral home, where Catherine Gabbett now provides friendly B&B accommodation. Set in informal gardens, the house is within a 500-acre farm producing cereals and Christmas trees; there is a ruined Norman church opposite. Refurbished country house-style rooms are decorated in soothing colours and furnished with paintings and antiques; generous breakfasts are served at a large table in the elegant dining room. Drawing room, dining room, study, conservatory. Free Wi-Fi. No background music. Tennis, croquet, clock golf. Children and dogs welcomed. 10 miles from Kilkenny. 3 bedrooms. Per person B&B €50–€60. Closed Nov–Mar.

CARLINGFORD Co. Louth
Map 6:B6

GHAN HOUSE. Tel 00 353 42-937 3682, www.ghanhouse.com. In walled gardens with views of Carlingford Lough, this listed Georgian house is run in 'hands-on' style by Paul Carroll and his mother, Joyce. Traditionally furnished rooms have family antiques alongside modern equipment (iPod dock, flat-screen internet-enabled TV); they look out over the gardens to the mountains beyond. There is a grand piano in the 'very elegant' dining room, where menus are based on the abundant supply of shellfish from the lough, and vegetables and herbs from the kitchen garden. Breakfast has home-made jams and marmalade, and home-baked bread. Stephane Le Sourne is the new chef. Sitting room, bar, restaurant (3 dining areas; closed Mon, Tues in low season). Free Wi-Fi. 'Easy listening' background music. Civil wedding licence. 3-acre garden. Parking; bicycle storage. Children welcomed. Dogs welcomed (in stables only). 12 bedrooms (8 in annexe). Per person B&B €65–€95, D,B&B €99–€125.

CASTLEBALDWIN Co. Sligo
Map 6:B5

CROMLEACH LODGE, Lough Arrow. Tel 00 353 71-916 5155, www.cromleach. com. 'We were refreshed by our experience.' Moira and Christy Tighe's hotel in the hills above Lough Arrow is surrounded by 'beautiful Sligo scenery'. Modern bedrooms are divided between the main building and a new block accessible via enclosed walkways (some rooms are 'a considerable distance' from the public areas); deluxe rooms have a private balcony with views to the Bricklieve Mountains. Moira Tighe cooks 'superb' modern Irish dishes in the restaurant; sandwiches and light meals are served in the bar. Lounge, bar, restaurant; spa (sauna, steam room, outdoor whirlpool; treatment rooms). Free Wi-Fi (in public rooms only). Background music. 30-acre grounds: forest walks, private access to Lough Arrow (fishing, boating, surfing), hill climbing. Wedding/function facilities. Good walks from the front door; packed lunches available. Children and dogs welcomed (dog-grooming parlour). 57 bedrooms (1 suitable for ⅏). Per room B&B €80–€258. Closed Mon and Tues, May–June, Sept–Dec; Christmas.

COBH Co. Cork
Map 6:D5

KNOCKEVEN HOUSE, Rushbrooke. Tel 00 353 21-481 1778, www. knockevenhouse.com. Pam and John Mulhaire greet B&B guests with afternoon tea or coffee and home-made scones in the comfortable drawing room of their richly furnished Victorian home. On the outskirts of town, the house is in tranquil, well-kept gardens; displays of magnolias, azaleas and camellias can be seen from the large windows in the elegant bedrooms. Generous breakfasts are taken at a large mahogany table; Pam Mulhaire serves three-course Aga-cooked meals by arrangement. Drawing room, dining room. Free Wi-Fi. Classical background music. Children welcomed. 2-acre grounds. 1 mile from town. 4 bedrooms. Per room B&B single €75, double €100. D,B&B €85 per person.

CONG Co. Mayo
Map 6:C4

LISLOUGHREY LODGE, The Quay. Tel 00 353 94-954 5400, www. lisloughreylodge.com. Overlooking Lough Corrib on the Ashford Castle estate, this country hotel, in a former gamekeeper's home, has welcomed fishermen, huntsmen and nature walkers since the late 19th century. Spacious bedrooms are located in a quiet courtyard, linked to the main house by a covered walkway. They are decorated with striking fabrics, feature wallpaper and stylish furniture; duplex suites have a fireplace and private terrace. The *Quay* bar and brasserie has a wood-burning open fire; overlooking Lisloughrey Quay, *Wilde's at Lisloughrey* serves 'contemporary country cuisine'. Bar, restaurant; vault with pool table, games room; private screening room. Free Wi-Fi. Background music. Spa suite, beauty treatments; gym. Wedding/function facilities. Children welcomed (playroom). 50 bedrooms (family suites). Per room B&B from €130, D,B&B from €170.

CORK Co. Cork
Map 6:D5

CAFÉ PARADISO, 16 Lancaster Quay. Tel 00 353 21-427 7939, www.cafeparadiso.ie. Acclaimed chef and cookbook author Denis Cotter owns this vegetarian restaurant-with-rooms, which he runs with Geraldine O'Toole. Mr Cotter's inventive meat-free dishes in the quayside restaurant are based on seasonal, organic produce from the nearby Gort na Nain Farm (visits arranged). Upstairs, the spacious bedrooms have an iPod dock, coffee machine and supply of board games and books; no TV. Breakfast, with baked pastries, yogurt, granola, farmhouse cheeses, preserves and juice, is served in the room. Background music. Free Wi-Fi. Restricted parking. 2 bedrooms (1 faces the river). Per person D,B&B €100. Closed 24–31 Dec.

DERRY Co. Londonderry
Map 6:B6

SERENDIPITY HOUSE, 26 Marlborough Street, BT48 9AY. Tel 028-7126 4229, www.serendipityrooms.co.uk. On a hill overlooking the city walls, this good-value, no-frills B&B is within walking distance of the restaurants, bars and tourist sites of the centre; top-floor bedrooms have good views. It is run by father-and-son team Paul and Stephen Lyttle, who are knowledgeable about the area and helpful with recommendations. Lounge, dining room (background music at breakfast; jukebox); sun deck with city views. Free Wi-Fi. Parking. Children welcomed. 5 bedrooms (1 with private bathroom).

Per room B&B (continental) £32–£75. Full Irish breakfast £3.50.

DONEGAL Co. Donegal
Map 6:B5

HARVEY'S POINT, Lough Eske. Tel 00 353 74-972 2208, www.harveyspoint.com. At the foot of the Bluestack Mountains, this peaceful country hotel overlooks Lough Eske. The Gysling family have been long-standing owners; Mark Gysling and Deirdre McGlone are now in charge. Large bedrooms in the main house are traditionally designed (dark wood furniture, oriental rugs); some have a four-poster bed. A turf fire burns in the cocktail bar, where locals and guests gather; there are lovely views of the lake from large windows in the elegant restaurant. Chef Paul Montgomery's Irish dishes have a French influence. Activity breaks (fishing, canoeing, golf, walks, archery) available. Lounge, drawing room, bar, restaurant (closed Sun–Tues, Nov–Mar), ballroom (resident pianist; Irish/classical background music). Free Wi-Fi. Beauty treatments; massage. Lift. Ramps. Civil wedding licence; conference facilities. 20-acre grounds. 4 miles from town. Children (babysitting, early supper), and dogs (in some bedrooms) welcomed. 64 bedrooms (8 lakeside suites). Per person B&B €99–€140, D,B&B €149–€189.
25% DISCOUNT VOUCHERS

DUBLIN
Map 6:C6

THE CLIFF TOWNHOUSE, 22 St Stephen's Green, Dublin 2. Tel 00 353 1-638 3939, www.theclifftownhouse.com. On St Stephen's Green, this handsome Georgian house – once home to one of the oldest private members' clubs in Ireland – is now a stylish town house hotel and seafood and oyster restaurant run by owners Gerri and Barry O'Callaghan. It is decorated in pleasing heritage shades, and furnished with a mix of antique and modern pieces. Bedrooms have reproduction period prints and Donegal tweed blankets; some of the marble bathrooms have a quirky hip bath and vintage fittings. Most deluxe rooms overlook the green. In the smart restaurant, with its high ceilings and leather booths, chef Sean Smith's menus showcase local seafood (Galway oysters, native lobster, dressed Yawl Bay crab) and hearty salads. Bar, restaurant (pre- and post-theatre service); private dining room. 'Subtle' background music. Free Wi-Fi. Wedding/function facilities. Children welcomed. 9 bedrooms. Per room B&B single €115–€135, double €135–€155. Dinner €45.

WATERLOO HOUSE, 8–10 Waterloo Road, Dublin 4. Tel 00 353 1-660 1888, www.waterloohouse.ie. 'Very central', in a quiet, tree-lined area near St Stephen's Green, Evelyn Corcoran's B&B occupies two Georgian town houses with distinctive red doors. Some bedrooms are compact, though 'more than adequate' for a short stay. Served in the raspberry dining room or adjoining conservatory, the 'good' breakfast has a 'catch of the day', home-made traditional Irish soda bread and freshly baked croissants. Lounge (classical background music), dining room, conservatory; garden. Free Wi-Fi. Lift; ramp. Parking. Children welcomed. 20 bedrooms (some suitable for &.). Per person B&B €40–€90.

DUNFANAGHY Co. Donegal
Map 6:A5
THE MILL, Figart. Tel 00 353 74-913 6985, www.themillrestaurant.com. On the outskirts of a small resort town, this former 19th-century flax mill is run as an unpretentious restaurant-with-rooms by Susan Alcorn and her husband, Derek. She is the granddaughter of Frank Egginton, the watercolour artist, whose work is displayed throughout. A 'vivacious' host, she takes dinner orders in the conservatory overlooking the lake, and in the drawing room, which has an open fire on cool evenings. Bedrooms are simply furnished; guests, who are asked to arrive after 4 pm, are offered a cup of coffee or tea and home-made shortbread. Derek Alcorn, the chef, cooks an 'imaginative' modern Irish menu using local produce (served 7 pm–9 pm, Tues–Sun; popular with non-residents; booking is advisable). Breakfast, with home-made breads and preserves, is 'equally good'. Free Wi-Fi. Background music. Children welcomed. ½ mile W of town. 6 bedrooms. Per person B&B €48–€60. Closed Jan–mid-Mar.

DUNGARVAN Co. Waterford
Map 6:D5
THE CASTLE COUNTRY HOUSE, Millstreet, Cappagh, Tel 00 353 58-68049, www.castlecountryhouse.com. On a working dairy farm, the Nugent family offers B&B accommodation in the restored wing of a 16th-century fortified tower house. (Guests may lend a hand with milking the cows, should they choose to.) There is an open fire and plenty of reading matter in the sitting room; spacious bedrooms have period furniture and views over the gardens. The River Finisk runs at the

bottom of the garden; reels and rods are provided for anglers to fish for trout. Joan Nugent serves a set evening meal, by arrangement, with produce that comes mostly from the farm. Complimentary afternoon teas with home baking (baking demonstrations); packed lunches and picnic baskets on request. No background music. Free Wi-Fi. Children welcomed. 15 mins' drive from Dungarvan. 5 rooms. Per person B&B €40–€50. Dinner €25. Closed Nov–Apr.
25% DISCOUNT VOUCHERS

GALWAY Co. Galway
Map 6:C4

THE G HOTEL, Wellpark. Tel 00 353 91-865200, www.theghotel.ie. Overlooking Lough Atalia, this style-conscious Philip Treacy-designed hotel has swirly carpets, rich wallpaper and gumdrop-coloured seating. It is managed by Triona Gannon for Edward Hotels; staff are notably 'calm and helpful'. Bedrooms are spacious; those overlooking the Zen garden are 'particularly quiet and private'. Chef Pauline Reilly's menus focus on Irish dishes with a European influence. 3 lounges, cocktail bar, *gigi's* restaurant; spa (indoor swimming pool, sauna, steam room, treatments); bamboo Zen garden. Free Wi-Fi. Background music. Lift. Wedding/function facilities. Parking. On the outskirts of town. Children welcomed (milk and cookies on arrival, DVD and games library; babysitting). 101 rooms. Per room B&B €150–€500, D,B&B €212–€590.

GLASLOUGH, Co. Monaghan
Map 6:B6

CASTLE LESLIE. Tel 00 353 47-88100, www.castleleslie.com. 'Everything was excellent.' In 1,000 acres of rolling countryside, ancient woods and lakes, this luxury hotel still remains in the hands of the Leslie family, who founded the estate in the 1660s. It is managed by Brian Baldwin. Rooms in the main house are furnished in sumptuous country house style with antiques and old paintings; there is much interesting family history here. Near the main gate, the *Lodge* has been sympathetically restored and extended to include the restaurant, the spa and further accommodation. Drawing room, bar, *Snaffles* restaurant (Andrew Bradley is chef); conservatory, billiard room, library, cinema. Background music in *Lodge* only. Free Wi-Fi. Spa (treatment rooms, relaxation area; outdoor hot tub). Civil wedding licence. Children welcomed (special menu). Equestrian centre; fishing, boating, kayaking, clay-pigeon shooting, hot air balloon rides, walking trails, picnics. 6 miles from Monaghan. 61 bedrooms (29 in the *Lodge*, 12 in mews and cottages with self-catering facilities). Per room B&B €130–€310, D,B&B €210–€420.

KENMARE Co. Kerry
Map 6:D4

BROOK LANE HOTEL. Tel 00 353 64-664 2077, www.brooklanehotel.com. An ideal base for exploring the Ring of Kerry, Una and Dermot Brennan's modern, small hotel is in a pretty heritage town on the bay. Superior bedrooms are simply decorated in earth tones; deluxe rooms have bold colours and striking wallpaper. In the restaurant, chef Brendan Scannell serves contemporary Irish dishes; sister restaurant *No. 35* is a 15-minute walk away. Sustaining full Irish breakfasts.

Library, bar/restaurant; private dining room; garden. Free Wi-Fi (in public areas). Lift. Background music. Wedding/conference facilities. Golf, walking, cycling. Parking. 20 bedrooms (1 suitable for ♿), plus *Studio* 2-bedroom apartment. Per person B&B €50–€90, D,B&B €85–€130.
25% DISCOUNT VOUCHERS

KILKENNY Co. Kilkenny
Map 6:D5
ROSQUIL HOUSE, Castlecomer Road. Tel 00 353 56-772 1419, www.rosquilhouse. com. There are copious breakfasts to be had at Phil and Rhoda Nolan's guest house: bread, scones and cakes are home baked; fruit compotes, jam and granola are home made. Good-sized bedrooms have biscuits, tea and coffee; a comfortable sitting room has large windows, and books to browse. 20 mins' walk from the town. Lounge; small garden. No background music. Free Wi-Fi. Children welcomed. Close to Kilkenny Golf Club. 7 bedrooms (1 suitable for ♿), plus *The Mews* self-catering apartment. Per person B&B €35–€50.

KILLARNEY Co. Kerry
Map 6:D4
THE DUNLOE, Beaufort. Tel 00 353 64-664 4111, www.thedunloe.com. Surrounded by stunning scenery overlooking the Gap of Dunloe, this family- and dog-friendly hotel sits in extensive grounds with gardens, farmland and the ruins of the 12th-century Dunloe Castle. It is managed by Jason Clifford. There is complimentary fishing on the River Laune; the kitchen will prepare and cook guests' catch for their dinner. Children are made very

welcome, with movie nights, a kids' club and many other facilities (playground, games room, indoor tennis; pony riding). 3 lounges, bar, *Garden* café, *Oak* restaurant: 64-acre grounds. Free Wi-Fi. Background music. Heated indoor pool; tennis courts; sauna, steam room, treatment rooms. Wedding/function facilities. 102 bedrooms (20 smoking; 1 suitable for ♿). Per person B&B €90–€287.50, D,B&B €130–€159. Closed mid-Oct–mid-Apr.

KINSALE Co. Cork
Map 6:D5
THE OLD PRESBYTERY, 43 Cork Street. Tel 00 353 21-477 2027, www.oldpres. com. On a quiet street in the centre of town, this 200-year-old house was once a priests' residence attached to the nearby St John the Baptist church. Restored by Philip and Noreen McEvoy, it is today a modern B&B full of period charm. Traditionally decorated bedrooms have antiques and a brass or cast iron bed; some superior rooms have a balcony. Philip McEvoy, a professional chef, cooks substantial breakfasts using organic produce (vegetarian options available). Lounge, dining room; patio. Free Wi-Fi. Classical/Irish background music. Parking. Children welcomed. 9 bedrooms (3 suites; 2 self-catering). Per person B&B €45–€90. Closed mid-Nov–Feb.

LAHINCH Co. Clare
Map 6:C4
MOY HOUSE. Tel 00 353 65-708 2800, www.moyhouse.com. With uninterrupted views over Lahinch Bay, this 19th-century country house sits in extensive grounds with mature woodland and a river. Bedrooms are

individually decorated; the Signature Suite has a private conservatory, and an original well in the bathroom. In the drawing room, guests help themselves to the honesty bar in front of an open fire; daily-changing five-course menus are served in the candlelit conservatory restaurant overlooking the ocean. Library, drawing room, restaurant (background music). Free Wi-Fi; computer provided. 15-acre grounds. Children welcomed. 9 bedrooms. Per person B&B €92.50–€180. Dinner €55. Closed Nov–Mar. Restaurant closed Sun and Mon off-season.

LONGFORD Co. Longford
Map 6:C5
VIEWMOUNT HOUSE, Dublin Road. Tel 00 353 43-334 1919, www. viewmounthouse.com. 'The accommodation was very comfortable, the welcome warm, the breakfasts wonderful.' Less than a mile from the town centre, this restored Georgian house, the former home of the Earl of Longford, sits in large landscaped gardens adjoining Longford Golf Club. It is run as a guest house and restaurant by Beryl and James Kearney. Colourful, individually decorated bedrooms have an antique bed and country views; the former kitchen, with its vaulted ceiling, is now a cosy sitting room with chesterfields in front of an open fire. Dinner is served (6.30 pm–9 pm Wed–Sat) in the candlelit *VM* restaurant, converted from old stables in the grounds; chef Gary O'Hanlon serves seasonal Irish meals with a modern twist. Reception room, library, sitting room, breakfast room, restaurant (background music); courtyard. Free Wi-Fi. 4-acre gardens (Japanese garden,

knot garden, orchard). Wedding facilities. Children welcomed. 12 bedrooms (7 in modern extension; some on ground floor). Per room B&B €110–€130. Dinner (4 courses) €53.

MAGHERAFELT Co. Londonderry
Map 6:B6
LAUREL VILLA TOWNHOUSE, 60 Church Street, BT45 6AW. Tel 028-7930 1459, www.laurel-villa.com. The atmosphere at Eugene and Gerardine Kielt's elegant B&B is decidedly literary, with a rich collection of Seamus Heaney memorabilia on display, and comfortable bedrooms named after Ulster poets. Guests are offered coffee and home-made scones on arrival; Eugene Kielt, a Blue Badge guide, arranges poetry readings and tours of 'Heaney country'. In the centre of town. No background music. Free Wi-Fi. 2 lounges, dining room. Children welcomed. 4 bedrooms. Per person B&B single £60, double £40–£45.

MOYARD Co. Galway
Map 6:C4
CROCNARAW COUNTRY HOUSE. Tel 00 353 95-41068, www.crocnaraw.co.uk. In 20 acres of wooded gardens and meadows, and with 'a great, easy atmosphere', this small guest house is run by Lucy Fretwell in her Georgian country home. Individually decorated bedrooms are quaint and 'full of light'; one has an old-fashioned claw-footed bath. Afternoon tea with home-made scones and strawberry jam is taken in front of the peat fire in the drawing room. Generous breakfasts include home-made Irish bread and produce from the kitchen garden. Fishing, angling, golf nearby. Dining room,

drawing room, snug; garden, orchard. Free Wi-Fi. No background music. Children (no babies) welcomed. Dogs allowed in some bedrooms. 4 bedrooms. Per person B&B £35–£58. Dinner £35. Closed Nov–May.

NEWPORT Co. Mayo
Map 6:B4

NEWPORT HOUSE. Tel 00 353 98-41222, www.newporthouse.ie. Overlooking the estuary of the River Newport, this grand Georgian country house has extensive fishing rights and is popular with fisherfolk. It is owned by Kieran Thompson; Catherine Flynn, the manager, is 'the heart and soul of the place'. Public rooms are traditionally decorated, and have high ceilings, comfy seating and open fires; a Regency drawing room upstairs overlooks the park. Long-serving chef John Gavin's noteworthy seven-course menus include produce from the fishery, garden and farm, and home-smoked salmon; an extensive wine list. No background music. Free Wi-Fi (in public areas and some bedrooms). Children, and dogs (in courtyard bedrooms) welcomed. 14 bedrooms (4 in courtyard). Per person B&B €95–€140, D,B&B €160–€205. Closed Nov–20 Mar.
25% DISCOUNT VOUCHERS

NEWTOWNARDS Co. Down
Map 6:B6

BEECH HILL COUNTRY HOUSE, 23 Ballymoney Road, Craigantlet, BT23 4TG. Tel 028-9042 5892, www.beech-hill.net. With panoramic views over the north Down countryside, this white Georgian-style house in the Holywood hills is convenient for Belfast City Airport and the ferries. Victoria

Brann, the owner, has decorated it in period style with antiques and lots of comfortable seating. The stunning entrance hall, painted a vivid red, has a chandelier and fresh flowers; bedrooms are spacious. Water is heated by solar power; extensive breakfasts consist of locally sourced produce. Drawing room, dining room, conservatory. Free Wi-Fi. No background music. Parking. Dogs welcomed. 3 bedrooms (on ground floor; *The Colonel's Lodge* is available for self-catering). Per person B&B £55–£60.

PORTSTEWART Co. Londonderry
Map 6:A6

THE YORK, 2 Station Road, BT55 7DA. Tel 028-7083 3594, www.theyorkport stewart.co.uk. 'We would stay again.' On the seafront, this modern bar and restaurant has views of the water and the Inis Eoghain peninsula. Bedrooms are 'spacious, well equipped, clean and comfortable, with pleasant modern furniture'. Several rooms have sea views; superior suites have a private balcony as well. The *York Grill Bar* restaurant (piano, jukebox) serves pub classics; a children's menu is available. Bar, dining room; terrace/conservatory. Free Wi-Fi. Lift. Small wedding/function facilities. Children welcomed. 8 bedrooms (1 suitable for ♿). Per room B&B single £79, double £115. Dinner from £22.

RAMELTON Co. Donegal
Map 6:B5

FREWIN, Rectory Road. Tel 00 353 74-915 1246, www.frewinhouse.com. On the outskirts of a historic Georgian port, Regina and Thomas Coyle's carefully restored Victorian rectory stands in mature wooded grounds. Decorated 'with flair', the family home has stained-glass windows, an elegant staircase, and antiques. Three of the spacious country house-style bedrooms have their own sitting room; bathrooms are compact. Regina Coyle greets B&B guests with afternoon tea, served by a big open fire in the cosy library; copious breakfasts are taken communally at a large table. Candlelit dinners are by arrangement. No background music. Sitting room, library, dining room; 2-acre garden. Free Wi-Fi. Children welcomed. 4 bedrooms (1 with private bathroom; plus 1-bedroom cottage in the grounds). Per person B&B €50–€75, D,B&B €95–€110.

25% DISCOUNT VOUCHERS

RATHNEW Co. Wicklow
Map 6:C6

HUNTER'S HOTEL, Newrath Bridge. Tel 00 353 404 40106, www.hunters.ie. Full of old-world charm, this former coaching inn is in two acres of beautiful gardens on the banks of the River Vartry; it is said to be the oldest in Ireland. Currently run by brothers Richard and Tom Gelletlie, it has been in the same family for five generations. Bedrooms have antiques, prints and creaking floorboards; many overlook the gardens. The public areas are traditionally decorated and have chintzy sofas, polished brass and open fires. In warm weather, the garden is a pleasant place in which to take afternoon tea and drinks. Set lunch and dinner menus are based on traditional Irish/French cooking, and freshly picked garden produce. Sitting room, lounge, bar, restaurant; garden. Free Wi-Fi. No background music. Children welcomed. 16 bedrooms (1 suitable for &). Per

person B&B €65–€85, D,B&B €95–€115. Closed Christmas.

25% DISCOUNT VOUCHERS

RECESS Co. Galway
Map 6:C4

LOUGH INAGH LODGE, Connemara. Tel 00 353 95-34706, www.loughinagh lodgehotel.ie. Overlooking the lough, there are 'warm fires and delicious food' at this 'lovely, peaceful lodge' surrounded by the Twelve Bens and Mam Turk mountain ranges. It is run with 'a pleasant informality' by owner Máire O'Connor and manager Dominic O'Morain. Each of the country house-style bedrooms has a comfortable seating area; all have views of the lough and the mountains. Chef Julie Worley's four-course Irish country menus, served in the elegant dining room, feature seafood and wild game; a good bar menu is also available. Good walks, fishing. Bar, sitting room, library, dining room. Free Wi-Fi. No background music. 5-acre grounds. Wedding facilities. Children and dogs welcomed. 13 bedrooms (4 on ground floor). Per room B&B €180–€250. Dinner €50. Closed mid-Dec–Mar.

ROSSLARE Co. Wexford
Map 6:D6

KELLY'S. Tel 00 353-53 91-32114, www.kellys.ie. On a five mile stretch of beautiful sandy beach, this large resort hotel and spa has been run by the 'hands-on' Kelly family for four generations. Family-friendly, it has plenty to suit all ages, from Ayurvedic treatments to volleyball. Exercise, and leisure pool (swimming jet, waterfall with hydromassage); spa (steam room, sauna, outdoor hot tub, treatments; open to non-residents); badminton, tennis, basketball, bowls, table tennis, crazy golf, boules; gym; jogging track. *Pirates Club* for children over four; activities for teenagers; golf nearby. *La Marine Bistro and Bar* serves brasserie food; menus in *Beaches* restaurant are more sophisticated. Eugene Callaghan is chef. Bedrooms are airy and modern. Public areas have an 'eclectic, but very impressive' collection of modern art. Live entertainment. Free Wi-Fi. Children welcomed (high tea; childminding). Reading room with open fire, library, TV room, bar (background music). 118 bedrooms (35 family rooms). B&B per person €60–€90, D,B&B €110–€160.

STRANGFORD Co. Down
Map 6:B6
THE CUAN, 6–10 The Square, BT30 7ND. Tel 028-4488 1222, www.thecuan.com. In a conservation village on the shores of Strangford Lough (a World Heritage site), this guest house is owned by Peter and Caroline McErlean. Some of the simply decorated bedrooms overlook the village square; breakfast has home-baked bread and scones, and locally smoked haddock. Peter McErlean cooks plenty of locally sourced seafood for the restaurant, including langoustines freshly caught from the lough. 2 lounges, bar, restaurant (traditional background music). Wedding/function facilities. Free Wi-Fi. Children welcomed. 9 bedrooms (1 suitable for &). Per person B&B €42.50–€65, D,B&B €58–€80.

THOMASTOWN Co. Kilkenny
Map 6:D5
BALLYDUFF HOUSE. Tel 00 353 56-775 8488, www.ballyduffhouse.ie.

In a 'fabulous situation' amid farmland and gardens, this classic Georgian house lies on the banks of the River Nore. It is run by the owner, Brede Thomas, who looks after guests with 'grace and warmth'. Comfortable bedrooms are prettily decorated in traditional country house style; each has views of the river or rolling parkland. An elegant lounge, with open fire, is furnished with family antiques; a book-lined library is 'a gem'. 'Delicious' breakfasts are taken in the dining room. Lounge, library, dining room. Free Wi-Fi. No background music. Children are welcomed; pets allowed by arrangement. Fishing, canoeing. 6 bedrooms. Per person B&B €50.

WATERFORD Co. Waterford
Map 6:D5
FOXMOUNT COUNTRY HOUSE, Passage East Road. Tel 00 353 51-874308, www.foxmountcountryhouse.com. At the end of a long drive bordered by greenery, Margaret and David Kent's creeper-covered 17th-century house is on a working dairy farm with manicured lawns, mature trees and a profusion of azaleas and rhododendrons. B&B accommodation is in homely, 'well-decorated' rooms overlooking the extensive grounds; tea and home-made cakes are served in the drawing room beside an open fire. At breakfast, home-grown produce is used in Margaret Kent's fruit compotes and preserves; bread is home baked. Free Wi-Fi. No background music. Children welcomed. Dogs stay in kennels in the grounds. 4 bedrooms (all with a private bathroom). Per room B&B €110–€130. Closed Nov–Mar.

WESTPORT Co. Mayo
Map 6:C4

ARDMORE COUNTRY HOUSE, The Quay.
Tel 00 353 98-25994, www.ardmore
countryhouse.com. Overlooking Clew
Bay, the Hoban family's yellow-painted
hotel and restaurant is a short walk
from the lively town and harbour.
David Hoban is the manager.
Traditional and comfortably furnished,
most of the 'fine, spacious and well-
equipped' rooms have a large sleigh bed,
separate walk-in shower and bath, and
views of Croagh Patrick and the bay. As
chef, Pat Hoban specialises in locally
caught fish and shellfish; Noreen, his
wife, is the helpful, friendly front-of-
house. Sitting room, bar, dining room.
Free Wi-Fi. Classical background
music. 1½-acre garden. Small
conference facilities. Parking. Children
welcomed. 13 bedrooms (some on
ground floor). Per room B&B €90–€160,
D,B&B €140–€200. Closed Nov–Mar.

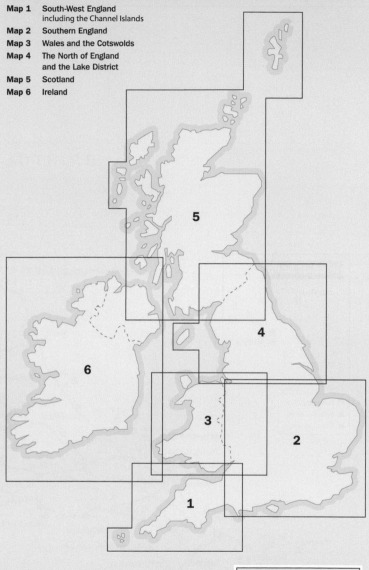

Channel Islands

1

Not to scale

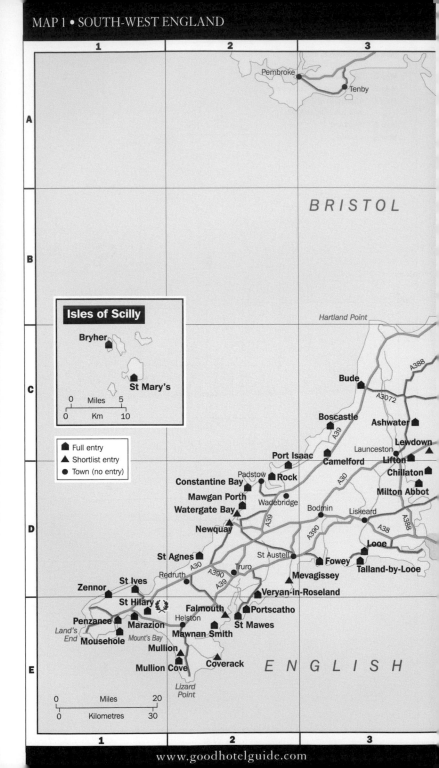

MAP 1 • SOUTH-WEST ENGLAND

1   **2**   **3**

A

Pembroke

Tenby

BRISTOL

B

Isles of Scilly

Bryher

St Mary's

0   Miles   5

0   Km   10

■ Full entry
▲ Shortlist entry
● Town (no entry)

C

Hartland Point

Bude

A388

A3072

Boscastle

Ashwater

A39

Launceston

Lewdown

Port Isaac   **Camelford**   **Lifton**

Padstow   **Rock**   **Chillaton**

Constantine Bay   A30

Milton Abbot

Mawgan Porth   Wadebridge

Watergate Bay   Bodmin   Liskeard   A38   A388

A39

Newquay   A390

A390

St Agnes   St Austell   **Looe**

D

Redruth   A30   Truro   **Fowey**   **Talland-by-Looe**

A390   **Mevagissey**

Zennor   **St Ives**   A39   **Veryan-in-Roseland**

St Hilary   **Falmouth**   **Portscatho**

Penzance   Helston   **St Mawes**

Marazion   **Mawnan Smith**

Mousehole   *Mount's Bay*   **Mullion**

Land's End   **Mullion Cove**   **Coverack**

Lizard Point   *ENGLISH*

E

0   Miles   20

0   Kilometres   30

1   **2**   **3**

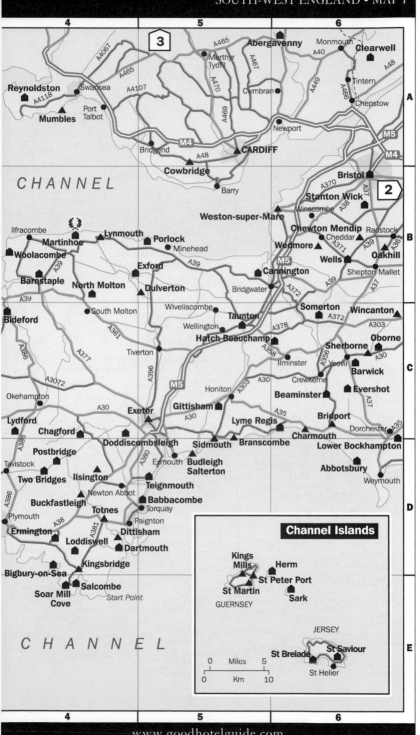

MAP 2 • SOUTHERN ENGLAND

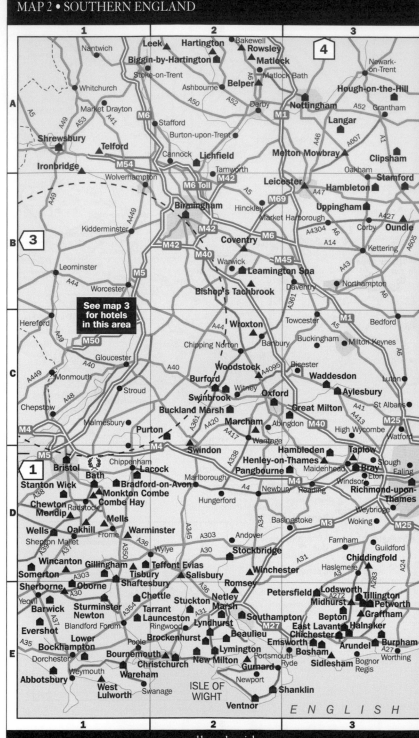

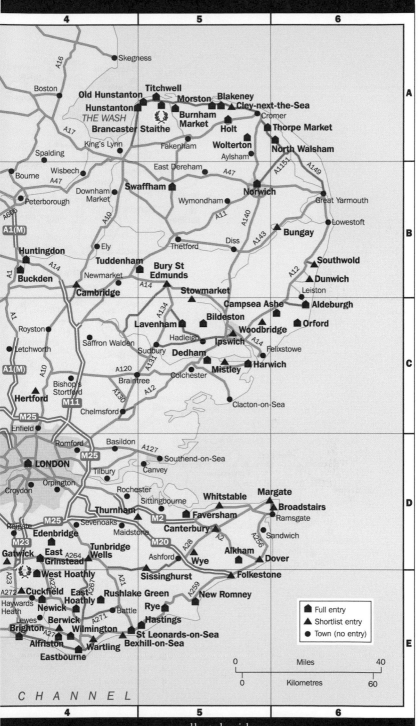

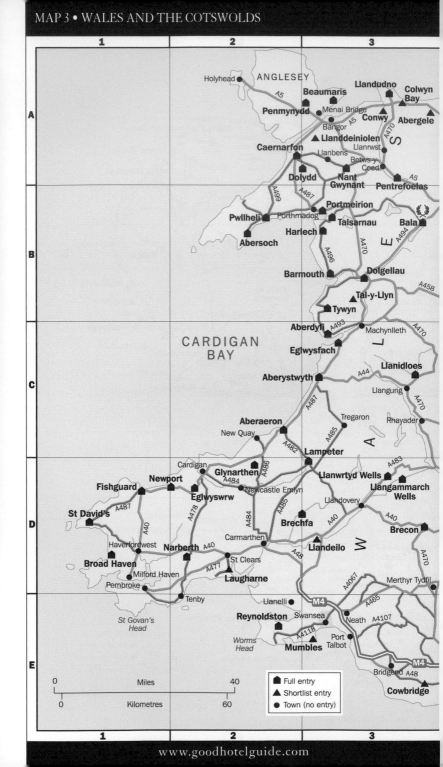

MAP 3 • WALES AND THE COTSWOLDS

ANGLESEY

Holyhead

Beaumaris

Penmynydd

Menai Bridge

Bangor

Llanddeiniolen

Caernarfon

Llanberis

Llanrwst

Betws-y-Coed

Dolydd

Nant Gwynant

Llandudno

Colwyn Bay

Conwy

Abergele

S

Pentrefoelas

Portmeirion

Pwllheli

Porthmadog

Talsarnau

Bala

Harlech

Abersoch

Barmouth

Dolgellau

E

Tal-y-Llyn

Tywyn

CARDIGAN BAY

Aberdyfi

Machynlleth

Eglwysfach

Llanidloes

L

Aberystwyth

Llangurig

Aberaeron

New Quay

Tregaron

Rhayader

Lampeter

A

Cardigan

Glynarthen

Llanwrtyd Wells

Newport

Newcastle Emlyn

Llangammarch Wells

Fishguard

Eglwyswrw

Llandovery

St David's

Brechfa

Brecon

Haverfordwest

Narberth

Carmarthen

Broad Haven

St Clears

Llandeilo

W

Milford Haven

Laugharne

Pembroke

Merthyr Tydfil

Tenby

Llanelli

M4

St Govan's Head

Reynoldston

Swansea

Neath

Worms Head

Port Talbot

Mumbles

Bridgend

M4

Cowbridge

| 0 | Miles | 40 |
| 0 | Kilometres | 60 |

■ Full entry
▲ Shortlist entry
● Town (no entry)

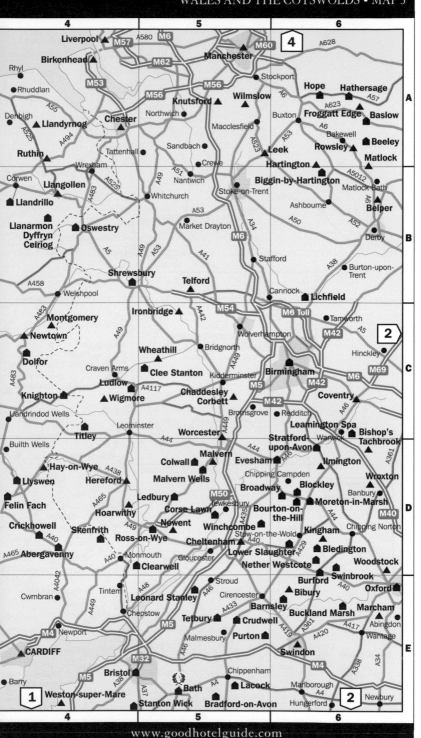

MAP 4 • THE NORTH OF ENGLAND AND THE LAKE DISTRICT

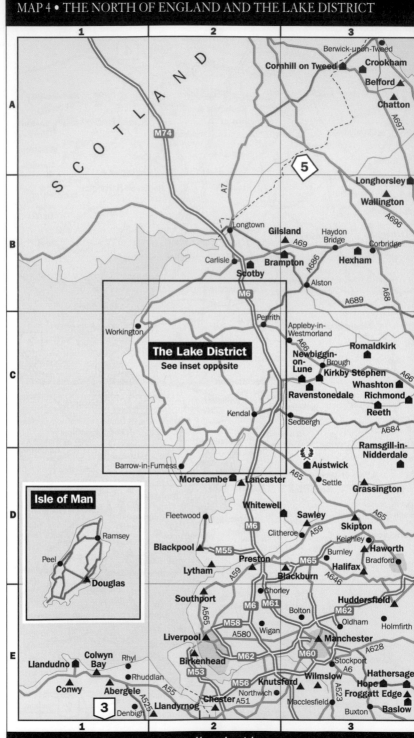

Berwick-upon-Tweed
Cornhill on Tweed
Crookham
Belford
Chatton

SCOTLAND

M74

5

Longhorsley
Wallington

A7

Longtown
Gilsland
Haydon Bridge
Corbridge
Carlisle
Brampton
Hexham
Scotby
Alston

M6

A689

Workington

Penrith

Appleby-in-Westmorland

The Lake District
See inset opposite

Newbiggin-on-Lune
Brough
Kirkby Stephen
Ravenstonedale

Romaldkirk
Whashton
Richmond
Reeth

A66

Kendal
Sedbergh

A684

Ramsgill-in-Nidderdale

Barrow-in-Furness

Austwick
Settle
Grassington

Morecambe
Lancaster

A65

Isle of Man

Ramsey

Peel

Douglas

Whitewell
Sawley
Skipton

Fleetwood
Clitheroe
A59
Keighley
Haworth
Bradford

Blackpool
M55
Preston
Burnley
Halifax

Lytham
A59
Blackburn
A646

Chorley
Huddersfield

Southport
M6
M61
Bolton
M62
Oldham
Holmfirth

M58
A580
Wigan
Stockport
A6

Liverpool
M62
M60
Manchester
A628

Birkenhead
M53
Hathersage

Llandudno
Colwyn Bay
Rhyl
Wilmslow
Hope
Froggatt Edge

Conwy
Abergele
Rhuddlan
Knutsford
Northwich
Macclesfield
Baslow

Llandyrnog
Chester
A51
Buxton

Denbigh

3

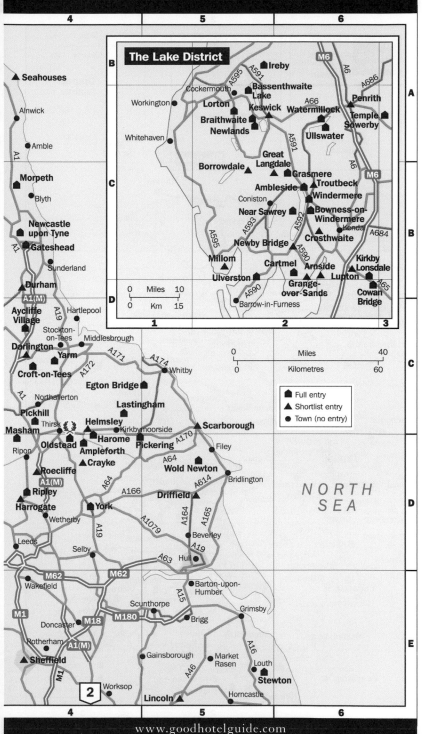

The Lake District

Ireby
Cockermouth
Bassenthwaite Lake
Workington
Lorton
Keswick
Watermillock
Penrith
Braithwaite
Temple Sowerby
Whitehaven
Newlands
Ullswater
Great Langdale
Borrowdale
Grasmere
Ambleside
Troutbeck
Coniston
Windermere
Near Sawrey
Bowness-on-Windermere
Newby Bridge
Crosthwaite
Kendal
Millom
Cartmel
Arnside
Kirkby Lonsdale
Ulverston
Lupton
Grange-over-Sands
Cowan Bridge
Barrow-in-Furness

| 0 | Miles | 10 |
| 0 | Km | 15 |

Seahouses
Alnwick
Amble
Morpeth
Blyth
Newcastle upon Tyne
Gateshead
Sunderland
Durham
Aycliffe Village
Hartlepool
Stockton-on-Tees
Middlesbrough
Darlington
Yarm
Whitby
Croft-on-Tees
Northallerton
Egton Bridge
Pickhill
Lastingham
Masham
Thirsk
Helmsley
Kirkbymoorside
Scarborough
Ripon
Oldstead
Harome
Pickering
Filey
Ampleforth
Crayke
Wold Newton
Roecliffe
Bridlington
Ripley
Driffield
Harrogate
Wetherby
NORTH SEA
Leeds
York
Beverley
Selby
Hull
Wakefield
Barton-upon-Humber
Scunthorpe
Grimsby
Doncaster
Brigg
Rotherham
Gainsborough
Market Rasen
Louth
Sheffield
Stewton
Worksop
Lincoln
Horncastle

◼ Full entry
▲ Shortlist entry
● Town (no entry)

| 0 | Miles | 40 |
| 0 | Kilometres | 60 |

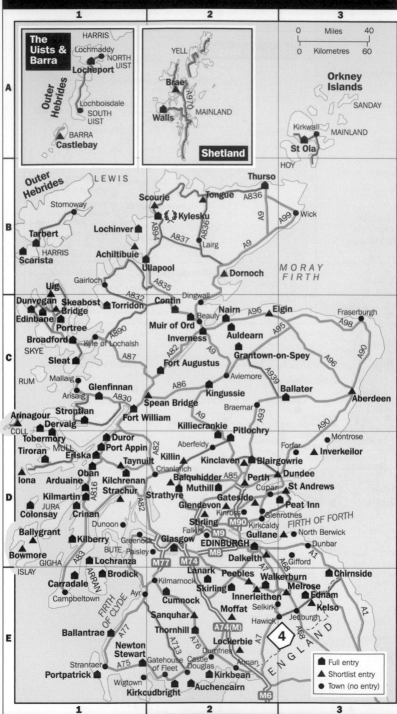

MAP 5 • SCOTLAND

The Uists & Barra

HARRIS
Lochmaddy
NORTH UIST
Locheport
Outer Hebrides
Lochboisdale
SOUTH UIST
▲ BARRA
Castlebay

YELL
Brae
A970
MAINLAND
Walls
Shetland

0 — Miles — 40
0 — Kilometres — 60

Orkney Islands
SANDAY
Kirkwall
MAINLAND
St Ola
HOY

Outer Hebrides
LEWIS
Stornoway
Scourie
Tarbert
HARRIS
Scarista
Lochinver
Kylesku
A894 A837 A836
Lairg
Achiltibuie
Ullapool
A835
Gairloch
A832
Dingwall
Thurso
Tongue A836
A9 A99 Wick
A9
MORAY FIRTH
Dornoch

Uig
Dunvegan **Skeabost Bridge** **Torridon** **Contin**
Edinbane
Portree A890
Broadford
SKYE Kyle of Lochalsh
A87
Sleat
RUM Mallaig
A82
Arisaig A830
Glenfinnan
Strontian
Arinagour
COLL **Dervaig**
Tobermory
Tiroran MULL
Eriska
Port Appin
Iona **Arduaine**
Oban
Kilchrenan
Kilmartin
Colonsay A816
JURA
Crinan
Ballygrant
Kilberry
Bowmore
GIGHA
Lochranza
ISLAY
Carradale
ARRAN **Brodick**
Campbeltown
FIRTH OF CLYDE
Ballantrae
Newton Stewart
Stranraer A75
Portpatrick
Wigtown

Muir of Ord
Beauly **Nairn** A96 **Elgin**
Inverness
A9 **Auldearn**
Fort Augustus
Grantown-on-Spey A96
Aviemore A939
A86 **Kingussie**
Spean Bridge
Fort William
A9 Braemar A93 **Ballater**
Killiecrankie
Duror
Aberfeldy **Pitlochry**
Taynuilt
Killin
Crianlarich
Balquhidder A85
Strachur
Strathyre
Dunoon
Stirling
Falkirk
Glasgow
EDINBURGH M9
M8
Paisley M74
Greenock
BUTE
Ayr
Kilmarnock
Cumnock
Sanquhar
Thornhill
A76
A713
Gatehouse of Fleet
Castle Douglas
Dumfries
Lockerbie
A74(M)
Annan
Kirkbean
Auchencairn
Kirkcudbright

Fraserburgh
A98
A90
Aberdeen
Montrose
Forfar
Inverkeilor
A90
Blairgowrie
Kinclaven
Dundee
Perth
Cupar **St Andrews**
Muthill
Gateside
Peat Inn
Glendevon
Kinross Glenrothes
M90 Kirkcaldy
FIRTH OF FORTH
Gullane
North Berwick
Dunbar
A1
Dalkeith
A68
Gifford
Lanark
Peebles
Walkerburn
Chirnside
Skirling
Innerleithen
Melrose
Moffat
Selkirk
Ednam
Hawick Jedburgh
Kelso
A68
A1
ENGLAND
4
M6

Full entry
▲ **Shortlist entry**
● **Town (no entry)**

www.goodhotelguide.com

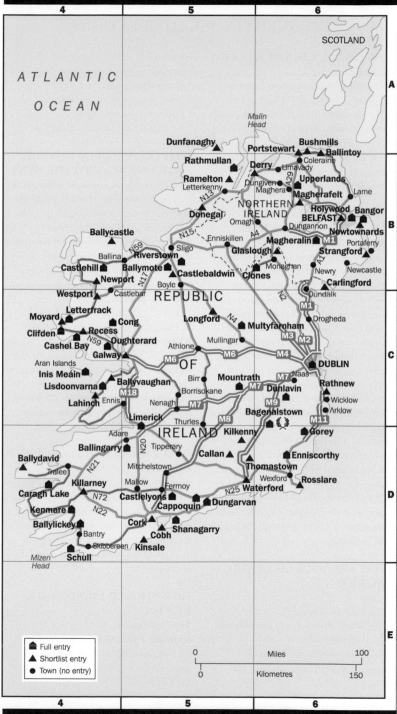

SCOTLAND

ATLANTIC

OCEAN

Malin
Head

Dunfanaghy
Portstewart Bushmills
Rathmullan Ballintoy
Derry Coleraine
Ramelton Limavady
Letterkenny Dungiven Upperlands
Donegal Maghera Larne
NORTHERN Magherafelt
IRELAND Holywood Bangor
Omagh BELFAST
Dungannon Newtownards
Ballycastle Enniskillen Portaferry
Sligo Magheralin
Riverstown Glaslough Strangford
Ballina Newry Newcastle
Castlehill Ballymote Castlebaldwin Monaghan
Newport Clones Carlingford
Boyle Dundalk
Westport Castlebar REPUBLIC Drogheda
Letterfrack Longford
Moyard Cong Multyfarnham
Recess Mullingar
Clifden Oughterard Athlone
Cashel Bay Galway OF DUBLIN
Aran Islands Rathnew
Inis Meáin Ballyvaughan Birr Mountrath Naas
Lisdoonvarna Borrisokane Dunlavin Wicklow
Lahinch Ennis Nenagh Arklow
Limerick Bagenalstown
Thurles IRELAND Kilkenny Gorey
Adare Tipperary
Ballingarry Callan Enniscorthy
Ballydavid Mitchelstown Thomastown
Tralee Mallow Fermoy Wexford
Killarney Castlelyons Waterford Rosslare
Caragh Lake Cappoquin Dungarvan
Kenmare Cork
Ballylickey Bantry Shanagarry
Skibbereen Cobh
Mizen Schull Kinsale
Head

N59, N15, N13, N29, A29, A4, A1, M1, N2, N4, M6, M3, M2, M4, M7, M9, M11, M18, N20, N21, N72, N22, N25, M8, N17

Full entry
▲ **Shortlist entry**
● **Town (no entry)**

0 Miles 100
0 Kilometres 150

FREQUENTLY ASKED QUESTIONS

HOW DO YOU CHOOSE A GOOD HOTEL?

The hotels we like are relaxed, unstuffy and personally run. We do not have a specific template: our choices vary greatly in style and size. Most of the hotels in the *Guide* are family owned and family run. These are places where the needs and comfort of the guest are put ahead of the convenience of the management.

YOU ARE A HOTEL GUIDE – WHY DO YOU INCLUDE SO MANY PUBS AND B&BS?

Attitudes and expectations have changed considerably since the *Guide* was founded in the 1970s. Today's guests expect more informality, less deference. There has been a noticeable rise in the standards of food and accommodation in pubs and restaurants. This is demonstrated by the number of such places suggested to us by our readers. While pubs may have a more relaxed attitude than some traditional hotels, we ensure that only those that maintain high standards of service are included in our selections. The best B&Bs have always combined a high standard of accommodation with excellent value for money. Expect the bedrooms in a pub or B&B listed in the *Guide* to be well equipped, with thoughtful extras. B&B owners invariably know how to serve a good breakfast.

WHAT ARE YOUR LIKES AND DISLIKES?

We like
* Flexible times for meals.
* Two decent armchairs in the bedroom.
* Good bedside lighting.
* Proper hangers in the wardrobe.
* Fresh milk with the tea tray in the room.

We dislike
* Intrusive background music.
* Stuffy dress codes.
* Bossy notices and house rules.
* Hidden service charges.
* Packaged fruit juices at breakfast.

WHY DO YOU DROP HOTELS FROM ONE YEAR TO THE NEXT?

Readers are quick to tell us if they think standards have slipped at a hotel. If the evidence is overwhelming, we drop the hotel from the *Guide* or perhaps downgrade it to the Shortlist. Sometimes we send inspectors just to be sure. When a hotel is sold, we look for reports since the new owners took over, otherwise we inspect or omit it.

WHY DO YOU ASK FOR 'MORE REPORTS, PLEASE'?

When we have not heard about a hotel for several years, we ask readers for more reports. Sometimes readers returning to a favourite hotel may not send a fresh report. Readers often respond to our request.

WHAT SHOULD I TELL YOU IN A REPORT?

How you enjoyed your stay. We welcome reports of any length. We want to know what you think about the welcome, the service, the building and the facilities. Even a short report can tell us a great deal about the owners, the staff and the atmosphere.

HOW SHOULD I SEND YOU A REPORT?

You can email us at editor@goodhotelguide.com. Or you can write to us at the address given on the report forms at the back of the *Guide*.

Please send your reports to:

The *Good Hotel Guide*, Freepost PAM 2931, London W11 4BR

NOTE: No stamps needed in the UK.

Letters/report forms posted outside the UK should be addressed to:

The *Good Hotel Guide*, 50 Addison Avenue, London W11 4QP, England, and stamped normally.

Unless asked not to, we assume that we may publish your name. If you would like more report forms please tick ☐

NAME OF HOTEL: _____

ADDRESS: _____

_____

Date of most recent visit: _____ Duration of stay: _____

☐ New recommendation   ☐ Comment on existing entry

REPORT:

Please continue overleaf

I am not connected directly or indirectly with the management or proprietors

Signed:

Name: (CAPITALS PLEASE)

Address:

Email address:

Please send your reports to:

The *Good Hotel Guide*, Freepost PAM 2931, London W11 4BR

NOTE: No stamps needed in the UK.

Letters/report forms posted outside the UK should be addressed to:

The *Good Hotel Guide*, 50 Addison Avenue, London W11 4QP, England, and stamped normally.

Unless asked not to, we assume that we may publish your name. If you would like more report forms please tick ☐

NAME OF HOTEL: _____

ADDRESS: _____

_____

Date of most recent visit: _____ Duration of stay: _____

☐ New recommendation ☐ Comment on existing entry

REPORT:

Please continue overleaf

I am not connected directly or indirectly with the management or proprietors

Signed: _____

Name: (CAPITALS PLEASE) _____

Address: _____

_____

Email address: _____

Please send your reports to:

The *Good Hotel Guide*, Freepost PAM 2931, London W11 4BR

NOTE: No stamps needed in the UK.

Letters/report forms posted outside the UK should be addressed to:

The *Good Hotel Guide*, 50 Addison Avenue, London W11 4QP, England, and stamped normally.

Unless asked not to, we assume that we may publish your name. If you would like more report forms please tick ☐

NAME OF HOTEL: _____

ADDRESS: _____

_____

Date of most recent visit: _____ Duration of stay: _____

☐ New recommendation   ☐ Comment on existing entry

REPORT:

Please continue overleaf

I am not connected directly or indirectly with the management or proprietors

Signed: _____

Name: (CAPITALS PLEASE) _____

Address: _____

_____

Email address: _____

INDEX OF HOTELS BY COUNTY
(S) indicates a Shortlist entry

ALPHABETICAL LIST OF HOTELS
(S) indicates a Shortlist entry